PERGAMON INTERNATION
of Science, Technology, Engineering

The 1000-volume original paperback libr
industrial training and the enjoyment of leisure

Publisher: Robert Maxwell, M.C.

THEORETICAL MECHANICS FOR SIXTH FORMS

IN TWO VOLUMES

VOLUME 2

SECOND (SI) EDITION

Other Titles of Interest

CHIRGWIN & PLUMPTON:
A Course of Mathematics for Engineers and Scientists (six volumes)
Elementary Classical Hydrodynamics

CHIRGWIN *ET AL.*:
Elementary Electromagnetic Theory (three volumes)

PLUMPTON & TOMKYS:
Sixth Form Pure Mathematics (two volumes)

ROMAN:
Some Modern Mathematics for Physicists and Other Outsiders
(two volumes)

THEORETICAL MECHANICS FOR SIXTH FORMS

IN TWO VOLUMES

VOLUME 2

C. PLUMPTON
Queen Mary College, London

W. A. TOMKYS
Belle Vue Boys' Grammar School
Bradford

SECOND (SI) EDITION

PERGAMON PRESS
OXFORD · NEW YORK · TORONTO
SYDNEY · PARIS · FRANKFURT

U.K.	Pergamon Press Ltd., Headington Hill Hall, Oxford OX3 0BW, England
U.S.A.	Pergamon Press Inc., Maxwell House, Fairview Park, Elmsford, New York 10523, U.S.A.
CANADA	Pergamon of Canada, Suite 104, 150 Consumers Road, Willowdale, Ontario M2J 1P9, Canada
AUSTRALIA	Pergamon Press (Aust.) Pty. Ltd., P.O. Box 544, Potts Point, N.S.W. 2011, Australia
FRANCE	Pergamon Press SARL, 24 rue des Ecoles, 75240 Paris, Cedex 05, France
FEDERAL REPUBLIC OF GERMANY	Pergamon Press GmbH, 6242 Kronberg-Taunus, Hammerweg 6, Federal Republic of Germany

First edition 1964

Second (SI) edition 1972

Reprinted 1973, 1974, 1979, 1980

Library of Congress Catalog Card No. 77-131995

Printed in Great Britain by A. Wheaton and Co. Ltd., Exeter.

ISBN 0 08 016591 5 flexi net
0 08 016592 3 flexi non-net

CONTENTS

PREFACE

THIS volume completes the revised edition of the course in Theoretical Mechanics for sixth-form pupils taking mathematics as a double subject using SI units throughout. We believe that some of the chapters, notably Chapters XXI and XXII on Virtual Work and Stability, Chapter XVI on the free motion of a rigid lamina in a plane, and Chapter XXV on the motion of bodies with variable mass are useful material for pupils in the third year of a sixth-form course and as preparation for their first year at University or at one of the Polytechnics. The chapters of the book are arranged in a logical order of development, but exercises, sections of chapters, and whole chapters, consideration of which might well be postponed until the third year of the course, are marked with an asterisk.

Many of the topics discussed in Volume I are reintroduced in this volume where they are considered in more detail and with more rigour. In particular the ideas of vectors are developed further in Chapters XVIII and XIX and, because of the importance of vectors in modern mathematics, we have included Chapter XXVI on vector algebra and its applications. We hope that this will serve as a useful introduction to more advanced work.

The first two chapters of this book concern the motion of a rigid lamina in a plane. We then discuss the dynamics of a particle under the action of variable forces and follow with a chapter concerning the uniplanar motion of a particle with two degrees of freedom. The next group of chapters develops the ideas of Statics which were introduced in Volume I. After a new consideration of the theoretical aspects of force analysis, the sets of conditions of equilibrium for a body under the action of coplanar forces are reclassified and applied to more difficult problems of equilibrium. We then consider stability and introduce the special technique of *Virtual Work*. Then graphical statics applied particularly to light frameworks is considered and finally in this group we discuss continuously distributed forces in the particular cases of loaded beams and the catenary.

In this volume, as in Volume I, references are made wherever necessary to the authors' *Sixth Form Pure Mathematics* and particularly to Volume II of that book. In *A Course of Mathematics, Volume III* by Chirgwin and Plumpton, the topics of the present volume are developed further and third year sixth-form pupils in particular would be well advised to read that book.

We wish to thank the Authorities of the University of London, the Cambridge Syndicate, the Oxford and Cambridge Joint Board, the Northern Universities Joint Board, the Oxford Colleges and the Cambridge Colleges for permission to include questions (marked L., C., O.C., N., O.S. and C.S., respectively) from papers set by them. We also thank Mr. J. A. Croft who read the proofs and made valuable suggestions.

C. PLUMPTON
W. A. TOMKYS

CHAPTER XV

THE MOTION OF A RIGID BODY ABOUT A FIXED AXIS

15.1. The Definition of a Rigid Body

We define a rigid body here as an aggregate of particles in which the distance between any two particles is invariable. A rigid body, thus defined, is a mathematical ideal which is unattainable in practice; most bodies are distorted under the action of external forces, but the mathematical models which are produced on the basis of the assumption of rigidity give results of value in applications to practical problems.

We assume further that the particles of a rigid body thus defined, are held together by internal forces between them and that the action and reaction between any pair of particles are equal in magnitude and opposite in direction. We also assume that, because the distance between any two particles of a rigid body remains constant and because the action and reaction between them are equal and opposite, the total work done by these internal forces in a displacement of the body is zero and that therefore the increase of the kinetic energy of a rigid body in any period is equal to the work done by the external forces in that period.

15.2. The Kinetic Energy of a Rigid Body Rotating about a Fixed Axis

Figure 15.1 represents a section perpendicular to the axis of a rigid body rotating about a fixed axis at right angles to the section and meeting the section at O. The rigid body is considered as consisting of an aggregate of particles, each of which is in one such section, and in which a particle of mass m_P is distant r_P from the axis. When the body is rotating about the axis with angular velocity ω, the linear velocity of the particle of mass m_P is $r_P\omega$ and the kinetic energy of this particle is $\frac{1}{2}m_P r_P^2 \omega^2$.

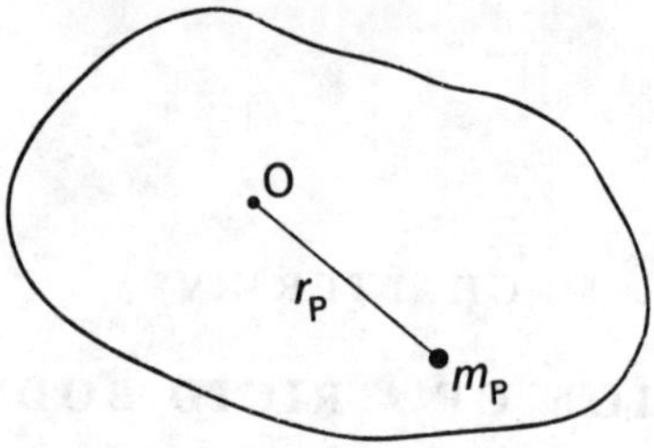

FIG. 15.1

The kinetic energy of the whole body is therefore

$$\Sigma \tfrac{1}{2} m_P r_P^2 \omega^2 = \tfrac{1}{2}\omega^2 \Sigma m_P r_P^2. \tag{15.1}$$

The summation sign indicates summation over all the particles of the body.

The quantity $\Sigma m_P r_P^2$ is defined as the *moment of inertia of the rigid body about the given axis*. The quantity k, where $\Sigma m_P r_P^2 = Mk^2$ and M is the total mass of the body, is defined as the *radius of gyration* of the body about the given axis.

15.3. Calculation of Moments of Inertia in Particular Cases

1. *The moment of inertia of a thin uniform rod of length 2l and mass M about an axis through its centre perpendicular to its length.* Let the line density of the rod be ϱ (Fig. 15.2). Then the M. of I. of a small increment δx of the rod, distance x from the axis, is approximately $\varrho\delta x . x^2$. Hence

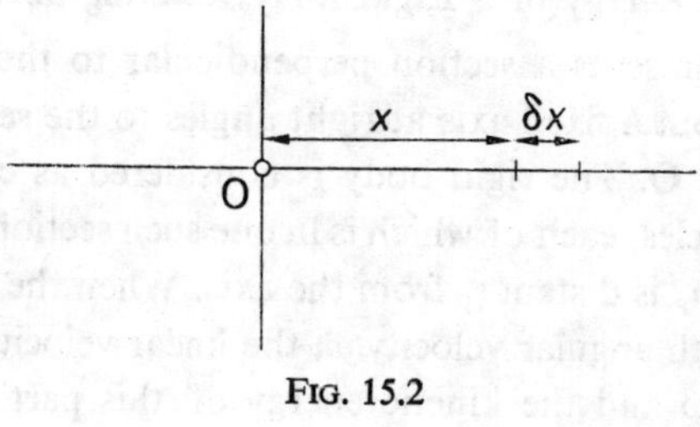

FIG. 15.2

the total M. of I. of the rod about the axis is

$$I = \int_{-l}^{l} \varrho x^2 \, dx = \frac{2\varrho l^3}{3} = \frac{Ml^2}{3}. \tag{15.2}$$

2. *The moment of inertia of a thin uniform rod of length 2l and mass M about an axis through its centre at an angle θ with its length.* Let the line density of the rod be ϱ and let its mid-point be O (Fig. 15.3). Then

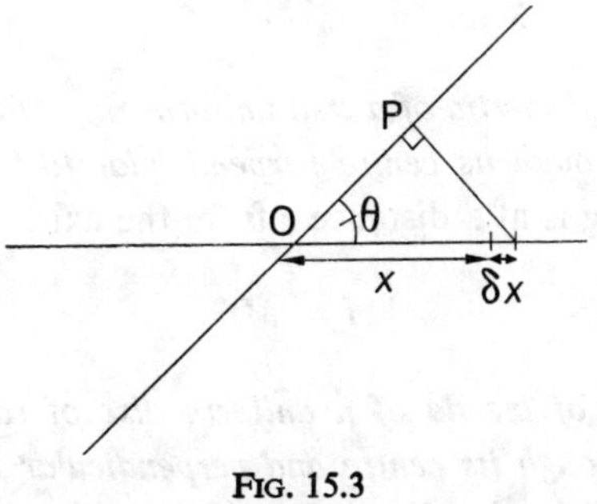

FIG. 15.3

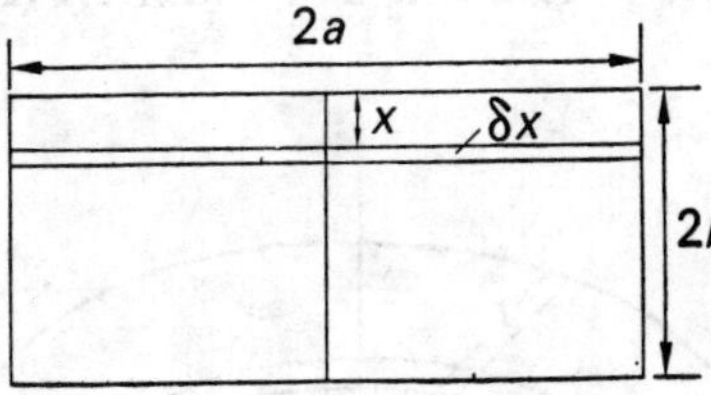

FIG. 15.4

the M. of I. about the given axis of a small increment δx of the rod, distance x from O, is approximately $\varrho \delta x . x^2 \sin^2 \theta$. Hence the total M. of I. of the rod about the axis is

$$I = \int_{-l}^{+l} \varrho x^2 \sin^2 \theta \, dx = \frac{2\varrho l^3 \sin^2 \theta}{3} = \frac{Ml^2 \sin^2 \theta}{3}. \tag{15.3}$$

3. *The moment of inertia of a lamina in the shape of a rectangle of length 2a, breadth 2b, and mass M about the axis in its plane, through its centre and parallel to the side of length 2b.* Figure 15.4 shows that the rectangle can be divided into thin strips each parallel to a side of length $2a$, a typical strip being distance x from that side and of width δx. Then if the surface density of the lamina is ϱ, the M. of I. of the lamina about the axis is

$$I = \int_0^{2b} 2\varrho a \cdot \frac{a^2}{3}\,\mathrm{d}x = \frac{4\varrho a^3 b}{3} = \frac{Ma^2}{3}. \tag{15.4}$$

4. *The moment of inertia of a thin uniform ring of mass M and radius r about the axis through its centre perpendicular to its plane.* Since every particle of the ring is at a distance r from the axis,

$$I = Mr^2. \tag{15.5}$$

5. *The moment of inertia of a uniform disc of radius r and mass M about the axis through its centre and perpendicular to its plane.* Let the surface density of the disc be ϱ. Consider a thin ring of the disc, concentric with the disc, of radius x and width δx (Fig. 15.5). Then the

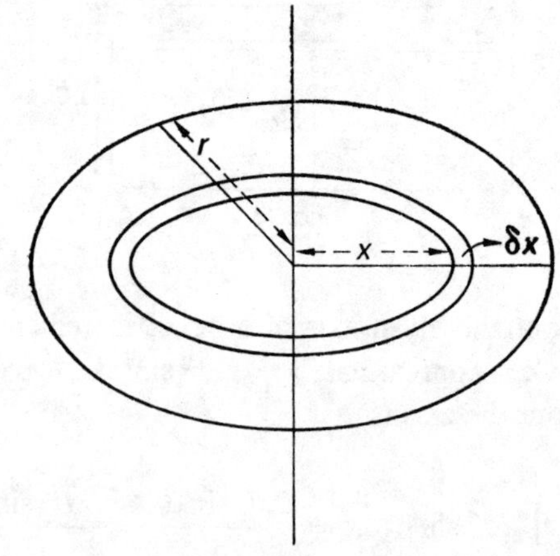

FIG. 15.5

M. of I. of this thin ring about the axis is approximately $2\pi\varrho x\delta x.x^2$,

$$\therefore\ I = \int_0^r 2\pi\varrho x.x^2\,dx = \frac{\pi\varrho r^4}{2} = \frac{Mr^2}{2}. \tag{15.6}$$

6. *The moment of inertia of a uniform sphere of radius R and mass M about a diameter.* Let the density of the sphere be ϱ (Fig. 15.6). Consider a thin disc (of the sphere) whose plane faces are perpendicular to

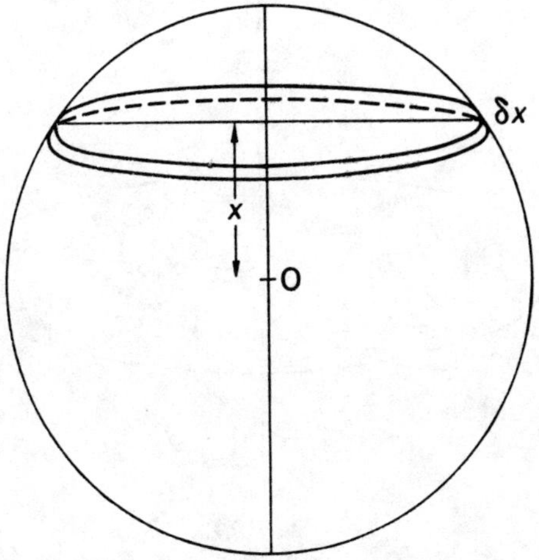

FIG. 15.6

the axis at a distance x from the centre of the sphere. Let the thickness of the disc be δx. Then the mass of the disc is approximately $\pi(R^2-x^2)\varrho\delta x$ and hence the M. of I. of the disc about the axis is approximately $\pi(R^2-x^2)\varrho\delta x.\frac{1}{2}(R^2-x^2)$. Hence the M. of I. of the sphere about the axis is

$$I = \int_{-R}^{+R} \frac{1}{2}\pi\varrho(R^2-x^2)^2\,dx = \frac{1}{2}\pi\varrho\left[R^4x-\frac{2R^2x^3}{3}+\frac{x^5}{5}\right]_{-R}^{+R}$$

$$= \frac{8\pi\varrho R^5}{15} = \frac{2MR^2}{5}. \tag{15.7}$$

Two Theorems

(a) *The theorem of perpendicular axes.* If Ox and Oy are any two rectangular axes in the plane of a *lamina* and Oz is an axis at right angles to the plane, then the moment of inertia of the lamina about Oz is equal to the sum of the moments of inertia of the lamina about Ox and Oy.

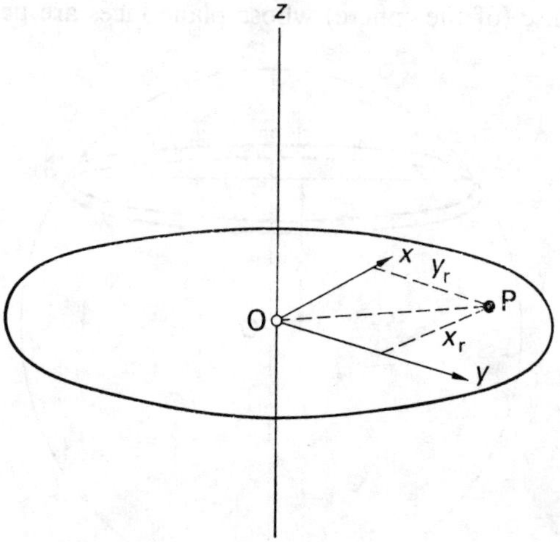

FIG. 15.7

For, with reference to Fig. 15.7, if m_r is the mass of a particle P whose coordinates referred to Ox, Oy are (x_r, y_r), the M. of I. of the particle about Ox is $m_r y_r^2$ and the M. of I. of the particle about Oy is $m_r x_r^2$. But $m_r y_r^2 + m_r x_r^2 = m_r(y_r^2 + x_r^2) = m_r \text{OP}^2$ and this is equal to the M. of I. of P about Oz. Hence, for the whole lamina, the sum of the moments of inertia about Ox and Oy is equal to the moment of inertia about Oz.

(b) *The theorem of parallel axes.* The moment of inertia of a body about any axis is equal to the moment of inertia about a parallel axis through the centre of mass together with the mass of the whole body multiplied by the square of the distance between the axes.

Figure 15.8 shows a section of the body through the centre of mass G. This section is at right angles to the axis and meets the axis at T where

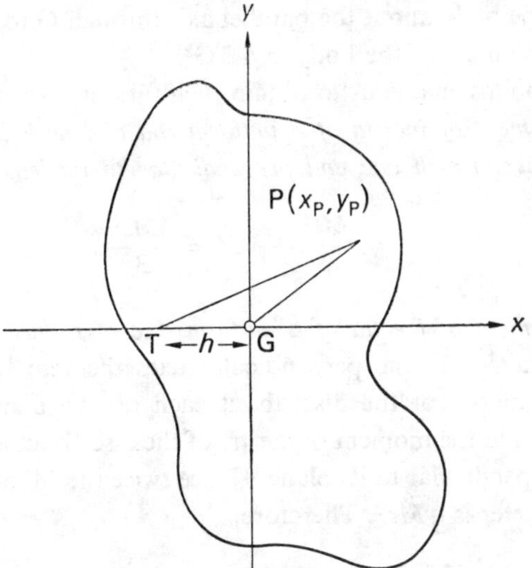

FIG. 15.8

GT $= h$. Take G as the origin and TG produced as the x-axis. A linear element of the solid of mass m_P which is parallel to the axis meets the section at $P(x_P, y_P)$. Then

$$m_P \, PT^2 = m_P\{y_P^2 + (h + x_P)^2\}.$$

Hence the M. of I. of the body about the axis through T is

$$\begin{aligned} \Sigma m_P \, PT^2 &= \Sigma m_P y_P^2 + \Sigma m_P h^2 + 2\Sigma m_P h x_P + \Sigma m_P x_P^2 \\ &= \Sigma m_P(x_P^2 + y_P^2) + \Sigma m_P h^2 + 2\Sigma m_P h x_P . \end{aligned}$$

But

$\Sigma m_P(x_P^2 + y_P^2) =$ M. of I. of the body about a parallel axis through G,

$\Sigma m_P h^2 = Mh^2$, where M is the mass of the body,

$\Sigma m_P h x_P = h\Sigma m_P x_P = 0$ because the x-coordinate of the centre of mass of the system is given by $\bar{x} = \Sigma m_P x_P / \Sigma m_P$ and in this case $\bar{x} = 0$ since G is the origin of coordinates.

Hence the M. of I. of the body about the axis through T is equal to the

M. of I. of the body about the parallel axis through G together with the product of the mass of the body and TG^2.

These theorems enable us to obtain such further results as:

7. *The moment of inertia of a uniform rod of length 2l and mass M about an axis through one end perpendicular to its length* is given by

$$I = \frac{Ml^2}{3} + Ml^2 = \frac{4Ml^2}{3}. \tag{15.8}$$

8. *The moment of inertia of a uniform disc of radius r and mass M about a diameter.* By the perpendicular axes theorem the sum of the moments of inertia of the disc about each of two diameters at right angles is equal to the moment of inertia of the disc about an axis through its centre perpendicular to its plane. Hence twice the M. of I. for the disc about a diameter is $\frac{1}{2}Mr^2$. Therefore,

$$\text{the M. of I. for the disc about a diameter is } \tfrac{1}{4}Mr^2. \tag{15.9}$$

Example 1. Find the radius of gyration about an axis through the centre perpendicular to the plane of a system consisting of an equilateral triangle of side $2a$, together with its circumcircle, all made of thin uniform wire.

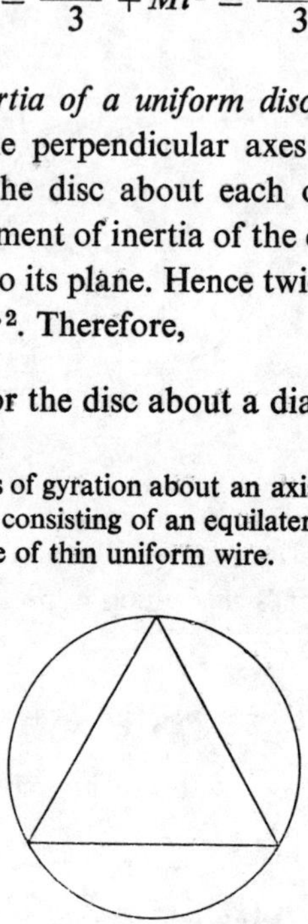

FIG. 15.9

Figure 15.9 shows the system. The M. of I. of each side of the triangle about an axis through its mid-point perpendicular to its plane is $\frac{2}{3}\varrho a^3$, where ϱ is the line density of the wire. The total M. of I. of the three rods about an axis through the centre of the circle perpendicular to the plane, from the parallel axes theorem, is therefore

$$3\left\{\frac{2\varrho a^3}{3} + 2\varrho a \cdot \frac{a^2}{3}\right\} = 4\varrho a^3.$$

The M. of I. of the circle about the axis is

$$2\pi \cdot \frac{2a}{\sqrt{3}}\,\varrho \cdot \frac{4a^2}{3} = \frac{16\sqrt{3}\varrho\pi a^3}{9}.$$

The M. of I. of the whole system about the axis is therefore $(4\varrho a^3/9)(4\sqrt{3}\pi+9)$, and the total mass of the system is $[(4\sqrt{3}\pi/3)+6]a\varrho$.

Therefore the radius of gyration of the system about the axis is

$$a\sqrt{\left\{\frac{2(4\sqrt{3}\pi+9)}{3(2\sqrt{3}\pi+9)}\right\}}.$$

Example 2. Find the M. of I. of a square lamina, of diagonal $2a$ and mass M, about an axis through one vertex perpendicular to its plane.

The M. of I. of the lamina about an axis through its centre parallel to one of its sides is

$$\frac{M(a\sqrt{2})^2}{12} = \frac{Ma^2}{6} \qquad \text{[from (15.4)].}$$

The M. of I. of the lamina about the axis in its plane which is perpendicular to the axis first chosen is also $Ma^2/6$ and therefore, by the theorem of perpendicular axes, the M. of I. of the lamina about an axis through its centre perpendicular to the plane is

$$\frac{Ma^2}{6} + \frac{Ma^2}{6} = \frac{Ma^2}{3}.$$

By the theorem of parallel axes the M. of I. of the lamina about an axis though one vertex perpendicular to its plane is, therefore,

$$\frac{Ma^2}{3} + Ma^2 = \frac{4Ma^2}{3}.$$

Example 3. Find the moment of inertia of a uniform solid cone of height h, base radius r and mass M, about a diameter of its base.

Figure 15.10 shows a section of the cone parallel to the base and distant x from the vertex. The radius of the section is y, where $y = xr/h$. The M. of I. about a diameter of a disc of thickness δx with this section as base, from equation (15.9) is

$$\frac{1}{4}\pi\varrho\frac{x^2r^2}{h^2}\,\delta x \cdot \frac{x^2r^2}{h^2},$$

where ϱ is the density of the cone, and therefore the M. of I. of the disc about a diameter of the base of the cone, from the theorem of parallel axes, is

$$\left\{\frac{\pi\varrho x^4r^4}{4h^4} + \frac{\pi\varrho x^2r^2}{h^2}(h-x)^2\right\}\delta x.$$

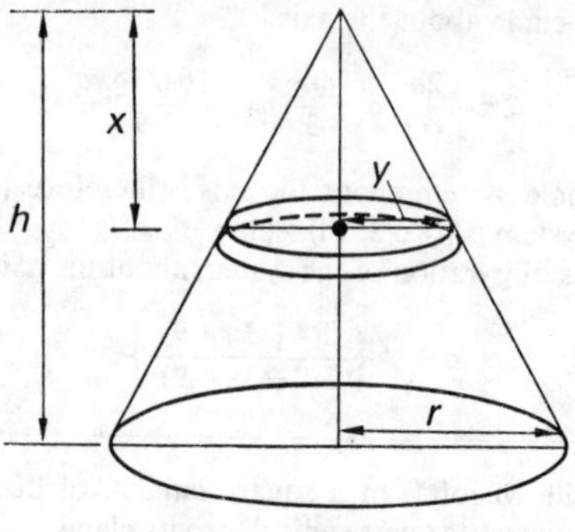

FIG. 15.10

Therefore the M. of I. of the whole cone about a diameter of the base is

$$\frac{\pi\varrho r^2}{h^2}\int_0^h\left(\frac{x^4r^2}{4h^2}+x^2h^2-2x^3h+x^4\right)dx = \frac{\pi\varrho r^2}{h^2}\left(\frac{r^2h^3}{20}+\frac{h^5}{3}-\frac{h^5}{2}+\frac{h^5}{5}\right)$$

$$= \pi\varrho r^2h\left(\frac{r^2}{20}+\frac{h^2}{30}\right) = M\left(\frac{3r^2+2h^2}{20}\right).$$

Example 4. An equilateral triangular lamina ABC of side 2*a* has a variable surface density so that the density at a point P of the lamina is proportional to the distance of P from the side BC. Find the M. of I. of the lamina (a) about BC, (b) about AB.

(a) Figure 15.11 shows a thin strip of the lamina distant x from BC and width δx. The mass of this strip is approximately

$$\frac{(a\sqrt{3}-x)\,2akx\delta x}{a\sqrt{3}},$$

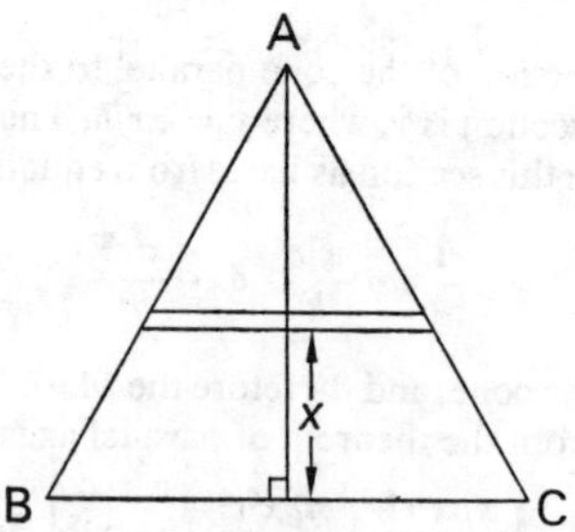

FIG. 15.11

where k is the constant of density variation. The M. of I. of the strip about BC is therefore approximately

$$\frac{(a\sqrt{3}-x)\,2akx\delta x}{a\sqrt{3}}\times x^2.$$

Therefore the M. of I. of the whole lamina about BC is

$$\int_0^{a\sqrt{3}} \frac{(a\sqrt{3}-x)\,2akx^3\,dx}{a\sqrt{3}} = \frac{2k}{\sqrt{3}}\left[\frac{ax^4\sqrt{3}}{4}-\frac{x^5}{5}\right]_0^{a\sqrt{3}} = \frac{9ka^5}{10}.$$

The mass of the lamina is

$$\int_0^{a\sqrt{3}} \frac{(a\sqrt{3}-x)\,2akx\,dx}{a\sqrt{3}} = \frac{2k}{\sqrt{3}}\left[\frac{ax^2\sqrt{3}}{2}-\frac{x^3}{3}\right]_0^{a\sqrt{3}} = ka^3 = M \quad \text{(say)}.$$

The M. of I. of the lamina about BC is therefore $\frac{9}{10}Ma^2$.

(b) From (15.3) and from the parallel axes theorem, the M. of I. of a thin uniform rod, of length l and mass m, about an axis through one end at an angle θ with the rod is $\frac{1}{3}ml^2\sin^2\theta$. Therefore the M. of I. of the strip about AB is approximately

$$\frac{1}{3}\left\{\frac{(a\sqrt{3}-x)\,2akx\delta x}{a\sqrt{3}}\right\}\left\{\frac{(a\sqrt{3}-x)\,2a}{a\sqrt{3}}\right\}^2\frac{3}{4}.$$

Therefore the M. of I. of the whole lamina about AB is

$$\frac{2k}{3\sqrt{3}}\int_0^{a\sqrt{3}}(a\sqrt{3}-x)^3x\,dx = \frac{2k}{3\sqrt{3}}\int_0^{a\sqrt{3}}x^3(a\sqrt{3}-x)\,dx$$

$$= \frac{2k}{3\sqrt{3}}\left[\frac{ax^4\sqrt{3}}{4}-\frac{x^5}{5}\right]_0^{a\sqrt{3}} = \frac{3ka^5}{10} = \frac{3}{10}Ma^2.$$

**Equimomental systems.* Two bodies are said to be equimomental when they have equal moments of inertia about an arbitrary line in space.

Example. A uniform plane triangular lamina of mass M is equimomental with three equal masses $\frac{1}{3}M$ at the mid-points of its sides.

Figure 15.12 shows a triangular lamina ABC and perpendicular axes Ax, Ay in the plane of the lamina so that B and C are at distances β and γ from Ax and BC produced meets Ax at D where AD = a.

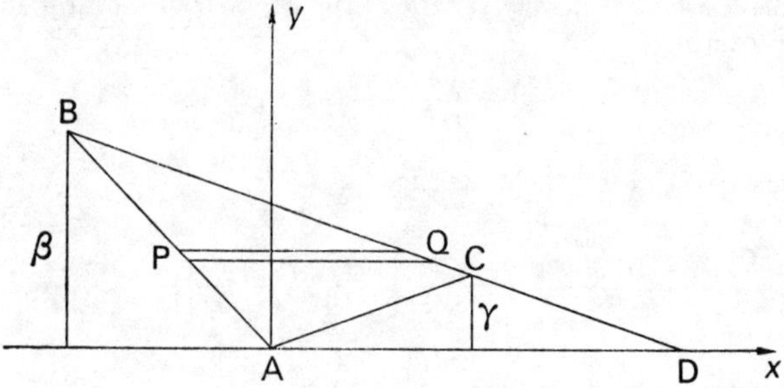

FIG. 15.12

PQ is a strip of the triangular lamina ABD parallel to Ax and distance y from it, and of width δy. The mass of this strip is approximately equal to

$$\frac{\beta-y}{\beta}\cdot a\varrho\,\delta y$$

where ϱ is the surface density of the lamina. Therefore the M. of I. of a lamina ABD of surface density ϱ about Ax is

$$\int_0^\beta \left(1-\frac{y}{\beta}\right) a\varrho y^2\,\mathrm{d}y = a\varrho\left[\frac{y^3}{3}-\frac{y^4}{4\beta}\right]_0^\beta = \frac{a\varrho\beta^3}{12}.$$

Similarly the M. of I. of a triangular lamina ACD of surface density ϱ about Ax is

$$\frac{a\varrho\gamma^3}{12}.$$

Therefore, by subtraction, the M. of I. of lamina ABC about Ax is

$$\frac{a\varrho}{12}(\beta^3-\gamma^3).$$

But the mass of ABC is $\frac{1}{2}a(\beta-\gamma)\varrho$.
Therefore the M. of I. of lamina ABC about Ax is

$$\frac{M}{6}(\beta^2+\beta\gamma+\gamma^2) = \frac{M}{3}\left\{\left(\frac{\beta}{2}\right)^2+\left(\frac{\gamma}{2}\right)^2+\left(\frac{\beta+\gamma}{2}\right)^2\right\}.$$

This is the same as the M. of I. of three equal particles of mass $\frac{1}{3}M$ about Ax when they are placed at the mid-points of the sides of the triangle ABC. (When Ax cuts BC internally a similar proof involving addition instead of subtraction of the laminas ABD, ACD shows the proposition still to be true.)

It can easily be shown that the centre of mass of these three particles is the same as the centre of mass of the lamina ABC and their combined mass is equal to that of the lamina. Therefore, by the theorem of parallel axes, the system of particles has the same M. of I. about all lines parallel to Ax as the lamina has. But the direction Ax was arbitrary. The particles therefore have the same M. of I. as the lamina about any axis in the plane of the lamina. From the theorem of perpendicular axes the statement can be extended to include any axis at right angles to the plane of the lamina. It can further be proved, but it will not be proved here, that the particles have the same M. of I. as the lamina has about an axis inclined to the plane of the lamina.

This particular result is so frequently useful that the student is advised to remember it and quote it when necessary. Example 2 of this section could have been worked with its help as follows:

The square lamina is considered as the two triangles each of mass $\frac{1}{2}M$ into which it is divided by one of its diagonals. The equimomental system consists of two particles each of mass $M/6$ distant $a\sqrt{(5/2)}$ from the axis, two particles each of mass $M/6$ distant $a\sqrt{\frac{1}{2}}$ from the axis and one particle of mass $\frac{1}{3}M$ distant a from the axis. The M. of I. of the lamina about the axis is therefore

$$\frac{1}{3}M\frac{5a^2}{2}+\frac{1}{3}M\frac{a^2}{2}+\frac{1}{3}Ma^2 = \frac{4}{3}Ma^2.$$

EXERCISES 15.3

In each of questions 1–7 find the moment of inertia of the body defined about the axis named. In each case give the answer in the form Mk^2 where M is the mass of the body.

1. A uniform rectangular lamina of length $2a$ and breadth $2b$ about an axis through one vertex perpendicular to its plane.

2. A uniform disc of radius r about a tangent.

3. A uniform equilateral triangular lamina of side $2a$ about an axis through its centre of mass perpendicular to its plane. (Use the equimomental system of particles.)

4. A uniform lamina in the shape of a regular hexagon of side $2a$ about an axis through its centre perpendicular to its plane.

5. A uniform triangular lamina ABC about an axis through A perpendicular to its plane (in terms of a, b, c the lengths of the sides of the triangle).

6. A hollow sphere, of external and internal radii a and b respectively, about a diameter.

7. A uniform solid cylinder of radius r and length l about a diameter of one end.

8. A wheel consists of a uniform disc of mass 20 kg and radius 0·5 m on to which is shrunk a thin uniform rim of mass 2 kg. Find the moment of inertia of the wheel about a diameter.

9. A uniform hollow sphere of mass M has external and internal radii $2a$ and a respectively. Show that its moment of inertia about a tangent to its outer surface is $\frac{202}{35}Ma^2$. (L.)

10. (i) Four equal uniform rods, each of mass M and length $2l$, form a square frame. Find its moment of inertia about an axis through its centre and perpendicular to its plane.

(ii) Twelve equal uniform rods, each of mass M and length $2l$, form a skeleton cube. Find its moment of inertia about an axis through its centre and parallel to one of its edges. (O.C.)

11. Prove that the moment of inertia of a uniform solid right circular cone about its axis is $3Mr^2/10$, where M is the mass of the cone and r is the radius of its base.

A frustum of this cone is formed by removing a conical portion whose height is one-half that of the original cone. If m is the mass of the frustum, prove that its moment of inertia about its axis is $93mr^2/280$. (C.)

12. A uniform body consists of a solid hemisphere of radius a, with a solid right circular cone of the same base radius a and height a, attached to the hemisphere so that the circular bases of the cone and hemisphere coincide. Show that the moment of inertia of the body about its axis of symmetry is $11Ma^2/30$, where M is the total mass. (L.)

13. A plane lamina in the form of an isosceles triangle ABC has AB = AC = b, BC = a. Find its radius of gyration about the axis in its plane through its centroid and parallel to BC. (L.)

14. The density of a thin rod OA of length l at a point P is λOP where λ is a constant. Show that its centre of gravity is distant $2l/3$ from O and find its radius of gyration about an axis through O perpendicular to OA. (L.)

15. From a homogeneous square lamina ABCD, of mass 10 kg and side 10 m, a square piece XYZW of 8 m side is removed. The side XY lies along AB and AX = YB. Find the moment of inertia of the remaining part of the lamina (i) about AB, (ii) about a line parallel to AB through its centre of gravity. (L.)

15.4. Conservation of Energy

When a rigid body moves under the action of a conservative system of forces the sum of its potential and kinetic energies remains constant.

The potential energy of a rigid body. If m_P is the mass of a particle of the rigid body at a distance y_P from a fixed horizontal plane, the potential energy of the particle referred to the plane as origin is $m_P g y_P$ and the potential energy of the whole body is $g\Sigma m_P y_P$, the summation being over the whole body. But $\Sigma m_P y_P = M\bar{y}$, where $\bar{y}$ is the height of the centre of mass of the body above the fixed plane and M is the mass of the body. The potential energy of the rigid body is therefore $Mg\bar{y}$.

The principle of conservation of energy for a rigid body rotating freely under gravity about a fixed axis about which its moment of inertia is I can therefore be stated, in the usual notation, as

$$\tfrac{1}{2}I\dot{\theta}^2+Mg\bar{y} \quad \text{is constant.}$$

The work done by a force acting on a body rotating about a fixed axis. In § 14.8 of Volume I we obtained for two particles, and in the usual notation, the equations

$$X_1+X_2 = m_1\ddot{x}_1+m_2\ddot{x}_2,$$
$$Y_1+Y_2 = m_1\ddot{y}_1+m_2\ddot{y}_2.$$

These results can be extended to the aggregate of particles we have defined as a rigid body, i.e.

$$\Sigma X_P = \Sigma m_P\ddot{x}_P,$$
$$\Sigma Y_P = \Sigma m_P\ddot{y}_P,$$

where ΣX_P, ΣY_P are the sums of the components in the x, y directions of the external forces acting on the rigid body. It follows that *the resultant of the external forces acting on the body is equal to the vector sum of the forces acting on all the particles of the body,* and it follows from this statement that *for a body rotating about a fixed axis the moment-sum of the external forces about the axis is equal to the moment-sum of all the forces acting on the particles about the axis.* Figure 15.13 shows the components of the resultant force acting on a particle of mass m_P at a

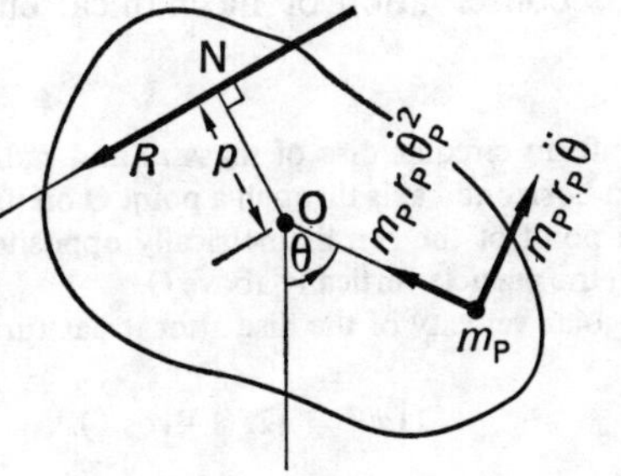

FIG. 15.13

distance r_P from the axis. These are $m_P r_P \dot{\theta}^2$ in a direction towards the axis and $m_P r_P \ddot{\theta}$ in a direction at right angles to this.

The work done by all such forces in a small angular displacement $\delta\theta$ of the body is approximately equal to

$$\Sigma(m_P r_P \ddot{\theta} \times r_P \delta\theta) = I\ddot{\theta}\delta\theta$$

and the total work done in a displacement from $\theta = \alpha$ to $\theta = \beta$ is therefore

$$I\int_{\alpha}^{\beta} \ddot{\theta}\,\mathrm{d}\theta = \left[\frac{I\dot{\theta}^2}{2}\right]_{\theta=\alpha}^{\theta=\beta}.$$

In Fig. 15.13, R is the resultant of the external forces acting on the body, including the weight of the body and the action of the hinge on the body. The line of action of R is assumed to be in the plane of rotation of the section of the body through R. The perpendicular from the axis through O on to the line of action of R meets it at N and ON $= p$. The work done by R in a small displacement $\delta\theta$ of the body is approximately $Rp\delta\theta$ and the total work done by R in the displacement from $\theta = \alpha$ to $\theta = \beta$ is $\int_{\alpha}^{\beta} L\,\mathrm{d}\theta$ where $L = Rp$ is the moment of R about the axis.

We state, therefore, that the work done by the external forces, $\int_{\alpha}^{\beta} L\,\mathrm{d}\theta$, is equal to the increase in kinetic energy $[I\dot{\theta}^2/2]_{\theta=\alpha}^{\theta=\beta}$ gained in the displacement from $\theta = \alpha$ to $\theta = \beta$. This statement includes the statement of the principle of conservation of mechanical energy with which this section begins.

Example 1. A uniform circular disc of mass m and radius a can turn freely in a vertical plane about a horizontal axis through a point O on its rim. A particle P of mass m is attached to the point of the rim diametrically opposite to O. The system is disturbed from rest with the particle vertically above O.

Show that the angular velocity of the disc after it has turned through an angle θ is given by

$$11a\dot{\theta}^2 = 12g(1-\cos\theta).$$

Find the magnitude of the force exerted by the disc on the particle when $\theta = \pi$. (L.)

The combined M. of I. of the disc and particle P about the axis of rotation is

$$\left(\frac{ma^2}{2}+ma^2\right)+m(2a)^2 = \frac{11ma^2}{2}.$$

The energy equation for the system when it has fallen through an angle θ from its initial position is therefore

$$\frac{1}{2}\frac{11ma^2}{2}\dot{\theta}^2+3mga\cos\theta = 3mga,$$

where potential energy is measured from a horizontal plane through O as origin.

$$\therefore\ 11a\dot{\theta}^2 = 12g(1-\cos\theta). \qquad (1)$$

The particle rotates about O in a circle of radius $2a$ and has, therefore, components of acceleration $2a\dot{\theta}^2$ towards O and $2a\ddot{\theta}$ perpendicular to OP. The acceleration of the particle is provided by the resultant of the force which the disc exerts on the particle and the weight of the particle. Differentiation of (1) with respect to t gives

$$11a\ddot{\theta} = 6g\sin\theta.$$

Therefore, when $\theta = \pi$, $\dot{\theta}^2 = 24g/(11a)$, $\ddot{\theta} = 0$ and the force exerted by the disc on the particle is a vertically upward force R where $R-mg = 2ma\dot{\theta}^2$.

Hence $$R = 2ma\dot{\theta}^2+mg = \frac{59mg}{11}$$

vertically upwards.

Example 2. A light inextensible string passes round the rim of a rough pulley, which is supported with its axis horizontal, and carries masses of 5 kg and 4·5 kg at its ends. It is found that the 5 kg mass descends a distance of 1·25 m from rest in 2·5 s. Assuming that the pulley is a uniform disc of radius 0·1 m and mass 2 kg, find the frictional couple, assumed constant, acting on the pulley at the supports.

If the string and masses are removed and the pulley is made to rotate at the rate of 4 revolutions per second, find how many revolutions it will make before coming to rest, assuming that the frictional couple is now reduced to 1/7 of its value when the masses are in motion.

Figure 15.14 shows the pulley and the masses with their respective velocities at the time when the angular displacement of the pulley from its initial position is θ. Because the string does not slip on the pulley, each of the speeds of the 5 kg mass downwards and that of the 4·5 kg mass upwards is equal to the linear speed of a point on the circumference of the pulley, i.e. $0{\cdot}1\dot{\theta}$ m/s. If each of the particles has moved a distance x m

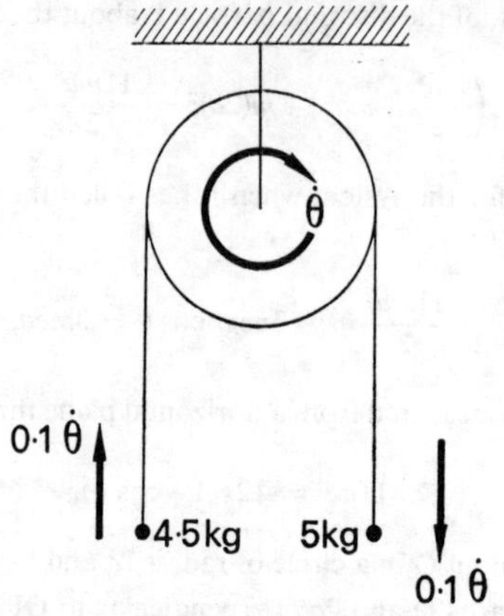

FIG. 15.14

from rest when the pulley has moved through an angle θ from rest, the energy equation for the motion is

$$\frac{1}{2}I\dot\theta^2+\frac{1}{2}\frac{9}{2}\frac{\dot\theta^2}{100}+\frac{1}{2}5\frac{\dot\theta^2}{100}-5gx+\frac{9}{2}gx+M\theta = 0,$$

where I kg m² is the M. of I. of the pulley about the axis, M joules is the frictional couple acting on the pulley, and $x = 0{\cdot}1\theta$.

Since
$$I = \tfrac{1}{2}\times 2\times(0{\cdot}1)^2 = 0{\cdot}01,$$

the energy equation reduces to

$$0{\cdot}0525\dot\theta^2+(M-0{\cdot}49)\theta = 0.$$

Differentiation with respect to t gives

$$0{\cdot}105\,\dot\theta\,\ddot\theta+(M-0{\cdot}49)\,\dot\theta = 0,$$

i.e.
$$0{\cdot}105\ddot\theta+(M-0{\cdot}49) = 0.$$

Therefore $\ddot\theta$ is constant and, since the masses each move 1·25 m from rest in 2·5 s,

$$\ddot x = 0{\cdot}4, \quad \ddot\theta = 4.$$

$$\therefore M = 0{\cdot}49-0{\cdot}42 = 0{\cdot}07.$$

The frictional couple acting on the pulley is 0·07 J.

$$4 \text{ rev/s} = 8\pi \text{ radians/s}.$$

Therefore, if a constant frictional couple of 0·01 J reduces the pulley to rest in n revolutions, the work-energy equation for the motion is

$$0{\cdot}01 \times 2n\pi = \tfrac{1}{2} \times 0{\cdot}01 \times (8\pi)^2.$$
$$\therefore\ n = 16\pi.$$

The pulley makes 16π revolutions before coming to rest.

Example 3. A uniform circular disc of mass M and radius a is free to rotate about a horizontal axis through its centre normal to its plane. A particle P of mass m is placed on the rim of the disc at its highest point, the coefficient of friction between P and the disc being μ. The system is slightly disturbed from rest, and θ is the angle turned through by the disc at time t. Show that, so long as there is no relative motion between P and the disc,

$$(M+2m)a(d\theta/dt)^2 = 4mg(1-\cos\theta)$$

and

$$(M+2m)a(d^2\theta/dt^2) = 2mg\sin\theta.$$

Find the radial and tangential components of the force exerted on P by the disc. Deduce that P will slip before it loses contact with the disc and show that slipping will occur when

$$M\sin\theta = \mu\{(M+6m)\cos\theta - 4m\}. \qquad \text{(N.)}$$

Figure 15.15 shows the forces acting on the particle when the disc has turned through an angle θ.

The energy equation for the system is

$$\tfrac{1}{2}I\dot{\theta}^2 = mga(1-\cos\theta),$$

where

$$I = \frac{Ma^2}{2} + ma^2.$$

$$\therefore\ (M+2m)a\dot{\theta}^2 = 4mg(1-\cos\theta). \qquad (1)$$

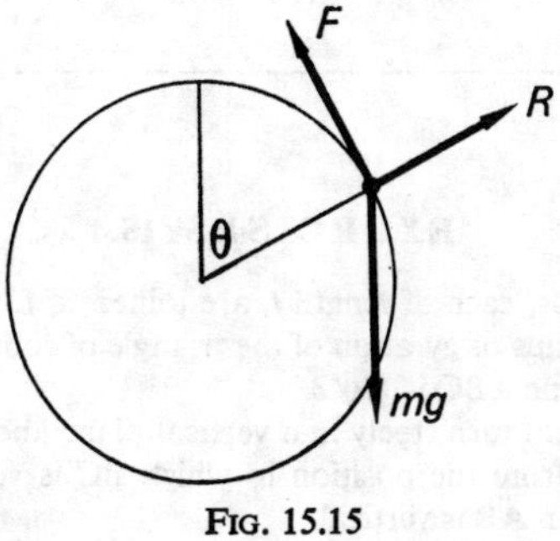

FIG. 15.15

Differentiating with respect to t we have

$$2(M+2m)a\dot{\theta}\ddot{\theta} = 4mg\,\dot{\theta}\sin\theta.$$

$$\therefore\ (M+2m)a\ddot{\theta} = 2mg\sin\theta. \qquad (2)$$

The equations of motion for the particle are,
in the radial direction

$$R = mg\cos\theta - ma\dot{\theta}^2$$

$$= mg\cos\theta - \frac{4m^2g(1-\cos\theta)}{M+2m} \quad \text{[from (1)]}, \qquad (3)$$

in the tangential direction

$$F = mg\sin\theta - ma\ddot{\theta}$$

$$= mg\sin\theta - \frac{2m^2g\sin\theta}{M+2m} \quad \text{[from (2)]}. \qquad (4)$$

$$\therefore\ R = \frac{mg\{(M+6m)\cos\theta - 4m\}}{M+2m},$$

$$F = \frac{Mmg\sin\theta}{M+2m}.$$

Hence F increases and R decreases as θ increases and so the ratio F/R, as given by these values, increases from 0 to ∞ as θ increases from 0 to $\cos^{-1}\{4m/(M+6m)\}$. But for equilibrium $F/R \leqq \mu$, and so F/R will equal the finite value μ before R becomes zero and the particle slips before leaving the disc.

When the particle slips $F/R = \mu$,

i.e.
$$\frac{Mmg\sin\theta}{M+2m} \Big/ \left[\frac{mg\{(M+6m)\cos\theta-4m\}}{M+2m}\right] = \mu.$$

$$\therefore\ M\sin\theta = \mu\{(M+6m)\cos\theta - 4m\}.$$

EXERCISES 15.4

1. Three uniform rods, each of length l, are joined to form an equilateral triangle ABC. Prove that the radius of gyration of the triangle of rods about an axis through A perpendicular to the plane ABC is $\frac{1}{2}l\sqrt{2}$.

The triangle, which can turn freely in a vertical plane about a fixed horizontal axis through A, is released from the position in which BC is vertical and C is above B. Find the speed of B when AB is vertical.

2. A heavy thin uniform rod AB of length 1 m and mass 6 kg has a particle of mass 1 kg attached to it at B. The rod can rotate in a vertical plane about a smooth pivot at A. It is released from rest with B vertically above A. Find the force between the mass and the rod when B is vertically below A.

3. A flywheel is mounted on a horizontal axle of diameter 0·2 m which can turn freely. A thin string is wrapped round the axle, one end being fixed to the axle. The other end of the string hangs vertically and carries a mass of 2 kg which is allowed to move from rest. The mass is observed to move through 1 m in 10 s. Calculate the angular velocity acquired by the flywheel in this time and use the principle of energy to calculate the combined moment of inertia of the flywheel and axle.

If at the end of the 10 s the 2 kg mass falls off, find what constant braking couple will bring the flywheel to rest in 6 s more.

4. Calculate I for a flywheel of mass M in the form of a disc of uniform thickness and radius a.

The flywheel is rotating at the rate of n revolutions per minute, and is braked by a constant force F applied tangentially to the rim. Find the number of revolutions of the wheel before it is brought to rest.

5. Find the moment of inertia of a uniform circular disc of mass M and radius a, about an axis perpendicular to its plane through a given point of its rim.

This axis is fixed horizontally and the disc rotates freely about it in a vertical plane. If the greatest angular velocity of the disc is $\sqrt{(3g/a)}$, find its least angular velocity. (L.)

6. A uniform circular disc of radius 1 m is pivoted about a horizontal axis through its centre perpendicular to its plane. A particle of twice the mass of the disc is fixed to a point P on the disc 0·5 m from the axis. The disc is held with P almost vertically above the axis, and then released. Find the maximum angular velocity of the disc in the subsequent motion.

7. One end of a uniform rod of length l is smoothly hinged to a fixed point. While it is hanging freely, the rod is given an angular velocity $\sqrt{(6g/l)}$. Show that it describes a complete circle. (L.)

8. A uniform semicircular lamina, of radius a, can swing freely in a vertical plane about one end of its bounding diameter AB. Show that, if the lamina is released from rest when AB is horizontal and lowermost, its angular velocity when AB is again horizontal is

$$\frac{4}{3}\sqrt{\left(\frac{2g}{\pi a}\right)}.$$

[The centre of gravity of the lamina is distant $4a/3\pi$ from AB.] (L.)

9. Two uniform rods AB and CD, of lengths $2a$ and a respectively, are each of the same mass per unit length. The rods are rigidly joined together at right angles so that C coincides with the mid-point of AB. If the system is pivoted at D so that it can move in a vertical plane, and it starts to move from rest with AB vertical, prove that when this rod is horizontal the angular velocity of the system is $\sqrt{(5g/3a)}$. (L.)

10. Find the moment of inertia of a uniform rod AB, of mass m and length $2l$, about one end.

The rod is freely hinged to a fixed point at A, and a particle of mass M is fixed to the end B. If the rod is just displaced from the position of unstable equilibrium in which B is vertically above A, show that the angular velocity ω of the rod when it becomes horizontal is given by

$$\omega^2 = \frac{3(m+2M)}{2(m+3M)} \cdot \frac{g}{l}. \qquad \text{(O.C.)}$$

11. A uniform disc, of diameter 2·4 m, is mounted on a smooth horizontal axle of negligible diameter, the disc being in a vertical plane and the axle at a distance of 0·1 m from the centre of the disc. If the disc is allowed to move from rest in the unstable position of equilibrium, find its greatest angular velocity in the subsequent motion.

12. Find the moment of inertia of a uniform circular disc, of mass M and radius a, about an axis perpendicular to its plane through its centre.

This axis is fixed horizontally and the disc can rotate freely about it in a vertical plane. A particle of mass m is attached to the disc at a distance $\frac{1}{2}a$ from the centre, and in one revolution the greatest and least angular velocities of the disc are $\sqrt{(g/4a)}$ and $\sqrt{(g/8a)}$, respectively. Show that $m/M = 2/63$. (L.)

13. Prove that the moment of inertia of a uniform circular disc of mass M and radius a about the axis through its centre normal to its plane is $\frac{1}{2}Ma^2$.

The disc is mounted so as to be free to revolve without friction about the axis, which is fixed horizontally. A particle P of mass m is attached to the highest point of the disc, and the system is slightly disturbed from rest. Show that the angular momentum at the instant when P is vertically below the centre of the disc is $\sqrt{[2m(M+2m)ga^3]}$. At this instant a constant retarding couple is applied so that the disc comes to rest after rotating through a further 60°. Find the magnitude of the couple. (N.)

14. A uniform rod, of weight W and of length $2a$, is pivoted at one end. It is released from rest when it is horizontal and the only resistance to motion is a constant friction couple of magnitude $3Wa/5\pi$. Show that it will rise through an angle of 60° on the other side of the vertical and find its angular velocity when it is vertical for the first time. (N.)

15. Prove that the moment of inertia of a uniform circular disc of radius a and mass M, about an axis OQ through the centre O and perpendicular to the plane of the disc, is $\frac{1}{2}Ma^2$.

The circular disc can rotate freely about the axis OQ, which is horizontal. A light inextensible string is wound round the rim with one end attached to the rim; to the other end is attached a particle P, of mass m, which hangs vertically. When the system is released from rest prove, by the principle of conservation of energy, that the velocity of P, when it has descended through a distance b, is

$$2\sqrt{\left(\frac{bmg}{M+2m}\right)}.$$

Find also the tension in the string. (O.C.)

16. Prove that the moment of inertia of a uniform rod AB, of length $2a$ and mass M, about an axis through the end A and perpendicular to AB is $\frac{4}{3}Ma^2$.

AB is welded to a uniform circular disc of radius a and mass M, its end A coinciding with the centre O of the disc and AB being in the plane of the disc. The system can rotate freely about a horizontal axis through O and perpendicular to the plane of the disc. Prove that, if the system is released from rest when AB is horizontal, then

$$\omega^2 = \frac{12g}{11a} \sin \theta,$$

where θ denotes the angle between AB and the horizontal and ω is the angular velocity.

Prove also that the angular acceleration is greatest when AB is horizontal. (O.C.)

17. Four thin uniform rigid rods, each of mass m and length $2a$, are joined together at their ends to form a rigid square frame ABCD which can turn freely about a fixed horizontal axis through A perpendicular to the plane ABCD. Show that the moment of inertia of the frame about this axis is $40ma^2/3$.

The frame executes complete revolutions. If the greatest and least angular velocities are $(1+p)\omega$ and $(1-p)\omega$, where $0 < p < 1$, show that

$$10pa\omega^2 = 3\sqrt{2}g. \qquad \text{(N.)}$$

15.5. The Compound Pendulum

A rigid body constrained to rotate about a fixed horizontal axis and making small oscillations under gravity about its position of stable equilibrium is called a *compound pendulum*.

The Period of Small Oscillations of a Compound Pendulum

Figure 15.16 represents a rigid body of mass M rotating about a horizontal axis through P and displaced through an angle θ from its position of stable equilibrium. G is the centre of mass of the body, PG $= h$, and the M. of I. of the body about the axis is I.

The energy equation is

$$\tfrac{1}{2}I\dot{\theta}^2 - Mgh\cos\theta = C,$$

where C is constant and potential energy is measured with reference to a horizontal plane through P as origin. Differentiation of the energy equation with respect to t gives

$$I\dot{\theta}\ddot{\theta} + Mgh\sin\theta\,\dot{\theta} = 0.$$

$$\therefore\ \ddot{\theta} = -\frac{Mgh\sin\theta}{I}.$$

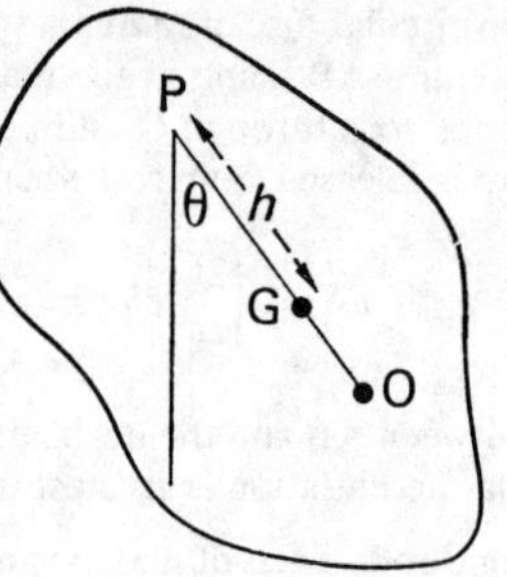

FIG. 15.16

If θ is small and terms involving higher powers of θ than the second are neglected, this equation becomes

$$\ddot{\theta} \approx -\frac{Mgh}{I}\theta.$$

This is the equation of an approximate SHM of period

$$T = 2\pi\sqrt{\left(\frac{I}{Mgh}\right)}. \tag{15.10}$$

If k is the radius of gyration of the body about an axis parallel to the given axis and through G, then $I = M(k^2+h^2)$ and the formula for the period of small oscillations becomes

$$T = 2\pi\sqrt{\left(\frac{k^2+h^2}{gh}\right)}. \tag{15.11}$$

The length l of the equivalent simple pendulum is thus given by the equation

$$l = \frac{k^2+h^2}{h}. \tag{15.12}$$

The centre of oscillation. If O is the point in PG produced such that $GO = k^2/h$ and the pendulum makes small oscillations about a horizontal axis through O, the length of the E.S.P. is

$$\left(k^2+\frac{k^4}{h^2}\right)\bigg/\frac{k^2}{h} = \frac{k^2+h^2}{h}.$$

The period of small oscillations of the pendulum about the axis through O is therefore the same as the period of small oscillations about the axis through P. The point O is called the *Centre of Oscillation* corresponding to P. Note that OP has the length of the E.S.P. about either axis.

There are also two points P′ and O′ in PG and on opposite sides of G from P and O so that GP′ = GP and GO′ = GO about a horizontal axis through each of which the period of small oscillations is the same as that about the axis through P.

The Minimum Period of Small Oscillations as the Position of the Axis Varies

The period of small oscillations $2\pi\sqrt{[(k^2+h^2)/gh]}$ is a minimum when $(k^2+h^2)/h$ is a minimum, i.e. if

$$\frac{d}{dh}\left(\frac{k^2}{h}+h\right) \text{ is zero and } \frac{d^2}{dh^2}\left(\frac{k^2}{h}+h\right) > 0.$$

These conditions are satisfied when $h = k$. The period of oscillation is therefore a minimum when the distance between the axis and the centre of gravity of the body is equal to its radius of gyration about a parallel axis through the centre of gravity.

Example 1. A compound pendulum consists of a uniform rod CD, of mass m and length $2a$, rigidly clamped at its centre O to a similar rod AB; the rods are at right angles and OA = x. Find the length of the equivalent simple pendulum for free oscillations in the plane of the rods about a horizontal axis through A.

Find the values of x for which the length of the equivalent simple pendulum is unaltered by removal of the rod CD. (L.)

The M. of I. of AB about the axis is $\frac{4}{3}ma^2$, Fig. 15.17. The M. of I. of CD about the axis is $\frac{1}{3}ma^2+mx^2$.

Therefore the total M. of I. of the pendulum about the axis is

$$\frac{5ma^2}{3}+mx^2.$$

Therefore, in the usual notation,

$$k^2+h^2 = \left(\frac{5ma^2}{3}+mx^2\right)\Big/2m = \frac{5a^2+3x^2}{6}.$$

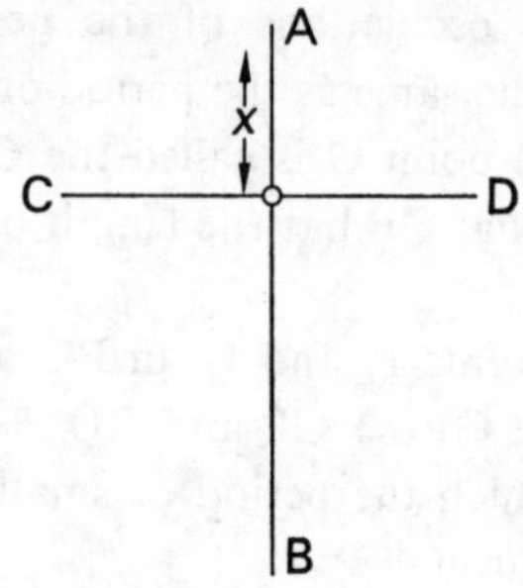

FIG. 15.17

Also $$h = (ma+mx)/(2m) = \tfrac{1}{2}(a+x).$$

Therefore the length of the E.S.P. is $(5a^2+3x^2)/\{3(a+x)\}$.

When the rod CD is removed the length of the E.S.P. is $4a/3$. The length of the E.S.P. is therefore unaltered by the removal of CD if

$$\frac{5a^2+3x^2}{3(a+x)} = \frac{4a}{3}, \quad \text{i.e. if} \quad 3x^2-4ax+a^2 = 0,$$

$$\text{i.e. if} \quad x = a \quad \text{or} \quad \tfrac{1}{3}a.$$

Example 2. A uniform circular disc, of mass m and radius a, can turn freely in its own vertical plane about a horizontal axis through a point O on the rim. A particle of mass $2m$ is attached to the disc at P, where P is on the diameter through O, and $OP = x$. Show that the period of small oscillations of the whole system is the same as that of a simple pendulum of length l, given by

$$l = \frac{3a^2+4x^2}{2(a+2x)}.$$

Show also that $a \leq l \leq 1{\cdot}9a$. (N.)

The M. of I. about the axis is $(3ma^2/2)+2mx^2$. Fig. 15.18 (i). Therefore in the usual notation

$$k^2+h^2 = (3ma^2+4mx^2)/(6m) = (3a^2+4x^2)/6,$$
$$h = (ma+2mx)/(3m) = (a+2x)/3.$$

$$\therefore\ l = \frac{k^2+h^2}{h} = \frac{3a^2+4x^2}{2(a+2x)}.$$

The stationary value of l occurs when $dl/dx = 0$ for positive values of x.

$$\frac{dl}{dx} = \frac{(2x+3a)(2x-a)}{(a+2x)^2},$$

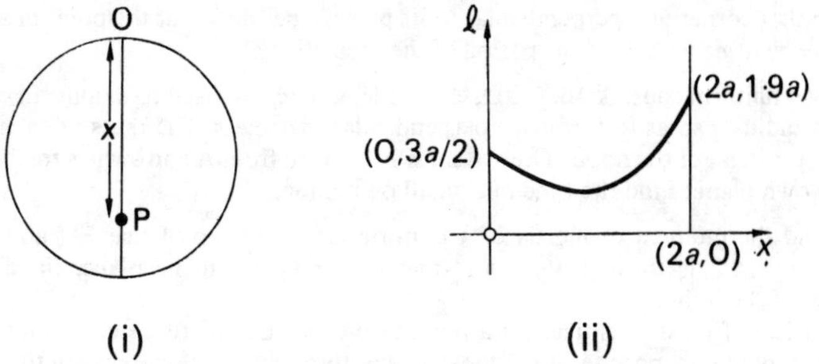

FIG. 15.18

and therefore l is stationary when $x = \frac{1}{2}a$, $l = a$. This stationary value of l is a minimum value because dl/dx is negative for $-3a/2 < x < \frac{1}{2}a$ and positive for $x > \frac{1}{2}a$.

Figure 15.18 (ii) is a sketch of the graph of l against x for physically possible values of x. This sketch shows that the greatest value of l for values of x in the range $0 \leqq x \leqq 2a$ is the value of l when $x = 2a$, i.e. $1{\cdot}9a$.

$$\therefore\ a \leqq l \leqq 1{\cdot}9a.$$

EXERCISES 15.5

1. Four uniform thin rods, each of mass m and length $2a$, are joined rigidly together to form a square frame of side $2a$. Show that the moment of inertia of the frame about a horizontal axis through the mid-point of one of the rods and perpendicular to the plane of the frame is $28ma^2/3$. The frame performs, under gravity, small oscillations in its plane about this axis. Find the period of these oscillations. (L.)

2. Find the moment of inertia of a uniform thin rod, of mass m and length $2a$, about an axis through one end perpendicular to its length.

If such a rod is pivoted freely about an end, so that it can execute small oscillations in a vertical plane, find the period of these oscillations. Hence determine the length of the rod, in metres, if this period is to be 1 second. (L.)

3. Three particles of the same mass m are fixed to a uniform circular hoop of mass M and radius a at the corners of an equilateral triangle. The hoop is free to swing in a vertical plane about any point in its circumference. Prove that the equivalent simple pendulum is equal in length to the diameter of the circle. (O.C.)

4. Four equal uniform rods, each of mass M and length $2l$, form a rigid square frame. Prove that the moment of inertia about an axis through the centre of the frame and perpendicular to its plane is $16Ml^2/3$.

The frame is suspended by one corner and makes small oscillations about an axis through that corner and perpendicular to its plane. The friction at the point of suspension may be neglected. Find the period of the oscillations. (O.C.)

5. Two uniform rods, AOB, COD, each of length $2a$, are fixed to a uniform circular hoop of radius a so as to form two perpendicular diameters. The mass of each rod is equal to the mass of the hoop. The system is suspended from A and swings freely about A in its own plane. Find the time of a small oscillation. (O.C.)

6. Find the moment of inertia of a uniform circular hoop of mass M and radius a (i) about an axis through its centre and perpendicular to its plane, (ii) about a diameter of the hoop.

A particle of mass m is fixed to a point A on the circumference of this hoop and O is the point at the opposite end of the diameter through A. The system can turn freely about a horizontal axis through O and perpendicular to the plane of the hoop. Prove that the periodic time of small oscillations of the system about its position of stable equilibrium is $2\pi\sqrt{(2a/g)}$. (N.)

7. A uniform rod, of mass m and length $2a$, is rigidly fastened at its middle point A to a uniform circular disc, of mass M and radius a, so that the rod is in the plane of the disc and tangential to it. If the system can swing freely in the vertical plane of the disc about a horizontal axis through the point O, which is on the circumference of the disc at the other end of the diameter passing through A, prove that the periodic time of a small oscillation is

$$2\pi\sqrt{\left(\frac{9M+26m}{6M+12m}\cdot\frac{a}{g}\right)}. \qquad \text{(N.)}$$

8. A uniform circular disc of radius a has a particle of mass equal to that of the disc fixed to a point of its circumference. The disc can turn freely about a fixed horizontal axis through its centre at right angles to its plane. Assuming that the radius of gyration of the disc about this axis is $a/\sqrt{2}$, show that the length of the equivalent simple pendulum for small oscillations of the system about its position of stable equilibrium is $3a/2$. (O.C.)

9. A thin uniform wire is in the form of a semicircular arc of radius a. Find its radius of gyration about an axis through one end perpendicular to its plane. The wire is free to swing about this axis which is horizontal. Find the period of small oscillations about the position of stable equilibrium.

If the wire is slightly disturbed from its position of unstable equilibrium find the angular velocity with which it passes through its position of stable equilibrium. (L.)

10. A uniform circular disc of radius a swings in its own plane about a point of its circumference. Prove that the length of the equivalent simple pendulum is $3a/2$.

If any point of the disc may be taken as the point of suspension, prove that the time of a small oscillation is least when the distance of the point of suspension from the centre of the disc is $a/\sqrt{2}$. (O.C.)

11. Prove that the moment of inertia of a uniform thin rod of mass m and length $2a$ about an axis through its middle point perpendicular to its length is $ma^2/3$.

If such a rod is pivoted freely about a point of its length at distance x from its middle point so that it can oscillate in a vertical plane, find the length of the equivalent simple pendulum and determine the value of x in order that this shall be as small as possible. (L.)

12. A thin uniform wire of length $6a$ is bent into the form of a plane rectangle ABCD whose longer side, AB, is of length $2a$. Find the radius of gyration about (i) AB and (ii) XY (the line joining the mid-points of AB and CD).

Hence, or otherwise, find the length of the equivalent simple pendulum, for small oscillations of the rectangle under gravity in a vertical plane about a horizontal axis through X. (L.)

13. A compound pendulum consists of a thin uniform rigid rod of length $2a$ and mass m, with a heavy particle of mass $2m$ at its middle point. Show that there are two points of suspension on each side of the mid-point of the rod, about each of which the small oscillations will have the same period as those of a simple pendulum of length a, and show that the distance between these points is $0{\cdot}745a$ approximately. (N.)

14. Find the moment of inertia of a uniform thin circular disc, of radius a and mass m, about an axis through its centre perpendicular to its plane.

Two such discs, in the same plane, have their centres connected by a light rigid bar of length $4a$. Find the period of small oscillations in a vertical plane, when the system is freely pivoted at a point of the bar distant x from its middle point.

For what value of x is this period least? (L.)

15. A thin uniform rod AB, of mass m and length $2a$, can turn freely in a vertical plane about a fixed horizontal axis through the end A. A uniform thin circular disc, of mass $24m$ and radius $\frac{1}{3}a$, has its centre C clamped to the rod so that AC $= x$ and the plane of the disc passes through the axis of rotation. Show that the moment of inertia of the system about this axis is $2m(a^2+12x^2)$.

The system oscillates under gravity. Write down the energy equation when AB makes an angle θ with the downward vertical. Find the period T of small oscillations. Show that, if x is varied, the least value of T is $2\pi(a/2g)^{1/2}$. (N.)

16. A uniform rod AB, of length $2l$ and mass M, is welded to a uniform circular disc, of radius $a\ (< 2l)$ and mass M, in the plane of the disc and with the end B coinciding with the centre of the disc. The system can rotate freely in a vertical plane about a horizontal axis through A perpendicular to the plane of the disc. If θ denotes the angle between AB and the downward vertical and the system is released from rest when $\theta = \alpha$, prove that the angular velocity ω of the system in the subsequent motion is given by

$$(32l^2+3a^2)\omega^2 = 36gl(\cos\theta-\cos\alpha).$$

Find also the period of small oscillations if $4l = 3a$. (O.C.)

17. Show that the moment of inertia of a uniform thin rod OA, of mass m and length a, about an axis OB is $\frac{1}{3}ma^2\sin^2\theta$, where θ is the angle AOB.

Two uniform metal rods AC, BC, each of mass m and length a are welded together at C to form a letter V with angle 60°. If the system is pivoted freely at A and B to a horizontal axis, find the period of small oscillations about the position of equilibrium. (N.)

18. A mass m is attached to the centre of a uniform square lamina of side $2a$ and mass M. A circle of radius x and centre the centre of the lamina is marked on it and the system can turn freely in a vertical plane about a horizontal axis through any point on the circle. Show that the period of small oscillations about the axis is independent of the position of the point on the circle.

Find also the value of m/M if this time is least when $x = a/\sqrt{2}$. (L.)

19. A lamina, of mass M, rotates freely about a horizontal axis through O and perpendicular to the lamina; the centre of gravity, G, of the lamina is at a distance h from O; OG is produced to L at a distance l from O, and at L a particle of mass m is attached. Prove that if, at time t, OG makes an angle θ with the downward vertical, then

$$(I+ml^2)\dot{\theta}^2-2g(Mh+ml)\cos\theta = C,$$

where C is a constant.

Hence find the period, P, of small oscillations about the axis.

When the particle is detached it is found that the period of small oscillations is again P; prove that

$$I = Mhl. \qquad \text{(O.C.)}$$

20. (i) The lengths of the equivalent simple pendulums corresponding to oscillations of a rigid body about parallel horizontal axes AP and BQ whose plane passes through the centre of gravity G are a and b respectively. The axes are on the same side of G, with BQ nearer to G, and are at a distance d apart. Show that the distance of G from the axis BQ is $d(a-d)/(2d-a+b)$.

(ii) A uniform square lamina is of side a and mass m. Find the period of small oscillations of the lamina under gravity about a horizontal line perpendicular to the lamina and passing through a corner of the square. (L.)

15.6. The Equation of Motion for a Rigid Body Rotating about a Fixed Axis

We have shown in § 15.4 that the moment-sum about the axis of the external forces acting on a rigid body rotating about a fixed axis is equal to the moment-sum about that axis of all the forces acting on the particles which constitute the rigid body. In the notation we have used in § 15.4, we now state the equation of motion for a rigid body rotating about a fixed axis.

$$\text{The moment of the external forces about the axis} = \Sigma(m_P r_P^2 \ddot{\theta}) = I\ddot{\theta}. \qquad (15.13)$$

The relation between the work-energy equation and the equation of motion. The equation of motion can be derived from the energy equation when the body is moving freely under gravity, or from the work-energy equation when there are other external forces acting on the body, by differentiation with respect to time. Thus we derived the equation of motion from the energy equation for the compound pendulum in § 15.5. Conversely we could derive the energy equation from the equation of motion by integration. As a result of this interrelation between the two equations we have, in many problems, a choice of methods between the approach through energy and the approach through the equation of motion. Either of the examples which follow could be solved from the work-energy principle.

Example 1. A wheel and axle can rotate freely about a fixed horizontal axis. A light cord, wound round the axle which is of radius r, carries a mass M hanging at its free end. If, when the system is allowed to move from rest, the mass M moves through a distance H in a time t_0, show that the moment of inertia of the wheel and axle about its axis is

$$\frac{Mr^2}{2H}(gt_0^2 - 2H). \qquad \text{(L.)}$$

Figure 15.19 shows the forces acting on the wheel and axle and the forces acting on the mass M. We denote the angular acceleration of the wheel and axle by $\ddot{\theta}$. Since the string does not slip on the axle the linear acceleration of the mass M is equal to the linear acceleration of a point on the circumference of the axle, i.e. $r\ddot{\theta}$.

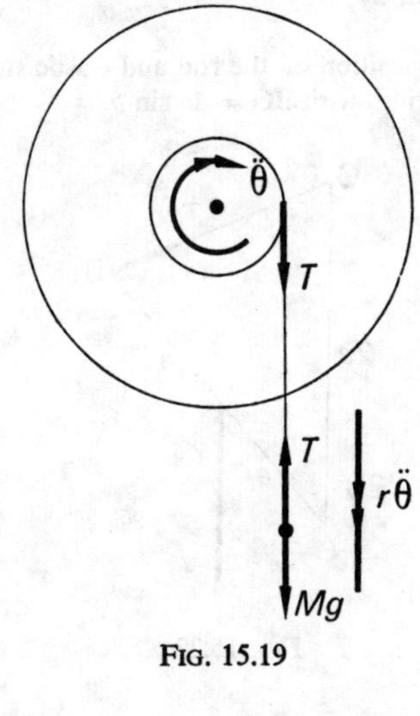

FIG. 15.19

The equation of motion for the mass M is

$$Mg - T = Mr\ddot{\theta}.$$

The equation of motion for the wheel and axle is

$$Tr = I\ddot{\theta},$$

where I is the M. of I. of the wheel and axle.

From these equations, eliminating T, $\ddot{\theta} = Mgr/(I+Mr^2)$. Since $\ddot{\theta}$ is constant and M moves through a distance H in time t_0,

$$H = \frac{\frac{1}{2}Mgr^2}{I+Mr^2}t_0^2.$$

$$\therefore\ IH = \tfrac{1}{2}Mgr^2t_0^2 - HMr^2.$$

$$\therefore\ I = \frac{Mr^2}{2H}(gt_0^2 - 2H).$$

Example 2. A uniform rod AB of length $2a$ and mass m is freely pivoted to a fixed point at A. One end of a light elastic string of natural length a and modulus mg is attached to B and the other to a fixed point C distant $2a$ vertically above A. Denoting the angle BAC by 2θ show that there is a position of equilibrium in which $\theta = \alpha$ where $3 \sin \alpha = 1$.

Calculate the moment of the forces about A when $\theta = \alpha + \varepsilon$, and by approximating to the first order in ε, where ε is small, show that the period of small oscillations of the rod in the plane BAC is $2\pi(a/2g)^{1/2}$. (N.)

Figure 15.20 shows the position of the rod and elastic string when $\angle$ BAC $= 2\theta$ and the system is in equilibrium with BC $= 4a \sin \theta$.

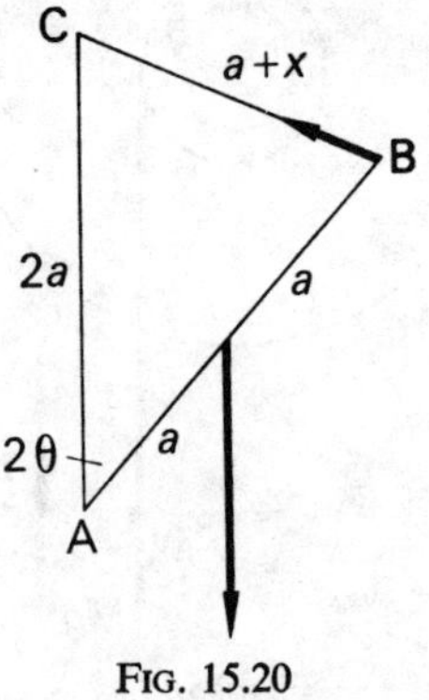

FIG. 15.20

The forces acting on the rod are the tension in the elastic string, the weight of the rod and the action of the hinge on the rod. The sum of the moments about A of the forces acting on the rod is zero.

$$\therefore\ amg\sin 2\theta = \frac{mg(4a\sin\theta - a)}{a}\,2a\cos\theta.$$

$$\therefore\ \sin 2\theta = 8\sin\theta\cos\theta - 2\cos\theta.$$

$$\therefore\ 2\sin\theta\cos\theta = 8\sin\theta\cos\theta - 2\cos\theta.$$

$$\therefore\ 2\cos\theta(3\sin\theta - 1) = 0.$$

Therefore there is a position of equilibrium in which $\theta = \alpha$ where $3\sin\alpha = 1$. When $\theta = \alpha+\varepsilon$, the sum of the moments of the forces about A is

$$mga\sin 2(\alpha+\varepsilon) - \frac{mg\{4a\sin(\alpha+\varepsilon) - a\}\,2a\cos(\alpha+\varepsilon)}{a}$$

$$= mga\sin 2\alpha\cos 2\varepsilon + mga\cos 2\alpha\sin 2\varepsilon$$
$$- mg(4\sin\alpha\cos\varepsilon + 4\cos\alpha\sin\varepsilon - 1)(2a\cos\alpha\cos\varepsilon - 2a\sin\alpha\sin\varepsilon).$$

Therefore, when ε is small so that $\sin\varepsilon \approx \varepsilon$, $\sin 2\varepsilon \approx 2\varepsilon$, $\cos\varepsilon \approx \cos 2\varepsilon \approx 1$, the sum of the moments of the forces about A is approximately

$$mga(\sin 2\alpha + 2\varepsilon\cos 2\alpha) - mga(4\sin\alpha + 4\varepsilon\cos\alpha - 1)(2\cos\alpha - 2\varepsilon\sin\alpha).$$

But $\sin\alpha = \dfrac{1}{3}$; $\therefore\ \cos\alpha = \dfrac{2\sqrt{2}}{3}$, $\sin 2\alpha = \dfrac{4\sqrt{2}}{9}$ and $\cos 2\alpha = \dfrac{7}{9}$.

Therefore the sum of the moments of the forces about A is approximately

$$mga\left(\frac{4\sqrt{2}}{9} - \frac{16\sqrt{2}}{9} + \frac{12\sqrt{2}}{9}\right) - mga\varepsilon\left(-8\cdot\frac{1}{9} + 8\cdot\frac{8}{9} + \frac{2}{3} - \frac{14}{9}\right) = -\frac{16mga\varepsilon}{3}.$$

Hence

$$(2\ddot{\varepsilon}) \approx \frac{-\dfrac{16mga\varepsilon}{3}}{\dfrac{4ma^2}{3}} = -\frac{2g(2\varepsilon)}{a}.$$

The motion is therefore approximately SHM of period

$$T = 2\pi\sqrt{\left(\frac{a}{2g}\right)}.$$

EXERCISES 15.6

1. Two masses of 1·3 kg and 1·2 kg are hung at the ends of a light inextensible string which passes over a pulley, in the form of a uniform thin circular disc, free to rotate about a fixed horizontal axle. If the mass of the pulley is 0·3 kg and the pulley sufficiently rough to prevent the string slipping, show that the acceleration of the masses is $2g/53$.

2. A wheel and axle has a moment of inertia I about its axis which is fixed horizontally and about which it can turn freely. Light strings are wrapped round the wheel and the axle and masses m_1, m_2 hang from their respective free ends. If the radius of the wheel is a and that of the axle is b, show that, after the system is released from rest, its angular acceleration is

$$\frac{(m_1a-m_2b)g}{m_1a^2+m_2b^2+I}$$

until one string is fully unwound. (L.)

3. A wheel of radius 0·2 m can rotate in a vertical plane about a fixed smooth horizontal axis which passes through the centre of the wheel. A light inextensible string which passes over the wheel carries at its ends masses of 1 kg and 0·5 kg the parts of the string not in contact with the wheel being vertical. The heavier particle is observed to descend from rest through 0·4 m in 1 s. Assuming that the string does not slip on the wheel, show that the moment of inertia of the wheel about the axis of rotation is 0·185 kg m² approximately.

4. A uniform circular disc, of mass m and radius a, is free to rotate without friction about a horizontal axis OA through its centre O and perpendicular to its plane. One end of a light string is attached to a point on the circumference of the disc and part of the string is wound on the circumference. The other end of the string carries a particle of mass km hanging freely. The system is released from rest. Show that, when the disc has rotated through an angle θ, the velocity of the particle will be

$$2\{kga\,\theta/(1+2k)\}^{1/2}.$$

Find the tension in the vertical part of the string. (N.)

5. A pulley, of mass M and radius a, can rotate freely about a horizontal axis through its centre and perpendicular to its plane. A string, placed over the pulley, supports two particles of masses $2M$ and M, the pulley being sufficiently rough to prevent the string from slipping. The system is released from rest with the particles hanging vertically; prove that, when the pulley has rotated through an angle θ, its angular velocity ω is given by the formula

$$7a\omega^2 = 4g\theta.$$

Show also that the tension of that part of the string supporting the mass of $2M$ is $\frac{10}{7}Mg$. (O.C.)

6. A circular disc of mass M and radius a is free to turn in its own plane (which is vertical) about a horizontal axis through its centre. A light string passes over the disc and masses M and $\frac{1}{2}M$ hang at its ends. The free portions of the string are vertical, and there is no slipping of the string over the disc. Show that the acceleration of the masses is $\frac{1}{4}g$. (O.C.)

7. A pulley consists of a uniform circular disc of mass 100 g and radius 3 cm mounted on a smooth horizontal axle. A string passing over the pulley has masses of 400 g and 300 g attached to its ends. The string does not slip on the pulley. Find the acceleration of the larger mass when the system is released from rest.

If the pulley, instead of being on a smooth axle, is subject to a frictional retarding couple of amount 5×10^{-3} J, find the work done on the system by gravity and friction when the larger mass descends 1 cm. Hence deduce the acceleration in this case.

8. A light inextensible string, carrying masses M and m ($< M$), passes over a uniform solid pulley, of mass $2m$, which can rotate freely about a fixed horizontal axis through its centre O and perpendicular to its plane; the groove of the pulley is sufficiently rough to prevent the string from slipping. The system is released from rest when the mass M is at a distance b vertically below O. Prove that, when the mass M is at a distance x below O,

$$(M+2m)\,\dot{x}^2 = 2(M-m)\,g(x-b).$$

Hence find the ratio of the tensions in the parts of the string carrying the masses M and m. (O.C.)

*15.7. The Force Exerted on the Axis of Rotation

In § 14.8 of the last chapter (Vol. I) we established the fact that the motion of the centre of mass of two particles of masses m_1 and m_2 is the same as that of a single particle of mass (m_1+m_2) under the action of a force which is the vector sum of the external forces acting on the system of two particles. This result can be generalized to refer to the aggregate of particles constituting a rigid body.

In the case of a rigid body of mass M rotating in a vertical plane under gravity about a fixed horizontal axis, Fig. 15.21, the external forces acting on the body are its weight and the action of the hinge upon it. If the components of this force are X, Y in directions at right angles to and along GP, then, since the corresponding accelerations of G are $h\ddot{\theta}$ and $h\dot{\theta}^2$,

$$X - Mg\sin\theta = Mh\ddot{\theta}, \tag{15.14}$$

$$Y - Mg\cos\theta = Mh\dot{\theta}^2. \tag{15.15}$$

Together with the energy equation and the initial (boundary) condi-

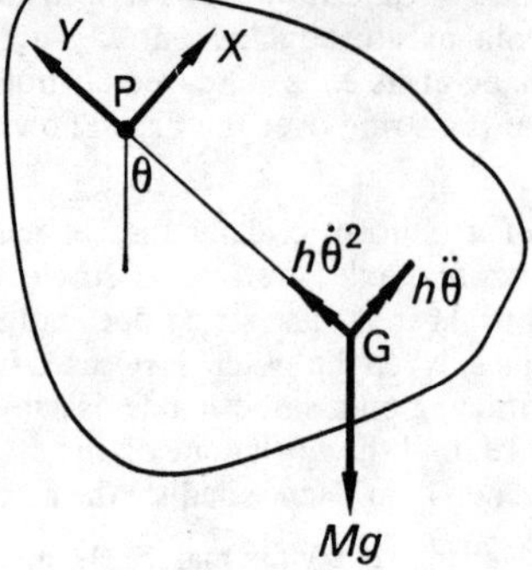

FIG. 15.21

tions these two equations are sufficient to determine X and Y. In practice the use of the equation of motion discussed in § 15.6 obviates the necessity of differentiating the energy equation and may shorten the calculation.

Example 1. A thin uniform rod swings in a vertical plane about a smooth pivot at one end, through an angle $\frac{1}{2}\pi$ on each side of the vertical. Prove that when the rod makes an angle θ with the vertical, the reaction on the pivot makes an angle φ with the rod, such that

$$\tan\theta = 10\tan\varphi. \qquad \text{(L.)}$$

The moment of inertia of the rod about the axis is $4\,ml^2/3$, where $2l$ is the length of the rod and m is the mass of the rod.

The equations of motion for the centre of mass of the rod are

$$X - mg\sin\theta = ml\ddot{\theta},$$

$$Y - mg\cos\theta = ml\dot{\theta}^2,$$

where θ is the angle made by the rod with the downward vertical.

The energy equation is

$$\frac{2ml^2}{3}\dot{\theta}^2 - mgl\cos\theta = C,$$

where C is a constant such that $\dot{\theta} = 0$ when $\theta = \frac{1}{2}\pi$.

$$\therefore\ C = 0, \quad \text{and} \quad \dot{\theta}^2 = \frac{3g\cos\theta}{2l}.$$

The equation of motion for the rod is

$$\frac{4ml^2}{3}\ddot{\theta} = -mgl \sin \theta.$$

$$\therefore \ddot{\theta} = -\frac{3g \sin \theta}{4l}.$$

$$\therefore X = \frac{mg \sin \theta}{4}, \quad Y = \frac{5mg \cos \theta}{2}.$$

$$\therefore \tan \varphi = \frac{X}{Y} = \frac{\tan \theta}{10}.$$

$$\therefore \tan \theta = 10 \tan \varphi.$$

Example 2. A light rod of length $4a$ has particles of masses m and $2m$ attached to its ends A and B respectively. The rod can rotate freely in a vertical plane about C, where C is the point on the rod such that AC $= a$. The rod is released from rest when AB is horizontal. Show that when the rod has turned through an angle θ, $19a(d\theta/dt)^2 = 10g \sin \theta$. Find the stresses in the parts AC and CB of the rod when it is passing through the vertical position. (N.)

The M. of I. of the rod and particles about the axis is

$$ma^2 + 2m(3a)^2 = 19ma^2.$$

The energy equation is, therefore,

$$\frac{19ma^2}{2}\dot{\theta}^2 + mga \sin \theta - 2mg\, 3a \sin \theta = K,$$

where K is a constant such that $\dot{\theta} = 0$ when $\theta = 0$.

$$\therefore K = 0 \quad \text{and} \quad 19a\dot{\theta}^2 = 10g \sin \theta.$$

Therefore when $\theta = \frac{1}{2}\pi, \quad \dot{\theta}^2 = \frac{10g}{19a}.$

Figure 15.22 shows the forces acting on the particles at A and B respectively, and the accelerations of those particles when the rod is vertical. The equation of motion for the particle at A is

$$mg + T_1 = \frac{ma \, . \, 10g}{19a}; \quad \therefore T_1 = -\frac{9mg}{19}.$$

The equation of motion for the particle at B is

$$T_2 - 2mg = 2m \, . \, 3a \, . \frac{10g}{19a}; \quad \therefore T_2 = \frac{98mg}{19}.$$

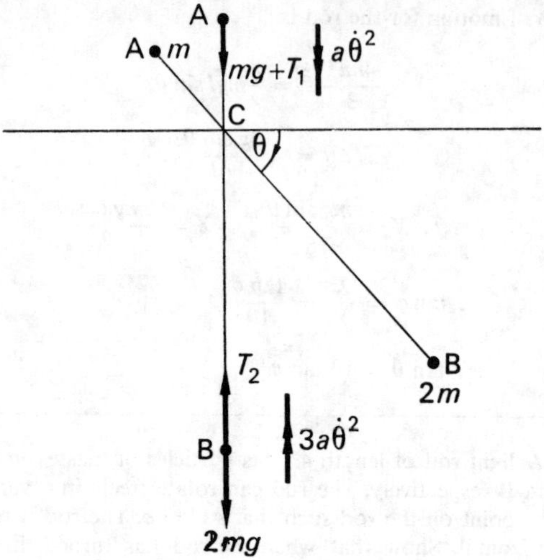

FIG. 15.22

The rod AC is in compression with a force $9mg/19$ and BC is in tension with a force $98mg/19$.

---

*EXERCISES 15.7

***1.** A light rod, which can turn freely in a vertical plane about one end A, carries masses P and Q at distances a and b from A. If the rod is held in a horizontal position and released, prove that its angular velocity when vertical is given by

$$\omega^2 = 2g\left(\frac{Pa+Qb}{Pa^2+Qb^2}\right).$$

If the masses P and Q, instead of being attached at different points, are attached at the same point, prove that the pull on the point of support when the rod is vertical is $3(P+Q)g$.

***2.** Prove that the moment of inertia of a uniform rod, of length $2a$ and mass m, about an axis perpendicular to the rod at a distance x from its mid-point is

$$\tfrac{1}{3}m(a^2+3x^2).$$

A uniform rod, of weight W and length $6b$, is smoothly pivoted to a fixed point at a distance $2b$ from one end and is free to swing in a vertical plane. The rod is held horizontal and released. Prove that after it has rotated through an angle θ its angular velocity is

$$\sqrt{\left(\frac{g \sin \theta}{2b}\right)},$$

and that when the rod is vertical the reaction on the pivot is $3W/2$. (N.)

***3.** A uniform circular lamina, centre C, is freely pivoted at a point O of the circumference and is held with its plane vertical and with OC making an angle of 60° with the downward vertical through O. If the lamina is released, prove that, when OC is vertical, the reaction on the pivot at O is 5/3 of the weight of the lamina. (N.)

***4.** A uniform rectangular lamina ABCD of mass m in which $AB = 2a$, $BC = 4a$ is free to rotate about a fixed horizontal axis which is perpendicular to its plane and passes through O, the mid-point of AB. Show that the moment of inertia of the lamina about this axis is $17ma^2/3$.

When the lamina is at rest with AB horizontal and uppermost, a particle of mass $2m$ is attached to it at B without impulse. Show that in the subsequent motion the lamina will be momentarily at rest when AB is vertical, and find an expression for ω, the angular velocity of the lamina when AB is inclined at angle θ to the horizontal. Show also that when AB is vertical, the vertical component of the reaction at O is $57mg/23$, and find the horizontal component. (N.)

***5.** A light rod OA of length $2a$ is rigidly fixed at A to a uniform square plate ABCD of mass m and side $2a$, so that OAB is a straight line. The end O of the rod is pivoted to a fixed horizontal axis which is perpendicular to the plane of the square and the system can swing freely about this axis. If the system is released from rest when OAB is horizontal and CD is below AB, show that when OA has turned through an angle θ, the angular velocity of OA is ω, where

$$16a\omega^2 = 3g(3 \sin \theta + \cos \theta - 1).$$

Show also that when the centre of gravity of the square plate is vertically below O, the action at O is vertical and of magnitude $mg(46 - 3\sqrt{10})/16$. (N.)

***6.** A uniform rod AB, of mass m and length $2a$, is free to rotate in a vertical plane about a horizontal axis through A. The rod is slightly disturbed from the position in which B is vertically above A. Show that in the subsequent motion

$$2a\dot{\theta}^2 = 3g(1 - \cos \theta)$$

where θ is the angle made by AB with the *upward* vertical. Calculate the horizontal and vertical components of the force exerted by the rod on the axis of rotation. (L.)

***7.** Prove that the moment of inertia of a straight uniform rod AB, of mass M and length $2a$, about an axis through A and perpendicular to AB is $\frac{4}{3}Ma^2$.

If the rod, which is free to rotate in a vertical plane about a horizontal axis through A, is released from rest when AB is horizontal, prove that the angular velocity ω of the rod about A when AB has moved through an angle θ is given by

$$a\omega^2 = \tfrac{3}{2}g \sin \theta$$

and find the component of the reaction on the rod at A perpendicular to AB. (O.C.)

***8.** A rod of length $2l$ is held almost vertically with one end resting on a horizontal plane, which is rough enough to prevent slipping, and is then released. Prove that in the subsequent motion the normal reaction of the plane vanishes when the rod makes an angle $\cos^{-1}(1/3)$ with the vertical, and that the angular velocity of the rod is then $\sqrt{(g/l)}$. (N.)

***9.** A uniform rod AB of mass m and length $2a$ has a particle of mass m fixed to the end B. It is held in a horizontal position with its middle point resting on a fixed small rough peg. If the rod is allowed to move, prove that it will turn through an angle $\tan^{-1}(5\mu/14)$, where μ is the coefficient of friction, before slipping takes place. (N.

15.8. Impulse and Momentum

The equation of motion of a rigid body rotating about a fixed axis was established in § 15.6 as $L = I\ddot{\theta}$, where L is the moment about the axis of the external forces acting on the body and I is the moment of inertia of the body about the axis. By integration with respect to t,

$$\int_{t_1}^{t_2} L\,\mathrm{d}t = \int_{t_1}^{t_2} I\ddot{\theta}\,\mathrm{d}t = [I\dot{\theta}]_{t_1}^{t_2}.$$

The quantity $I\dot{\theta}$ is defined as the *angular momentum* of the body about the axis. When the external force acting on the body acts for a short interval only, so that we can write $L = Pa$, where a is the constant distance from the axis at which the variable force P acts, the quantity $\int_{t_1}^{t_2} L\,\mathrm{d}t$ is equal to $a\int_{t_1}^{t_2} P\,\mathrm{d}t$ and $a\int_{t_1}^{t_2} P\,\mathrm{d}t$ is *the moment of the impulse about the axis*, since $\int_{t_1}^{t_2} P\,\mathrm{d}t$ is the impulse of the force in the interval t_1 to t_2.

Thus we have established the general principle, for a rigid body rotating about a fixed axis and acted upon by an impulsive force,

Moment of impulse about the axis = change in angular momentum.

Note. $I\dot{\theta} = \Sigma(m_P r_P^2\dot{\theta}) = \Sigma\{(m_P r_P\dot{\theta})r_P\}$. But $m_P r_P\dot{\theta}$ is the magnitude of the linear momentum of the particle of mass m_P, and $m_P r_P^2\dot{\theta}$ is the angular momentum of the particle about the axis. Thus

(i) the angular momentum of a particle about an axis is equal to the product of its linear momentum and the perpendicular distance of the axis from the path of the particle, and

(ii) the angular momentum of a rigid body about a fixed axis is equal to the sum of the angular momenta of its particles about that axis.

Angular momentum is sometimes called *Moment of Momentum.*

Conservation of angular momentum. When two bodies interact on each other with impulsive forces and there are no external impulses which have moments about a particular axis, then the total angular momentum about that axis remains constant. This is a direct consequence of Newton's third law. The impulsive forces between the bodies are equal in magnitude, opposite in direction, and act for the same time. The changes in the angular momenta about the axis of the two bodies are therefore equal and opposite and the total change in angular momentum about the axis is zero.

Centre of percussion. From the definition of an impulse in the form $\int_{t_1}^{t_2} P\,dt$ it follows at once from the principle stated in § 14.8 that:

The initial motion of the centre of mass of an aggregate of particles is the same as that of a particle of mass equal to the sum of the masses of the constituent particles acted upon by an impulse which is the vector sum of the external impulses acting on the particles.

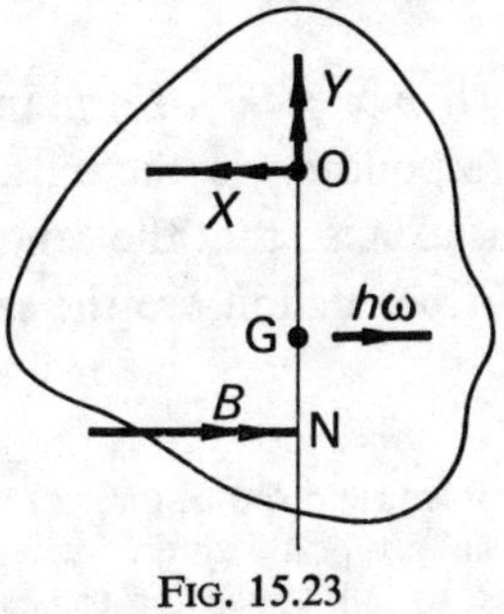

FIG. 15.23

Figure 15.23 represents a rigid body capable of rotation under gravity about a horizontal axis through a fixed point O. The body hanging freely at rest receives a *horizontal* blow B (i.e. it is acted upon by a horizontal impulse B) in the vertical plane containing G, its centre of mass. There will, in general, be an impulsive reaction of the axis on the body, denoted in the diagram by components X and Y in directions at right angles to and along GO. The line of action of B meets OG at N and ON $= x$. Then

(i) the moment of the impulse of B about the axis is equal to the change in the angular momentum about the axis of the rigid body, i.e.

$$Bx = M(k^2+h^2)\,\omega,$$

where M is the mass of the body, k its radius of gyration about a parallel axis through G, GO $= h$ and ω is the angular velocity of the body immediately after receiving the blow, and

(ii) the initial motion of G is the same as that of a particle of mass M acted upon by a horizontal impulse $B-X$, a vertical impulse Y and starting to move horizontally with velocity $h\omega$, i.e.

$$B-X = Mh\omega, \quad Y = 0.$$

Therefore eliminating B,

$$X = \frac{M(k^2+h^2)\omega}{x} - Mh\omega = M\omega\left\{\frac{k^2+h^2}{x} - h\right\}.$$

It follows that $X = 0$ when $x = (k^2+h^2)/h$. In this case N is called the *centre of percussion* corresponding to the axis. The distance ON is the length of the ESP for this axis, so that the centre of oscillation discussed in § 15.5 and the centre of percussion are the same point for a particular axis.

Example 1. A straight uniform rigid rod of mass m and length l is freely hinged at one end and is held in a vertical position with the free end uppermost. The rod is now slightly displaced and allowed to fall. When the rod has turned through an angle θ prove that the angular velocity is

$$\sqrt{\left\{\frac{3g(1-\cos\theta)}{l}\right\}}.$$

At the instant when $\theta = \frac{1}{3}\pi$ the rod is brought suddenly to rest by an impulse applied at the free end at right angles to the rod. Calculate this impulse in terms of m and l. (N.)

The M. of I. of the rod about the axis is $\frac{1}{3}ml^2$. When the rod has turned through an angle θ, the equation of energy is

$$\tfrac{1}{2}mgl(1-\cos\theta) = \tfrac{1}{2}\cdot\tfrac{1}{3}ml^2\dot{\theta}^2.$$

$$\therefore\ \dot{\theta} = \sqrt{\{3g(1-\cos\theta)/l\}}.$$

Therefore when $\theta = \frac{1}{3}\pi$, $\dot{\theta} = \sqrt{\{3g/2l\}}$.

If B is the impulse which brings the rod to rest,

$$Bl = \frac{ml^2}{3}\sqrt{\left(\frac{3g}{2l}\right)}; \quad \therefore\ B = m\sqrt{\left(\frac{gl}{6}\right)}.$$

Example 2. A thin uniform disc, of centre O, radius r and mass M, is free to rotate in a vertical plane about a horizontal axis through a point P of its circumference. When the disc is hanging freely at rest it is struck an impulsive blow B in its plane and along a radius QO where $\angle$ POQ $= 3\pi/4$. Calculate, in terms of B, the impulsive reaction of the axis on the disc, and the angular velocity with which the disc begins to move.

Figure 15.24 shows the impulses (double arrows), and the initial velocity (single arrow) of the centre of mass O of the disc. The moment of inertia of the disc about the axis is $3Mr^2/2$.

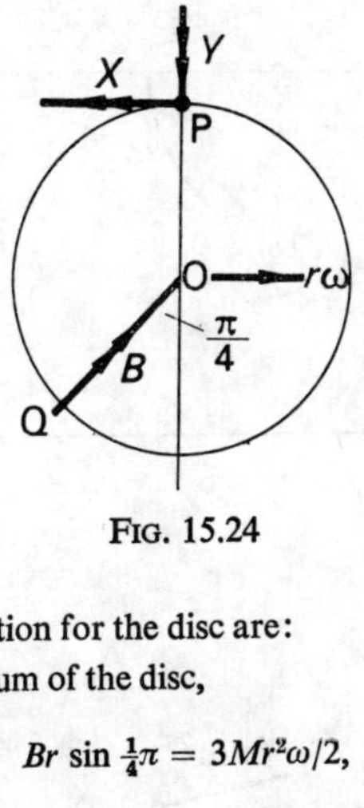

FIG. 15.24

The equations of initial motion for the disc are:
(a) for the angular momentum of the disc,

$$Br\sin\tfrac{1}{4}\pi = 3Mr^2\omega/2,$$

(b) for the initial motion of O,

$$B\sin\tfrac{1}{4}\pi - X = Mr\omega,$$
$$B\cos\tfrac{1}{4}\pi - Y = 0.$$

These equations give

$$X = \frac{B\sqrt{2}}{6}, \quad Y = \frac{B\sqrt{2}}{2}, \quad \omega = \frac{B\sqrt{2}}{3Mr}.$$

Therefore the impulsive reaction of the axis on the disc is

$$B\sqrt{[2\{(\tfrac{1}{6})^2+(\tfrac{1}{2})^2\}]} = B\sqrt{(\tfrac{5}{9})}$$

at an angle $\tan^{-1}\frac{1}{3}$ with the downward vertical at the same side of PO as Q. The initial angular velocity of the disc is $\omega = (B\sqrt{2})/(3Mr)$.

Example 3. A smooth heavy uniform rod of length l is free to rotate about one end in a horizontal plane. A small ring of the same mass is free to slide on the rod and is placed at its middle point. If the rod is given an initial angular velocity ω, show that the ring will leave the rod with a speed $l\omega\sqrt{(133)}/16$.

If, with the same initial condition, the rod is maintained at a uniform angular velocity ω, show that the ring will leave with a speed $l\omega\sqrt{(7)}/2$.

Explain why the two results are different. (N.)

Figures 15.25 (i) and 15.25 (ii) show the velocities of the rod and the ring (i) initially and (ii) when the ring is leaving rod. The M. of I. of the rod about its axis is $ml^2/3$.

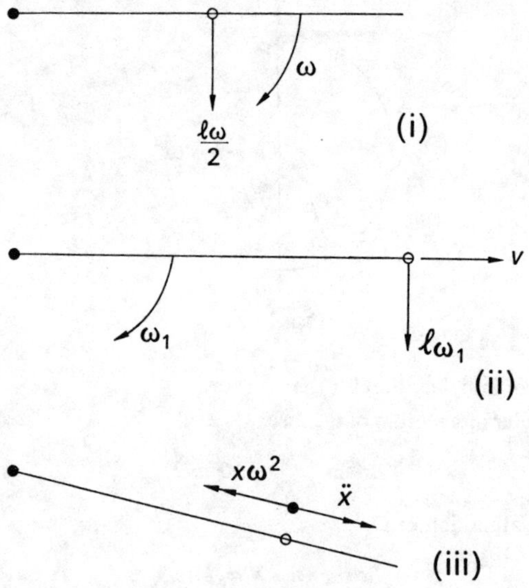

FIG. 15.25

In the first case, when the ring is leaving the rod its velocity has two components, the component $l\omega_1$ at right angles to the rod and the component v along the rod which is the velocity of the ring relative to the rod. In this case, energy is conserved, and the energy equation is

$$\frac{1}{2}mv^2+\frac{1}{2}\frac{ml^2}{3}\omega_1^2+\frac{1}{2}ml^2\omega_1^2 = \frac{1}{2}\frac{ml^2}{3}\omega^2+\frac{1}{2}m\frac{l^2}{4}\omega^2.$$

$$\therefore\ \tfrac{1}{2}mv^2+\tfrac{2}{3}ml^2\omega_1^2 = \tfrac{7}{24}ml^2\omega^2.$$

There are no external forces with moments about the axis of rotation and therefore angular momentum about this axis is conserved.

$$\therefore\ \left(\frac{ml^2}{3}+\frac{ml^2}{4}\right)\omega = \left(\frac{ml^2}{3}+ml^2\right)\omega_1; \qquad \therefore\ \omega_1 = \frac{7}{16}\omega.$$

$$\therefore\ v^2 = \frac{7}{12}l^2\omega^2-\frac{4}{3}l^2\omega_1^2 = l^2\omega^2\left(\frac{7}{12}-\frac{49}{192}\right) = \frac{21l^2\omega^2}{64}.$$

Therefore the ring leaves the rod with component velocities $l\omega\sqrt{(\frac{21}{64})}$ and $\frac{7}{16}l\omega$, i.e. with a resultant velocity of magnitude

$$l\omega\sqrt{\left(\frac{21}{64}+\frac{49}{256}\right)} = \frac{l\omega\sqrt{133}}{16}.$$

In the second case, because the rod is kept at a uniform angular velocity, necessarily by means of an external force which has a moment about the axis, neither energy nor angular momentum is conserved and in consequence the result will be different from that obtained in the first case.

Figure 15.25 (iii) shows the accelerations of the particle when it is at a distance x from the axis, $x\omega^2$ towards the centre of rotation since it is moving instantaneously in a circle of radius x about the hinge and $\ddot{x}$ relative to the rod in the direction along the rod and away from the hinge. The equation of motion of the ring relative to the rod is, therefore,

$$\ddot{x}-\omega^2x = 0, \quad \text{i.e.} \quad v\frac{dv}{dx} = \omega^2x,$$

where v is the velocity of the ring relative to the rod. Hence, if u is the velocity *relative to the rod* at which the ring leaves the rod,

$$\frac{u^2}{2} = \left[\frac{\omega^2x^2}{2}\right]_{l/2}^{l} = \frac{3\omega^2l^2}{8}, \qquad \therefore\ u^2 = \frac{3\omega^2l^2}{4},$$

and so the magnitude of the resultant velocity with which the ring leaves the rod is

$$\sqrt{\left(\frac{3\omega^2l^2}{4}+\omega^2l^2\right)} = \frac{l\omega\sqrt{7}}{2}.$$

Example 4. Two gear wheels are spinning about parallel axles. Their moments of inertia about the axles and their effective radii are I_1, I_2, r_1, r_2, and their angular velocities measured in the same sense are ω_1, ω_2. The axles are then moved so that the gears engage. Find the resultant angular velocity of each wheel, and show that the impulse acting upon the first at the instant of contact has a moment

$$-\frac{I_1 I_2(r_1\omega_1+r_2\omega_2)r_1}{r_1^2 I_2+r_2^2 I_1}$$

about the axle of this wheel. (N.)

Let the impulse acting on each wheel at the instant of contact be B and let the final, common, linear velocity of the point of contact of the two wheels be v, Fig. 15.26. (After the wheels enmesh they will continue to move so that their angular velocities are in opposite senses.)

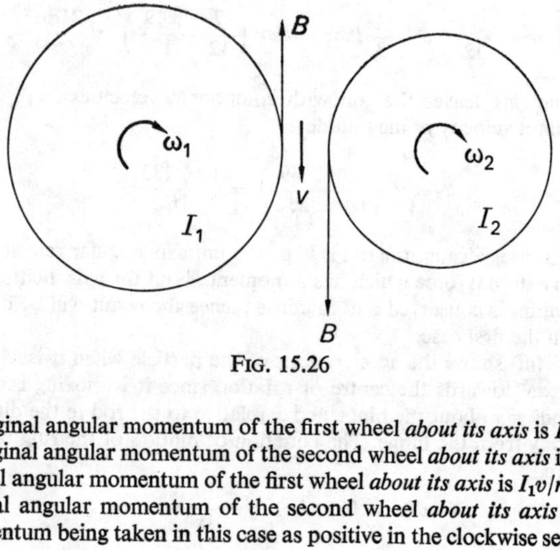

FIG. 15.26

1. The original angular momentum of the first wheel *about its axis* is $I_1\omega_1$.
2. The original angular momentum of the second wheel *about its axis* is $I_2\omega_2$.
3. The final angular momentum of the first wheel *about its axis* is $I_1 v/r_1$.
4. The final angular momentum of the second wheel *about its axis* is $-(I_2 v/r_2)$, angular momentum being taken in this case as positive in the clockwise sense.

$$\therefore\ Br_1 = I_1\omega_1-\frac{I_1 v}{r_1},$$

$$Br_2 = I_2\omega_2+\frac{I_2 v}{r_2}.$$

Hence, equating values of B,

$$\frac{I_1\omega_1}{r_1}-\frac{I_1 v}{r_1^2}=\frac{I_2\omega_2}{r_2}+\frac{I_2 v}{r_2^2}.$$

$$\therefore\ v=\frac{r_1 r_2(I_1\omega_1 r_2-I_2\omega_2 r_1)}{I_2 r_1^2+I_1 r_2^2}.$$

Therefore the new angular velocities of the wheels are

$$\frac{r_2(I_1\omega_1r_2-I_2\omega_2r_1)}{I_1r_2^2+I_2r_1^2} \quad \text{and} \quad -\frac{r_1(I_1\omega_1r_2-I_2\omega_2r_1)}{I_1r_2^2+I_2r_1^2}.$$

The moment of the impulse about its axle acting on the first wheel at the instant of contact is

$$-Br_1 = -\left\{I_1\omega_1-\frac{I_1r_2(I_1\omega_1r_2-I_2\omega_2r_1)}{I_1r_2^2+I_2r_1^2}\right\}$$

$$= -\frac{I_1I_2(\omega_1r_1+\omega_2r_2)r_1}{r_1^2I_2+r_2^2I_1}$$

the negative sign indicating that the sense of the impulse-moment is opposite to the sense of the original rotation.

EXERCISES 15.8

1. A uniform circular lamina of mass M and radius a is free to move in its own plane (which is vertical) about the extremity A of a diameter AB. The lamina hangs in equilibrium with B vertically below A, and is struck by a blow applied horizontally at B in the plane of the lamina. If the lamina first comes to rest when AB has turned through an angle of 60°, calculate, in terms of M and a, the impulse of the blow. (N.)

2. A uniform lamina of mass m in the form of a square ABCD of diagonal $2d$ is suspended freely from a corner A. An impulsive force P is applied to the lamina at C in the direction CB. Prove that the kinetic energy communicated to the lamina is $3P^2/4m$. Show also that the lamina will come to instantaneous rest after turning through an angle α, where

$$\sin\frac{\alpha}{2} = \frac{P}{2m}\sqrt{\left(\frac{3}{2gd}\right)}. \qquad \text{(N.)}$$

3. A particle of mass m is fixed to one end of a uniform rod of mass m and length $2a$, the other end of the rod being smoothly pivoted to a point O. The rod is released from rest when it is horizontal; find its angular velocity when it is vertical.

If, at the instant when the rod is vertical, its angular velocity is suddenly changed by the action of a horizontal impulsive force, prove that there will be no impulsive action at O if the line of action of the impulse is at a depth $16a/9$ below O. (N.)

4. A uniform circular disc of mass M and radius a is freely mounted on a fixed horizontal axis normal to its plane and passing through its centre O, and is rotating with angular velocity ω. The disc picks up a stationary particle P of mass m at the lowest point of its circumference. Find the angular velocity immediately after the particle is picked up. Show that the disc will come to rest in the subsequent motion if

$$M^2a\omega^2 \leq 8m(M+2m)g,$$

and if this condition is satisfied, find the angle which OP makes with the vertical at the moment when the disc comes to rest. (N.)

5. A pendulum consists of a thin uniform rod OE of mass M and length $2a$ rigidly attached at E to the mid-point of the side AB of a uniform square lamina ABCD of mass $5M$ and side $2a$; the rod EO is in the line FE produced, where F is the mid-point of CD. The pendulum is free to rotate about a fixed horizontal axis through O, parallel to AB, and initially is hanging at rest in the equilibrium position. A particle of mass m moving with velocity v in a line perpendicular to the plane of the lamina then strikes it at the centre of the square and remains embedded in it. Find the angular velocity of the pendulum immediately after the impact, and the magnitude of the impulse at O. Show also that if in the subsequent motion the greatest inclination of OEF to the vertical is α, then

$$v^2 = \frac{2ga}{3}\left(\frac{16M+3m}{m}\right)^2(1-\cos\alpha). \qquad \text{(N.)}$$

6. A rod of mass M can swing freely in a vertical plane about one end A. The distance of the centre of gravity of the rod (not necessarily uniform) from A is h, and the radius of gyration about A is K.

While the rod is hanging in equilibrium, it is struck by a horizontal impulse of magnitude P at a point X at a depth x below A. (i) Find the angular velocity with which the rod begins to move. (ii) Prove that the kinetic energy imparted to the rod is $\frac{1}{2}Pv$, where v is the velocity with which the point X begins to move. (iii) If the rod just reaches the upward vertical, prove that $Px = 2MK\sqrt{(gh)}$. (N.)

7. A particle of mass m is placed at the lowest point of a smooth circular tube of mass M and radius a, which is free to turn about a fixed vertical axis coincident with a diameter. The tube is given an initial angular velocity and the particle is slightly displaced from its position of rest. In the subsequent motion the radius to the particle when it reaches its highest point makes an angle α with the downward vertical. Find the initial angular velocity of the tube. (N.)

8. A uniform rod AB, of mass m and length $2a$, is freely pivoted to a fixed point at A and is initially hanging in equilibrium. A particle of mass m, moving horizontally with speed u, strikes the rod at its middle point and rebounds from it. If there is no loss of energy at the impact, show that immediately afterwards the speed of the particle is $u/7$, and find the angular velocity with which the rod begins to rotate. Deduce that, if $u^2 < 49ag/12$, the rod will come to rest at an inclination θ to the downward vertical at A, where

$$\cos\theta = 1-\frac{24}{49}\frac{u^2}{ag}. \qquad \text{(N.)}$$

9. A target consists of a uniform plane square lamina, of side a and mass M, freely hinged along one edge to a fixed horizontal axis. The target hangs at rest with its plane vertical and is struck in its centre by a bullet of mass m moving with speed v perpendicular to the plane of the target. If the bullet becomes embedded in the target, prove that the velocity of the bullet is instantaneously reduced to $3mv/(3m+4M)$ and that the fractional loss of kinetic energy in the impact is $4M/(3m+4M)$.

Prove that the target and bullet will make complete revolutions about the hinge in the subsequent motion if

$$3m^2v^2 > 2ag(m+M)(3m+4M). \qquad \text{(N.)}$$

10. Two uniform rods AB and BC, each of length $2a$ and of masses m and $3m$ respectively, are smoothly pivoted to a fixed point B. The rods are initially in a horizontal straight line ABC and are released from rest so that they collide when A and C are vertically below B. Find the angular velocities of the rods just before the collision. If the rods adhere to each other on meeting, find the angle which the combined rod makes with the vertical when its angular velocity is zero. (N.)

11. Show that the moment of inertia of a uniform rod, of mass m and length $2a$, about an axis through its mid-point O and perpendicular to its length, is $\frac{1}{3}ma^2$.

The rod is free to rotate in a horizontal plane about O which is fixed. Two smooth small rings, each of mass $\frac{1}{2}m$, are free to slide on the rod. The rings are initially on opposite sides of O and are each at a distance $a/\sqrt{3}$ from O. The rod is given an initial angular velocity $2\sqrt{(g/a)}$, the rings being initially at rest relative to the rod. Show that, when the rings are about to slip off the rod, its angular velocity is $\sqrt{(g/a)}$. Show also that at this instant the speed of either ring is $\frac{1}{3}\sqrt{(21ga)}$. (N.)

12. Two equal wheels, mounted on the same horizontal axis, have each radius a and moment of inertia ma^2 about the axis, on which they can rotate independently of each other. To the rim of one wheel a particle P of mass m is attached at a point on the same level as the axis. This wheel then starts rotating from rest, the other meanwhile rotating uniformly in the opposite direction with angular velocity ω. When P reaches the position vertically below the axis, the two wheels are suddenly locked together. Find the value of ω if the wheels are brought to rest immediately after the locking.

If, however, the value of ω is so great that the locked wheels just carry P back to its starting point show that

$$\omega = (2+\sqrt{6})\sqrt{(g/a)}. \qquad \text{(N.)}$$

13. A smooth straight tube of length a and mass m is free to rotate on a smooth table about one end. A particle also of mass m is placed in the tube at its middle point and the system is given an initial angular velocity Ω. Find the angular velocity of the tube when the particle reaches the end of the tube, and show that the speed of the particle relative to the tube at that instant is $\frac{1}{8}a\Omega\sqrt{21}$. (N.)

14. A uniform circular wire ring of radius a is free to revolve about a vertical diameter. A small bead of the same mass as the ring can slide upon the ring without friction. When the bead is at the uppermost point of the ring the latter is given an angular velocity Ω about a vertical diameter, and the bead is slightly displaced from its position. Find the angular velocity of rotation of the ring when the bead is at the extremity of a horizontal diameter, and show that the square of its speed relative to the ring is then $\frac{1}{3}(a^2\Omega^2+6ag)$. (N.)

15.9. Note on the Relationship between the Equations of Motion of Rotation of a Rigid Body and the Equations of Motion for a Particle moving in a Straight Line

The dynamical equations for a particle moving in a straight line are transformed into the corresponding equations for a rigid body rotating about a fixed axis if *mass* is replaced by *moment of inertia about the axis*, *force* by *moment of force about the axis* and the linear quantities *displacement*, *velocity* and *acceleration* by the quantities *angular displacement*, *angular velocity*, and *angular acceleration*.

Thus:

	For a particle moving in a straight line	For a rigid body rotating about an axis
Force-Acceleration	$P = m\ddot{x}$	$M = I\ddot{\theta}$
Work-Energy	$\int_{x_1}^{x_2} P\,dx =$ Change in $\frac{1}{2}mv^2$ (Change in kinetic energy)	$\int_{\theta_1}^{\theta_2} M\,d\theta =$ Change in $\frac{1}{2}I\dot{\theta}^2$ (Change in kinetic energy)
Impulse-Momentum	$\int_{t_1}^{t_2} P\,dt =$ Change in mv (Change in linear momentum)	$\int_{t_1}^{t_2} M\,dt =$ Change in $I\dot{\theta}$ (Change in angular momentum about the axis)

Note on dimensions. It is of interest at this point to consider the dimensions of the quantities with which we have been concerned in this chapter.

Angles (measured in circular measure) have zero dimensions.

Angular Velocity has dimensions s^{-1}.

Angular Acceleration has dimensions s^{-2}.

Moment of Inertia has dimensions kg m^2.

Kinetic Energy. The quantity expressed by $\frac{1}{2}mv^2$ has dimensions kg $(m\,s^{-1})^2$, i.e. kg $m^2\,s^{-2}$; the quantity expressed by $\frac{1}{2}I\dot{\theta}^2$ has dimensions kg $m^2(s^{-1})^2$, i.e. kg $m^2\,s^{-2}$.

Linear Momentum (mv) has dimensions kg m s^{-1}.

Angular Momentum ($I\dot{\theta}$) has dimensions kg $m^2\,s^{-1}$.

MISCELLANEOUS EXERCISES XV

1. A light rod of length $2l$ is freely movable about one end which is fixed. The rod carries two particles of equal mass, one fastened at the middle point and the other at the free end. Find the time of a small oscillation and the length of the equivalent simple pendulum. (N.)

2. A uniform rod of length $a+b$ is bent to form a right angle with arms of length a and b. If it is suspended from its angular point and makes small oscillations in its own plane, show that the length of the equivalent simple pendulum is

$$\frac{2}{3}\cdot\frac{a^3+b^3}{\sqrt{(a^4+b^4)}}. \qquad \text{(N.)}$$

3. A square lamina ABCD of diagonal d and mass M and a circular disc of diameter d and mass m are rigidly joined together so that a diameter of the disc coincides with the diagonal AC of the square, the planes of the disc and square being at right angles. The system can swing freely about a horizontal axis passing through A and perpendicular to the circular disc, the motion of the disc being in its own vertical plane. Show that the period of a small oscillation of the system about its equilibrium position is

$$\pi\sqrt{\left\{\frac{(9m+7M)\,d}{3(m+M)\,g}\right\}}. \qquad \text{(N.)}$$

4. The points A, B, C, D, on a uniform circular ring of mass M, are the vertices of a square. Particles, each of mass m, are fastened to the ring at B, C, D and the system is mounted to rotate freely about a horizontal axis which is the tangent to the ring at A. The system is released from rest when its plane makes an angle α with the vertical. Show that the angular velocity when this angle has become β is independent of M/m.

Find also the time for a complete small oscillation about the equilibrium position if a is the radius of the ring. (L.)

5. Prove that the moment of inertia of a uniform straight rod AB, of length $2a$ and mass M, about an axis through A and perpendicular to AB is $\frac{4}{3}Ma^2$.

The rod AB can rotate about a smooth horizontal axis through A and perpendicular to the vertical plane ABC, where C is a point on the same horizontal level as A and at a distance $2a$ from A. One end of a string, of length greater than $2a\sqrt{2}$, is attached to B and the string passes over a small smooth peg at C carrying at the other end a particle P of mass m which hangs vertically. The system is released from rest when B is at C, the subsequent motion being such that P rises and AB reaches the vertical position. Prove that the angular velocity ω of AB when the rod is vertical is given by

$$\omega^2 = \frac{3g(M-2m\sqrt{2})}{a(2M+3m)}. \qquad \text{(O.C.)}$$

6. Prove that the moment of inertia of a uniform square lamina, of mass M and side $2a$, about an axis through its centre parallel to one side is $\frac{1}{3}Ma^2$. Deduce the moment of inertia of the lamina about an axis through one corner perpendicular to its plane.

The lamina oscillates in its own plane, which is vertical, about an axis through one corner which is perpendicular to its plane. In the positions of instantaneous rest, a side of the square is vertical and directed downwards; find the speed of the lowest corner of the lamina when it is at the lowest point of its path. (L.)

7. A uniform lamina, of mass M, is in the form of the portion of the parabola $y^2 = 4ax$ cut off by the latus rectum $x = a$. Find the moment of inertia of the lamina about (i) the line $x = 0$; (ii) the line through the vertex A $\equiv (0, 0)$ of the parabola perpendicular to its plane.

The tangent at the vertex of the above parabola is fixed and horizontal, and the lamina is free to rotate about it. Prove that the period of small oscillations is $2\pi\sqrt{(5a/7g)}$. (O.C.)

8. AB is a diameter of a uniform circular disc of radius a and mass M, which can rotate freely in its plane about a horizontal axis through A; a particle of mass m is attached at B and, with B vertically above A, the system is slightly disturbed. Prove that the velocity v of the particle at B, when AB makes an angle θ with the upward vertical, is given by

$$v^2 = 16ag(M+2m)(1-\cos\theta)/(3M+8m).$$

Find also the horizontal and vertical components of the linear acceleration of the particle when AB is horizontal and $M = 4m$. (O.C.)

9. A wheel of radius a and moment of inertia I, mounted on a vertical axis, starts rotating from rest under the action of a constant driving couple N which acts for a time t and then ceases. The rotation is subject also to a constant frictional couple R. Find the total time which elapses before the wheel comes to rest again, and the total angle through which it turns.

If, at the moment when N ceases to act, the wheel picks up on its rim a particle of mass m, originally at rest, find what the total time of motion will now be. (N.)

10. A rigid body of mass M oscillates about a fixed horizontal axis. Its moment of inertia about the axis is I, and its centre of gravity G is at a distance h from the axis. The perpendicular from G to the axis makes an angle θ with the downward vertical at time t. If the maximum value of θ is α, prove that

$$\frac{1}{2}I\left(\frac{d\theta}{dt}\right)^2 = Mgh(\cos\theta - \cos\alpha),$$

and deduce that the motion is the same as that of a simple pendulum of length (I/Mh).

A uniform square lamina of side $2a$ oscillates about a horizontal axis which passes through the mid-points of two adjacent edges. Find the length of the equivalent simple pendulum. (C.)

11. A uniform rod OA of mass m and length $2a$ hangs from O where it is freely pivoted to a fixed support. A horizontal blow $m\sqrt{(ga)}$ is applied to the rod at the end A. Prove that the initial angular velocity of the rod is $\frac{3}{2}\sqrt{(g/a)}$.

Show also that the rod will swing through an angle of 120° before it reaches its first position of instantaneous rest. Find the components, along and perpendicular to the rod, of the reaction at O in this position of instantaneous rest. (N.)

12. One end of a uniform rod, of length $2a$ and mass m, is smoothly hinged to a pivot fixed on a smooth horizontal table. The other end of the rod is in contact with a vertical face of a rectangular block of mass M, which rests on the table and which is pushed forward as the rod falls. Initially the rod is inclined at an angle α to the horizontal. Show that, in the subsequent motion, so long as the rod remains in contact with the block the velocity of the block is $2a\omega \sin\theta$, where ω is the angular velocity of the rod and θ its inclination to the horizontal.

From considerations of energy show that

$$a\omega^2(2m+6M\sin^2\theta) = 3mg(\sin\alpha-\sin\theta). \qquad \text{(L.)}$$

***13.** A rough uniform circular disc of radius a is free to rotate about a vertical axis through its centre and perpendicular to its plane, and is initially rotating with angular velocity ω. A uniform rod of length $2a$ is gently placed on the disc so that it is initially at rest and coincident with a diameter of the disc. The coefficient of friction between the two bodies is μ and the middle point of the rod remains at rest during the motion. The mass per unit length of the rod is σ and the moment of inertia of the disc about the vertical axis is $2\sigma a^3$. By considering the forces acting on elements of the rod show that while slipping occurs the couple between the disc and the rod has moment $\mu g\sigma a^2$. Deduce that the time during which slipping takes place is $a\omega/2\mu g$, and find the final common angular velocity. (N.)

***14.** A uniform rough rigid wire of length $8a$ and mass $4m$, bent into the form of a square ABCD, is pivoted to a fixed point at O, the middle point of AB, and is free to rotate about a horizontal axis through O normal to its plane. Show that the moment of inertia of the wire about this axis is $28ma^2/3$.

A small ring of mass m is threaded on the portion CD of the wire and rests at its middle point. The system is released from rest with AB inclined at an acute angle α to the horizontal, B being uppermost. If θ denotes the inclination of AB to the horizontal in the subsequent motion, show that, so long as the ring does not slip,

$$10a(d\theta/dt)^2 = 9g(\cos\theta-\cos\alpha),$$
$$20a(d^2\theta/dt^2) = -9g\sin\theta.$$

Find the components along and perpendicular to CD of the force exerted on the ring by the wire, and deduce that the ring will not slip if the coefficient of friction exceeds $(\tan\alpha)/10$. (N.)

***15.** A uniform rod AB of mass m and length $2a$ is freely pivoted to a fixed point at A. The point A is at a distance $2a$ vertically above the mid-point of a horizontal line CD of length $4a$. Two elastic strings, each of modulus mg and natural length a, have one end of each attached to B and their other ends to C and D. The rod is released from rest in a horizontal position at right angles to CD. Show that the angular acceleration of the rod immediately after the release is

$$\frac{g}{a}\cdot\frac{\sqrt{3}(9\sqrt{3}-4)}{4}.$$

Find the angular velocity of the rod when it reaches the vertical position. (N.)

***16.** A uniform circular disc of mass m and radius a is free to rotate about a fixed horizontal axis passing through its centre and normal to its plane. A light inextensible string AB rests on the upper half of the circumference of the disc and hangs down vertically at each side. A particle of mass m is attached to the string at A, and to B is attached one end of a light elastic string BC of natural length c and modulus λ. To C is attached another particle of mass m. The inextensible string does not slip on the pulley, the particles move in vertical lines and BC remains vertical throughout. The system is released from rest with the elastic string at its natural length. If x is the displacement of A below its initial position and y is the extension of the elastic string, show that

$$2\, d^2y/dt^2 = 5\, d^2x/dt^2.$$

Show also that the particles move with simple harmonic motion of period $2\pi\sqrt{(3mc/5\lambda)}$. (N.)

***17.** A rough uniform lath of mass M and length $2a$ can move freely in a vertical plane about one end which is fixed. It is held in a horizontal position and a particle of mass m is placed on top of its middle point. If the system is released from rest and μ is the coefficient of friction between the lath and the particle, prove that the particle will remain at the middle point of the lath until the lath has turned through an angle α, where $\tan\alpha = \mu M/(10M+9m)$. (N.)

***18.** A uniform square lamina of mass m and side $2a$ is free to turn about the middle point of one side, and hangs in equilibrium. An impulse P is delivered along the lower horizontal side of the square just sufficient to cause it to rotate through 180°. Show that $P = \frac{1}{3}m\sqrt{(15ag)}$. Find the horizontal and vertical components of the reaction at the pivot when the lamina has turned through 90°. (N.)

***19.** A uniform circular pulley of radius a is mounted on a horizontal axle. A light inextensible string, attached to the rim of the pulley, passes round part of the rim and then vertically downwards to a hanging particle of mass m to which the other end of the string is attached. The moment of inertia of the pulley about the axis of rotation is Mk^2. Show that in the absence of friction at the axle the downward acceleration of the particle is

$$mga^2/(ma^2+Mk^2).$$

If, however, the rotation of the pulley is subject to a frictional couple $p\omega$, where ω is the angular velocity and p is a constant, and if the system starts from rest, show that the greatest possible angular velocity ω_1 in the subsequent motion is given by $p\omega_1 = mga$. Obtain the equation of motion of the system in the form

$$(Mk^2+ma^2)\,\omega_1\frac{d\omega}{dt} = mga(\omega_1-\omega).$$

Deduce that the angular velocity of the pulley acquired in a time t after the start is

$$\omega_1(1-e^{-\lambda t}),$$

where λ is $p/(Mk^2+ma^2)$.

(Assume that a part of the string is wrapped round the rim of the pulley throughout the motion.) (N.)

***20.** Three equal uniform rods are rigidly connected at their ends to form a triangular frame ABC of mass M. The frame swings in a vertical plane about a smooth hinge at the corner C and starts from rest with AB vertical. Show that the component of the reaction perpendicular to AB is $\frac{7}{3}Mg\cos\theta$, where θ is the angle of inclination of AB to the horizontal.

If the angular velocity of the frame is suddenly changed by an impulsive force, find its line of action if there is no impulsive action at C. (N.)

CHAPTER XVI

*FREE MOTION OF A RIGID BODY IN TWO DIMENSIONS

*16.1. Angular Velocity and Angular Acceleration

In Fig. 16.1, P_1, P_2, P_3 are three particles of a rigid lamina which is free to move in its own plane and AB is an arbitrary line, *fixed in the frame of reference*, in the plane of the lamina. The angle between AB and P_1P_2 is θ, the angle between AB and P_1P_3 is φ, and the angle between P_1P_3 and P_1P_2 is α, each angle being measured in the anticlockwise sense from the first-named direction.

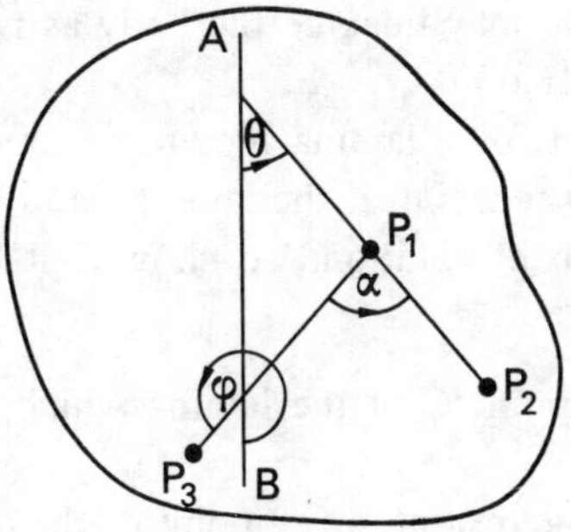

FIG. 16.1

We have, in this case, $\varphi-\theta = 2\pi-\alpha$, and from the definition of a rigid body, α is constant. (In general, for all positions of P_1, P_2, P_3 relative to the axis $\varphi-\theta$ is constant.)

$$\therefore\ \dot{\varphi} = \dot{\theta} \quad \text{and} \quad \ddot{\varphi} = \ddot{\theta}.$$

Similarly it can be shown that $\dot{\theta}$ and $\ddot{\theta}$ are each independent of the choice of the fixed direction AB. It follows that all lines of the lamina have the same angular velocity and the same angular acceleration and these quantities are respectively defined as the *angular velocity* and the *angular acceleration* of the lamina.

*16.2. Instantaneous Centre of Rotation

Translation and Rotation. If the angular velocity of a rigid lamina moving in its plane is zero, the motion is described as *translation.* In the case of the motion of a rigid lamina about a fixed axis discussed in the last chapter, each particle of the lamina moves in a circle about the fixed axis and the motion in this case is described as *rotation.* For the purposes of this discussion the moving lamina is assumed to be of infinite extent; the motion we consider resembles the sliding of a sheet of glass on a table top. If we wish to consider the motion of a special body, such as a rod, or a wheel, this body is imagined to be part of an extensive lamina and the rod, or wheel, is imagined to be drawn on the sheet of glass. (The discussion also applies to the motion of a three-dimensional body when every particle of the body moves parallel to one plane; in this case we may imagine the body as rigidly attached to the sheet of glass. See § 16.6.)

We show now that for a lamina moving in any manner in its plane there is *at any instant* a point of the lamina about which the motion of the lamina is motion of rotation. To show that this point exists it is necessary to show

(i) that there is a point C of the lamina which, instantaneously, has zero velocity,

(ii) that, at the same instant, every point of the lamina is moving in a circle about C.

If condition (i) is satisfied, condition (ii) is satisfied directly from the definition of a rigid body which states that the distance between any two particles Q_1, Q_2 of the body is constant and so each describes a circle relative to the other, i.e. the velocity of Q_2 relative to Q_1 is perpendicular to Q_1Q_2.

Figure 16.2 shows points A and P of the lamina. Referred to rectangu-

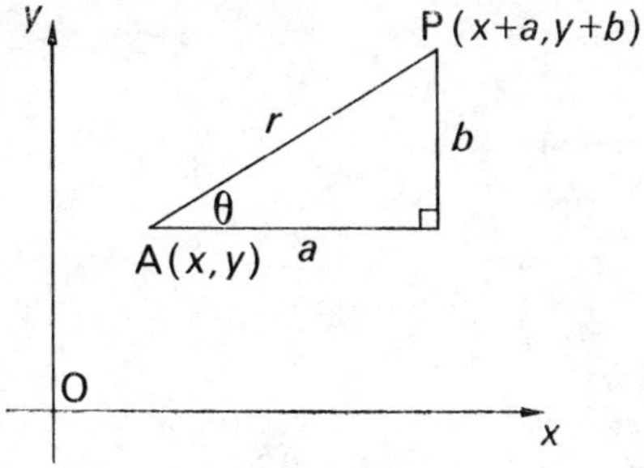

FIG. 16.2

lar axes in the plane of the lamina, and fixed in the frame of reference, the coordinates of A are (x, y) and the coordinates of P are $(x+a, y+b)$. The angle between the positive direction of the x-axis and AP is θ so that $\dot{\theta}$ is the angular velocity of the lamina at any instant. If AP$=r$, $a=r\cos\theta$ and $b = r\sin\theta$, and, *from the definition of a rigid body*, r is constant. Therefore, at any instant, the components of the velocity of P parallel to the axes are $\dot{x}-r\dot{\theta}\sin\theta$ and $\dot{y}+r\dot{\theta}\cos\theta$, and thus the velocity of P at this instant is zero if

$$\dot{x}-b\dot{\theta} = 0 \quad \text{and} \quad \dot{y}+a\dot{\theta} = 0.$$

This argument establishes the fact that, unless $\dot{\theta}=0$ when the motion is one of translation, there is a point C in the plane of the lamina whose coordinates are $(x-\dot{y}/\dot{\theta},\ y+\dot{x}/\dot{\theta})$ which is instantaneously at rest. This point of the body is defined as the *instantaneous centre of rotation of the body* (associated with one particular motion of the body). The instantaneous centre of rotation is unique. This follows at once from the fact that only one point of the lamina can be instantaneously at rest. (The velocity of Q_1 relative to Q_2 is $Q_1Q_2 . \dot{\theta}$ perpendicular to Q_1Q_2 and, unless $\dot{\theta} = 0$, this relative velocity cannot vanish.)

The Instantaneous Centre of Rotation of a Body which Rolls without Slipping

Figure 16.3 illustrates three cases of a body able to *roll* on a fixed surface. In each case there is a point of the body *instantaneously* in contact with the fixed surface. If, throughout a finite period of the motion,

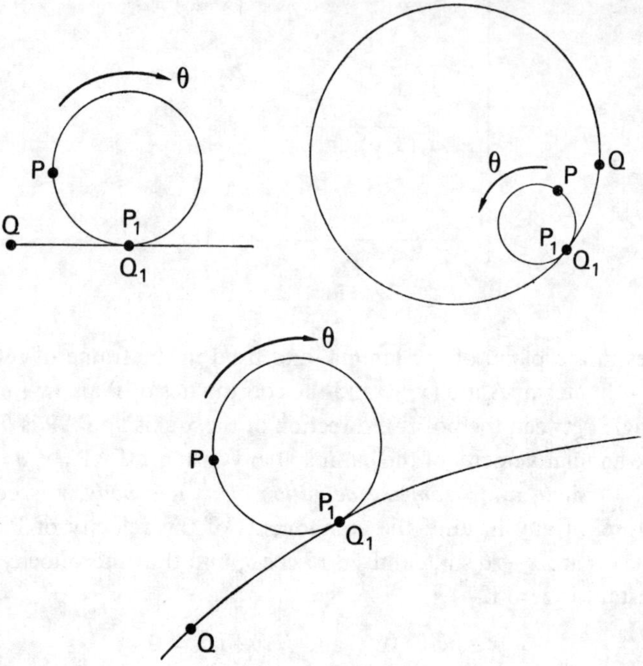

FIG. 16.3

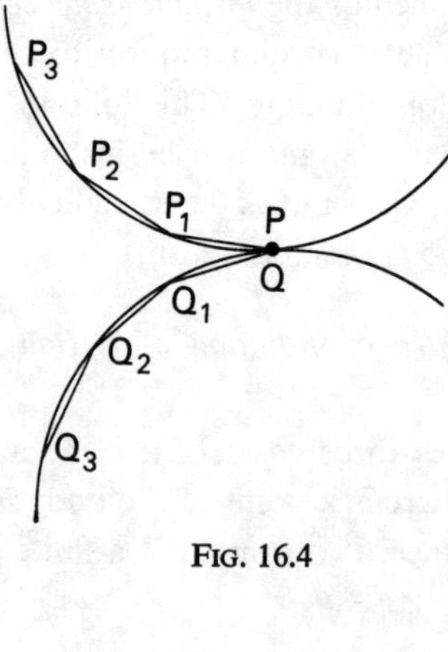

FIG. 16.4

the particle of the body instantaneously in contact with the fixed surface has no velocity relative to the surface at that instant, the body is said to roll without slipping on the surface. This definition implies the statement that when a body rolls without slipping over a fixed surface *the point of the body in contact with the surface at any instant is the instantaneous centre of rotation of the body.*

It follows from this definition and from the definition of arc length as the limiting sum of lengths of chords (Fig. 16.4) that, if the point P of the body was in contact with the point Q of the surface at a particular instant, and if, at a later instant, the point P_n of the body was in contact with the point Q_n of the surface, then arc PP_n = arc QQ_n. (See *Sixth Form Pure Maths.*, Vol. II, § 14.2.)

In each of the cases illustrated in Fig. 16.3 the velocity of P is $PP_1 . \dot{\theta}$ in a direction at right angles to PP_1.

Example. A rod passes through a small fixed ring at O and is constrained so that one end A moves on a fixed straight line. The distance of O from the line is c. Find the instantaneous centre of rotation C of the rod, and show that the path of C in the plane containing the straight line and O is a parabola.

If the rod is turning with uniform angular velocity ω, show that the speed of C, at the instant when the angle between the rod and the fixed line is $\frac{1}{4}\pi$, is $2c\omega\sqrt{5}$. (N.)

Consider the rod in a position inclined at an angle θ to the given straight line, Fig. 16.5. The instantaneous centre is found by drawing perpendiculars to the direction of motion of the rod at the points A and O of the rod. This centre, C, is thus at the inter-

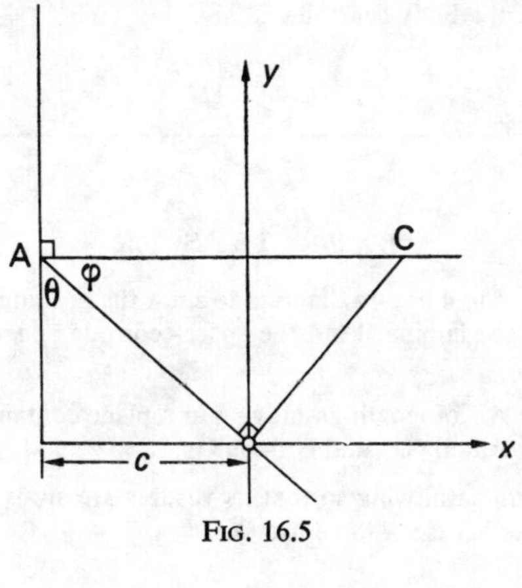

FIG. 16.5

section of the perpendicular to the rod at O, where the rod is moving along OA, and the perpendicular to the given straight line at A. If rectangular axes perpendicular and parallel respectively to the given straight line are taken through O and if (x, y) are the coordinates of C,

$$y = c \cot \theta, \qquad x = y \cot \theta = c \cot^2 \theta.$$

$$\therefore\ y^2 = cx$$

is the equation of the locus of C. Therefore the path of C in the plane containing the straight line and O is a parabola.

Also we have

$$\dot{y} = -c\dot{\theta} \operatorname{cosec}^2 \theta, \qquad \dot{x} = -2c\dot{\theta} \operatorname{cosec}^2 \theta \cot \theta.$$

Hence the speed of C is

$$\sqrt{(\dot{y}^2+\dot{x}^2)} = \dot{\theta} \sqrt{(c^2 \operatorname{cosec}^4 \theta + 4c^2 \operatorname{cosec}^4 \theta \cot^2 \theta)},$$

and when $\dot{\theta} = \omega$ and $\theta = \frac{1}{4}\pi$ the speed of C is

$$\omega\sqrt{(4c^2+16c^2)} = 2c\, \omega \sqrt{5}.$$

Note. For a lamina moving in its own plane the locus of the instantaneous centre in space is called the *space-locus* or *space-centrode*, the locus relative to the moving lamina is called the *body-locus* or *body-centrode*.

In the above example the space-centrode is the parabola $y^2 = cx$. To find the equation of the body-centrode we must find the locus of C referred to axes *fixed relative to the rod*. We let $r =$ AC, $\varphi = \angle$ OAC be the polar coordinates of C referred to A as pole and AO as initial line (both fixed relative to the rod). Then, since

$$AC = c+x = c(1+\cot^2 \theta) = c \operatorname{cosec}^2 \theta, \qquad \varphi = \tfrac{1}{2}\pi - \theta,$$

the polar equation of the body-centrode is

$$r = c \sec^2 \varphi.$$

---

*EXERCISES 16.2

In each of exercises 1 to 4 draw a diagram to show the position of the instantaneous centre of rotation of the lamina. Find the space-centrode and the body-centrode in each case.

***1.** A uniform rod AB of length $2a$ moving in a plane containing rectangular axes Ox, Oy so that A moves along Ox and B along Oy.

***2.** A triangular lamina moving so that its vertices are always in contact with the circumference of a fixed circle with centre O.

***3.** A triangular lamina moving so that two of its sides always touch a fixed circle with centre O.

***4.** PX is a tangent at P to a fixed circle with centre O. A rod AB moves in the plane of the circle so that it is always a tangent to the circle and so that A moves on PX.

***5.** A rod AB moves with its extremities upon two fixed perpendicular lines Ox, Oy so that the mid-point C of AB describes a circle about O with uniform angular velocity ω. Describe the motions of A and B.

Find the instantaneous centre of rotation of AB, and show that, if D, E are two points on AB such that AD = EB, the velocity of D at any instant is perpendicular to OE. (N.)

*16.3. The Motion of a Rigid Lamina Referred to its Centre of Mass

From the analysis of p. 461 it follows that:

The instantaneous motion of a rigid lamina can be analysed into a motion of translation of any one point of the body together with a rotation of the body about that point as centre. When the chosen point of the body is the centre of mass, dynamical problems can be solved by considering these two parts of the motion separately.

This fundamental principle is briefly justified as follows:

We established in § 14.8 of Vol. I and § 15.7 for the two-dimensional motion of a rigid body of mass M,

$$\Sigma X = M\ddot{\bar{x}}, \quad \Sigma Y = M\ddot{\bar{y}}, \tag{16.1}$$

where ΣX and ΣY are the sums of the components in the x, y directions of the external forces acting on the body and $\ddot{\bar{x}}$, $\ddot{\bar{y}}$ are the accelerations in these directions of the centre of mass of the body.

Consider a lamina moving in its own plane. Let the coordinates of a particle of mass m referred to rectangular axes in the plane of the lamina and fixed in the frame of reference be (x, y), let the coordinates of the centre of mass of the lamina be $(\bar{x}, \bar{y})$, and let $x = \bar{x}+x'$, $y = \bar{y}+y'$.

Then $\ddot{x} = \ddot{\bar{x}}+\ddot{x}'$ and $\ddot{y} = \ddot{\bar{y}}+\ddot{y}'$, and therefore the sum of the moments of the forces acting on the separate particles of the lamina about a *fixed* axis perpendicular to its plane through the origin (Fig. 16.6) is

$$\begin{aligned}\Sigma\{m(\ddot{\bar{y}}+\ddot{y}')(\bar{x}+x')-m(\ddot{\bar{x}}+\ddot{x}')(\bar{y}+y')\}\\ = \Sigma m(\bar{x}\ddot{\bar{y}}-\bar{y}\ddot{\bar{x}})+\Sigma m(x'\ddot{y}'-y'\ddot{x}')\\ +\Sigma(m\ddot{y}'\bar{x}+mx'\ddot{\bar{y}}-m\ddot{x}'\bar{y}-my'\ddot{\bar{x}}).\end{aligned}$$

But

(i) $$\Sigma m(\bar{x}\ddot{\bar{y}}-\bar{y}\ddot{\bar{x}}) = \bar{x}\Sigma Y-\bar{y}\Sigma X,$$

where ΣX and ΣY are the sums of the components in the x, y directions of the external forces acting on the lamina,

(ii) and because $$\bar{x} = \frac{\Sigma m(\bar{x}+x')}{\Sigma m} = \bar{x}+\frac{\Sigma mx'}{\Sigma m},$$

$\therefore \Sigma mx' = 0$ and by differentiation with respect to t, $\Sigma m\ddot{x}' = 0$ and similarly $\Sigma my' = 0$, $\Sigma m\ddot{y}' = 0$.

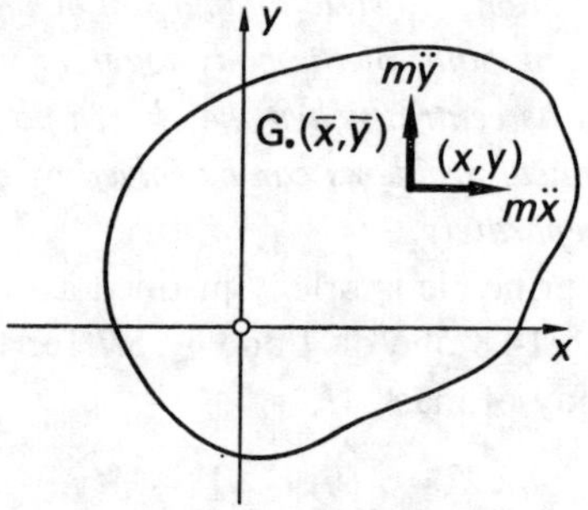

FIG. 16.6

Therefore the sum of the moments of the forces acting on the separate particles about this fixed axis is

$$(\bar{x}\Sigma Y-\bar{y}\Sigma X)+\Sigma m(x'\ddot{y}'-y'\ddot{x}').$$

This quantity is equal to the sum of the moments of the external forces acting on the body which we write as

$$\Sigma\{Y(\bar{x}+x')-X(\bar{y}+y')\}.$$

$$\therefore\ \Sigma m(x'\ddot{y}'-y'\ddot{x}') = \Sigma(Yx'-Xy'). \tag{16.2}$$

Since

$$\frac{\mathrm{d}}{\mathrm{d}t}(x'\dot{y}'-y'\dot{x}') = x'\ddot{y}'-y'\ddot{x}',$$

equation (16.2) can be written

$$\frac{d}{dt}\{\Sigma m(x'\dot{y}'-y'\dot{x}')\} = \Sigma(Yx'-Xy'). \tag{16.3}$$

But, if $x' = r'\cos\theta'$, $y' = r'\sin\theta'$, so that r', θ' are the polar coordinates of a typical particle of mass m referred to G as pole and a line through G parallel to Ox as initial line,

$$x'\dot{y}'-y'\dot{x}' = r'^2\dot{\theta}'\cos^2\theta'+r'^2\dot{\theta}'\sin^2\theta' = r'^2\dot{\theta}'$$

and equation (16.3) can be written

$$\frac{d}{dt}(\Sigma mr'^2\dot{\theta}') = \Sigma(Yx'-Xy'), \tag{16.4}$$

i.e.

$$I_G\ddot{\theta}' = \Sigma(Yx'-Xy'), \tag{16.4a}$$

where I_G is the moment of inertia of the lamina about an axis through G perpendicular to the plane of the lamina.

This is the same result as that obtained in § 15.6 for the motion of a body about a *fixed* axis.

We summarize our conclusions thus:

1. *The motion of a rigid lamina in its plane can be analysed into a motion of translation of the centre of mass, together with a motion of rotation about the centre of mass.*

2. *The motion of translation of the centre of mass is the same as that of a particle of mass equal to the total mass of the lamina acted upon by a force which is the vector sum of the external forces acting on the body.*

3. *The motion of rotation about the centre of mass is the same as the motion of rotation would be if the lamina rotated about a fixed axis through the centre of mass and the same external forces acted on the body.*

*16.4. The Kinetic Energy of a Lamina Moving in its Plane

With the notation of § 16.3 the kinetic energy of the lamina is

$$\begin{aligned}\Sigma\tfrac{1}{2}m(\dot{x}^2+\dot{y}^2) &= \Sigma\tfrac{1}{2}m\{(\dot{x}'+\dot{\bar{x}})^2+(\dot{y}'+\dot{\bar{y}})^2\}\\ &= \Sigma\tfrac{1}{2}m(\dot{\bar{x}}^2+\dot{\bar{y}}^2)+\Sigma\tfrac{1}{2}m(\dot{x}'^2+\dot{y}'^2)+\dot{\bar{x}}\Sigma m\dot{x}'+\dot{\bar{y}}\Sigma m\dot{y}'.\end{aligned}$$

But

(i) $\Sigma mx' = 0$ and therefore $\Sigma m\dot{x}' = 0$; similarly $\Sigma m\dot{y}' = 0$,

(ii) $\Sigma\frac{1}{2}m(\dot{\bar{x}}^2+\dot{\bar{y}}^2) = \frac{1}{2}MV^2$ where M is the mass of the lamina and V is the speed of translation of the centre of mass of the lamina,

(iii) the quantity

$$\Sigma\tfrac{1}{2}m(\dot{x}'^2+\dot{y}'^2) = \Sigma\tfrac{1}{2}mr'^2\dot{\theta}'^2(\cos^2\theta'+\sin^2\theta')$$
$$= \Sigma\tfrac{1}{2}mr'^2\dot{\theta}'^2 = \tfrac{1}{2}I_G\dot{\theta}'^2$$

is the kinetic energy of a similar lamina fixed at the centre of mass and rotating with the same angular velocity about the centre of mass.

We state, therefore, that:

The kinetic energy of a lamina moving freely in its own plane is equal to the kinetic energy due to the motion of translation of the centre of mass together with the kinetic energy due to the motion of rotation relative to the centre of mass about the centre of mass:

$$\text{K.E} = \tfrac{1}{2}MV^2+\tfrac{1}{2}I_G\omega^2, \tag{16.5}$$

where I_G is the M. of I. about an axis through the centre of mass perpendicular to the plane of the lamina, ω is the angular velocity of the lamina about this axis, M is the mass of the lamina and V is the speed of translation of the centre of mass of the lamina.

Note. If C is the instantaneous centre of the lamina and P is a point of the lamina distant R from C, the velocity of the particle of mass m at P is $R\omega$ and the kinetic energy of the lamina is

$$T = \Sigma\tfrac{1}{2}mR^2\omega^2 = \tfrac{1}{2}\omega^2\Sigma mR^2 = \tfrac{1}{2}I_C\omega^2. \tag{16.6}$$

Example 1. A uniform rod AB, of length $2a$ and mass M, moves in a vertical plane with the upper end A against a smooth vertical wall and the lower end B on a smooth horizontal floor. Initially the rod was at rest in a vertical position against the wall and the end B was slightly displaced. Calculate the angular velocity ω of the rod when it makes an angle $\frac{1}{4}\pi$ with the wall.

The instantaneous centre of rotation C is at the intersection of the perpendicular to the wall at A with the perpendicular to the floor at B, Fig. 16.7.

When $\angle$ OAB $= \frac{1}{4}\pi$, the moment of inertia of the rod about a horizontal axis through C is

$$\frac{Ma^2}{3}+Ma^2 = \frac{4Ma^2}{3}.$$

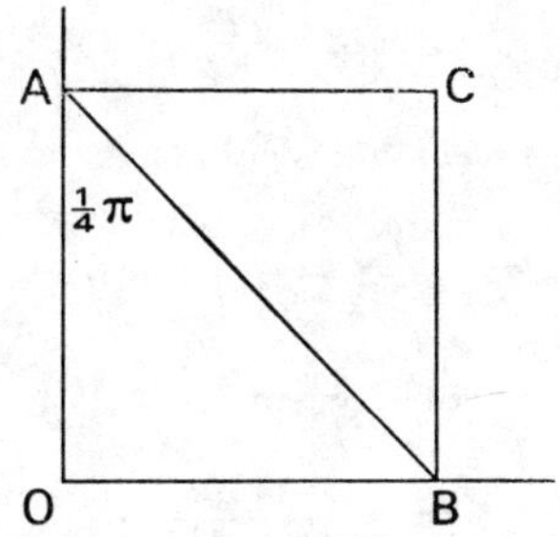

FIG. 16.7

Therefore the energy equation for the rod in this position is

$$Mga\left(1-\frac{1}{2}\sqrt{2}\right) = \frac{2Ma^2}{3}\omega^2.$$

$$\therefore\ \omega = \sqrt{\left\{\frac{3g(2-\sqrt{2})}{4a}\right\}}.$$

Example 2. A uniform thin disc, of centre O, radius a and mass m, has a particle of mass M attached to a point P of its circumference. The disc stands at rest in a vertical plane and on a rough horizontal plane. P is its highest point. The disc is now slightly displaced from rest so as to continue to move in contact with the plane and in a vertical plane. Find an expression for the velocity of the particle when OP is horizontal. (Assume that the disc rolls on the plane.)

The instantaneous centre of the motion is at N the point of contact of the disc with the horizontal plane, Fig. 16.8. The moment of inertia of the disc and particle combined about a horizontal axis through N is $\frac{3ma^2}{2}+M.PN^2$.

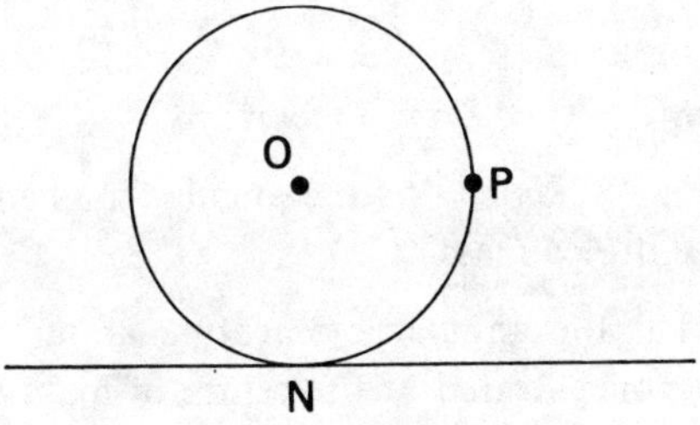

FIG. 16.8

Therefore, when $\angle \text{PON} = \frac{1}{2}\pi, \quad I_N = \frac{3ma^2}{2}+2Ma^2.$

The energy equation for the system in this position is

$$Mga = \frac{1}{2}\left(\frac{3ma^2}{2}+2Ma^2\right)\omega^2,$$

where ω is the angular velocity of the system.

$$\therefore\ \omega^2 = \frac{4Mg}{(3m+4M)a}\,.$$

Therefore the velocity of the particle when OP is horizontal is

$$a\omega\sqrt{2} = 2\sqrt{\left(\frac{2Mga}{3m+4M}\right)}$$

in a direction at right angles to NP.

---

*16.5. The Angular Momentum about an Arbitrary Axis Perpendicular to its Plane of a Lamina Moving in its Own Plane

Take the point of intersection of the *fixed* arbitrary axis with the plane of the lamina as the origin of coordinates. With the notation of the previous sections, the angular momentum of the lamina about the origin is

$$\begin{aligned}\Sigma m\{(\bar{x}+x')(\dot{\bar{y}}+\dot{y}')-(\bar{y}+y')(\dot{\bar{x}}+\dot{x}')\}\\ = \Sigma m(x'\dot{y}'-y'\dot{x}')+\Sigma m(\bar{x}\dot{\bar{y}}-\bar{y}\dot{\bar{x}})\\ +\Sigma m\dot{y}'\bar{x}+\Sigma mx'\dot{\bar{y}}-\Sigma m\dot{x}'\bar{y}-\Sigma my'\dot{\bar{x}}.\end{aligned}$$

But

(i) $\Sigma mx' = \Sigma my' = 0 = \Sigma m\dot{x}' = \Sigma m\dot{y}'$,

(ii) $\Sigma m(x'\dot{y}'-y'\dot{x}') = \Sigma mr'^2\dot{\theta}'$ is the angular momentum of the body about the centre of mass,

(iii) $\Sigma m(\bar{x}\dot{\bar{y}}-\bar{y}\dot{\bar{x}})$ is the angular momentum about the origin of the whole mass concentrated at the centre of mass and moving with the velocity of the centre of mass.

We state, therefore, that:

The angular momentum of a lamina moving in its own plane about a fixed origin in that plane is equal to the sum of the angular momentum relative to the centre of mass about the centre of mass and the angular momentum about the origin of the whole mass concentrated at the centre of mass and moving with the velocity of translation of the centre of mass.

$$\text{Angular momentum about the origin} = I_G\omega + MVp, \qquad (16.7)$$

where I_G is the moment of inertia of the lamina about the axis perpendicular to the plane of the lamina *through its centre of mass*, ω is the angular velocity about this axis, M is the mass of the lamina, V is the speed of translation of its centre of mass and p is the perpendicular distance from the origin to the vector representing the velocity of translation of the centre of mass.

*16.6. Three-dimensional Motion

We have confined the above discussion to the motion of a lamina in its plane. The principles we have stated can be extended to include three-dimensional motion. We shall use the principles in a few problems of two-dimensional motion applied to three-dimensional bodies but only in cases in which the direction of translation of the centre of mass lies in the plane of rotation about the axis through the centre of mass, i.e. when every particle moves parallel to a fixed plane, e.g. a cylinder rolling down an inclined plane.

*16.7. Impulsive Motion

Suppose a lamina moving in its own plane is acted upon by a set of simultaneously applied impulses. Then the results corresponding to those of § 16.3 for the change in motion due to the impulses are as follows:

1. *The change in velocity of* G *is the same as the change in velocity of a particle of mass M at* G *under the action of all the external impulses transferred to act at* G.

2. *The change in the moment of momentum (angular momentum) of the system about any point* A *equals the moment of the external impulses about* A.

[Result (1) follows at once on writing down the equations of motion of each separate particle, integrating over the (infinitesimally) short period of the impulses, adding for the system and using the fact that the sum of the internal impulses is zero.

Result (2) follows similarly on taking moments.]

The following examples illustrate the above results.

Example 1. A uniform rod AB, of mass m and length $2a$, lies at rest on a smooth horizontal table. A horizontal impulse P, making an angle β with AB, is applied to the end A. Find the kinetic energy generated by the impulse.

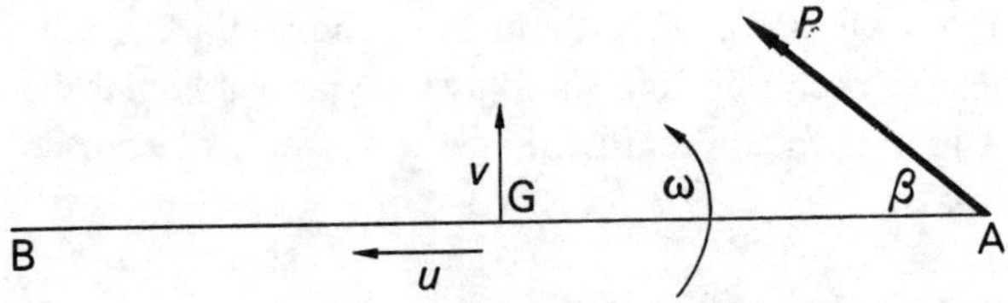

FIG. 16.9

Let the velocity components of the centre of mass G be u, v and the angular velocity be ω just after the application of the impulse, Fig. 16.9. Then the (impulsive) equations of motion of G along and perpendicular to AB are respectively

$$mu = P\cos\beta, \quad mv = P\sin\beta. \tag{1}$$

The equation for the (impulsive) change of angular momentum about G is

$$\tfrac{1}{3}ma^2\omega = aP\sin\beta.$$

$$\therefore\ u = \frac{P\cos\beta}{m}, \quad v = \frac{P\sin\beta}{m}, \quad \omega = \frac{3P\sin\beta}{ma}$$

and the kinetic energy generated by the impulse is

$$\frac{1}{2}m(u^2+v^2)+\frac{1}{2}\frac{ma^2}{3}\omega^2 = \frac{(1+3\sin^2\beta)P^2}{2m}.$$

Note. Instead of taking moments about G we could take moments about A, writing down the fact that the change in angular momentum about A (§ 16.5) is zero, thus

$$\tfrac{1}{3}ma^2\omega - amv = 0.$$

This technique can be useful in avoiding the introduction of unknown internal impulses into the equations of a problem. See examples 4, p. 478, and 6, p. 481.

Example 2. A uniform circular disc, of radius a and mass m, is rolling along a horizontal line with velocity V and its plane is vertical. The highest point of the disc is then suddenly fixed by passing a smooth spindle parallel to the axle of the disc through a small hole at the circumference. Show that the disc will make complete revolutions about the spindle if $V^2 > 24ga$.

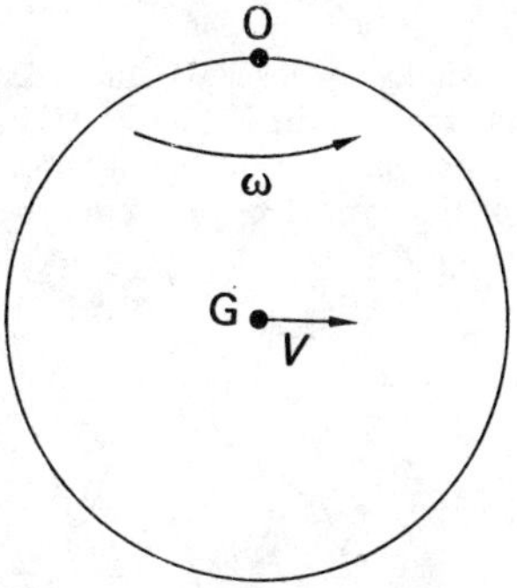

FIG. 16.10

Let ω, Fig. 16.10, be the angular velocity of the disc about the spindle, O. Just before the spindle is inserted the counter-clockwise angular momentum about O is

$$amV-\tfrac{1}{2}ma^2(V/a) = \tfrac{1}{2}amV.$$

(The first term on the l.h. side is the angular momentum due to the motion of G, the second is that due to the motion about G.) When the disc begins to turn about O, its angular momentum about O is $3ma^2\omega/2$ counter-clockwise. Since there is no moment of the impulsive forces about O, angular momentum about O is conserved and

$$\tfrac{1}{2}maV = \tfrac{3}{2}ma^2\omega.$$
$$\therefore\ \omega = \tfrac{1}{3}V/a.$$

The disc will execute complete revolutions about O if the kinetic energy just after the spindle is inserted is *more than sufficient* to raise the centre of mass through a height $2a$, i.e. if

$$\frac{1}{2}\frac{3ma^2}{2}\omega^2 > 2mga$$

which leads to

$$V^2 > 24ga.$$

*16.8. Application to Problems

The principles of motion, kinetic energy and momentum stated in this chapter make possible the solution of problems concerning the motion of a rigid body. In general, the motion is analysed into motion of the centre of mass and motion about an axis through the centre of mass. The principles of particle dynamics are applied to the former and the principles discussed in Chapter XV are applied to the latter. In some cases, use can be made of the instantaneous centre of rotation.

Example 1. A uniform cylinder, of mass M and radius r, rolls, without slipping, down a fixed plane of inclination α to the horizontal. Use the energy equation to find the time taken by the cylinder to move through a distance x from rest down the plane. Find the minimum value of the coefficient of friction between the cylinder and the plane for which the motion is possible.

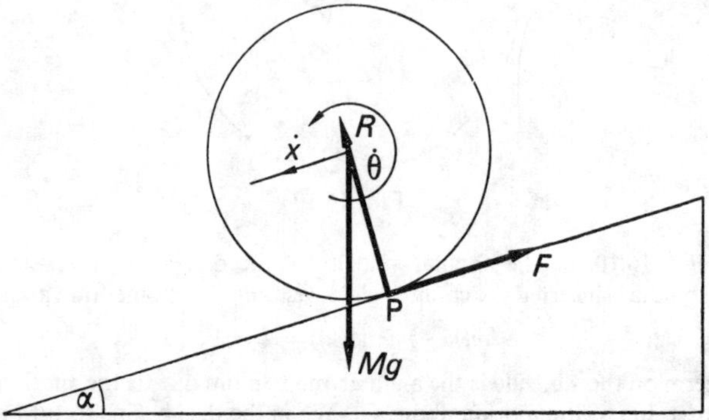

FIG. 16.11

Figure 16.11 shows the forces acting on the cylinder, the angular velocity $\dot{\theta}$ of the cylinder about its axis, and the linear velocity $\dot{x}$ of the axis. The direction of $\dot{x}$ is determined by the geometrical constraints of the system. Further, since the generator of the cylinder in contact with the plane is instantaneously at rest, $\dot{x} = r\dot{\theta}$.

The energy equation is

$$\frac{1}{2}M\dot{x}^2 + \frac{1}{2}\frac{Mr^2}{2}\dot{\theta}^2 = Mgx\sin\alpha.$$

$$\therefore\ \tfrac{3}{4}M\dot{x}^2 = Mgx\sin\alpha.$$

$$\therefore\ \dot{x}^2 = \frac{4gx\sin\alpha}{3}.$$

Differentiating this equation with respect to t we get

$$2\dot{x}\ddot{x} = \frac{4g\sin\alpha}{3}\dot{x}.$$

$$\therefore\ \ddot{x} = \tfrac{2}{3}g\sin\alpha.$$

The time taken for the axis of the cylinder to move through a distance x from rest with this constant acceleration is given by

$$x = \frac{1}{2}\frac{2g\sin\alpha}{3}t^2,$$

$$\text{i.e.,}\qquad t = \sqrt{\left(\frac{3x}{g\sin\alpha}\right)}.$$

The equations of motion for the cylinder are:

(1) for the motion of *translation* of its axis *parallel to the plane*,

$$Mg\sin\alpha - F = M\ddot{x},$$

where F is the force of friction, not necessarily limiting, acting on the cylinder up the plane,

(2) for the motion of *translation* of its axis *perpendicular* to the plane

$$Mg\cos\alpha - R = 0,$$

where R is the normal action of the plane on the cylinder,

(3) for the motion of rotation about the axis

$$Fr = \frac{Mr^2}{2}\ddot{\theta}.$$

From these equations and from the values of $\ddot{x}$ and $\ddot{\theta}$ obtained above we have,

$$R = Mg\cos\alpha, \qquad F = \tfrac{1}{3}Mg\sin\alpha.$$

For the motion to be possible $F/R \leqq \mu$, i.e. $\mu \geqq \frac{1}{3}\tan\alpha$.

Note. Here we do not assume limiting friction; the frictional force brought into play is just sufficient to prevent slipping. It should only be assumed that friction is limiting if slipping is known to be taking place (and the direction of this limiting frictional force must then oppose the direction of relative slipping).

Example 2. A circular disc AB rolls without slipping up a line of greatest slope of an inclined plane, being drawn up by a light string which is wound round the disc. The string passes over a smooth peg P and carries a heavy particle of mass m' at its free end C. If AP is parallel to the plane and the motion takes place in a vertical plane through the line of greatest slope, find the acceleration of the disc. The plane is inclined at an angle α to the horizontal, the mass of the disc is m, its radius is a, and the radius of gyration about an axis through its centre and perpendicular to its plane is k. (N.)

Figure 16.12 shows the forces acting on the disc, the linear acceleration, $\ddot{x}$, of its centre and the angular acceleration, $\ddot{\theta}$, about its centre. The downward acceleration of C is f and the tension in the string is T. The equations of motion for the disc are

$$Ta - Fa = mk^2\ddot{\theta}, \qquad (1)$$

$$T + F - mg\sin\alpha = m\ddot{x}, \qquad (2)$$

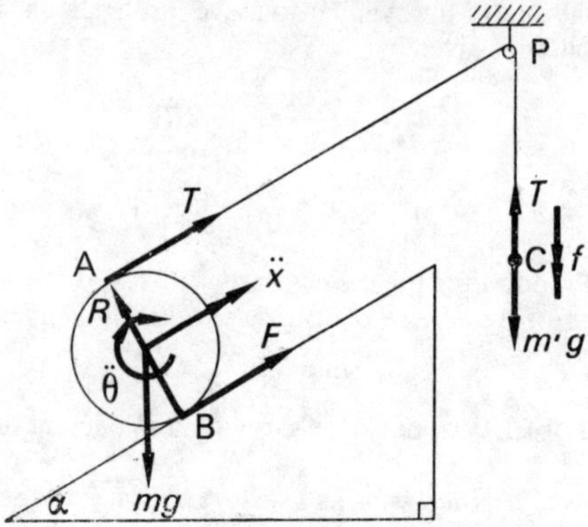

FIG. 16.12

where F is the force of friction between the plane and the disc. The equation of motion for the particle is

$$m'g - T = m'f. \tag{3}$$

Since B is the instantaneous centre of rotation of the disc,

$$a\ddot{\theta} = \ddot{x}. \tag{4}$$

Since the acceleration of C is equal to the linear acceleration of A,

$$f = \ddot{x} + a\ddot{\theta} = 2a\ddot{\theta}. \tag{5}$$

From these equations,

$$m'g - T = 2m'a\ddot{\theta},$$

$$T - F = \frac{mk^2\ddot{\theta}}{a},$$

$$T + F = ma\ddot{\theta} + mg\sin\alpha.$$

$$\therefore\ 2T = \ddot{\theta}\left(\frac{mk^2}{a} + ma\right) + mg\sin\alpha.$$

$$\therefore\ 2m'g - 4m'a\ddot{\theta} = \theta\left(\frac{mk^2}{a} + ma\right) + mg\sin\alpha.$$

$$\therefore\ \ddot{\theta} = (2m'g - mg\sin\alpha)\,a/(4m'a^2 + mk^2 + ma^2).$$

Hence the acceleration of the disc is

$$(2m'g - mg\sin\alpha)\,a^2/(4m'a^2 + mk^2 + ma^2).$$

Example 3. A uniform rod is held inclined to the vertical at an angle β, with one end on a smooth horizontal table, and is released. Find the angular velocity of the rod just before it strikes the plane, and show that the angular acceleration at that instant is independent of β.

Prove also that, at the same instant, the reaction of the plane on the rod is one quarter of the weight of the rod.

Because there is no horizontal force acting on the rod, its centre of gravity G does not acquire any horizontal velocity and therefore remains in the same vertical line Oy, Fig. 16.13. If m is the mass of the rod, $2a$ the length of the rod, y the height of G above

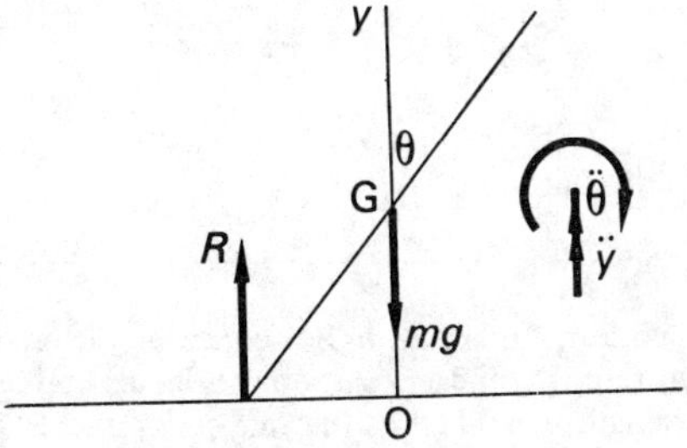

FIG. 16.13

the plane and θ the inclination of the rod to the vertical, the kinetic energy of the rod is

$$\tfrac{1}{2}m(\dot{y}^2+k^2\dot{\theta}^2),$$

where $k^2 = \tfrac{1}{3}a^2$ and $y = a\cos\theta$. Also

$$\dot{y} = -a\dot{\theta}\sin\theta.$$

Therefore the kinetic energy of the rod is $\tfrac{1}{2}ma^2(\tfrac{1}{3}+\sin^2\theta)\dot{\theta}^2$.

The energy equation is therefore

$$\tfrac{1}{2}ma^2(\tfrac{1}{3}+\sin^2\theta)\dot{\theta}^2+mga\cos\theta = C,$$

where C is constant and, since $\dot{\theta} = 0$ when $\theta = \beta$, therefore $C = mga\cos\beta$ and the energy equation becomes

$$\tfrac{1}{2}ma^2(\tfrac{1}{3}+\sin^2\theta)\dot{\theta}^2+mga(\cos\theta-\cos\beta) = 0. \tag{1}$$

Therefore when

$$\theta = 90°, \quad \dot{\theta} = \sqrt{\left(\frac{3g\cos\beta}{2a}\right)},$$

i.e. the angular velocity of the rod just before it strikes the plane is

$$\sqrt{\left(\frac{3g\cos\beta}{2a}\right)}.$$

The equations of motion for the rod are

$$R - mg = m\ddot{y} = -ma(\dot{\theta}^2 \cos\theta + \ddot{\theta} \sin\theta),$$

$$Ra \sin\theta = \tfrac{1}{3}ma^2\ddot{\theta}.$$

When the rod is about to strike the plane $\theta = \frac{1}{2}\pi$, and if the appropriate variables are indicated by the suffix $\pi/2$,

$$R_{\pi/2} - mg = -ma\ddot{\theta}_{\pi/2},$$

$$R_{\pi/2} = \tfrac{1}{3}ma\ddot{\theta}_{\pi/2}.$$

$$\therefore \; R_{\pi/2} = \frac{1}{4}mg, \qquad \ddot{\theta}_{\pi/2} = \frac{3g}{4a},$$

both being independent of β. Note that $\ddot{\theta}_{\pi/2}$ can be obtained at once by differentiating (1) with respect to t and putting $\theta = \frac{1}{2}\pi$,

---

Example 4. Two uniform rods AB, BC of equal lengths and masses are smoothly hinged at B and laid in a straight line on a smooth horizontal table. A horizontal impulse perpendicular to its length is applied at the mid-point of AB. Determine the subsequent initial motions, and show that C moves off with one-fifth the initial speed of A and in the opposite direction. (N.)

Let each rod be of mass m and length $2a$ and let the horizontal impulse be P. At the hinge there is an impulsive action and an equal and opposite impulsive reaction between the rods and because initial relative motion in the direction parallel to the rods is not possible these impulses ($= Y$, say) are at right angles to the rods.

The initial velocity of the centre of mass of each rod is at right angles to its length. In Fig. 16.14 initial velocities are marked with a single arrow and impulses with a double arrow.

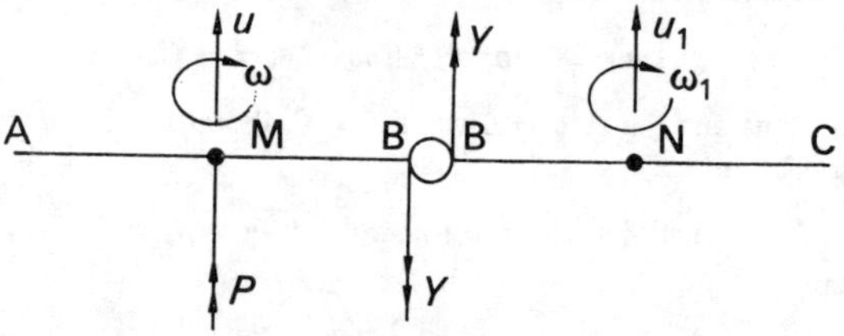

FIG. 16.14

The equations of motion for the rods are:
for the rod AB, and for the initial motion of translation of its centre of mass,

$$P - Y = mu; \tag{1}$$

for the rod AB, and for the initial motion of rotation about its centre of mass,

$$Ya = \frac{ma^2}{3}\omega; \tag{2}$$

for the rod BC and for the initial motion of translation of its centre of mass,

$$Y = mu_1; \tag{3}$$

for the rod BC and for the initial motion of rotation about its centre of mass,

$$Ya = \frac{ma^2}{3}\omega_1. \tag{4}$$

In addition, there is an equation which expresses the fact that the initial linear velocities of the ends of the rods at B are equal,

$$u_1 + a\omega_1 = u - a\omega. \tag{5}$$

From equations (2) and (4), $\omega = \omega_1$.

From equations (3) and (4), $u_1 = \dfrac{a\omega_1}{3} = \dfrac{a\omega}{3}$.

Therefore from equation (5), $u = \dfrac{7a\omega}{3}$.

Therefore from equation (1), $u = \dfrac{7P}{8m}$.

$$\therefore\ u_1 = \frac{P}{8m}, \qquad \omega = \omega_1 = \frac{3P}{8am}.$$

Hence the linear velocity of A is

$$u + a\omega = \frac{5P}{4m},$$

and the linear velocity of C is

$$u_1 - a\omega_1 = -\frac{P}{4m}.$$

Therefore C starts to move with one-fifth of the initial speed of A in the opposite direction.

Note that this problem can be solved without introducing the internal impulses at B as follows:

Linear momentum of the whole system perpendicular to the line of the rods gives

$$mu + mu_1 = P. \tag{6}$$

The equations expressing the change of angular momentum about B of AB and BC are respectively

$$amu + \tfrac{1}{3}ma^2\omega = aP, \tag{7}$$

$$amu_1 - \tfrac{1}{3}ma^2\omega_1 = 0. \tag{8}$$

Equations (6), (7), (8) together with the kinematical condition (5) are sufficient to determine u, u_1, ω and ω_1.

Example 5. A hollow cylinder of internal radius a is fixed with its axis horizontal. A uniform solid cylinder of radius b, with its axis also horizontal, rolls without slipping on the inner surface of the hollow cylinder. If initially the plane through the two axes is horizontal and the inner cylinder is released, find the angular velocity of this plane when it is vertical. Show that the motion of this plane is the same as that of a simple pendulum of length $3(a-b)/2$ swinging through the same angle. (N.)

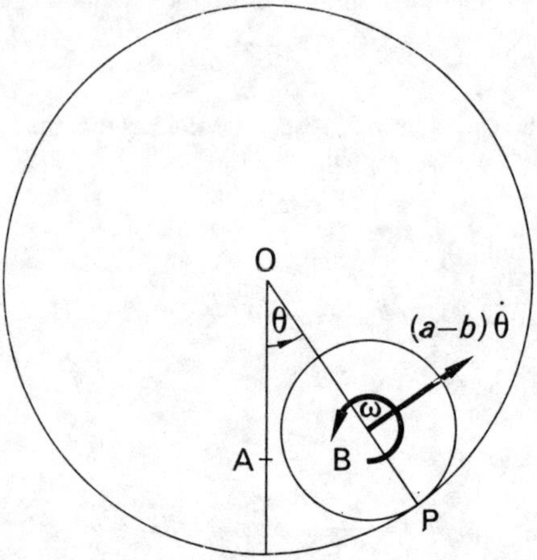

FIG. 16.15

Figure 16.15 shows the cylinders when the angle between the plane of the axes and the vertical is θ. The velocity of the axis of the rolling cylinder is $(a-b)\dot{\theta}$ in the direction at right angles to the plane of the axes, and the angular velocity of this cylinder about its axis is ω (say).

Because the generator of contact between the two cylinders is instantaneously at rest

$$b\omega+(a-b)\dot{\theta} = 0.$$

The kinetic energy of the rolling cylinder is

$$\frac{1}{2}m(a-b)^2\dot{\theta}^2+\frac{1}{2}\frac{mb^2}{2}\omega^2,$$

where m is its mass and this is equal to

$$\tfrac{1}{2}m(b^2\omega^2+\tfrac{1}{2}b^2\omega^2) = \tfrac{3}{4}mb^2\omega^2 \quad \text{or} \quad \tfrac{3}{4}m(a-b)^2\dot{\theta}^2.$$

The energy equation for the rolling cylinder is therefore

$$\tfrac{3}{4}m(a-b)^2\dot{\theta}^2-mg(a-b)\cos\theta = \text{constant}.$$

Therefore, differentiating with respect to t,

$$\tfrac{3}{2}m(a-b)^2\dot{\theta}\,\ddot{\theta}+mg(a-b)\dot{\theta}\sin\theta = 0.$$

$$\therefore\ \ddot{\theta} = \frac{-2g}{3(a-b)}\sin\theta.$$

The equation of motion for a simple pendulum of length l obtained in § 14.10 is $\ddot{\theta} = -(g/l)\sin\theta$. The motion is therefore the same as that of a simple pendulum of length $3(a-b)/2$ swinging through the same angle.

Example 6. A uniform hoop, of mass m, radius a and centre A, rolling upright on a horizontal plane with velocity v collides with a fixed perfectly rough inelastic rail which is perpendicular to the plane of the hoop and at a height $h(< a)$ above the horizontal plane. Show that, for the hoop to surmount the rail without jumping,

$$\frac{2a\sqrt{\{g(a-h)\}}}{2a-h} \geqq v > \frac{2a\sqrt{(gh)}}{2a-h}.$$

After impact the hoop will begin to turn about the rail; let the angular velocity just after the impact be ω. Then, since the angular momentum of the hoop about the rail is unaltered by the impact,

$$m(a-h)v+ma^2\frac{v}{a} = 2ma^2\omega.$$

$$\therefore\ a^2\omega = \tfrac{1}{2}(2a-h)v. \qquad (1)$$

Let O be the point of the rail about which the hoop turns and suppose that the hoop remains in contact with the rail and that at time t after the impact OA makes the angle θ with the upward vertical, Fig. 16.16. Then the energy equation for rotation about O is

$$\tfrac{1}{2}2ma^2\dot{\theta}^2+mg(h+a\cos\theta) = \tfrac{1}{2}2ma^2\omega^2+mga. \qquad (2)$$

Also, if R is the component along OA of the reaction between the rail and the hoop, the equation of motion of A resolved along AO, is

$$mg\cos\theta-R = ma\dot{\theta}^2. \qquad (3)$$

Equations (2) and (3) give

$$a^2\dot{\theta}^2 = a^2\omega^2-g(h+a\cos\theta-a), \qquad (4)$$

$$R = m\{g(2a\cos\theta+h-a)-a^2\omega^2\}/a. \qquad (5)$$

In order that the hoop should surmount the rail without jumping we must have both $\dot{\theta}^2 > 0$ and $R \geqq 0$ for

$$\frac{a-h}{a} \leqq \cos\theta \leqq 1.$$

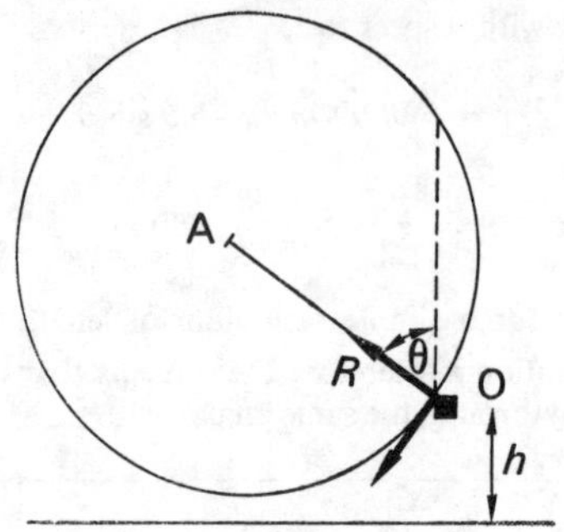

FIG. 16.16

Therefore, from (4) and (5),

$$a^2\omega^2 > gh, \tag{6}$$

$$g(a-h) \geqq a^2\omega^2. \tag{7}$$

Here (6) expresses the condition that the hoop has sufficient energy to surmount the rail and (7) expresses the condition that the hoop is not moving so fast *that it leaves the rail immediately after the impact* (when R is least). Substitution for ω^2 from (1) gives the required inequalities.

---

*MISCELLANEOUS EXERCISES XVI

***1.** Find the energy equation for a sphere which rolls, without slipping, down a fixed plane of inclination α to the horizontal. Deduce the acceleration of the centre, the time taken for the sphere to move through a distance x from rest and the velocity of the centre in this position.

If the sphere moves through 2 m in the first second of its motion from rest, and completes the distance in two more seconds, find the total length of the plane.

***2.** Find the moment of inertia of a uniform circular cylinder 0·3 m long, 0·1 m in diameter, and of mass 4 kg, about (i) its axis, (ii) a diameter of one of its ends.

A roller of the above dimensions and mass rolls down a plane inclined at 30° to the horizontal, and rough enough to prevent slipping. The handle of the roller, whose mass may be neglected, is parallel to the plane and is attached to a cord also parallel to the plane, which passes over a smooth fixed pulley attached to the highest point of the plane and carries a weight of 1 kg at its other end. Find the acceleration of the weight as the roller rolls down the plane.

***3.** A thin uniform rod AB of mass m and length $2l$ lies on a smooth horizontal table. A particle of mass m moving with velocity v in the direction making an angle

$\frac{1}{4}\pi$ with AB collides with and adheres to the rod at the end B. Find the initial velocity of the end A of the rod.

***4.** Prove that the moment of inertia of a uniform rod of length $2a$ about an axis intersecting the rod at right angles at a distance b from its centre is $M(\frac{1}{3}a^2+b^2)$, where M is the mass of the rod.

A wheel of radius a is formed of a thin uniform rim of mass M and n uniform spokes of length $a-b$, each of mass m, which are fastened to the rim and to an axle of radius b and mass m'. The wheel rolls down an inclined plane of inclination α. Find the acceleration of its centre. (O.C.)

***5.** A uniform plank AB, of mass m and of length $2a$, rests with A on a smooth horizontal floor and B against a smooth vertical wall. The plank is initially vertical and at rest, and is slightly disturbed so that A slides in a direction at right angles to the wall and B slides vertically downwards. Find the angular velocity and angular acceleration of the plank when it has turned through the angle $\tan^{-1}(3/4)$. Find also the reactions at A and B when the plank is in this position. (N.)

***6.** A uniform rod of mass m and length $2l$ has a small light ring attached to one end and the ring is free to slide on a smooth horizontal wire. When the rod is at rest in the vertical position, it receives at the lower end a horizontal blow of magnitude $2mV$ parallel to the wire. Show that the lower end of the rod starts off with a speed $8V$, and that when it is inclined at an angle θ to the vertical,

$$(1+3\sin^2\theta)l^2\dot{\theta}^2 = 36V^2-6gl(1-\cos\theta). \qquad \text{(N.)}$$

***7.** Prove that the moment of inertia of a uniform cylindrical tube of mass M, about its axis, is equal to

$$\tfrac{1}{2}M(a^2+b^2),$$

where a, b are the internal and external radii of the tube.

The tube starts from rest and rolls, with its axis horizontal, down an inclined plane (making an angle β with the horizontal). By applying the principle of energy, or otherwise, show that T, the time occupied in travelling a distance l along the plane, is given by

$$l\left(3+\frac{a^2}{b^2}\right) = gT^2\sin\beta. \qquad \text{(O.C.)}$$

***8.** A uniform rod of length $2a$ is held at an angle α to the vertical with its lower end on a smooth horizontal plane, and is then released. Show that the angular velocity of the rod when it becomes horizontal is

$$\sqrt{\{(3g\cos\alpha)/(2a)\}}. \qquad \text{(N.)}$$

***9.** A uniform circular disc of mass m and radius a rolls (without slipping) down a plane inclined at an angle α to the horizontal; the coefficient of friction between the plane and the disc is μ. Prove that the acceleration of the centre of the disc is $\frac{2}{3}g\sin\alpha$ and that $\mu \geqq \frac{1}{3}\tan\alpha$.

If a constant braking couple of moment G is applied to the disc prove that it will continue to roll down the plane if

$$\mu \geqq \frac{1}{3}\tan\alpha+\frac{2G\sec\alpha}{3mag}. \qquad \text{(N.)}$$

***10.** A circular disc of radius a rolls without slipping in a vertical plane on a horizontal table. The centre of gravity G of the disc is at a distance $\frac{1}{2}a$ from the centre O and the radius of gyration of the disc about an axis through G perpendicular to its plane is k. When G is at the same level as O the disc starts rolling with an angular velocity ω so that G begins to move downward. Form the equation of energy and show that when G is at its lowest position the angular velocity is

$$\sqrt{\left\{\frac{(\frac{5}{4}a^2+k^2)\omega^2+ga}{\frac{1}{4}a^2+k^2}\right\}}. \qquad \text{(N.)}$$

***11.** A uniform circular disc of radius a is free to roll in a vertical plane on a rough horizontal table. To the middle point of a radius of the disc is attached a particle whose mass is half that of the disc. If the system is just started rolling from the position in which the particle is vertically above the centre, prove that when the disc has rolled through an angle θ, its angular speed is

$$\sqrt{\left(\frac{4g}{a}\cdot\frac{1-\cos\theta}{17+4\cos\theta}\right)}.$$

Prove also that when the particle is at the level of the centre, the force of friction is 92/867 of the total weight of the system. (N.)

***12.** An inextensible string, attached to and wrapped round a pulley mounted on a fixed smooth horizontal axis, passes vertically downwards to a cylindrical reel round which it is wrapped and to which its other end is attached. The pulley and reel are each of mass m, their radii are a_1 and a_2, and their radii of gyration about their axes k_1 and k_2 respectively. Find the angular accelerations of the reel and pulley, assuming the axis of the reel to remain horizontal. Show also that the tension of the string is

$$mgk_1^2k_2^2/(a_1^2k_2^2+a_2^2k_1^2+k_1^2k_2^2). \qquad \text{(N.)}$$

***13.** A string connects a particle of mass m to the end B of a uniform rod AB of mass M. The system is at rest on a smooth horizontal table with the particle at B. If the particle is projected horizontally with velocity V perpendicular to AB, prove that its velocity immediately after the string becomes taut is $4mV/(M+4m)$.

Show also that the loss of kinetic energy of the system due to the tightening of the string is $\frac{1}{2}mMV^2/(M+4m)$. (N.)

***14.** A circular hoop of radius a is rotating and sliding in a vertical plane along a straight line on a rough horizontal table. After a time t the velocity of its centre is $V-\mu gt$ and the velocity of its highest point is V in the same direction as that of the centre, V being constant. Find the locus of the instantaneous centre of the hoop referred to horizontal and vertical axes through the initial position of its centre. Prove that the hoop will begin to roll after its centre has described a distance $3V^2/8\mu g$. (N.)

***15.** A uniform rod of length $2a$ has a small ring of the same mass attached to one end. The ring is free to slide on a smooth horizontal wire. Initially the ring is at instantaneous rest and the rod is vertically below the ring, swinging in a vertical plane through the wire with an angular velocity $\sqrt{(g/a)}$. Describe the subsequent motion, show that the angular velocity of the rod vanishes instantaneously when the rod is inclined at an angle $\cos^{-1}(7/12)$ to the vertical, and determine the speed of the ring at that instant. (N.)

***16.** A uniform circular disc, of mass m and radius a, is at rest with its plane vertical on a rough horizontal table; the coefficient of friction at the point of contact is μ. A constant couple λmga, acting in the plane of the disc, is applied to the disc. Assuming that the disc rolls on the plane show that the acceleration of its centre is $2\lambda g/3$. Show also that in this case $\mu \geqq 2\lambda/3$. (L.)

***17.** A uniform rod AB of mass m and length $2a$ slides with its ends on a fixed smooth vertical circular wire whose centre is O. If b denotes the distance of the centre C of the rod from O, and θ the angle which OC makes with the downward vertical, prove that

$$\dot{\theta}^2 = \frac{6bg}{3b^2+a^2}(\cos\theta - \cos\varphi),$$

where $\varphi \left(< \frac{\pi}{2}\right)$ is the maximum value of θ during the motion. (L.)

***18.** A particle of mass m rests on a smooth fixed plane inclined at an angle α to the horizontal. A light inextensible string attached to the particle passes up the line of greatest slope of the plane, over a fixed smooth peg at the highest point of the plane, and then vertically downwards to a reel of mass M and radius a round which it is wrapped and to which its end is attached. The reel has symmetry about an axis about which its radius of gyration is k, and the string is free to unwind with this axis remaining horizontal. Find the tension of the string and the acceleration of the particle. If the system is released from rest, show that the subsequent motion of the reel will be upwards if

$$\sin\alpha > \frac{M}{m} + \frac{a^2}{k^2}. \qquad \text{(N.)}$$

***19.** A uniform sphere, of radius a, is projected with velocity u and without rotation up a rough plane of inclination α. The coefficient of friction between the sphere and the plane is $\frac{1}{7}\tan\alpha$. Show that friction acts down the plane for a time $2u/(3g\sin\alpha)$, and then up the plane, and that the angular velocity of the sphere when its centre is reduced to rest is $5u/36a$. (O.C.)

***20.** A sphere of mass M, of radius a and radius of gyration k about any diameter, is such that its centre of gravity coincides with its geometrical centre. The sphere is placed on a rough plane inclined at angle α to the horizontal and is initially at rest. A constant horizontal force $P\,(> Mg\tan\alpha)$ acts on the sphere in a line passing through its centre and in a vertical plane normal to the inclined plane, the sense of P tending to make the sphere move upwards. Show that the sphere will roll up the plane if the coefficient of friction, μ, is greater than μ_0, where

$$\mu_0 = \frac{k^2}{a^2+k^2}\cdot\frac{P - Mg\tan\alpha}{P\tan\alpha + Mg}.$$

If $\mu < \mu_0$, find the angular acceleration and the linear acceleration of the centre of the sphere, and show that the velocity of the point of the sphere momentarily in contact with the plane will always be directed up the plane. (N.)

***21.** A uniform heavy sphere of radius a, rolls without slipping, inside a fixed rough cylinder of inner radius $5a$ and with its axis horizontal. The sphere rolls from the equilibrium position, in a vertical plane perpendicular to the axis of the cylinder, with initial angular velocity $2\sqrt{(ng/a)}$.

Show that the sphere will roll completely round the inner surface of the cylinder if $n > 27/7$. Show also that if $n = 4$ the coefficient of friction between the sphere and the cylinder is $\geqq 2/\sqrt{35}$. (L.)

***22.** A uniform sphere of radius a, rotating with angular velocity ω about a horizontal diameter is placed on a rough plane inclined at angle α to the horizontal so that the axis of rotation is parallel to the plane and the direction of rotation is such that the sphere tends to roll up the plane. If μ, the coefficient of friction, is greater than $\tan\alpha$ and if the centre of the sphere is initially at rest, show that the sphere will slip for a time $2a\omega/(7\mu\cos\alpha - 2\sin\alpha)g$ before rolling begins, and find the distance through which the centre of the sphere moves while slipping is taking place. Find also the angular velocity at the moment when rolling begins. (N.)

***23.** A uniform solid cylinder of mass M and radius a has a particle of mass m embedded in its curved surface at a point of the circumference of the central cross-section. The cylinder is placed on a perfectly rough horizontal plane with its axis horizontal, and rolls on the plane so that its angular velocity is ω at the moment when the particle is in contact with the plane. Find the angular velocity of the cylinder at the moment when the radius to the particle is inclined at angle θ to the downward vertical, and show that, in order that the cylinder may make complete revolutions, the value of ω must exceed $\sqrt{(8mg/3Ma)}$.

If ω is small, show that the cylinder performs small oscillations about the position of stable equilibrium, and that the period of oscillation is

$$2\pi\sqrt{\left(\frac{3Ma}{2mg}\right)}. \qquad \text{(N.)}$$

***24.** A uniform rod AB of mass m and length $2a$ is held in the horizontal position and is then allowed to fall freely. After falling through a height $8a$ the end A engages with a fixed smooth hinge. Prove that the rod begins to turn about A with angular velocity $3\sqrt{(g/a)}$.

Find the velocity of B when it is vertically below A. (L.)

***25.** A uniform rod of length $2l$ rests on a smooth table and passes through a small smooth ring which is freely hinged to the table. Initially the rod is rotating with angular velocity ω about a vertical axis through the ring and the ring is at a distance a from the mid-point of the rod. Find the angular velocity when the rod is just leaving the ring and show that the speed of the mid-point of the rod is then

$$\omega\sqrt{\left\{\frac{5}{16}l^2 + \frac{7}{8}a^2 - \frac{3}{16}\frac{a^4}{l^2}\right\}}. \qquad \text{(N.)}$$

CHAPTER XVII

MOTION WITH VARIABLE ACCELERATION

17.1. Kinematics

In Chapter III of Volume I we discussed the graphical relationships among the quantities distance, velocity, acceleration and time for a particle moving in a straight line. Graphical interpretations of the definitions

$$v = \frac{ds}{dt}, \qquad f = \frac{dv}{dt} = v\frac{dv}{ds}$$

(in the usual notation) enabled us to estimate any two of the quantities s, v, f and t within the range involved if a number of corresponding values of the other two were known. In each of the examples which follow a *functional* relationship between two of the quantities is known, necessary boundary conditions are given, and the remaining quantities are calculated.

Example 1. A particle moves in a straight line so that at time t from the beginning of the motion its displacement from a fixed point O in the line is s and its velocity is v where $v = ks$, k being constant, and $s = a$ when $t = 0$. Find

(a) the initial acceleration of the particle,
(b) the value of s when $t = 2$ seconds,
(c) the equation of motion of the particle relating v and t.

(a) From $v = ks$, $dv/ds = k$ and the acceleration of the particle is

$$v\frac{dv}{ds} = k^2 s.$$

Therefore, since $s = a$ when $t = 0$, the initial acceleration of the particle is $k^2 a$.

(b)
$$v = \frac{ds}{dt} = ks.$$

$$\therefore \int \frac{ds}{s} = \int k\, dt.$$

$$\therefore \ln s = kt + A,$$

where A is constant.

But $s = a$ when $t = 0$; $\quad A = \ln a$.

$$\therefore \ln s - \ln a = kt.$$

$$\therefore \ln\left(\frac{s}{a}\right) = kt.$$

$$\therefore s = a\,e^{kt}.$$

Therefore, when $t = 2$ seconds, $s = a\,e^{2k}$.

(c) *First Method.* $v = ks$ and $s = a\,e^{kt}$.

Eliminating s we have $v = ka\,e^{kt}$.

Second Method. $s = a\,e^{kt}$.

$$\therefore v = \frac{ds}{dt} = ka\,e^{kt}.$$

Example 2. In the usual notation, the equation of motion of a particle moving in a straight line is $f = k/s^2$, for $s \geqq 1$, and $s = 1$, $v = 0$ when $t = 0$. Show that v cannot exceed $\sqrt{(2k)}$ and find the time taken by the particle to move from $s = 2$ to $s = 4$.

$$v\frac{dv}{ds} = \frac{k}{s^2}.$$

$$\therefore \int v\, dv = \int \frac{k}{s^2}\, ds.$$

$$\therefore \frac{v^2}{2} = A - \frac{k}{s},$$

where A is constant.

But $s = 1$ when $v = 0$; $\quad \therefore A = k$.

$$\therefore v^2 = 2k\left(1 - \frac{1}{s}\right),$$

i.e. $v = \sqrt{\left\{2k\left(1 - \frac{1}{s}\right)\right\}}$ and therefore $v < \sqrt{(2k)}$ for all values of s.

Also
$$v = \frac{ds}{dt} = \sqrt{\left\{2k\left(1 - \frac{1}{s}\right)\right\}}.$$

Hence the time to move from $s = 2$ to $s = 4$ is T, where

$$T = \frac{1}{\sqrt{(2k)}} \int_2^4 \sqrt{\left(\frac{s}{s-1}\right)}\, ds.$$

Consider $$I = \int \sqrt{\left(\frac{s}{s-1}\right)}\, ds.$$

Put $s = \cosh^2 u$, then $ds/du = 2 \cosh u \sinh u$.

$$\therefore\ I = \int \frac{\cosh u}{\sinh u} 2 \cosh u \sinh u\, du = \int 2 \cosh^2 u\, du$$

$$= \int (1+\cosh 2u)\, du = u + \tfrac{1}{2} \sinh 2u.$$

$$\therefore\ T = \frac{1}{\sqrt{(2k)}} \left[u + \frac{1}{2} \sinh 2u\right]_{s=2}^{s=4}.$$

When $s = 4$, $\cosh^2 u = 4$; $\therefore\ \sinh u = \sqrt{3}$; $\therefore\ \tfrac{1}{2} \sinh 2u = 2\sqrt{3}$.

When $s = 2$, $\cosh^2 u = 2$; $\therefore\ \sinh u = 1$; $\therefore\ \tfrac{1}{2} \sinh 2u = \sqrt{2}$.

When $s = 4$, $u = \cosh^{-1} \sqrt{s} = \ln (2+\sqrt{3})$.

When $s = 2$, $u = \ln (1+\sqrt{2})$.

$$T = \frac{1}{\sqrt{(2k)}} \left\{2\sqrt{3} - 2 + \ln\left(\frac{2+\sqrt{3}}{1+\sqrt{2}}\right)\right\}.$$

Example 3. A particle is projected with speed V from a fixed point O, and moves in a straight line OX. The retardation is proportional to v^3, where v is the speed of the particle when its distance from O is x. Show that

(a) $\dfrac{1}{v} = \dfrac{1}{V} + ax$, where a is a positive constant,

(b) $t = \dfrac{x}{V} + \dfrac{1}{2} ax^2$, where t is the time taken to travel the distance x. (N.)

The equation of motion of the particle is

$$v \frac{dv}{dx} = -bv^3,$$

where b is a positive constant.

$$\therefore\ \int \frac{v\, dv}{v^3} = \int -b\, dx.$$

$$\therefore\ -\frac{1}{v} = -bx + k,$$

where k is constant.

But $v = V$ when $x = 0$; $\quad \therefore\; k = -1/V$; $\quad \therefore\; 1/v = (1/V)+bx$.

$$\therefore \int \frac{dt}{dx} = \frac{1}{V}+bx.$$

$$\therefore\; t = \int \left(\frac{1}{V}+bx\right) dx.$$

$$\therefore\; t = \frac{x}{V}+\frac{bx^2}{2}+C,$$

where C is constant.

But $x = 0$ when $t = 0$; $\quad \therefore\; C = 0$.

$$\therefore\; t = \frac{x}{V}+\frac{bx^2}{2},$$

i.e. $\quad t = (x/V)+(ax^2/2)$ where a is a positive constant.

Example 4. A particle moves in a straight line so that its acceleration at any instant is kv, where k is a constant. Find equations of motion for the particle relating (a) v and t, (b) s and v, (c) s and t. All the quantities are expressed in the usual notation.

An equation of motion for the particle is

$$\frac{dv}{dt} = kv. \tag{1}$$

[This is the differential equation of the law of natural growth (see *Pure Mathematics*, Vol. II, § 17.5) concerning a quantity whose rate of growth at any instant is proportional to its magnitude. Newton's law of cooling and the rate of radioactive decay are among the many examples of the incidence of the law in the physical world.]

(a) From (1),

$$\int \frac{dv}{v} = kt.$$

$$\therefore\; t = \frac{1}{k}\ln v+C, \quad \text{where } C \text{ is constant.}$$

If $v = v_0$ when $t = 0$, $C = -(1/k)\ln v_0$.

$$\therefore\; t = \frac{1}{k}\ln\left(\frac{v}{v_0}\right).$$

$$\therefore\; v = v_0\, e^{kt}.$$

(b) Another form of the equation of motion for the particle is

$$v\frac{dv}{ds} = kv.$$

$$\therefore\; v = ks+A,$$

where A is constant.

If $s = 0$ when $v = v_0$, then $A = v_0$.

$$\therefore \quad s = \frac{1}{k}(v - v_0).$$

(c) From result (a) $ds/dt = v_0 e^{kt}$.

$$\therefore \quad s = \frac{v_0}{k} e^{kt} + B,$$

where B is constant.

But $s = 0$ when $t = 0$; $\quad \therefore \; B = -v_0/k$.

$$\therefore \quad s = \frac{v_0}{k}(e^{kt} - 1).$$

This result could have been obtained by eliminating v between (a) and (b).

EXERCISES 17.1

In each of questions 1–7 the equation of motion of a particle moving in a straight line and the boundary conditions for the motion are given in the usual notation.

1. $v^2 = 36 - 4s^2$; $s = 3$ when $t = 0$.
Calculate f when $s = 1$ and calculate f when $t = \frac{1}{3}\pi$.

2. $f = k/s$ where k is a positive constant; $v = 0$ when $s = 1$. Find s in terms of v and k.

3. $v = 2 - 3s$, $s = 0$ when $t = 0$. Calculate f when $s = \frac{1}{2}$ and calculate s when $t = 1$. Show that s cannot exceed the value $\frac{2}{3}$.

4. $f = -(a + bv^2)$ where a and b are positive constants; $s = 0$ and $v = v_0$ when $t = 0$. Prove that $v = 0$ when

$$t = \frac{1}{\sqrt{(ab)}} \tan^{-1}\left(v_0 \sqrt{\frac{b}{a}}\right), \qquad s = \frac{1}{2b} \ln\left(1 + \frac{bv_0^2}{a}\right).$$

5. $f = -\lambda v^3$, where λ is a positive constant; $v = 20$ and $s = 0$ when $t = 0$; $v = 10$ when $t = 15$. Show that $\lambda = \frac{1}{4000}$ and find v when $s = 600$.

6. $f = \frac{1}{100}v$; $v = 1$ when $t = 0$. Find v when $t = 10$ and find t when $v = 100$.

7. $f = 2 + \frac{1}{5}v$; $v = 0$, $s = 0$ when $t = 0$. Find v and s when $t = 1$.

8. A particle moves in a straight line so that its distance s from a fixed point of the line at time t is given by the equation $s^2 = a^2 + V^2t^2$, where a and V are constants. Find in terms of s its velocity and acceleration at time t. (O.C.)

9. A car is travelling along a straight road. When it is passing a certain position O the engine is switched off. At time t after the car has passed O the speed v is given by the formula

$$\frac{1}{v} = A+Bt,$$

where A and B are positive constants. Show that the retardation is proportional to the square of the speed.

If when $t = 0$ the retardation is 1 m/s^2 and $v = 80$ m/s, find A and B.

If x is the distance moved from O in time t, express

(i) x in terms of t, (ii) v in terms of x.

10. The velocity v of a particle along a straight line OX is increasing with respect to its distance x from O at a rate which is proportional to x/v. When the particle is at O its velocity is 10 m/s; after it has travelled 10 m from O its velocity is 20 m/s. What further distance will the particle have travelled by the time it attains the velocity of 30 m/s?

11. A particle is moving in a straight line and its distance at time t from a fixed point O in the line is x. Its velocity is given by

$$50\frac{dx}{dt} = (40-x)(x-20)$$

and $x = 25$ when $t = 0$. Find an expression for x in terms of t.

Find the greatest velocity in the interval $20 < x < 40$ and the value of t when the greatest velocity is attained. (N.)

12. A particle moving along a straight line OX is at a distance x from O at time t, and its velocity is given by

$$8t^2\frac{dx}{dt} = (1-t^2)x^2.$$

If $x = 4$ when $t = 1$, prove that $x = 8t/(1+t^2)$.

Find

(i) the velocity when $t = 0$,
(ii) the maximum distance from O,
(iii) the maximum speed *towards* O for positive values of t. (N.)

13. A particle is moving along a straight line away from a fixed point O in the line so that when its distance from O is x its velocity v is given by $v = k/x$, where k is a constant. Show that the particle has a retardation which is inversely proportional to the cube of its distance from O.

If P, Q, R, S are points in that order on the straight line such that the distances PQ, QR, RS are all equal, show that the times taken to traverse these successive distances increase in arithmetical progression.

14. A car of mass 500 kg travelling along a straight road passes a point A at a velocity of 10 m/s and subsequently passes a point B, distant 25 m from A, at 20 m/s.

When the car is distant x m from A its velocity is v m/s and the graph of v against x is a straight line. Express v as a function of x and show that the resultant force acting on the car is $(2000+80\,x)$ newtons. Show also that the time taken from A to B is $\frac{5}{2}\ln 2$ seconds.

15. A particle moving in a straight line is at a distance x from a fixed point O of the line at time t, and is then moving with velocity v. Prove that the acceleration of the particle can be expressed in the form

$$v\frac{dv}{dx}.$$

If, further, the particle is moving in such a way that its acceleration is directed towards O, and varies as the cube of the velocity, obtain differential equations connecting

$$\text{(i)}\ \frac{dv}{dt}\ \text{with } v, \qquad \text{(ii)}\ \frac{dv}{dx}\ \text{with } v.$$

If the particle is initially projected from O with velocity u, and if the velocity is $\frac{1}{2}u$ when it has travelled a distance a, prove that a time

$$\frac{3a}{2u}$$

has then elapsed. (C.)

***16.** The only force acting on a particle moving in a straight line is a resistance $mk(c^2+v^2)$ acting in that line; m is the mass of the particle, v its velocity and k, c are positive constants. The particle starts to move with velocity U and comes to rest in a distance s; its speed is $\frac{1}{3}U$ when it has moved a distance $\frac{1}{2}s$. Show that $63c^2 = U^2$. Show also that when the distance moved is x,

$$63\frac{v^2}{U^2} = 64\,e^{-2kx}-1. \qquad \text{(N.)}$$

***17.** A particle moves in a straight line and its displacement from the origin at time t is given by the equation

$$x = e^{-kt}\sin pt.$$

Prove that, if $\tan\varepsilon = p/k$ and ε is a positive acute angle, the particle is at rest at instants given by the formula

$$t = \frac{n\pi+\varepsilon}{p},$$

where $n = 0, 1, 2, \ldots$; and that the corresponding coordinates of the particle are given by the formula

$$x = (-1)^n e^{-k(n\pi+\varepsilon)/p}\sin\varepsilon.$$

Also show that the *total distance* travelled by the particle in the time from $t = 0$ to $t = \infty$ is

$$\frac{2\,e^{-k\varepsilon/p}\sin\varepsilon}{1-e^{-k\pi/p}}. \qquad \text{(O.C.)}$$

17.2. Dynamical Problems

The examples which follow illustrate problems in which the equation of motion of a body is derived from an analysis of the force system acting upon the body.

Example 1. The motion of a body of mass m (moving in a straight line) is resisted by a constant force ma and a variable force mv^2/k. Show that the body is brought to rest by the resistances from speed u in a distance $(k/2)\ln\{1+u^2/(ak)\}$ and in a time $\sqrt{(k/a)}\tan^{-1}\{u/\sqrt{(ak)}\}$.

From the equation $P = mf$ for the body, we derive the equation of motion either as

$$\text{(a)} \qquad v\frac{dv}{ds} = -a - \frac{v^2}{k}$$

or as

$$\text{(b)} \qquad \frac{dv}{dt} = -a - \frac{v^2}{k}.$$

Each of these equations is a differential equation with variables separable.

From (a), the distance in which the body is brought to rest is

$$k\int_u^0 \frac{-v\,dv}{ka+v^2} = k\int_0^u \frac{v\,dv}{ka+v^2} = \frac{1}{2}k\Big[\ln(ka+v^2)\Big]_0^u$$

$$= \frac{1}{2}k\{\ln(ka+u^2)-\ln(ka)\} = \frac{1}{2}k\ln\left(\frac{ka+u^2}{ka}\right)$$

$$= \frac{1}{2}k\ln\left(1+\frac{u^2}{ka}\right).$$

From (b), the time in which the body is brought to rest is

$$k\int_0^u \frac{dv}{ka+v^2} = \frac{k}{\sqrt{(ka)}}\left[\tan^{-1}\left\{\frac{v}{\sqrt{(ka)}}\right\}\right]_0^u = \sqrt{\left(\frac{k}{a}\right)}\tan^{-1}\left\{\frac{u}{\sqrt{(ka)}}\right\}.$$

Example 2. A body is projected vertically upwards from the earth's surface with velocity u. Neglecting atmospheric resistance and assuming the gravitational attraction between the body and the earth to be inversely proportional to the square of the distance of the body from the centre of the earth, calculate the smallest value of u for which the body does not return to the earth.

The equation of motion for the body is

$$mv\frac{dv}{ds} = -\frac{mgR^2}{s^2};$$

where R is the radius of the earth and s is the distance of the body from the centre of the earth. Therefore

$$v\frac{dv}{ds} = -\frac{gR^2}{s^2}$$

$$\therefore \frac{v^2}{2} = \frac{gR^2}{s} + A,$$

where A is constant.

Since $v = u$ when $s = R$, $A = (u^2/2) - gR$.

$$\therefore \frac{v^2}{2} = \frac{gR^2}{s} + \frac{u^2}{2} - gR,$$

so that v will never become zero if $u^2 > 2gR$, i.e. the required least value of u is $\sqrt{(2gR)}$.

Taking R as 6400 km and g as 9·8 m/s², this result gives about 40,000 km/h as the minimum "velocity of escape".

Motion under Gravity in a Resisting Medium

Physical experience tends to indicate that for bodies moving under gravity in the atmosphere, or in fluids generally, the resistance to motion is dependent on the velocity of the body. We consider here two cases in each of which the resistance is assumed to be a simple function of the velocity.

I. *Resistance Proportional to the Velocity*

Let the resistance $= mkv$, where k is a positive constant, m is the mass of the body and v its velocity.

(a) For a particle of mass m falling vertically from rest, one form of the equation of motion is

$$m\frac{dv}{dt} = mg - mkv.$$

Here we measure v and s *downward* from the point of release.

[We note that, if and when v reached the value g/k the acceleration would become zero and the particle would continue to descend with uniform speed.] Integrating this equation of motion, we have

$$\int \frac{dv}{g-kv} = t.$$

$$\therefore t = -\frac{1}{k}\ln(g-kv) + A,$$

where A is constant.

But $v = 0$ when $t = 0$; $\quad \therefore \; A = \dfrac{1}{k} \ln g.$

$$\therefore \; t = \frac{1}{k} \ln \left(\frac{g}{g-kv} \right),$$

i.e.

$$v = \frac{g}{k}(1-e^{-kt}). \tag{17.1}$$

Since $\lim\limits_{t \to \infty} (1-e^{-kt}) = 1$, v increases continuously with t and, for sufficiently large values of t, v can take any positive value less than g/k however near to g/k. The quantity g/k is called the *terminal velocity* of the particle.

(Note that the *dimensions* of k in this discussion are time^{-1} [s^{-1}].) A second form of the equation of motion of the particle is

$$mv \frac{dv}{ds} = mg - mkv.$$

$$\therefore \int \frac{v \, dv}{g-kv} = s.$$

$$\therefore \; s = -\frac{1}{k} \int \left(1 - \frac{g}{g-kv} \right) dv.$$

$$\therefore \; s = -\frac{v}{k} - \frac{g}{k^2} \ln (g-kv) + B,$$

where B is constant.

But $v = 0$ when $s = 0$; $\quad \therefore \; B = (g/k^2) \ln g.$

$$\therefore \; s = \frac{g}{k^2} \ln \left(\frac{g}{g-kv} \right) - \frac{v}{k}. \tag{17.2}$$

Also from (17.1),

$$\frac{ds}{dt} = \frac{g}{k}(1-e^{-kt}).$$

$$\therefore \; s = \frac{gt}{k} + \frac{g}{k^2} e^{-kt} + C,$$

where C is constant.

But $s = 0$ when $t = 0$; $\therefore\ C = -(g/k^2)$.

$$\therefore\ s = \frac{g}{k^2}(kt+e^{-kt}-1). \tag{17.3}$$

(b) The equation of motion for a particle projected vertically upwards with velocity u in such a medium is

$$\frac{dv}{dt} = -g-kv.$$

Here v and s are measured *upward* from the point of projection.

$$\therefore\ t = -\int \frac{dv}{g+kv}.$$

$$\therefore\ t = -\frac{1}{k}\ln(g+kv)+C,$$

where C is a constant.

Since $v = u$ when $t = 0$; $\therefore\ C = (1/k)\ln(g+ku)$.

$$\therefore\ t = \frac{1}{k}\ln\left(\frac{g+ku}{g+kv}\right). \tag{17.4}$$

The time to reach the highest point of the path, where $v = 0$, is thus

$$\frac{1}{k}\ln\left(1+\frac{ku}{g}\right). \tag{17.5}$$

Another form of the equation of motion is

$$v\frac{dv}{ds} = -g-kv,$$

from which the greatest height reached is given by

$$-\int_u^0 \frac{v\,dv}{g+kv} = \int_0^u \frac{v\,dv}{g+kv}$$

$$= \frac{1}{k}\int_0^u \left(1-\frac{g}{g+kv}\right)dv = \frac{1}{k}\left[v-\frac{g}{k}\ln(g+kv)\right]_0^u$$

$$= \frac{1}{k}\left\{u-\frac{g}{k}\ln\left(1+\frac{ku}{g}\right)\right\}. \tag{17.6}$$

II. *Resistance Proportional to the Square of the Velocity*

Let the resistance $= mkv^2$, where m is the mass of the particle and v its velocity.

(a) For a particle of mass m falling vertically from rest, one form of the equation of motion is

$$m\frac{dv}{dt} = mg - mkv^2.$$

Here v and s are measured *downward* from the point of release.

[We note that, if and when v reached the value $\sqrt{(g/k)}$, the acceleration would become zero and the particle would continue to descend with uniform speed $\sqrt{(g/k)}$.]

Integrating the equation of motion, we have

$$t = \int \frac{dv}{g-kv^2} \quad [(v < \sqrt{(g/k)}].$$

$$\therefore\ t = \frac{1}{2\sqrt{(kg)}} \ln\left(\frac{\sqrt{\left(\frac{g}{k}\right)}+v}{\sqrt{\left(\frac{g}{k}\right)}-v}\right) + A,$$

where A is constant.

But $v = 0$ when $t = 0$; $\quad \therefore\ A = 0.$

$$\therefore\ e^{2t\sqrt{(kg)}}\left\{\sqrt{\left(\frac{g}{k}\right)}-v\right\} = \sqrt{\left(\frac{g}{k}\right)}+v.$$

$$\therefore\ v = \sqrt{\left(\frac{g}{k}\right)}\left\{\frac{e^{2t\sqrt{(kg)}}-1}{e^{2t\sqrt{(kg)}}+1}\right\} = \sqrt{\left(\frac{g}{k}\right)} \tanh\{t\sqrt{(kg)}\}. \quad (17.7)$$

Since

$$\lim_{t\to\infty}\left\{\frac{e^{2t\sqrt{(kg)}}-1}{e^{2t\sqrt{(kg)}}+1}\right\} = \lim_{t\to\infty}\left\{\frac{1-e^{-2t\sqrt{(kg)}}}{1+e^{-2t\sqrt{(kg)}}}\right\} = 1,$$

v increases continuously with t, and, for sufficiently large values of t, v can take any positive value less than $\sqrt{(g/k)}$, however near to $\sqrt{(g/k)}$. The quantity $\sqrt{(g/k)}$ is the *terminal velocity* of the particle.

(Note that the *dimensions* of k in this discussion are distance^{-1}, i.e. m^{-1}). A second form of the equation of motion is

$$mv\frac{\mathrm{d}v}{\mathrm{d}s} = mg-mkv^2.$$

$$\therefore\ s = \int \frac{v\,\mathrm{d}v}{g-kv^2}.$$

$$\therefore\ s = -\frac{1}{2k}\ln(g-kv^2)+A,$$

where A is constant.

But $s = 0$ when $v = 0$; $\quad \therefore\ A = \dfrac{1}{2k}\ln g.$

$$\therefore\ s = \frac{1}{2k}\ln\left(\frac{g}{g-kv^2}\right), \tag{17.8}$$

i.e.

$$v^2 = \frac{g}{k}(1-\mathrm{e}^{-2ks}). \tag{17.8a}$$

(b) The equation of motion for a particle projected vertically upwards in such a medium with velocity u is

$$\frac{\mathrm{d}v}{\mathrm{d}t} = -g-kv^2,$$

where v and s are measured *upward* from the point of projection.

$$\therefore\ t = -\int\frac{\mathrm{d}v}{g+kv^2}.$$

$$t = -\frac{1}{\surd(kg)}\tan^{-1}\left\{v\sqrt{\left(\frac{k}{g}\right)}\right\}+B,$$

where B is constant.

But $v = u$ when $t = 0$; $\quad \therefore\ B = \dfrac{1}{\surd(kg)}\tan^{-1}\left\{u\sqrt{\left(\dfrac{k}{g}\right)}\right\}.$

$$\therefore\ t = \frac{1}{\surd(kg)}\left[\tan^{-1}\left\{u\sqrt{\left(\frac{k}{g}\right)}\right\}-\tan^{-1}\left\{v\sqrt{\left(\frac{k}{g}\right)}\right\}\right].$$

The time to reach the highest point of the path (where $v = 0$) is thus

$$\frac{1}{\sqrt{(kg)}} \tan^{-1}\left\{u\sqrt{\left(\frac{k}{g}\right)}\right\}. \tag{17.9}$$

Also
$$v\frac{dv}{ds} = -g-kv^2.$$

$$\therefore \quad -\int \frac{v\, dv}{g+kv^2} = s.$$

$$\therefore \quad s = -\frac{1}{2k}\ln(g+kv^2)+C,$$

where C is constant.

Since $s = 0$ when $v = u$; $\quad \therefore \; C = \{1/(2k)\}\ln(g+ku^2)$.

$$\therefore \quad s = \frac{1}{2k}\ln\left(\frac{g+ku^2}{g+kv^2}\right).$$

The greatest height reached by the particle is thus

$$\frac{1}{2k}\ln\left(1+\frac{ku^2}{g}\right). \tag{17.10}$$

[When the resistance to the motion is proportional to the velocity, the particle is projected vertically upwards and the upward direction is taken as the positive direction, the whole of the motion *both upwards and downwards* is described by the equation

$$\frac{dv}{dt} = -g-kv.$$

When the resistance to the motion is proportional to the square of the velocity, *separate equations for the upward and downward motions are required.*]

Example. A particle is projected vertically upwards with speed nu. Show that, if the resistance of the medium in which it is projected is assumed to vary as the square of the velocity of the particle and if the terminal velocity when the particle is allowed to fall from rest in this medium is u, then (a) the particle returns to the ground with its original kinetic energy reduced in the ratio $1/(1+n^2)$, (b) the time taken by the particle to return to its starting point is T, where

$$T = \frac{u}{g}[\tan^{-1} n + \ln\{\sqrt{(n^2+1)}+n\}].$$

(To avoid repetition, results obtained above are used in the work which follows. The reader is not, however, advised to quote these results in his own work, but to obtain them from first principles whenever necessary.)

An equation of motion for the particle projected upwards is

$$\frac{dv}{dt} = -g - kv^2,$$

where $u = \sqrt{(g/k)}$ and $v = nu$ when $t = 0$, from which we have obtained the result (17.9),

$$t_1 = \frac{1}{\sqrt{(kg)}} \tan^{-1}\left\{nu\sqrt{\left(\frac{k}{g}\right)}\right\} = \frac{u}{g}\tan^{-1} n,$$

where t_1 is the time taken to reach the highest point of the path.

Another equation of motion for the particle projected vertically upwards is

$$v\frac{dv}{ds} = -g - kv^2,$$

from which we obtain the result (17.10),

$$s_1 = \frac{1}{2k}\ln\left(1+\frac{kn^2u^2}{g}\right) = \frac{u^2}{2g}\ln(1+n^2)$$

for the greatest height s_1 reached by the particle.

An equation of motion for the particle on its return fall to the earth is

$$v\frac{dv}{ds} = g - kv^2,$$

from which we obtain the result (17.8),

$$s = \frac{1}{2k}\ln\left(\frac{g}{g-kv^2}\right) = \frac{u^2}{2g}\ln\left(\frac{u^2}{u^2-v^2}\right)$$

relating the distance s fallen from the highest point to the velocity v at that point. Therefore, when the particle strikes the ground,

$$\frac{u^2}{2g}\ln(1+n^2) = \frac{u^2}{2g}\ln\left(\frac{u^2}{u^2-v^2}\right).$$

$$\therefore\ 1+n^2 = \frac{u^2}{u^2-v^2},$$

i.e.

$$v^2 = \frac{n^2u^2}{1+n^2}.$$

The initial kinetic energy of the particle was $\frac{1}{2}mn^2u^2$ and the final kinetic energy of the particle is $\frac{1}{2}mn^2u^2/(1+n^2)$. Therefore the ratio in which the kinetic energy is reduced is $1/(1+n^2)$.

Another equation of motion for the particle on its return fall to earth is

$$\frac{dv}{dt} = g-kv^2,$$

from which we obtain the result (17.7),

$$t_2 = \frac{1}{2\sqrt{(kg)}} \ln \left\{ \frac{\sqrt{\left(\frac{g}{k}\right)}+v}{\sqrt{\left(\frac{g}{k}\right)}-v} \right\} = \frac{u}{2g} \ln \left(\frac{u+v}{u-v} \right)$$

for t_2 the time taken on the downward journey, where $v^2 = n^2u^2/(1+n^2)$.

$$\therefore\ t_2 = \frac{u}{2g} \ln \left\{ \frac{\sqrt{(n^2+1)}+n}{\sqrt{(n^2+1)}-n} \right\} = \frac{u}{g} \ln \{\sqrt{(n^2+1)}+n\}$$

$$\therefore\ T = t_1+t_2 = \frac{u}{g} [\tan^{-1} n + \ln \{\sqrt{(n^2+1)}+n\}].$$

**Note on the two-dimensional motion of a projectile in a medium, the resistance to motion of which is proportional to the velocity.*

A particle of mass m is projected from O (Fig. 17.1) in a vertical plane with velocity u at an angle α with the horizontal in a medium whose resistance $\mathbf{R}$ to the motion of the particle is $mk\mathbf{v}$, where $\mathbf{v}$ is the velocity of the particle and k is constant. It is assumed that $\mathbf{R}$ acts instantaneously in the direction opposite to that of the particle's motion. The figure shows the forces acting on the particle at an instant of its flight.

When the coordinates of the particle referred to horizontal and vertical axes through the point of projection are (x, y) the equations of the resolved parts of the motion, parallel to the x and y-axes respectively, are

$$m\ddot{x} = -mkv \cos \psi, \tag{17.11}$$

$$m\ddot{y} = -mkv \sin \psi - mg, \tag{17.12}$$

where ψ is the angle which the direction of motion of the particle makes with Ox.

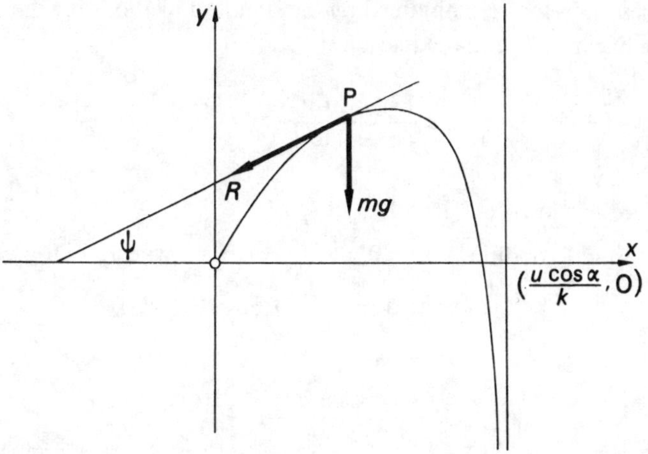

FIG. 17.1

If s is the length of the arc of the trajectory from O to P, (x, y), then $v = \mathrm{d}s/\mathrm{d}t$, $\cos\psi = \mathrm{d}x/\mathrm{d}s$ and $\sin\psi = \mathrm{d}y/\mathrm{d}s$. (See *Pure Maths.*, Vol. II, § 14.2.) Hence equations (17.11) and (17.12) can be written

$$\ddot{x}+k\frac{\mathrm{d}s}{\mathrm{d}t}\frac{\mathrm{d}x}{\mathrm{d}s} = 0,$$

i.e.

$$\ddot{x}+k\dot{x} = 0, \tag{17.13}$$

and

$$\ddot{y}+k\frac{\mathrm{d}s}{\mathrm{d}t}\frac{\mathrm{d}y}{\mathrm{d}s}+g = 0,$$

i.e.

$$\ddot{y}+k\dot{y} = -g. \tag{17.14}$$

The solutions of these equations are

$$x = A\,\mathrm{e}^{-kt}+B,$$

where A and B are constants, and

$$y = C\,\mathrm{e}^{-kt}+D-\frac{gt}{k},$$

where C and D are constants.

(These solutions are obtained by the standard methods for the solution of the linear differential equation

$$a\frac{d^2y}{dx^2}+b\frac{dy}{dx}+cy = P.$$

See *Pure Maths.*, Vol. II, §§ 17.9 et seq.)

The initial conditions $x = 0$, $dx/dt = u \cos \alpha$ when $t = 0$ give

$$A+B = 0 \quad \text{and} \quad u \cos \alpha = -kA,$$

i.e.

$$A = -(u \cos \alpha)/k, \quad B = (u \cos \alpha)/k.$$

$$\therefore\ x = \frac{u \cos \alpha}{k}(1-e^{-kt}). \tag{17.15}$$

The initial conditions $y = 0$, $dy/dt = u \sin \alpha$ when $t = 0$ give

$$C+D = 0, \quad -kC-\frac{g}{k} = u \sin \alpha,$$

i.e.

$$C = -\frac{u \sin \alpha}{k}-\frac{g}{k^2}, \quad D = \frac{u \sin \alpha}{k}+\frac{g}{k^2}.$$

$$\therefore\ y = \left(\frac{u \sin \alpha}{k}+\frac{g}{k^2}\right)(1-e^{-kt})-\frac{gt}{k}. \tag{17.16}$$

The equation of the path of the projectile obtained by eliminating t from (17.15) and (17.16) is

$$y = x\left(\tan \alpha+\frac{g}{ku \cos \alpha}\right)+\frac{g}{k^2}\ln\left(1-\frac{kx}{u \cos \alpha}\right). \tag{17.17}$$

Equation (17.15) shows that as

$$t \to \infty, \quad x \to \frac{u \cos \alpha}{k},$$

and it follows that the path has a vertical asymptote.

EXERCISES 17.2

1. A car of mass 500 kg stands at rest on a hill inclined at an angle θ to the horizontal, where $\sin\theta = \frac{1}{20}$. When the brakes are released it descends under a resistance which at any instant is proportional to the speed. If this resistance is equal to the weight of 10 kg when the speed is 24 km/h, show that the speed cannot exceed 60 km/h and that the equation of motion may be written

$$\frac{5000}{147} v \frac{dv}{dx} = \frac{50}{3} - v,$$

where v is the speed of the car in m/s.

Hence find the distance travelled by the car from rest before its speed is 36 km/h.

2. The tractive force on a car, of mass 1000 kg and moving in a straight line, is fixed in direction and increases uniformly in magnitude from zero to 700 N in 10 s. The force remains constant at 700 N for the next 10 s and then diminishes uniformly from 700 N to -1050 N in 10 s. By means of a time-force diagram or otherwise find the greatest speed of the car and its speed after 10, 20 and 30 seconds of the motion respectively.

3. A 10,000 kg lorry moves from rest in a straight line under the action of a propulsive force P newtons whose magnitude at time t seconds from the start is given in the following table:

P	5350	7800	6600	5000	3250	2000	1250
t	0	5	10	15	20	25	30

If the resistances to the motion are equivalent to a constant force of 100 N per 1000 kg, find, graphically or otherwise, the speed acquired in km/h at the end of 30 s. Find also the acceleration of the lorry when $t = 20$.

4. A mass of 8 kg is attached to a point A on a smooth horizontal table by a light inextensible string of length 1 m. The mass is released from rest at A and is attracted towards a point B on the table, $2\frac{1}{2}$ m from A, by a force equal to $2x$ N when its distance from B is x m for all values of x. Find the impulse in the string when it becomes taut, assuming the mass is brought to rest.

5. A particle of mass 10 kg starts from rest and is acted upon by a force in a constant direction and increasing uniformly in 5 s from zero to 6 N. Prove that t seconds after the start of the motion the acceleration of the particle is $0{\cdot}12\,t$ m/s². Find the distance the particle moves in the first 5 s and show that when it has moved a distance x m its speed is v m/s where $50v^3 = 27x^2$.

6. A load W is raised through a vertical height h, starting from rest and coming to rest under gravity, by a chain incapable of supporting a load greater than P where $P > W$. Show that the shortest time in which this can be done is

$$\sqrt{\left\{\frac{2hP}{g(P-W)}\right\}}.$$

(P.T.O).

If a large cargo is to be discharged in this way, show that the time occupied by upward journeys from rest to rest will be least if the cargo is sent up in loads of $\frac{2}{3}P$. (L.)

7. The net accelerating force acting on a train of mass W varies with the speed, being $F(v)$ when the speed is v. Show that the time t required to reach a speed of V from rest is given by

$$t = \int_0^V \frac{5W\,dv}{18F(v)}.$$

8. A train of mass W kg moves on the level under the action of a pull P newtons against a resistance of R newtons. The speed of the train at any instant is v m/s. Show that the distance travelledb y the train whilst its speed varies from v_0 m/s to v_1 m/s is $W\int_{v_0}^{v_1} v\,dv/(P-R)$ metres. If $W = 3\times10^5$ and $R = 9000+70v^2$ show that the distance travelled by the train in slowing down, with the engine shut off, from 72 km/h to 54 km/h is about 860 m.

9. A car of mass M moves from rest on a horizontal road against a constant resistance R. The pull exerted by the engine decreases uniformly with the distance from the starting point, being initially P and falling to R after the car has travelled a distance a. Derive an expression for the accelerating force when the car has moved a distance x from rest ($x \leqq a$), and show that, if t is the time taken to describe the distance x,

$$\left(\frac{dx}{dt}\right)^2 = k^2(2ax-x^2),$$

where $k^2 = (P-R)/(Ma)$.

Verify by differentiation that $x = a(1-\cos kt)$ is a solution of the above equation, and show that it satisfies the initial conditions.

10. A particle of mass 0·5 kg is moving in a horizontal straight line under a retardation of $0{\cdot}4t^2$ m/s², where t seconds is the time which has elapsed since the particle passed a fixed point A of the line. The particle comes to rest at B, 5 seconds after passing A. Calculate the distance AB, and the work done by the force causing the retardation.

11. A car of mass 250 kg stands at rest on a gradient of 1/10. When the brakes are released it descends under a resistance which is proportional to the velocity at any instant. This resistance is equal to the weight of 5 kg when the velocity is 18 km/h. Show that the velocity can never exceed 90 km/h and find, to the nearest metre, how far the car descends before the velocity reaches 36 km/h.

12. The resistance to motion of a particle is proportional to the square of its velocity v, being equal to the weight of the particle when $v = V$. If the particle is projected vertically upwards with speed u_1, show that it will return to the point of projection with speed u_2, given by

$$\frac{1}{u_2^2} = \frac{1}{u_1^2}+\frac{1}{V^2}. \qquad \text{(L.)}$$

13. A particle is shot vertically downwards under gravity with speed u and the resistance of the atmosphere is kv^2 per unit mass, where k is a constant and v is the speed of the particle. If $c^2 = g/k$, show that when the particle has moved a distance x,

$$v^2 = c^2-(c^2-u^2)\,e^{-2kx}.$$

If $u = \frac{1}{2}c$ show that the time taken by the particle to attain a speed $\frac{3}{4}c$ is

$$\frac{1}{2kc}\ln\frac{7}{3}. \qquad \text{(L.)}$$

14. A particle of mass 1 kg is projected from a point O with velocity u m/s along a smooth horizontal table in a medium whose resistance is Rv^2 newtons when the particle has any velocity v m/s, R being constant. Find its velocity after t seconds.

An equal particle is projected from O simultaneously with the first particle but vertically upward under gravity with velocity u m/s in the same medium. Show that the velocity V m/s of the first particle when the second is momentarily at rest is given by

$$\frac{1}{V} = \frac{1}{u}+\frac{1}{a}\tan^{-1}(u/a) \quad \text{where} \quad Ra^2 = g.$$

15. A particle of mass m can move in a resisting medium in which the resistance varies as the square of the speed, the magnitude of the terminal velocity being V. If it is projected vertically upwards with a speed $V\tan\alpha$, show that it will return to the point of projection with a speed $V\sin\alpha$.

Show also that the amount of energy, kinetic and potential together, which is lost in its ascent is

$$\tfrac{1}{2}mV^2(\tan^2\alpha-2\ln\sec\alpha). \qquad \text{(L.)}$$

16. A particle of mass m falls from rest under gravity and the resistance to its motion is kmv^2 when its speed is v, the factor k being a constant. Prove that, if the distance fallen is then x,

$$v^2 = \frac{g}{k}(1-e^{-2kx}).$$

If as x increases from d to $2d$ the speed increases from V to $5V/4$, find, in terms of V only, the greatest possible speed of the particle. (N.)

17. A particle is released from rest at a height a above a horizontal plane. The resistance to the motion of the particle is kv^2 per unit mass, where v is its velocity and k is a constant. Show that the particle strikes the plane with velocity V where

$$kV^2 = g(1-e^{-2ka}).$$

If the particle rebounds from the plane without loss of energy and reaches a maximum height b in the subsequent motion, show that

$$e^{-2ka}+e^{2kb} = 2. \qquad \text{(L.)}$$

18. A particle moves under gravity in a medium in which the resistance to motion per unit mass is k times the velocity where k is a constant. The particle is projected vertically upwards with velocity g/k. Show that the velocity v and height x reached after time t are given by

$$kv = g(2e^{-kt}-1) \quad \text{and} \quad k^2x = g(2-2e^{-kt}-kt).$$

Show that the greatest height H the particle can attain is given by

$$k^2H = g(1-\ln 2). \qquad \text{(N.)}$$

19. A particle of mass m is projected with speed V vertically upwards from a point on horizontal ground. Its subsequent motion is subject to gravity and to a resistance kmv^2, where v is the speed and k is a constant. Show that the greatest height attained is

$$\frac{1}{2k}\ln\left(1+k\frac{V^2}{g}\right).$$

Find an expression for the work done against the resistance during the whole of the upward motion. (N.)

20. A body of mass 1 kg falls from rest under gravity in a medium exerting a resistance 0·01 gv^2 newtons when the speed is v m/s. State the terminal velocity.

Taking the value of g to be 9·8 m/s² show that the speed attained after falling 5 m is 7·9 m/s approximately.

***21.** A particle of mass m is projected with a velocity of magnitude u inclined to the horizontal at an angle α, in a medium in which the horizontal component of resistance is mkv, where v is the horizontal component of the velocity of the particle, and in which the vertical component of the resistance is negligible compared with gravity. Show that the range of the particle on the horizontal plane through the point of projection is

$$\frac{u\cos\alpha}{k}\left(1-e^{-\frac{2ku\sin\alpha}{g}}\right).$$

If this range is R, show that the horizontal distance travelled by the particle before reaching the highest point of its path is greater than $\frac{1}{2}R$. (L.)

***22.** A particle is projected in a vertical plane in a medium the resistance of which to the motion of the particle varies as the velocity of the particle and is equal to n times the weight of the particle when the speed of the particle is V. The initial horizontal and vertical components of the velocity of the particle are U, V respectively. Show that the particle reaches its maximum height after a time

$$\frac{V}{ng}\ln(n+1)$$

from the instant of projection and that the horizontal displacement of the particle from the point of projection is then

$$\frac{UV}{(n+1)g}. \qquad \text{(L.)}$$

17.3. Rate of Working by a Variable Force

When a force which is exerted by a machine moves a body against a resistance which is a function of the velocity there are upper limits imposed by the mechanical detail of the machine on the magnitude of the force and on the rate of working of the force. Cases which arise frequently in practice are

(a) the case in which the force exerted is constant,
(b) the case in which the rate of working is constant and the force varies.

In the first of these cases the problems involved are solved by integrating the equation of motion $P = mf$, and in the second case the *power equation* of the motion provides the differential equation from which the solution is obtained.

Example 1. The engine of a train of total mass 4×10^5 kg works at a rate of 360 kW, when pulling a train on the level at a steady speed of 54 km/h. The resistance to the motion of the train is proportional to its speed and while that speed is less than or equal to 54 km/h the engine exerts a constant tractive force. Calculate the time taken by the train to acquire a speed of 36 km/h from rest and calculate the distance covered by the train in this time.

Suppose the resistance to the motion of the train to be kv newtons, where k is constant and v m/s is the speed of the train. Then, since there is no acceleration when the speed is 15 m/s, the tractive force is equal to the resistance at this speed, i.e. the constant tractive force is $15k$ newtons. The power at this speed is 360 kW and therefore the power equation is

$$360\times1000 = k\times15\times15.$$

$$\therefore\ k = 1600.$$

Therefore the resistance to the motion of the train at speed v m/s is $1600v$ newtons.

An equation of motion for the train is therefore,

$$1600\times15-1600v = 4\times10^5\frac{dv}{dt}.$$

The time taken to acquire a speed of 36 km/h (= 10 m/s) from rest is therefore

T seconds where

$$T = \frac{4\times 10^5}{1600}\int_0^{10} \frac{dv}{15-v}$$

$$= \frac{4\times 10^5}{1600}\Big[\ln(15-v)\Big]_{10}^{0}$$

$$= 250 \ln 3$$

$$\approx 275.$$

The train acquires a speed of 36 km/h in 4 min 35 s.

Another equation of motion for the train is

$$1600\times 15 - 1600v = 4\times 10^5 v\frac{dv}{ds}.$$

Therefore the distance in which the train acquires a speed of 36 km/h is S m where

$$S = 250\int_0^{10} \frac{v\,dv}{15-v}$$

$$= 250\int_0^{10}\left(-1+\frac{15}{15-v}\right)dv$$

$$= 250\Big[-v-15\ln(15-v)\Big]_0^{10}$$

$$= 250(15\ln 3 - 10)$$

$$\approx 1620.$$

The train acquires a speed of 36 km/h in 1620 m.

Example 2. An engine pulls a train along a level track against a resistance which at any time is k times the momentum. The engine works at constant power $9mkv_0^2$ where m is the total mass of the engine and the train. Show that the speed increases from v_0 to $2v_0$ in a time $\{\ln(8/5)\}/(2k)$.

The power is cut off when the train has speed U and a constant braking force F then acts in addition to the resistance. Show that the train will stop after a further time $(1/k)\ln\{(F+mkU)/F\}$. (N.)

The total force exerted by the engine at time t, when the speed is v and the acceleration is dv/dt is

$$mkv + m\frac{dv}{dt}.$$

Therefore the power equation of the motion is

$$9mkv_0^2 = \left(mkv+m\frac{dv}{dt}\right)v,$$

i.e.

$$v\frac{dv}{dt} = k(9v_0^2-v^2).$$

$$\therefore \frac{1}{k}\int_{v_0}^{2v_0} \frac{v\,dv}{9v_0^2-v^2} = T_1,$$

where T_1 is the time during which the speed increases from v_0 to $2v_0$.

$$\therefore T_1 = \frac{1}{2k}\Big[\ln(9v_0^2-v^2)\Big]_{2v_0}^{v_0} = \frac{1}{2k}\{\ln(8v_0^2)-\ln(5v_0^2)\}$$

$$= \frac{1}{2k}\ln\left(\frac{8}{5}\right).$$

After the power is cut off the equation of motion of the train becomes

$$-(F+mkv) = m\frac{dv}{dt}.$$

$$\therefore T_2 = -\int_U^0 \frac{m\,dv}{F+mkv},$$

where T_2 is the further time required for the train to stop.

$$\therefore T_2 = \frac{1}{k}\Big[\ln(F+mkv)\Big]_0^U = \frac{1}{k}\ln\{(F+mkU)/F\}.$$

EXERCISES 17.3

1. The engine of a train of mass M pulls the train against a variable resistance of $M\,kv$, where k is constant and v is the speed of the train. The time taken to reach the speed v from rest is

$$\frac{1}{2k}\ln\left(\frac{H}{H-Mkv^2}\right), \quad \text{where} \quad v < \sqrt{\left(\frac{H}{Mk}\right)}$$

and H is constant. Prove that the engine is working at a constant rate.

2. A train of mass M is being pulled by its engine against a constant resistance R. The engine works at a constant rate H. Prove that the time taken to reach a velocity $v(< H/R)$ from rest is

$$\frac{MH}{R^2}\ln\left(\frac{H}{H-Rv}\right)-\frac{Mv}{R}.$$

3. The effective power of a ship of mass M kg is H kW and its full speed is V m/s. Assuming that the resistance to motion varies as the square of the speed and that the power is constant, show that the ship travels a distance of $(MV^3/3000\,H)\ln(8/7)$ metres in attaining half speed from rest.

4. A light locomotive of mass 20,000 kg works at a constant effective rate of 100 kW. The total resistance to its motion is constant and is equal to 6000 N. Show that for high speeds, if v is the velocity in m/s and x is the distance travelled in metres, $10v^2\,dv/dx = 50-3v$. Find the maximum speed and the distance travelled while the speed increases from 36 to 54 km/h.

5. A train of mass 3×10^5 kg travels on the level at a uniform speed of 25 m/s against a resistance of 2×10^4 N. The train then climbs an incline of 1 in 147. Assuming the power and the resistance to be constant show that when the speed has dropped to v m/s the retardation is $(2v-25)/(15v)$ m/s². Find the time taken for the speed to fall from 25 m/s to 20 m/s.

6. The engine of a car of mass 1000 kg works at the constant rate of 10 kW. The frictional resistance varies as the square of the speed, and the maximum speed of the car on the level is 72 km/h. Find the distance which the car covers on a level road while accelerating from rest to 45 km/h.

Find also the rate at which energy is being used in overcoming friction at the speed of 45 km/h.

7. A train of total mass M is drawn on the level by an engine working at a constant rate H, and the resistance varies as the square of the speed. Show that the speed has a certain limiting value.

If the limiting speed is V, show that when the speed of the train is v the acceleration is

$$\frac{H(V^3-v^3)}{MV^3v}.$$

Show also that the distance moved while the speed is increased from $\frac{1}{2}V$ to $\frac{3}{4}V$ is

$$\frac{MV^3}{3H}\ln\frac{56}{37}. \qquad \text{(N.)}$$

8. A cyclist working at 100 W rides at a steady speed of 45 km/h down a slope of inclination $\sin^{-1}(1/70)$. If the total mass of the rider and his machine is 100 kg, show that the resistance opposing his motion is 22 N.

If the resistance varies directly as his velocity and his rate of working is unaltered, show that, when the cyclist is riding along a level road at speed v m/s, his acceleration is

$$\frac{625-11v^2}{625v}\ \text{m/s}^2.$$

Hence show that the interval of time during which his speed increases from 9 km/h to 18 km/h is

$$\frac{625}{22}\ln\left(\frac{89}{56}\right) \quad \text{seconds.}$$

9. The total resistance to the motion of a car when the speed is v m/s is $(a+bv^2)$ newtons, where a and b are constants. A car of mass 1500 kg travels at a steady speed of 72 km/h when the power exerted is 12 kW and at 54 km/h when the power is 6 kW. Calculate the values of a and b.

If the engine is switched off, show that the distance covered while the speed falls from 72 km/h to 54 km/h is

$$\frac{2625}{4}\ln\frac{3}{2} \quad \text{metres.}$$

10. A train of total mass m moves from rest against a resistance which at any time is k times the momentum. Assuming the power P of the engine to be constant, show that the speed v of the train at time t after the start of the motion is given by

$$mkv^2 = P(1-e^{-2kt}).$$

The power is cut off when the train has speed V and the train is stopped in a further time T by means of a constant braking force F. Show that

$$F = mkV/(e^{kT}-1). \qquad \text{(L.)}$$

11. A lorry of mass M kg moves along a level road against a resistance proportional to the speed. The engine works at a constant rate H kW and the maximum speed attainable is v_0 m/s. Show that the equation of motion reduces to the form

$$1000H(v_0^2-v^2) = Mv_0^2v^2\frac{dv}{dx}.$$

Show that the distance covered by the lorry while its speed increases from $\frac{1}{4}v_0$ m/s to $\frac{1}{2}v_0$ m/s is

$$\frac{Mv_0^3}{4000H}\left\{2\ln\left(\frac{9}{5}\right)-1\right\} \quad \text{metres.}$$

12. The engine of a train of total mass 3×10^4 kg works at the constant rate of 500 kW. The train is moving along a level track and its motion is resisted by a constant force of 10^4 N. Show that the acceleration of the train is

$$\frac{50-v}{3v} \quad \text{m/s}^2$$

when the speed is v m/s.

Show that the time taken for the speed to increase from 45 km/h to 72 km/h is

$$15\{20\ln(\tfrac{5}{4})-3\}/2 \quad \text{seconds.}$$

13. A motor-cycle with its rider has a mass of 150 kg and is able to attain a speed of 15 m/s up a hill of inclination $\sin^{-1}(\frac{1}{15})$ and a speed of 30 m/s down the hill. The power H W is constant, and the resistance is kvg N when the speed is v m/s. Show that $H = 2940$ and $k = \frac{2}{3}$.

Show also that it would take (1125/98) ln 2 seconds starting from rest, to reach a speed of 15 m/s on a level road.

14. A train of mass M moves along a straight level track with constant speed u. The engine works at a constant rate K and the resistance to motion is constant and of magnitude F. Write down the equation connecting K, F and u.

The rate of working of the engine is now increased to λK, where λ is a constant and > 1; the resistance is unaltered. At time t after the change the speed of the train has changed to v. Show that

$$Muv\, \mathrm{d}v/\mathrm{d}t = K(\lambda u - v)$$

and deduce that

$$M\lambda u^2 \ln \{(\lambda-1)u/(\lambda u-v)\} - Mu(v-u) = Kt. \qquad \text{(N.)}$$

17.4. Equations of Motion Deduced from the Energy Equation

In previous chapters of this book we have discussed methods in which the motion of a particle, or of a rigid lamina, is analysed by reference, in the first instance, to the equation of energy. The example, and the exercises which follow, illustrate this method further.

Example. Two particles A and B, of masses m and $2m$ respectively, are joined by a light inextensible string of length exceeding $\frac{1}{2}\pi b$. The particle A is held at rest at the highest point of a fixed smooth solid sphere, of centre O and radius b. The particle B hangs freely in equilibrium. If A is now released and OA makes an angle θ with the upward vertical at time t after release, show that, so long as A remains in contact with the sphere,

$$3b(\mathrm{d}\theta/\mathrm{d}t)^2 = 2g(1+2\theta-\cos\theta).$$

Deduce that A leaves the sphere when $\theta = \alpha$, where

$$5 \cos\alpha = 2+4\alpha.$$

Find, in terms of θ, the tension in the string before A leaves the sphere. (N.)

At time t when OA makes an angle θ with the upward vertical, Fig. 17.2, the velocity of A is $b\dot{\theta}$ in the direction of the tangent to the circle and the velocity of B is $b\dot{\theta}$ vertically downwards. In this position A is displaced a vertical distance $b(1-\cos\theta)$ below its original position and B is displaced a vertical distance $b\theta$ below its original position. The equation of energy for the particles is therefore

$$\tfrac{1}{2}mb^2\dot{\theta}^2+\tfrac{1}{2}2mb^2\dot{\theta}^2 = mgb(1-\cos\theta)+2mgb\theta.$$

$$\therefore\ 3b\dot{\theta}^2 = 2g(1+2\theta-\cos\theta). \qquad (1)$$

The forces acting on the particles are shown in Fig. 17.2. The equation of motion of A in the direction of the centre of the sphere is

$$mg\cos\theta - R = mb\dot{\theta}^2.$$

$$\begin{aligned}\therefore\ R &= mg\cos\theta-\tfrac{2}{3}mg(1+2\theta-\cos\theta)\\ &= \tfrac{1}{3}mg(3\cos\theta-2-4\theta+2\cos\theta)\\ &= \tfrac{1}{3}mg(5\cos\theta-2-4\theta).\end{aligned}$$

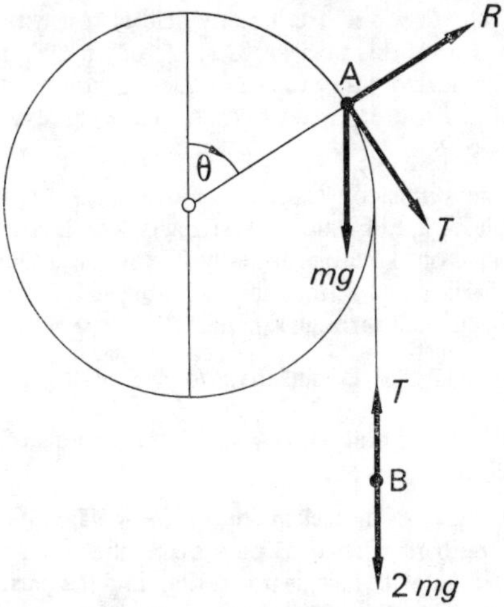

FIG. 17.2

Particle A therefore leaves the sphere when $\theta = \alpha$, where

$$5 \cos \alpha = 2+4\,\alpha.$$

Differentiating (1) with respect to t we have

$$6b\dot{\theta}\ddot{\theta} = 2g(2\dot{\theta}+\dot{\theta} \sin \theta).$$

$$\therefore\ \ddot{\theta} = \frac{g}{3b}(2+\sin \theta). \qquad (2)$$

The equation of motion for B is

$$2mg-T = 2mb\ddot{\theta}.$$

$$\therefore\ T = 2mg-\tfrac{2}{3}mg(2+\sin \theta) = \tfrac{2}{3}mg(1-\sin \theta). \qquad (3)$$

The tension in the string is $\frac{2}{3}mg(1-\sin \theta)$. Results (2) and (3) hold for $\theta \leqq \alpha$.

EXERCISES 17.4

1. A small ring P of mass m is threaded on a fixed smooth horizontal bar OX, and an equal ring Q is threaded on a fixed smooth vertical bar OY, where Y is below the meeting point O of the two bars. The rings are connected to each other by a light inextensible string of length a, and are initially held at rest with Q at O and P distant a from O. After release from this position Q slides down OY and P along XO. If the inclination of PQ to the horizontal in the subsequent motion is denoted by $\theta (0 \leqq \theta \leqq \frac{1}{2}\pi)$, find an expression for $(d\theta/dt)^2$ in terms of θ. Deduce an expression for the tension of the string in terms of θ. (N.)

2. A particle P of mass m is constrained to move in a straight smooth groove on a smooth horizontal table. A light inextensible string of length $2a$ connects it to a particle Q of mass m free to move on the table. Initially P is at rest, PQ is perpendicular to the groove and Q is moving parallel to the groove with speed u, the string being taut. Show that when the string has turned through an angle $\theta (\leqq \frac{1}{2}\pi)$

$$4a^2(1+\sin^2\theta)(d\theta/dt)^2 = u^2.$$

Show also that when $\theta = 0$ and when $\theta = \frac{1}{2}\pi$ the tensions of the string are $mu^2/2a$ and $mu^2/8a$ respectively. (N.)

3. Two particles A and B, of masses m and M, $(m < M < 3m)$, are joined by a light inextensible string of length πa. The string passes over the upper half of a smooth circular cylinder of radius a, fixed with its axis horizontal, and the particles are released from rest in a position in which the line AB is horizontal and passes through a point O on the axis of the cylinder. If the particle A is still in contact with the cylinder after OA has turned through an angle θ, prove that

$$(M+m)\,a\left(\frac{d\theta}{dt}\right)^2 = 2g(M\theta - m\sin\theta).$$

Prove also that the particle A will leave the surface of the cylinder when θ satisfies the equation

$$2M\theta = (M+3m)\sin\theta,$$

and that this will occur before $\theta = \pi$.

Explain briefly what happens in the case when $3m < M$. (N.)

***4.** A small bead B of mass m is threaded on a smooth wire bent into the form of a circle, of radius a and centre O, fixed in a vertical plane. The bead is connected to the highest point A of the wire by an elastic string, of natural length $a\sqrt{2}$ and modulus kmg, and is released from rest when at the same level as O. Show that the speed v of B when $\angle$ OAB $= \theta$ is given by

$$v^2/ag = (4-2k\sqrt{2})\cos^2\theta + 4k\cos\theta - (2+k\sqrt{2}).$$

Show that if B comes to rest before it reaches the position vertically below O, then $k > 3\sqrt{2}+4$. (N.)

***5.** A bead P of mass m is threaded on a smooth wire which has the form of a circle of radius a, centre O, and is fixed in a vertical plane. A light inextensible string, attached at one end to P, passes through a small smooth ring B fixed at a distance $2a$ vertically below O and then down to a hanging particle Q of mass m attached to the other end of the string. Initially Q is at rest and P is at the lowest point A of the wire and is moving with speed $\sqrt{(3ga)}$. If the angle POA is denoted by θ and the distance PB by r, show that in the subsequent motion

$$(\mathrm{d}r/\mathrm{d}t)^2+a^2(\mathrm{d}\theta/\mathrm{d}t)^2 = g(3a+2a\cos\theta-2r).$$

Express r as a function of θ and deduce that when θ reaches the value $\frac{1}{3}\pi$ the velocity of Q is

$$\{ga(2-\sqrt{3})\}^{1/2}. \qquad \text{(N.)}$$

*17.5. Damped Harmonic Oscillations

The equation of motion of a particle moving in a straight line under the action of a force directed towards a fixed point in the line and proportional to the displacement of the particle from the point is

$$\frac{\mathrm{d}^2x}{\mathrm{d}t^2}+\omega^2x = 0 \qquad \text{(Volume I, Chapter XIV, § 14.1).}$$

This motion is one example of Simple Harmonic Motion which we defined in that chapter by the equation

$$\frac{\mathrm{d}^2z}{\mathrm{d}t^2}+\omega^2z = 0.$$

When the particle is also subject to a resistance which is proportional to its velocity, the equation of motion becomes

$$\frac{\mathrm{d}^2x}{\mathrm{d}t^2} = -\omega^2x-2\lambda\frac{\mathrm{d}x}{\mathrm{d}t},$$

where x is the directed displacement of the particle from the fixed point and ω, λ are constants.

This equation of motion is a linear equation of the second order with constant coefficients. [The method of solution of such equations is discussed in *Pure Maths.*, Vol. II, §§ 17.9–17.11.] The nature of the motion of the particle as determined by its equation of motion is dependent on the nature of the roots of the auxiliary equation used in solving the equation of motion. The example below illustrates the different cases which can arise.

Example. A particle of mass m moves in a straight line under the action of a force directed towards a fixed point O of the line. This force varies as the distance of the particle from O and is equal to $4mx$ at a distance x from O. There is a resistance to the motion of the particle which is proportional to its velocity and which is equal to $2\lambda mv$ when the velocity of the particle is v. The particle starts from rest at the point $x = a$. Discuss the motion of the particle in each of the three cases

$$\text{(a) } \lambda = 2\tfrac{1}{2}, \quad \text{(b) } \lambda = 2, \quad \text{(c) } \lambda = 1.$$

The force $4mx$ is equivalent to a force $-4mx$ in the direction of x increasing on whichever side of O the particle is. The resistance to the motion of the particle is equivalent to a force $-2\lambda m\dot{x}$ in the direction of x increasing in whichever direction the particle is moving. Hence the equation of motion of the particle is

$$\frac{d^2x}{dt^2}+2\lambda\frac{dx}{dt}+4x = 0.$$

(a) When $\lambda = 2\frac{1}{2}$, this equation becomes

$$\frac{d^2x}{dt^2}+5\frac{dx}{dt}+4x = 0.$$

The auxiliary equation is $m^2+5m+4 = 0$ and the roots of this equation are $m_1 = -4$, $m_2 = -1$. The solution of the equation of motion is therefore

$$x = A\,e^{-4t}+B\,e^{-t}.$$

Since $x = a$ when $t = 0$, $A+B = a$. Also

$$\frac{dx}{dt} = -4A\,e^{-4t}-B\,e^{-t}$$

and since $dx/dt = 0$ when $t = 0$, $-4A-B = 0$,

$$\therefore\ A = -\frac{a}{3}, \quad B = \frac{4a}{3}.$$

$$\therefore\ x = -\tfrac{1}{3}a(e^{-4t}-4e^{-t}),$$

i.e.

$$x = \tfrac{1}{3}a\,e^{-4t}(4e^{3t}-1).$$

This expression for x is positive for all values of t and $\lim_{t\to\infty} x = 0$.

It follows from this analysis that the particle never passes through the origin $x = 0$ but approaches it asymptotically. The x–t graph of the motion is shown in Fig. 17.3 (i).

(b) When $\lambda = 2$, the equation of motion becomes

$$\frac{d^2x}{dt^2}+4\frac{dx}{dt}+4 = 0.$$

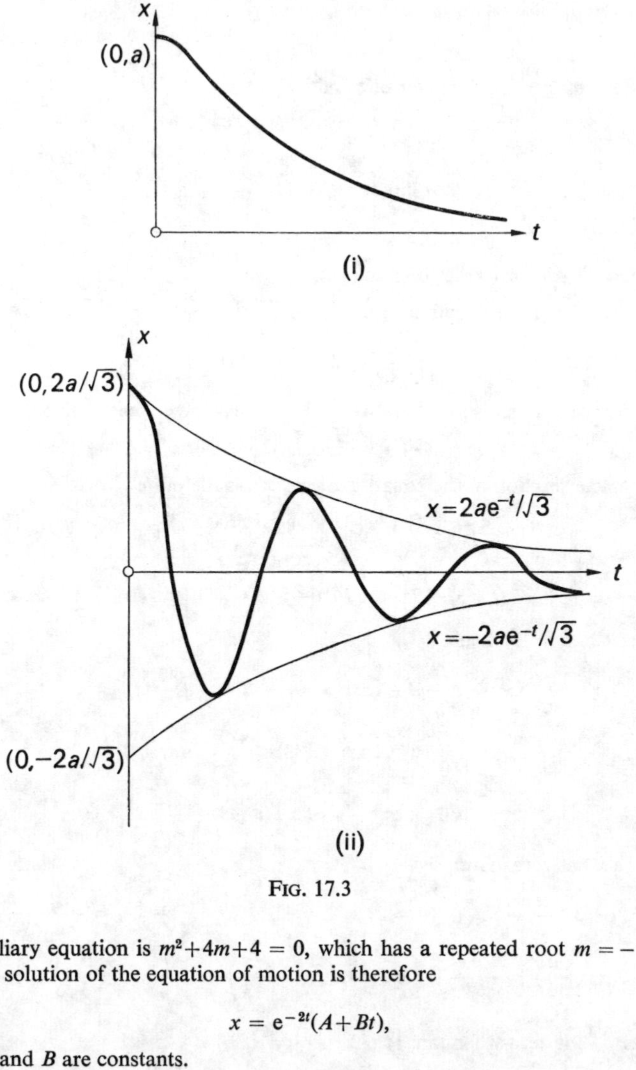

FIG. 17.3

The auxiliary equation is $m^2+4m+4 = 0$, which has a repeated root $m = -2$. The complete solution of the equation of motion is therefore

$$x = e^{-2t}(A+Bt),$$

where A and B are constants.

Since $x = a$ when $t = 0$, $\therefore\ A = a.$ Also

$$\frac{dx}{dt} = -2e^{-2t}(A+Bt)+B\,e^{-2t}$$

and since $dx/dt = 0$ when $t = 0$, $\quad \therefore \ -2A+B = 0, \quad B = 2a.$

$$\therefore \ x = a\,e^{-2t}(1+2t).$$

Again x is positive for all values of t and

$$\lim_{t\to\infty} x = a \lim_{t\to\infty} \{e^{-2t}+2t/(1+2t+2t^2+\ldots)\}$$

$$= a \lim_{t\to\infty} \left\{e^{-2t}+1\Big/\left(\frac{1}{2t}+1+2t+\ldots\right)\right\}$$

$$= 0.$$

The motion is similar to that of case (a).

(c) When $\lambda = 1$ the equation of motion becomes

$$\frac{d^2x}{dt^2}+2\frac{dx}{dt}+4 = 0.$$

The auxiliary equation is $m^2+2m+4 = 0$, which has the complex roots

$$m_1 = -1+i\sqrt{3}, \quad m_2 = -1-i\sqrt{3}.$$

The complete solution of the equation of motion is therefore

$$x = e^{-t}\{A\cos(t\sqrt{3})+B\sin(t\sqrt{3})\}.$$

Since $x = a$ when $t = 0$, $\quad \therefore \ A = a.$ Also

$$dx/dt = -e^{-t}\{A\cos(t\sqrt{3})+B\sin(t\sqrt{3})\}+e^{-t}\{-\sqrt{3}A\sin(t\sqrt{3})+\sqrt{3}B\cos(t\sqrt{3})\}$$

and since $dx/dt = 0$ when $t = 0$,

$$\therefore \ -A+\sqrt{3}B = 0, \quad B = \frac{a\sqrt{3}}{3}.$$

$$\therefore \ x = a\,e^{-t}\left\{\cos(t\sqrt{3})+\frac{\sqrt{3}}{3}\sin(t\sqrt{3})\right\},$$

i.e.

$$x = a\,e^{-t}\frac{2}{\sqrt{3}}\sin\left\{(t\sqrt{3})+\frac{\pi}{3}\right\}.$$

Therefore x has zeros given by

$$t\sqrt{3}+\frac{\pi}{3} = n\pi, \quad (n = 1, 2, 3, \ldots), \quad \text{i.e. by} \quad t = \frac{\pi}{\sqrt{3}}\left(\frac{3n-1}{3}\right).$$

Also

$$\frac{dx}{dt} = \frac{2a\,e^{-t}}{\sqrt{3}}\left\{\sqrt{3}\cos\left(t\sqrt{3}+\frac{\pi}{3}\right)-\sin\left(t\sqrt{3}+\frac{\pi}{3}\right)\right\}$$

and thus $\dfrac{dx}{dt}$ is zero when $\tan\left(t\sqrt{3}+\dfrac{\pi}{3}\right) = \sqrt{3}$,

i.e. when

$$t\sqrt{3}+\frac{\pi}{3} = n\pi+\frac{\pi}{3}, \quad (n = 0, 1, 2, \ldots),$$

i.e. when

$$t = \frac{n\pi}{\sqrt{3}}.$$

Therefore x has stationary values (which are alternately maxima and minima) for values of t given by $t = n\pi/3$. Because of the factor e^{-t} in the expression for x, the numerical values of these maxima and minima decrease progressively as t increases and the decrease is in geometrical progression. For all values of t, $|x| \leqq 2a\,e^{-t}/\sqrt{3}$. For values of t given by $t\sqrt{3}+\pi/3 = \frac{1}{2}(4n+1)\pi$, $(n = 0, 1, 2, \ldots)$, $x = 2a\,e^{-t}/\sqrt{3}$ and for values of t given by $t\sqrt{3}+\pi/3 = \frac{1}{2}(4n+3)\pi$, $(n = 0, 1, 2, \ldots)$, $x = -2a\,e^{-t}/\sqrt{3}$. The x–t graph of the function is therefore as shown in Fig. 17.3 (ii).

At the common points of the graph of the function and each of the graphs $x = \pm 2ae^{-t}/\sqrt{3}$ the gradients of the two curves are equal and the curves therefore touch. These common points do not coincide with the maxima and minima of x.

We conclude that, in this case, the particle oscillates with constantly decreasing amplitude of oscillation, but always passing through the "centre" $x = 0$.

In general, it can be shown by the method applied to the particular cases of the above example, that if the equation of the motion is

$$\frac{d^2x}{dt^2}+2\lambda\frac{dx}{dt}+\omega^2x = 0,$$

then (a) when $\lambda \geqq \omega$, the particle approaches the position $x = 0$ asymptotically (the particle, in some cases, passes through the origin before returning to approach the origin asymptotically),

(b) when $\lambda < \omega$, the particle oscillates about $x = 0$ with oscillations, the amplitudes of which decrease in geometrical progression.

Motion of a simple pendulum. When a simple pendulum (Chapter XIV, § 14.1) oscillates in a medium of which the resistance varies as the velocity, its equation of motion can be reduced to the form

$$\frac{d^2\theta}{dt^2}+\lambda\frac{d\theta}{dt}+\frac{g}{l}\sin\theta = 0$$

which, when θ is small so that terms involving the third and higher powers of θ can be neglected, becomes

$$\frac{d^2\theta}{dt^2}+\lambda\frac{d\theta}{dt}+\frac{g}{l}\theta = 0.$$

Forced oscillations. If the particle is subjected to a force which is a function of the time, its equation of motion takes the form

$$\frac{d^2x}{dt^2}+\lambda\frac{dx}{dt}+\omega^2x = f(t).$$

In these cases the solution of the equation of motion involves the finding of a particular integral in addition to the complementary function.

Example 1. A particle of mass m is attached to one end, B, of a light spring, AB, of natural length l and modulus mln^2. At time $t = 0$ the spring and particle are lying at rest on a smooth horizontal table, with the spring straight but unstretched. The end A is then moved in a straight line in the direction BA with constant acceleration f, so that, after t seconds, its displacement in this direction from its initial position is $\frac{1}{2}ft^2$. Show that the displacement, x, of the particle at time t in the direction BA from its initial position satisfies the equation

$$\frac{d^2x}{dt^2}+n^2x = \frac{1}{2}n^2ft^2.$$

By using the substitution $y = \frac{1}{2}ft^2-x$, or otherwise, find the value of x at time t and show that the tension in the spring never exceeds $2mf$. [N.]

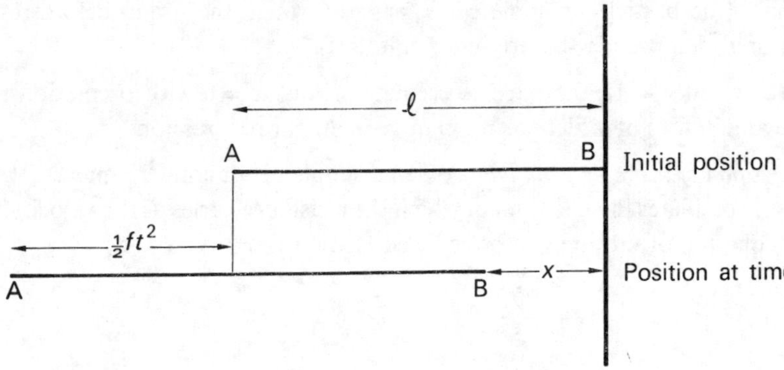

FIG. 17.4

At time t the length of the spring is $l-x+\frac{1}{2}ft^2$ (Fig. 17.4). The only force acting in the direction of motion on the particle is the elastic tension in the spring. The equation of motion for the particle is therefore:

$$m\frac{d^2x}{dt^2} = mln^2\left(\frac{1}{2}ft^2-x\right)\Big/l,$$

i.e.

$$\frac{d^2x}{dt^2}+n^2x = \frac{1}{2}n^2ft^2.$$

Substitute $y = \frac{1}{2}ft^2-x$, so that $d^2y/dt^2 = f-(d^2x/dt^2)$ and the equation is transformed into

$$\frac{d^2y}{dt^2}+n^2y = f.$$

The general solution of this equation is

$$y = A\cos nt+B\sin nt+\frac{f}{n^2},$$

where A and B are constants. Therefore

$$x = \frac{1}{2}ft^2-A\cos nt-B\sin nt-\frac{f}{n^2}.$$

But $x = 0$ when $t = 0$; therefore $A = -(f/n^2)$.
Also, $\dot{x} = 0$ when $t = 0$; therefore $B = 0$, and the value of x at time t is given by

$$x = \frac{1}{2}ft^2+\frac{f}{n^2}\cos nt-\frac{f}{n^2}.$$

Therefore, if T is the tension in the spring, and considering the motion of the particle,

$$T = m\frac{d^2x}{dt^2}.$$

$$\therefore\ T = m(f-f\cos nt).$$

The maximum value of T occurs when $\cos nt = -1$, and then $T = 2mf$.

Example 2. A particle P of mass m moves along a straight line so that OP $= x$, where O is a fixed point on the line. The forces acting on P are

(i) a force mn^2x directed towards O,
(ii) a resistance $2mnv$, where v is the speed of P,
(iii) a force $F = ma\cos nt$ acting along the direction x increasing.

Write down the differential equation satisfied by x and solve this equation given that at time $t=0$ the particle is at rest at O.
Find the rate at which the force F is doing work at time t. [L.]

The equation of motion for the particle is

$$m\ddot{x} = -mn^2x-2mn\dot{x}+ma\cos nt,$$

or

$$\ddot{x}+2n\dot{x}+n^2x = a\cos nt.$$

The complementary function is $e^{-nt}(A+Bt)$, where A and B are constants.

Particular integral. If x = the real part of $C\,e^{int}$ is a solution,

$$-Cn^2+2in^2C+n^2C = a,$$

i.e.

$$C = \frac{a}{2in^2}.$$

The particular integral is, therefore, the real part of $(a/2in^2)\,e^{int}$, i.e.

$$\frac{a}{2n^2}\sin nt.$$

Therefore

$$x = e^{-nt}(A+Bt)+\frac{a}{2n^2}\sin nt.$$

But $x = 0$ when $t = 0$, therefore $A = 0$.

Also $\dot{x} = 0$ when $t = 0$, therefore $B = -a/(2n)$.

Therefore

$$x = -\frac{a}{2n}t\,e^{-nt}+\frac{a}{2n^2}\sin nt.$$

At time t, the force is doing work at the rate $F\dot{x}$, i.e. at the rate

$$\frac{ma^2}{2n}\cos nt\,(\cos nt+nt\,e^{-nt}-e^{-nt}).$$

[That part of the motion of the particle which is represented by $-(a/2n)te^{-nt}$ in the equation for x, and which dies away as t increases, is called the *transient* part of the motion. That part which is represented by $(a/2n^2)\sin nt$ is the *forced oscillation*.]

---

*EXERCISES 17.5

In questions 1–4 the differential equation is the equation of motion of a particle moving in a straight line under the action of a restoring force directed towards a fixed point O of the line and proportional to the displacement of the particle from O and also of a resistance to its motion which is proportional to its velocity. In each case state the nature of the motion.

***1.** $\ddot{x}+2\dot{x}+2x = 0$; $x = 1$, $\dot{x} = 0$ when $t = 0$.

Calculate x when $t = \frac{1}{4}\pi$.

***2.** $\ddot{x}+2\dot{x}+x = 0$; $x = 2$, $\dot{x} = 0$ when $t = 0$.

Calculate each of x and $\dot{x}$ when $t = 1$, giving your answers correct to 2 significant figures.

*3. $\ddot{x}+2\dot{x}+5x = 0$; $x = 2$, $\dot{x} = 0$ when $t = 0$.

Calculate each of x and $\dot{x}$ when $t = \frac{1}{2}\pi$.

*4. $\ddot{x}+3\dot{x}+2x = 0$; $x = 1$, $\dot{x} = 0$ when $t = 0$.

Show that x is always positive and that for $x < \frac{1}{10}$, $t > \ln(10+3\sqrt{10})$.

*5. Show that the general solution of the differential equation $a\ddot{y}+b\dot{y}+cy = 0$ in the case when $4ac > b^2$ is

$$y = e^{-kt}(P\cos\omega t+Q\sin\omega t),$$

where $k = b/2a$ and $4a^2\omega^2 = 4ac-b^2$, and P, Q are arbitrary constants.

A particle P of mass 0·25 kg on a horizontal table is connected by an elastic string, of natural length 1 metre and modulus 8 N, to a point A on the table. The particle, initially at rest with the string at its natural length, is projected in the direction AP with speed u m/s, and the motion is subject to a resistance $2v$ newtons when the speed is v m/s. Write down and solve the equation of motion of P, and show that until the string slackens, the distance AP at time t seconds after projection is $1+\frac{1}{4}u\,e^{-4t}\sin 4t$ metres.

Find the maximum value of AP.

*6. A particle of mass m moves in a straight line and x is its displacement at time t from a fixed point of the line. Explain the nature of the forces acting on the particle, given that the equation of motion is

$$\frac{d^2x}{dt^2}+2k\frac{dx}{dt}+5k^2x = 0,$$

where k is a positive constant.

Solve the equation of motion given that $x = 0$, $dx/dt = u$ when $t = 0$.

Show that, when x is next zero,

$$\frac{dx}{dt} = -u\,e^{-\pi/2}$$

and find the corresponding value of d^2x/dt^2. (N.)

*7. A particle moves in a straight line so that its distance x from a fixed point in the line satisfies the differential equation

$$\frac{d^2x}{dt^2}+4\frac{dx}{dt}+4x = 0.$$

The particle starts from rest at time $t = 0$ when $x = a$. Prove that its greatest speed in the ensuing motion is $2a\,e^{-1}$. (N.)

*8. A body of mass 5 kg is suspended from a spring of stiffness 2 N/cm and there is a resistance to motion proportional to the velocity of the body which is 0·5 N at 0·025 m/s. The displacement of the body is x m from the unstretched position after

t seconds and the body starts from rest with $x = 0{\cdot}545$. Show that the differential equation for x is

$$\ddot{x}+4\dot{x}+40x = 9{\cdot}8.$$

Find x in terms of t and the period of damped oscillations.

***9.** A particle P of mass m moves in a straight line under the action of a force mn^2 OP, which is always directed towards a fixed point O in the line. If the resistance to motion is $2\lambda mnv$, where v is the speed and $0 < \lambda < 1$, write down the equation of motion, and find x in terms of the time t, given that when $t = 0$, $x = 0$ and

$$\frac{dx}{dt} = u, \quad \text{where} \quad x = \text{OP}. \qquad \text{(N.)}$$

***10.** A simple pendulum whose period of small oscillations *in vacuo* is $\pi/2$ sec is made to perform small oscillations under gravity in a fluid which offers resistance to the motion of the bob. The force of resistance is $2mkv$ where m is the mass and v the speed of the bob: k is a constant whose value depends on the fluid being used. Prove that the angular displacement, θ, of the pendulum from the vertical during the small oscillations satisfies the following differential equation,

$$\frac{d^2\theta}{dt^2}+2k\frac{d\theta}{dt}+16\theta = 0.$$

If the resistance is such that $k = 3$, show that

$$\theta = a\,e^{-3t}\sin\sqrt{7}t$$

gives a possible motion, where a is arbitrary but small. If the fluid is such that the resistance is greater, $k = 5$, show that $\theta = a\,e^{-5t}\sinh 3t$ is a possible motion. By means of rough graphs of θ against the time t point out the chief characteristics of these two motions. (O.C.)

***11.** A body is attached by a spring to a point which is oscillating with sinusoidal motion. The displacement s of the body from a fixed reference point at any time t is given by the differential equation

$$\frac{d^2s}{dt^2}+4s = \lambda \sin t,$$

where λ is a constant. Given that $s = 0$ when $t = 0$, and $ds/dt = 2\lambda/3$ when $t = 0$, solve the equation for s in terms of t. (L.)

***12.** A particle P moves along the straight line Ox so that, at time t, OP $= x$ where O is a fixed point on the line. The particle starts from rest at O at time $t = 0$ and its equation of motion is

$$\frac{d^2x}{dt^2}+4\omega^2x = f(t),$$

where $f(t) = 3\omega^2 c \sin \omega t$ for $0 \leqq t \leqq \pi/\omega$, $f(t) = 0$ for $\pi/\omega \leqq t \leqq 2\pi/\omega$, and c, ω are constants. Calculate x for $0 \leqq t \leqq 2\pi/\omega$. Sketch the graph of x against t for $0 \leqq t \leqq 2\pi/\omega$. (L.)

***13.** A particle of mass m lies in a rough fixed horizontal tube and is attached to one end of a light spiral spring. The spring lies along the tube and its other end is attached to a fixed point in the tube. When the length of the spring is changed from its natural length by x, the restoring force is mn^2x. Initially the spring is compressed by an amount a. If the coefficient of friction between the particle and the tube is $n^2a/6g$ show, by consideration of energy or otherwise, that the particle will first come to instantaneous rest with the spring extended by an amount $2a/3$.

Find the position of the particle when it is next instantaneously at rest, and show that it finally comes to rest with the spring neither extended nor compressed. (L.)

***14.** A light spring AB of natural length a and modulus of elasticity $3amn^2$, initially lies straight and at its natural length on a horizontal table, and a particle of mass m is attached to it at B. Starting at time $t = 0$, the end A is moved in the direction BA with constant speed V. The motion of the particle is resisted by a force equal to $4mn$ times the speed of the particle. If x is the extension of the spring at time t, prove that

$$\frac{d^2x}{dt^2}+4n\frac{dx}{dt}+3n^2x = 4nV.$$

Find x in terms of t, and deduce the value of the force applied at A at time t. (N.)

***15.** A particle of mass m is suspended from a fixed point by a spring of natural length a and modulus λ, and a periodic force equal to $mf \sin pt$ acts downwards on it. The motion of the particle is resisted by a force equal to k times its speed. If x is the downward displacement from the equilibrium position at time t, show that

$$\frac{d^2x}{dt^2}+\frac{k}{m}\frac{dx}{dt}+\frac{\lambda}{ma}x = f \sin pt.$$

If $k = 4m$ and $\lambda = 5ma$, show that the amplitude of the periodic forced oscillations is

$$\frac{|f|}{\sqrt{\{(5-p^2)^2+16p^2\}}}.$$

Show that this amplitude decreases steadily as p^2 increases. (N.)

MISCELLANEOUS EXERCISES XVII

1. A particle of mass m is projected vertically from the ground, its motion being subject to gravity and to an air resistance $R(v)$, a function of its speed v. When the particle is at a height x and moving upwards its speed v is given by

$$v^2 = a\,e^{-2gx/b}-b, \quad (a > b > 0),$$

where a, b are constants and g is the constant acceleration due to gravity. Calculate, in terms of m, a and b, the work done against air resistance during the entire upward motion.

Find the acceleration as a function of v and deduce an expression for $R(v)$.

Show that in a downward motion of the particle starting from rest the speed can never exceed $\sqrt{b}$. (N.)

2. A train of mass M moves on a straight horizontal track. At speeds less than V the resultant force on the train is constant and equal to P; at speeds not less than V the rate of working of the force is constant and equal to PV. Show that a speed $v\,(>V)$ is attained from rest in the time

$$\frac{M(V^2+v^2)}{2PV},$$

and find the corresponding distance travelled. (N.)

3. A lorry of mass M kg moves along a straight level road with its engine shut off. When the lorry is travelling at v m/s the resistance to its motion is $a(v^2+V^2)/V^2$ newtons, where a and V are positive constants. Find, in m/s^2, the retardation of the lorry. Prove that the distance in which the lorry is brought to rest from a speed of V m/s is

$$\frac{MV^2 \ln 2}{2a} \quad \text{metres}$$

and that the corresponding time is

$$\frac{\pi MV}{4a} \quad \text{seconds.}$$

4. The acceleration of a motor car at a speed of v metres/second is

$$\frac{80^2-v^2}{80^2} \quad \text{m/s}^2.$$

If the car starts from rest, state the greatest speed of which it is capable.

Find by integration the distance in which half this speed is acquired from rest, and the time taken to travel this distance.

5. The only force acting on a particle of mass m, moving in a straight line, is a resistance $kv(V^2+3v^2)$ where v is the velocity of the particle and k and V are constants. The particle is given an initial velocity V, which is reduced to $\frac{1}{3}V$ after a time T during which the particle travels a distance L. Prove that $2kV^2T = m \ln 3$ and

$$6\sqrt{3kVL} = \pi m. \qquad \text{(L.)}$$

6. A particle of mass m falls from rest in a medium which produces a resistance mkv^2 at speed v. Show that after time t, $v = c \tanh (gt/c)$ where c is the terminal velocity.

Show also that the distance x fallen in time t is given by $kx = \ln(\cosh gt/c)$. (L.)

7. Two particles P and Q move along a line AB, both starting from A with speed u and coming instantaneously to rest at B. The particle P moves with constant retardation and Q moves with a retardation proportional to the distance AQ. Prove that the times taken by P and Q to reach B are in the ratio $4:\pi$. (L.)

8. A light spring AB is constrained to be in a vertical line and is fixed at its lower end B. At its upper end A the spring carries a cup of mass m. In the equilibrium state the cup compresses the spring, which obeys Hooke's law, by the amount a. Show that if a particle of mass m is gently placed in the cup, the ensuing motion is governed by the equation

$$2\,d^2x/dt^2 + gx/a = 2g$$

where x is the compression of the spring.

If the system is released from rest with $x = 6a$, show that the particle will leave the cup at time $(2\pi/3)\sqrt{(2a/g)}$ after the start of the motion. (L.)

9. A particle of mass m moves in a straight line, the only force acting on it being a frictional resistance mkv^2, where v is its speed and k is a constant. At time $t = 0$ the particle is at a point O and has speed v_0. When a time t has elapsed the particle is distant x from O and its speed is v. Show that

$$kt = \frac{1}{v} - \frac{1}{v_0} \quad \text{and} \quad kx = \ln\left(\frac{v_0}{v}\right).$$

When the particle reaches a point A on the line its speed is $\frac{1}{2}v_0$. Show that the average speed between O and A is $v_0 \ln 2$. If B is the point on the line such that OA = AB, show that at B the speed is $v_0/4$. (N.)

10. A particle of mass m is moving vertically in a medium which exerts a resistance mgv^2/V^2, where v is the speed of the particle. If the particle is projected upwards with speed $V \tan\alpha$, show that it rises to a height

$$(V^2/g) \ln \sec\alpha,$$

and returns to its point of projection with speed $V \sin\alpha$.

Show further that the total time of flight is

$$(V/g)\left\{\alpha + \ln\cot\left(\frac{\pi}{4} - \frac{\alpha}{2}\right)\right\}. \qquad \text{(L.)}$$

***11.** A body of mass m moves in a straight line under a constant propelling force and a resistance mkv, where v is its velocity and k is a constant. The body starts from rest at time $t = 0$ and the velocity tends to a limiting value V as t increases. Write down differential equations connecting (i) v with t, (ii) v with the distance covered. Solve these equations.

Show that the average velocity during the interval from the start to the instant when $v = \frac{1}{2}V$ is

$$V\left(1 - \frac{1}{2\ln 2}\right). \qquad \text{(N.)}$$

12. A particle of mass m moves in a straight line from rest under the action of a force mp and a resistance mqv^4 where p and q are positive constants and v is the speed of the particle. Show that, when the time t is small, v is approximately equal to $pt-\frac{1}{5}qp^4t^5$. (N.)

***13.** The engines of a ship are stopped when its speed is u. While the speed is dropping from u to v the resistance may be taken to be proportional to the cube of the speed. During this interval the ship travels a distances s in time T. Show that

$$\frac{2T}{s}=\frac{1}{u}+\frac{1}{v}.$$

Show that when the ship has travelled a distance $\frac{1}{2}s$ from the instant when the engines are shut off the time which has elapsed is

$$\frac{(u+3v)T}{4(u+v)}.$$ (N.)

***14.** The engine of a train of mass M kg can exert a maximum pull of pM newtons, and the greatest power that it can develop is hMV kilowatts, where V is a velocity; h and V are constants. The train experiences a constant resistance rM newtons. In a certain test the train is started from rest and the engine is brought up to its full power as quickly as possible. Show that this takes a time t minutes, where

$$t=\frac{50hV}{3p(p-r)}.$$

If the engine continues to develop its full power for a further t minutes, find the total work done by the engine in joules.

15. A body of mass 20 kg is pulled along a smooth horizontal plane by a horizontal force which is constant in direction and which diminishes uniformly with the distance the body has moved. The force is initially 20 N and falls to 10 N when the body has moved 8 m. If the body starts from rest, find its speed when it has moved 16 m.

***16.** A particle moves with velocity v in a horizontal straight line against a resistance $v^{3/2}$ per unit mass. Its initial velocity is V, and after time t this has been reduced to kV; its distance from the initial position is then s.

Prove that $s = k^{1/2}\,Vt$.

Show that the particle is never brought to rest, and that its distance from the initial position is always less than $2V^{1/2}$. (C.)

17. A vehicle starts from rest and accelerates uniformly at the rate of 1 m/s² for the first 20 s, and after that the acceleration is $(2500-v^2)/2100$ m/s², where v metres/second is the velocity. Show that a speed of 40 m/s is attained in about 1090 m.

18. A particle of mass m moves in a straight line, and its distance from a fixed point O in the line is $ut\,e^{-nt}$ at time t, where n and u are constants. Prove that u is its velocity when $t = 0$.

It is known that the particle is acted on by a restoring force towards O of magnitude mn^2 times its distance from O and a certain resistance. Prove that the resistance is proportional to the velocity of the particle. (L.)

***19.** A particle of mass m falls from rest in a medium exerting a resistance mgv^4/c^4 where v is the speed and c is a constant. Show that it acquires a speed $c/2$ after falling a distance

$$\{c^2 \ln(5/3)\}/4g \quad \text{in a time} \quad c\{2\tan^{-1}(\tfrac{1}{2})+\ln 3\}/4g. \qquad \text{(L.)}$$

20. A car of mass 1000 kg is travelling at a uniform speed of 20 m/s along a straight level road, the total resistance being 800 N. The car's engine then begins to fail so that the tractive force exerted becomes zero after 16 s. During these 16 s the graph of the force against the time is a straight line. Show that t s after the engine begins to fail the velocity is $(800-t^2)/40$ m/s, assuming that the total resistance is constant.

Show also that, during these 16 s, the car travels about 286 m.

At the end of this time the driver puts on the brakes and pulls up in 20 m. Find the total retarding force, assuming it to be constant during this last stage.

21. Two particles are connected by an elastic spring, of modulus λ and natural length a. They also attract one another with a force of magnitude $\lambda a^2/8r^2$ when at a distance r apart. Show that the resultant force F acting on each particle towards the other is given by

$$F = \frac{\lambda}{ar^2}\left(r^3 - ar^2 + \frac{a^3}{8}\right).$$

Deduce that there are two values of r for which equilibrium is possible and find these values. (N.)

22. A particle of mass m is projected downwards, under gravity, in a medium whose resistance is equal to the velocity of the particle multiplied by mg/V, where V is constant. Show that the velocity tends asymptotically to the value V.

A particle is projected vertically upwards in the above medium with velocity u. Show that it attains a height

$$\frac{uV}{g} + \frac{V^2}{g}\ln\left(\frac{V}{u+V}\right)$$

above the point of projection. (N.)

***23.** A balloon of mass m, moving in a vertical line, is acted on by (i) its weight, (ii) a force $(1-k)mg$ vertically upwards and (iii) a resisting force due to the air of magnitude $m\lambda$ times the speed of the balloon. If the balloon starts to descend from rest at a height h above the ground, show that after falling through a distance $a\,(< h)$ its speed is v_0, where

$$v_0 = \frac{kg}{\lambda}\{1 - e^{-\lambda(v_0+\lambda a)/kg}\}.$$

At this point a weight $2\,kmg$ is thrown overboard. Show that the balloon will come to rest at the ground if

$$h - a = \frac{v_0}{\lambda} - \frac{kg}{\lambda^2}\ln\left(1 + \frac{\lambda v_0}{kg}\right). \qquad \text{(L.)}$$

24. A particle is projected vertically upwards in a medium whose resistance varies as the square of the velocity and whose terminal velocity is U. If the initial velocity of the particle is U, show that it rises to a height $(U^2/2g)\ln 2$ above the point of projection, and find its velocity when it returns to the point of projection. (L.)

25. A car of mass m travelling along a horizontal road has a maximum attainable speed c. When moving with speed $v(<c)$ the engine works at a rate $(mk/c^2)(2vc-v^2)$, where k is a constant. If the frictional resistances may be neglected in the range $0<v<\frac{1}{2}c$, show that the time taken for the car, starting from rest, to attain half its maximum speed is $(c^2/k)\ln(\frac{4}{3})$. Show also that the distance travelled in that time is

$$(c^3/k)[2\ln(\tfrac{4}{3})-\tfrac{1}{2}]. \qquad \text{(L.)}$$

***26.** A particle of mass m moving in the line Ox is subject to a force $m\omega^2 x$ towards O and a resistance of magnitude $mk\dot{x}^2$, where x is the displacement of the particle from O and ω, $k\,(>0)$ are constants. Show that the equation of motion is

$$\ddot{x}+k\dot{x}^2+\omega^2 x = 0, \quad (\text{when} \quad \dot{x}>0),$$

and

$$\ddot{x}-k\dot{x}^2+\omega^2 x = 0, \quad (\text{when} \quad \dot{x}<0).$$

Deduce that

$$e^{2kx}\left\{\dot{x}^2+\frac{\omega^2}{2k^2}(2kx-1)\right\} = \text{constant}, \quad (\dot{x}>0)$$

and write down the corresponding result when $\dot{x}<0$.

The particle is projected from O with speed u, reaches a maximum distance a, and returns to O with speed v. Show that

$$k^2(u^2-v^2) = \omega^2(2ka\cosh 2ka-\sinh 2ka). \qquad \text{(L.)}$$

***27.** A particle moves in a straight line under a force $\omega^2 x$ per unit mass towards a point O fixed in the line, where x is the distance of the particle from O after time t. In addition a damping force $k(dx/dt)$ per unit mass $(k>0)$ acts in the direction opposite to the motion and an applied force $F\cos pt$ per unit mass is applied in the direction of motion. Set up the differential equation of the motion.

If $k^2<4\omega^2$, show that as t tends to infinity x tends to

$$\frac{F\sin(pt+\alpha)}{[(\omega^2-p^2)^2+k^2p^2]^{1/2}},$$

where $\tan\alpha = (\omega^2-p^2)/(kp)$. (L.)

***28.** The displacement x at time t of a mechanical system satisfies

$$\frac{d^2x}{dt^2}+2a\frac{dx}{dt}+(\omega^2+a^2)x = F$$

where a and ω are positive constants of the system and F is a constant external force. At $t=0$ the system starts from rest at $x=0$. Determine x in terms of t and find where the system ultimately comes to rest. (L.)

***29.** A particle of mass m moving in a line Ox is subject to a restoring force to the origin of magnitude $\omega^2 mx$ and a resistance $2mk(\mathrm{d}x/\mathrm{d}t)$, where ω, k are positive constants ($k < \omega$) and x is the displacement of the particle at time t. If an additional force $mf(t)$ is applied in the direction Ox show that

$$\frac{\mathrm{d}^2x}{\mathrm{d}t^2}+2k\frac{\mathrm{d}x}{\mathrm{d}t}+\omega^2 x = f(t).$$

Find the value of x at time t, given that $f(t) = \cos \omega t$ and that $x = 0$, $\mathrm{d}x/\mathrm{d}t = 0$ at time $t = 0$. Show that after a sufficiently long time the motion is sinusoidal, with amplitude $1/(2k\omega)$. (L.)

***30.** A particle of mass m is suspended from a fixed point above a tank of water by means of a light spring of natural length l and elastic modulus mn^2l. The particle moves in a vertical line, its equilibrium position being in the surface of the water. There is no significant air resistance to its motion but the water resistance is mn times its speed. Show that, during an excursion of the particle into the water, its depth x at time t is given by

$$x = \mathrm{e}^{-nt/2}\left(A\cos\frac{\sqrt{3}}{2}nt+B\sin\frac{\sqrt{3}}{2}nt\right),$$

where A and B are constants.

Given that the particle starts from the water surface with an upward velocity that carries it to a height a, show that in its first excursion into the water it descends to a depth $a\,\mathrm{e}^{-\pi/(3\sqrt{3})}$, and determine the total distance it travels before finally coming to rest.

(Assume that there is no change of either momentum or energy when the particle enters or leaves the water.) (N.)

CHAPTER XVIII

MOTION OF A PARTICLE IN TWO DIMENSIONS

18.1. A Note on Vectors

In previous chapters we have distinguished between *scalar* quantities, such as mass, temperature, energy, which are completely specified by their magnitudes, and *vector* quantities, such as displacement, velocity, force, which require both magnitude and direction (and also position if they are not free vectors) for their complete specification. We have postulated the following laws in relation to vector quantities represented in magnitude and direction by straight lines:

1. $\overrightarrow{AB} = \overrightarrow{CD}$, if AB is equal in length to CD and also AB is parallel to CD in the same sense.

2. $\overrightarrow{AB} = -\overrightarrow{BA}$.

3. $\overrightarrow{AB}+\overrightarrow{BC} = \overrightarrow{AC}$ (the triangle of vectors).

4. $\overrightarrow{AB}+\overrightarrow{BC}+\overrightarrow{CD}+ \ldots +\overrightarrow{HK} = \overrightarrow{AK}$ (the polygon of vectors).

5. $\overrightarrow{AB}-\overrightarrow{CD} = \overrightarrow{AB}+(-\overrightarrow{CD})$.

We have also discussed the *parallelogram law* of vectors. This law, stating that $\mathbf{a}+\mathbf{b} = \mathbf{c}$, is illustrated in Fig. 18.1 in which vectors are denoted by single symbols in heavy bold-face type.

In this notation, the positive number which represents the length of a vector $\mathbf{a}$ is called the *modulus* of $\mathbf{a}$ and is written either as $|\mathbf{a}|$ or as a.

A unit vector is defined as a vector with modulus 1. The unit vector whose direction is that of $\mathbf{a}$ is written $\hat{\mathbf{a}}$.

The zero vector $\mathbf{0}$ *(null vector)* is a vector whose modulus is 0.

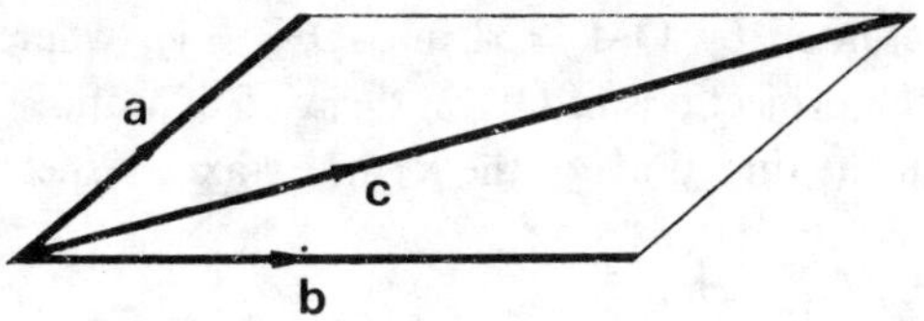

FIG. 18.1

Multiplication and Division of a Vector by a Real Number. Definitions

1. The result of multiplying the vector $\mathbf{a}$ by the positive number k is the vector $k\mathbf{a}$ which has the direction of the vector $\mathbf{a}$ and modulus ka. An immediate consequence of this definition is the relation $\mathbf{a} = a\hat{\mathbf{a}}$.

2. The result of multiplying the vector $\mathbf{a}$ by the negative number $-k$ is the vector $-k\mathbf{a}$ which has the direction opposite to that of the vector $\mathbf{a}$ and modulus ka.

3. $\mathbf{a} \div n = \mathbf{a}/n$ is a vector which has the direction of $\mathbf{a}$ and modulus a/n.

From these definitions:

$$m(n\mathbf{a}) = mn(\mathbf{a}) = n(m\mathbf{a}),$$
$$(m+n)\,\mathbf{a} = m\mathbf{a}+n\mathbf{a},$$
$$m(\mathbf{a}+\mathbf{b}) = m\mathbf{a}+m\mathbf{b}.$$

Components of a Vector

In Fig. 18.2, the position of a vector $\mathbf{r}$ represented by $\overrightarrow{\text{OP}}$ is defined by reference to rectangular axes in its plane with O as origin. The components of the vector in the directions of the axes are uniquely determined

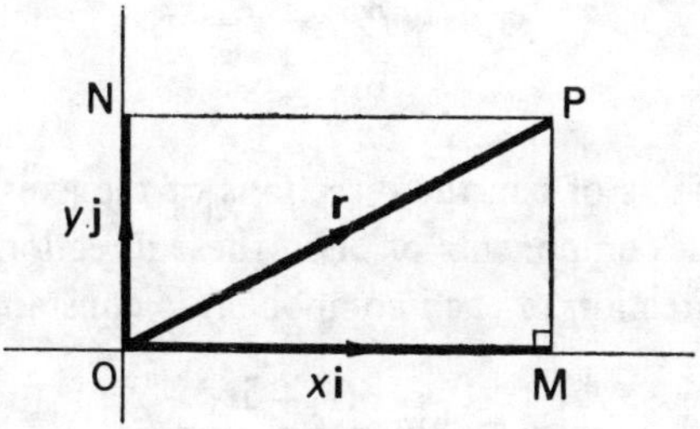

FIG. 18.2

and are represented by $\overrightarrow{OM} = x\mathbf{i}$ and $\overrightarrow{ON} = y\mathbf{j}$, where $x = OM$ and $y = ON$ are the projections of OP on the axes of x and y, and $\mathbf{i}$ and $\mathbf{j}$ are unit vectors in the directions of the x- and y-axes respectively.

Differentiation of a Vector

Consider a vector $\mathbf{r}$ which can be expressed in the form $\mathbf{f}(t)$ where $\mathbf{f}(t)$ is a function of a scalar parameter t in terms of vector quantities. [For example: $\mathbf{r} = \mathbf{f}(t) = \mathbf{a}t^2+\mathbf{b}$.] In Fig. 18.3, $\mathbf{r} = \overrightarrow{OP}$ referred to rectangular axes through O, and $\mathbf{r}$ is called the *position vector* of P relative to O.

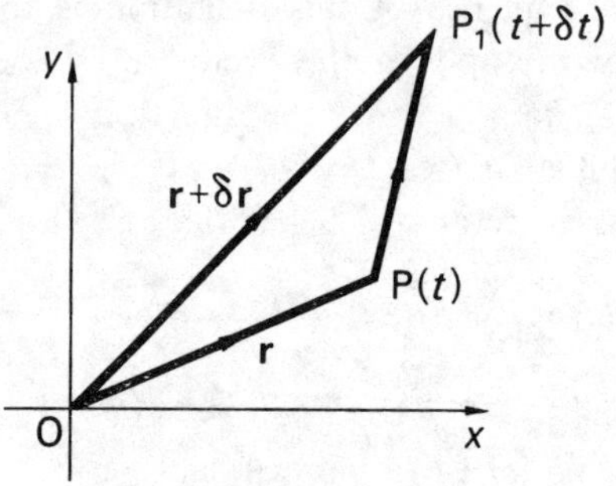

FIG. 18.3

As t varies, P moves on a curve relative to O. Let P_1 be the position of P corresponding to the parameter $t+\delta t$. Then $\overrightarrow{OP_1} = \mathbf{r}+\delta\mathbf{r}$, where $\delta\mathbf{r}$ is the change in $\mathbf{r}$ resulting from the increment δt in t. Then we have $\overrightarrow{OP}+\overrightarrow{PP_1} = \overrightarrow{OP_1}$.

$$\therefore\ \mathbf{r}+\overrightarrow{PP_1} = \mathbf{r}+\delta\mathbf{r}.$$

$$\therefore\ \overrightarrow{PP_1} = \delta\mathbf{r}.$$

If the components of $\mathbf{r}$ in the directions of the axes are $\mathbf{r}_1$ and $\mathbf{r}_2$ respectively, and the components of $\delta\mathbf{r}$ in these directions are $\delta\mathbf{r}_1$ and $\delta\mathbf{r}_2$, then since the direction of each component is constant as t varies,

$$\frac{d\mathbf{r}_1}{dt} = \lim_{\delta t\to 0} \frac{(\mathbf{r}_1+\delta\mathbf{r}_1)-\mathbf{r}_1}{\delta t},$$

and
$$\frac{d\mathbf{r}_2}{dt} = \lim_{\delta t \to 0} \frac{(\mathbf{r}_2 + \delta\mathbf{r}_2) - \mathbf{r}_2}{\delta t}.$$

We now *define* $d\mathbf{r}/dt$ as the vector which has $d\mathbf{r}_1/dt$ and $d\mathbf{r}_2/dt$ as its respective components parallel to the axes. This definition implies that

$$\frac{d\mathbf{r}}{dt} = \lim_{\delta t \to 0} \frac{\mathbf{f}(t+\delta t) - \mathbf{f}(t)}{\delta t}. \tag{18.1}$$

It must be emphasized that in general $d\mathbf{r}/dt$ *has a direction different from that of* $\mathbf{r}$.

If we now assume that certain limit theorems which are true of scalar quantities are true also of vectors, we can easily obtain the following results.

1. $$\frac{d}{dt}(\mathbf{a}+\mathbf{b}) = \frac{d\mathbf{a}}{dt} + \frac{d\mathbf{b}}{dt}. \tag{18.2}$$

2. If λ, $\mathbf{a}$ both depend on t and $\mathbf{b} = \lambda\mathbf{a}$, then

$$\frac{d\mathbf{b}}{dt} = \frac{d\lambda}{dt}\mathbf{a} + \lambda\frac{d\mathbf{a}}{dt}. \tag{18.3}$$

The vector $\overrightarrow{OP} = \mathbf{r}$ in Fig. 18.3 has components in the directions of the axes $x\mathbf{i}$ and $y\mathbf{j}$, respectively, so that

$$\mathbf{r} = x\mathbf{i} + y\mathbf{j}$$

and therefore from (18.2) and (18.3), since $\mathbf{i}$ and $\mathbf{j}$ are constant,

$$\frac{d\mathbf{r}}{dt} = \mathbf{i}\frac{dx}{dt} + \mathbf{j}\frac{dy}{dt}. \tag{18.4}$$

Equation (18.4) is equivalent to the statement that,

the components in two given fixed directions of the derivative of a vector are the derivatives of its components.

Note that it is not a necessary condition of the foregoing that the two directions should be at right angles.

The Derivative of a Unit Vector

In Fig. 18.4, X is a fixed point and P is a moving point on a circle of unit radius: $\angle$ XOP $= \theta$ at time t. Then $\overrightarrow{OP}\,(=\hat{\mathbf{r}})$ represents a unit vector.

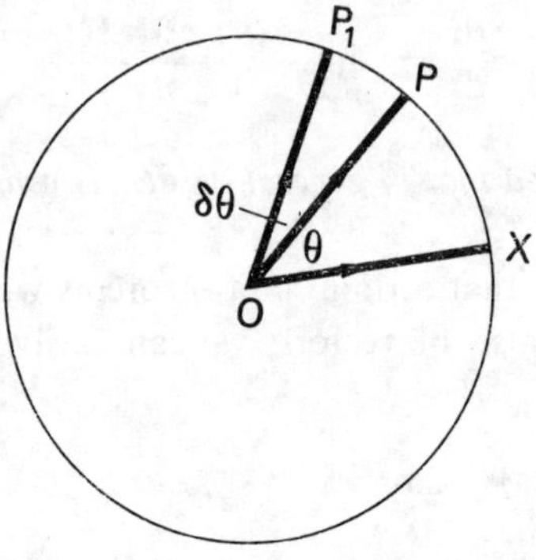

FIG. 18.4

If now, θ is increased in time δt by an increment $\delta\theta$ so that the new direction of $\overrightarrow{OP}$ becomes $\overrightarrow{OP_1}$, then from (18.1),

$$\left|\frac{d\hat{\mathbf{r}}}{dt}\right| = \lim_{\delta t \to 0}\left|\frac{PP_1}{\delta t}\right| = \lim_{\delta t \to 0}\left|\frac{PP_1}{\delta\theta}\frac{\delta\theta}{\delta t}\right|$$

$$= \lim_{\delta t \to 0}\left|\frac{2\sin(\frac{1}{2}\delta\theta)}{\delta\theta}\frac{\delta\theta}{\delta t}\right| = \left|\frac{d\theta}{dt}\right|,$$

and the direction of $d\hat{\mathbf{r}}/dt$ is the limiting direction of $\overrightarrow{PP_1}$ as δt and therefore $\delta\theta \to 0$, i.e. the direction of $d\hat{\mathbf{r}}/dt$ is the direction of the tangent to the circle.

The derivative of $\hat{\mathbf{r}}$ is therefore given by

$$\frac{d\hat{\mathbf{r}}}{dt} = \frac{d\theta}{dt}\hat{\mathbf{s}}, \tag{18.5}$$

where $\hat{\mathbf{s}}$ is the unit vector which makes an angle $\theta+\frac{1}{2}\pi$ with Ox.

Application to Kinematics

When the position of a point $P(x, y)$ in a plane is defined in relation to rectangular axes Ox and Oy in the plane, and if $\overrightarrow{OP} = \mathbf{r}$, then the *velocity* of P is defined to be the vector

$$\mathbf{v} = \frac{d\mathbf{r}}{dt}. \tag{18.6}$$

We denote the components of $\mathbf{v}$ by (v_1, v_2) so that

$$v_1 = \frac{dx}{dt}, \quad v_2 = \frac{dy}{dt}. \tag{18.7}$$

Similarly the *acceleration* of a point is *defined* to be the vector

$$\mathbf{f} = \frac{d\mathbf{v}}{dt} = \frac{d^2\mathbf{r}}{dt^2} \tag{18.8}$$

and therefore, if f_1, f_2 are the cartesian components of the acceleration,

$$f_1 = \frac{d^2x}{dt^2}, \quad f_2 = \frac{d^2y}{dt^2}.$$

*18.2. Motion of a Particle in Two Dimensions—Special Representations

Here we consider the components of the velocity and acceleration of a point in terms of different representations of its position.

(a) *Cartesian coordinates.* The position vector $\mathbf{r}$ of a point P can be represented in the form $x\mathbf{i}+y\mathbf{j}$ and therefore the velocity of P can be represented in the form

$$\mathbf{v} = \frac{d\mathbf{r}}{dt} = \frac{dx}{dt}\mathbf{i}+\frac{dy}{dt}\mathbf{j} \tag{18.9}$$

since $\mathbf{i}$ and $\mathbf{j}$ are constant. Also, the acceleration of P can be represented in the form

$$\mathbf{f} = \frac{d\mathbf{v}}{dt} = \frac{d^2x}{dt^2}\mathbf{i}+\frac{d^2y}{dt^2}\mathbf{j}. \tag{18.10}$$

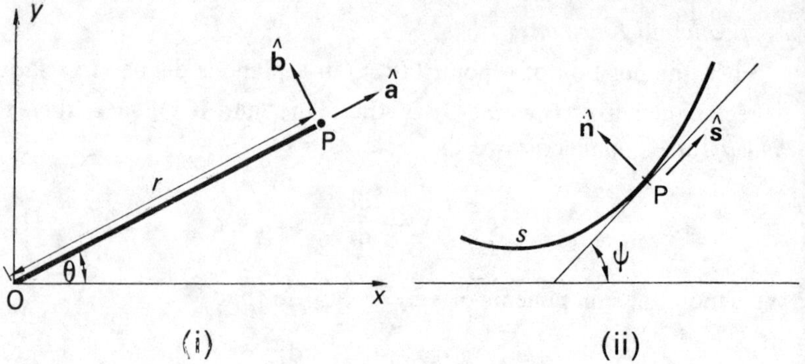

FIG. 18.5

(b) *Polar coordinates.* In Fig. 18.5 (i) the coordinates of P referred to initial line O*l* (i.e. O*x*) and pole O are (r, θ). The vector $\overrightarrow{OP}$ can be represented as $\mathbf{r} = r\hat{\mathbf{a}}$, where $\hat{\mathbf{a}}$ is the unit vector in the direction $\overrightarrow{OP}$ and therefore $\hat{\mathbf{a}} = \mathbf{i}\cos\theta + \mathbf{j}\sin\theta$. Then, by differentiation, using (18.3)

$$\mathbf{v} = \frac{dr}{dt}\hat{\mathbf{a}} + r\frac{d\hat{\mathbf{a}}}{dt}$$

and therefore from (18.5)

$$\mathbf{v} = \dot{r}\hat{\mathbf{a}} + r\dot{\theta}\hat{\mathbf{b}}, \tag{18.11}$$

where $\hat{\mathbf{b}}$ is the unit vector in the direction at right angles to $\overrightarrow{OP}$, i.e. in the *transverse* direction.

By differentiating equation (18.11) again we obtain the acceleration

$$\mathbf{f} = \frac{d\mathbf{v}}{dt} = \ddot{r}\hat{\mathbf{a}} + \dot{r}\frac{d\hat{\mathbf{a}}}{dt} + (\dot{r}\dot{\theta} + r\ddot{\theta})\,\hat{\mathbf{b}} + r\dot{\theta}\frac{d\hat{\mathbf{b}}}{dt}\,.$$

But, from (18.5) $d\hat{\mathbf{b}}/dt = -\dot{\theta}\hat{\mathbf{a}}$, and hence

$$\mathbf{f} = (\ddot{r} - r\dot{\theta}^2)\,\hat{\mathbf{a}} + (2\dot{r}\dot{\theta} + r\ddot{\theta})\,\hat{\mathbf{b}}. \tag{18.12}$$

The radial component of this acceleration is

$$\ddot{r} - r\dot{\theta}^2. \tag{18.13}$$

and the transverse component is

$$2\dot{r}\dot{\theta}+r\ddot{\theta} = \frac{1}{r}\frac{\mathrm{d}}{\mathrm{d}t}(r^2\dot{\theta}). \tag{18.14}$$

Note that when the particle is moving in a circle the radial component of the acceleration is $-r\dot{\theta}^2$ and the transverse (in this case tangential) component of acceleration is $r\ddot{\theta}$, these results being those which we used in Chapter XIII of Volume I of this book.

(c) *Intrinsic coordinates.* This representation is used when a particle moves in a plane along a curve, Fig. 18.5 (ii). One of the intrinsic coordinates is the arc length s along the curve from some fixed point to P, and the other is the angle ψ between the tangent and a fixed direction. The direction of the tangent at P is denoted by the unit vector $\hat{\mathbf{s}}$ and the direction of the normal towards the centre of curvature (see *Pure Maths.*, Vol. II, § 14.2 and § 14.6) by $\hat{\mathbf{n}}$. [In Fig. 18.5 (ii) the curvature $\varkappa$ is such that ψ increases as s increases, i.e.

$$\frac{\mathrm{d}\psi}{\mathrm{d}s} = \varkappa = \frac{1}{\varrho} > 0.]$$

The velocity vector is given by

$$\mathbf{v} = v\hat{\mathbf{s}} = \frac{\mathrm{d}s}{\mathrm{d}t}\hat{\mathbf{s}}. \tag{18.15}$$

Differentiation with respect to t gives the acceleration

$$\mathbf{f} = \frac{\mathrm{d}\mathbf{v}}{\mathrm{d}t} = \frac{\mathrm{d}v}{\mathrm{d}t}\hat{\mathbf{s}}+v\frac{\mathrm{d}\hat{\mathbf{s}}}{\mathrm{d}t}.$$

But from (18.5)

$$\frac{\mathrm{d}\hat{\mathbf{s}}}{\mathrm{d}t} = \frac{\mathrm{d}\psi}{\mathrm{d}t}\hat{\mathbf{n}} = \frac{\mathrm{d}s}{\mathrm{d}t}\cdot\frac{\mathrm{d}\psi}{\mathrm{d}s}\hat{\mathbf{n}}$$

$$= \frac{v}{\varrho}\hat{\mathbf{n}}.$$

$$\therefore\ \mathbf{f} = \frac{\mathrm{d}v}{\mathrm{d}t}\hat{\mathbf{s}}+\frac{v^2}{\varrho}\hat{\mathbf{n}}. \tag{18.16}$$

The *normal* component of this acceleration is v^2/ϱ towards the centre of curvature and the *tangential* component is

$$\frac{dv}{dt}\left(=\frac{d^2s}{dt^2}=v\frac{dv}{ds}\right).$$

If the curvature is in the opposite direction so that $d\psi/ds < 0$, provided that $\hat{\mathbf{n}}$ is directed towards the centre of curvature, the same formula holds.

Example 1. A particle moves in a plane so that its accelerations parallel to cartesian axes of coordinates in its plane are λa parallel to Ox and $-\mu y$ parallel to Oy where λ, μ, a are positive constants. The particle starts from rest at the point (0, a). Find the equation of the path of the particle.

$$\ddot{x} = \lambda a.$$

$$\therefore\ \dot{x} = \lambda at+C, \quad \text{where } C \text{ is constant.}$$

$$\dot{x} = 0 \quad \text{when} \quad t = 0; \quad \therefore\ C = 0.$$

$$\therefore\ \dot{x} = \lambda at.$$

$$\therefore\ x = \tfrac{1}{2}\lambda at^2+K, \quad \text{where } K \text{ is constant.}$$

$$x = 0 \quad \text{when} \quad t = 0; \quad \therefore\ K = 0.$$

$$\therefore\ x = \tfrac{1}{2}\lambda at^2. \tag{1}$$

Also $$\ddot{y} = -\mu y$$

and the general solution of this differential equation (see *Pure Maths.*, Chapter XVII, § 17.8) is

$$y = A\cos(t\sqrt{\mu})+B\sin(t\sqrt{\mu}),$$

where A and B are constants.

$$y = a \quad \text{when} \quad t = 0; \quad \therefore\ A = a.$$

Also, $$\dot{y} = -A\sqrt{\mu}\sin(t\sqrt{\mu})+B\sqrt{\mu}\cos(t\sqrt{\mu})$$

and $$\dot{y} = 0 \quad \text{when} \quad t = 0; \quad \therefore\ B = 0.$$

The particular solution of the differential equation is therefore

$$y = a\cos(t\sqrt{\mu}). \tag{2}$$

Eliminating t between (1) and (2) we find

$$y = a\cos\sqrt{\{2\mu x/(a\lambda)\}}$$

is the equation of the path of the particle.

Example 2. A particle describes the curve $r = a \sin 2\theta$ in such a manner that the radius vector from the origin rotates with uniform angular velocity ω. Find, in terms of ω, expressions for the radial and transverse components of acceleration of the particle and find the component of acceleration perpendicular to the initial line when $\theta = \frac{1}{4}\pi$.

Because the radius vector rotates with uniform angular velocity ω, $\dot{\theta} = \omega =$ constant and therefore, since $r = a \sin 2\theta$,

$$\dot{r} = 2a\dot{\theta}\cos 2\theta = 2a\omega\cos 2\theta \quad \text{and} \quad \ddot{r} = -4a\omega^2 \sin 2\theta.$$

Therefore, from (18.13) the radial component of acceleration is $-4a\omega^2 \sin 2\theta - r\omega^2$, and from (18.14) and since $\ddot{\theta} = 0$ the transverse component of acceleration is $4a\omega^2 \cos 2\theta$. The component of acceleration perpendicular to the initial line is therefore

$$(-4a\omega^2 \sin 2\theta - r\omega^2)\sin\theta + 4a\omega^2 \cos 2\theta \cos\theta.$$

When $\theta = \frac{1}{4}\pi$, $r = a$. Hence when $\theta = \frac{1}{4}\pi$ this component of acceleration is $-5a\omega^2/\sqrt{2}$. The negative sign implies that this acceleration component is in fact towards the initial line.

Example 3. A particle describes the curve (catenary) whose intrinsic equation is $s = c \tan\psi$ with uniform speed u. Find expressions for the normal and tangential components of the acceleration of the particle at the point $(c, \frac{1}{4}\pi)$ of the curve.

The tangential component of acceleration is zero since the particle is describing the curve with uniform speed [equation (18.16)]. For this curve $\varrho = |\mathrm{d}s/\mathrm{d}\psi| = c\sec^2\psi$, and therefore ϱ at the point $(c, \frac{1}{4}\pi)$ is $2c$. Hence the normal component of acceleration at $(c, \frac{1}{4}\pi)$ is $u^2/\varrho = u^2/(2c)$.

---

*EXERCISES 18.2

In each of questions 1–4 the motion of a particle is defined in a conventional notation. In each case, find the equation of the path.

***1.** $\ddot{x} = 0, \ddot{y} = -g$; $x = 0, y = 0, \dot{x} = v, \dot{y} = u$ when $t = 0$.

***2.** $\ddot{x} = 2$, $\ddot{y} = 1$; $x = 0$, $y = 0$, $\mathbf{v} = \hat{\mathbf{s}}u\sqrt{2}$ when $t = 0$, where the direction of $\hat{\mathbf{s}}$ bisects the angle between the axes.

***3.** $\ddot{x} = \omega^2 a \sin\omega t$, $\ddot{y} = \omega^2 a \cos\omega t$; $x = 0$, $y = -a$, $\dot{y} = 0$, $\dot{x} = -\omega a$ when $t = 0$.

***4.** $\ddot{x} = -\omega^2 x$, $\ddot{y} = -\omega^2 y$; $x = a$, $y = 0$, $\dot{x} = 0$, $\dot{y} = \omega b$ when $t = 0$.

***5.** Given that $\overrightarrow{OP} = \mathbf{r}$ and $\mathbf{r} = t^2\mathbf{i} + 2kt\mathbf{j}$, show that the locus of P is a parabola. [Resolve $\mathbf{r}$ into its components parallel to the cartesian coordinate axes.]

***6.** Given that $\overrightarrow{OP} = \mathbf{r}$ and $\mathbf{r} = t\mathbf{i} + (1/t)\mathbf{j}$, find the equation of the locus of P.

***7.** A particle starts from the origin with velocity 2 in the direction of the x-axis and moves with unit accelerations in the directions of the x- and y-axes respectively. Find an expression for the distance travelled by the particle in the first second of its motion. [Use $(\mathrm{d}s/\mathrm{d}t)^2 = (\mathrm{d}x/\mathrm{d}t)^2+(\mathrm{d}y/\mathrm{d}t)^2$. See *Pure Maths.*, Vol. II, § 14.2.]

***8.** The motion of a particle P, whose coordinates are (x, y) referred to a pair of fixed axes through a point O, satisfies the equations

$$\frac{\mathrm{d}^2x}{\mathrm{d}t^2} = -\omega^2 x, \qquad \frac{\mathrm{d}^2y}{\mathrm{d}t^2} = -\omega^2 y;$$

the initial conditions are

$$x = a, \quad y = 0, \quad \frac{\mathrm{d}x}{\mathrm{d}t} = 0 \quad \text{and} \quad \frac{\mathrm{d}y}{\mathrm{d}t} = b\omega \quad \text{when} \quad t = 0,$$

where ω, a and b are positive constants. Prove that the path of the particle is the ellipse $(x/a)^2+(y/b)^2 = 1$.

Find, in terms of OP, the magnitude of the component perpendicular to OP of the velocity of P. Hence, or otherwise, show that the angular speed of OP is

$$\frac{\omega ab}{\mathrm{OP}^2}.$$ (N.)

***9.** A particle is describing the ellipse $l/r = 1+e\cos\theta$ with uniform angular velocity ω about the pole. Show that when the particle is at one end of the latus rectum through the pole, the component of acceleration towards the pole is $(1-2e^2)l\omega^2$. (L.)

10. A particle describes the curve $r = a\,\mathrm{e}^{\theta\sqrt{3}}\cosh 2\theta$ in such a manner that the angular velocity about the origin is constant. Show that the resultant acceleration of the particle at any instant makes an angle of 30° with the radius vector from the origin. (L.)

*18.3. Motion of a Particle on a Smooth Curve

Note on some properties of curves. (See *Pure Maths.*, Vol II, § 14.2 et seq.)

In the section which follows we use the following facts concerned with curves:

In Fig. 18.6 the tangent at P(x, y) to the curve makes an angle ψ with the positive direction of the x-axis. The point A is fixed on the curve and the arc-length AP is s. Then,

$$\tan\psi = \frac{\mathrm{d}y}{\mathrm{d}x}, \quad \sin\psi = \frac{\mathrm{d}y}{\mathrm{d}s}, \quad \cos\psi = \frac{\mathrm{d}x}{\mathrm{d}s}.$$

The radius of curvature $\varrho = \left|\dfrac{\mathrm{d}s}{\mathrm{d}\psi}\right| = \left|\dfrac{\left\{1+\left(\dfrac{\mathrm{d}y}{\mathrm{d}x}\right)^2\right\}^{3/2}}{\dfrac{\mathrm{d}^2y}{\mathrm{d}x^2}}\right|.$

Figure 18.6 also shows the forces acting on a particle P of mass m which is free to move under gravity on the inside of a smooth curve which is fixed in a vertical plane. These forces are the weight of the particle and the normal reaction R of the curve on the particle. The particle is at the point $P(x, y)$ at time t from the beginning of the motion.

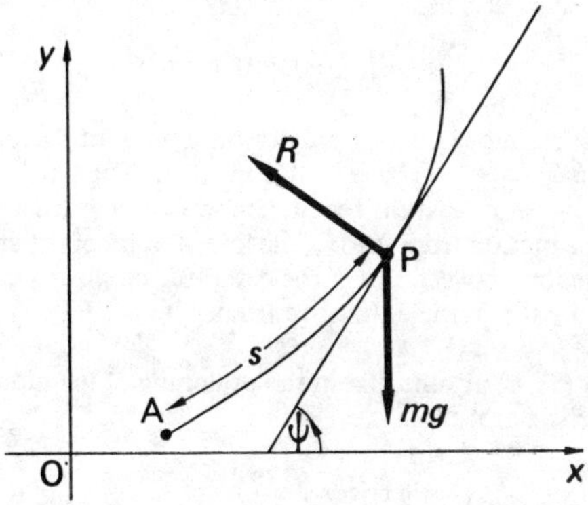

FIG. 18.6

The equations which determine the motion of the particle are

$$R - mg\cos\psi = \frac{mv^2}{\varrho} \tag{18.17}$$

and the energy equation

$$\tfrac{1}{2}mv^2 + mgy = k, \tag{18.18}$$

where v is the speed of the particle at P and k is a constant depending upon the boundary conditions of the motion.

The energy equation could be replaced by the equation of motion for the particle in the *tangential* direction

$$-mg\sin\psi = m\ddot{s}, \tag{18.19}$$

where the length of the arc AP is s. This equation (18.19) can be obtained directly from the energy equation by differentiation with respect to s, thus:

$$\tfrac{1}{2}mv^2+mgy = k.$$

$$\therefore\ mv\frac{dv}{ds}+mg\frac{dy}{ds} = 0.$$

But
$$v\frac{dv}{ds} = \ddot{s} \quad\text{and}\quad \frac{dy}{ds} = \sin\psi.$$

$$\therefore\ \ddot{s}+g\sin\psi = 0.$$

Example 1. A particle moves under gravity on a smooth cycloid whose intrinsic equation is $s = 4a\sin\psi$; $s = 0$ when $\psi = 0$, Fig. 18.7. The particle starts from rest at the point A, $\psi = \frac{1}{4}\pi$. Show that the reaction between the particle and the curve is positive throughout the motion from A to O, the lowest point of the curve, and calculate

(a) the normal reaction between the particle and the curve at O,

(b) the time taken by the particle to move from A to O.

If the particle is at P(s, ψ) at time t from the beginning of the motion, the equations of motion for the particle are:

(1) $$R-mg\cos\psi = \frac{mv^2}{\varrho},$$

(2) $$v^2 = 2g(y_A-y_P),$$

where v is the speed of the particle at P and y_A, y_P are respectively the heights of A and P above the horizontal through O.

Also
$$dy/ds = \sin\psi.$$

$$\therefore\ y = \int \sin\psi\, ds = \int \sin\psi\frac{ds}{d\psi}\, d\psi = \int \sin\psi\,.\,4a\cos\psi\, d\psi$$
$$= -a\cos 2\psi+K,$$

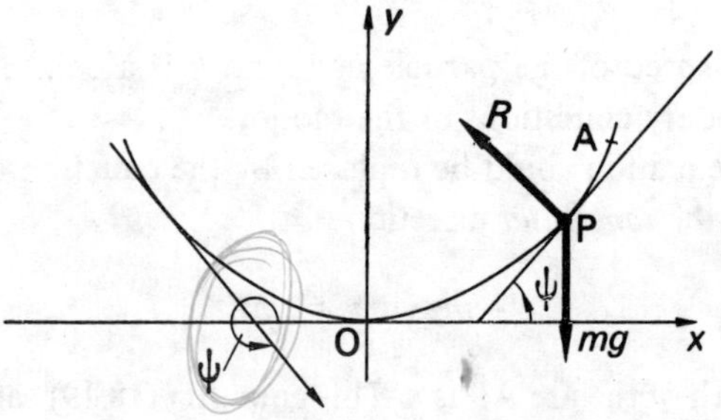

FIG. 18.7

where K is constant. At A, $\psi = \frac{1}{4}\pi,$

$$\therefore\ y_A - y_P = a\cos 2\psi.$$

$$\therefore\ v^2 = 2ga\cos 2\psi.$$

But $$\varrho = \frac{ds}{d\psi} = 4a\cos\psi.$$

$$\therefore\ R = mg\cos\psi + \frac{2mga\cos 2\psi}{4a\cos\psi} = \frac{mg(4\cos^2\psi - 1)}{2\cos\psi}.$$

But, for $0 \leqq \psi \leqq \frac{1}{4}\pi$, $4\cos^2\psi > 1$ and therefore R is positive for all values of ψ in this range.

[The symmetry of the motion about O shows that when the particle is on the negative side of O, R remains positive. This result is apparent from the value of R obtained above since the definitions involved here give $-\frac{1}{4}\pi \leqq \psi \leqq 0$ for values of ψ on the x negative side of the origin.]

At O, $\psi = 0$ and so the normal reaction there is $3mg/2$.

Also, for the tangential component of the motion of the particle at P,

$$m\ddot{s} = -mg\sin\psi.$$

$$\therefore\ \ddot{s} = -\frac{gs}{4a}.$$

The general solution of this equation is

$$s = A\cos\left\{t\sqrt{\left(\frac{g}{4a}\right)}\right\} + B\sin\left\{t\sqrt{\left(\frac{g}{4a}\right)}\right\}$$

and the boundary conditions $s = 2a\sqrt{2}$, $\dot{s} = 0$ when $t = 0$ give $A = 2a\sqrt{2}$, $B = 0$.

$$\therefore\ s = 2a\sqrt{2}\cos\left\{t\sqrt{\left(\frac{g}{4a}\right)}\right\}.$$

Therefore, when $s = 0$,

$$0 = \cos\left\{t\sqrt{\left(\frac{g}{4a}\right)}\right\}, \quad \text{i.e.} \quad t = \pi\sqrt{\left(\frac{a}{g}\right)}.$$

The particle moves from A to O in time $\pi\sqrt{(a/g)}$.

[*Note*. It is an important characteristic of the cycloid that the motion discussed here is a simple harmonic motion whatever its amplitude, see § 14.1.]

Example 2. Show that the radius of curvature of the parabola $x^2 = 4ay$ at the point $(2ap, ap^2)$ is $2a(1+p^2)^{3/2}$.

A small heavy bead can slide freely along a fixed smooth wire in the form of this parabola, the axis of y being directed vertically upwards. The bead is projected from the origin with speed U. Show that when the direction of motion has turned through an angle ψ the speed of the bead is

$$\sqrt{(U^2 - 2ga\tan^2\psi)}$$

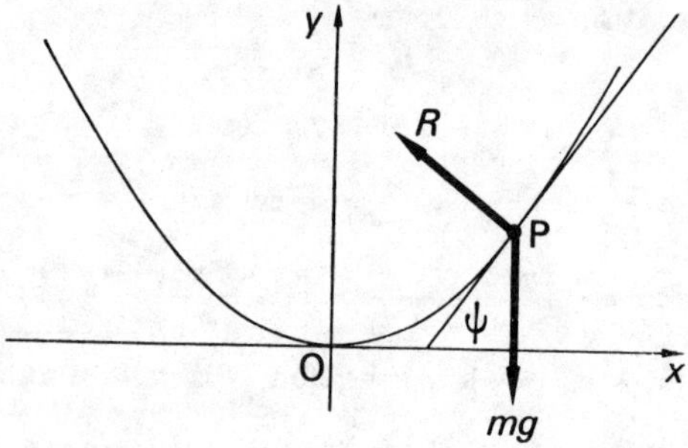

FIG. 18.8

and that the force exerted by the bead on the wire is proportional to $\cos^3 \psi$. (N.)

$$x^2 = 4ay.$$

$$\therefore \quad \frac{dy}{dx} = \frac{x}{2a}; \qquad \frac{d^2y}{dx^2} = \frac{1}{2a}.$$

Therefore at $(2ap, ap^2)$,

$$\varrho = \left| \frac{\left\{1+\left(\frac{dy}{dx}\right)^2\right\}^{3/2}}{\frac{d^2y}{dx^2}} \right| = \frac{(1+p^2)^{3/2}}{\frac{1}{2a}} = 2a(1+p^2)^{3/2}.$$

Figure 18.8 shows the forces acting on the bead when it is at P, where the gradient of the parabola is $\tan \psi$ and the direction of motion has turned through an angle ψ.

The equations of motion for the particle are,

(1) $$R - mg \cos \psi = \frac{mv^2}{\varrho},$$

(2) $$v^2 = U^2 - 2gap^2.$$

But $$\tan \psi = \frac{dy}{dx} = p, \quad \therefore \cos \psi = \frac{1}{\sqrt{(1+\tan^2 \psi)}} = \frac{1}{\sqrt{(1+p^2)}},$$

$$\therefore \varrho = 2a \sec^3 \psi.$$

Then, from equation (1),

$$R = \frac{m(U^2 - 2ga \tan^2 \psi) \cos^3 \psi}{2a} + mg \cos \psi$$

$$= m\left(\frac{U^2}{2a} \cos^3 \psi - g \sin^2 \psi \cos \psi + g \cos \psi\right) = m\left(\frac{U^2}{2a} + g\right) \cos^3 \psi.$$

The force exerted by the bead on the wire is therefore proportional to $\cos^3 \psi$.

*EXERCISES 18.3

*1. A small bead of mass m slides on a smooth wire bent in the form of a parabola with its axis vertical and its vertex at the lowest point. The bead is released from rest at one end of the latus rectum. Find the reaction of the wire on the bead when the bead is at the vertex of the parabola.

*2. A small bead moves on a smooth wire in the shape of one branch of the rectangular hyperbola $y^2-x^2 = a^2$. The wire is held with its real axis vertical and its vertex downwards and the bead is released from rest at a point where $y = 3a/2$. Prove that when the bead passes through the vertex, the magnitude of the reaction between the bead and the wire is twice the weight of the bead.

*3. A small bead moves on a smooth wire in the shape of the curve $y = \cos x$ from $x = 0$ to $x = \frac{1}{2}\pi$, the wire being held in a vertical coordinate plane in which the axis of y is vertical. Show that, if the bead is displaced slightly from rest at $x = 0$, the reaction of the wire on the bead is outward (i.e. away from the origin) throughout the motion from $x = 0$ to $x = \frac{1}{2}\pi$. Calculate the speed of the bead when it reaches the point $(\frac{1}{2}\pi, 0)$ and the reaction of the wire on the bead there.

*4. A smooth wire in the shape of the curve $y = \ln \sec x$ from $x = 0$ to $x = \frac{1}{3}\pi$ is held in a vertical coordinate plane in which the axis of y is vertical. A small bead can move on the wire. The bead starts from rest at the point $x = \frac{1}{3}\pi$ and slides down the wire.

(i) Calculate the reaction of the wire on the bead at the point $x = \alpha$, $(\frac{1}{3}\pi > \alpha > 0)$.

(ii) Show that if the bead reaches the origin with speed v, and if the reaction of the wire on the bead there is R, then

$$R = mv^2+mg.$$

*5. A smooth plane curve, in the shape of the cycloid $s = 4a \sin \psi$, is fixed in a vertical plane with its vertex as lowest point. Prove that the time taken for the particle to slide from rest at any point on the curve to the vertex is independent of its initial displacement from the vertex.

Prove also that if the curve is fixed with its vertex at its highest point, a particle slightly disturbed from rest at the vertex will leave the curve when its vertical displacement from the vertex is a. (L.)

*6. Show that the radius of curvature at the point t of the parabola $x = 2at$, $y = at^2$ is

$$2a(1+t^2)^{3/2}.$$

A smooth rigid wire bent into the form of this parabola is fixed with the y-axis vertical and the vertex at the lowest point. A bead of mass m threaded on the wire is released from rest at the point $t = t_0$. Show that when the bead reaches the point $t = t_1$ in the subsequent motion its speed is $\{2ga(t_0^2-t_1^2)\}^{1/2}$, and prove that the force exerted by the wire on the bead is

$$mg\,\frac{1+t_0^2}{(1+t_1^2)^{3/2}}.$$ (N.)

***7.** A particle of mass m slides on a smooth cycloid $s = 4a \sin \psi$ which is held fixed with axis vertical and vertex downwards. If the particle is released from rest at a point whose distance from the vertex, measured along the arc, is c, prove that it passes through the vertex with speed $c\sqrt{(g/4a)}$ and that the thrust on the curve is then $mg(1+c^2/16a^2)$. (L.)

***8.** A smooth curve having the form of the catenary $y = c \cosh (x/c)$ is fixed with the positive direction of the y-axis pointing vertically downwards. A particle of mass m, initially resting on the curve at its highest point, is projected along the curve with speed $\sqrt{(gc/2)}$. Show that the speed v of the particle when it is moving on the curve in a direction inclined at an angle ψ to the horizontal is given by $2v^2 = gc(4 \sec \psi - 3)$. Find an expression for the reaction between the particle and the curve in terms of ψ, and show that the particle leaves the curve when $\cos \psi = 2/3$. (N.)

***9.** For the parabola $4ay = x^2+4a^2$, prove that the radius of curvature, ϱ, at any point is given by

$$a\varrho^2 = 4y^3.$$

A small bead slides on a smooth parabolic wire fixed in a vertical plane with its axis vertical and vertex downwards. If y is the height of the bead above the directrix of the parabola, prove that the normal reaction on the wire is proportional to $y^{-3/2}$. (N.)

***10.** A small bead P of mass m is threaded on a smooth circular wire, of radius a and centre O, fixed in a vertical plane. The bead is initially at the lowest point A of the circle and is projected along the wire with a velocity which is just sufficient to carry it to the highest point. Denoting the angle POA by θ find the reaction between the wire and the bead in terms of θ.

Deduce from the energy equation by means of integration that the time taken for the bead to reach the position $\theta = \frac{1}{2}\pi$ is $\sqrt{(a/g)} \ln (1+\sqrt{2})$. (N.)

18.4. The Angular Momentum of a Particle about an Axis

We have discussed angular momentum with particular reference to the rotation of a rigid body about a fixed axis (in § 15.8). We now discuss the fundamental theorem of *conservation of angular momentum* for a particle in a *central field of force*. In such a field the resultant force acting on a particle is directed towards a fixed point in the field and that force is usually a function of the position of the particle.

The Conservation of Angular Momentum

(a) *Cartesian coordinates.* Figure 18.9 shows a particle of mass m at P(x, y) in a central field of force, with the origin O as the centre of force and $\angle$ PO$x = \theta$.

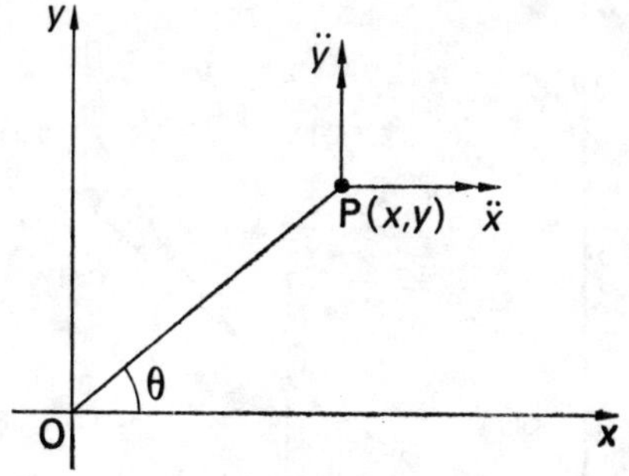

FIG. 18.9

The component accelerations of P are $\ddot{x}$ and $\ddot{y}$ in the directions of the axes, and the resultant acceleration of P in the direction at right angles to OP is zero.

$$\therefore\ \ddot{y}\cos\theta - \ddot{x}\sin\theta = 0,$$

i.e.
$$\frac{\ddot{y}x}{\sqrt{(x^2+y^2)}} - \frac{\ddot{x}y}{\sqrt{(x^2+y^2)}} = 0,$$

i.e.
$$x\ddot{y} - y\ddot{x} = 0.$$

But
$$x\ddot{y} - y\ddot{x} = \frac{\mathrm{d}}{\mathrm{d}t}(x\dot{y} - y\dot{x}).$$

$$\therefore\ x\dot{y} - y\dot{x} = k,$$

where k is constant. The quantity $m(x\dot{y} - y\dot{x})$, where m is the mass of the particle, is defined as the *angular momentum* or *moment of momentum* of the particle about the origin.

Thus in a central field of force the moment of momentum about the origin is constant.

If the perpendicular from O to the tangent to the path of the particle at P, Fig. 18.10, is equal to p and if this tangent makes an angle ψ with the x-axis,

$$\dot{x} = v\cos\psi, \quad \dot{y} = v\sin\psi,$$

where v is the resultant velocity of the particle in its path.

$$\therefore\ m(x\dot{y} - y\dot{x}) = mv(x\sin\psi - y\cos\psi).$$

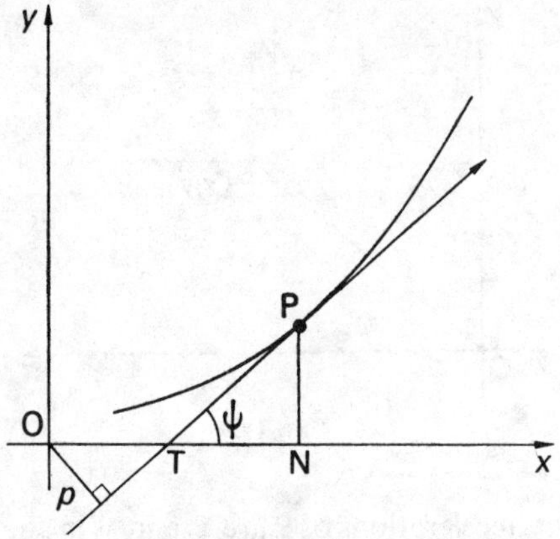

FIG. 18.10

Also $\quad p = \text{OT} \sin \psi = (x - y \cot \psi) \sin \psi = x \sin \psi - y \cos \psi.$

$$\therefore \; m(x\dot{y} - y\dot{x}) = mvp.$$

Thus the angular momentum of a particle (which is constant in a central field of force) is the product of the magnitude of the linear momentum of the particle and the perpendicular distance of the centre of force from the instantaneous path of the particle. This quantity is *the moment about the origin of the momentum* ($m\dot{x}$, $m\dot{y}$) *of the particle localized at* P(x, y).

*(b) *Polar coordinates.* From equation (18.14), if the polar coordinates of P referred to O as pole and a *fixed* line through O as initial line are (r, θ), the transverse acceleration of P is $(1/r)(\mathrm{d}/\mathrm{d}t)(r^2\dot{\theta})$. Therefore, *in a central field,*

$$\frac{1}{r}\frac{\mathrm{d}}{\mathrm{d}t}(r^2\dot{\theta}) = 0.$$

By integration with respect to t,

$$r^2\dot{\theta} = C,$$

where C is constant,
i.e. $mr(r\dot{\theta})$ is constant or, mvp is constant as before.

**The theorem of areas.* The area of the sector bounded by $r = f(\theta)$, $\theta = \theta_1$ and $\theta = \theta_2$, $(\theta_2 > \theta_1)$, is $\int_{\theta_1}^{\theta_2} \frac{1}{2} r^2 \, d\theta$. When a particle is moving in a central field the area swept out by the radius vector joining the centre of force to the particle, from time t_1 to time t_2, is

$$\int_{t_1}^{t_2} \frac{1}{2} r^2 \frac{d\theta}{dt} \, dt = \int_{t_1}^{t_2} \frac{1}{2} r^2 \dot{\theta} \, dt = \frac{1}{2} r^2 \dot{\theta} (t_2 - t_1),$$

since $\frac{1}{2} r^2 \dot{\theta}$ is a constant for this field.

Therefore *for a particle moving in a central field* the rate of sweeping out of area by the radius vector is constant.

This law, in relation to the motion of the planets around the sun, was discovered by Kepler and stated as his Second Law in a book published in 1609. Kepler's discovery formed a substantial part of the foundation upon which Newton developed his Laws of Universal Gravitation published in the *Principia* in 1687.

Example 1. A particle of mass m on a smooth horizontal table is connected to a fixed point of the table by an elastic spring of natural length a and modulus λ. The particle is projected horizontally with velocity $2a\omega$ in a direction perpendicular to the spring when the length of the latter is $2a$. Show that when the length of the spring is r in the subsequent motion, its angular velocity will be $4a^2\omega/r^2$. Write down the energy equation and show that, if the maximum length of the spring is $4a$, then $\lambda = 3ma\omega^2/8$. (N.)

After the particle is projected the only force acting upon it is the tension in the elastic spring and this is directed towards O (and is a function of the distance of the particle from O). Therefore the angular momentum about O is conserved. Hence, in the subsequent motion, when the length of the spring is r, if the angular velocity of the particle is then Ω,

$$mr^2\Omega = m(2a)^2\omega.$$

$$\therefore \; \Omega = \frac{4a^2\omega}{r^2}.$$

Also, since, *after the particle is projected*, the system of forces acting on the particle is a conservative system, the energy of the system is conserved,

i.e. (Elastic P.E. of spring + K.E. of particle) is constant,

i.e. $$\frac{\lambda(r-a)^2}{2a} + \frac{1}{2} m(r^2\Omega^2 + \dot{r}^2) = \frac{1}{2} m(2a\omega)^2 + \frac{\lambda a^2}{2a},$$

where $\dot{r}$ is the velocity of the particle in the direction of the spring.

When the spring reaches its maximum length $r = 4a$ and $\dot{r} = 0$,

$$\therefore \quad \frac{\lambda(4a-a)^2}{2a} + \frac{1}{2} m(4a)^2 \frac{16a^4\omega^2}{(4a)^4} = 2ma^2\omega^2 + \frac{\lambda a^2}{2a}.$$

Hence $$\lambda = 3ma\omega^2/8.$$

Example 2. A particle P, of mass m, lies on a smooth table and is attached by a string of length l passing through a small hole O in the table and carries an equal particle Q hanging vertically. The former particle is projected along the table at right angles to the string with velocity $\sqrt{(2gh)}$ when at a distance a from the hole. If r is the distance from the hole at time t, prove the following results:

(α) $$\dot{r}^2 = gh\left(1 - \frac{a^2}{r^2}\right) + g(a-r),$$

(β) the lower particle will be pulled up to the hole if

$$l \leqq \frac{h}{2} + \sqrt{\left(ah + \frac{1}{4}h^2\right)},$$

(γ) the tension in the string is

$$T = \frac{mg}{2}\left(1 + \frac{2a^2h}{r^3}\right). \qquad \text{(L.)}$$

After projection, the only force acting on the particle P is towards the hole and the angular momentum of this particle is therefore conserved (Fig. 18.11). Also, the energy of the whole system is conserved. At time t, the velocity of the hanging particle Q is $\dot{r}$ upwards, where OP $= r$.

Conservation of angular momentum for P gives

$$ma\sqrt{(2gh)} = mr^2\dot{\theta}. \qquad (1)$$

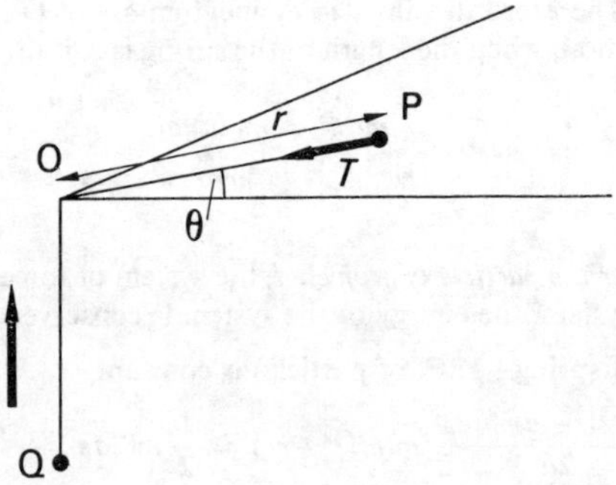

FIG. 18.11

Conservation of energy gives

$$\tfrac{1}{2}m(r^2\dot{\theta}^2+\dot{r}^2)+\tfrac{1}{2}m\dot{r}^2-mg(a-r) = mgh.$$

$$\therefore\ m\dot{r}^2+\frac{1}{2}mr^2\frac{m^2a^2 2gh}{m^2r^4}-mg(a-r) = mgh.$$

$$\therefore\ \dot{r}^2 = gh\left(1-\frac{a^2}{r^2}\right)+g(a-r).$$

$$\therefore\ \dot{r}^2 = \frac{g}{r^2}(r-a)\{h(r+a)-r^2\},$$

i.e.

$$\dot{r}^2 = -\frac{g}{r^2}(r-a)(r-\lambda_1)(r-\lambda_2), \qquad (2)$$

where λ_1, λ_2 are the roots of $r^2-hr-ah = 0$ and $\lambda_1 > 0 > \lambda_2$. Since $\dot{r}^2 \geqq 0$, it follows from (2) that $(r-a)(r-\lambda_1) \leqq 0$, i.e. that r lies in the range a to λ_1 inclusive. Note that steady motion of P in a circle of radius a is only possible when $m(2gh)/a = mg$, i.e. when $h = \frac{1}{2}a$. If this is not the case r will vary from a to λ_1 and Q will be pulled up to O if $l \leqq \lambda_1$. But $\lambda_1 = \frac{1}{2}h+\sqrt{(ah+\frac{1}{4}h^2)}$ and therefore result (β) follows.

The equation of motion for the hanging particle Q in the direction of the string is

$$mg-T = m\frac{d^2}{dt^2}(l-r) = -m\ddot{r},$$

and the equation of motion in the radial direction for the particle P on the table is

$$-T = m(\ddot{r}-r\dot{\theta}^2).$$

$$\therefore\ mg-2T = -m\ddot{r}+m\ddot{r}-mr\dot{\theta}^2.$$

$$\therefore\ 2T = m(g+r\dot{\theta}^2).$$

But, from (1),

$$\dot{\theta}^2 = 2a^2gh/r^4.$$

$$\therefore\ T = \frac{mg}{2}\left(1+\frac{2ha^2}{r^3}\right).$$

Example 3. Two particles A and B, each of mass m kg, attached to the ends of an inextensible string of length $5a$ m are initially at rest on a smooth horizontal table at points whose coordinates referred to axes in the table are (0, 0) and ($3a$, 0) respectively, the unit of length being 1 m. The particle A is projected along the y-axis with such speed that the string becomes taut after 4 s. Describe the subsequent motion, finding the angular velocity of AB and the tension of the string. Show that AB is first parallel to the y-axis at time 9·36 s approximately after the initial projection of A. (N.)

Just before the string tightens the coordinates of A are (0, $4a$), Fig. 18.12 (i), and the velocity of A is a m/s in the positive y-direction. Fig. 18.12 (i) is the impulse diagram for the motion at the instant when the string tightens. Here I is the impulsive

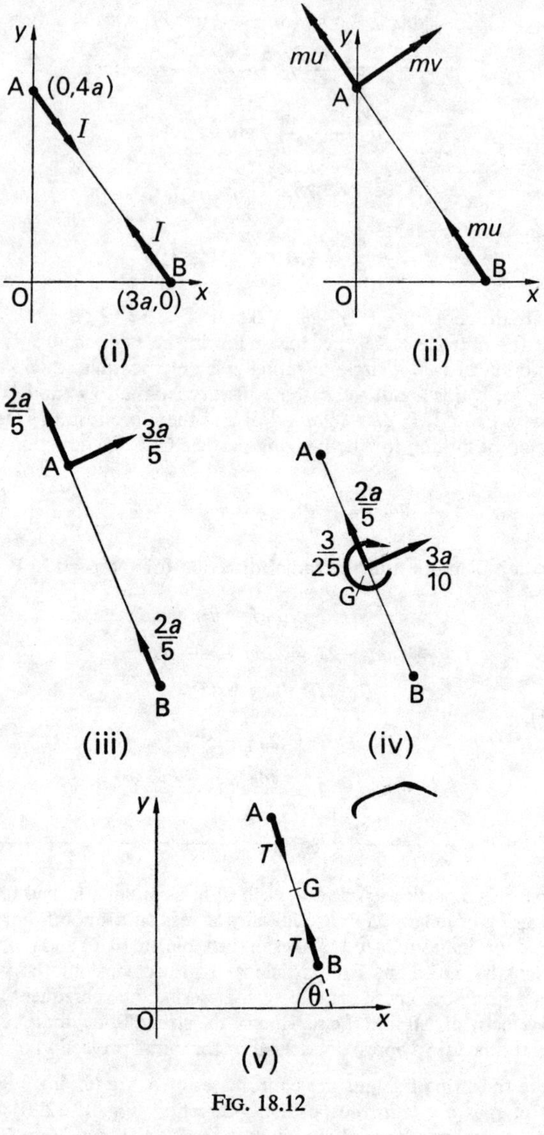
y
A
(0,4a)
I
I
B
O
(3a,0)
x
(i)
mu
y
mv
A
mu
B
O
x
(ii)
2a/5
3a/5
A
2a/5
B
(iii)
A
2a/5
3/25
3a/10
G
B
(iv)
y
A
T
G
T
B
θ
O
x
(v)

FIG. 18.12

tension in the string. Figure 18.12 (ii) is the momentum diagram for the motion immediately after the string tightens. The initial velocity u of B must be in the direction BA. The component of the initial velocity of A in the direction BA must also be u. Let the component of the initial velocity of A in the direction at right angles to BA be v.

The impulse-momentum equations for the particles at the instant when the string tightens are:

For B $$I = mu,$$

For A $$\tfrac{4}{5}ma - I = mu,$$

$$\tfrac{3}{5}ma = mv.$$

Hence, $u = \frac{2}{5}a$, $v = \frac{3}{5}a$. The velocities of the particles immediately after the string tightens are shown in Fig. 18.12 (iii).

The centre of mass *G* of the particles (at the mid-point of the line joining them) has initial velocities $u = \frac{2}{5}a$ along BA and $\frac{1}{2}v = \frac{3}{10}a$ at right angles to BA.

The angular velocity of the string is obtained by applying the following two theorems (§ 16.5, § 16.6):

1. The change in the angular momentum of a system of particles about any point equals the moment of the external impulses about that point.

2. The angular momentum of a system of particles moving in its own plane about a fixed origin in that plane is equal to the sum of the angular momentum relative to the centre of mass and the angular momentum about the origin of the whole mass concentrated at the centre of mass and moving with the velocity of translation of the centre of mass.

In this case there is no external impulse with a moment about an origin taken at the instantaneous position of G. Just before the string becomes taut the angular momentum about G of the two particles together is

$$m\,\frac{3a}{5}\times 2\,\frac{1}{2}\,a$$

(i.e. that of A above). Just after the string becomes taut, and if its angular velocity is then ω, the angular momentum about G is $2\times m2\frac{1}{2}a\omega\times 2\frac{1}{2}a = \frac{25}{2}ma^2\omega$.

$$\therefore \quad \frac{25ma^2\omega}{2} = \frac{3ma^2}{2}.$$

$$\therefore \quad \omega = \tfrac{3}{25} \text{ radians/second.}$$

This result is illustrated in Fig. 18.12 (iv).

Because after the string tightens, there are no forces acting on the particles which do not act through their centre of mass, the angular momentum of the system about the centre of mass relative to the centre of mass remains constant and therefore the angular velocity of the string remains constant and equal to ω (§ 16.6). At the moment when the string tightens, AB makes an angle $\tan^{-1}\frac{3}{4} = 36°52' = 0{\cdot}6435^c$ with the vertical. Assuming that the string remains taut (see p. 558), it follows that the time taken from this instant for the string to become vertical is $0{\cdot}6435\times\frac{25}{3} \approx 5{\cdot}36$ s. AB is therefore first parallel to the y-axis 9·36 s approximately after the initial projection of A.

Assuming that the string remains taut, that the tension in it is of magnitude T and that the string makes an angle θ with xO at time t s, Fig. 18.12 (v), the y-coordinate of G is $(2+\frac{1}{2}t)a$ and so the y-coordinate of A is $(2+\frac{1}{2}t+2\frac{1}{2}\sin\theta)\,a$. The only force acting on A is the tension of the string and so the equation of motion of A resolved parallel to Oy is

$$m\frac{d^2}{dt^2}\left\{\left(2+\frac{1}{2}t+\frac{5}{2}\sin\theta\right)a\right\} = -T\sin\theta,$$

i.e.

$$T\sin\theta = 2\tfrac{1}{2}ma\,(-\ddot{\theta}\cos\theta+\dot{\theta}^2\sin\theta).$$

But $\dot{\theta} = \omega$, $\ddot{\theta} = 0$ and therefore

$$T = 2\tfrac{1}{2}ma\omega^2 = 9ma/250.$$

[*Note* that this result could be obtained by assuming that the motion of A about G relative to G is the same as if G were fixed and the same forces acted, for A describes a circle with constant angular velocity relative to G. *This is possible only because* G *moves with constant velocity*.]

---

*EXERCISES 18.4

***1.** A particle P of mass m lies at rest in a smooth straight tube AB which is free to rotate in a horizontal plane about a fixed vertical axis through A. The particle is attached to A by an elastic string, of modulus mg, which is initially at its natural length l. If the tube is now set rotating with constant angular velocity $\omega = \sqrt{\{g/(2l)\}}$, show that after time t, AP $= l(2-\cos\omega t)$ and find the magnitude of the action of the particle on the tube then.

***2.** A particle of mass m is held on a smooth table. A string attached to this particle passes through a hole in the table and supports a mass $3m$. Motion is started by the particle on the table being projected with velocity v at right angles to the string. If a is the original length of the string on the table, show that, when the hanging mass has descended a distance $\frac{1}{2}a$ (assuming this to be possible) its velocity will be $\frac{1}{2}\{3(ga-v^2)\}^{1/2}$. (L.)

***3.** Two particles each of mass M are attached to the ends of a taut string of length $2a$ which lies at rest on a smooth horizontal table, passing through a small ring attached to the table; the ring is at the middle point of the string. An impulse I is applied to one of the particles in a direction perpendicular to the string. Prove that, when the other particle reaches the ring, the velocities of the particles are in the ratio $\sqrt{5}:\sqrt{3}$. (O.C.)

***4.** A long tube is pivoted at a point O, about which it can move freely in a horizontal plane. Its moment of inertia about O is I. A particle of mass m can move, without friction, in the tube. It is initially at a distance a from O, and both tube and particle are at rest. An angular velocity ω_0 is suddenly given to the tube. Show that when the particle is at distance r from O, its velocity along the tube is

$$\omega_0(r^2-a^2)^{1/2}\left(\frac{I+ma^2}{I+mr^2}\right)^{1/2}. \qquad \text{(L.)}$$

***5.** An elastic string of modulus mg and natural length a is attached at one end to a point O on a smooth horizontal table and at the other to a particle of mass m on the table. The particle is projected with speed v in a horizontal direction perpendicular to the string when the length of the string is $3a$. If the maximum length of the string in the subsequent motion is $5a$, show that $v^2 = 75ga/4$. (N.)

***6.** Two particles A, B of the same mass are connected by a light inextensible string, of length $2a$, and lie on a smooth horizontal table at a distance $2a$ apart. If A is projected with velocity v perpendicular to the string, show that the angular velocity of the system remains constant. Find the velocity of each particle when the string has turned through an angle θ, and prove that each particle describes a cycloid. (L.)

7. A light inextensible string of length $2a$, has particles of mass m fixed at each end. Initially the string is taut and vertical, the lower particle is moving downwards with velocity v and the velocity of the upper particle has horizontal and vertical (downward) components both equal to v. Show that in the subsequent motion the angular velocity is constant and equal to $v/(2a)$. Show also that when the string is horizontal for the first time the centre of gravity is at a distance $a\pi(2v^2+ga\pi)/(2v^2)$ below its initial position. (L.)

18.5. The Motion of a Projectile

In Volume I, Chapter IV we considered some elementary problems concerning the motion of a projectile in a vertical plane and in a non-resisting medium. We derived the equation of the path of a particle projected with initial velocity u at an angle α with the horizontal and referred to horizontal and vertical axes through the point of projection, in the form

$$y = x\tan\alpha - \frac{gx^2}{2u^2}(1+\tan^2\alpha). \qquad (18.20)$$

The position of the particle at time t from the instant of projection is given by the equations

$$x = ut\cos\alpha,$$
$$y = ut\sin\alpha - \tfrac{1}{2}gt^2.$$

Eliminating α from these equations we obtain

$$x^2+(y+\tfrac{1}{2}gt^2)^2 = u^2t^2,$$

i.e.

$$g^2t^4-4(u^2-gy)\,t^2+4(x^2+y^2) = 0. \tag{18.21}$$

The bounding parabola. From equation (18.20) the possible angles of projection for a particle projected from the origin O with speed u to pass through the point P(h, k) are given by the quadratic equation in tan α,

$$k = h\tan\alpha-\frac{gh^2}{2u^2}(1+\tan^2\alpha).$$

According as this equation has real distinct roots, equal roots, or complex roots, there are two, one, or no possible paths for the particle from O to P. When the roots of the equation are equal, the point P is the point of maximum range for the particle on the line OP.

We consider now the geometric problem of finding the possible trajectories for a particle projected from O with speed u to pass through P. In either case the path of the particle is a parabola with directrix $y = u^2/(2g)$ (Vol. I, § 4.4).

Since O is a point on the parabola, the focus of the parabola must lie on the circle with centre O and radius $u^2/(2g)$, Fig. 18.13 (i). The focus must also lie on the circle with central P and radius PN, where PN is the perpendicular from P to the directrix. The focus must therefore be either at S or S′, where S and S′ are the points of intersection of the circles, if these points exist. If there are two such points, the possible trajectories of the particles are:

1. The parabola through O and P with focus S and directrix $y = u^2/(2g)$.
2. The parabola through O and P with focus S′ and directrix $y = u^2/(2g)$.

If the two circles do not intersect, it is not possible to project the particle from O through P with initial speed u.

If the circles touch [Fig. 18.13 (ii)] there is only one such path for the particle from O to P and in this case the point P is a point of maximum range on the line OP.

It is a proposition of geometry that the tangent to a parabola at a point K on the parabola bisects the angle between the perpendicular

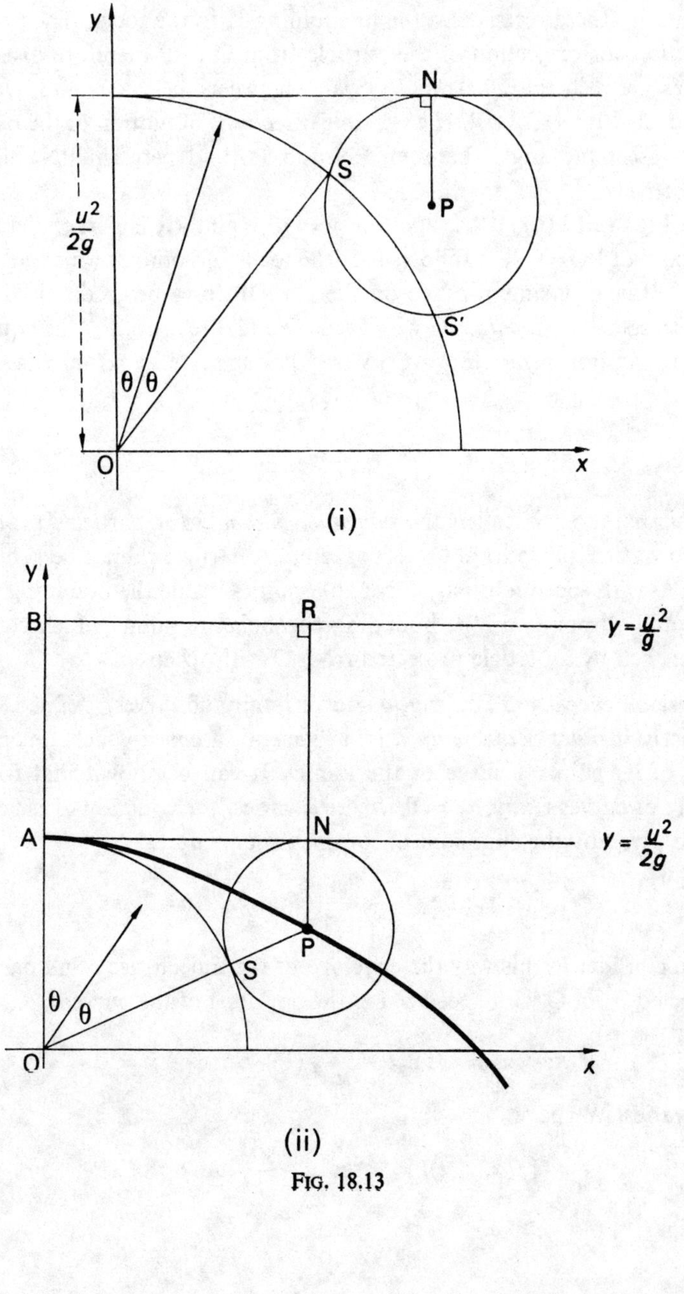

FIG. 18.13

from K to the directrix and the line joining K to the focus. The possible directions of projection of the particle from O to P therefore bisect the angles between the y-axis and OS and between the y-axis and OS′ respectively [Fig. 18.13 (i)]. The possible directions of motion of the particle at P bisect the angles between PN and PS and between PN and PS′ respectively.

In Fig. 18.13 (ii), BR is the line $y = u^2/g$ and PR is perpendicular to BR so that PO=PR. It follows that the locus of points P which are such that OP is a maximum range on the line OP for a projectile fired from O with speed u is a *parabola* with focus O and directrix BR. The equation of this parabola *referred to* AO *as axis of x and* AN *as axis of y* is

$$y^2 = 4 \,.\, \mathrm{OA} \,.\, x,$$

i.e.

$$y^2 = \frac{2u^2}{g}\, x. \tag{18.22}$$

This parabola is called the *bounding parabola* for particles projected in the vertical plane from O with speed u. A particle cannot be projected from O with speed u to pass through a point outside the bounding parabola and all points on the bounding parabola are points which can just be reached by a particle projected from O with speed u.

Note on envelopes. The *envelope* of a family of curves, defined more precisely in *Pure Mathematics*, is, in general, a curve which touches at each of its points a curve of the family. It can be shown that for the family of curves $f(x, y, \alpha) = 0$, where α varies, the equation of the envelope is given by the eliminant of α from the equations

$$f(x, y, \alpha) = 0, \quad \frac{\mathrm{d}}{\mathrm{d}\alpha}\{f(x, y, \alpha)\} = 0.$$

We consider in this way the envelope of the trajectories of all particles projected from O with speed u, i.e. the envelope of the curves

$$f(x, y, \alpha) = x \tan\alpha - \frac{gx^2}{2u^2}(1+\tan^2\alpha) - y = 0$$

as α varies. We have

$$\frac{\mathrm{d}}{\mathrm{d}\alpha}\{f(x, y, \alpha)\} = x\sec^2\alpha - \frac{gx^2}{u^2}\tan\alpha\sec^2\alpha,$$

and the required envelope is therefore given by eliminating α between $f(x, y, \alpha) = 0$ and $\tan\alpha = u^2/(gx)$. The eliminant is

$$\frac{xu^2}{gx} - \frac{gx^2}{2u^2}\left(1+\frac{u^4}{g^2x^2}\right) - y = 0,$$

i.e.
$$x^2 = -\frac{2u^2}{g}\left(y-\frac{u^2}{2g}\right).$$

Referred to horizontal and vertical axes of x and y this is the equation of a parabola with latus rectum $(2u^2)/g$ and vertex $\{0, u^2/(2g)\}$, i.e. the equation of the bounding parabola we have defined above.

The bounding parabola is sometimes called the *enveloping parabola* or the *parabola of safety*.

Equations (18.20), (18.21) and the enveloping parabola between them afford a choice of methods for the solution of certain problems concerning projectiles. These methods are illustrated in the examples which follow.

Example 1. A shot is fired with speed V from a point O which is distance d vertically above a plane inclined to the horizontal at an angle β. Find the maximum range down the plane.

In Fig. 18.14, P is the point $V^2/(2g)$ vertically above O. The equation of the bounding parabola referred to vertically downwards and horizontal axes of x and y through P is

$$y^2 = \frac{2V^2}{g}x.$$

The section of the inclined plane in the plane of projection is the straight line through $\{d+V^2/(2g), 0\}$ inclined at $(\frac{1}{2}\pi-\beta)$ to the x-axis and the equation of this line is

$$y = \left(x-d-\frac{V^2}{2g}\right)\cot\beta.$$

The line meets the bounding parabola where

$$y^2 = \frac{2V^2}{g}\left\{\frac{y}{\cot\beta}+d+\frac{V^2}{2g}\right\},$$

i.e. where
$$y^2-\frac{2V^2y}{g\cot\beta}-\frac{V^4}{g^2}-\frac{2V^2d}{g} = 0.$$

The maximum range of the particle on the inclined plane is therefore $y_1\sec\beta$, where y_1

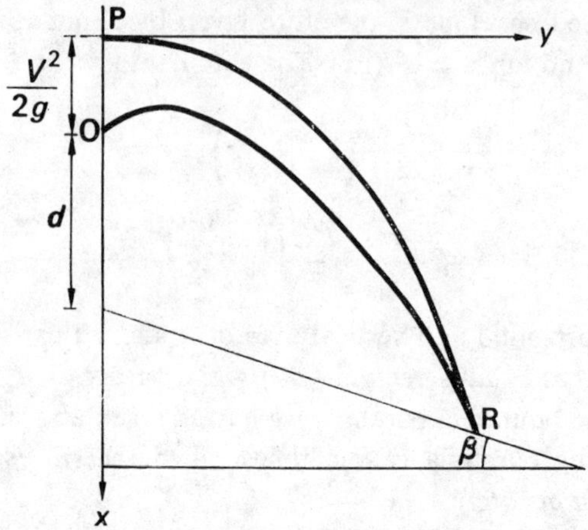

FIG. 18.14

is the positive root of this equation in y. This maximum range is therefore

$$\left\{\frac{V^2}{g\cot\beta}+\sqrt{\left(\frac{V^4}{g^2\cot^2\beta}+\frac{V^4}{g^2}+\frac{2V^2d}{g}\right)}\right\}\sec\beta$$

$$=\frac{V^2}{g\cos\beta}\left\{\tan\beta+\sqrt{\left(\sec^2\beta+\frac{2\,dg}{V^2}\right)}\right\}.$$

Example 2. A particle is to be projected with velocity v from a point O to strike an object at a vertical distance h below O and at a horizontal distance d from O. Find the least value of v for which this is possible and show that for larger values of v there are two possible directions of projection. Show also that the values of v for which the two possible directions of projection are at right angles is $d\sqrt{(g/h)}$.

Let the angle of projection be α. Then the equation of the path of the projectile is

$$y = x\tan\alpha-\frac{gx^2}{2v^2}(1+\tan^2\alpha)$$

referred to horizontal and upward vertical axes Ox and Oy through O. Therefore, since the projectile passes through $(d, -h)$,

$$-h = d\tan\alpha-\frac{gd^2}{2v^2}(1+\tan^2\alpha),$$

i.e.

$$gd^2\tan^2\alpha-2v^2d\tan\alpha+(gd^2-2v^2h) = 0.$$

If the point $(d, -h)$ is a point of limiting range for the particle, this equation in $\tan\alpha$

has equal roots. Hence, in this case,

$$v^4 d^2 = gd^2(gd^2 - 2v^2 h),$$

i.e.

$$v^4 + 2ghv^2 - g^2 d^2 = 0.$$

The least value of v^2 for which it is possible to reach $(d, -h)$ is therefore the positive root of this equation in v^2, i.e. $-gh + g\sqrt{(h^2+d^2)}$. The least value of v for which it is possible to reach $(d, -h)$ is thus $+\sqrt{\{-gh+g\sqrt{(h^2+d^2)}\}}$.

The equation in $\tan\alpha$ is a quadratic and gives two values of $\tan\alpha$ for values of v above the minimum value. There are therefore two possible directions of projection for such values of v. If the directions of projection (say α_1 and α_2 with the horizontal) are at right angles, one direction is above the horizontal and one is below the horizontal so that $\alpha_1 - \alpha_2 = 90°$. Therefore $\tan\alpha_1 \tan\alpha_2 = -1$, and from the equation in $\tan\alpha$,

$$\tan\alpha_1 \tan\alpha_2 = 1 - \frac{2v^2 h}{gd^2}.$$

$$\therefore\ -1 = 1 - \frac{2v^2 h}{gd^2},$$

$$\therefore\ v = d\sqrt{(g/h)}.$$

Example 3. A ball is to be thrown with speed u from a point O on the ground distance d from a high vertical cliff face so as to strike the cliff at the point P which is at a vertical height d above O. Calculate the difference between the two possible times of flight from O to P and show that if P is the highest point on the cliff face that can be reached with a ball thrown at speed u from O then $u^2 = gd(1+\sqrt{2})$ and find the time of flight from O to P in this case, in terms of d and g only.

The coordinates of P referred to horizontal and vertical axes in the plane of projection are (d, d). Let P be the point reached in time t from the instant of projection from O (at angle α with the horizontal). Then $d = ut\cos\alpha$ and $d = ut\sin\alpha - \frac{1}{2}gt^2$. Hence, eliminating α, we have

$$g^2 t^4 - 4(u^2 - gd)\, t^2 + 8d^2 = 0,$$

and, if t_1 and t_2 are the possible times of flight from O to P,

$$t_1^2 + t_2^2 = \frac{4(u^2 - gd)}{g^2}, \quad t_1^2 t_2^2 = \frac{8d^2}{g^2}.$$

$$\therefore\ (t_1 - t_2)^2 = \frac{4(u^2 - gd)}{g^2} - 4\sqrt{2}\frac{d}{g}$$

$$= \frac{4}{g^2}\{u^2 - (1+\sqrt{2})\, dg\}.$$

$$\therefore\ t_1 - t_2 = \frac{2}{g}\sqrt{\{u^2 - (1+\sqrt{2})\, dg\}}.$$

If P is the highest point that can be reached with a projectile fired at speed u from O, then $t_1 = t_2$ and therefore $u^2 = (1+\sqrt{2})\,dg$.

The time of flight from O to P in this case is given by $t = 2^{3/4}\sqrt{(d/g)}$ since the roots of the equation in t^2 are equal.

EXERCISES 18.5

1. From a point on a plane, inclined at an angle α to the horizon, a particle is projected with speed V at an angle β to the plane in the vertical plane through the line of greatest slope. Find for what angle β the range up the plane is greatest and the length of this range.

For this trajectory show that the direction of projection and the direction of impact upon the inclined plane are perpendicular. (N.)

2. A particle is projected from a given point so as just to pass over a wall of height h which is in such a position that the *top* of the wall is at a distance r from the point of projection. Show that the least speed of projection necessary for this purpose is $\sqrt{\{g(h+r)\}}$, and that with this speed the particle will have reached its greatest height before grazing the wall.

Find also the angle of projection. (N.)

***3.** The angle of elevation of a point P from an origin O is θ, and a particle is projected under gravity from O with given speed V to pass through P. Show that in general there are two possible trajectories, and that if α_1 and α_2 are the two angles of projection $\alpha_1+\alpha_2 = 90°+\theta$.

Prove also that if T_1 and T_2 are the corresponding times required to reach P, then gT_1T_2 depends only on the distance OP. (C.S.)

***4.** If a particle is projected under gravity from a point A with given initial velocity U in a fixed vertical plane, show that all the points that can just be reached by the particle lie on a parabola of latus rectum $2U^2/g$.

If the point A lies on a plane inclined at an angle β to the horizontal, show that the product of the distances from A of the highest and lowest point of the plane that can be reached is $U^4/g^2\cos^2\beta$. (C.S.)

***5.** A particle is projected with velocity V from a point P so as to pass through a small ring at a horizontal distance a and a vertical distance b (upwards) from P. Prove that the angle of projection θ must satisfy

$$\tan^2\theta-\frac{2V^2}{ga}\tan\theta+\left(\frac{2V^2b}{ga^2}+1\right) = 0.$$

Hence find the least possible value of V and the corresponding angle of projection, and prove that for these conditions of projection the range on the horizontal plane through P is

$$a\left\{1+\frac{b}{\sqrt{(b^2+a^2)}}\right\}. \qquad \text{(C.S.)}$$

6. If a particle is projected horizontally with a speed V from a point A at height $V^2/2g$ above another point O, show that it will describe the enveloping parabola of the family of trajectories obtained by projecting particles from O with speed V in varying directions in the same vertical plane.

A particle is projected horizontally from A with speed V, and another is projected from O with the same speed at any angle to the horizontal and in the vertical plane containing the first trajectory. Prove that the difference of the squares of their speeds at the common point of their paths is V^2. (N.)

***7.** A stone is thrown with speed V from a point at height h above the ground. Show that, in order to hit the ground as far away as possible, the stone must be thrown at an angle of elevation

$$\tan^{-1}\sqrt{\left(\frac{V^2}{V^2+2gh}\right)}. \qquad \text{(C.S.)}$$

***8.** A gun, whose maximum range on a horizontal plane is r, is mounted at the top of a vertical cliff at a height h above the sea. A ship at sea has a gun whose maximum range on a horizontal plane is R. Show that it is possible for the ship to engage the cliff-top gun while remaining out of its range if $R > r+2h$. (C.S.)

*MISCELLANEOUS EXERCISES XVIII

***1.** A smooth curve has the form given by the equations

$$x = a(\theta+\sin\theta), \qquad y = a(1-\cos\theta)$$

and is fixed with the y-axis directed vertically downwards. Show that the gradient of the curve is $\tan(\theta/2)$ and the radius of curvature is $4a\cos(\theta/2)$.

A particle placed on the curve at the origin is projected along the curve with velocity $\sqrt{(2ga)}$. Show that while the particle is in contact with the curve its velocity v is given by the equations

$$v^2 = 2ga\left(1+2\sin^2\frac{\theta}{2}\right) = 4a^2\left(\frac{d\theta}{dt}\right)^2\cos^2\frac{\theta}{2}.$$

Show that the particle will leave the curve when it reaches the point $\theta = \pi/3$. (N.)

***2.** A smooth wire has the form of the parabola $x^2 = 4ay$ and is fixed with the y-axis vertical and the vertex uppermost. A small ring of mass m sliding on the wire has speed v_0 when at the vertex. Prove that when the ring is at a depth y below the vertex the reaction between the ring and the wire is

$$m\left(g-\frac{v_0^2}{2a}\right)\left(\frac{a}{a+y}\right)^{3/2}. \qquad \text{(N.)}$$

***3.** An aeroplane is flying horizontally at height k with velocity U. An anti-aircraft gun is situated on the ground at a distance h from the vertical plane in which the aeroplane is flying. The gun can fire shells with velocity V. Prove that the aeroplane is within range of the gun for a time

$$\frac{2}{gU}(V^4-2V^2gk-g^2h^2)^{1/2},$$

provided that $$g^2h^2+2V^2gk < V^4.$$ (C.S.)

*4. A fine smooth cycloidal tube, whose intrinsic equation is $s = 4a \sin \psi$, is fixed in a vertical plane with its vertex uppermost. Two equal particles, each of mass m, are connected by a light inextensible string of length $2a$ and are placed inside the tube so that the upper particle is at the vertex and the string is fully extended and inside the tube. If the upper particle is released, show that the tension of the string throughout the motion is $mg/4$ and that the time taken for the lower particle to reach the nearest cusp is

$$2\sqrt{\left(\frac{a}{g}\right)}\ln(3+\sqrt{8}).$$ (L.)

*5. A light rod is rotating with constant angular velocity ω about a fixed end A in a horizontal plane, when a smooth ring of mass m is projected from the end A with speed V along the rod. Simultaneously a couple is applied to the rod to maintain its angular velocity ω whilst the ring is sliding on the rod.

Find the distance of the ring from A at any time t of this period and show that, at this instant, the couple has the value $mV^2 \sinh 2\omega t$. (L.)

*6. A particle describes the cardioid $r = a(1-\cos\theta)$ in such a manner that the radius vector from the origin rotates with constant angular velocity ω. Show that its acceleraion can be resolved into a component $2a\omega^2$ parallel to the initial line and a component $4r-3a)\omega^2$ towards the origin. (L.)

*7. A particle is projected under gravity from a point O to pass through a certain point P at distance R from it and elevation α above it. Prove that its trajectory will meet OP at right angles if the speed of projection is

$$\sqrt{\{gR(\operatorname{cosec}\alpha+3\sin\alpha)/2\}}.$$ (C.S.)

*8. Two particles A and B each of mass m are connected by a light inextensible string of length $2a$ and lie at rest on a smooth horizontal table with the string taut. If the particle A is projected along the table with velocity V perpendicular to the string, prove that the centre of mass of the particles moves with uniform velocity and that the angular velocity of the string is constant. Show also that at time t the distance of A from the initial position of the middle point of the string is

$$\frac{1}{2}\sqrt{\left(V^2t^2+4a^2+4Vta\sin\frac{Vt}{2a}\right)}.$$ (N.)

*9. A particle moves on a smooth curve under the action of gravity and the reaction of the curve only. Prove that the square of its velocity is proportional to its depth below a certain fixed level. Explain why the reaction of the curve does not enter into this result.

A particle of mass m is attached to one end of a light rod of length a. The other end of the rod is attached to a small bead of mass m threaded on a rough fixed horizontal wire. The system is released from rest with the particle in contact with the wire. Find the velocity of the particle when the rod is inclined at angle θ to the horizontal, assuming that slipping has not taken place. Find also the horizontal and vertical components of the force exerted on the bead by the wire, and show that if the coefficient of friction exceeds $\frac{3}{4}$ the bead will never slip. (N.)

***10.** A smooth curve in the form of a cycloid is fixed in a vertical plane with its vertex uppermost. The equations of the curve are

$$x = a(2\psi+\sin 2\psi), \quad y = a(1-\cos 2\psi),$$

the positive direction of the y-axis being vertically downwards; it may be assumed that the length of arc, s, measured from the origin is $4a \sin \psi$. A particle placed at rest on the curve at the origin is slightly disturbed and slides down the arc. Show that the particle will lose contact with the curve where $y = a$. If the particle subsequently moves freely under gravity, find the value of x at the point where it meets the line $y = 2a$, and the angle which its direction of motion then makes with the horizontal. (N.)

***11.** A small sphere is projected with velocity V in a vertical plane from a point O and subsequently strikes a plane through O, with the line of greatest slope in the vertical plane and inclined at angle θ to the horizontal. Find the range x up the plane when α is the inclination of the velocity of projection to the line of greatest slope of the plane.

If e is the coefficient of restitution of the impact of the sphere and the plane, prove that if $2 \tan \theta = (1-e) \cot \alpha$, the distances between successive impacts are in the decreasing ratio e^2. (C.S.)

***12.** Three equal particles each of mass m are attached to the ends and mid-point respectively of a taut, inextensible, light string. They rest on a smooth horizontal table in a straight line. By means of a sharp blow the middle particle is set in motion with a velocity u at right angles to the line of the string. In the subsequent motion the end particles will eventually collide.

Find the components of the velocity along and perpendicular to the string of one of the end particles immediately before the collision. Prove also that, if the particles are inelastic, the kinetic energy lost in the impact is $mu^2/3$. (L.)

***13.** Two equal particles A and B are connected by a light inextensible string of length l. Initially A is on a smooth table, the string being taut and perpendicular to the edge of the table, while B hangs just over the edge. Describe the motion when A has left the table, and show that the string will be horizontal when at a depth $\frac{1}{8}l(\pi^2+2\pi+4)$ below the edge of the table. (N.)

***14.** A region of V-shaped cross-section is formed by two planes at right angles to each other, each of them inclined at an angle of 45° to the vertical, the line of intersection being horizontal. A particle is projected from a point P on one of the planes into the V-shaped region, the velocity of projection being normal to the plane and of magnitude v. The distance of P from the line of intersection is h. Show that the particle hits the other plane at a distance

$$2v\sqrt{\left(\frac{h}{g}\right)}-h$$

from the line of intersection provided $v > 2^{-3/4}\sqrt{(hg)}$.

Find v if the particle is to hit the line of intersection after one rebound, assuming that the coefficient of restitution of the planes is $\frac{3}{4}$. (C.S.)

***15.** A particle can be projected with fixed speed V from a given point O of a plane inclined to the horizontal at an angle α. Prove that the area within range is an ellipse, with O as focus and of area $\pi V^4/(g^2 \cos^3 \alpha)$, where g is the acceleration of gravity. (C.S.)

***16.** Particles are projected under gravity in a vertical plane from a point O on level ground with initial velocity v at all angles of elevation. Show that the region above the ground covered by all the trajectories is bounded by the trajectory of a particle which, at a certain point vertically above O, moves horizontally with velocity v.

Find also the region covered by the ascending parts of all trajectories and the region covered by all trajectories with angle of elevation less than 45°. Indicate the position of the various regions on a diagram. (C.S.)

***17.** Two particles of masses m and $2m$ are connected by a light inextensible string of length l, and are placed in a smooth straight tube which is kept rotating in a horizontal plane with constant angular velocity ω about a fixed end. Initially the particles are at rest relative to the tube and are at distances a and $a+l$ from the fixed end. Show that at time t the distance of m from its starting point is $(a+\frac{2}{3}l)(\cosh \omega t-1)$. Show also that the tension in the string is constant and find the horizontal component of the reaction of the tube on the first particle in terms of t. (L.)

***18.** A small ring of mass m can slide freely on a fixed smooth horizontal rod. To the ring is attached one end of a light inextensible string of length l, the other end of which carries a particle of mass $3m$. The particle is held, with the string taut, at the level of the rod and then allowed to fall from rest. Show that when the string is vertical the velocity of the ring along the rod is

$$\frac{3}{2}\sqrt{(2lg)}. \qquad \text{(L.)}$$

***19.** A smooth circular wire of radius a is fixed horizontally. A small ring can slide freely along the wire, and is attached to a point O of the wire by an elastic string of natural length a. Initially the ring is slightly disturbed from rest at the other end of the diameter through O. Show that the sense of the component along the radius to the ring of the pressure of the wire upon the ring will change from outwards to inwards where the length of the string is $5a/3$. (L.)

***20.** A particle of unit mass moves under the action of a force whose components parallel to the axes of coordinates are given by $X = -n^2x$, $Y = -4n^2y$, where n is a constant; find expressions for the rectangular coordinates (x, y) of the particle as functions of the time, having given that its initial position is (a, b) and initial velocity components are u and v parallel to the x- and y-axes respectively. If b and u are both zero, show that the equation of the path of the particle is

$$v^2x^2(a^2-x^2) = n^2a^4y^2. \qquad \text{(L.)}$$

***21.** A square field OABC has side of unit length. A man starts at the point A and walks along the side AB with constant speed c, and a dog starts simultaneously at the point O and moves with unit speed always directly towards the instantaneous position of the man. Taking OA as the axis of x and OC as the axis of y, show that the path of the dog satisfies the differential equation

$$(1-x)\frac{dp}{dx} = c\sqrt{(1+p^2)},$$

where $p = dy/dx$.

Hence show that the dog will not overtake the man within the field if $2c > \sqrt{5}-1$. (L.)

CHAPTER XIX

SYSTEMS OF COPLANAR FORCES

19.1. Forces Acting on a Particle

The Resultant. In Volume I, Chapter II we considered the methods of addition of forces acting on a particle, treating a force as a localised vector through the particle, i.e. *as a vector having the particle as origin.* In that chapter we postulated laws of vector addition, which we interpreted in the case of two forces acting on a particle to obtain

(a) the Parallelogram of Forces for the addition of two non-parallel forces,

(b) the Polygon of Forces (including the special case of the Triangle of Forces) for the addition of a number of forces,

(c) the law of the resolved parts, which we now state formally as follows:

If $P_1, P_2, P_3, \ldots, P_n$ are coplanar forces acting on a particle at O and if these forces have components $X_1, X_2, X_3, \ldots, X_n$ and $Y_1, Y_2, Y_3, \ldots, Y_n$ respectively in directions parallel to rectangular axes Ox, Oy in the plane of the forces, then the resultant **R** of the forces acts through O, and has components ΣX_r, ΣY_r parallel to Ox, Oy respectively. Therefore, in the vector notation used in the last chapter,

$$\mathbf{R} = \mathbf{i}\Sigma X_r + \mathbf{j}\Sigma Y_r,$$
$$|\mathbf{R}| = \sqrt{\{(\Sigma X_r)^2 + (\Sigma Y_r)^2\}},$$

and the direction of **R** is θ with Ox, where

$$\cos\theta = \frac{\Sigma X_r}{|\mathbf{R}|} \quad \text{and} \quad \sin\theta = \frac{\Sigma Y_r}{|\mathbf{R}|}, \quad 0 \leqq \theta < 2\pi.$$

The angle θ thus has a unique value in this range.

The Conditions of Equilibrium

Newton's first law states that a particle remains in a state of rest or of uniform speed in a straight line, unless it is acted upon by a force. It is not reasonable to postulate a particle which is absolutely at rest; we can only postulate a particle which has no acceleration *relative to a chosen origin* within an arbitrary frame of reference. Such a particle is said to be in *equilibrium.*

From Newton's law it now follows that if the particle is acted upon by forces having a resultant **R**, the necessary and sufficient condition for the equilibrium of the particle is

$$\mathbf{R} = \mathbf{0}.$$

This condition can be interpreted to give the alternative sets of conditions,

(i) the force polygon is closed,

(ii) $\Sigma X_r = 0, \quad \Sigma Y_r = 0.$

[For if $\mathbf{R} = \mathbf{0}$, then $|\mathbf{R}| = 0$, i.e. $\sqrt{\{(\Sigma X_r)^2 + (\Sigma Y_r)^2\}} = 0$ and this condition can be satisfied only if $\Sigma X_r = 0$, $\Sigma Y_r = 0$. Conversely, if $\Sigma X_r = 0$, $\Sigma Y_r = 0$, then $R = 0$ and therefore $\mathbf{R} = \mathbf{0}$.]

Special Cases

(a) A particle is in equilibrium under the action of two forces only if these forces are equal in magnitude and opposite in direction.

(b) If a particle is in equilibrium under the action of three forces, these forces can be represented by the sides of a triangle taken in order round the triangle. This condition is interpreted by Lami's Theorem which states that if a particle is in equilibrium under the action of three forces, each force is proportional to the sine of the angle between the other two.

19.2. Coplanar Forces Acting on a Rigid Body

The Moment of a Force about an Axis

When a system of coplanar forces acts on a rigid body, each force tends to move the whole body in its own direction and, in general, the force also tends to rotate the body. In order for the body to be in equilibrium there must be no *total* tendency either for rotation or for translation. In Volume I we defined the *turning effect*, i.e. the moment of a force about an axis, as being either positive (anticlockwise) or negative (clockwise) and of magnitude equal to the product of the magnitude of the force and the distance of the force from the axis. This definition of the moment of a force was based upon the Principle of the Lever, established by Archimedes, which stated that the lever is in equilibrium when the moments about the fulcrum of the "load" and the "effort" are equal and opposite.

(The moment of a force about a point can be defined as a *vector*. This definition is discussed in § 19.6. In the discussion which follows, each system of forces considered is a coplanar system and the axis about which moments are taken is in each case perpendicular to the plane of the forces. In these circumstances we shall refer to "the moment of a force about a point", the point in question being the intersection of the axis with the plane of the forces.)

The sum of the moments about any point of two forces acting on a particle is equal to the moment of their resultant about that point

Let the coordinates of the position of the particle be (x, y) referred to coordinate axes through O, where O is the point about which moments are to be taken, Fig. 19.1. Let the components, parallel to the axes, of

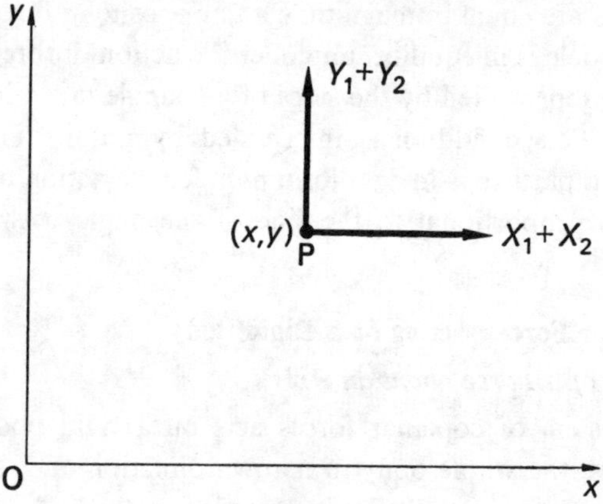

FIG. 19.1

the forces acting at P be (X_1, Y_1) and (X_2, Y_2). Then the sum of the moments of the two forces about O is $(Y_1x-X_1y)+(Y_2x-X_2y)$ and this is equal to $(Y_1+Y_2)x-(X_1+X_2)y$.

The components of the resultant of the two forces parallel to the axes are (X_1+X_2, Y_1+Y_2) and the moment of this resultant about O is

$$(Y_1+Y_2)x-(X_1+X_2)y,$$

which establishes the principle stated above.

The Equivalence of Two Sets of Coplanar Forces

Two sets of coplanar forces acting on a body are *defined* as equivalent sets if,

(i) the vector sum of the forces of the first set is equal to the vector sum of the forces of the second set, *and*

(ii) the sum of the moments of the forces of the first set is equal to the sum of the moments of the forces of the second set *about every point in the plane.*

Parallel Forces

$P_1, P_2, P_3, \ldots, P_n$ and $Q_1, Q_2, Q_3, \ldots, Q_n$ are two sets of parallel forces in a plane, the forces of each set being parallel to the forces of the other, and each force being a directed quantity. The axes Ox and Oy are taken through an arbitrary point O in the plane, so that Oy is parallel to the forces of each set, and so that P_r meets the x-axis at $(p_r, 0)$ and Q_r meets the x-axis at $(q_r, 0)$.

The sum of the moments of the forces of the set P_r about O is $\Sigma P_r p_r$, and the sum of the moments of the forces of the set P_r about an arbitrary point (x, y) in the plane is $\Sigma P_r(p_r-x)$. (This statement takes into account the directed nature of the moments concerned.)

If now,

$$\Sigma P_r = \Sigma Q_r, \quad \text{and} \quad \Sigma P_r p_r = \Sigma Q_r q_r,$$

then

$$\Sigma P_r(p_r-x) = \Sigma P_r p_r - x\Sigma P_r = \Sigma Q_r q_r - x\Sigma Q_r = \Sigma Q_r(q_r-x).$$

Thus we have shown that two such sets of parallel forces are equivalent if

(1) *the sum of the forces of the first set is equal to the sum of the forces of the second set,*

(2) *the sum of the moments of the forces of the first set about any one point in the plane is equal to the sum of the moments of the forces of the second set about that point.*

Also, if

$$\Sigma P_r p_r = \Sigma Q_r q_r \quad \text{and} \quad \Sigma P_r(p_r - x) = \Sigma Q_r(q_r - x),$$

then

$$\Sigma P_r x = \Sigma Q_r x,$$

and therefore

$$\Sigma P_r = \Sigma Q_r \quad \textit{unless} \quad x = 0.$$

Thus we have shown that sufficient conditions for the equivalence of two such sets of parallel forces are:

(1) the sum of the moments of the forces of the first set about an arbitrary point O in the plane is equal to the sum of the moments of the forces of the second set about that point, *and*

(2) the sum of the moments of the forces of the first set about a second point A in the plane, *where* OA *is not parallel to the forces of the set*, is equal to the sum of the moments of the second set about A.

Couples

A system of forces consisting of two equal and opposite parallel forces has no single force equivalent. Such a system is called a couple. In Volume I, § 6.2 we showed that a couple has a constant moment about all the points in its plane. The definition of equivalence given above shows that two couples are equivalent if their moments are equal.

19.3. The Equivalence of Sets of Coplanar Forces

If a set of coplanar forces contains more than two forces, then it must contain at least two forces which can be replaced by a single force. The system can thus be successively reduced either to a single force or to a pair of equal, parallel, and unlike forces constituting a couple. A special case occurs when the system reduces in this way to two equal and opposite forces in the same line. In this case the system of forces is said to be "in equilibrium".

Consider the system of forces with components parallel to the axes $(X_1, Y_1), (X_2, Y_2), \ldots, (X_n, Y_n)$ acting respectively through the points $(x_1, y_1), (x_2, y_2), \ldots, (x_n, y_n)$. Then,

(a) from the definition of equivalence, the single force with components $(\Sigma X_r, \Sigma Y_r)$ acting through (h, k) where $h\Sigma Y_r - k\Sigma X_r = \Sigma Y_r x_r - \Sigma X_r y_r$ is an equivalent system, unless $\Sigma X_r = \Sigma Y_r = 0$,

(b) if $\Sigma X_r = \Sigma Y_r = 0$ there is no single force which is equivalent to the system. In this case there is a couple which is equivalent to the system, or the system has zero moment about every point in the plane and is therefore in equilibrium.

In case (a) if $\Sigma X_r = X$, $\Sigma Y_r = Y$, and $\Sigma(Y_r x_r - X_r y_r) = G$, the magnitude of the resultant force is $\sqrt{(X^2+Y^2)}$ and the equation of its line of action is the equation of a line of gradient Y/X at a perpendicular distance $G/\{\sqrt{(X^2+Y^2)}\}$ from the origin, i.e. $Yx - Xy - G = 0$.

In general a system of coplanar forces is equivalent to a single force acting at an arbitrary point in the plane of the forces together with a couple.

Unless the system is in equilibrium it is equivalent either to a single force or to a couple. If the system reduces to a single force $\mathbf{R}$ in a line of action l which does not pass through the arbitrary point P, then the system is equivalent to

$$(\mathbf{R} \text{ in } l) + (\mathbf{R} \text{ through } P) - (\mathbf{R} \text{ through } P),$$

i.e. to the system $(\mathbf{R}$ through $P) + \{(\mathbf{R}$ in $l) - (\mathbf{R}$ through $P)\}$, i.e. to the force ($\mathbf{R}$ at P) and a couple of moment Rp where p is the distance of P from l.

Special cases occur,

(a) when P lies in l, in this case there is no couple;

(b) when the original system reduces to a couple, in this case there is no force;

(c) when the system is in equilibrium.

The system (X_r, Y_r) through (x_r, y_r), etc., which we discussed above, is equivalent to a force of magnitude $\sqrt{(X^2+Y^2)}$ acting through the arbitrary point (a, b) in the line $Yx - Xy + (Xb - Ya) = 0$ and a couple of moment equal to the moment-sum of the system about (a, b), i.e. of moment $Xb-Ya+G$.

By applying the principles of equivalence discussed in this section, equivalent systems of coplanar forces of varying patterns which involve three degrees of freedom can be found for any system of forces. The method involved is illustrated in the examples which follow.

Example 1. Forces P, $-7P$, $8P$, $-7P$, $-3P$ act along the sides AB, BC, CD, DE, EF of a regular hexagon. Find the magnitude and direction of the resultant, and the point at which its line of action meets AF (produced if necessary). (O.C.)

With reference to Fig. 19.2, the resultant has components (X, Y) parallel and perpendicular respectively to AB, such that

$$X = P-7P\cos 60°-8P\cos 60°+7P+3P\cos 60° = 2P,$$

$$Y = (7P-8P-3P)\sin 60° = -2\sqrt{3}P.$$

Hence the resultant has magnitude $\sqrt{(4P^2+12P^2)} = 4P$ and is in a direction making an anticlockwise angle of $\tan^{-1}\{(-2\sqrt{3})/2\}$ with AB and therefore lies in the *fourth quadrant*, at 300° with AB.

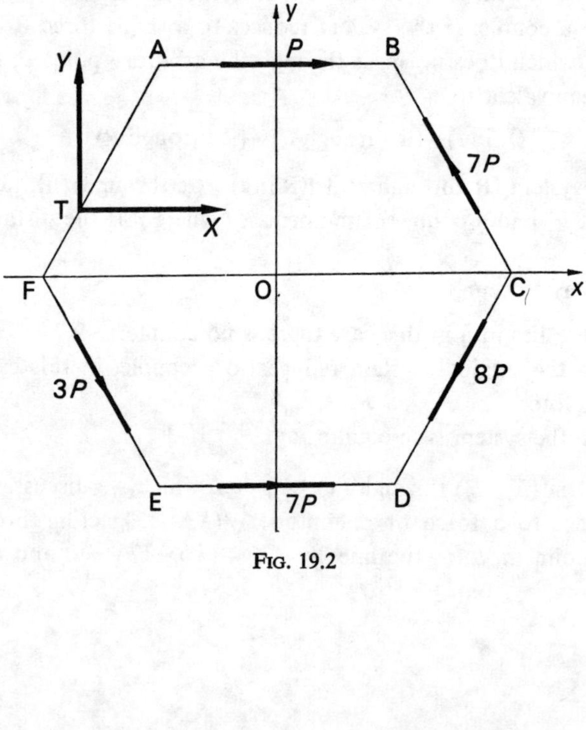

FIG. 19.2

The moment of the resultant about O, the centre of the hexagon, is equal to the sum of the moments of the forces of the system about O. Hence, if the length of the side of the hexagon is a, and if AT $= h$,

$$X(a-h)\sin 60° + Y\left(\frac{a}{2}+h\cos 60°\right) = -8Pa\sin 60°.$$

$$\therefore\ P(a-h)\sqrt{3}-P(a+h)\sqrt{3} = -4Pa\sqrt{3}.$$

$$\therefore\ h = 2a.$$

The resultant meets AF produced at T where AF = FT.

Example 2. The moment of a system of coplanar forces about each of three non-collinear points in the plane of the forces is zero. Prove that the system is in equilibrium.

The angle B of an isosceles triangle ABC is a right angle. A system of forces acts in the plane of ABC and the moments of the system about A, B, C are M_1, M_2, M_3 respectively, these moments not being all equal. Prove that the resultant of the system is a single force; find its magnitude and direction and the point at which it intersects BC. (N.)

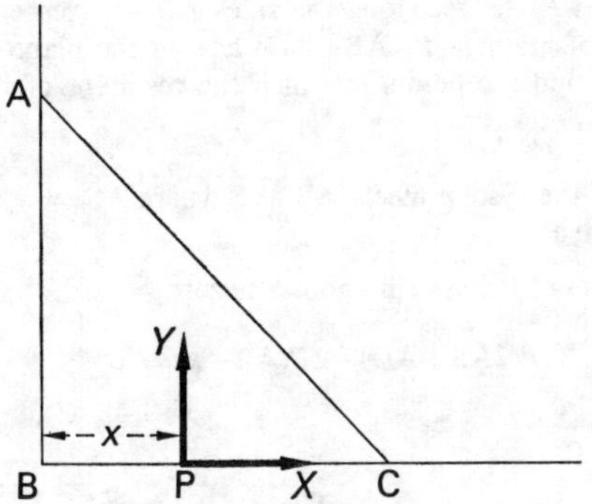

FIG. 19.3

Suppose the moment of the system about each of the non-collinear points A, B and C is zero. Then the system cannot have a single force equivalent, because such a force would have to act in the line AB and have no moment about C, which is contrary to the hypothesis that A, B and C are non-collinear points. Nor can the system reduce to a couple, because the moment of the system is zero about a point in the plane. The system is therefore in equilibrium.

Figure 19.3. Because the moment of the system about the points of the plane is not constant, the system is not equivalent to a couple, nor is it in equilibrium. The system is therefore equivalent to a single force. If the components of this force are

(X, Y) in the directions BC, BA and if the force intersects BC at P where BP $= x$, then

(1) moments about A, $M_1 = Yx + Xa$,

(2) moments about B, $M_2 = Yx$,

(3) moments about C, $M_3 = -Y(a-x)$,

where the sense of each of M_1, M_2, M_3 is taken as ABC and AB $=$ BC $= a$. From these equations,

$$X = \frac{M_1 - M_2}{a}, \quad Y = \frac{M_2 - M_3}{a}, \quad x = \frac{aM_2}{M_2 - M_3}.$$

The resultant force is therefore

$$\frac{1}{a}\sqrt{\{(M_1 - M_2)^2 + (M_2 - M_3)^2\}}$$

in a direction θ with BC where $\tan\theta = (M_2 - M_3)/(M_1 - M_2)$ and intersecting BC at P where BP $= aM_2/(M_2 - M_3)$.

Example 3. Forces P, $2P$ act along the sides $\overrightarrow{AB}$, $\overrightarrow{BC}$ respectively of a rectangle ABCD. If a couple of moment P(2AB+AD) acts in the plane of the rectangle and in the sense ADCB, find the points in which the resultant of the system meets AB and AD, produced if necessary. (N.)

If the resultant of the system meets AB at S where AS $= x$, and AD at T where AT $= y$, Fig. 19.4, then

(a) the moment-sum of the system about S is zero,

$$\therefore \; P(2\text{AB} + \text{AD}) - 2P(\text{AB} - x) = 0$$

$$\therefore \; x = -\tfrac{1}{2}\text{AD},$$

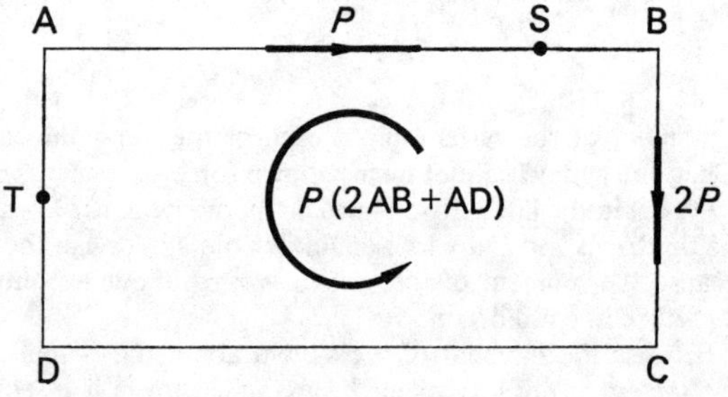

FIG. 19.4

(b) the moment-sum of the system about T is zero,

$$\therefore\ P(2AB+AD)-Py-2P\,.\,AB = 0,$$

$$\therefore\ y = AD.$$

The resultant passes through D and meets BA produced at S where AS = $\frac{1}{2}$AD.

Example 4. Forces of magnitudes 13, 5, 3, 10 units act along the sides AB, CB, DC, AD respectively of a square ABCD in the directions indicated by the order of the letters. Reduce the system to forces along AB, AD together with a couple; show also that the system may be replaced by a force acting along DC and a force through B, and find the components of the latter force along and perpendicular to AB. (O.C.)

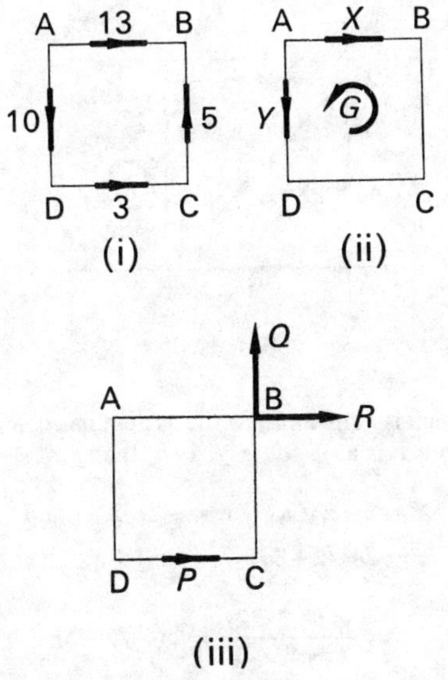

FIG. 19.5

Figure 19.5 comprises diagrams of the three equivalent force systems.
(a) From the equivalence of systems (i) and (ii),

$$X = 16; \quad Y = 5; \quad G = 8AB.$$

The system is equivalent to forces of 16 units and 5 units along AB, AD respectively together with an anti-clockwise couple of moment 8AB units.

(b) From the equivalence of systems (i) and (iii),

$$P+R = 16; \quad Q = -5; \quad P \times BC = 13 \times BC.$$
$$\therefore P = 13, \quad Q = -5, \quad R = 3.$$

The system is equivalent to a force of 13 units along DC and a force through B with components 3 units along AB and 5 units along BC.

Example 5. A square lamina ABCD is acted on by forces of 5 units along BA, 4 units along DB, 8 units along DC (in the directions indicated by the orders of the letters) together with a couple of $7a$ units, where a is the side of the square, in the sense ABCD. Find the equation of the line of action of the resultant of the system, taking AB and AD as coordinate axes. (L.)

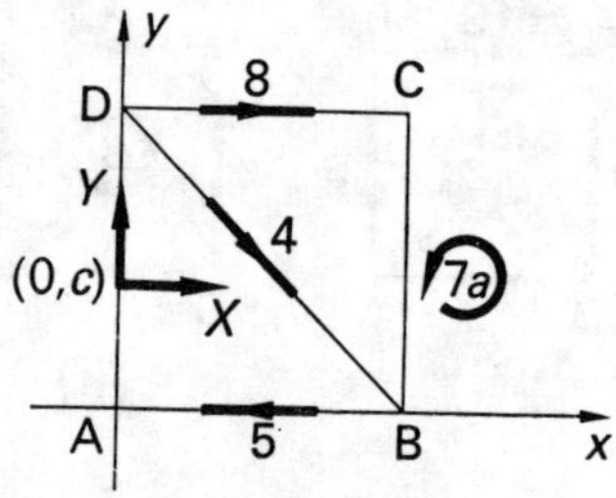

FIG. 19.6

If the single force which is equivalent to the system has components (X, Y) parallel to the axes and cuts the y-axis at $(0, c)$, Fig. 19.6, then

$$X = 3+2\sqrt{2}, \quad Y = -2\sqrt{2}, \quad \text{and}$$
$$Xc = 2a\sqrt{2}+8a-7a = a(1+2\sqrt{2}).$$

Hence,

$$c = \frac{a(1+2\sqrt{2})}{(3+2\sqrt{2})} = a(4\sqrt{2}-5).$$

The line of action of the resultant therefore has a gradient

$$\frac{-2\sqrt{2}}{3+2\sqrt{2}} = 8-6\sqrt{2},$$

and passes through $(0, c)$. Hence, the equation of the line of action of the resultant is

$$y = (8-6\sqrt{2})x+a(4\sqrt{2}-5).$$

Example 6. Forces acting at O are represented by the lines OA, OB, OC where ABC is a straight line whose mid-point is B. Prove that the sum of the resolved parts of the forces in the direction ABC is represented by 3MB, where M is the foot of the perpendicular drawn from O to AC. (N.)

This is an example which is best approached through the geometrical laws of vector addition. With reference to Fig. 19.7,

$$\overrightarrow{OA} = (\overrightarrow{OB}+\overrightarrow{BA}) \qquad \text{(at O)},$$

$$\overrightarrow{OC} = (\overrightarrow{OB}+\overrightarrow{BC}) \qquad \text{(at O)}.$$

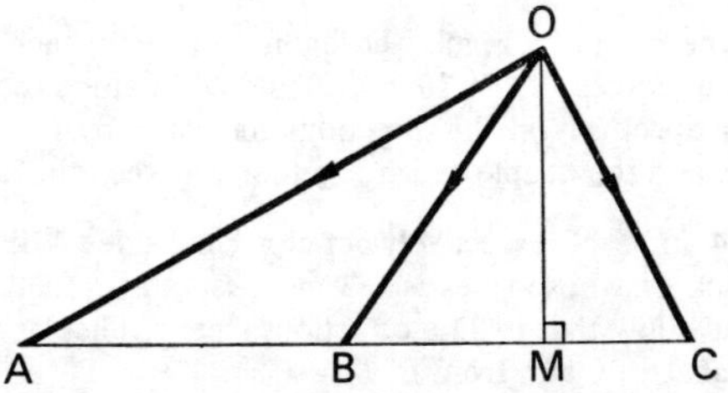

FIG. 19.7

But $$\overrightarrow{BA} = -\overrightarrow{BC}.$$

$$\therefore\ \overrightarrow{OA}+\overrightarrow{OC}+\overrightarrow{OB} = 3\overrightarrow{OB}.$$

$$3\overrightarrow{OB} = (3\overrightarrow{OM}+3\overrightarrow{MB}) \qquad \text{(at O)}.$$

Therefore the sum of the resolved parts of the forces at O in the direction ABC is $3\overrightarrow{MB}$.

EXERCISES 19.3

1. Forces of 8 N, 5 N, 4 N, and 2 N act along the sides AB, BC, CD, and DA respectively of a square ABCD in directions indicated by the order of the letters. Calculate the magnitude and direction of the resultant. If AB = a m, calculate the distance from A of the point where the line of action of the resultant intersects AB (produced if necessary).

2. Forces of 3, 4, 5 N act along the sides AB, BC, AC respectively of an equilateral triangle ABC. Find the magnitude of the resultant and the position of its line of action.

3. Along the sides AB, BC, CA of an equilateral triangle of side 6 m act forces of 2 N, 1 N, 1 N, respectively.

Find the resultant of the three forces in magnitude, direction, and position.

4. Forces P, $4P$, $2P$, $6P$ act along the sides AB, BC, CD, DA of a square ABCD of side a. Find the magnitude of their resultant, and prove that the equation of its line of action, referred to AB and AD as coordinate axes, is

$$2x-y+6a = 0. \qquad \text{(O.C.)}$$

5. ABC is an equilateral triangle of side $2a$ and D is the mid-point of BC. A force, of magnitude $6\sqrt{3}$W, acts at A parallel to $\overrightarrow{BC}$, and forces of magnitude 9W and 3W, parallel to $\overrightarrow{AD}$, act at B and C respectively. Find the distance from A of the point of intersection of AD with the line of action of the resultant of the three forces, and prove that this line of action passes through C. (O.C.)

6. A lamina in the form of a regular hexagon ABCDEF, each side being of length 1 m, is acted upon by forces 10, 20, 30, 40, 50 and 60 N along the sides AB, BC, CD, DE, EF, and FA respectively in the directions indicated by the order of the letters. Find the force at A and the couple which together will keep the lamina at rest.

7. Forces of 3, 4 and 5 N respectively act along the sides AB, BC, CA of an equilateral triangle, each of whose sides is 0·2 m in length. Find the magnitude of the resultant force; and show that its line of action is perpendicular to BC, and cuts BC produced at a distance of 0·5 m from B.

8. An equilateral triangle ABC has the mid-points of the sides BC, CA, AB at D, E, F respectively. Forces of 1, 1, 2, 2 N act respectively along AD, BC, BE, CA in the directions indicated. Find the magnitude and direction of the resultant of the system, and the point in which its line of action cuts BC. (N.)

9. The points A, B, C, D, E, F are the vertices of a regular hexagon of side a m. Forces of magnitude 6, 5, 4, 4, 5, 6 N act along the lines AB, BC, CA, DC, AD, DE in the directions indicated by the order of the letters. Find the magnitude and direction of the single force acting at A and the moment of the couple to which the given system is equivalent.

10. An isosceles triangle ABC is right-angled at A and the side BC is of length $2a$. The sense of description of the triangle, ABC, is counter-clockwise. The moments of a system of forces in the plane of this triangle about the vertices A, B, C are $2M$, M, M in the counter-clockwise sense. Prove that the system is equivalent to a single force, and find its magnitude and line of action.

If all the forces of the system are turned counter-clockwise through a right angle, and if the moment of the system about B is now $\frac{1}{2}M$ (counter-clockwise), find the moments of the system about C and A. (N.)

11. A system of coplanar forces is equivalent to forces X and Y along Ox and Oy respectively and a couple of moment G. The axes being rectangular, show that the equation of the line of action of the resultant of the system is $G-xY+yX = 0$.

The sums of the moments of a system of forces about the points (10, 6), (−5, 8) and (5, −4) are 40, 100 and −4 joules respectively, the coordinates being measured in metres. Find the components of the resultant force and the coordinates of the points in which its line of action cuts the axes.

12. Forces of magnitude 2, 3, 5, P, 4 and Q newtons act along the sides of a regular hexagon taken in order. Determine the values of P and Q in order that the forces may reduce to a couple.

If the side of the hexagon is 1 m, calculate the moment of this couple.

13. Forces of magnitude 1, 3, 3, 2, 5 N act along the sides AB, BC, CD, ED, FE, respectively, of a regular hexagonal lamina in the directions indicated by the order of the letters. Prove that the resultant is a force acting through A, and find its magnitude and line of action. (O.C.)

14. The length of each side of the square ABCD is 2 m, and E is the middle point of AD. Forces of magnitude 2, 9, 2, $\sqrt{5}$, and $2\sqrt{5}$ N act along the lines AB, BC, CD, EC, and EB. Find the force acting through A and the couple to which the system is equivalent. Find also the line of action of the single force to which the system is equivalent.

15. Forces represented by $2\overrightarrow{AB}$, $4\overrightarrow{CB}$, $2\overrightarrow{CD}$, and $\overrightarrow{AD}$ act along the sides AB, BC, CD, DA of a trapezium ABCD in which AD is parallel to BC. Show that the resultant is parallel to AD and, if it cuts the diagonals BD and AC in the points K and L, show that it is represented by $9\overrightarrow{LK}$. Find the ratio of the length of BC to that of AD if the system of forces is in equilibrium. (N.)

16. Prove that, if three forces kBC, kCA, kAB act along the sides BC, CA, AB of a triangle ABC, their resultant is a couple of magnitude $2k\Delta$, where Δ is the area of the triangle.

Three forces kBC, $2k$CA, $2k$AB act along the sides BC, CA, AB of a triangle; find the single force at A and the couple to which the system is equivalent. Also find the magnitude and direction of the resultant force and the point where its line of action meets AB. (N.)

17. Forces $4P$, P, and $2P$ act along the sides $\overrightarrow{BC}$, $\overrightarrow{CA}$, and $\overrightarrow{BA}$ respectively of an equilateral triangle ABC of side a. Prove that the system is equivalent to a force $3\sqrt{3}P$ in the direction $\overrightarrow{DE}$, where D is the point in BC at a distance $\frac{1}{3}a$ from B and E is the point in CA at a distance $\frac{1}{3}a$ from C.

Prove also that, if the given system of forces is equivalent to a certain force R along $\overrightarrow{BA}$ and a force S along $\overrightarrow{AC}$ together with a couple G in the sense ABC, then $R = 6P$, $S = 3P$, and $G = 2\sqrt{3}aP$. (O.C.)

18. ABCD is a plane quadrilateral in which the angles A and B are each right angles, the angle ADC is 60°, and the sides AD and DC are equal. A force P acts along BC in the direction from B to C. Find graphically or otherwise the magnitudes and directions of three forces along CD, DA, AB respectively, which will be in equilibrium with P. (O.C.)

19. The moments of a force about the vertices of an equilateral triangle of side 3 m are 20, -10 and -10 joules respectively. Prove that the force passes through the centroid of the triangle, and find its magnitude and direction.

20. Forces of magnitudes 3, 4, 6, 7 units act along the sides AB, BC, CD, DA of a square ABCD of side a, the directions of the forces being indicated by the order of the letters. In addition a couple acts in the plane of the square. If the whole system is equivalent to a force acting through the centre of the square, find the magnitude and sense of this couple. Find also the magnitude and line of action of this force. (L.)

21. The points O, A, B, C have coordinates (0, 0), (3, 0), (3, 4), (0, 4) respectively. Forces of magnitudes 4, 7, 2, 3, 10 units act along OA, AB, BC, CO, OB respectively in the senses indicated by the order of the letters and a couple of moment 11 units acts in the sense OABC. Find the magnitude of the resultant of the five forces and the couple, and show that the equation of its line of action is $3x-2y-10 = 0$. (N.)

22. A system of coplanar forces has anticlockwise moments M, $\frac{1}{2}M$, $\frac{3}{2}M$ about the points (0, 0), $(2a, 0)$, (a, a) respectively. Find the magnitude of the resultant of the system and show that the equation of its line of action is $3y-x+4a = 0$. (L.)

23. A system of coplanar forces has anticlockwise moments M_1, M_2, M_3 about the points (0, 0), $(a, 0)$ and (b, c) respectively. If X is the sum of the resolutes of the forces in the positive direction of the x-axis and Y the corresponding sum for the y-axis, obtain the values of X and Y.

Hence find the magnitude of the resultant of the system and the equation of its line of action. (L.)

24. Three forces are represented completely by the sides BC, CA and AB of a triangle ABC. Show that their resultant is a couple and state the magnitude of its moment. (You may assume any property of concurrent forces.)

If three forces are represented completely by BC, CA and kAB (where $k \neq 1$), show that their resultant is a force whose line of action is parallel to AB. If the perpendicular from C on to AB has length h, find, in terms of h and k only, the distance of the line of action of the resultant force from AB.

Give sketches to illustrate the two cases in which $k = 2$ and $k = -2$ respectively. (N.)

25. Forces of magnitudes 1, 5, 9, 11, 7, 3 act in the sides AB, BC, CD, DE, EF, FA of a regular hexagon of side a in the senses indicated by the order of the letters. Taking as axes OA and OH, where O is the centre of the hexagon and H is the middle point of BC, find the forces along the axes and the couple by which the system may be replaced. Prove also that the system is equivalent to a single force which meets the axes at the points

$$(-9a/4,\ 0) \quad \text{and} \quad (0,\ -9\sqrt{3}a/2). \qquad \text{(O.C.)}$$

19.4. The Equilibrium of a Rigid Body under the Action of a System of Coplanar Forces

The results of § 19.3 show that a system of coplanar forces acting on a rigid lamina can be reduced to a force acting through the centre of mass of the lamina together with a couple. In § 16.3 we showed that the motion of a rigid lamina acted upon by forces in its plane could be reduced to a motion of translation of its centre of mass and a motion of rotation about the centre of mass. Using Newton's laws of motion, we showed that these two motions are determined respectively by the vector sum of the forces acting on the lamina and the moment of those forces about the centre of mass. It follows from this that if a system of forces acting on a lamina is in equilibrium, as defined in § 19.3, then the lamina is in equilibrium. We use this result in Chapter XX.

19.5. A Law of Vector Addition

$$\lambda\overrightarrow{OA}+\mu\overrightarrow{OB} = (\lambda+\mu)\,\overrightarrow{OG},$$

where G divides AB in the ratio $\mu : \lambda$. See Fig. 19.8.

$$\lambda\overrightarrow{OA} = \lambda\overrightarrow{OG}+\lambda\overrightarrow{GA}.$$

$$\mu\overrightarrow{OB} = \mu\overrightarrow{OG}+\mu\overrightarrow{GB}.$$

But $$\lambda\overrightarrow{GA} = -\mu\overrightarrow{GB}.$$

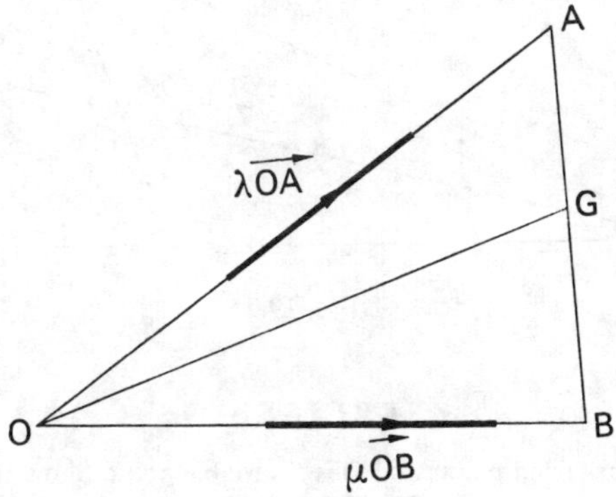

Fig. 19.8

Therefore, by addition,

$$\lambda\overrightarrow{OA}+\mu\overrightarrow{OB} = (\lambda+\mu)\overrightarrow{OG}.$$

Note. Here G is the centre of mass of particles of masses λ, μ at A, B respectively. It follows, by induction, that the resultant of forces

$$k_1\overrightarrow{OA_1},\ k_2\overrightarrow{OA_2},\ \dots,\ k_n\overrightarrow{OA_n}$$

is a force $(k_1+k_2+\ldots+k_n)\,\overrightarrow{OG}$, where G is the centre of mass of particles of masses $k_1, k_2, \ldots, k_n$ at $A_1, A_2, \ldots, A_n$ respectively.

Example. If I is the incentre of the triangle ABC, prove that the forces represented by $a\overrightarrow{IA}$, $b\overrightarrow{IB}$, $c\overrightarrow{IC}$ are in equilibrium. (L.)

With reference to Fig. 19.9,

$$a\overrightarrow{IA}+b\overrightarrow{IB} = (a+b)\,\overrightarrow{IF}$$

because F divides AB in the ratio $b:a$.

$$(a+b)\overrightarrow{IF}+c\overrightarrow{IC} = 0$$

because I divides FC in the ratio $(AF/AC) = [bc/(a+b)]\times 1/b = [c/(a+b)]$. Forces represented by $a\overrightarrow{IA}+b\overrightarrow{IB}+c\overrightarrow{IC}$ are therefore in equilibrium.

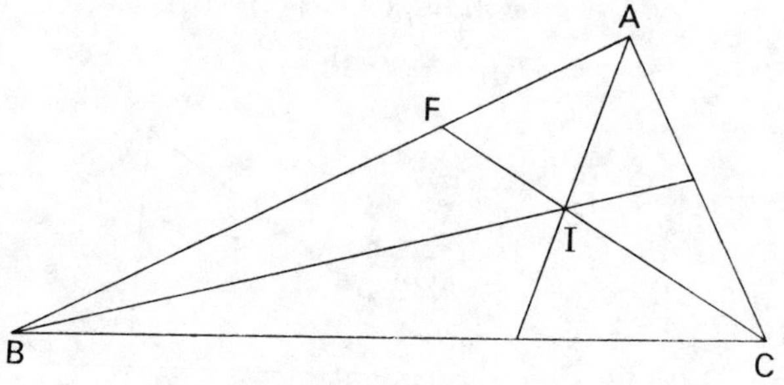

FIG. 19.9

EXERCISES 19.5

1. A, B, C, D are fixed points and O is a variable point. Show that the resultant of forces completely represented by $\overrightarrow{AO}$, $\overrightarrow{BO}$, $\overrightarrow{OC}$, $\overrightarrow{OD}$ is fixed in magnitude and direction. (L.)

2. If G is the centre of mass of a uniform triangular lamina ABC, prove that forces acting at a point and represented in magnitude and direction by GA, GB, GC are in equilibrium.

Prove that the resultant of forces at a point represented by GA, 2GB, 4GC is a force represented by 4GD, where D is a point on BC such that BD = 3DC. (O.C.)

*3. Forces of magnitudes pAB, qBC act along the sides AB, BC of a triangle ABC. If X is a point dividing AC in the ratio m:1 prove that the given forces are equivalent to a force of magnitude $(q-p)$BX along BX and a force of magnitude $(mp+q)/(m+1)$AC at B in the direction AC.

Forces of magnitudes pAB, qBC, rCD, sDA act along the sides AB, BC, CD and DA of a quadrilateral ABCD whose diagonals AC, BD meet at the point X. If the forces are equivalent to a couple, prove that X divides AC in the ratio $(r-q)/(p-s)$ and BD in the ratio $(s-r)/(q-p)$.

Prove also that the moment of the couple is $2S(pr-qs)/(p-q+r-s)$, where S is the area of the quadrilateral. (O.C.)

4. A particle P of mass M on a horizontal table is attracted towards four points A, B, C, D on the table by forces $k_1\overrightarrow{PA}$, $k_2\overrightarrow{PB}$, $k_3\overrightarrow{PC}$, $k_4\overrightarrow{PD}$ respectively. Show that the resultant of the four forces is

$$(k_1+k_2+k_3+k_4)\,\overrightarrow{PG},$$

where G is the centre of mass of particles of masses proportional to k_1, k_2, k_3, k_4 placed at A, B, C, D respectively.

If the table is rough, the coefficient of friction between it and the particle being μ, show that P can rest in equilibrium at any point of the table whose distance from G is not greater than

$$\mu Mg/(k_1+k_2+k_3+k_4). \qquad \text{(N.)}$$

5. Forces $p\overrightarrow{AB}$, $q\overrightarrow{BC}$, $p\overrightarrow{CD}$, $q\overrightarrow{DA}$ act in the corresponding sides of a plane quadrilateral ABCD of area S. Show that the four forces are equivalent to a single force unless (i) $p = q$ or (ii) ABCD is a parallelogram.

Show that the moments of the equivalent couples in cases (i) and (ii) are $2pS$ and $(p+q)S$ respectively. (N.)

6. PQRS is a plane quadrilateral in which the lines joining the mid-points of opposite sides meet at Y. The point X is any point in the plane of the quadrilateral. Show that forces represented by XP, XQ, XR and XS have a resultant represented by 4XY. (L.)

7. EFG is an equilateral triangle. Three forces are represented in magnitude and line of action by $\overrightarrow{FE}$, $\overrightarrow{GE}$, $2\overrightarrow{FG}$ respectively. Prove that the three forces are equivalent to a single force whose line of action cuts EG at H, where EH = 2HG. Find the magnitude of this single force. (O.C.)

*19.6. The Moment of a Force as a Vector

In this section we give to the student a short introduction to the theory of moments applied to three-dimensional problems by means of vector algebra. [See also Chapter XXVI.]

The Vector Product

The vector product of two vectors $\mathbf{a}$ and $\mathbf{b}$ is written $\mathbf{a}\times\mathbf{b}$ and is defined as a vector $\mathbf{v}$ of modulus $|\mathbf{a}|\,|\mathbf{b}|\sin\theta$, where θ is the angle between the positive directions of $\mathbf{a}$ and $\mathbf{b}$. [Sometimes the notation $\mathbf{a}\wedge\mathbf{b}$ is used for the vector product.] The vector $\mathbf{v}$ is perpendicular to the plane of $\mathbf{a}$ and $\mathbf{b}$, in a direction which is determined by the following rule:

If θ is the angle of rotation from the positive direction of $\mathbf{a}$ to the positive direction of $\mathbf{b}$, the direction of $\mathbf{v}$ is the direction in which the point of a right-handed corkscrew would move when the corkscrew was rotated through the angle θ, Fig. 19.10. Thus

$$\mathbf{a}\times\mathbf{b} = \hat{\mathbf{v}}ab\sin\theta,$$

where $\hat{\mathbf{v}}$ is the unit vector in the direction shown in Fig. 19.10.

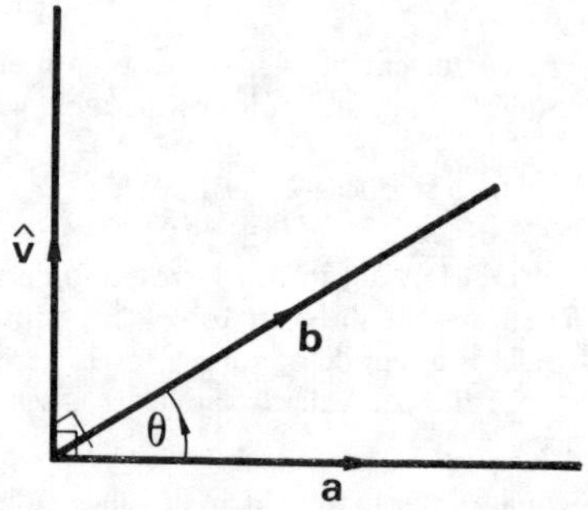

FIG. 19.10

With this definition it is clear that the vector product is *non-commutative*, i.e.

$$\mathbf{a}\times\mathbf{b} \neq \mathbf{b}\times\mathbf{a}$$

but
$$\mathbf{a}\times\mathbf{b} = -(\mathbf{b}\times\mathbf{a}).$$

The distributive law

$$\mathbf{a}\times(\mathbf{b}+\mathbf{c}) = \mathbf{a}\times\mathbf{b}+\mathbf{a}\times\mathbf{c}$$

can be shown to hold for vector products.

The Moment of a Force

In Fig. 19.11, O is a fixed point, $\mathbf{P}$ is a force vector through a point A where $\overrightarrow{OA} = \mathbf{r}$ and the angle from $\overrightarrow{OA}$ to $\mathbf{P}$ is θ. The line ON is the perpendicular from O on to the line of action of $\mathbf{P}$. *The moment of* $\mathbf{P}$

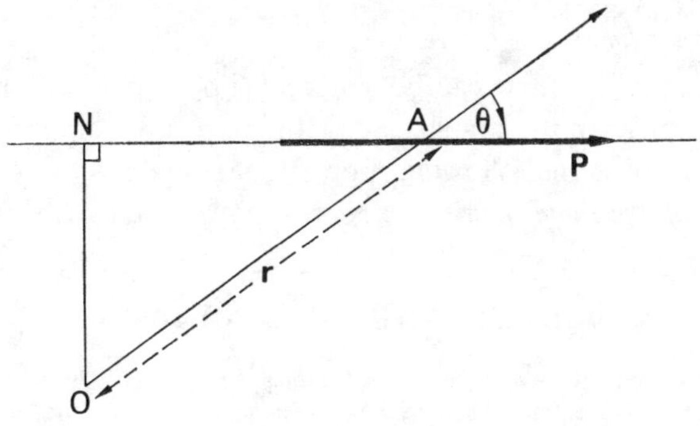

FIG. 19.11

about O *is defined as the vector* $\mathbf{r}\times\mathbf{P}$. In the case shown in Fig. 19.11 this vector is perpendicular to the paper and directed into the paper.

The magnitude of the moment so defined is $Pr \sin\theta = P\,.\,\mathrm{ON}$, a result which is independent of the choice of A and which is consistent with the definition of moment about an axis given in § 19.2. With this definition the moment of a force about a point can be represented by a vector at right angles to the plane containing the force and the point.

Varignon's theorem. If **P** and **Q** are two forces acting through the point A and **R** is their resultant, and if **r** is the position vector of A with respect to O, then the moment of **R** about O is

$$\mathbf{r}\times\mathbf{R} = \mathbf{r}\times(\mathbf{P}+\mathbf{Q}) = \mathbf{r}\times\mathbf{P}+\mathbf{r}\times\mathbf{Q}.$$

This result implies that *the moment of the vector sum of two forces about a point is equal to the sum of the moments of the forces about the point.* The result can be extended by induction to relate to the vector sum of any number of forces, and it is the three-dimensional extension of the result obtained for coplanar forces in § 19.2.

The moment of a force about a point can therefore be represented by a free vector in a direction at right angles to the plane containing the force and the point, and the sum of such moments can be obtained by the laws of vector addition.

Couples as Vectors

It follows that a couple can be represented by a free vector perpendicular to the plane of the couple, and, with this method of representation, we deduce at once the following property of couples:

Couples of the same moment in parallel planes are equivalent.

MISCELLANEOUS EXERCISES XIX

1. Forces of magnitudes P, Q, R, S act along the sides $\overrightarrow{AB}$, $\overrightarrow{BC}$, $\overrightarrow{CD}$, $\overrightarrow{DA}$ of a square of side $2a$. Prove that the sum of the moments about (x, y) of the forces is

$$a(P+Q+R+S)-(Q-S)\,x-(R-P)\,y,$$

where the origin is at the centre of the square, and the axes of x, y are parallel to the sides $\overrightarrow{AB}$, $\overrightarrow{AD}$ respectively.

Deduce that, if the forces are not in equilibrium, the equation of the line of action of their resultant is

$$(Q-S)\,x+(R-P)\,y = a(P+Q+R+S),$$

and that, if the forces are in equilibrium then

$$P = -Q = R = -S. \qquad \text{(O.C.)}$$

2. ABCD is a rectangle in which AB is 4 m and BC is 3 m. Forces p, q, r newtons act along DC, CB and BD respectively, the directions of the forces being indicated by the order of the letters. The sum of the moments of the forces about B is 15 J, the sum of the moments of the forces about C is 24 J and the sum of the resolved parts of the forces parallel to BC is zero. Calculate p, q and r and find the resultant of the three forces p, q and r in magnitude and direction. Find where the resultant of the three forces cuts AD produced.

3. Forces P, $2P$, $3P$, $4P$ act along the sides AB, BC, CD, DA of a square of side a. Determine the point of BC about which the moment of these forces is zero and find the magnitude and line of action of the single force which is statically equivalent to them. (O.C.)

4. Forces $4P$, P, and $2P$ act along the sides $\overrightarrow{BC}$, $\overrightarrow{CA}$, and $\overrightarrow{BA}$ respectively of an equilateral triangle ABC of side a. Prove that the system is equivalent to a force $3\sqrt{3}P$ in the direction $\overrightarrow{DE}$, where D is the point in BC at a distance $\frac{1}{3}a$ from B and E is the point in CA at a distance $\frac{1}{3}a$ from C.

Prove also that, if the given system of forces is equivalent to a certain force R along $\overrightarrow{BA}$ and a force S along $\overrightarrow{AC}$ together with a couple G in the sense ABC, then $R = 6P$, $S = 3P$, and $G = 2\sqrt{3}aP$. (O.C.)

5. Two vectors are represented by $\overrightarrow{AB}$, $\overrightarrow{AC}$, and D is the point on BC such that $\overrightarrow{BD} = k\overrightarrow{DC}$, where k is a scalar. Show that

$$\overrightarrow{AB}+k\overrightarrow{AC} = (1+k)\,\overrightarrow{AD}.$$

(i) In a triangle ABC the points D, E, F divide BC, CA, AB so that

$$\overrightarrow{BD} = k\overrightarrow{DC}, \quad \overrightarrow{CE} = k\overrightarrow{EA}, \quad \overrightarrow{AF} = k\overrightarrow{FB}.$$

Prove that $\overrightarrow{AD}+\overrightarrow{BE}+\overrightarrow{CF} = \mathbf{0}$.

(ii) Three forces are represented by $\overrightarrow{AL}$, $\overrightarrow{BM}$, $\overrightarrow{CN}$, where L, M, N are the points in the sides BC, CA, AB of a triangle such that

$$\overrightarrow{BL} = 2\overrightarrow{LC}, \quad 2\overrightarrow{CM} = 3\overrightarrow{MA}, \quad \overrightarrow{AN} = 2\overrightarrow{NB}.$$

Show that the resultant force is parallel to AC. (N.)

6. The moments of a system of coplanar forces about the points (2, 1), (−3, 4) and (1, −3) are 11, −15 and 15 units respectively. Find the magnitude and the equation of the line of action of the force acting at the point (3, 2) which, together with the given system, constitute a couple.

Show that the moment of the couple is 13 units. (O.C.)

7. The lines of action of two forces P and Q are along $\overrightarrow{OA}$ and $\overrightarrow{OB}$; prove that the component along $\overrightarrow{OC}$ of the resultant of the two forces is equal to the algebraic sum of the components of P and Q along $\overrightarrow{OC}$.

ABC is a triangular lamina in which AB $= 7a$, BC $= 3a$ and CA $= 5a$; forces $3P$, P and $3P$ act along the sides $\overrightarrow{AB}$, $\overrightarrow{CB}$, and $\overrightarrow{CA}$ respectively. Find the magnitude of the resultant of the forces, the angle which its line of action makes with $\overrightarrow{AB}$, and the point O in which its line of action meets AB.

If the lamina can rotate freely in its own plane about A, find the magnitude of the couple which can maintain the lamina at rest. (O.C.)

8. ABCD is a trapezium with AB parallel to DC. Show that forces represented in magnitude, direction and line of action by the sides AD, DC, CB, BA and the diagonals AC and BD have a resultant represented in magnitude and direction by 2EF, where E and F are the middle points of AB and CD respectively. (L.)

9. Given a constant k and a triangle ABC with sides of lengths a, b, c, find (i) the resultant of a force ka along BC and a force kc along AB, (ii) the resultant of a force ka along BC and a force kc along BA. Give the magnitude and line of action in each case.

Prove that a force $2ka$ along BC and a force kc along BA are equivalent to a force $3k$BD along BD, where D is a point on CA such that AD $=$ 2DC. (O.C.)

10. A square ABCD has its vertices at the points $(-a, -a)$, $(a, -a)$, (a, a), $(-a, a)$; forces P, Q, R, S act along and in the directions AB, BC, CD, DA. Prove that the forces are equivalent to two forces, parallel to the axes and acting at the point (x, y), together with a couple of moment

$$a(P+Q+R+S)-x(Q-S)+y(P-R).$$

Prove that, unless $P = R$ and $Q = S$, the forces P, Q, R, S are equivalent to a single force and find the equation of the line along which this force acts. (O.C.)

11. Two forces P and Q acting at a point have a resultant whose magnitude is Q. If P is reversed in direction, the magnitude of the resultant is $\frac{5}{3}Q$. Find

(i) the ratio of P to Q,

(ii) the cosine of the original angle between the forces. (O.C.)

12. Forces of P and Q newtons act along the diagonals $\overrightarrow{AC}$ and $\overrightarrow{BD}$ respectively of a square ABCD, and a force of 2 N acts along $\overrightarrow{AB}$. The resultant of the three forces is a couple. Find the values of P and Q.

The resultant of these three forces, together with an additional force whose line of action passes through the centre of the square, is a force whose line of action bisects BC and CD. Find the magnitude and direction of the additional force.

13. Forces of magnitudes pb, qa, rb, and sa act along the sides $\overrightarrow{AB}$, $\overrightarrow{BC}$, $\overrightarrow{CD}$, and $\overrightarrow{DA}$, respectively, of a rectangle ABCD in which the lengths of AD and AB are respectively a and b; E is the mid-point of AD and F is a point on DC such that DF $= b/3$. If the resultant of the forces acts along $\overrightarrow{FE}$, prove that $q+r$ is positive and find p and s in terms of q and r. (O.C.)

14. Forces P, $4P$, $2P$, $6P$ act along the sides AB, BC, CD, DA of a square ABCD. Find the magnitude of their resultant, and prove that it meets AD produced at a point E, such that

$$\text{AE} : \text{DE} = 6 : 5. \qquad \text{(O.C.)}$$

15. A rigid rhombus ABCD has acute angles θ at A and C. Forces each of magnitude F act on the rhombus along AD and DC, and a force P acts along BA. Show that the resultant R of these three forces acts through the point E on BA produced, where AE $=$ BA.

If the force P is varied in magnitude while the forces F remain fixed, find the value of P when R is least, and show that R is then of magnitude $F \sin \theta$. (N.)

16. A horizontal square plate ABCD lies on a smooth horizontal table and is kept in equilibrium by a force P parallel to CB through the point of intersection of the diagonals and in the direction C to B, by a force Q along the edge CD in the direction C to D, and by a horizontal force R at A. Find, in terms of P, the magnitudes of the forces Q and R. (N.)

17. OAB is an equilateral triangle of side a; C is the midpoint of OA. Forces $4P$, P, and P act along the sides $\overrightarrow{OB}$, $\overrightarrow{BA}$, and $\overrightarrow{AO}$ respectively. If $\overrightarrow{OA}$ and $\overrightarrow{OY}$ (parallel to CB) are taken as x and y axes prove that the resultant R of the forces is $3P$ and that the equation of its line of action is

$$3y = \sqrt{3}(3x+a).$$

Prove also that R is equivalent to a like parallel force R through the centroid of the triangle together with a couple of moment $aP\sqrt{3}$, and state the sense of the latter. (O.C.)

18. ABC and A′B′C′ are two coplanar triangles, whose centroids are at G and G′. Forces represented in magnitude and *direction* by AA′, BB′, and CC′ act at A, B, C respectively. Show that they are equivalent to a single force represented in magnitude and *direction* by 3GG′. (O.C.)

19. Forces $5P$, $6P$, $7P$ act along the sides $\overrightarrow{BC}$, $\overrightarrow{CA}$, $\overrightarrow{AB}$ of an equilateral triangle ABC of side $6a$. If the system is replaced by a single force F acting through the middle point of BC together with a couple, find the moment of the couple and show that the magnitude of F is $P\sqrt{3}$. Show also that the line of action of F makes an angle of 30° with CB. (N.)

20. Forces of magnitude $3P$, $8P$, $2P$, and $4P$ act along the sides $\overrightarrow{AB}$, $\overrightarrow{BC}$, $\overrightarrow{DC}$, and $\overrightarrow{AD}$ respectively of a square lamina of side $2a$. Find the magnitude of the resultant and the point of intersection of its line of action with AB.

The lamina is laid on a smooth horizontal table and it can turn freely about a point X on BD. Prove that, if it is in equilibrium under the system of forces, the distance of X from B is $\frac{12}{17}a\sqrt{2}$. (O.C.)

CHAPTER XX

THE EQUILIBRIUM OF RIGID BODIES

20.1. Conditions of Equilibrium

In Volume I, § 2.8 we discussed the conditions of equilibrium for a body acted upon by three forces only and in § 6.3 we discussed the equilibrium of a rigid body acted upon by a system of coplanar forces. From the conclusions of Chapter XIX of this volume, together with the statement concerning the equilibrium of a rigid body made in § 19.4, we now classify sets of conditions, each necessary and sufficient to ensure the equilibrium of a rigid body, as follows.

1. *For a Rigid Body Acted Upon by Two Forces Only*

The forces must be equal in magnitude and opposite in direction, and they must act in the same straight line.

2. *For a Rigid Body Acted Upon by Three Non-parallel Forces Only*

(a) The forces must act at a point, and

(b) The vector sum of the forces must be zero.

Condition (b) may be tested by any one of: the triangle of vectors, Lami's theorem, the law of the resolved parts.

3. *For a Rigid Body Acted Upon by Any System of Parallel Forces*

EITHER (a) the sum of the forces, considered as directed quantities, must be zero, and

(b) the sum of the moments of the forces about an arbitrary point in the plane must be zero,

OR the sum of the moments of the forces about any two points of the plane, which do not lie in a line parallel to the forces, separately vanish.

4. *For a Rigid Body Acted Upon by Any System of Forces*

(This is the general case which includes the three special cases discussed above.)

EITHER (a) the vector sum of the forces must be zero, and

(b) the sum of the moments of the forces about an arbitrary point in the plane must be zero,

OR the sum of the moments of the forces about any three non-collinear points in the plane must separately vanish [example 2, § 19.3],

OR any other set of conditions, which ensure that the vector sum of the forces is zero and that the moment-sum of the forces about *every point* in the plane is zero, must be satisfied.

The examples and exercises which follow involve these principles and also, in some cases, the principles of friction enunciated in Volume I, Chapter IX.

Example 1. A uniform straight rod has one end resting on a fixed smooth horizontal cylinder and the other end in contact with a smooth vertical wall whose plane is parallel to the axis of the cylinder. In equilibrium the rod makes an angle φ with the horizontal and the radius of the cylinder through the point where the rod rests on the cylinder makes an angle θ with the horizontal. Prove that $\tan\theta = 2\tan\varphi$. (C.S.)

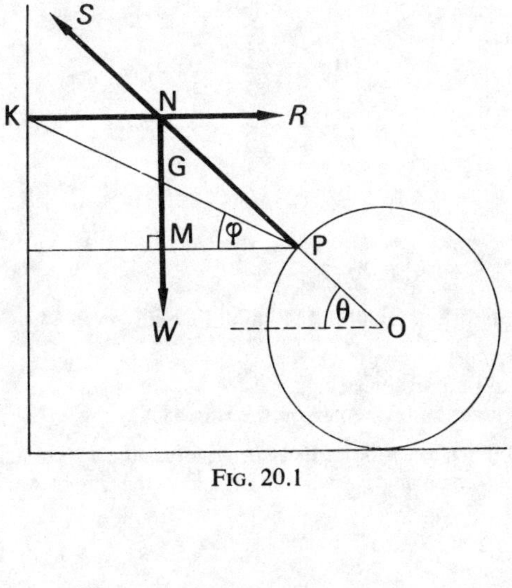

FIG. 20.1

The rod PK is in equilibrium under the action of the following three forces, as illustrated in Fig. 20.1,

(a) its weight W acting through its mid-point G,
(b) the normal reaction R of the wall on the rod at K,
(c) the normal reaction S of the cylinder on the rod at P.

The lines of action of these three forces are therefore concurrent.
If these lines meet at N and NG produced meets the horizontal through P at M,

$$\tan\theta = \text{NM/MP}, \quad \tan\varphi = \text{GM/MP},$$

and, since triangles KNG and PMG are congruent, NG = GM.
Therefore, NM = 2GM and hence $\tan\theta = 2\tan\varphi$.

Example 2. A thin uniform heavy ring hangs in equilibrium over a small rough peg. To the lowest point of the ring a string is attached and pulled in a horizontal direction with steadily increasing force, the ring and string being in one vertical plane. The angle of friction at the peg being λ ($< \sin^{-1}\frac{1}{3}$), show that slipping is about to commence there when the diameter through the peg is inclined at an angle $\frac{1}{2}\{\sin^{-1}(3\sin\lambda)+\lambda\}$ to the vertical, and that if $\lambda > \sin^{-1}\frac{1}{3}$, slipping will never occur whatever the tension in the string. (N.)

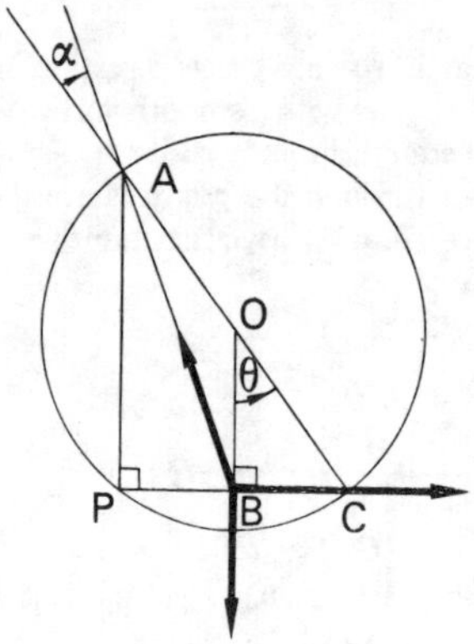

FIG. 20.2

The ring is in equilibrium under the action of three forces:

(a) its weight through its centre O, Fig. 20.2,
(b) the horizontal pull on the string,
(c) the *resultant* reaction of the peg on the ring at A.

For equilibrium the lines of action of these three forces must be concurrent and, if the resultant reaction makes an angle α with the normal to the ring at A, and OA makes an angle θ with the vertical,

$$\sin(\theta-\alpha) = \mathrm{PB/AB}, \quad (\Delta\mathrm{APB})$$

and

$$\frac{\mathrm{PB}}{\mathrm{AB}} = \frac{\mathrm{BC}}{\mathrm{AB}} = \frac{\sin\alpha}{\cos\theta}, \quad (\Delta\mathrm{ABC}).$$

$$\therefore \sin(\theta-\alpha)\cos\theta = \sin\alpha.$$

$$\therefore \tfrac{1}{2}\{\sin(2\theta-\alpha)-\sin\alpha\} = \sin\alpha.$$

$$\therefore \sin(2\theta-\alpha) = 3\sin\alpha.$$

$$\therefore \theta = \tfrac{1}{2}\{\sin^{-1}(3\sin\alpha)+\alpha\}.$$

Slipping is about to commence when $\alpha = \lambda$ (the angle of friction), i.e. when

$$\theta = \tfrac{1}{2}\{\sin^{-1}(3\sin\lambda)+\lambda\}.$$

In order that this value of θ should exist $3\sin\lambda \leq 1$. [The equation $\sin^{-1}x = a$ has no real solution when $x > 1$.] Therefore, if $\lambda > \sin^{-1}(\frac{1}{3})$, slipping will never occur however large the tension in the string may be.

Example 3. A uniform rod of length $2l$ rests on a rough horizontal table. A steadily increasing horizontal force T is applied to the rod perpendicular to its length at a point P distant y from its mid-point O. Show that, if the pressure between the table and the rod be assumed to be uniformly distributed along the rod, the rod will begin to turn about a point Q of itself at a distance x from O, where P and Q are on opposite sides of O, and x satisfies the equation $x^2+2yx-l^2 = 0$.

Show also that, as y varies, the least value of x is $l(\sqrt{2}-1)$. (N.)

If the point about which the rod AB begins to turn is the instantaneous centre of rotation I, Fig. 20.3 (i), and N is the foot of the perpendicular from I to AB, the small element K of the rod, between N and B, begins to move in a direction KC at right angles to IK as shown in that figure. *Before motion begins*, the direction of friction acting on this element is therefore in the direction CK. The component parallel to AB of this force is therefore in the direction A to B. Therefore the component parallel to AB of the force of friction acting on every element of the rod between N and B is in the direction A to B. Similarly the component parallel to AB of the force of friction acting on every element of the rod between N and A is in the direction A to B. Therefore, for equilibrium, the component parallel to AB of the force of friction acting on each element of the rod is zero. This can only be so if I is in AB or AB produced.

Figure 20.3 (ii) shows the forces acting on the rod AB in the vertical plane through the rod. These are the weights of the portions AQ, QB of the rod and the corresponding actions R and S of the table on AQ, QB. Because the rod is uniform and the pressure of the table is uniformly distributed along the rod, R and S will act at the mid-points N and M of AQ and QB respectively and

$$R = \frac{l+x}{2l}W, \quad S = \frac{l-x}{2l}W.$$

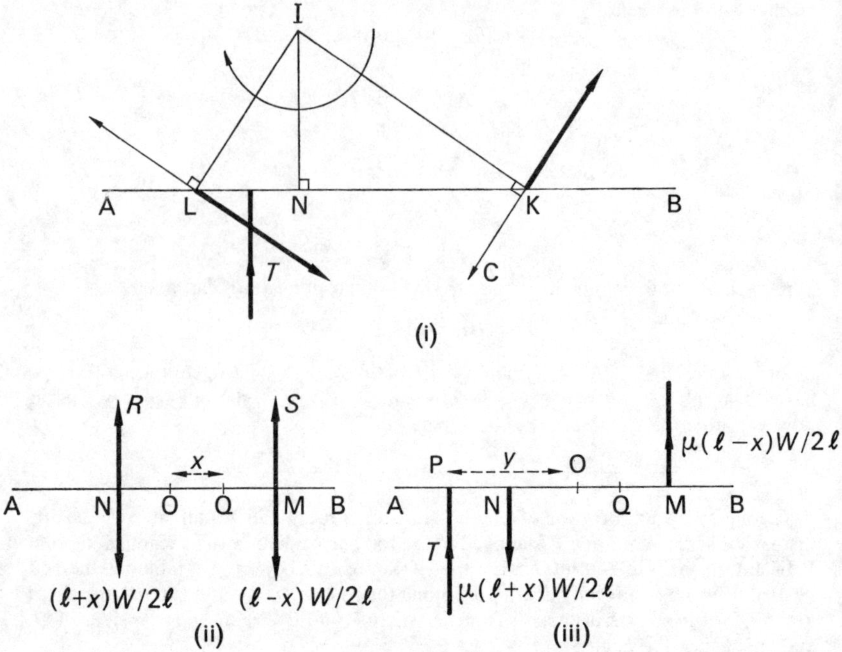

FIG. 20.3

Figure 20.3 (iii) shows the forces acting on the rod AB in the plane of the table, when the rod is on the point of rotating about Q. Since the portion QB will start to rotate in a clockwise direction about Q, limiting friction

$$\frac{\mu(l-x)W}{2l},$$

where μ is the coefficient of friction between the rod and the table, will act as shown at M, and similarly limiting friction

$$\frac{\mu(l+x)W}{2l}$$

will act as shown at N. Since the rod is in equilibrium, the sum of the moments of the forces in this plane about P is zero, and therefore

$$\frac{\mu(l-x)W}{2l} \cdot \text{MP} - \frac{\mu(l+x)W}{2l} \cdot \text{NP} = 0,$$

i.e.

$$l(\text{MP}-\text{NP}) - x(\text{MP}+\text{NP}) = 0.$$

But $$\text{MP} = (l+x+2y)/2, \quad \text{NP} = (x+2y-l)/2.$$

$$\therefore\ l^2-x(x+2y) = 0,$$

i.e. $$x^2+2xy-l^2 = 0.$$

Hence, since x must be positive,

$$x = -y+\sqrt{(y^2+l^2)},$$

$$\therefore\ \frac{dx}{dy} = -1+\frac{y}{\sqrt{(y^2+l^2)}}$$

and is, therefore, < 0 for all values of y. It follows that x decreases as y increases and the least value of x corresponds with the greatest possible value of y, i.e. with $y = l$.

The least value of x is therefore $-l+\sqrt{(2l^2)} = l(\sqrt{2}-1)$.

Example 4. A uniform solid hemisphere rests with its curved surface against a rough horizontal plane and against a rough vertical plane, the radius through the mass-centre being in a vertical plane perpendicular to each of the other planes. If the coefficient of friction at the horizontal plane is μ, and that at the vertical plane μ', show that in the position of limiting equilibrium the radius through the mass-centre will be inclined to the vertical at an angle θ given by

$$\sin\theta = \frac{8\mu(1+\mu')}{3(1+\mu\mu')}.$$

Show also that, when $\mu = \mu'$, the hemisphere will rest at any inclination if $\mu \geqq \frac{1}{5}(\sqrt{31}-4)$. (N.)

Figure 20.4 shows the forces acting on the hemisphere in the position of limiting equilibrium. Since slipping at one contact involves slipping also at the other contact,

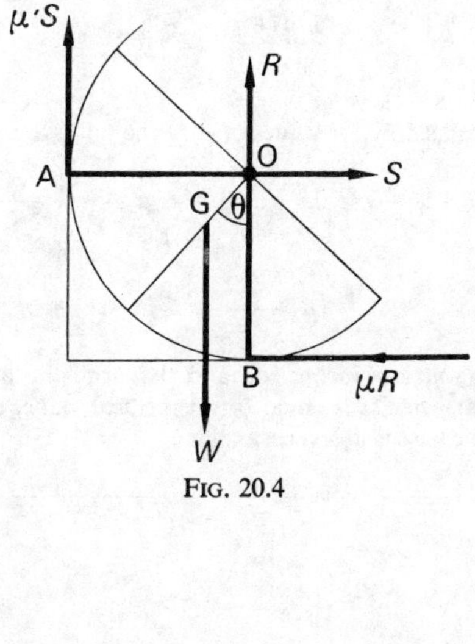

FIG. 20.4

friction is limiting at both contacts in the position of limiting equilibrium. Necessary and sufficient conditions of equilibrium are:

1. The sum of the vertical components vanishes; i.e.

$$R+\mu' S = W.$$

2. The sum of the horizontal components vanishes, i.e.

$$S = \mu R.$$

3. The sum of the moments about O vanishes; i.e.

$$\mu' Sr+\mu Rr = W.\tfrac{3}{8}r \sin\theta,$$

where r is the radius of the hemisphere. (The weight of the hemisphere acts through the centre of gravity G on the axis of symmetry distant $\frac{3}{8}r$ from the centre of the hemisphere.)

From (1) and (2),

$$R = \frac{W}{1+\mu\mu'}, \quad S = \frac{\mu W}{1+\mu\mu'}.$$

Therefore from (3),

$$\frac{\mu\mu' W}{1+\mu\mu'}+\frac{\mu W}{1+\mu\mu'} = \frac{3}{8} W \sin\theta.$$

$$\therefore \sin\theta = \frac{8\mu(1+\mu')}{3(1+\mu\mu')}.$$

If $\mu = \mu'$, the position of limiting equilibrium is given by

$$\sin\theta = \frac{8\mu(1+\mu)}{3(1+\mu^2)}.$$

Since $\sin\theta \leqq 1$ this position can only exist provided that

$$\frac{8\mu(1+\mu)}{3(1+\mu^2)} \leqq 1,$$

i.e. provided that $5\mu^2+8\mu-3 \leqq 0$.

This inequality obtains only for values of $\mu \leqq$ the positive root of

$$5\mu^2+8\mu-3 = 0, \quad \text{i.e. for} \quad \mu \leqq \frac{-4+\sqrt{31}}{5}.$$

It follows that if

$$\mu > \frac{-4+\sqrt{31}}{5}$$

friction is not limiting at any inclination and therefore the hemisphere rests at all inclinations. Note that when μ is equal to this critical value, equilibrium is limiting at $\theta = \frac{1}{2}\pi$, i.e. when the base is in a vertical plane.

EXERCISES 20.1

1. Two horizontal wires inclined to one another at an angle 2α are attached to the top of a vertical post movable about its lower end, which is fixed. The post is supported by a stay inclined at an angle β to the vertical and fastened to a point two-thirds of the way up the post. Find the tension in the stay when the tensions in the wires are both T. Find also the horizontal and vertical components of reaction at the lower end of the post. (O.C.)

2. A uniform lamina in the form of an equilateral triangle of side l rests in a vertical plane perpendicular to a smooth vertical wall, one vertex being in contact with the wall and another attached to a point in the wall by a string of length l. Show that in the position of equilibrium the angle between the string and the vertical is $\cot^{-1}(3\sqrt{3})$. (L.)

3. A uniform rod, of mass M, rests partly within and partly without a thin smooth hemispherical bowl, of mass $3M\sqrt{3}$ and radius a, which itself rests on a horizontal plane. The centre of gravity of the bowl is at the middle point of its radius of symmetry. If the rod is inclined at an angle of 30° to the horizontal, prove that the plane of the rim of the bowl is inclined at an angle θ to the horizontal, where $\cot\theta = 4\sqrt{3}$. Show also that the length of the rod is $12a/7$. (N.)

4. A thin rod AB, whose centre of gravity G is not at its midpoint, rests inside a rough spherical bowl in a vertical plane through the centre O of the bowl. If the rod is horizontal when it is in limiting equilibrium with B about to slip down, show that

$$AG : GB = \tan(\alpha+\lambda) : \tan(\alpha-\lambda),$$

where λ is the angle of friction at each end of the rod and 2α is the angle AOB. (L.)

5. A uniform rod PQ, of weight w, rests in contact with a smooth fixed right circular cylinder whose axis is horizontal, the vertical plane through the rod being perpendicular to the axis. The ends P, Q of the rod are fastened by strings to the cylinder and, when the rod is in equilibrium, the strings are *horizontal* and tangential to the cylinder. The string with the shorter horizontal length is uppermost. If the rod makes an angle $\theta\,(<\pi/2)$ with the horizontal, show that the lower string will not be taut unless

$$\cos^2\theta+\cos\theta < 1. \qquad \text{(L.)}$$

6. The angles B, C of a triangular lamina ABC, of negligible mass, are 45° and 30° respectively. The lamina hangs freely in a vertical plane from the vertex A, which is fixed. When masses M_1, M_2 are attached to the vertices B and C respectively the internal bisector of the angle A is vertical. If $M_2 = 5$ kg, find the reaction at the vertex A.

7. A uniform rod of mass M and length l rests on a rough horizontal table, the coefficient of friction between the rod and the table being μ. A gradually increasing horizontal force is applied perpendicularly at one end of the rod. Assuming that the vertical reaction is distributed uniformly along the rod, show that the rod begins to turn about a point distant $l/\sqrt{2}$ from the end at which the force is applied, and find the corresponding magnitude of the applied force. (N.)

8. A uniform circular hoop of mass M rests on a rough rail which is inclined at an angle of 30° to the horizontal. The hoop and the rail are in the same vertical plane. The hoop is held in equilibrium by means of a string which leaves the hoop tangentially and is inclined at 60° to the horizontal, this angle being measured in the same sense as the angle of inclination of the rail. Show that the coefficient of friction between the rail and the hoop is not less than $\frac{1}{2}(\sqrt{3}-1)$, and find the tension in the string. (N.)

9. The extremities of a light string are attached to the ends A and B of a rod AB, whose centroid is at G, where AG > GB. The string is placed over a smooth peg C and the rod hangs in equilibrium, inclined at an angle θ to the vertical. Prove that CG is the internal bisector of the angle ACB and that A is below the level of B.

BC and AC make an angle φ with the vertical. Prove that

$$\text{AB} \tan \varphi = (\text{AG}-\text{GB}) \tan \theta. \qquad \text{(O.C.)}$$

10. A light inextensible string of length $a\sqrt{3}$ has its ends A, B fastened to the ends of a light rod AB of length $a\sqrt{2}$. A particle C of weight W is attached to A and B by means of two equal strings AC and BC, each of length a. The string of length $a\sqrt{3}$ passes over a fixed smooth peg P, from which the system hangs in a vertical plane, the particle being below the rod. Prove that PA and PB make equal angles with the vertical.

By taking each of these equal angles to be 45°, prove that there is an unsymmetrical position of equilibrium in which the string AC makes an angle of 15° with the vertical. (O.C.)

11. A uniform circular cylinder with its plane ends normal to its axis rests horizontally upon two equally rough inclined planes which are fixed in opposite senses at an angle θ to the horizontal, the axis of the cylinder being parallel to the line of intersection of the planes. A couple G is applied to the cylinder tending to turn it about its axis. If w is the weight of the cylinder, a its radius and λ the angle of friction, show that when the cylinder is about to slip

$$G = \tfrac{1}{2}wa \sin 2\lambda \sec \theta. \qquad \text{(N.)}$$

12. An elastic string of natural length $3a$ and modulus of elasticity kW has its ends fixed at the same horizontal level at a distance $3a$ apart, and equal weights W are suspended from points distant a and $2a$ from one end. Show that in the position of equilibrium the two end portions of the string are inclined at an angle θ to the horizontal given by $3 \cot \theta = 2k(1-\cos \theta)$, and that the length of the middle portion is $a(5-2\cos\theta)/3$.

Show that if k is large θ is approximately $(3/k)^{1/3}$. (L.)

20.2. Hinged Bodies

Smooth Hinges

In § 2.9 of Volume I we stated that a body is smoothly hinged when the action of the hinge on the body is a single force through the centre of the hinge. Fig. 20.5 (i) shows two rods AB and AC smoothly hinged

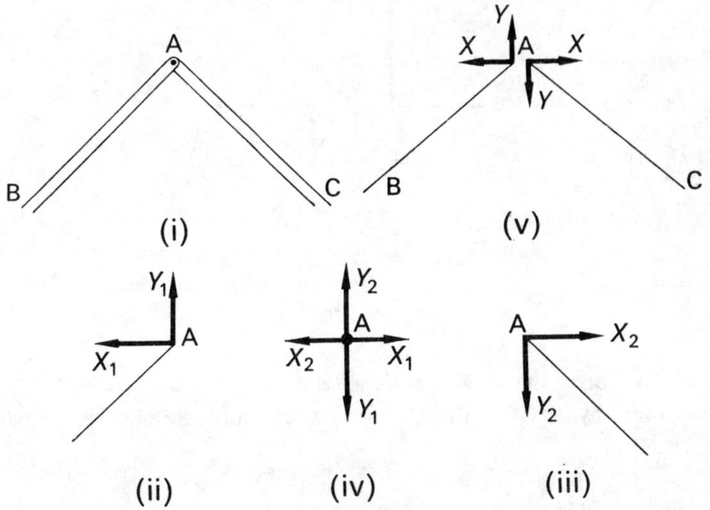

FIG. 20.5

together at A. The hinge acts on the rod AB at A with a force, the components X_1, Y_1 of which are shown in Fig. 20.5 (ii), and the rod AB reacts on the hinge with an equal and opposite force. Similarly the hinge acts on the rod AC at A with a force of components X_2, Y_2, Fig. 20.5 (iii), and the rod AC reacts on the hinge with an equal and opposite force. It follows that if the hinge is in equilibrium, Fig. 20.5 (iv), $X_1 = X_2$ and $Y_1 = Y_2$ *provided that no other force is acting on the hinge.* If this latter condition is fulfilled, the forces can be represented as an action and an equal and opposite reaction between the rods themselves, Fig. 20.5 (v).

Rough Hinges

If one body is joined to another by a hinge which is not smooth, the forces on the hinge at the surface of contact between the hinge and the body do not pass through the centre of the hinge and the resultant of these forces does not, in general, pass through the centre of the hinge. This resultant can, however, be replaced *by a single force acting through the centre of the hinge and a couple* (§ 19.3). In cases where no other forces

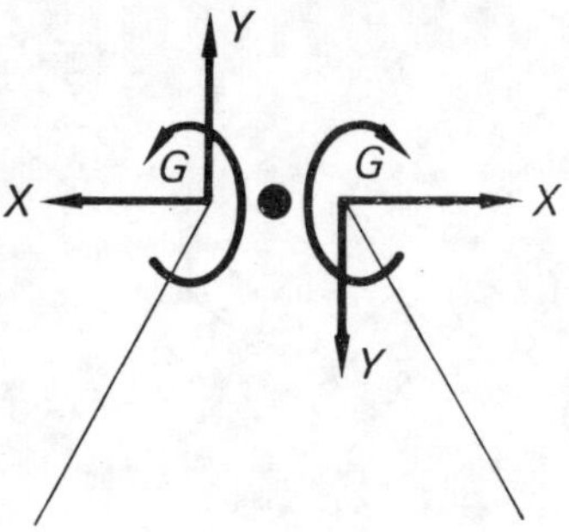

FIG. 20.6

act on the hinge, the action of the hinge on the two bodies can then be represented by equal and opposite forces and couples as shown in Fig. 20.6.

The Action of One Part of a Body on Another

Figure 20.7 shows a uniform horizontal rod AB fixed to a vertical wall at A. The part CB of the rod is in equilibrium under the action of

(i) its weight acting through its mid-point, and
(ii) the action of the part AC.

Equilibrium is only possible in this case if (ii) consists of an upward vertical force w at C and a couple of moment $\frac{1}{2}w$. CB counterclockwise, where w is the weight of the part CB. The part of the rod CB will act

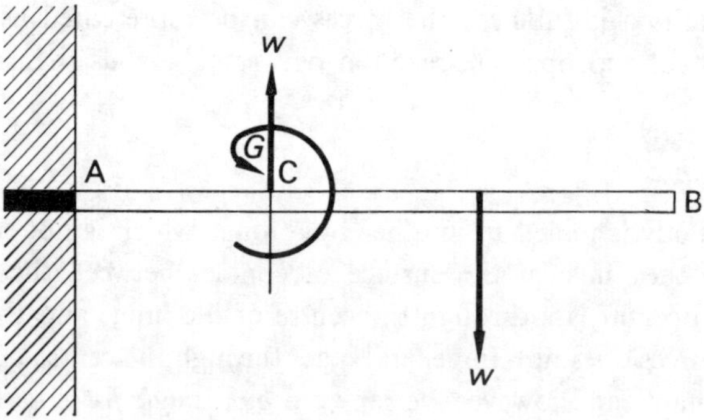

FIG. 20.7

with an equal and opposite force and an equal and opposite couple on the part of the rod AC. This is a particular case which illustrates the general principle which must be applied in considering equilibrium in such problems (see Chapter XXIV, § 24.1).

20.3. Problems of Equilibrium Involving More than One Body

When there are two or more bodies concerned in a problem of equilibrium, there are, in general, three conditions of equilibrium for each of the bodies. There are also three conditions of equilibrium for the system as a whole, and there are three conditions of equilibrium for any part of the system considered as a whole. Clearly, all these sets of conditions are not independent sets, since, for example, the equilibrium of each body of the system, separately, implies the equilibrium of the system as a whole. In consequence, the solution of problems involving two or more bodies involves the careful selection from the equations of equilibrium of those equations which are independent and which constitute the minimum number necessary to determine whatever factors of the system are required.

Example 1. Two uniform rods AB, BC, of lengths $2a$, $2b$, and of weights $2W$, $3W$ respectively, are smoothly jointed at B. They are in equilibrium in a vertical plane with A resting on a rough horizontal plane and C resting against a smooth vertical guide. The point A is further from the vertical guide than B and α is the acute angle between AB and the horizontal plane. The angle between CB and the downward vertical at C is β. Show that

$$3 \tan \alpha \tan \beta = 8.$$

If μ is the coefficient of friction between the rod AB and the horizontal plane, show that $\beta \leqq \tan^{-1}(10\mu/3)$. (N.)

Figure 20.8 shows the forces acting on each of the rods.

For the equilibrium of the whole system,

(1) the sum of the vertical components is zero, $T = 5W$,

(2) the sum of the horizontal components is zero, $S = F$,

(3) the sum of the moments about A is zero,

$$2Wa \cos \alpha + 3W(2a \cos \alpha + b \sin \beta) = S(2a \sin \alpha + 2b \cos \beta).$$

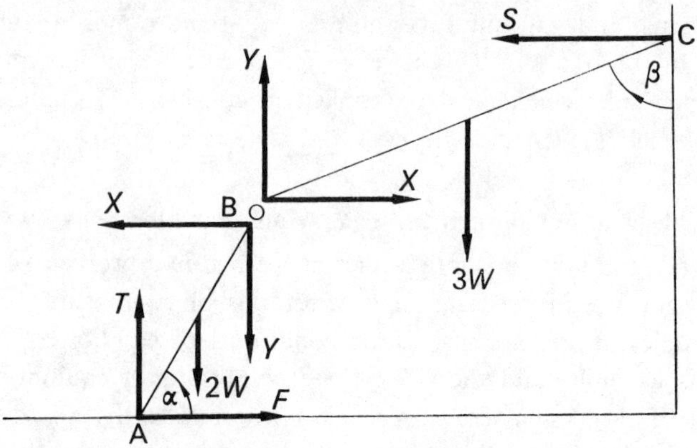

FIG. 20.8

For the equilibrium of the rod BC,

(4) the sum of the moments about B is zero,

$$S2b\cos\beta = 3Wb\sin\beta,$$

$$\therefore\ S = \frac{3W}{2}\tan\beta.$$

From equations (3) and (4),

$$2a\cos\alpha + 6a\cos\alpha + 3b\sin\beta = \tfrac{3}{2}(2a\sin\alpha + 2b\cos\beta)\tan\beta$$

and this simplifies to the result $3\tan\alpha\tan\beta = 8$.

Also, for the equilibrium of BC, $F/T \leqq \mu$.

$$\therefore\ \left(\frac{3W\tan\beta}{2}\right)\bigg/(5W) \leqq \mu,$$

i.e.

$$\tan\beta \leqq \frac{10\mu}{3},$$

and since for $0 \leqq \beta < \frac{1}{2}\pi$, $\tan\beta$ increases with β,

$$\therefore\ \beta \leqq \tan^{-1}(10\mu/3).$$

Example 2. A uniform circular cylinder of weight W, whose axis is horizontal, rests on a fixed plane inclined to the horizontal at an angle α. A uniform rod, also of weight W, rests in a horizontal position with one end on the highest generator of the cylinder and the other smoothly hinged to the plane. The rod lies in a vertical plane through the centre of gravity of the cylinder and perpendicular to its axis. The system is in equilibrium and the coefficient of friction between the rod and cylinder and also between the cylinder and inclined plane is μ. Show that the normal reaction of the rod on the cylinder has magnitude $\frac{1}{2}W$. Show also that the frictional forces acting on the cylinder are equal in magnitude.

Hence show that $\mu \geqq 3 \tan \frac{1}{2}\alpha$. (N.)

Figure 20.9 shows the forces acting on each of the rod and the cylinder. The rod is tangential to the cylinder, since the radius at the highest generator is vertical. At the point of contact of the rod with the cylinder, the forces exerted by the rod on the cylinder are equal and opposite to the forces exerted by the cylinder on the rod.

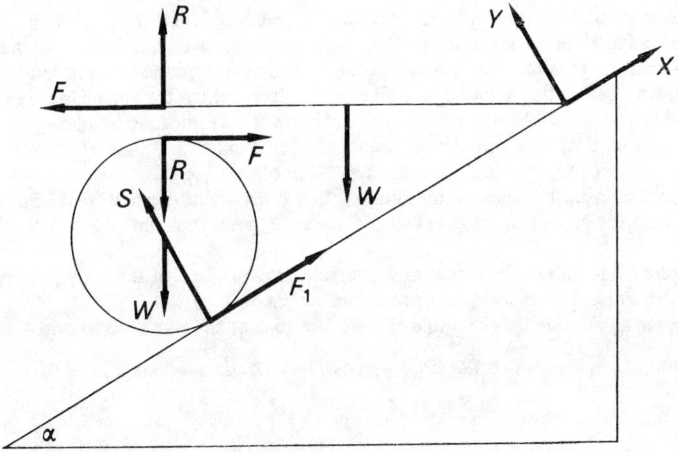

FIG. 20.9

For the equilibrium of the cylinder,
the sum of the moments about the axis is zero,

$$\therefore \; F = F_1.$$

For the equilibrium of the rod,
the sum of the moments about the hinge is zero,

$$\therefore \; R = \tfrac{1}{2}W.$$

Also, *for the equilibrium of the cylinder,* the sum of the components parallel to the plane is zero,

$$\therefore \; F_1 + F\cos\alpha = W\sin\alpha + R\sin\alpha,$$

i.e.

$$F_1(1+\cos\alpha) = \frac{3W}{2}\sin\alpha.$$

$$\therefore \; F_1 = \frac{3W\sin\alpha}{2(1+\cos\alpha)} = \frac{3W}{2}\tan\left(\frac{1}{2}\alpha\right).$$

Taking moments for the cylinder about its highest point,

$$Sa \sin\alpha = F_1 a(1+\cos\alpha); \quad \therefore\ S = \frac{3W}{2}.$$

Also for the equilibrium of the cylinder $F/R \leqq \mu$, $F_1/S \leqq \mu$.

$$\therefore\ \mu \geqq \text{the greater of} \quad \frac{F}{R} \quad \text{and} \quad \frac{F_1}{S},$$

$$\therefore\ \mu \geqq 3\tan(\tfrac{1}{2}\alpha).$$

***Example 3.** Two uniform rods AB and BC, each of length $2a$ and weight W, are maintained at right angles to each other by a stiff hinge at B. The friction at the hinge is such that the greatest couple which either rod can exert on the other has moment K. The end A is smoothly pivoted to a fixed point from which the rods hang. A vertical force F acting at C holds the rods in equilibrium with AB inclined at an angle φ to the downward vertical at A, and with C higher than B. Find F, and show that the moment of the reaction couple at B is $2Wa \sin\varphi/(1+\tan\varphi)$.

By considering the maximum value of this function of φ, show that equilibrium is possible for any value of φ between 0 and $\pi/2$, provided that $K \geqq Wa/\sqrt{2}$. (N.)

Figure 20.10 shows the forces and couple acting on each of the rods. The rod BC makes an angle $\frac{1}{2}\pi-\varphi$ with the upward vertical at B.

For the equilibrium of the whole system, the sum of the moments about A is zero,

$$\therefore\ Wa\sin\varphi + W(2a\sin\varphi + a\cos\varphi) - F(2a\sin\varphi + 2a\cos\varphi) = 0,$$

$$\therefore\ F = W(3\tan\varphi+1)/(2+2\tan\varphi).$$

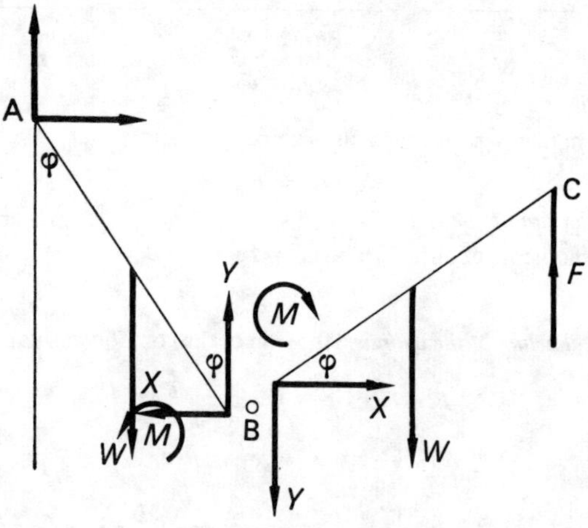

FIG. 20.10

For the equilibrium of the rod BC, the sum of the moments about B is zero,

$$\therefore\ M = F2a\cos\varphi - Wa\cos\varphi = Wa\left\{\frac{3\sin\varphi+\cos\varphi}{1+\tan\varphi} - \frac{\cos\varphi+\sin\varphi}{1+\tan\varphi}\right\}$$
$$= 2Wa\sin\varphi/(1+\tan\varphi).$$

$$\frac{dM}{d\varphi} = 2Wa\left\{\frac{\cos\varphi+\sin\varphi-\sin\varphi\sec^2\varphi}{(1+\tan\varphi)^2}\right\}$$
$$= 2Wa\left\{\frac{\cos^3\varphi-\sin^3\varphi}{(1+\tan\varphi)^2}\right\}\sec^2\varphi.$$

M therefore has a stationary value when $\tan^3\varphi = 1$, i.e. when $\varphi = \frac{1}{4}\pi$ for $0 \leqq \varphi \leqq \frac{1}{2}\pi$, and this stationary value is a maximum since $dM/d\varphi$ is positive when $\varphi < \frac{1}{4}\pi$ and negative when $\varphi > \frac{1}{4}\pi$ for values of φ in this range. This maximum value of M is $(2Wa\sin\frac{1}{4}\pi)/(1+\tan\frac{1}{4}\pi) = Wa/\sqrt{2}$. It follows that provided $K \geqq Wa/\sqrt{2}$ equilibrium is possible for all values of φ between 0 and $\frac{1}{2}\pi$.

***Example 4.** Two equal uniform solid rough cylinders, each of weight W, lie on a rough horizontal plane in contact along a generator of each. A horizontal force P is applied to one of the cylinders in a line through and at right angles to the axes of both cylinders. This line passes through the centres of gravity of the cylinders. The coefficient of friction between the cylinders is equal to μ and that between either cylinder and the plane is μ'. Show that while equilibrium is not broken the force of friction between each cylinder and the plane is equal to the force of friction between the two cylinders. Find the forces exerted by the cylinders on one another and the force exerted on each cylinder by the plane. Deduce that for equilibrium to be possible for any value of P, $\mu \geqq 1$, and find how equilibrium will be broken as P is gradually increased.

Figure 20.11 shows the vertical section through the centres of gravity A and B of the cylinders and also shows the forces acting on each of the cylinders.

For the equilibrium of each cylinder separately, the sum of the moments about the axis is zero,

$$\therefore\ F_1 = F_3 \quad \text{and} \quad F_2 = F_3.$$

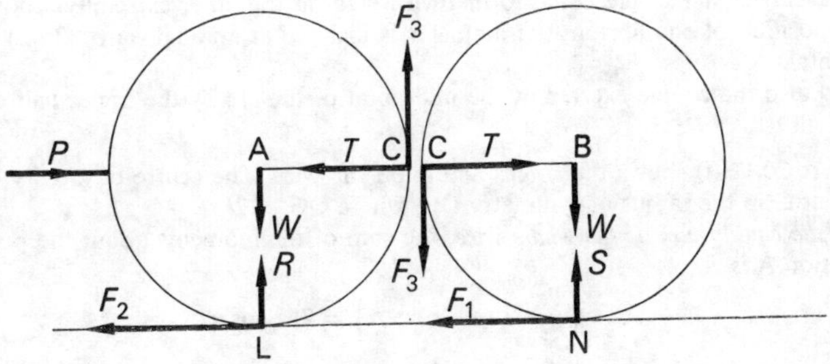

FIG. 20.11

Therefore the forces of friction at all contacts are equal and equal to F (say). Consideration of the horizontal components of the forces acting on the whole system shows that the frictional forces at the plane must act in the direction shown in order to balance P. Also, the sum of the horizontal components for each cylinder is zero and therefore

$$T = F = \tfrac{1}{2}P.$$

It follows that, whatever the value of P, for equilibrium at C, we must have $\mu \geqq F/T$, i.e. $\mu \geqq 1$. Further, if this condition obtains, there will not be slipping between the cylinders at C whatever the value of P. Equilibrium is therefore broken first by slipping at either L or N, the cylinder A rolling on the cylinder B at C.

The sum of the vertical components of the forces acting on each of the cylinders is zero, and therefore

$$R = W - F = W - \tfrac{1}{2}P,$$

$$S = W + F = W + \tfrac{1}{2}P.$$

$$\therefore \frac{F}{R} = \frac{x}{2-x} = \frac{2}{2-x} - 1, \quad \frac{F}{S} = \frac{x}{2+x} = 1 - \frac{2}{2+x},$$

where $x = P/W$. Therefore as x increases from 0 to 2, F/R increases from 0 without limit and F/S increases from 0 to $\frac{1}{2}$. Also

$$\frac{F}{R} - \frac{F}{S} = \frac{2x^2}{4-x^2}$$

and this expression is positive for $0 < x < 2$. It follows that, as P increases, friction becomes limiting and slipping takes place at L. In fact, as P increases, F/R approaches the critical value μ' at L and equilibrium is broken when

$$\frac{x}{2-x} > \mu', \quad \text{i.e. when} \quad P > \frac{2\mu' W}{1+\mu'}.$$

When equilibrium is broken, the cylinder A rotates counter-clockwise slipping at L, while the cylinder B rolls clockwise on the plane and the spheres roll on one another at C.

Example 5. A wire in the form of a semicircular arc hangs freely from one extremity and carries a particle equal to its own weight at the other extremity. Show that in the position of equilibrium the diameter is inclined at an angle $\tan^{-1}(3\pi/2)$ to the horizontal.

Find also the couple exerted at the mid-point of the arc by the upper half on the lower half. (N.)

Figure 20.12 (i) shows the forces acting on the wire. The centre of gravity of the wire is at G in the radius of symmetry OC, where $OG = 2r/\pi$.

For the equilibrium of the whole wire, the sum of the moments about the point of suspension A is zero,

$$\therefore w\left(\frac{2r}{\pi}\sin\alpha - r\cos\alpha\right) = 2wr\cos\alpha.$$

$$\therefore \tan\alpha = 3\pi/2.$$

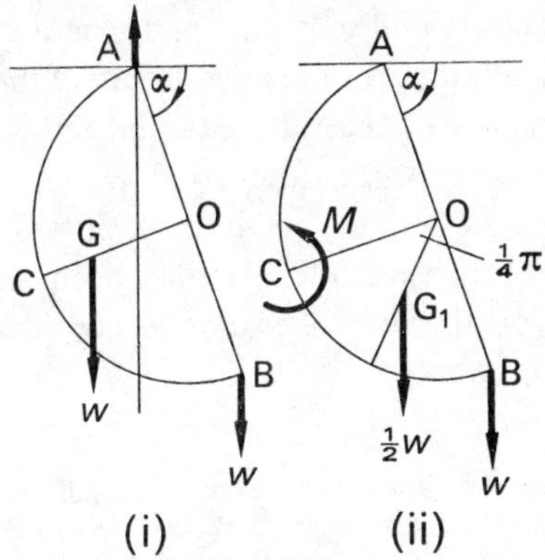

FIG. 20.12

Figure 20.12 (ii) shows those forces acting on the lower half of the wire which have a moment about C, together with the couple M exerted at C by the upper half of the wire on the lower half. The centre of gravity of the lower half of the wire is at G_1 on its radius of symmetry distant $(r2\sqrt{2})/\pi$ from O. The distance of G_1 from the vertical through C is

$$r\sin\alpha + \frac{r2\sqrt{2}}{\pi}\cos\left(\alpha+\frac{1}{4}\pi\right).$$

The distance of B from the vertical through C is $r(\sin\alpha+\cos\alpha)$. Therefore *for the equilibrium of the lower half* of the wire, the sum of the moments about C is zero, i.e.

$$M = \frac{1}{2}w\left\{r\sin\alpha+\frac{r2\sqrt{2}}{\pi}\cos\left(\alpha+\frac{1}{4}\pi\right)\right\}+wr(\sin\alpha+\cos\alpha).$$

But $$\sin\alpha = \frac{3\pi}{\sqrt{(4+9\pi^2)}}, \qquad \cos\alpha = \frac{2}{\sqrt{(4+9\pi^2)}}.$$

$$\therefore\ M = \frac{wr}{\sqrt{(4+9\pi^2)}}\left(\frac{9\pi}{2}+\frac{2}{\pi}-1\right).$$

20.4. The Equilibrium of the Hinge

In § 20.2 we discussed the actions on the hinge of each of two rods connected by the hinge in the case in which no other forces acted on it. In this case Newton's third law operated between the two rods through the agency of the hinge. When, however, there are other forces acting on the hinge, the actions of the hinge on the two rods connected by it are not necessarily equal and opposite, and separate equations expressing the necessary conditions for the equilibrium of the hinge are required to complete the analysis of the total equilibrium. The examples which follow illustrate the use of this method.

In the next chapter, where the method of Virtual Work is discussed, we consider an alternative method for such problems in which the actions of the hinges on the rods need not be considered unless they are specifically required.

Example 1. Four equal uniform rods, each of weight W, are smoothly jointed together at their ends to form a rhombus ABCD. The rhombus is suspended from A and is maintained in equilibrium, with C below A and with $\angle$ DAB $= 2\theta$, by a light string connecting the joints at A and C. Find the horizontal and vertical components of the force exerted by AB on BC. Hence, or otherwise, find the tension in the string. (N.)

The system is symmetrical both geometrically and mechanically about AC. *The forces exerted by the hinge at* C *on the rods* CB *and* CD are therefore as shown in Fig. 20.13 (i) which also shows the weights of the rods AB and BC and the forces exerted by the hinge B on those rods. Figure 20.13 (ii) shows the forces acting on the hinge C. We denote by T the tension in the string AC.

For the equilibrium of the rod AB, the sum of the moments about A is zero,

$$\therefore\ 2X\cos\theta + 2Y\sin\theta = W\sin\theta,$$

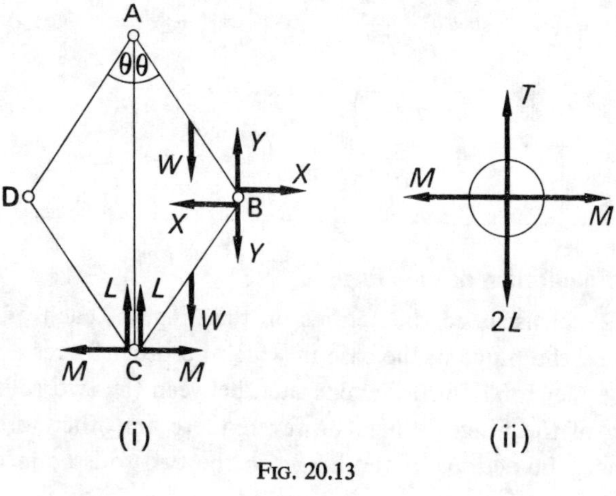

FIG. 20.13

and for the equilibrium of the rod BC, the sum of the moments about C is zero,

$$\therefore\ 2X\cos\theta - 2Y\sin\theta = W\sin\theta.$$

Hence,

$$X = \tfrac{1}{2}W\tan\theta, \quad Y = 0.$$

For the equilibrium of the rod BC, the sum of the vertical components is zero,

$$\therefore\ L = W+Y = W.$$

Finally, for the equilibrium of the hinge C, the sum of the vertical components is zero,

$$\therefore\ T = 2L = 2W.$$

The tension in the string is $2W$.

Note that this result follows also by resolving vertically for the equilibrium of the whole of the framework below the line BD.

Example 2. We solve the same problem as in 1 above except that the string AC is removed and equilibrium is maintained by a light string joining the mid-points E, F of AD, CD respectively.

As before C is vertically below A and the components of reaction at B are the same as in example 1. However, the system is not symmetrical about AC. The tension T' in EF can be found by taking moments about D for the portion BCD of the framework. We find

$$T' = 4W.$$

Example 3. Six equal uniform rods, each of weight W, are smoothly jointed so as to form the hexagon ABCDEF. They are suspended from the vertex A and kept in the shape of a regular hexagon by means of a light horizontal rod PQ, of length $AB\sqrt{3}$, the ends P and Q being smoothly hinged to points of BC and EF respectively. If the action at the hinge D is X, and the thrust in PQ is T, express the horizontal and vertical components of the actions at C and B in terms of X, T, W, and show that $T = 6X = 3W\sqrt{3}$.

Show also that BC = 6BP. (L.)

Since the system is symmetrical about AD, the action at D is horizontal, X say, Fig. 20.14. Then by considering the equilibrium of the hinges at C and B, and resolving horizontally and vertically for the rods DC, CB (starting at the bottom of the framework) the forces are as shown.

Taking moments about C for CD gives

$$X.\,CD\cos 60° = W.\tfrac{1}{2}CD\sin 60°.$$

$$\therefore\ X = \tfrac{1}{2}W\sqrt{3}.$$

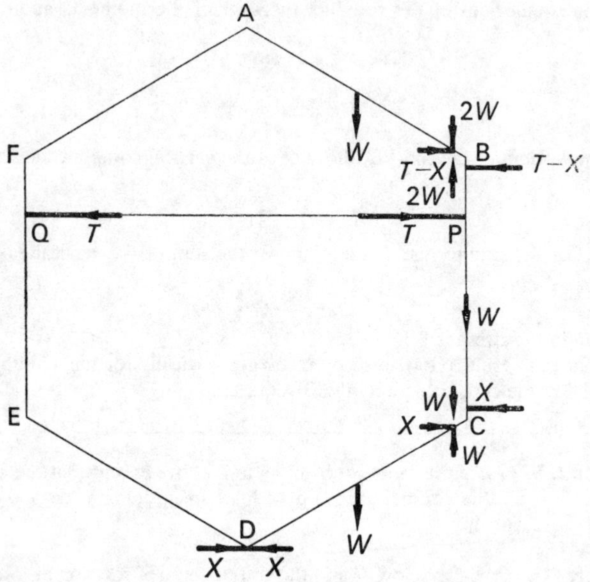

FIG. 20.14

Taking moments about A for AB gives

$$W.\tfrac{1}{2}\text{AB}\sin 60°+2W.\text{AB}\sin 60° = (T-X).\text{AB}\cos 60°.$$

$$\therefore\ T-X = 5\sqrt{3}W/2.$$

$$\therefore\ T = 3\sqrt{3}W.$$

Taking moments about B for BC gives

$$X.\text{BC} = T.\text{BP}.$$

$$\therefore\ \text{BC} = 6\text{BP}.$$

EXERCISES 20.4

1. A smooth uniform circular cylinder of weight W is kept in equilibrium with its curved surface in contact with a smooth inclined plane and its axis horizontal by means of a smooth uniform rod AB of weight $2W$ freely hinged to the inclined plane below the cylinder at A, the rod being tangential to the cylinder at its upper end B. The vertical plane through AB intersects the inclined plane in a line of greatest slope and passes through the centre of gravity of the cylinder. If α is the inclination of the plane to the horizontal and θ the acute angle which the rod makes with the inclined plane, show that

$$\tan \alpha = \frac{\sin 2\theta}{3-\cos 2\theta}. \qquad \text{(N.)}$$

2. Two equal uniform rods, AB and BC, each of weight W are freely jointed at B. The system is suspended freely from A and horizontal force P is applied at the lowest point C. If, in the equilibrium position, the inclination of AB to the downward vertical is 30°, find the corresponding inclination of BC and show that $P = \frac{1}{2}W\sqrt{3}$.

Determine the resultant action at B. (L.)

3. Two small rings A, B, each of weight W, are threaded on a fixed rough horizontal wire. The rings are connected by a light inelastic string, of length $2a$, to the mid-point C of which is attached a particle of weight $2W$. The system rests in equilibrium with $\angle \text{ACB} = 2\beta$.

(i) Find the tension in each part of the string.

(ii) Find, in terms of W and β, the normal reactions and the frictional forces between the wire and the rings. (The directions of the frictional forces acting on the rings must be clearly shown in a diagram.)

If the coefficient of friction between each ring and the wire is $\frac{3}{8}$, show that AB $\leqq 6a/5$. (N.)

4. Two planes each making an angle φ with the horizontal form a V-groove. Three equal uniform cylinders, each of radius a and weight W, are laid symmetrically in the groove with their axes horizontal and parallel to the line of intersection of the planes. The two lower cylinders touch one another and each touches one of the planes and the third cylinder rests on the other two. There is no friction at any point of contact. Show that equilibrium is not possible unless $\tan \varphi \geqq \sqrt{3}/9$. (N.)

5. A rough heavy uniform sphere of radius a and centre C rests in contact with a horizontal floor at D. A uniform rod AB of length $2b$ and weight W is smoothly hinged at A to a fixed point on the floor and rests on the sphere, touching it at E. The rod is inclined at an angle 2θ to the horizontal (with $2b > a \cot \theta$) and is in the vertical plane ACD. If the contacts at D and E are rough enough to prevent slipping, prove that the mutual action and reaction at E act in the line ED and are each of magnitude $Wb \sin \theta(1-\tan^2 \theta)/a$.

The angle of friction at both D and E is λ. Prove that if $\lambda > \theta$ the friction is not limiting at either contact but that if $\lambda = \theta$ then the friction is limiting at E and not at D. (N.)

***6.** Two equal uniform circular cylinders B and C, each of weight W, rest side by side on a rough horizontal plane; their axes are horizontal and parallel and the cylinders are almost in contact. A third equal cylinder A is gently placed so as to rest in equilibrium upon them and in contact with each of them along a generator. Show, by considering the equilibrium of C, that the force of friction between C and A and that between C and the plane are equal in magnitude. Show also that their common magnitude is $\frac{1}{2}W(2-\sqrt{3})$.

If μ is the coefficient of friction at all contacts, show that $\mu > 2-\sqrt{3}$. (N.)

*7. A uniform solid cube stands on a rough horizontal plane and an exactly similar cube is placed on it so that the faces coincide. The coefficient of friction between the two cubes is $\mu'(<1)$ and the coefficient of friction between the lower cube and the plane is μ. A gradually increasing horizontal force is applied to the upper cube at right angles to one of its faces at the centre of that face. Prove that, when equilibrium is broken, the upper cube will slide on the lower, while the lower remains at rest, or both cubes will move together as a single rigid body according as 2μ is greater or less than μ'. (O.C.)

8. A uniform ladder AB, of weight W and length $2a$, is placed at an inclination θ to the horizontal with A on a rough horizontal floor and B against a rough vertical wall. The ladder is in a vertical plane perpendicular to the wall and the coefficients of friction at A and B are μ and μ' respectively. Show that the ladder will be in equilibrium if

$$\tan\theta \geqq (1-\mu\mu')/2\mu.$$

If this condition is not satisfied and a couple of moment K is applied in the vertical plane so that the ladder is just prevented from slipping down, show that

$$K = Wa\cos\theta(1-\mu\mu'-2\mu\tan\theta)/(1+\mu\mu'). \quad \text{(N.)}$$

9. The cross-section ABC of a uniform solid right prism has AC = CB = a and the angle ACB = 90°. The prism is placed with the edge through A resting on a *smooth* horizontal table, the face through AC vertical, and the face through AB in contact with a generator of a *rough* semicircular cylinder of radius a, which is fixed with its rectangular plane face on the table. Show that for equilibrium to be possible the coefficient of friction must be at least unity.

If there is equilibrium, find the ratio of the reaction at the edge through A to the weight of the prism. (N.)

10. Two uniform rods AB, BC, each of length $2a$ and respectively of weights $2W$ and W, are rigidly jointed at B so that the angle ABC is a right angle. The rod AB is smoothly pivoted at A to a fixed point and the rods hang in equilibrium in a vertical plane. Show that AB makes an angle $\tan^{-1}(\frac{1}{4})$ with the vertical.

If instead of being rigidly jointed the rods are smoothly hinged at B, with A and C connected by a light inextensible string of length $2\sqrt{2}a$ and the rod AB pivoted as before at A, show that the tension in the string is $4W/\sqrt{34}$. Find the horizontal and vertical components of the force exerted by AB on BC. (N.)

11. Two equal uniform rods AB, AC, each of length $2a$, are freely jointed at A. They rest symmetrically over two small smooth pegs at the same level and at a distance $2c$ apart. Prove that, if the rods make an angle α with the horizontal, $c = a\cos^3\alpha$. (O.C.)

12. Two uniform rods AB, BC of equal lengths, but of masses 4 kg and 3 kg respectively, are freely hinged at B and rest with A and C on a rough horizontal plane with B vertically above AC. The ends A and C are originally near together and the angle 2θ between AB and BC is gradually increased. Assuming the coefficient of friction between each rod and the plane to have the same value μ, show that slipping will first occur at the point C and when θ reaches the value given by $7\tan\theta = 13\mu$. (L.)

13. Two uniform rods, AB and BC, are each 2 m long and their masses are 2 kg and 4 kg respectively. They are freely jointed at B. Small light rings are attached at the ends A and C, and through the rings passes a fixed rough horizontal bar. The coefficient of friction between each ring and the bar is μ. Show that, if the rods are in equilibrium with B below the bar when the angle between them is 90°, then μ cannot be less than 3/5.

If $\mu = \frac{1}{2}$, find the magnitude of the least couple applied to the rod AB which will prevent slipping at A and verify that, when this couple is applied, there is no slipping at C. (N.)

***14.** Two equal uniform planks AB, CD have their lower ends B, D on rough horizontal ground and their upper ends A, C resting against one another. A third equal plank is now inserted between A and C and is held in a vertical position, not touching the ground, by friction at A and C. The coefficient of friction at A and C is μ, that at B and D is μ', and AB, CD are inclined to the horizontal at an angle θ. Find, in terms of μ and μ', the limits between which $\tan\theta$ must lie.

Deduce that equilibrium in this position is possible only if $\mu\mu' \geqq 1/3$. (N.)

15. A rhombus ABCD of side $2a$ is composed of four freely jointed rods, and lies on a smooth horizontal plane. The rod AB is fixed and the mid-points of the rods BC and CD are joined by a string which is kept taut by a couple of moment M applied to the rod DA. If the angle ABC is 2θ, find the tension in the string and show that it is twice the reaction at the joint C. (L.)

16. Three uniform rods AB, BC, CD, each of length $2a$ and of weights W, $4W$, W respectively, are smoothly jointed at B and C. The rods are in equilibrium in a vertical plane with A and D resting on rough horizontal ground and AB, CD each inclined at 60° to the horizontal so that AD $= 4a$.

(i) Calculate the vertical components and the frictional components of the forces at A and D.

(ii) Calculate the horizontal and vertical components of the force exerted by BC on AB.

(iii) If μ is the coefficient of friction at A and D, find the inequality satisfied by μ.

(The directions of the forces acting on each rod must be clearly indicated in a diagram.) (N.)

***17.** Four uniform rods AB, BC, CD, DE, each of length a and mass m, are freely hinged to one another at B, C, D and freely hinged to fixed points A, E which are in the same horizontal plane at a distance $a \operatorname{cosec} \pi/8$ apart. Prove that the rods will hang in equilibrium in the form of half of a regular octagon if equal and opposite couples are applied either to AB and DE, or to BC and CD.

Prove that the ratio of the moments of the couples in the two cases is $-\cot\pi/8$. (N.)

18. Four equal uniform rods, each of weight W, are smoothly jointed to form a square framework ABCD. They hang freely from the corner A and the shape of the square is maintained by a light string joining the mid-points of the rods AB and BC. Prove that the reaction at the joint D is horizontal and of magnitude $\frac{1}{2}W$, and that the tension in the string is $4W$.

Find the magnitude and the direction of the reaction at each of the joints B and C. (N.)

***19.** Two uniform rods AB, BC, of lengths l_1, l_2 and weights w_1, w_2 respectively, are stiffly hinged at B. The rods rest in equilibrium in a vertical plane with the ends A, C on a smooth horizontal table. If the reactions at A and C are w_1, w_2 respectively and the frictional couple at B is G, prove that

$$G = \tfrac{1}{2}w_1w_2\sqrt{\left(\frac{l_2^2-l_1^2}{w_1^2-w_2^2}\right)}. \qquad \text{(N.)}$$

20. Two uniform beams AB and AC, equal in length and of weights $3W$ and W respectively, are smoothly jointed at A; the system rests in a vertical plane with the ends B and C in contact with a rough horizontal plane, the coefficients of limiting friction at B and C being the same and equal to μ.

If R and S are the vertical reactions of the plane on AB and AC respectively and 2θ denotes the angle BAC, prove that

(i) $R = \frac{5}{2}W$, $S = \frac{3}{2}W$,
(ii) $\tan\theta \leq \frac{3}{2}\mu$,

stating at which point, B or C, the friction first becomes limiting as θ is increased from zero.

Prove also that, when $\tan\theta = \frac{3}{2}\mu$, the reaction of one beam on the other makes an angle of $\tan^{-1}(3\mu)$ with the vertical. (O.C.)

21. Four equal uniform rods each of length a and weight w are freely jointed together to form a framework ABCD which is suspended from the joint A. It is kept in the form of a square by a light string connecting A and C. A load of weight $2w$ is suspended from B and D by two equal light strings each of length $2a$. Show that the tension in the string AC is $w(3+1/\sqrt{7})$. (L.)

22. Two equal uniform rods AB and BC, each of weight w, are smoothly hinged at B. They are placed in a vertical plane with the ends A and C on a rough horizontal table ($\mu = \frac{2}{3}$), the angle at B being $\pi/2$. A string is attached to B and is pulled with a horizontal force P in the direction AC. Show that, as the force P is increased from zero, slipping will take place first at C, and that this will occur when P is just greater than w. (N.)

***23.** Two uniform beams, AB and BC, of equal lengths but of different weights, W_1 and W_2, of which W_1 is the greater, are freely jointed together at B and rest in a vertical plane with the ends A and C on a rough horizontal plane, the angle ABC being a right angle. If the coefficients of friction between the beams and the plane are the same, show that their common value must not be less than

$$(W_1+W_2)\div(W_1+3W_2).$$

If the common value is as great as unity, show that a weight of any magnitude may be suspended from the joint without disturbing equilibrium. (L.)

***24.** A uniform rod AC of weight w and length $4a$ is bent into two straight parts at right angles at the midpoint B. It is hung from a smooth hinge at A and a horizontal force $P(>\frac{1}{4}w)$ is applied at C in a direction away from AB. In the position of equilibrium AB is inclined to the downward vertical through A at an acute angle θ. Show that

$$\tan\theta = (4P-w)/(4P+3w),$$

and find the couple exerted at the end B of the portion AB. (N.)

MISCELLANEOUS EXERCISES XX

1. A non-uniform rigid beam AB, of length $3a$ and weight nW, rests on supports P and Q at the same level, where AP = PQ = QB = a. When a load of weight W is hung from A, the beam is on the point of tilting about P. Find the distance of the centre of gravity of the beam from A. When an additional load of weight W_1 is hung from B, the forces exerted on the supports at P and Q are equal. Find W_1 in terms of n and W.

If a couple, of moment L and acting in the vertical plane through AB, is now applied to the loaded beam, the reaction at P is increased in the ratio 3 : 2. Show that

$$L = \tfrac{1}{3}(n+1)Wa. \qquad \text{(N.)}$$

2. Two uniform rods AB, BC, alike in all respects and each of weight W, are rigidly jointed at B so that ABC is a right angle, and the end A is hinged freely to a fixed point, from which the two rods hang in equilibrium. Show that AB makes an angle $\tan^{-1}(\frac{1}{3})$ with the vertical.

If the rods are freely jointed at B but A and C are connected by a light inextensible string of such a length that ABC is a right angle, show that the tension in this string is $3W/(2\sqrt{5})$. (O.C.)

3. Two uniform straight rods AB, BC are smoothly jointed at B and rest in a horizontal position on two supports D and E, with A, B, C collinear. The length of AB is 4 m and its mass 4 kg; the length of BC is 6 m and its mass 6 kg. The support E is between B and C and distant 4 m from B. The support D is between A and B and distant x m from A. Find x and the reaction at D.

If the support D is moved to the mid-point of AB and the joint at B is no longer smooth, find what frictional couple one rod exerts on the other if equilibrium is still maintained. (N.)

4. A uniform circular cylinder of weight W and radius a rests between two fixed rough planes each inclined to the horizontal at an angle α. Prove that the least couple required to rotate the cylinder about its axis has moment

$$\frac{\mu Wa}{(1+\mu^2)\cos\alpha},$$

where μ is the coefficient of friction between the cylinder and each plane. (L.)

5. A small rough bead of weight $4W$ is movable on a circular hoop of radius a and weight W. The hoop hangs on a rough peg at a point P on its circumference, the bead being at a point Q of the circumference, and the system being in equilibrium. The radii to P and Q from the centre of the hoop are on the same side of the vertical diameter and make angles θ, φ respectively with this diameter. Prove that $4\sin\varphi = 5\sin\theta$ and determine in terms of θ and φ the ratio of the force of friction to the normal reaction at each of the points P and Q. (N.)

6. Two uniform rods AB, BC, of equal lengths and weights $2W$, W respectively, are smoothly hinged at B. The rods rest in a vertical plane with the ends A and C on a rough horizontal plane and the coefficient of friction at A and C is μ. If the system is in equilibrium when the angle ABC is 2θ, and the vertical components of the reactions at A and

C are R and S respectively, prove that $R > S$. If θ is gradually increased, show that slipping will occur first at C.

Prove that, when the rod BC is on the point of slipping at C, $3 \tan \theta = 5\mu$. (N.)

7. A chain of four equal uniform rods, AB, BC, CD, DE, each of weight W and freely jointed together at B, C, D, hangs symmetrically from two fixed points A and E in the same horizontal line. The angles of inclination of AB and BC to the vertical are θ and φ respectively. Prove that $\tan \varphi = 3 \tan \theta$.

Show also that the resultant reaction at B is

$$W\sqrt{(1+\tfrac{1}{4}\tan^2 \varphi)}.$$ (L.)

8. Two equal uniform rods AB and BC each of weight W are freely jointed at B. The end A is attached to a smooth pivot and the rods are in equilibrium under the action of a horizontal force P acting at C. Prove that the angles of inclination of AB and BC to the vertical are $\tan^{-1}(2P/3W)$ and $\tan^{-1}(2P/W)$, and find the reactions at A and B on the rod AB. (N.)

9. The axis of a fixed right circular cylinder, whose surface is smooth, is horizontal and a section perpendicular to the axis is of radius a and centre O. A smoothly jointed framework consisting of three rods AB, BC and CD, each of length a and weight W, is placed symmetrically over the cylinder in the plane of the section, the mid-point, G, of BC being vertically above O. Prove that the reaction of the cylinder on BC is $57W/25$, and find the magnitude and direction of the reaction of the hinge at B on AB. (O.C.)

***10.** A cylinder of weight W and radius $4a$ lies on a smooth floor and against a smooth wall. A smooth cylinder of radius a lies on the floor in contact with the first cylinder along a generator. A horizontal force P is applied symmetrically to the smaller cylinder so as to push the system against the wall, its line of action being at a height a above the floor. Prove that as P is increased, the larger cylinder will cease to exert pressure on the floor when $P = \frac{4}{3}W$.

The two cylinders are removed and bound together by an endless cord at tension T passing round them in a plane perpendicular to their axes. The system is placed on the floor away from the wall. Show that each cylinder exerts on the floor a pressure equal to its own weight. (O.C.)

11. Four uniform rods AB, BC, CD, DA each of length $2a$ and weight W are freely hinged at their ends, and rest with the upper rods AB, AD in contact with two smooth pegs in the same horizontal line at a distance $2c$ apart. Prove that β, the inclination of the rods to the vertical in the equilibrium position, is given by the equation $c = 2a \sin^3 \beta$, and determine the horizontal and vertical components of the reaction at B in terms of W and β. (O.C.)

12. Three equal uniform rods AB, BC, CD, each of length $2c$ and weight W, are smoothly jointed at B and C and rest with AB, CD in contact with two smooth pegs at the same level. In the position of equilibrium AB and CD are inclined at an angle α to the vertical, BC being horizontal. Prove that the distance between the pegs is $2c(1+\frac{2}{3}\sin^3 \alpha)$.

If β is the angle which the reaction at B makes with the vertical, prove that $\tan \alpha \tan \beta = 3$. (O.C.)

13. Two equal smooth cylinders of radius a and weight W lie in contact along generators on a horizontal table. A third equal cylinder is placed symmetrically upon them, and the system is kept in equilibrium by a band which passes round the cylinders in a plane perpendicular to the generators. Find the tension of the band if the lower cylinders are just about to separate.

If the band is elastic and its natural length is $12a$, prove that the tension of the band at any extension x would be

$$\frac{Wx}{4\sqrt{3}(\pi-3)a}. \qquad \text{(O.C.)}$$

14. Three equal smooth circular cylinders each of weight W are placed with their axes parallel, each cylinder in contact with the other two. A light smooth continuous elastic band, whose modulus of elasticity is λ, is placed round them in a plane perpendicular to the axes. In this position the band is just unstretched. The cylinders are then placed so that the curved surfaces of two of them rest on a smooth horizontal table. If T is the tension in the elastic band in the position of equilibrium, θ the inclination to the vertical of the plane passing through the axis of the upper cylinder and one of the lower cylinders, show that

$$T = \tfrac{1}{2}W \tan\theta$$

and

$$\frac{W}{\lambda} = \frac{2\cot\theta(2\sin\theta - 1)}{3+\pi}. \qquad \text{(N.)}$$

15. AB, BC, and CD are three uniform rods of lengths $2a$, $2b$, and $2a$ respectively and of weights proportional to their lengths, freely jointed at B and C; P and Q are small smooth pegs on the same horizontal level at a distance $2d$ apart. The system is in equilibrium with AB in contact with P and CD in contact with Q, AB and CD each making an angle θ with the horizontal and BC being below the level of the pegs. Prove that

$$\text{(i) } b < d < b + a\cos\theta,$$

$$\text{(ii) } \cos^3\theta = (2a+b)(d-b)/(2a^2). \qquad \text{(O.C.)}$$

***16.** Inside a smooth hollow cylinder of radius a, the axis of which is horizontal, are placed two equal smooth uniform solid cylinders of radius b with their axes parallel to the axis of the hollow cylinder. Another smooth uniform solid cylinder of the same dimensions and weight is now placed symmetrically upon the other two. The axes of the cylinders are all parallel. Show that the lower cylinders will separate if $a > b(1+2\sqrt{7})$. (N.)

17. Two uniform smooth spheres, each of weight W and radius a, are placed in contact on a horizontal plane. A third equal sphere rests symmetrically on the other two. Equilibrium is maintained by an endless light elastic string, of modulus λ and natural length $2\pi a$, surrounding the lower spheres in the horizontal plane through their centres. Find the reaction between the lower spheres and deduce that this equilibrium configuration is only possible provided that $8\lambda \geqq \pi W/\sqrt{3}$. (N.)

18. A rough circular cylinder of radius r is fixed with its axis horizontal and a uniform rod of mass M and length $2l$ rests on it in a horizontal position perpendicular to its axis. If a particle of mass m is now attached to one end of the rod, show that the rod may be allowed to turn slowly, without slipping on the cylinder, into a position of equilibrium in which it is inclined to the horizontal, provided that the angle of friction between the rod and cylinder is greater than

$$ml/(M+m)r. \qquad \text{(N.)}$$

***19.** A uniform heavy rod AB of length $2a$ is in equilibrium in a horizontal position in contact with a rough plane of coefficient of friction μ inclined to the horizontal at an angle α. At the end A a gradually increasing force is applied up the plane in the direction of the line of greatest slope through A. Show that when the rod begins to move it turns about a point at distance

$$a\left(2-\frac{2\tan\alpha}{\mu}\right)^{1/2} \qquad \text{(C.S.)}$$

from A.

***20.** Two equal uniform ladders AB, BC, each of length $2l$ and weight W, are smoothly hinged together at B, while the ends A and C rest on a rough horizontal plane. The coefficient of friction is μ at A and C, and the angle ABC is 2α. Prove that a man of weight w can ascend a distance x given by

$$x = \frac{2lW(2\mu-\tan\alpha)}{w(\tan\alpha-\mu)},$$

provided that $x < 2l$ and $\mu < \tan\alpha < 2\mu$. (L.)

CHAPTER XXI

*THE PRINCIPLE OF VIRTUAL WORK

*21.1. The Work Done by a Force Acting on a Particle

In § 8.5 of Volume I we introduced the idea of mechanical work by considering the motion of a particle along a line. In this chapter we give a more formal definition of work and generalise the concept to include systems of forces acting on systems of rigid bodies.

Suppose that a force F acts on a particle and that, while the force is acting, the particle undergoes a small displacement from P to P′, Fig. 21.1, where $PP' = \delta s$ and the angle between PP′ and the direction of F is θ. Then the work done by F in the displacement δs is *defined to be*

$$\delta W = F\cos\theta \times PP' = F\delta s.\cos\theta, \tag{21.1}$$

i.e. the magnitude of the displacement multiplied by the component in the direction of the displacement of the force F. In particular δW vanishes when the displacement is perpendicular to the force. Note also that δW can be negative, i.e. work can be done against the force.

It follows from the above definition that

(1) the total work done by a number of forces on a particle in a given displacement is equal to the algebraic sum of the works done by the forces separately,

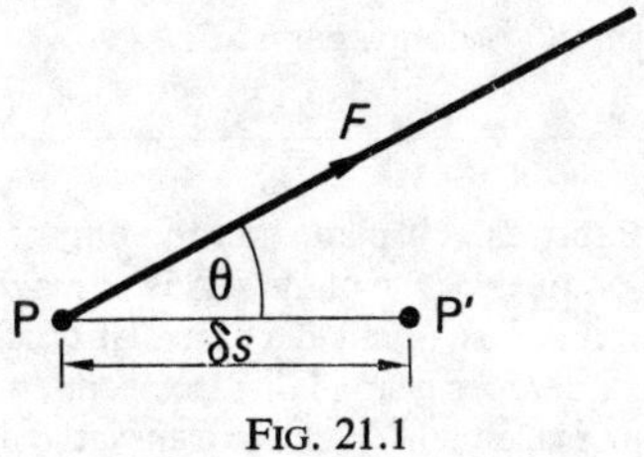

FIG. 21.1

(2) the total work done by a force in a number of displacements is the algebraic sum of the works done in the separate displacements.

Accordingly, when a variable force F acts on a particle, the total work done by the force when the particle moves along a path (not necessarily straight) from A to B, Fig. 21.2, is

$$\int F \cos \theta \, \mathrm{d}s, \tag{21.2}$$

where ds is an element of arc of the path at which the force makes an angle θ with the direction ds and the integral is evaluated between the points A and B.

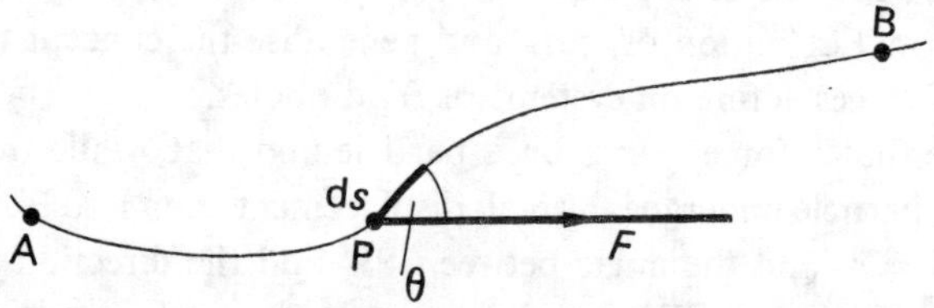

FIG. 21.2

Example 1. A force $F(x)$, acting along a straight line Ox, acts on a particle P. The work done by this force when P moves from $x = a$ to $x = b$ is

$$\int_a^b F(x) \, \mathrm{d}x.$$

For example, if $F(x) = -mn^2x$ and P moves from $x = 0$ to $x = c$, the work done by F is

$$\int_0^c -mn^2x \, \mathrm{d}x = -\tfrac{1}{2}mn^2c^2,$$

i.e. and amount of work $\frac{1}{2}mn^2c^2$ is done against F.

Example 2. A particle P moves in a plane and the only force acting on the particle is directed towards a fixed point O of the plane and is of magnitude $\varphi(r)$, where $r = \mathrm{OP}$. [The path described by P in this case is called a *central orbit*. See § 18.4.] Then the work done by the force when P undergoes a small displacement δs from A to A′, which can be analysed into a radial displacement δr and a transverse displacement $r\delta\theta$ (see Fig.

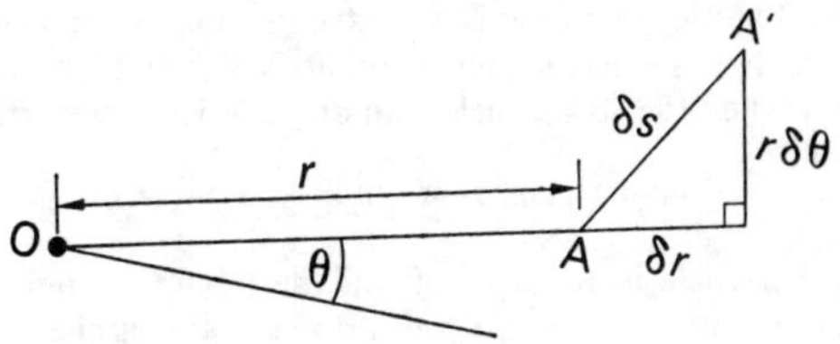

FIG. 21.3

21.3 and § 18.2) is approximately $-\varphi(r)\delta r$. Hence the work done by the force $\varphi(r)$ when P moves from $r = a$ to $r = b$ is

$$-\int_a^b \varphi(r)\,dr$$

and is independent of the path by which P *moves.*

---

*EXERCISES 21.1

***1.** A particle of mass m, situated in a rectangular coordinate plane, is attracted towards the origin O by a force km/x^2, where k is constant. Calculate the work done *by this force of attraction* in each of the following cases:

(a) the particle moves freely from (2, 0), to (1, 0),
(b) the particle moves from (1, 0), to (2, 0),
(c) the particle is moved in a straight line from (1, 0) to (1, 1).

***2.** The force of attraction on a body of mass m when at a distance x above the surface of the earth is $mga^2/(a+x)^2$, where g is the acceleration due to gravity at the surface and a is the radius of the earth. Show that the work which must be done against gravity in transporting the body from the earth's surface to a height h is $mgah/(a+h)$.

***3.** A small bead is threaded on a semicircular wire of radius r and is acted upon by a variable force at right angles to the bounding diameter of the semicircle. The magnitude of this force is kmy, where y is the distance of the particle from the diameter. Calculate the work done *by this force* when the particle moves from an extremity of the bounding diameter to the extremity of the radius at right angles to this diameter.

***4.** A small smooth ring of mass m is threaded on to a fixed straight wire and is attached by a light elastic string of natural length a and modulus mg to a fixed peg P distant a from the wire. The ring is held in a position in which the string makes an angle of 30° with the wire and is then released. Calculate the work done by the *elastic tension of the string* while the ring moves from its initial position to the position in which the string is at right angles to the wire.

***5.** One end of a light elastic string, of natural length a and modulus W, is attached to a fixed point O and the other end to a particle of weight W, which rests on a rough horizontal table $3a/2$ vertically below O, the string being vertical. A horizontal force P is applied to the particle so that it moves infinitely slowly along a straight line on the table. Show that when the string makes an angle θ with the vertical

$$P = W(\mu \cos \theta + \tfrac{3}{2} \tan \theta - \sin \theta - \tfrac{1}{2}\mu).$$

Show that when the particle is about to lift off the table the angle the string makes with the vertical is 60°, and that the total work done by the applied horizontal force is then

$$\tfrac{3}{8}Wa[5+2\mu\{2 \ln (2+\sqrt{3})-\sqrt{3}\}],$$

where μ is the coefficient of friction between the particle and the table. (N.)

***6.** A particle, of mass m, is supported by two light elastic strings each of natural length a and modulus of elasticity $15mg/16$, the other ends of which are fixed one at each of two points A, B in the same horizontal line and at a distance $2a$ apart. Verify that, in the position of equilibrium, each string is inclined to the vertical at an angle $\cos^{-1}(4/5)$, and find how much work must be done to raise the particle to the middle point of AB. (O.C.)

*21.2. The Potential Energy of a Particle

When a particle P moves very slowly under the action of a system of forces from A to B, Fig. 21.2, the work done by the system may be independent of the path by which the particle moves from A to B. In such cases the system of forces is said to be *conservative*. In this case the whole work which must be done *against* the system to take P from a standard position A to some other point B depends on the position of B only and can be taken as the *potential energy* at B. The standard position A can be chosen arbitrarily and hence the potential energy involves an arbitrary constant. However, it is only the difference in the potential energies of the particle as it moves from one position to another which is significant and this quantity does not involve the arbitrary constant. It is implicit in this definition of a conservative system of forces that when such a system is disturbed and subsequently returns to its original position no energy is lost or gained. Gravitational and electrical systems of forces are examples of conservative systems.

If a particle, subject to gravity, is displaced around a closed path returning to its starting point, the total work done by the gravitational force, the weight, is zero. On the other hand, if a particle is dragged around a closed curve on a rough surface, the total work done by the frictional force is negative (or the total work done by the dragging agent is positive).

With a conservative force the work done in one part of the circuit is "given back" in another part. A lifting agent does an amount of work mgy against uniform gravity in lifting a particle of mass m to a height y above ground-level. By allowing the particle to return to ground level this work can be "given back" to the agent. We say that the particle has *potential energy* of amount mgy in the raised position.

An agency does work against the tension in a string (or spring) when it stretches the string from its natural length a. When the length of the string is $a+s$ the tension is $\lambda s/a$, and the work done by the agent is

$$\int_0^x (\lambda s/a)\,\mathrm{d}s$$

in stretching the string to length $a+x$. This work is "given back" by allowing the string to contract. The potential energy of the string is V in its stretched state, where

$$V = \frac{1}{a}\int_0^x \lambda s\,\mathrm{d}s = \frac{\lambda x^2}{2a}.$$

[See Volume I, § 8.5.]

*21.3. Extension to Rigid Bodies

It follows, by extension of the results so far derived for a particle, that the total work done by a system of forces acting on a rigid body is the sum of the works done by the separate forces on the particles to which they are applied. Further, in finding this sum, the internal forces between the particles of the body can be neglected since any pair of internal reactions are equal and opposite (by Newton's third law) and do equal and opposite amounts of work. In fact, if the resultant of a system of forces acting on a rigid body has components X, Y referred to a set of plane cartesian axes Oxy and the body undergoes a translation without rotation with components δx, δy parallel to the coordinate axes, the work done by the system is

$$\delta W_1 = X\delta x + Y\delta y. \tag{21.3}$$

On the other hand, if the system of forces reduces to a couple of moment N and the body rotates through a small angle $\delta\theta$, the work done by the couple is

$$\delta W_2 = N\delta\theta. \tag{21.4}$$

In this case the work done by the couple in a finite rotation from $\theta = \alpha$ to $\theta = \beta$ is

$$W = \int_{\alpha}^{\beta} N \,\mathrm{d}\theta. \tag{21.5}$$

The result is independent of the precise forces constituting the couple; if N is independent of θ, then

$$W = N(\beta - \alpha).$$

In general, the forces acting on a rigid body are reduced to a force (X, Y) acting at the centre of mass G together with a couple N (see § 19.3). Then the work done in a displacement, which can be analysed into a displacement $(\delta\bar{x}, \delta\bar{y})$ of G together with a rotation $\delta\varphi$, is

$$W = X\delta\bar{x} + Y\delta\bar{y} + N\delta\varphi. \tag{21.6}$$

We give now examples of certain sets of forces which do no work in a displacement.

(i) When a wheel or other *rigid* body rolls on a stationary surface *without slipping*, the force acting on the wheel does no work in the course of the rolling because the point of contact, at which this force acts, is instantaneously stationary. If the wheel rolls on a moving surface, then the action of the wheel on the surface does work, and the reaction of the surface on the wheel does an equal and opposite amount of work.

(ii) If a particle or a body slides on a *smooth* stationary surface, the force exerted by the surface on the body does no work because the displacement of the point of application is always perpendicular to the force, which acts along the normal.

(iii) The action of a particle A of a rigid body on another particle B of the body acts along the line AB and is equal and opposite to the reaction of B upon A. Because the distance AB remains fixed, in any motion these two forces do no net work.

(iv) A *smooth* hinge is one which exerts no couple on a body attached at the hinge; it can, of course, exert a force on the body. When the body turns about a *fixed* hinge no work is done because the force acts at a fixed point.

Most of the examples cited above involve "internal" forces acting in some mechanical system, which do no work in the displacements specified. The reader, however, should not conclude that "internal" forces do no work in displacements of non-rigid bodies. For example, if a wheel is not rigid, then the forces exerted by the wheel do some work when the wheel rolls. If the distance between two interacting particles of a body alters, then their action and reaction do different amounts of work in a displacement.

When a system of rigid bodies interacts the work done on the system by the external forces is the sum of the works done on the bodies separately, to which must be added the work done in increasing the energy of any attachments, e.g. elastic strings, between the bodies.

Suppose now that a mechanical system acted upon by a conservative set of forces has one degree of freedom, i.e. its configuration is specified by one coordinate x say (see Vol. I, § 14.1). [Such a system is illustrated in examples 1 and 2 of pp. 633–4, where, in each case, the parameter is the angle θ.] Let F be the resultant "force" tending to increase the coordinate x and let δV, δW respectively be the change in potential energy and the work done by F when x increases by δx. Then, since the forces are conservative,

$$\delta V + \delta W = 0.$$

But $\delta W = F\delta x$ and therefore

$$F = -\frac{\mathrm{d}V}{\mathrm{d}x}. \tag{21.7}$$

This relation is very important. The minus sign implies that the "force" acts in a direction which tends to decrease the potential energy.

Note that, if x is an angle, then F as defined by (21.7) is the couple which tends to increase x.

Example 1. The potential energy of a stretched string is $V = \lambda x^2/2a$. The force tending to *increase* the coordinate x is

$$X = -\frac{\mathrm{d}V}{\mathrm{d}x} = -\frac{\lambda x}{a}.$$

This is the tension in the string.

Example 2. A uniform rod of weight W and length $2a$ can turn freely about one extremity A, which is fixed. A light inextensible string attached to the other extremity passes through a small smooth ring fixed at a point C, distant $2a$ from A and at the same level as A, and carries at its other end a weight w. When the rod is at an inclination θ to the horizontal and below it, determine the magnitude of the couple which tends to increase θ. (L.)

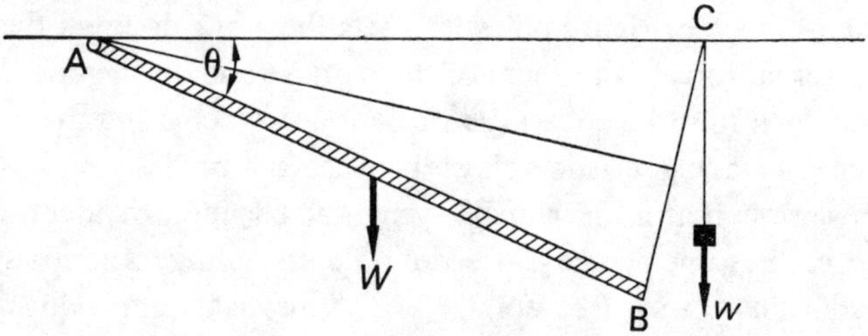

FIG. 21.4

In Fig. 21.4 the moment of the forces about A in the clockwise direction, i.e. in the sense of θ increasing, is

$$G(\mathrm{A}) = Wa\cos\theta - w\,.\,2a\cos\tfrac{1}{2}\theta.$$

If we take the standard position to be the one in which AB coincides with AC, the potential energy in the position shown is

$$V = -Wa\sin\theta + w\,.\,4a\sin\tfrac{1}{2}\theta.$$

(The centre of mass, where the weight W acts, is at a vertical distance $a\sin\theta$ below its standard position, and the weight w is distance BC above its standard position.)

$$\therefore\ \frac{\mathrm{d}V}{\mathrm{d}\theta} = -Wa\cos\theta + w\,.\,2a\cos\tfrac{1}{2}\theta = -G(\mathrm{A}).$$

This shows that the derivative of V gives the negative value of the "force" (torque) tending to increase θ.

When a system, which has one degree of freedom specified by the coordinate x, is acted upon by a conservative set of forces in equilibrium, the force F tending to increase x must vanish. Therefore, the possible positions of equilibrium are given by

$$\frac{dV}{dx} = 0. \tag{21.8}$$

Another way of expressing this result is to write down the condition $\delta V = 0$ to the first order in δx for small changes from the equilibrium position.

[To do this we use Taylor's theorem of pure mathematics which can be expressed in the form

$$\delta V = V(x+\delta x)-V(x) = \frac{dV}{dx}\,\delta x + \text{terms involving } (\delta x)^2$$

and higher powers of δx.]

Application of this result enables equilibrium positions to be determined *without the introduction of internal reactions* as illustrated in the following examples. It must be noted, however, that these examples can be solved by other methods (e.g. those of § 20.4).

Example 1. A uniform rod AB, of length $2a$ and weight W, rests with its ends A, B on two smooth planes inclined at angles α, β to the horizontal ($\alpha > \beta$). The vertical plane through the rod contains a line of greatest slope of each of the planes. Show that the inclination of the rod to the horizontal is θ where

$$2 \sin\alpha \sin\beta \tan\theta = \sin(\alpha-\beta).$$

The system is shown in Fig. 21.5; here O is the point where the line of intersection of the planes meets the vertical plane through the rod. In this case, since the planes are smooth, the reactions at A and B are normal to the planes and do no work in a displacement in which the ends A, B remain in contact with the planes. Hence the potential energy V of the rod, *considered as a function of* θ, must be stationary. But, taking O as the level of zero potential energy,

$$\begin{aligned} V &= \tfrac{1}{2}W(\text{OA} \sin\alpha + \text{OB} \sin\beta) \\ &= Wa\{\sin(\theta+\beta)\sin\alpha + \sin(\alpha-\theta)\sin\beta\}/\sin(\alpha+\beta). \end{aligned}$$

$$\therefore\ \frac{dV}{d\theta} = Wa\,\{\cos(\theta+\beta)\sin\alpha - \cos(\alpha-\theta)\sin\beta\}/\sin(\alpha+\beta).$$

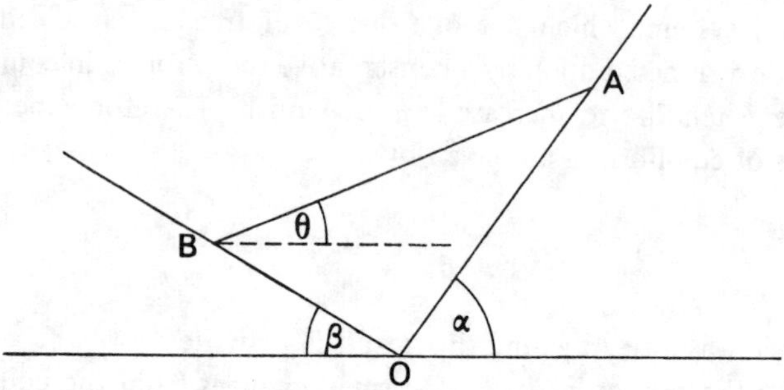

FIG. 21.5

The equilibrium position is given by $\mathrm{d}V/\mathrm{d}\theta = 0$,

i.e. by
$$\cos(\theta+\beta)\sin\alpha - \cos(\alpha-\theta)\sin\beta = 0,$$

and this condition reduces to

$$2\sin\alpha\sin\beta\tan\theta = \sin(\alpha-\beta).$$

Example 2. Two uniform rods AB, AC, each of weight W and length $2c$, are smoothly jointed at A. The rods rest on a smooth circular cylinder of radius a with their plane perpendicular to the axis of the cylinder which is horizontal. When the rods are in equilibrium in a vertical plane with A vertically above the axis of the cylinder, angle BAC $= 2\theta$. Show that $c\sin^3\theta = a\cos\theta$ and deduce that there is only one such position of equilibrium.

Let O, Fig. 21.6, be the point on the axis of the cylinder in the plane of the rods and N the point of contact of AB with the cylinder. Then the height of G, the centre of mass of AB, above the level of O is

$$\begin{aligned} h &= \text{ON}\sin\theta - \text{NG}\cos\theta \\ &= a\sin\theta - (c - a\cot\theta)\cos\theta \\ &= a\operatorname{cosec}\theta - c\cos\theta. \end{aligned}$$

Therefore the potential energy of the system, referred to O as the level of zero energy, is

$$V = 2W(a\operatorname{cosec}\theta - c\cos\theta).$$

$$\therefore \quad \frac{\mathrm{d}V}{\mathrm{d}\theta} = 2W(c\sin\theta - a\operatorname{cosec}\theta\cot\theta).$$

The equilibrium positions occur where $\mathrm{d}V/\mathrm{d}\theta = 0$, i.e. where

$$c\sin^3\theta = a\cos\theta. \tag{1}$$

As θ increases from 0 to $\frac{1}{2}\pi$ (within which range the equilibrium positions must lie) the l.h. side of (1) must increase steadily from 0 to c whereas the r.h. side decreases

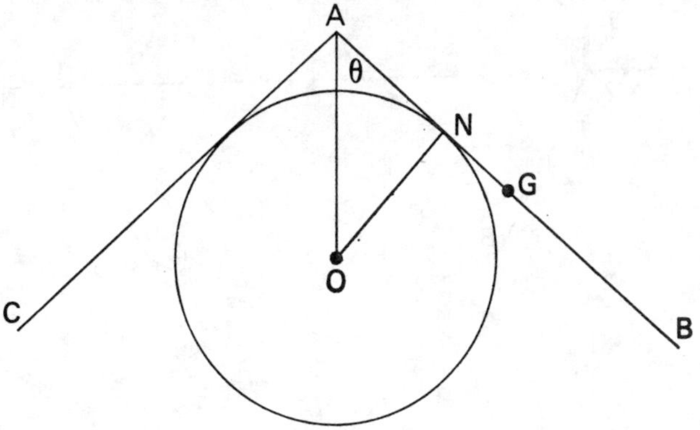

FIG. 21.6

steadily from a to 0. Hence the expressions $c \sin^3 \theta$ and $a \cos \theta$ must be equal for one and only one value of θ in the range $0 < \theta < \frac{1}{2}\pi$. Therefore there is just one position of equilibrium.

In the example below the system has only one degree of freedom but it is convenient to work with two dependent variables; the relation between them is obtained from the geometrical constraints of the system.

Example Four uniform rods AB, BC, CD, DE, each of length $2a$ and weight w, are freely hinged together at B, C and D, and the chain hangs in equilibrium from two supports at the same level to which the ends A and E are freely attached. If the rods AB, BC make angles θ, φ with the horizontal, prove that $\tan \theta = 3 \tan \varphi$.

If the horizontal component of the force exerted by a support is $3w/2$, prove that the distance AE is about $6 \cdot 6a$. (C.S.)

The equilibrium state is shown in Fig. 21.7. The potential energy of the system is

$$V = -2w\{\tfrac{1}{2}\text{AB} \sin \theta + (\text{AB} \sin \theta + \tfrac{1}{2}\text{BC} \sin \varphi)\}.$$

$$\therefore \; V = -2wa(3 \sin \theta + \sin \varphi).$$

Since A and E are fixed, the distance AE remains constant,

$$\therefore \; a(\cos \theta + \cos \varphi) = \text{constant}.$$

$$\therefore \; -\sin \theta - \sin \varphi \frac{d\varphi}{d\theta} = 0.$$

$$\therefore \; \frac{d\varphi}{d\theta} = -\frac{\sin \theta}{\sin \varphi}.$$

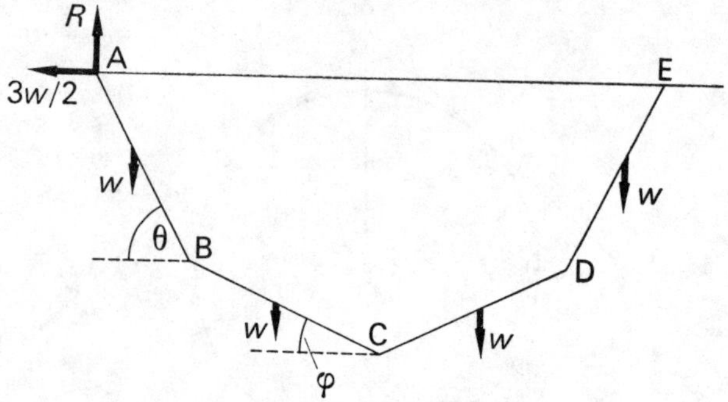

FIG. 21.7

Now,
$$\frac{dV}{d\theta} = -2wa\left(3\cos\theta + \cos\varphi\frac{d\varphi}{d\theta}\right)$$
$$= -2wa(3\cos\theta - \cot\varphi\sin\theta).$$

Hence the equilibrium position occurs where $dV/d\theta = 0$, i.e. where
$$\tan\theta = 3\tan\varphi. \tag{1}$$

The problem is now completed using the methods of § 20.4. The sum of the moments for AB about B is zero and therefore
$$R\,.\,2a\cos\theta = \frac{3w}{2}\cdot 2a\sin\theta + w\,.\,a\cos\theta. \tag{2}$$

The sum of the vertical components of the external forces acting on the whole system is zero and therefore
$$2R = 4w.$$

Substitution in (2) gives $\tan\theta = 1$. Then (1) gives $\tan\varphi = \frac{1}{3}$ and we find
$$AE = 4a(\cos\theta + \cos\varphi) = 4a\left(\frac{1}{\sqrt{2}} + \frac{3}{\sqrt{10}}\right) \approx 6{\cdot}6a.$$

[*Note* that this problem can be solved by introducing the internal reactions at B and C and using the methods of § 20.4. However, the method given above avoids the introduction of these forces which are not required to be calculated.]

---

*EXERCISES 21.3

***1.** Two uniform rods AB and BC, each of weight W and length $2l$, are smoothly hinged together at B. At A and C small light rings are attached to the rods and are threaded on a rough fixed horizontal bar below which the rods hang in equilibrium, the inclination of each rod to the horizontal being denoted by θ. The coefficient of friction between each ring and the bar is μ. Show that $\theta \geqq \alpha$ where $\cot \alpha = 2\mu$.

Two equal and opposite couples in the plane ABC are now applied, one to each rod, of moment just sufficient to cause A and C to slip towards each other. Find the moment K of either couple as a function of θ. If the couples are first applied when the rods are in the position given by $\theta = \alpha$ and continue to act so as just to cause slipping, show that the work they do in moving the system to the position $\theta = \frac{1}{2}\pi$ is

$$2Wl\{\sqrt{(4\mu^2+1)}-1\}. \qquad \text{(N.)}$$

***2.** A uniform rod AB, of length $2a$ and weight W, rests with the end B against a rough vertical wall and the end A smoothly hinged to a light rod AC, also of length $2a$. The end C of the light rod is smoothly hinged to a fixed point of the wall vertically below B. The plane ABC is perpendicular to the wall. A couple of moment K acts on the light rod AC in the plane ABC so that B is just on the point of slipping upwards. The coefficient of friction at B is μ, the angle ABC is θ and $\mu < \cot \theta$. Show that the horizontal component of the reaction at B is

$$\tfrac{1}{2}W/(\cot \theta - \mu)$$

and that

$$K = Wa\,\frac{\sin \theta(3 \cot \theta - \mu)}{\cot \theta - \mu}.$$

If the moment of the couple is so adjusted as to move the rods slowly from the position $\theta = \alpha$ to the position $\theta = \beta$ $(\alpha > \beta)$, show that the work done against friction is

$$2\mu a W \int_{\beta}^{\alpha} \frac{\sin \theta \, d\theta}{\cot \theta - \mu}. \qquad \text{(N.)}$$

***3.** A bead of mass M can slide on a smooth circular wire hoop of radius a whose plane is vertical, and another bead, of mass m, can slide on a smooth wire which coincides with the vertical diameter of the hoop. The beads are joined by a light inelastic string of length $l\,(< a)$, and rest in equilibrium in the upper half of the figure. Show that the radius to the bead M makes with the vertical an angle θ (assumed not zero), where

$$\left\{1-\left(\frac{m}{M+m}\right)^2\right\}\cos^2\theta = 1 - l^2/a^2.$$

[It is assumed that the conditions are such as to make this angle real.] (O.C.)

***4.** Four equal straight rods AB, BC, CD, and DA, each of length $2a$ and weight $\frac{1}{4}W$, are freely jointed at their ends to form a rhombus. The ends A and B are fixed to a wall, with A vertically above B. An elastic string of natural length a and modulus λ joins A and C. Show that when the angle BAC $= \theta$, the potential energy of the system is

$$-Wa\cos 2\theta + \tfrac{1}{2}\lambda a(4\cos\theta - 1)^2.$$

[P.T.O.]

Deduce that, if there is an equilibrium position in which the rhombus is not collapsed, the tension in the string is

$$\lambda W/(4\lambda - W). \qquad \text{(O.C.)}$$

***5.** Two small rings, each of weight w, slide on a smooth circular wire, of radius a, which is fixed in a vertical plane. The rings are joined by a light inextensible string of length a, and a particle of weight W ($< 2w$) is attached to the mid-point of the string. Show that there is a symmetrical position of equilibrium with the rings above the centre of the circle, and with the middle point of the string at a height c above the centre, where

$$4(W+w)c^2 = 3wa^2. \qquad \text{(N.)}$$

***6.** A heavy uniform isosceles triangular lamina of height h and vertical angle 2α rests in a vertical plane with the equal sides in contact with two smooth pegs at the same level and at a distance c apart. Show that there is an oblique position of equilibrium provided that $h \sin 2\alpha < 3c$, and determine the angle which the base of the lamina makes with the vertical in this case. (N.)

***7.** Two uniform equal heavy rods, each of weight w, are smoothly jointed at A and rest across a smooth horizontal cylinder. From A a weight W is suspended. If $2l$ is the length of each rod, r the radius of the cylinder, and θ the inclination of each rod to the horizontal, show that

$$Wr \sec \theta \tan \theta = 2w(l \cos \theta - r \sec \theta \tan \theta). \qquad \text{(L.)}$$

***8.** A uniform rod of weight w and length 8 m is smoothly hinged at one end to a fixed point O. The rod is supported by a small smooth light ring which slides on the rod and is attached by a light elastic string to a point 3 m vertically above O. The natural length of the string is 0·9 m and its modulus of elasticity is w. Show that there are two positions of equilibrium of the system in which the rod is inclined to the vertical, and that the inclinations are $\sin^{-1} \frac{3}{5}$ and $\frac{1}{3}(\pi - \sin^{-1} \frac{3}{5})$.

***9.** A solid hemisphere is supported by a string fixed to a point on its rim and to a point on a smooth vertical wall with which the curved surface of the hemisphere is in contact. If θ, φ are the inclinations of the string and the plane base of the hemisphere to the vertical, prove that

$$\tan \varphi = \tfrac{3}{8} + \tan \theta. \qquad \text{(C.S.)}$$

***10.** Two smooth wires OA and OB are fixed in a vertical plane and are inclined at equal angles α to the vertical. Two equal heavy uniform rods HC and KC are smoothly hinged at C and the ends H and K are constrained to slide along OA and OB respectively by means of small smooth weightless rings; the weight of each rod is W, and an additional weight W is attached at C. Show that in the symmetrical position of equilibrium each rod is inclined at an angle θ to the vertical given by

$$\tan \theta = \tfrac{3}{2} \cot \alpha. \qquad \text{(C.S.)}$$

***11.** A rhombus is formed of rods each of weight W and length l with smooth joints. It rests symmetrically with its two upper sides in contact with two smooth pegs at the same level and at a distance apart $2a$. A load of weight W' is hung at the lowest point. If the sides of the rhombus make an angle θ with the vertical show that

$$\sin^3 \theta = \frac{a(4W+W')}{l(4W+2W')}.$$

*21.4. The Principle of Virtual Work

The concept of work forms an essential part of an alternative method of investigating conditions of equilibrium or the equivalence of sets of forces. The adjective "virtual" is used because the work is done, or would be done, by the forces in displacements which the system on which they act is *imagined* to undergo.

The Equilibrium of a Particle

A particle is subject to the action of a number of forces which add up to a force F, see Fig. 21.1. We can *imagine* this particle given a small displacement δs; if it actually made this displacement, the forces would do an amount of work $F \cos \theta . \delta s$; this work is the *virtual work* of the forces.

If the particle is in equilibrium, $F = 0$ and the virtual work is zero. If the virtual work is zero *for all possible virtual displacements*, then F must be zero. (The product $F \cos \theta . \delta s$ cannot vanish for all possible displacements unless $F = 0$.) Hence a necessary and sufficient condition for the equilibrium of the particle is that the virtual work of the applied forces is zero for all possible displacements.

Expressed in terms of components referred to rectangular axes, if the forces have resultant sums (X, Y) and the displacement has components $(\delta x, \delta y)$, then the virtual work is

$$\delta W = X\delta x + Y\delta y.$$

If $X = 0$, $Y = 0$, then $\delta W = 0$; if $\delta W = 0$ for arbitrary values of δx, δy, we deduce that $X = 0$, $Y = 0$.

This result can be extended to the cases of a rigid body or system of bodies acted upon by a number of forces. In effect we take *as an axiom determining the equilibrium of a set of forces* the principle of virtual work or principle of virtual displacements in the following form.

If a set of forces acts upon a mechanical system, a necessary and sufficient condition for equilibrium is that the virtual work of the forces is zero, correct to the first order, when the system is given an arbitrary virtual displacement consistent with the constraints of the system.

The phrase "consistent with the constraints" needs some explanation. We have proved the principle for a particle. Most idealised mechanical systems consist of particles and rigid bodies which are connected by hinges, strings, etc. Conditions may also be imposed on the system such as one body remaining in contact with a given surface, a particle sliding on a smooth wire, and so on. When a system is given a virtual displacement "consistent with the constraints", the displacement is such that these conditions (constraints) are not violated and that any forces acting on the system because of these constraints (e.g. the reactions between surfaces, the tensions in inextensible strings, the interactions between particles of a rigid body) *do no work* in the displacement. If work is done in the displacement (perhaps a surface may be rough) it is usual to remove the constraint and add appropriate (initially unknown) forces to the given set acting on the system.

The principle of virtual work can be used to compare two sets of forces. If the two sets do the same work in an arbitrary virtual displacement, they are equivalent sets of forces, in the sense of § 19.3. The principle is capable of greater generalisation than the methods of resolution and is used extensively in more advanced mechanics to discuss very general systems and obtain results of wide applicability.

*21.5. Applications of the Principle of Virtual Work

The following examples illustrate the use of the principle of virtual work. Using the principle frequently avoids the necessity for the introduction of unknown internal actions and reactions unless a particular reaction or "force of constraint" is required. Such a force can often be determined by violating the corresponding constraint in the virtual displacement. (The force of constraint becomes one of the set of applied forces when the constraint is ignored.)

Example 1. A uniform rod AB, of length $2a$ and weight W, rests in equilibrium with the end A against a smooth vertical wall and the end B on rough horizontal ground. The vertical plane through the rod is perpendicular to the plane of the wall and AB makes the angle θ with the downward vertical. Calculate the force of friction at B.

This example can easily be solved by the methods of Volume I, Chapter IX. However, we give here a solution by using the Principle of Virtual Work to illustrate the method.

The only external forces acting on the rod AB are the normal reactions R, S, at A and B, the force of friction F at B and the weight W at G, as shown in Fig. 21.8. In a virtual displacement consistent with the geometrical constraints of the system, A, B remain in contact with the wall and ground respectively and so the displacements of A and B are perpendicular to the forces R and S, which, therefore, do no work in the displacement.

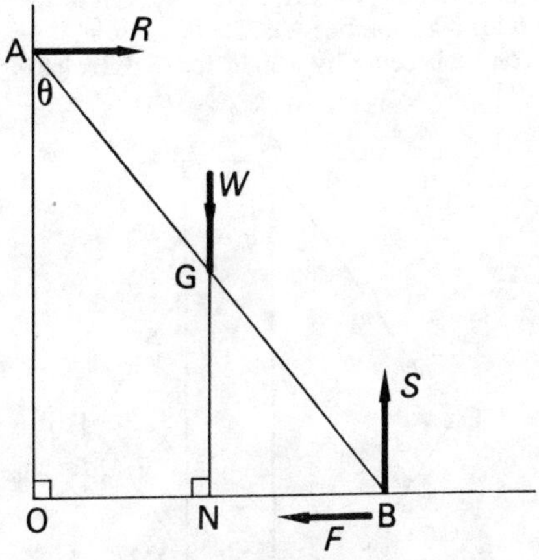

FIG. 21.8

The increase in the height of G above the (fixed) horizontal plane is $\delta(\text{NG})$ and so the virtual work of W is $-W\delta(\text{NG})$. The negative sign arises because an increase in NG moves G upwards against the direction of W which therefore does work $(-W)\times\delta(\text{NG})$. Similarly the work done by the force of friction F, corresponding to an increase $\delta(\text{OB})$ in the distance of its point of application from O, is $-F\delta(\text{OB})$. Therefore the equation of virtual work is

$$-W\delta(\text{NG})-F\delta(\text{OB}) = 0.$$

But NG $= a\cos\theta$, OB $= 2a\sin\theta$.

$$\therefore\quad -W\delta(a\cos\theta)-F\delta(2a\sin\theta) = 0.$$

To the first order in $\delta\theta$ this gives

$$Wa\delta\theta.\sin\theta-2Fa\delta\theta.\cos\theta = 0.$$

$$\therefore\quad F = \tfrac{1}{2}W\tan\theta.$$

Note: In the above example it is easy to see that, if θ is *increased* by $\delta\theta$, then OB increases and GN decreases so that the virtual works of F and W are $-2Fa\delta\theta \,.\, \cos\theta$ and $Wa\delta\theta \,.\, \sin\theta$ respectively and have correct signs. However, in more complicated cases this is not always apparent. In general it is best to use the fact that the increase of any length l is δl and to give the sign to the virtual work of a force, the point of application of which moves a distance δl, on the supposition that δl is positive. Correct use of the calculus will then ensure correct subsequent work.

Example 2. Four uniform rods AB, BC, CD, DA, each of weight W and length $2a$, are smoothly jointed to form a rhombus ABCD. The system is pivoted to a fixed point at A and prevented from collapsing by a light inextensible string AC. Calculate the tension in AC.

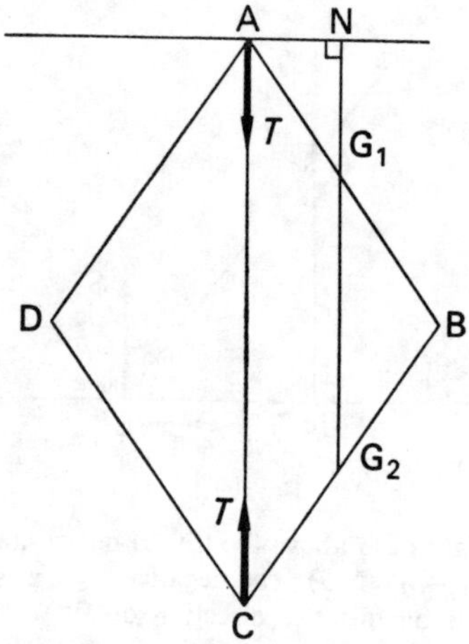

FIG. 21.9

The tension T in AC, Fig. 21.9, is an internal force of the system, so that, in order to find this force, we remove the "constraint" AC, replace it by the forces T acting at A, C, and use the principle of virtual work. In a virtual displacement of the system in which C remains vertically below A the centre G_1 of AB falls a distance $\delta(G_1N)$, since N is at the fixed level of A. Similarly G_2 falls a distance $\delta(G_2N)$ and so the virtual work of the weights of all the rods is

$$2\{W\delta(G_1N)+W\delta(G_2N)\} = 2W\delta(AC). \tag{1}$$

To find the virtual work of T we note that we have removed the "constraint" that AC is an inextensible string, i.e. is of fixed length, and have inserted the forces T acting at A and C in place of the constraint. The forces T each act in the line AC, so that contributions to the total work done will only arise from components of displacement which take place in the line AC. Whatever may be the displacements of A and C separately "in space", for the two forces T the virtual work is

$$-T\delta(\text{AC}).$$

[If T were a thrust, the virtual work would be $T\delta(\text{AC})$ because then the displacement $\delta(\text{AC})$ is in the direction of the forces T.]

The force at A and the reactions at the joints do no net work in the displacement. (This will be assumed without explicit statement in subsequent examples.) The equation of virtual work is, therefore,

$$2W\delta(\text{AC})-T\delta(\text{AC}) = 0.$$

$$\therefore\ T = 2W$$

and is independent of the angle BAD.

Example 3. We consider the same problem as 2 above except that the string AC is removed and the system maintained in the shape of a square by a light rigid rod joining BD.

We calculate the thrust in this special case after writing down the equation of virtual work of the system under consideration in the *general case*. We do not insert the value of θ corresponding to the specified configuration until the equation of virtual work has been written down and simplified.

Consider the general case in which angle BAD $= 2\theta$. Then, if P is the thrust in BD, the virtual work of P is $+P\delta(\text{BD})$. As before the virtual work of the weights of the rods is $2W\delta(\text{AC})$ and so the equation of virtual work is

$$P\delta(\text{BD})+2W\delta(\text{AC}) = 0.$$

$$\therefore\ P\delta(4a\sin\theta)+2W\delta(4a\cos\theta) = 0$$

and so, to the first order in $\delta\theta$,

$$P\delta\theta\,.\cos\theta-2W\delta\theta\,.\sin\theta = 0.$$

$$\therefore\ P = 2W\tan\theta.$$

Therefore, for a square, $(\theta = \frac{1}{4}\pi)$, $P = 2W$.

Example 4. A tripod is formed of three equal uniform rods OA, OB, OC, each of weight W and length a, smoothly jointed at O. The tripod is placed on a smooth horizontal table, and is prevented from collapsing by strings AB, BC, CA each of length a. Find the tension in the strings when a load of weight w is suspended from the joint. (O.S.)

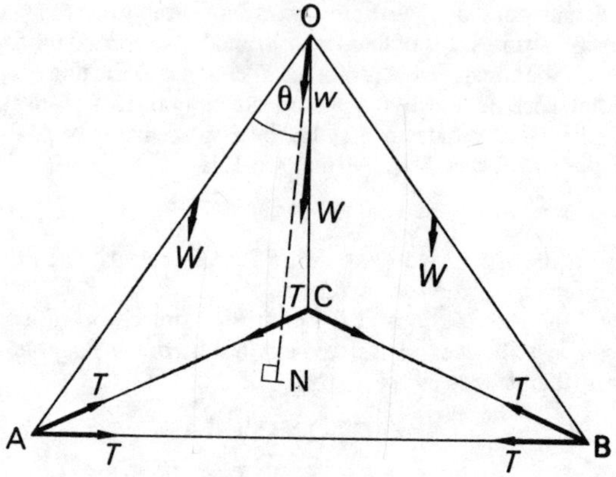

FIG. 21.10

Let N be the foot of the perpendicular from O to the table, Fig. 21.10. In a virtual displacement the virtual work of the weights of the rods and the load w is

$$-\{3W\delta(\tfrac{1}{2}\text{ON})+w\delta(\text{ON})\} = -(w+3W/2)\ \delta(\text{ON}).$$

By symmetry the tensions in the strings are equal and the total virtual work of the tensions is

$$-3T\delta(\text{AB}).$$

Therefore the equation of virtual work is

$$-(w+3W/2)\delta(\text{ON})-3T\delta(\text{AB}) = 0.$$

Let angle AON be θ in a general position. Then

$$\text{ON} = a\cos\theta, \qquad \text{AB} = a\sqrt{3}\sin\theta.$$

The equation of virtual work then gives to the first order in $\delta\theta$,

$$(w+3W/2)a\delta\theta.\sin\theta-3Ta\sqrt{3}\delta\theta.\cos\theta = 0.$$

$$\therefore\ T = \frac{(2w+3W)\tan\theta}{6\sqrt{3}}.$$

In the case when the strings are equal in length to the rods $\theta = \sin^{-1}(1/\sqrt{3})$ and

$$T = (2w+3W)/(6\sqrt{6}).$$

Note that here again the required internal force has been calculated after the solution in the general case has been obtained.

Example 5. A framework consists of four equal uniform rods, each of weight W, freely jointed at their ends to form a square ABCD, which hangs freely in equilibrium from the point A, being kept in shape by an endless light inextensible string passing through three light smooth rings, one fixed at C and the other two fixed at X and Y, the mid-points of AB and AD respectively. Show, by the principle of virtual work, that the tension in this string is $4(5+4\sqrt{10})\,W/27$. (L.)

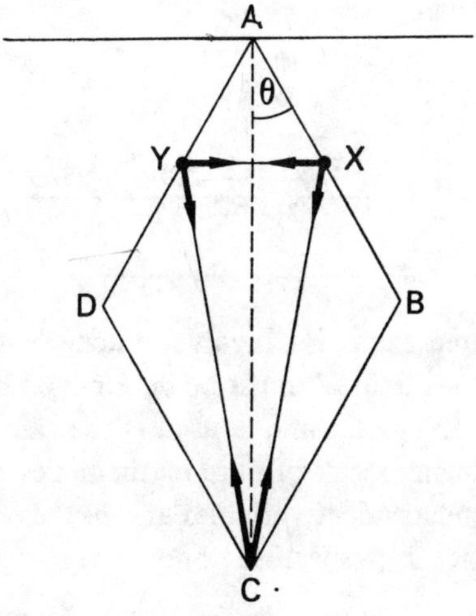

FIG. 21.11

Let angle BAD $= 2\theta$ in the general position, Fig. 21.11.

(We find the tension when the angle BAD $= 2\theta$ and then proceed to the case of a square by putting $\theta = \frac{1}{4}\pi$.)

As before the virtual work of the weights of the rods is $2W\delta(\text{AC})$. The virtual work of the tension in the string is

$$-T\delta(\text{CX}+\text{XY}+\text{YC}).$$

Therefore the equation of virtual work is

$$2W\delta(\text{AC})-T\delta(\text{CX}+\text{XY}+\text{YC}) = 0.$$

But, if each rod is of length $2a$,

$$\text{AC} = 4a\cos\theta, \quad \text{XY} = 2a\sin\theta, \quad \text{CX} = \text{CY} = a\sqrt{(1+8\cos^2\theta)}.$$

$$\therefore\ 2W\delta(4a\cos\theta)-T\delta\{2a\sin\theta+2a\sqrt{(1+8\cos^2\theta)}\} = 0.$$

To the first order in $\delta\theta$ this gives

$$-8W\delta\theta . \sin\theta - 2T\delta\theta . \left\{\cos\theta - \frac{8\cos\theta\sin\theta}{\sqrt{(1+8\cos^2\theta)}}\right\} = 0.$$

$$\therefore\ T = \frac{4W\sin\theta}{\cos\theta\left\{\frac{8\sin\theta}{\sqrt{(1+8\cos^2\theta)}} - 1\right\}}.$$

For a square, ($\theta = \frac{1}{4}\pi$), this result gives

$$T_{\theta=\frac{1}{4}\pi} = \frac{4W}{\left\{\frac{8}{\sqrt{2}\sqrt{5}} - 1\right\}} = \frac{4W\sqrt{10}}{8-\sqrt{10}}$$

$$= \frac{4W\sqrt{10}(8+\sqrt{10})}{8^2-10} = \frac{4(5+4\sqrt{10})W}{27}.$$

The following three examples involve systems with two degrees of freedom, i.e. two "coordinates" must be determined before the position of the system is fixed. The technique used is the same as before except that we use the following result of pure mathematics.

If x_1, x_2 are two independent variables and δx_1, δx_2 (independent) are small increments of x_1, x_2 respectively and

$$f_1(x_1, x_2)\,\delta x_1 + f_2(x_1, x_2)\,\delta x_2 = 0,$$

then

$$f_1(x_1, x_2) = 0, \quad f_2(x_1, x_2) = 0.$$

This result can be extended to any number of independent variables.

Example 1. Two uniform rods OA, AB, each of length $2a$ but of weights w_1, w_2 respectively, are freely jointed at A and OA is freely pivoted to a fixed hinge at O. When a horizontal force P is applied at B, the inclinations of OA, AB to the downward vertical in the position of equilibrium are θ, φ respectively. Show that

$$(w_1+2w_2)\tan\theta = w_2\tan\varphi = 2P. \qquad \text{(C.S.)}$$

This example can easily be solved by the methods of § 20.3; it is used here as a simple example to illustrate the application of the Principle of Virtual Work to a system with two degrees of freedom.

The system is illustrated in Fig. 21.12, where N_1, N_2 respectively are the feet of the perpendiculars from the mid-points of the rods on the (fixed) horizontal through O and L is the foot of the perpendicular from B on the (fixed) vertical through O. Then in a

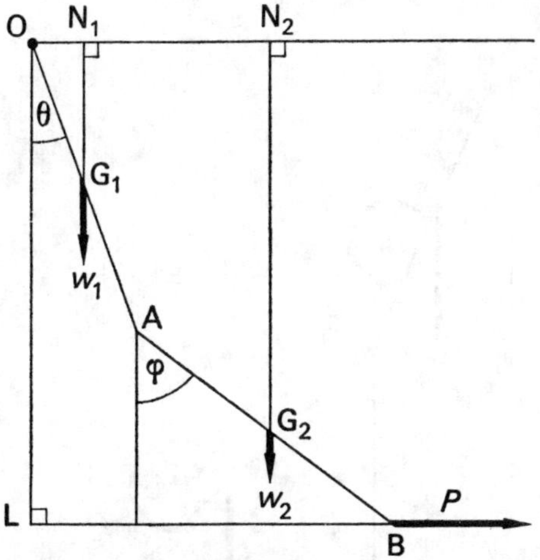

FIG. 21.12

virtual displacement the virtual work of the weights of the rods is

$$w_1\delta(N_1G_1)+w_2\delta(N_2G_2).$$

The corresponding virtual work of the force P is

$$P\delta(LB).$$

Therefore the equation of virtual work is

$$P\delta(LB)+w_1\delta(N_1G_1)+w_2\delta(N_2G_2) = 0.$$

But $$N_1G_1 = a\cos\theta,\quad N_2G_2 = a(2\cos\theta+\cos\varphi),$$

$$LB = 2a(\sin\theta+\sin\varphi).$$

$$\therefore\ 2aP\delta(\sin\theta+\sin\varphi)+aw_1\delta\cos\theta+aw_2\delta(2\cos\theta+\cos\varphi) = 0;$$

i.e. $$2P(\delta\sin\theta+\delta\sin\varphi)+w_1\delta\cos\theta+w_2(2\delta\cos\theta+\delta\cos\varphi) = 0,$$

i.e. $$2P(\delta\theta.\cos\theta+\delta\varphi.\cos\varphi)-w_1\delta\theta.\sin\theta-w_2(2\delta\theta.\sin\theta+\delta\varphi.\sin\varphi) = 0.$$

$$\therefore\ \{2P\cos\theta-(w_1+2w_2)\sin\theta\}\,\delta\theta+(2P\cos\varphi-w_2\sin\varphi)\,\delta\varphi = 0.$$

Since θ, φ are independent variables, the coefficients of $\delta\theta$, $\delta\varphi$ in this equation are separately zero.

$$\therefore\ 2P\cos\theta-(w_1+2w_2)\sin\theta = 0,$$

$$2P\cos\varphi-w_2\sin\varphi = 0,$$

which are equivalent to the required results.

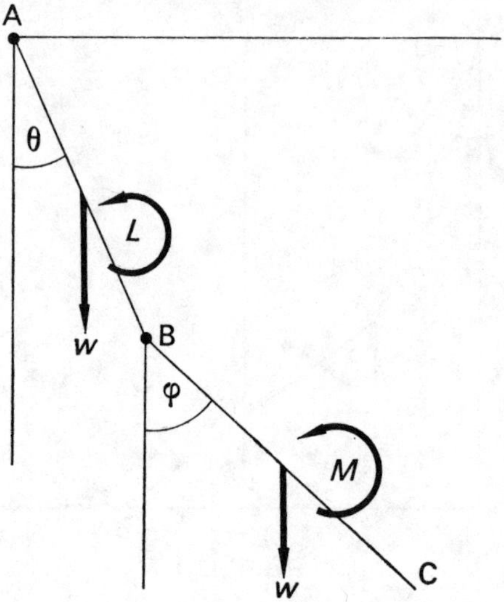

FIG. 21.13

Example 2. A uniform rod AB, of weight w and length $2l$, is supported by a smooth hinge at A, and an equal rod BC is smoothly hinged to the first at B. The hinges allow the rods to rotate freely in a vertical plane. A couple of moment L is applied to AB and a couple of moment M is applied to BC (the two couples lying in this vertical plane) and the system is maintained in a position of equilibrium with the rods inclined at angles θ and φ to the vertical. Prove that

$$3wl \sin \theta = L, \qquad wl \sin \varphi = M. \qquad \text{(C.S.)}$$

The configuration is shown in Fig. 21.13. Let the system undergo a virtual displacement so that θ, φ increase by $\delta\theta$, $\delta\varphi$ respectively. Then (see p. 630) the virtual work of the couples L, M are $L\,\delta\theta$, $M\,\delta\varphi$ respectively. As in example 1 the virtual work of the weights of the rods is

$$\delta(wl \cos \theta)+\delta\{wl(2 \cos \theta+\cos \varphi)\} = -wl(3\delta\theta\,.\sin \theta+\delta\varphi\,.\sin \varphi).$$

The equation of virtual work is, therefore,

$$L\,\delta\theta+M\,\delta\varphi-wl(3\delta\theta\,.\sin \theta+\delta\varphi\,.\sin \varphi) = 0,$$

i.e.

$$(L-3wl \sin \theta)\,\delta\theta+(M-wl \sin \varphi)\,\delta\varphi = 0.$$

$$\therefore\; L = 3wl \sin \theta, \qquad M = wl \sin \varphi.$$

Example 3. Six equal heavy rods, each of weight W and length $2a$, are freely hinged together to form a framework ABCDEF which is kept in the shape of a regular hexagon by two light rods BF and CE. The framework hangs from A in a vertical plane. Show that the thrusts in the rods BF and CE are $\frac{5}{2}W\sqrt{3}$ and $\frac{1}{2}W\sqrt{3}$ respectively. (O.S.)

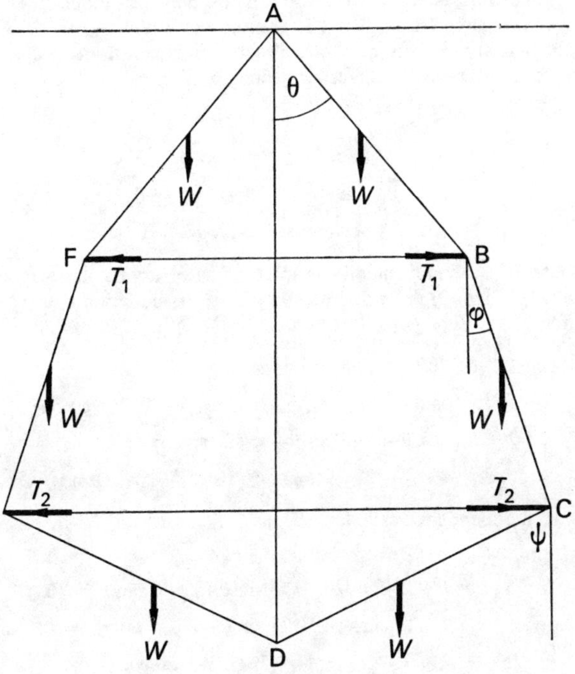

FIG. 21.14

Consider a general configuration, symmetrical about the vertical through A, as shown in Fig. 21.14. In a virtual displacement in which θ, φ, ψ increase by $\delta\theta$, $\delta\varphi$, $\delta\psi$ respectively the virtual work of the weights of the rods is

$$2W\delta\{a\cos\theta+a(2\cos\theta+\cos\varphi)+a(2\cos\theta+2\cos\varphi+\cos\psi)\}$$
$$=-2aW(5\delta\theta.\sin\theta+3\delta\varphi.\sin\varphi+\delta\psi.\sin\psi).$$

The virtual works of the thrusts T_1, T_2 in BF, CE respectively are

$$T_1\delta(\text{BF}) = T_1\delta(4a\sin\theta) = 4aT_1\delta\theta.\cos\theta,$$
$$T_2\delta(\text{CE}) = T_2\delta(4a\sin\theta+4a\sin\varphi) = 4aT_2(\delta\theta.\cos\theta+\delta\varphi.\cos\varphi).$$

Therefore the equation of virtual work is

$$2T_1\delta\theta.\cos\theta + 2T_2(\delta\theta.\cos\theta + \delta\varphi.\cos\varphi)$$
$$- W(5\delta\theta.\sin\theta + 3\delta\varphi.\sin\varphi + \delta\psi.\sin\psi) = 0. \quad (1)$$

The three "coordinates" (angles) θ, φ, ψ are not, however, independent. The system has only two degrees of freedom but it is more convenient to work with the three variables and then impose the (geometrical constraint) condition, which relates these variables, on them afterwards. In fact (projecting on CE)

$$\text{CE} = 4a(\sin\theta + \sin\varphi) = 4a\sin\psi.$$
$$\therefore \sin\theta + \sin\varphi - \sin\psi = 0. \quad (2)$$
$$\therefore \delta(\sin\theta + \sin\varphi - \sin\psi) = 0.$$
$$\therefore \delta\theta.\cos\theta + \delta\varphi.\cos\varphi - \delta\psi.\cos\psi = 0. \quad (3)$$

We now choose, θ, φ as independent variables. [If necessary ψ can be obtained in terms of θ, φ from (2)]. Then (3) gives $\delta\psi$ in terms of $\delta\theta, \delta\varphi$, and eliminating $\delta\psi$ between (1) and (3) we find

$$2T_1\delta\theta.\cos\theta + 2T_2(\delta\theta.\cos\theta + \delta\varphi.\cos\varphi)$$
$$- W\{5\delta\theta.\sin\theta + 3\delta\varphi.\sin\varphi + (\delta\theta.\cos\theta + \delta\varphi.\cos\varphi)\tan\psi\} = 0,$$

i.e. $$\{2T_1\cos\theta + 2T_2\cos\theta - W(5\sin\theta + \cos\theta\tan\psi)\}\,\delta\theta$$
$$+ \{2T_2\cos\varphi - W(3\sin\varphi + \cos\varphi\tan\psi)\}\,\delta\varphi = 0.$$

Since θ, φ are independent variables, the coefficients of $\delta\theta, \delta\varphi$ in this equation are separately zero, i.e.

$$2T_1\cos\theta + 2T_2\cos\theta - W(5\sin\theta + \cos\theta\tan\psi) = 0,$$
$$2T_2\cos\varphi - W(3\sin\varphi + \cos\varphi\tan\psi) = 0.$$
$$\therefore T_1 + T_2 = \tfrac{1}{2}W(5\tan\theta + \tan\psi),$$
$$T_2 = \tfrac{1}{2}W(3\tan\varphi + \tan\psi).$$
$$\therefore T_1 = \tfrac{1}{2}W(5\tan\theta - 3\tan\varphi).$$

In our case $\theta = \pi/3, \varphi = 0, \psi = \pi/3$ and so

$$T_1 = \tfrac{5}{2}W\sqrt{3}, \quad T_2 = \tfrac{1}{2}W\sqrt{3}.$$

---

*EXERCISES 21.5

***1.** A uniform rod AB, of weight W and length $2l$, has one end A in contact with a smooth horizontal plane and it rests against a small smooth peg C at a distance nl from the plane ($n < 2$). A horizontal force P is applied at the end B in a vertical plane through AB. Find the work done by the forces acting on the rod when the angle θ between AB and the horizontal is increased by a small amount $\delta\theta$.

If the rod is in equilibrium when $W = P\sqrt{3}$ and θ is 30° find the value of n. (L.)

***2.** Four smoothly jointed, weightless rods, each of length a, form a rhombus ABCD. It rests in a vertical plane with A vertically above C, the lower rods BC, CD supported on fixed smooth pegs which are on the same level and distant b apart. A light rod BD maintains an angle 2θ at A when a load W hangs from A. Show by the method of virtual work, or otherwise, that when BD acts as a strut, the thrust it exerts on the framework is

$$\frac{W}{4a\cos\theta}(b\operatorname{cosec}^2\theta - 4a\sin\theta).$$

Show also that if ABCD is a square, BD can only act as a tie and find the tension in BD. (L.)

***3.** Four uniform rods AB, BC, CD, DE, each of length a and weight W, are smoothly jointed together at their ends B, C, and D, and the ends A, E are smoothly jointed to fixed points at a distance $2a$ apart in the same horizontal line. If AB, BC make angles θ, φ respectively with the horizontal when the system hangs in equilibrium, show, by the principle of virtual work, that $3\cot\theta = \cot\varphi$.

Show also that if B and D are now connected by an inextensible string of length a, the tension in this string is $W/\sqrt{3}$. (L.)

***4.** Six uniform beams, each of weight W and length a, are freely jointed at their ends to form a hexagon ABCDEF and are placed in a vertical plane with AB resting on a horizontal plane; the middle points of the two upper slant beams CD and EF, which are each inclined at angle θ to the horizontal, are connected by a light string. Show that the tension in this string is $6W\cot\theta$. (C.S.)

***5.** Four uniform straight rods AB, BC, CD, DE, each of length $5l$ and weight W, are freely hinged together at B, C and D. The ends A and E are held at the same level at a distance $14l$ apart; B and D are joined by a light strut of length $8l$; and the system hangs in equilibrium in a vertical plane. Use the Principle of Virtual Work to find the stress in the strut BD. (L.)

***6.** Four uniform rods, each of length a and weight W, are freely jointed together to form a rhombus ABCD. A string of length $a\sqrt{3}$ is fastened at its ends to the joints A and C. If the system is suspended from A, prove that the tension of the string is $2W$ and find the force at C on the rod BC. (N.)

***7.** Four uniform heavy rods AB, BC, CD, DA are smoothly jointed together at their ends to form a framework. AB, AD are of length $2a$, BC, CD of length a, and each rod is of weight W. The framework is suspended from A, loaded with a particle of weight W at C, and kept from collapsing by an inextensible string of length a whose ends are attached to the middle points of CD and AD. Prove that the tension in the string is of magnitude $9W/2$, and find the horizontal and vertical components of the reaction at D. (L.)

***8.** Six uniform rods each of weight W and of the same length are freely jointed at their ends to form a hexagon ABCDEF. The rod AB is fixed in a horizontal position and the figure is kept in the form of a regular hexagon by means of a light rod connecting the middle point of AB to the middle point of the opposite rod DE which is below AB. Prove that the tension in the light rod is $3W$ and find the action of the rods BC and ED on the rod CD. (N.)

***9.** Four equal uniform rods each of weight W are freely jointed together at their ends and are kept in the form of a square ABCD by means of a rod BD of weight $2W$. The framework is suspended freely from A and particles of weight $2nW$ are attached to each of the joints B, C, and D. Prove that the horizontal stress in the rod BD is $(4n+3)W$. (N.)

***10.** Four uniform rods AB, BC, CD, DA, each of weight W and length $2a$, are freely jointed together to form a rhombus, which is suspended from A. A point E in AB and a point F in CD, at equal distances l (not equal to a) from B and D respectively, are joined by a light rod of length $2c$ which keeps the rhombus in the form in which the angle BAC is equal to α. Determine the condition that the rod EF should be in tension and find the magnitude of the tension. (C.S.)

***11.** Two uniform rods AB, AC, each of length a and weight W, are smoothly hinged at A. The ends B, C are joined by a light inelastic string of length $2l$ $(l < a)$. The system rests in a vertical plane on two smooth pegs X, Y at the same level so that AB is in contact with X, AC in contact with Y, XY $= 2c$ and A is above XY. If the string BC is horizontal and taut, show that it is in tension

$$\{(2a^2c-l^3)W\}/\{2l^2\sqrt{(a^2-l^2)}\}. \qquad \text{(O.S.)}$$

***12.** A framework consists of six equal uniform rods, each of weight W and of length $2a$, freely jointed at their ends to form a regular hexagon ABCDEF which hangs in equilibrium with AB fixed horizontally and DE below AB. Small smooth rings are attached at A, B and the mid-points H, K of CD and EF respectively. The framework is kept in shape by an endless, light inextensible string passing successively through the rings at A, B, H, and K. Show, by the principle of virtual work, that the tension in the string is

$$\frac{8\sqrt{21}+14\sqrt{3}}{9}W. \qquad \text{(L.)}$$

*MISCELLANEOUS EXERCISES XXI

***1.** Two smooth planes intersect in a horizontal line L. They lie on opposite sides of the vertical plane through L, making angles θ, φ $(< \pi/2)$ with this plane. Two smooth horizontal uniform circular cylinders, of equal weight and length but differing in radius, are in contact all along a generator and rest in equilibrium each with a single generator in contact with one inclined plane. Show that the plane through the axes makes an angle ψ with the vertical where

$$2\cot\psi = |\tan\theta - \tan\varphi|. \qquad \text{(L.)}$$

***2.** Four uniform rods AB, BC, CD, DA, each of weight W and length l, are smoothly jointed at A, B, C, and D, and rest in a vertical plane with A vertically above C and

BC, DC in contact with two smooth horizontal pegs, which are at the same horizontal level and distant $2b$ apart. A load of weight $4nW$ is attached to C, and equilibrium is maintained by a light rod joining A to C. If the angle between CB and CD is 2θ, show that the tension in the rod is

$$2W\left\{(n+1)\frac{b}{l}\operatorname{cosec}^3\theta-1\right\}. \qquad \text{(L.)}$$

***3.** Three equal uniform rods AB, BC, CD, each of weight W, are smoothly jointed to one another at B and C and to two fixed points A, D in the same horizontal line. A light inextensible string joining B to D maintains ABCD in the shape of a rhombus with angle BCD $= 60°$. Prove that when a weight $4W$ is suspended from B the tension in the string is $2\sqrt{3}W$. (L.)

***4.** Five equal uniform rods AB, BC, CD, DE, EA, each of weight W and length $2a$, are smoothly jointed together at A, B, C, D, E and rest in equilibrium in a vertical plane with the joint A uppermost, and AB, AE equally inclined to the vertical and in contact with two smooth fixed pegs, on the same horizontal level and distant $2c$ ($<2a$) apart. If E and B are joined by a light rod of length $2a$, show by the principle of virtual work that the compression in the rod is

$$2W\left(1-\frac{5c}{a}\right)\Big/\sqrt{3}. \qquad \text{(L.)}$$

***5.** Two uniform rods, AB, BC, of unequal lengths but equal weights W, smoothly hinged at B, rest in a vertical plane, the end A being smoothly pivoted at the point $(a, 0)$, B and C being above A, and C sliding on the smooth vertical constraint $x=0$. The system is kept from collapse by a light string of length l joining the point $(0, 0)$ to the hinge B, and $\overrightarrow{AB}$, $\overrightarrow{CB}$ make angles $+\beta$, $-\beta$ respectively, with $y=0$. Show that the tension in the string is given by $T = 2W(l/a)\cot\beta$. (L.)

***6.** Six equal uniform rods, each of weight W, are freely jointed at their ends to form a hexagon ABCDEF. The framework is maintained in the form of a regular hexagon by three light rods connecting B and D, B and F, and D and F respectively. If the framework rests in a vertical plane on two supports at A and B, so that AB is horizontal and below DE, prove that the tensions in the rods BF and DF are each of magnitude W and the thrust in BD is $2W$. (L.)

***7.** A rhombus ABCD consists of four equal uniform rods, of length a and weight W, freely jointed together at their ends. The corners A and C, B and D are joined by two light elastic strings under tension, of equal natural length and each having a modulus of elasticity equal to $2W$. The system is freely suspended from A so as to hang in a vertical plane. Show that in the position of equilibrium $AC = 4a/\sqrt{5}$, provided the natural length of each string is less than $2a/\sqrt{5}$. (L.)

***8.** Four equal uniform rods each of length a are freely jointed together to form a framework ABCD which is suspended from the joint A. The framework is kept in the form of a square by a light string joining A and C. The weight of the framework is W, and a load of weight w is suspended from B and D by two equal light strings each of length $b\,(> a/\sqrt{2})$. Show that the tension in the string AC is

$$\frac{1}{2}\left\{W+w+\frac{wa}{\sqrt{(2b^2-a^2)}}\right\}. \quad \text{(L.)}$$

***9.** A framework consists of six equal uniform rods, each of weight W, freely jointed at their ends to form a regular hexagon ABCDEF, which hangs freely in equilibrium from the point A, being kept in shape by three light rods AC, AD, and AE. Show that the tensions in the rods AC and AD are $W\sqrt{3}$ and $2W$ respectively. (L.)

***10.** A system of three uniform rods AB, BC, CD of unequal lengths freely jointed at B and C is suspended freely from points A and D not necessarily on the same horizontal level. If the weights of AB and CD are equal, show that in equilibrium the mid-point of BC is at its lowest possible position. (C.S.)

***11.** ABCD is a rhombus formed of light rods loosely jointed together; OB, OD are two equal rods jointed at O, B and D. If O is connected to A and C by strings in tension, prove that the tension of each string is inversely proportional to its length. (C.S.)

***12.** ABCD is a rhombus of freely jointed rods lying flat on a smooth table and P, Q are the middle points of AB, AD. Prove that if the system is held in equilibrium by tight strings joining P to Q and A to C, the tensions in these strings are in the ratio of 2BD to AC. (C.S.)

***13.** Three uniform rods AB, BC, CD each of weight W and length $2a$ are freely jointed at B and C. They rest in equilibrium with BC horizontal and uppermost, with AB, CD making equal angles of $\theta = 30°$ with the vertical and resting over two smooth pegs E and F respectively at the same horizontal level. Prove by the *principle of virtual work* that $EF = 13a/6$.

If θ is decreased to $\sin^{-1}\frac{5}{13}$ by means of a light elastic string of natural length $2a$ joining A and D, show that the modulus of the string is approximately $0{\cdot}32W$. (L.)

***14.** Four uniform rods, each of length a and weight w, are freely jointed to form a rhombus ABCD which is freely suspended from A. A smooth uniform disc, of radius r and weight w, rests between the rods CB and CD and in the same vertical plane. The joints B and D are connected by a light elastic string of natural length $3a/4$ and, in equilibrium, $BD = a$. Use the principle of virtual work to show that the modulus of elasticity of the string is $3(2r-\sqrt{3}a)\,w/a$ if $r > \sqrt{3}a/2$. (L.)

***15.** A framework of smoothly jointed rods in the form of a pentagon ABCDE of equal sides of length a is kept just stiff by rods AC, AD of length $b\,(a/2 < b < 2a)$, and rests flat on a smooth horizontal plane. If the rods AB, BC, CD, DE, EA are subject to a uniform normal inwards pressure p per unit length, apply the method of virtual work to show that the thrusts in AC and AD are

$$\frac{p}{4}\left[\frac{ab}{(b^2-\frac{1}{4}a^2)^{1/2}}+\frac{2a^2-b^2}{(a^2-\frac{1}{4}b^2)^{1/2}}\right]. \quad \text{(L.)}$$

***16.** Four uniform rods AB, BC, CD, DE, each of length $5a$ and weight W, are freely jointed at B, C, D. The joints B and D are connected by a light rod of length

$8a$; the ends A, E are attached to small fixed hinges at the same horizontal level and distant $14a$ apart. If the system hangs in equilibrium in a vertical plane with BD below AE and C below BD, show that the stress in the rod BD is $11W/24$. (L.)

***17.** Six equal rods, each of length $2a$ and weight W, are freely jointed together at their ends to form a hexagon ABCDEF, not necessarily regular. The joints B and F, and the joints C and E are joined by light struts, and the framework is freely suspended from A, the struts BF, CE being horizontal and inside the hexagon. If AB, BC, CD make acute angles θ, φ, ψ with the vertical, and CE is not greater than BF, prove that the thrusts in BF, CE are respectively

$$\tfrac{1}{2}W(5\tan\theta+3\tan\varphi), \quad \tfrac{1}{2}W(\tan\psi-3\tan\varphi).$$

Find the reaction at the joint D. (L.)

***18.** A framework consists of two uniform heavy rods AC, BC each of weight W and of length $2a$, and a light rod AB also of length $2a$, with AC horizontal and B below AC. The framework rests in equilibrium with A fixed to a vertical wall and is kept in position in a vertical plane by a horizontal rod BD, of weight $\frac{1}{2}W$ and length a, where D is fixed to the wall vertically below A. All the rods are pin-jointed at A, B, C and D and a weight w is attached to C.

A virtual displacement is made in the system such that the length of AB is increased, the others remaining constant in length. If $2\delta\theta$ is the increase in the angle ACB and $\delta\varphi$ is the increase in angle BAD, prove that $\delta\theta+\delta\varphi = 0$.

Hence prove that the tension in AB is $(7W+4w)/2\sqrt{3}$. (L.)

CHAPTER XXII

*STABILITY OF EQUILIBRIUM

*22.1. The Concept of Stability

In earlier chapters we have investigated the small oscillations of a system when it is slightly displaced from a position of equilibrium. [See § 14.10 and § 16.8, example 5.] In general, if a system is given an *arbitrary* small disturbance from a position of equilibrium, then either

(1) the deviation from the equilibrium state always remains small, or
(2) the deviation eventually becomes large.

The first case is the case of *stable* equilibrium; the second is the case of *unstable* equilibrium. If there is *any* small disturbance which causes the system to deviate largely from the steady state, that state is unstable. It may be possible to find certain disturbances which will not upset an unstable state; hence it is essential that the disturbance applied to a steady state is arbitrary.

Since the subsequent motion of a system after a disturbance is the criterion of stability or instability, we must investigate stability by means of the *equations of motion*. Stability is therefore a matter of dynamics and not strictly of statics, although associated closely with positions of equilibrium.

For systems having one degree of freedom the distinction between stability and instability depends upon the sign of one term in the equation of motion. The differential equation

$$\ddot{y}+n^2y = 0 \tag{22.1}$$

has a general solution

$$y = a\cos(nt+\varepsilon), \tag{22.2}$$

where a, ε are arbitrary constants. If a is small, y and all its derivatives remain small for all values of t, y performing an oscillatory, simple harmonic, variation with time. On the other hand, the differential equation

$$\ddot{y}-n^2y = 0 \tag{22.3}$$

has the general solution

$$y = A\,e^{nt}+B\,e^{-nt}. \tag{22.4}$$

For *arbitrary*, small values of A, B (or arbitrary, small initial values of y and $\dot{y}$), y does not remain small for all values of t. Although y is small initially the factor e^{nt} shows that eventually y increases without limit. (There are some solutions for which y is small and remains so, i.e. when $A=0$, but such solutions cannot satisfy arbitrary initial conditions.) Hence, if the equation of motion of a system approximates to equation (22.1) for small deviations from the steady state, that state is *stable*; if the equation of motion approximates to equation (22.3) for initially small deviations from the steady state, that state is *unstable*.

Consider now a system with one degree of freedom whose configuration is specified by a single parameter q, such as an angle or a length. *If the forces acting on the system are conservative*, the energy equation takes the form

$$\tfrac{1}{2}A(q)\dot{q}^2+V(q) = E, \tag{22.5}$$

where $V(q)$ is the potential energy, $\frac{1}{2}A(q)\dot{q}^2$ is the kinetic energy, and E is a constant, the total energy. Since the kinetic energy must be positive, $A(q) > 0$ for all possible values of q. The equation of motion of the system, obtained by differentiating equation (22.5) and cancelling through by $\dot{q}$, is

$$A(q)\ddot{q}+\tfrac{1}{2}A'(q)\dot{q}^2+V'(q) = 0. \tag{22.6}$$

This equation may also be obtained in many cases by direct application of the laws of motion.

Since all the terms in equation (22.6) are continuous functions of t, it holds when $\dot{q} = 0$ [despite the fact that (22.6) was obtained by cancelling $\dot{q}$ from an equation]. The position, or "motion", given by $q = q_0$ is a possible equilibrium, or steady, state if $\ddot{q} = \dot{q} = 0$, $q = q_0$ satisfy the equation of motion (22.6). Hence

$$V'(q_0) = 0,$$

i.e. V has a stationary value when $q = q_0$.

To investigate the stability of this position we substitute $q = q_0 + y$ into equation (22.6), obtaining

$$A(q_0+y)\ddot{y} + \tfrac{1}{2}A'(q_0+y)\dot{y}^2 + V'(q_0+y) = 0.$$

We assume that y and its derivatives are all small quantities of the first order (of smallness) and approximate this equation correct to the first order, using Taylor's expansion where necessary. Then

$$A(q_0+y)\ddot{y} + \tfrac{1}{2}A'(q_0+y)\dot{y}^2 + V'(q_0+y)$$
$$= V'(q_0) + A(q_0)\ddot{y} + V''(q_0)y + O(y^2) = 0. \qquad (22.7)$$

[Here we use the notation $O(y^2)$ to denote terms involving y^2 and higher powers of y.] The term $\frac{1}{2}A'(q_0+y)\dot{y}^2$ is included in $O(y^2)$ because $\dot{y}^2$ is of the second order. Since the condition for equilibrium is $V'(q_0) = 0$, the equation of motion (22.7), correct to the first order, becomes

$$A(q_0)\ddot{y} + V''(q_0)y = 0. \qquad (22.8)$$

Since $A(q_0) > 0$, equation (22.8) is of the form (22.1) if $V''(q_0) > 0$, and is of the form (22.3) if $V''(q_0) < 0$. We can therefore sum up:

(i) if $V'(q_0) = 0$ and $V''(q_0) < 0$, the equilibrium is unstable; in this case V has a maximum at $q = q_0$;

(ii) if $V'(q_0) = 0$ and $V''(q_0) > 0$, the equilibrium is stable; in this case V has a minimum at $q = q_0$.

The case for which $V''(q_0) = 0$ requires closer investigation; each particular problem is best treated on its merits. Although we have not proved that positions of minimum and maximum potential energy are positions of stable and unstable equilibrium respectively, we shall assume that this is so (and apply the "change in sign of the derivative" test).

*22.2. Stability of Equilibrium

For any system with one degree of freedom under the action of conservative forces the potential energy is a function, $V(q)$, of a single parameter. Excluding the case where $V''(q_0) = 0$, the results of § 22.1

show that the positions of stable and unstable (statical) equilibrium can be found by determining the minima and maxima, respectively, of the potential energy.

Example 1. A uniform rod AB, of weight $12w$ and length $2a$, can turn freely about one extremity A, which is fixed. A light inextensible string attached to the other extremity, B, passes through a small smooth ring fixed at a point C, distant $2a$ from A and at the same level as A, and carries at its other end a particle P of weight w. Show that the system is in stable equilibrium when $8\cos\theta = 1$, where θ is the inclination of AB to the horizontal (see Fig. 22.1).

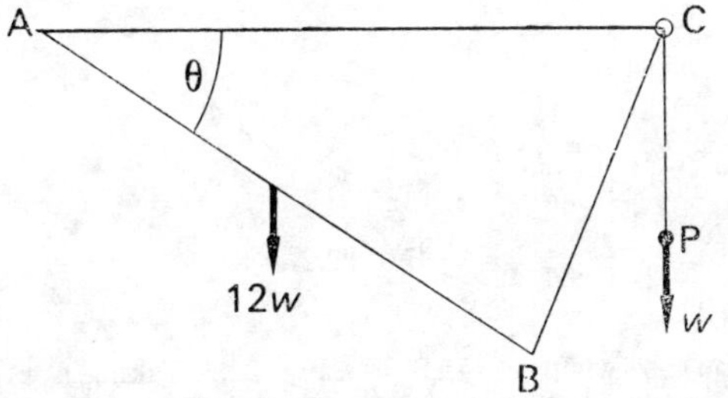

FIG. 22.1

The potential energy is

$$V = -12wa\sin\theta + 4wa\sin\tfrac{1}{2}\theta$$

measured from the configuration of the system when AB is horizontal as origin. We determine the stationary values of V and the nature of these stationary values.

$$\frac{dV}{d\theta} = -12wa\cos\theta + 2wa\cos\frac{1}{2}\theta = -2wa(12c^2 - c - 6),$$

$$\therefore\quad \frac{dV}{d\theta} = -2wa(4c-3)(3c+2),$$

where $c = \cos\frac{1}{2}\theta$. But $dV/d\theta$ vanishes where $c = \frac{3}{4}$ and $c = -\frac{2}{3}$. As θ increases through the value $2\cos^{-1}(\frac{3}{4}) = \cos^{-1}(\frac{1}{8})$, so that as c decreases through the value $\frac{3}{4}$, $dV/d\theta$ changes from negative to positive: hence V has a minimum and $c = \frac{3}{4}$ gives a position of stable equilibrium.

Example 2. A smooth wire in the shape of a circle of radius a is fixed with its plane vertical. A bead P of mass M slides on the wire, and is attached to one end of a light string PQ of length greater than $2a$; the string passes over a smooth peg A fixed at the highest point of the circle and carries a mass m, hanging freely, at its other end Q. Show that positions of unstable equilibrium exist in which the portion of the string between P and A is inclined to the vertical provided that $m < 2M$.

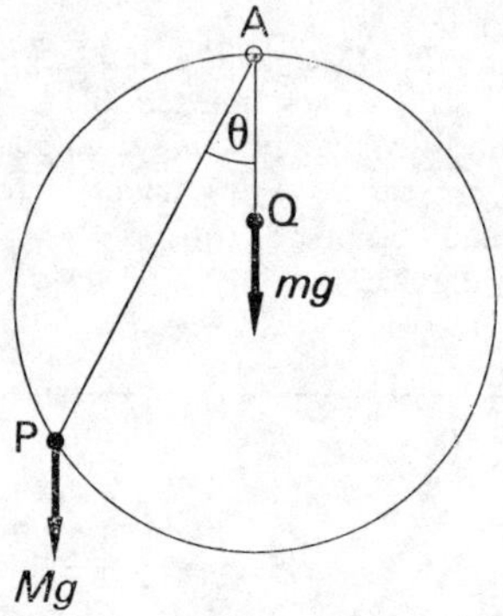

FIG. 22.2

We consider the case when $\angle$ QAP $= \theta$, Fig. 22.2. Taking A as the level of zero potential energy, the potential energy of the system is

$$V = -Mg.\text{AP}\cos\theta - mg.\text{AQ}.$$

But $\text{AP} = 2a\cos\theta, \quad \text{AQ} = l - \text{AP} = l - 2a\cos\theta,$

where l is the length of the string.

$$\therefore\ V = -2Mga\cos^2\theta + 2mga\cos\theta + \text{constant}$$

for $0 \leqq \theta \leqq \frac{1}{2}\pi$.

$$\therefore\ \frac{dV}{d\theta} = 4Mga\sin\theta\cos\theta - 2mga\sin\theta,$$

i.e.
$$\frac{dV}{d\theta} = 4Mga\sin\theta\left(\cos\theta - \frac{m}{2M}\right).$$

Equilibrium positions occur where $dV/d\theta = 0$, i.e. where

$$\sin\theta\left(\cos\theta - \frac{m}{2M}\right) = 0.$$

$$\therefore\ \sin\theta = 0 \quad \text{or} \quad \cos\theta = \frac{m}{2M}.$$

The only physically realizable position corresponding to $\sin\theta = 0$ is the position $\theta = 0$ in which P is vertically below A. The equation $\cos\theta = m/(2M)$ has a real root

$\theta = \alpha$ in the range $0 < \theta < \frac{1}{2}\pi$, i.e. an unsymmetrical position exists, if $m < 2M$. In this case

$$\frac{dV}{d\theta} = 4Mga \sin\theta\,(\cos\theta - \cos\alpha)$$

and, as θ *increases* through the value α, $dV/d\theta$ changes sign from positive to negative. Hence $\theta = \alpha$ gives a maximum value to V and the position of equilibrium is unstable.

There is also an intuitive method of determining the stability of a system without finding V explicitly.

In § 21.2, where the function V was introduced, we showed that

$$F = -\frac{dV}{dx},$$

where F is the resultant "force" acting on the system and x is the coordinate representing the one degree of freedom of the body.

This equation indicates that the sign of F determines the sign of dV/dx, and therefore that an examination of F for small displacements of the body from a predetermined equilibrium position will enable us to decide what kind of stationary value of V this equilibrium position represents. *If in the slightly displaced position the resultant tends to restore the position of equilibrium, the position is stable.* This is the intuitive method used when stability is regarded as a matter of statics instead of dynamics.

Example. A hollow vessel made of thin uniform material consists of a right circular cylinder of radius a and height h. One end of the vessel is closed by a plane face and the other end is closed by a hemispherical shell. Show that the vessel can rest in stable equilibrium with the hemisphere in contact with a horizontal table and the axis of symmetry of the vessel vertical provided $2h < (\sqrt{5}-1)a$. (C.S.)

The three possible cases which can arise are illustrated in Figs. 22.3 (i), (ii), (iii) in each of which the vessel has been displaced through a small angle θ from the vertical position. In each case the reaction between the hemisphere and the plane passes through its point of contact B with the plane. For stability the moment about B of the weight W must be in the sense (counter-clockwise) so as to diminish θ. Clearly the only case in which this condition is satisfied is shown in Fig. 22.3 (i), where G the centre of mass lies within OA where O is the centre of the plane base and A is the vertex of the hemisphere. In the critical case when G coincides with O, equilibrium is possible for any inclination of AO to the vertical and therefore the vertical position cannot be said to be stable. Therefore the condition for stability is

$$AG < AO.$$

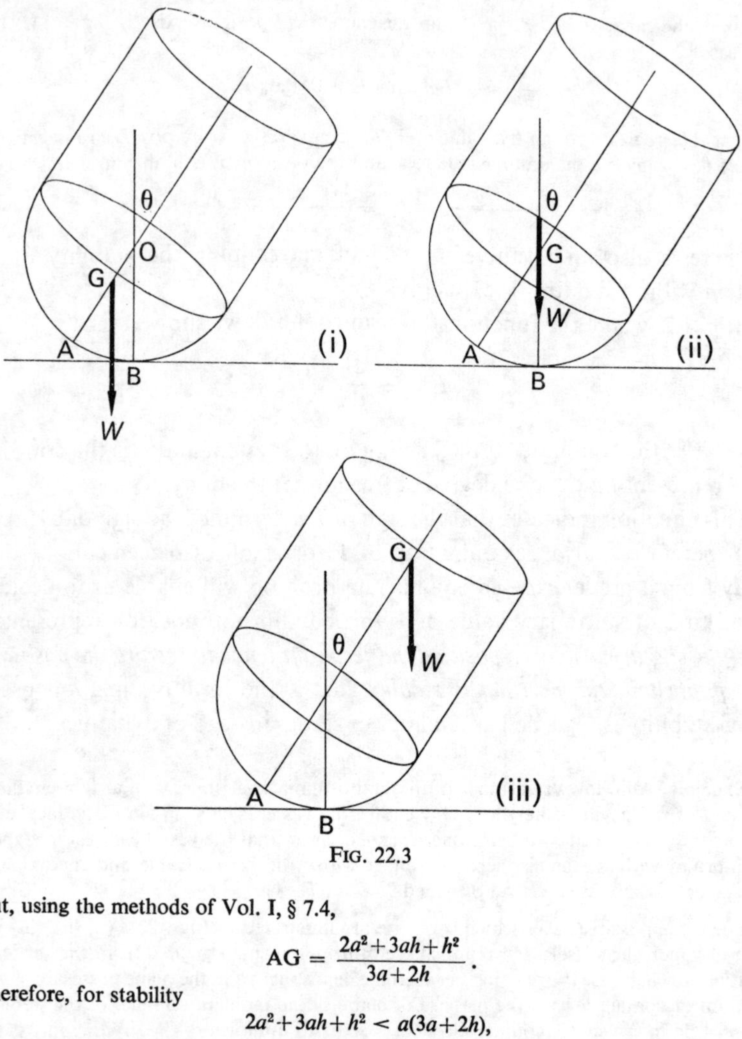

FIG. 22.3

But, using the methods of Vol. I, § 7.4,

$$AG = \frac{2a^2+3ah+h^2}{3a+2h}.$$

Therefore, for stability

$$2a^2+3ah+h^2 < a(3a+2h),$$

i.e.

$$h^2+ah-a^2 < 0.$$

Therefore h must lie between the roots of the equation $h^2+ah-a^2 = 0$,

i.e.

$$-(1+\sqrt{5})a < 2h < (\sqrt{5}-1)a$$

and since $h > 0$ this gives the required result.

For positions in which $V'(q_0) = 0$, $V''(q_0) = 0$ no statement about stability can be made on this evidence alone. A position of *neutral equilibrium* is such that on receiving a small disturbance the system neither tends to return to the equilibrium position nor to move further away but is in equilibrium in the disturbed position. Cases of strictly neutral equilibrium are rare, being typified by a uniform sphere resting with its curved surface on a rough horizontal plane. (However, if the sphere is given a small velocity it will continue to roll indefinitely; it can then hardly be said to "deviate slightly" from its original position, and so such a position could be called unstable.)

Since the determination of stability of equilibrium is effectively the same as the investigation of the nature of the stationary points of the function $V(q)$, those cases in which $V''(q_0) = 0$ are the mechanical counterparts of those cases of stationary points of functions for which some derivatives of higher order than the first vanish. These cases often arise from the coincidence of a number of stationary points. [See example (i) below.]

It remains true that, if V is a *minimum* at $q = q_0$, then this position is one of *stable* equilibrium and if V is a *maximum* at $q = q_0$ then this position is one of unstable equilibrium. Proofs of these statements will not be given here. [Proofs are given on pp. 299–300 of Vol. III, *A Course of Mathematics for Engineers and Scientists,* CHIRGWIN and PLUMPTON.]

Example 1. A uniform square lamina of side $2a$ rests in a vertical plane with two of its sides in contact with horizontal smooth pegs distant b apart, and in the same horizontal line. Find the positions of equilibrium and discuss their stability. Show in particular that, if $a/\sqrt{2} < b < a$, a non-symmetrical position of unstable equilibrium is possible in which

$$b(\sin\theta + \cos\theta) = a,$$

where θ is the inclination of a side of the square to the horizontal. (L.)

Figure 22.4 shows that the height of G above the fixed level PQ is

$$a\sqrt{2}\sin(\theta + \tfrac{1}{4}\pi) - x\cos\theta, \quad \text{where} \quad x = \text{AQ} = b\sin\theta.$$

$$\therefore \frac{V}{W} = a\sqrt{2}\sin\left(\theta + \frac{1}{4}\pi\right) - b\sin\theta\cos\theta.$$

$$\therefore \frac{1}{W}\frac{\mathrm{d}V}{\mathrm{d}\theta} = a\sqrt{2}\cos\left(\theta + \frac{1}{4}\pi\right) - b\cos 2\theta$$

$$= (\cos\theta - \sin\theta)\{a - b(\cos\theta + \sin\theta)\},$$

i.e.

$$\frac{1}{W}\frac{\mathrm{d}V}{\mathrm{d}\theta} = (\cos\theta - \sin\theta)\left\{a - b\sqrt{2}\sin\left(\theta + \frac{1}{4}\pi\right)\right\}.$$

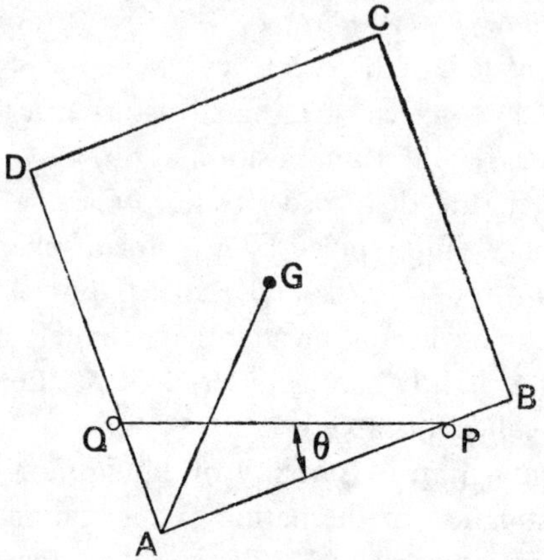

FIG. 22.4

Equilibrium positions occur when $\mathrm{d}V/\mathrm{d}\theta = 0$, i.e. when $\cos\theta = \sin\theta$ which gives the symmetrical position, $\theta = \frac{1}{4}\pi$, and when

$$\sin\left(\theta+\frac{1}{4}\pi\right) = \frac{a}{b\sqrt{2}},$$

i.e.

$$b(\sin\theta+\cos\theta) = a. \tag{1}$$

This latter value gives an unsymmetrical position. The corresponding value of $\theta(\neq \frac{1}{4}\pi)$ is real if $b > a/\sqrt{2}$. Moreover, $\theta > 0$ for equilibrium to be possible and hence for the existence of unsymmetrical positions

$$\frac{a}{b\sqrt{2}} > \frac{1}{\sqrt{2}},$$

i.e. $b < a$. Therefore unsymmetrical positions occur when

$$\frac{a}{\sqrt{2}} < b < a.$$

As θ is made to increase through $\frac{1}{4}\pi$, $\mathrm{d}V/\mathrm{d}\theta$ changes from positive to negative if $a \geqq b\sqrt{2}$. Hence if $b \leqq a/\sqrt{2}$ there is only one position of equilibrium and this position is unstable.

On the other hand, if $b > a/\sqrt{2}$, $\mathrm{d}V/\mathrm{d}\theta$ changes from negative to positive as θ increases through $\frac{1}{4}\pi$ and the symmetrical position is stable. In this case, too, the unsymmetrical positions exist (provided $b < a$) and, as θ increases through the values given by equation (1), $\mathrm{d}V/\mathrm{d}\theta$ changes from positive to negative showing that these positions are unstable.

If $a = b\sqrt{2}$, all three positions of equilibrium coincide in the position $\theta = \frac{1}{4}\pi$. Since

$$\frac{1}{W}\frac{d^2V}{d\theta^2} = -a\sqrt{2}\sin\left(\theta+\frac{1}{4}\pi\right)+2b\sin 2\theta,$$

we see that, in this case, $d^2V/d\theta^2 = 0$ in the equilibrium position. We have shown above that this is an unstable position.

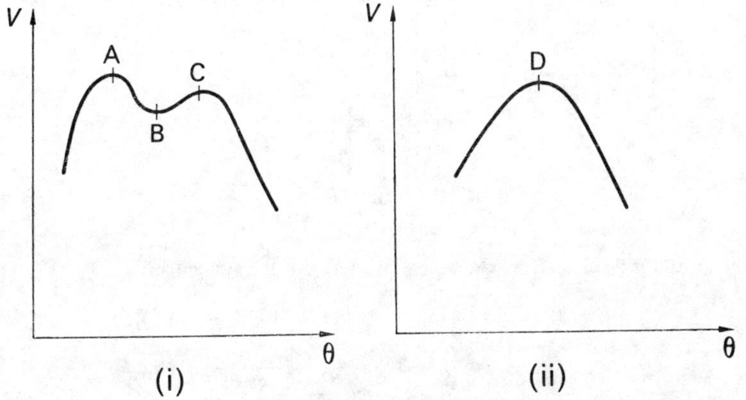

FIG. 22.5

This example illustrates two features which occur frequently when V is a function of a single parameter. Fig. 22.5 (i) shows that, in the graph of V, maxima and minima alternate, so that two positions of unstable equilibrium are separated by a position of stable equilibrium, and vice versa. This must be so for any function V which is continuous. The situation shown in Fig. 22.5 (ii) is the limiting case in which the three points A, B, C, of Fig. 22.5 (i) coincide in one stationary point D. Although $d^2V/d\theta^2 = 0$ at D the stationary value is nevertheless a maximum.

Example 2. One end A of a uniform rod AB of length $2a$ and weight W can turn freely about a fixed smooth hinge; the other end B is attached by a light elastic string of unstretched length a to a fixed support at the point O vertically above and distant $4a$ from A. If the equilibrium of the vertical position of the rod with B above A is stable, find the minimum modulus of elasticity of the string. (C.S.)

Consider the case in which $\angle$ OAB $= \theta$, Fig. 22.6. The potential energy of the rod (taking A as the level of zero energy) is $Wa\cos\theta$ and the potential energy of the elastic string is

$$\lambda(\text{OB}-a)^2/(2a) = \tfrac{1}{2}\lambda a\{2\sqrt{(5-4\cos\theta)}-1\}^2,$$

where λ is the modulus of the string. The string is always stretched since the least

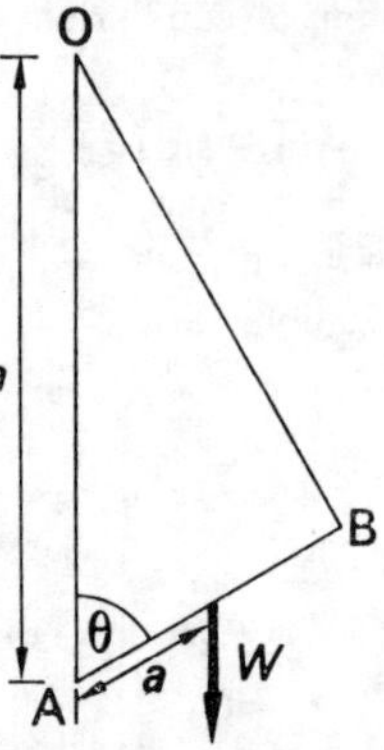

FIG. 22.6

value of OB is $2a$. Therefore the potential energy of the system is

$$V = Wa\cos\theta + \tfrac{1}{2}\lambda a\{21-16\cos\theta-4\sqrt{(5-4\cos\theta)}\}.$$

$$\therefore\ \frac{1}{a}\frac{dV}{d\theta} = \left\{8\lambda - W - \frac{4\lambda}{\sqrt{(5-4\cos\theta)}}\right\}\sin\theta. \qquad (1)$$

In order that the vertical position with B above A, $\theta=0$, should be stable V must be a minimum at $\theta=0$, i.e. $dV/d\theta$ must change from negative to positive as θ passes through 0. Since $\sin\theta$ changes sign from negative to positive as θ passes through 0, this is equivalent to the condition

$$8\lambda - W - \frac{4\lambda}{\sqrt{(5-4\cos\theta)}} > 0 \qquad (2)$$

for θ small but non-zero. Since the function on the l.h. side of inequality (2) increases as $|\theta|$ increases from zero, the required condition is obtained from the condition that the l.h. side of (2) is greater than or equal to zero when $\theta=0$,

i.e. $$8\lambda - W - 4\lambda \geqq 0,$$

i.e. $$\lambda \geqq \tfrac{1}{4}W.$$

The minimum modulus of the string is therefore $\frac{1}{4}W$.

Example 3. A thin smooth wire in the form of a circle, of radius a and centre O, is fixed with its plane vertical. At the ends A, B of the horizontal diameter AOB are fixed small smooth pulleys. A small smooth ring of weight W can slide on the wire, and attached to it are two light strings which pass one over each of the pulleys at A

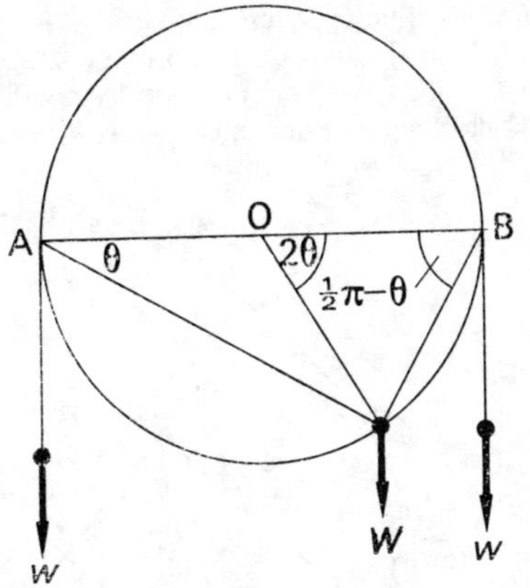

FIG. 22.7

and B, and support equal weights w. Show that, if $W < w < W\sqrt{2}$, there are three positions of equilibrium in which the ring is below AB. Discuss the stability of equilibrium. Discuss also the case $w \geqq W\sqrt{2}$. (O.S.)

In the position shown in Fig. 22.7 the potential energy, referred to AOB as zero level, is

$$V = -Wa\sin 2\theta + w(2a\cos\theta + 2a\sin\theta) + \text{constant}.$$

$$\therefore \quad \frac{dV}{d\theta} = -2Wa\cos 2\theta + 2wa(\cos\theta - \sin\theta),$$

i.e.
$$\frac{dV}{d\theta} = -2aW(\cos\theta - \sin\theta)\left(\cos\theta + \sin\theta - \frac{w}{W}\right),$$

i.e.
$$\frac{dV}{d\theta} = -2\sqrt{2}aW(\cos\theta - \sin\theta)\left\{\sin\left(\frac{1}{4}\pi + \theta\right) - \frac{w}{W\sqrt{2}}\right\}. \tag{1}$$

Hence the equilibrium positions are given by

$$\cos\theta = \sin\theta \quad \text{and} \quad \sin\left(\frac{1}{4}\pi + \theta\right) = \frac{w}{W\sqrt{2}},$$

i.e.
$$\theta = \frac{1}{4}\pi \quad \text{and} \quad \theta = \sin^{-1}\left(\frac{w}{W\sqrt{2}}\right) - \frac{\pi}{4}.$$

Therefore, if $w \geqq W\sqrt{2}$ there is only one position of equilibrium, the symmetrical case $\theta = \frac{1}{4}\pi$. [For $\sin^{-1}\{w/(W\sqrt{2})\}$ is only real *and different from* $\frac{1}{2}\pi$ provided $w < W\sqrt{2}$.] In this case $dV/d\theta$ changes sign from positive to negative as θ goes through $\frac{1}{4}\pi$ and so V is a maximum, i.e. when the symmetrical position alone exists it is unstable.

When $W < w < W\sqrt{2}$, $\frac{1}{4}\pi < \sin^{-1}\{w/(W\sqrt{2})\} < \frac{1}{2}\pi$ and unsymmetrical positions exist in addition to the symmetrical positions. In this case V is a minimum (equilibrium is stable) when $\theta = \frac{1}{4}\pi$ and V is a maximum (equilibrium is unstable) in the unsymmetrical positions.

Example 4. A uniform elliptic cylinder of weight W is loaded with a particle of weight kW at an end of the major axis of the normal cross-section through its centre of gravity, and is placed with its axis horizontal on a smooth horizontal table. Determine the possible positions of equilibrium and consider the stability of the symmetrical positions. (C.S.)

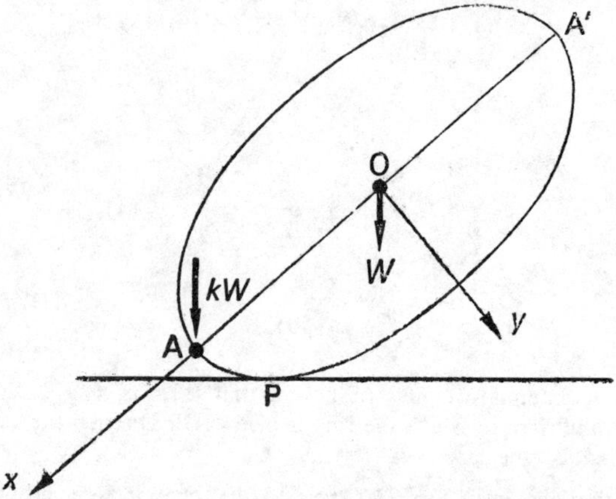

FIG. 22.8

With the usual notation for an ellipse, Fig. 22.8, let the point of contact P be the point of eccentric angle φ. Then the tangent at P has equation

$$\frac{x\cos\varphi}{a}+\frac{y\sin\varphi}{b}=1.$$

The perpendicular distances of O and A from this tangent are respectively

$$\frac{ab}{\sqrt{(a^2\sin^2\varphi+b^2\cos^2\varphi)}},\quad \frac{ab(1-\cos\varphi)}{\sqrt{(a^2\sin^2\varphi+b^2\cos^2\varphi)}}.$$

Therefore, taking the plane as the level of zero potential energy,

$$V=\frac{abW(1+k-k\cos\varphi)}{\sqrt{(a^2\sin^2\varphi+b^2\cos^2\varphi)}}.$$

$$\therefore\ \frac{1}{abW}\frac{dV}{d\varphi}=\frac{k\sin\varphi}{\sqrt{(a^2\sin^2\varphi+b^2\cos^2\varphi)}}$$

$$-\frac{(1+k-k\cos\varphi)(a^2-b^2)\sin\varphi\cos\varphi}{(a^2\sin^2\varphi+b^2\cos^2\varphi)^{3/2}},$$

i.e.

$$\frac{1}{abW}\frac{dV}{d\varphi}=\frac{\sin\varphi\{ka^2-(1+k)(a^2-b^2)\cos\varphi\}}{(a^2\sin^2\varphi+b^2\cos\varphi)^{3/2}}. \qquad (1)$$

Equilibrium positions occur where $\sin\varphi = 0$, i.e. $\varphi = 0$ and π, and

$$\cos\varphi = \frac{ka^2}{(1+k)(a^2-b^2)} = \frac{k}{(1+k)e^2},$$

where e is the eccentricity of the ellipse. This equation gives real values of φ (distinct from $\varphi = 0$) provided $e > \sqrt{\{k/(1+k)\}}$. Therefore there are

(1) two positions of equilibrium only when $e \leq \sqrt{\{k/(1+k)\}}$,
(2) four positions when $e > \sqrt{\{k/(1+k)\}}$.

Examination of the r.h. side of (1) shows that when the symmetrical positions alone exist the position $\varphi = 0$ is stable and the position $\varphi = \pi$ is unstable. On the other hand, when the unsymmetrical positions exist they are stable and both the symmetrical positions are unstable.

In some cases stability of equilibrium can be investigated by direct determination of the change in potential energy when a system is slightly disturbed. The technique is illustrated in the following example.

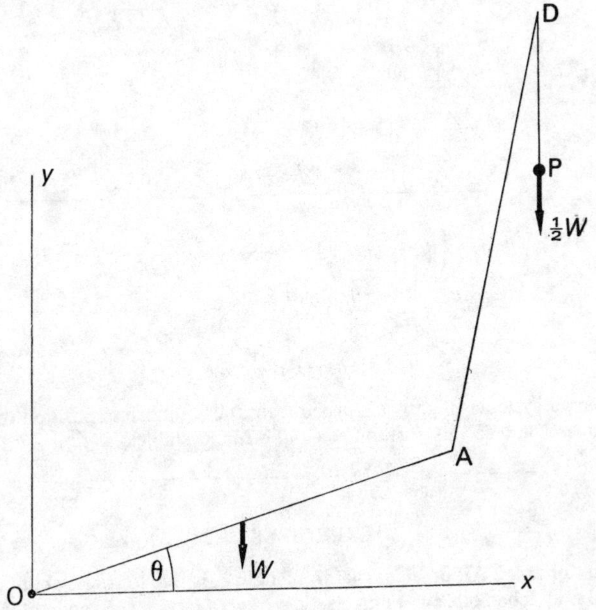

FIG. 22.9

Example. A uniform rod OA, of weight W and length $2a$, is free to turn about a smooth pivot at O. The rod is supported horizontally by a light inextensible string attached to A. The string passes over a small fixed smooth peg D vertically above A and at a height $2a$ above A, and carries a particle P of weight $\frac{1}{2}W$ at its other end. Find, correct to the fourth order in θ, the increase in potential energy when OA turns through a small angle θ and deduce that the equilibrium is stable. (O.S.)

We consider only disturbances for which the rod remains in the same vertical plane. When the rod is inclined at the angle θ to the horizontal, Fig. 22.9, the coordinates of A referred to horizontal and vertical axes Ox, Oy are $(2a\cos\theta, 2a\sin\theta)$. Since D is the point $(2a, 2a)$,

$$AD^2 = (2a-2a\cos\theta)^2+(2a-2a\sin\theta)^2 = 4a^2(3-2\cos\theta-2\sin\theta).$$

Hence P has fallen a distance $2a\{1-\sqrt{(3-2\cos\theta-2\sin\theta)}\}$. The gain in potential energy is, therefore,

$$\delta V = W.a\sin\theta-\tfrac{1}{2}W.2a\{1-\sqrt{(3-2\cos\theta-2\sin\theta)}\}.$$

Using the approximations

$$\sin\theta \approx \theta-\theta^3/6, \quad \cos\theta \approx 1-\theta^2/2+\theta^4/24,$$

where terms higher than θ^4 have been neglected, we find

$$\delta V \approx Wa\left\{\theta-\frac{\theta^3}{6}-1+\left(1-2\theta+\theta^2+\frac{\theta^3}{3}-\frac{\theta^4}{12}\right)^{1/2}\right\}$$

$$\approx Wa\left\{\theta-\frac{\theta^3}{6}-1+1+\frac{1}{2}\left(-2\theta+\theta^2+\frac{\theta^3}{3}-\frac{\theta^4}{12}\right)\right.$$

$$+\frac{\frac{1}{2}(-\frac{1}{2})}{2}\left(-2\theta+\theta^2+\frac{\theta^3}{3}\right)^2$$

$$\left.+\frac{\frac{1}{2}(-\frac{1}{2})(-\frac{3}{2})(-2\theta+\theta^2)^3}{6}+\frac{\frac{1}{2}(-\frac{1}{2})(-\frac{3}{2})(-\frac{5}{2})(-2\theta)^4}{24}\right\}$$

$$\approx Wa\left\{\theta-\frac{\theta^3}{6}-1+1-\theta+\frac{\theta^2}{2}+\frac{\theta^3}{6}-\frac{\theta^4}{24}-\frac{\theta^2}{2}\right.$$

$$\left.+\frac{\theta^3}{2}+\frac{\theta^4}{24}-\frac{\theta^3}{2}+\frac{3\theta^4}{4}-\frac{5\theta^4}{8}\right\}.$$

$$\therefore\ \delta V \approx Wa\theta^4/8.$$

Hence when the system is slightly disturbed from the equilibrium position the potential energy increases and so this position of equilibrium is stable.

---

*EXERCISES 22.2

*1. A uniform rod AB of weight W and length a, is free to rotate about A, which is fixed. To B is attached one end of an elastic string, of modulus W and natural length a. The rod is hung vertically downwards and the free end of the string is then attached to a fixed point, at a height b vertically above A. Show that the rod is in stable equilibrium if $b < a$. (O.C.)

***2.** A uniform rod AB, of weight W and length $2a$, is free to rotate in a vertical plane about the point A. A light elastic string, of modulus kW and natural length a, has one end attached to B and the other to a fixed point O which is vertically above A. If OA $= 2a$ show that when AB makes an angle θ with the downward vertical, the potential energy of the system, when the string is stretched, may be expressed in the form

$$Wa\{(4k-1)\cos\theta - 4k\cos(\theta/2)\} + \text{constant}.$$

Deduce that, if $k > \frac{1}{3}$, the equilibrium position in which the rod is vertical, with B below A, is unstable, and that there is an oblique position of equilibrium which is stable. (L.)

***3.** Two uniform rods AB, BC each of length a and of the same weight are smoothly hinged together at B and rest in equilibrium over two small smooth pegs in a horizontal line at a distance c ($< a$) apart. Prove that the angle of inclination of each rod to the vertical is

$$\sin^{-1}\left(\frac{c}{a}\right)^{1/3}.$$

Show also that the equilibrium is stable for displacements in which A moves in a vertical line passing through the middle point of the line joining the pegs. (N.)

***4.** Three equal uniform bars AB, BC, CD, each of length $2a$, are smoothly jointed at B, C and rest with BC horizontal and AB, CD each on small smooth pegs at the same level at a distance $2(a+b)$ apart.

Show that, if $2a > 3b$, there are two positions of equilibrium, and determine which of them is stable.

If $2a = 3b$, show that there is only one position of equilibrium and that it is unstable. (N.)

***5.** A smooth uniform wedge whose cross-section is an isosceles triangle of vertical angle 2α, with its centre of gravity at a distance h from its vertex, is placed with its equal slant sides in contact with the parallel edges of a slit in a horizontal table, these edges being at a distance c apart. Prove that there are unsymmetrical positions of equilibrium if

$$c < h\cos\alpha < c\operatorname{cosec}\alpha,$$

and that in this case the symmetrical position is stable.

Prove also, that if $h\cos\alpha = c\operatorname{cosec}\alpha$, the symmetrical position is the only position of equilibrium, and that it is unstable. It may be assumed that the wedge is too large to drop through the slit in any position. (O.C.)

***6.** A uniform rod can turn in a vertical plane about one end which is fixed. The rod is in equilibrium in the horizontal position, supported by a fine string attached to its other end passing over a smooth peg vertically above the middle point of the rod and then carrying a suitably chosen weight. Prove that the horizontal position is one of stable equilibrium if the inclination of the string to the horizontal is less than 45°. (O.C.)

*7. Four equal uniform rods, each of weight W and length $2a$, are smoothly jointed to form a rhombus ABCD which is smoothly pivoted to a fixed point at A. A uniform disc of radius $a/2$ and weight $8W$ is in the same plane as the rods and rests in smooth contact with the rods BC, CD, the whole hanging in a vertical plane. Show that there is an equilibrium position in which the rods are inclined at an angle $\tan^{-1}(\frac{1}{2})$ to the vertical. Discuss the stability of this position. (N.)

*8. Four uniform rods, each of weight W and length $2a$, are smoothly jointed together to form a rhombus ABCD, and a light elastic string of modulus $2W$ and natural length a connects A and C. The vertex A is smoothly pinned to a fixed support and the system hangs at rest. Show that there is a position of stable equilibrium in which the angle BCD of the rhombus is 120°. (L.)

*9. A rod AB of mass m and length $2a$ can move freely about an end A which is fixed. An elastic string of natural length a and modulus $\frac{1}{2}mg$ is attached to B and to a small ring which can move freely on a smooth horizontal wire at a height $3a$ above A and in the vertical plane through A. Find the positions of equilibrium and examine their stability. (N.)

*10. A heavy rod AB can turn freely in a vertical plane about one end A which is fixed. To the other end B is tied a light elastic string of natural length $\frac{3}{4}$ AB and of modulus equal to half the weight of the rod. The other end of the string is attached to a light ring which can slide on a smooth horizontal bar, which is fixed at a height equal to twice AB above A and in the vertical plane through AB. Find the equilibrium positions of the rod and discuss the stability in each case. (L.)

*11. A smooth ring P of mass m is free to slide on a smooth fixed vertical circular wire of radius a and centre O. A light elastic string, of natural length $2a$ and modulus kmg, passes through the ring, its ends being fixed to the ends A and B of the horizontal diameter of the wire. Find the potential energy of the system when OP makes an angle 2θ with AB, the ring being below AB. Show that if $k > 2+\sqrt{2}$ the ring is in unstable equilibrium when at the lowest point of the wire. Investigate the stability in this position when $k = 2+\sqrt{2}$. (L.)

*12. A uniform lamina in the shape of a rhombus consisting of two equilateral triangles of side a rests in a vertical plane with two adjacent sides on two smooth pegs in a horizontal line distance $\frac{1}{4}a\sqrt{3}$ apart. Prove that in equilibrium either a diagonal or a side is vertical, and find which of these is a position of stable equilibrium. (L.)

*13. A ring A of weight W slides on a smooth circular wire of radius a fixed with its plane vertical. A light inextensible string attached to A passes over a small smooth pulley at O, the end of a horizontal diameter, and supports a weight nW $(n < 1)$ hanging freely. If, when the system is in equilibrium, OA makes an angle θ above the horizontal prove that $\cos 2\theta = n \sin \theta$.

Prove that there are two positions of equilibrium and that the position with the ring on the upper half of the circle is unstable. (L.)

*14. A smooth circular wire of radius a and centre O is fixed with its plane vertical. A uniform rod PQ of length $6a/5$ and weight W has small light rings at its ends, which slide on the wire. A light elastic string of natural length a and modulus of elasticity

$6W/7$ has one end tied to C, the mid-point of PQ, and the other end to A, a fixed point at distance $2a$ vertically above O. Show that when the angle AOC is $\pi-\theta$, the potential energy of the system is

$$\frac{4}{35}Wa\{5\cos\theta-3\sqrt{(29+20\cos\theta)}\}+\text{ a constant.}$$

Deduce that there are four possible positions of equilibrium, and that the two in which the rod is horizontal are both unstable. (L.)

***15.** Four equal uniform rods, each of weight W and length $2a$, are smoothly jointed to form a rhombus ABCD. The rhombus is in equilibrium in a vertical plane with the lower rods, BC and DC, resting on two smooth pegs at the same level, distant $2c$ apart ($c < a$), and with AC vertical. A and C are joined by an elastic string of natural length $2a$ and modulus $2W$. Show that, if the angle DCB $= 2\theta$, then $4a\cos\theta\sin^3\theta = c$.

Verify that this equation has a root in θ between 0° and 45°, and investigate the stability of the corresponding equilibrium position. (N.)

***16.** A uniform rod AB of length l and weight W is placed with one end A against a smooth vertical wall OC and with the end B attached by a light ring to a fixed smooth wire in the form of a quadrant of a circle of radius a ($> l$), whose centre is O and whose lowest point is C. Find the couple which will keep the rod in equilibrium inclined at an angle φ to the vertical. Hence show that, if $2l > a$ and there is no couple acting, the rod is in equilibrium when $\varphi = 0$ and when $\cos^2\varphi = (a^2-l^2)/3l^2$. Prove that the equilibrium in the latter case is unstable. (N.)

***17.** A smooth semicircular wire is fixed in a vertical plane with its bounding diameter horizontal and above the wire. To a smooth bead, of mass m_1, which is free to slide on the wire, are attached light inextensible strings which pass over small smooth pulleys at the ends of the wire and carry equal masses m_2 at their other ends. Prove that there is always a position of equilibrium in which the ring is at the lowest point of the wire, and that this position is not stable if $m_1\sqrt{2} \leqq m_2$.

Prove also that, if $m_1\sqrt{2} > m_2$, there are positions of equilibrium in which the bead is not at the lowest point of the wire and that these positions are unstable. (O.C.)

***18.** Three equal uniform rods AB, BC, CD, each of weight W and length $2a$, are smoothly jointed together at B and C. The ends A and D are smoothly pivoted to two fixed points distant $2a$ apart in the same vertical line, with A uppermost. The middle points of AB and BC are joined by an elastic string of natural length a and modulus $12W$ and the rods rest in a vertical plane. Find the angles which AB makes with the vertical in the positions of equilibrium and discuss the stability of these positions. (N.)

***19.** Four equal uniform rods, each of length a, are rigidly jointed together to form a rhombus ABCD in which angle DAB $= 2\alpha$. The rhombus is free to move in a vertical plane with A uppermost and with the rods AB, AD resting on two smooth pegs, P and Q, fixed at the same level and distant c apart.

Show that if $a\sin\alpha\cos^2\alpha < c$ the equilibrium position in which AC is vertical is unstable, but that positions of stable equilibrium exist in which AC is inclined to the vertical. Find the inclination of AC to the vertical in these positions. It may be assumed that in these positions AP $< a$ and AQ $< a$. (N.)

***20.** Four equal uniform rods, each of weight W and length $2a$, are smoothly hinged together to form a rhombus ABCD, the hinge A being freely pivoted to a fixed point. The middle points of AB and BC are connected together by a light elastic string of modulus λ and natural length $a/3$, and the middle points of AD and DC are connected together by another, exactly similar, string. Find the inclinations of the rods to the vertical in the equilibrium positions in the cases $2W < 5\lambda$ and $2W > 5\lambda$. Discuss the stability of these positions. (N.)

***21.** A smooth cylinder of radius a is fixed with its axis horizontal and at a distance c from a smooth vertical wall. A uniform rod of length l rests at right angles to the axis of the cylinder with one end in contact with the cylinder and the other end in contact with the wall. Show that in the position of equilibrium the inclination φ of the rod to the vertical satisfies the equation

$$a \sin \varphi = (c - l \sin \varphi)\sqrt{(1+3\cos^2 \varphi)}.$$

Also show that the equilibrium is unstable. (O.C.)

*22.3. Rolling Stability—The Rocking Stone

We now discuss, by means of illustrative examples, the stability of equilibrium of a rigid body which rolls on a fixed surface so that each point of it moves parallel to a vertical plane. The theory covers the two-dimensional motion of a rocking stone. In the two examples below, both the rolling body and the fixed surface on which it rolls have circular cross-sections.

Example 1. Find the distance from the centre of a uniform solid sphere, of radius a, to the centre of mass of the smaller of the segments into which it is divided by a plane distant $\frac{1}{2}a$ from its centre.

This segment rests with its plane face horizontal and uppermost and its curved surface in contact with the highest point of a fixed sphere of radius a. Assuming that the surfaces are sufficiently rough to prevent sliding, show that the segment may be rolled through an angle $2\cos^{-1}(20/27)$ into a position of unstable equilibrium. (L.)

Integration shows that the centre of mass of the segment is at a distance $27a/40$ from the centre of the sphere from which it is cut. In the oblique position shown in Fig. 22.10 the segment has been turned through an angle 2θ. If W is the weight of the segment, the potential energy, V, is given by

$$\frac{V}{W} = 2a\cos\theta - \frac{27a}{40}\cos 2\theta.$$

$$\therefore \quad \frac{1}{W}\frac{dV}{d\theta} = -2a\sin\theta + \frac{27a}{20}\sin 2\theta = \frac{27a}{10}\sin\theta\left(\cos\theta - \frac{20}{27}\right).$$

Also
$$\frac{1}{W}\frac{d^2V}{d\theta^2} = -2a\cos\theta + \frac{27a}{10}\cos 2\theta.$$

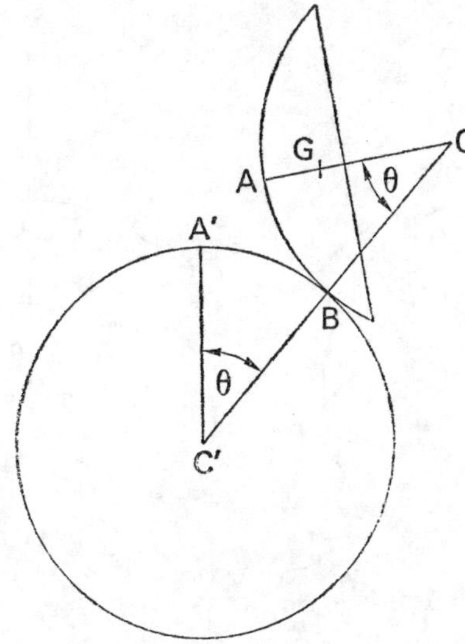

FIG. 22.10

Hence $dV/d\theta$ vanishes for $\theta = 0$ and $\cos\theta = 20/27$. When $\theta = 0$,

$$d^2V/d\theta^2 = W\left(-2a+\frac{27a}{10}\right) > 0.$$

Also, when $\cos\theta = 20/27$,

$$d^2V/d\theta^2 = Wa\left(-\frac{40}{27}+\frac{27}{5}\cdot\frac{400}{(27)^2}-\frac{27}{10}\right) < 0.$$

Therefore the position $\theta = 0$ is a position of stable equilibrium (V has a minimum there) and the oblique position, $\cos\theta = 20/27$, is a position of unstable equilibrium (V has a maximum there).

Example 2. A circular cylinder of radius r rests in equilibrium on the top of a rough circular cylinder, which is of radius R and is fixed with its axis horizontal. The vertical plane through the centre of gravity G of the upper cylinder cuts the axes of the cylinders in C′ and C, Fig. 22.11 (i). If A is the highest point of the fixed cylinder and AG = h, investigate the stability of this equilibrium.

In the displaced position [Fig. 22.11 (ii)] the weight of the upper cylinder acting through G will tend to restore equilibrium if G is to the left of the vertical through B. Since the displaced position is obtained by rolling the upper cylinder, arc A′B = arc AB and so

$$R\theta = r\varphi.$$

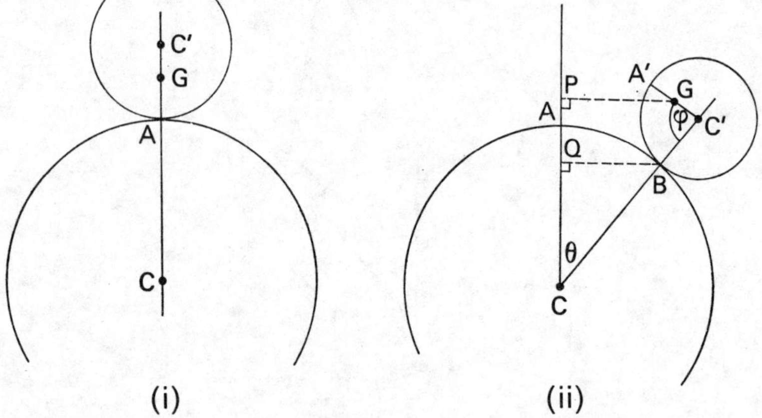

FIG. 22.11

The horizontal distance of B from the vertical CA is

$$R \sin \theta \approx R\theta,$$

and the horizontal distance of G from this vertical is

$$(R+r) \sin \theta-(r-h) \sin(\theta+\varphi) \approx (R+r)\, \theta-(r-h)\, (\theta+\varphi).$$

Hence the equilibrium of Fig. 22.11 (i) is stable provided

$$R\theta > (R+r)\theta-(r-h)\, (\theta+\varphi).$$

Utilizing the relation $R\theta = r\varphi$, the inequality gives

$$rR > (r+R)r-(r-h)\, (r+R),$$

i.e.

$$rR > h(r+R)$$

or

$$\frac{1}{h} > \frac{1}{r}+\frac{1}{R}$$

as a *sufficient condition for the equilibrium in the symmetrical position to be stable.*

When

$$\frac{1}{h} < \frac{1}{r}+\frac{1}{R}$$

the vertical through G passes to the right of B and *the symmetrical position is unstable.*

To investigate the critical case

$$\frac{1}{h} = \frac{1}{r}+\frac{1}{R}$$

we proceed as follows. With reference to Fig. 22.11 (ii),

$$\text{GP}-\text{BQ} = (R+r)\sin\theta-(r-h)\sin\left\{\frac{(R+r)\theta}{r}\right\}-R\sin\theta$$

$$= r\sin\theta-\frac{r^2}{R+r}\sin\left\{\frac{(R+r)\theta}{r}\right\}.$$

Using the approximate expansion $\sin\theta \approx \theta-\theta^3/6$ (in effect neglecting powers of θ above the fourth) we find

$$\text{GP}-\text{BQ} \approx r\left(\theta-\frac{\theta^3}{6}\right)-\frac{r^2}{R+r}\left\{\frac{(R+r)\theta}{r}-\frac{(R+r)^3\theta^3}{6r^3}\right\}$$

$$= \frac{R(R+2r)\theta^3}{6r}.$$

Hence GP > BQ and so the vertical through G passes to the right of B and *the symmetrical position is unstable in this critical case.*

Alternatively this problem can be solved by considering the potential energy (in the displaced position) given by

$$\frac{V}{W} = (r+R)\cos\theta-(r-h)\cos\left\{\frac{(r+R)\theta}{r}\right\},$$

where W is the weight of the moving cylinder. The reader should show, as an exercise, that V has a minimum at $\theta = 0$ if and only if

$$\frac{1}{h} > \frac{1}{r}+\frac{1}{R}$$

thereby recovering the condition for the equilibrium to be stable.

In the limiting cases where r or R become infinite the upper cylinder or the lower cylinder becomes a plane, and the condition determines the stability of a thick plank resting on the highest point of a cylinder or the stability of a cylinder resting on a plane.

---

*EXERCISES 22.3

***1.** A uniform cube of edge $2a$ rests in equilibrium on the top of a fixed rough cylinder of radius b whose axis is horizontal. Two of the faces of the cube are horizontal. By considering the potential energy when it is rolled over through an angle θ, show that the equilibrium is stable, if a is less than b.

Show also that, in this case, the cube can be rolled into another position of equilibrium, which is unstable. (C.S.)

***2.** A uniform hemisphere, of weight W and radius a, is placed symmetrically on top of a fixed sphere of radius b, the curved surfaces being sufficiently rough to prevent slipping. Show that when the hemisphere is rolled through a small angle θ the gain of potential energy is approximately

$$\frac{W(3b-5a)a\theta^2}{16(a+b)}.$$

Deduce that the symmetrical position is stable when $3b > 5a$. (C.S.)

***3.** A uniform rough plank of weight W and thickness $2b$ rests horizontally in equilibrium across a fixed rough cylinder of radius a, and a particle of weight w is fixed to the plank vertically above the axis of the cylinder. Prove that, if $(W+w)a > b(W+2w)$, equilibrium is stable, and that if $(W+w)a < b(W+2w)$ it is unstable. Show that in the former case there are two oblique positions of equilibrium which are unstable, provided that the friction is great enough to prevent slipping. (C.S.)

***4.** A uniform solid hemisphere of radius a rests with its plane face horizontal and its curved surface in contact with a fixed rough sphere of radius $2a$. Prove that the hemisphere can be rolled into a position of equilibrium with the plane face inclined to the horizontal and find the angle between the common normal and the vertical in this position.

Determine if this position of equilibrium is stable or unstable. (L.)

***5.** A uniform solid consists of a right circular cone of height h and a hemisphere with their bases, each of radius a, in contact and with their circular boundaries coinciding. The solid stands with its axis vertical and vertex upwards on the top of a rough sphere of radius $3a$. Prove that the equilibrium is stable if h is less than $\frac{1}{2}(\sqrt{5}-1)a$, but is unstable if h is greater than *or equal to* this value. (L.)

*MISCELLANEOUS EXERCISES XXII

***1.** A bead of mass m slides on a smooth circular hoop which is fixed in a vertical plane, and the bead is attached to a particle of mass M by a light inelastic string passing through a small smooth ring which is fixed at the highest point of the hoop. Show that the potential energy of the system is

$$C-\frac{1}{2}mga\left(x-\frac{M}{m}\right)^2,$$

where a is the radius of the circle, and ax is the distance of the bead from the ring.

Show that, if $M < 2m$, there is a position of unstable equilibrium in which $x = M/m$. (C.S.)

***2.** A uniform rod AB, of length l and mass m, is freely hinged to a horizontal floor at its lower end B so that it can turn in a fixed vertical plane; C and D are two points of the floor in this same vertical plane, and CB = BD = a. The end A is joined to C and D by two elastic strings, each of modulus λ and of unstretched length b [less than $\sqrt{(a^2+l^2)}$]. Show that the position in which AB is vertical is stable if $4a^2l\lambda$ is greater than $mg(a^2+l^2)^{3/2}$. (C.S.)

***3.** A heavy uniform rectangular lamina ABCD, in which the length of the diagonals is $16a$ and the angle ADB is α ($\cos^{-1}\frac{4}{5} < \alpha < 45°$), rests in a vertical plane with the sides AB, AD on two small smooth horizontal pegs E and F. EF has length $5a$ and makes an angle 2α with the upward vertical.

Prove that the lamina is in equilibrium when AC is vertical and when AC makes an angle $\cos^{-1}\frac{4}{5}$ with the vertical on either side. Prove that the first of these positions is stable and the others unstable. (L.)

***4.** A smooth circular wire centre O and radius a is held rigid in a vertical plane. An elastic weightless thread of natural length a has one end attached to the highest point of the wire and the other end to a bead P which can move freely on the wire. Show that if the tension in the string when the bead is at the lowest point is λ times the weight of the bead, there will be positions of equilibrium other than that with P at the lowest point of the wire, if $\lambda > 2$. Show that these positions are stable and that at the lowest point is unstable. (C.S.)

***5.** Two equal uniform rods AB and AC, each of length $2b$, are freely jointed at A. The rods rest on a smooth circular cylinder of radius a with their plane perpendicular to the axis of the cylinder, which is horizontal. Prove that if 2θ is the angle BAC when the rods are in equilibrium with A vertically above the axis of the cylinder, then $b\sin^3\theta = a\cos\theta$, and show that this equation has only one root in the range $0 < \theta < \pi/2$.

Show, also, that if the rods are constrained to move in a vertical plane and A is constrained to move vertically the position of equilibrium is stable. (L.)

***6.** A uniform bar AB of length l and weight W_1 is smoothly hinged to a fixed point A. The bar is supported by a light inextensible string attached to B and passing over a small light smooth pulley at a point C, which is vertically above A at a height $a\ (> l)$. The string carries a freely hanging weight W_2 at its other end. Show that there are three positions of equilibrium, provided that

$$\frac{2a}{a+l} < \frac{W_1}{W_2} < \frac{2a}{a-l}.$$

If $W_1 = 2W_2$ show that two of the positions of equilibrium are stable and one is unstable. (L.)

***7.** One end O of a uniform rod OA, of length a and mass m, is attached to a fixed smooth hinge, and the other end A is joined by a light elastic string, of natural length l and modulus of elasticity mg, to the point vertically above, and distant $2a$, from O. If $4a/5 < l < 12a/7$, prove that there is a stable configuration of equilibrium in which the rod is inclined to the vertical. (C.S.)

***8.** A light rod AB of length $2a$ is freely pivoted at A to a point of a vertical wall and carries a particle of mass M at B. A light spring of modulus λ and unstretched length l joins the mid-point of AB to a point of the wall a distance h vertically above A. If the system is in equilibrium with AB horizontal, show that $l = \lambda hs/(2Mgs+h\lambda)$, where $s^2 = a^2+h^2$, and show that this position of equilibrium is stable. (C.S.)

***9.** A uniform rod AB of mass m and length a can turn freely about a fixed point A. A small ring of mass m' slides smoothly along the rod, and is attached by a light inelastic string of length b ($b < a$) to a fixed point at height $2b$ vertically above A. Show that the position of equilibrium in which the rod is vertical is stable if $ma < 2m'b$ and unstable if $ma > 2m'b$. (C.S.)

***10.** A hemispherical cup, of radius r and mass m, has a particle of mass m attached to a point on its rim. The cup is placed in equilibrium with a point of its curved surface in contact with the highest point of a fixed rough sphere of radius R. Prove that the equilibrium is stable, if

$$R > r(4\sqrt{5}/5-1). \qquad \text{(N.)}$$

CHAPTER XXIII

LIGHT FRAMEWORKS

23.1. Graphical Method of Obtaining the Resultant of a System of Coplanar Forces

(a) *The Case when the Forces are not all Parallel*

In Chapter II of Volume I we discussed the use of the polygon of forces to obtain approximate values for the magnitude and direction of the resultant of a number of forces acting on a particle. Figure 23.1 illustrates a method of obtaining approximate values for the magnitude and direction of the resultant of a system of non-concurrent coplanar forces **P**, **Q**, **R**, **S**, **T** and of obtaining also an approximation to the position of the resultant.

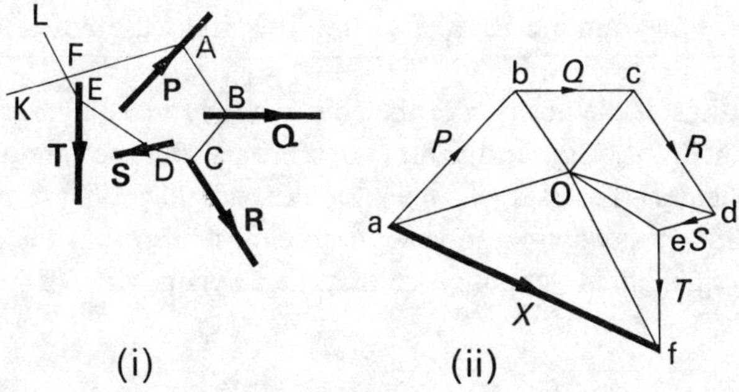

FIG. 23.1

Figure 23.1 (i) is the *space diagram* of the five forces represented in magnitude, direction and position by the vectors shown there. In Fig. 23.1 (ii), the polygon *abcdef* is the *force polygon* for the five forces and their resultant **X** which is represented in magnitude and direction *but not* *in position* by *af*. In this figure *o* is an *arbitrarily chosen* pole. In Fig. 23.1 (i), A is an *arbitrary* point on the line of action of **P** and AB parallel to *ob* meets the line of action of **Q** at B; AK is parallel to *oa*; the points C, D, E are on the lines of action of **R**, **S**, **T** so that BC, CD, DE are parallel respectively to *oc*, *od*, *oe*; EL parallel to *of* meets AK at F.

The line of action of the resultant **X** *of the five forces passes through* F. This statement is justified as follows:

$$\mathbf{P} \text{ through A} = (\overrightarrow{ao}+\overrightarrow{ob}) \text{ through A},$$
$$\mathbf{Q} \text{ through B} = (\overrightarrow{bo} \text{ through A})+(\overrightarrow{oc} \text{ through B}),$$
$$\mathbf{R} \text{ through C} = (\overrightarrow{co} \text{ through B})+(\overrightarrow{od} \text{ through C}),$$
$$\mathbf{S} \text{ through D} = (\overrightarrow{do} \text{ through C})+(\overrightarrow{oe} \text{ through D}),$$
$$\mathbf{T} \text{ through E} = (\overrightarrow{eo} \text{ through D})+(\overrightarrow{of} \text{ through E}).$$

Therefore, by addition, the resultant of **P**, **Q**, **R**, **S**, **T** is the resultant of ($\overrightarrow{ao}$ through A) and ($\overrightarrow{of}$ through E) and this resultant is therefore the force **X** through the intersection of AK and EL, i.e. through F. The polygon ABCDEF is called the *funicular polygon* for the forces. In the case in which *f* coincides with *a* in the force polygon, either the system of forces reduces to a couple or it is in equilibrium. In the former case, AK and EL in the space diagram are parallel, and in the latter case AK and EL coincide.

The choices of the position of the pole *o* in the force diagram and that of the point A in the space diagram are arbitrary, but the careful exercise of these choices is necessary if a manageable space diagram is to be obtained. The student is advised, in general, to choose *o* so that the angle *aof* is not too small and to choose A so that the polygon ABCDEF is not too large.

(b) *The Case when the Forces are all Parallel*

The method is essentially that used in case (a). Figure 23.2 (i) is a space diagram of the parallel forces **P**, **Q**, **R**, **S**, and Fig. 23.2 (ii) is a force diagram for these forces in which $\overrightarrow{ab}$, $\overrightarrow{bc}$, $\overrightarrow{cd}$, $\overrightarrow{de}$ represent **P**, **Q**, **R**, **S** in magnitude and direction only. The resultant **X** of **P**, **Q**, **R**, **S** is represented in magnitude and direction by $\overrightarrow{ae}$.

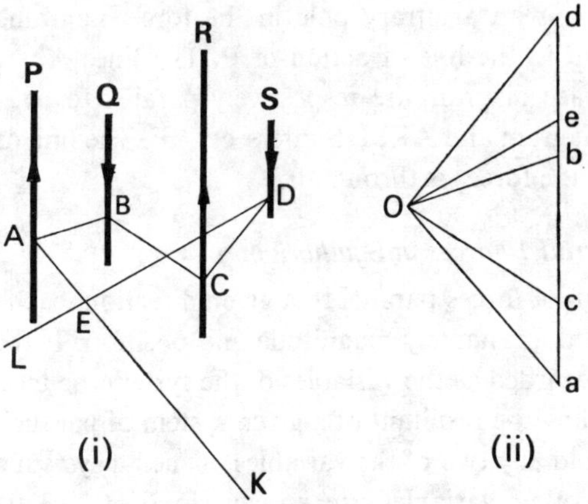

FIG. 23.2

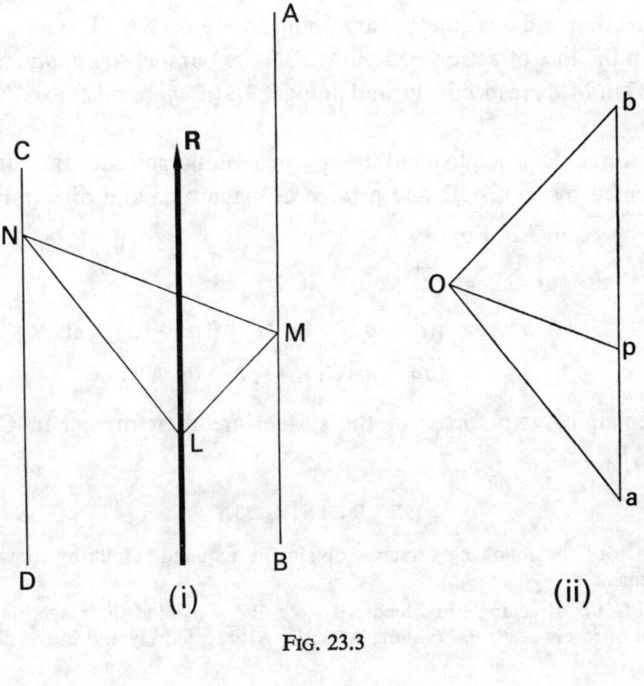

FIG. 23.3

The point o is an arbitrary pole in the force diagram, and A is an arbitrary point in the line of action of **P**. The lines AK, AB, BC, CD, DL in the space diagram are respectively parallel to oa, ob, oc, od, oe in the force diagram and AK, DL intersect at E. The line of action of the resultant **X** of the forces is through E.

Systems of Parallel Forces in Equilibrium

For a system of forces parallel to a given direction, each force has two degrees of freedom, namely magnitude and position. If these degrees of freedom are regarded as the variables of the system the method discussed above for finding the resultant of a given system of parallel forces can be used also to find any two of the variables of such a system in equilibrium when all the other variables are known. In Fig. 23.3 (i) the force **R** represents the resultant of all the forces but two in a system of parallel forces in equilibrium. The remaining two forces of the system act in the lines AB and CD. The line ab in Fig. 23.3 (ii) represents **R** in magnitude and direction and o is an arbitrary point. In Fig. 23.3 (i), L is an arbitrary point in the line of action of **R**; LM, LN are parallel to ob, oa and meet AB, CD in M, N respectively, and in Fig. 23.3 (ii) op parallel to MN meets ab at p.

The force **R** is equivalent to a force of magnitude and direction represented by $\overrightarrow{ap}$ in CD and a force of magnitude and direction represented by $\overrightarrow{pb}$ in AB. For

$$\begin{aligned} \overrightarrow{ab} \quad \text{at} \quad \text{L} &= (\overrightarrow{ao}+\overrightarrow{ob}) \quad \text{at L} \\ &= \{(\overrightarrow{ao}+\overrightarrow{op}) \quad \text{at N}\}+\{(\overrightarrow{po}+\overrightarrow{ob}) \quad \text{at M}\} \\ &= (\overrightarrow{ap} \quad \text{in CD})+(\overrightarrow{pb} \quad \text{in AB}). \end{aligned}$$

The remaining two forces of the system are therefore $\overrightarrow{pa}$ in CD and $\overrightarrow{bp}$ in AB.

EXERCISES 23.1

In each of the following exercises obtain the required results by drawing and measurement.

1. ABCD is a rectangle in which AB $= 2a$, BC $= a$. Find the magnitude of the resultant of forces of P, P, $2P$ along AC, BD, AB respectively and in the directions indicated by the order of the letters and find the points in which the line of action of this resultant cuts AB, AD.

2. Forces of 30, 20, 50, 40 N act along the sides AB, BC, DC, DA respectively of a square ABCD of side 1 m in the directions indicated by the order of the letters. Find the magnitude and direction of the resultant and the point at which it cuts CD.

3. ABC is an equilateral triangle of side 1 m and D is the point in AB produced so that AB = BD. Forces 30, 60, 40 N act along AB, BC and DC respectively. Find the point at which the line of action of the resultant cuts AD.

4. Forces of 2, 3, 2, 3, 2 N respectively act along the sides AB, CB, CD, DE, AE of a regular pentagon ABCDE of side 0·2 m in directions indicated by the order of the letters. Find the magnitude of the resultant and its distance from the centre of the pentagon.

5. ABCD is a trapezium in which the parallel sides AD and BC are in the ratio 2 : 3 and AB = AD = DC. Find the magnitude and direction of the resultant of forces $3P$ from B towards C, P from B towards A, $2P$ from D towards A, and $2\frac{1}{2}P$ from D towards C and find the point in which the resultant cuts BC.

6. Parallel forces of 3, −4, −2, 5 N act through the points A, B, C, D respectively of a line ABCD where AB = 0·2 m, BC = 0·4 m, CD = 0·3 m. Find the position of the resultant.

7. A uniform rod AB, of mass 50 g and length 1 metre, is supported in a horizontal position by thin vertical strings at P and Q where AP = 20 cm and AQ = 70 cm. A load of mass of 50 g is hung on the rod at S where AS = 60 cm. Find the tension in each of the strings.

8. PQRS is a rectangle in which PQ = 4 m, QR = 3 m. Forces of 20 N, 20 N, 5 N, 25 N act along SP, PQ, QR, QS in the directions indicated by the order of the letters. Show that the system of forces reduces to a couple and find the moment of the couple.

23.2. Light Frameworks

For the discussion which follows a light bar is defined as a rigid bar, the weight of which is so small as to be negligible compared with the other forces involved. A light framework is defined as a number of light bars smoothly hinged together to form a rigid system of bars in one plane.

We assume that the nature of each hinge is such that the force exerted by a hinge on a bar attached to it is a single force through the centre of the hinge. When the framework is in equilibrium each bar (or portion of bar between two hinges) is in equilibrium under the action of two forces only, the actions of the hinges at its two ends. These two forces must therefore be equal and opposite and in the same straight line, i.e. they must be equal and opposite and each must act along the bar. When the forces *with which the hinges act on the bar* tend to compress the bar as shown on the l.h. figure of Fig. 23.4 (i) the bar is said to be *in compression*, and it is called *a strut*. In this case the stress in the bar is defined as *positive*. When the forces *with which the hinges act on the bar* tend to stretch the bar as shown on the r.h. figure of Fig. 23.4 (i) the bar is said to be *in tension*, in this case the bar is called *a tie*, and the stress in the bar is defined as *negative*. The forces exerted by the bar on the hinges in the two cases are shown in Fig. 23.4 (ii). In this chapter, forces marked by arrows *on the bars*, indicate *the forces with which the bars act on the hinges.*

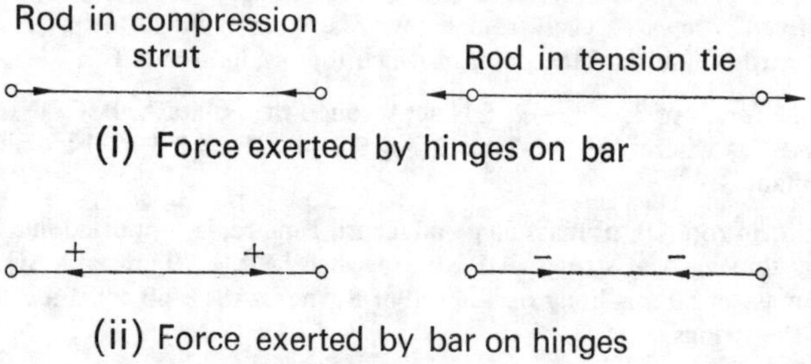

FIG. 23.4

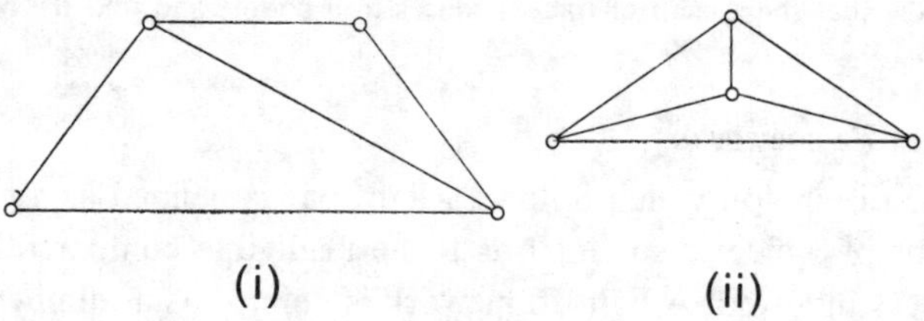

FIG. 23.5

A framework is said to be *stiff* if the number of bars in it is just sufficient to maintain its rigid shape; the framework is said to be *over-stiff* if there are more bars than are sufficient to maintain this shape. Figure 23.5 (i) shows a framework which is stiff and Fig. 23.5 (ii) a framework which is over-stiff. In general it is possible to determine the stresses in a framework which is just stiff but problems in which the framework is over-stiff are indeterminate. (A plane framework of n joints is just stiff with $2n-3$ bars, since the first two joints require one bar and each subsequent joint requires two bars to produce a stiff framework.)

23.3. Calculation of the Stresses in the Bars of a Light Framework

Example. Figure 23.6 (i) shows a framework of seven equal light bars in a vertical plane. The triangles ABC, BDC, DCE are equilateral and the bars BD, AC, CE are horizontal. The joints at B and D carry loads of 120 kg and 240 kg respectively and the framework is supported by vertical forces R and S at A and E. It is required to find the stress in each of the bars of the framework by calculation.

(a) In order to find the unknown external forces acting on the framework, i.e. the forces R and S at A and E respectively, we consider the equilibrium of the whole framework. The equal and opposite actions and reactions between the bars and the joints (the *internal* stresses of the framework) will not be involved in the equations of equilibrium of the whole framework considered as a rigid body. These equations are,

(1) the sum of the external forces is zero,

i.e. $$R+S = (240+120)g \text{ N},$$

(2) the sum of the moments about A is zero,

i.e. $$4S = (120+3\times 240)g \text{ N}.$$

$$\therefore\ R = 150g \text{ N}, \quad S = 210g \text{ N}.$$

(b) In order to find the forces exerted on the bars *by the joints*, we consider the equilibrium of each joint, thus finding first the forces exerted *on the joints by the bars*. In this case we are able to begin the analysis at a "*single*" *joint*, i.e. at a joint joining only two bars of the framework, and afterwards to proceed from joint to joint so that for each joint there are only two unknown quantities involved.

In *general* there are $2n$ equations available from the equilibrium conditions for the n joints considered separately. These equations involve the three conditions of equilibrium which must be satisfied by the external forces on the framework considered as a whole, so that there are $2n-3$ (independent) equations for the $2n-3$ bars. Exceptional cases can occur but we shall not consider them here. In § 23.5 we consider the case in which there is no "single" joint from which to begin the analysis.

For joint A, the forces acting *on the joint* are shown in Fig. 23.6 (ii), where T_1 and T_2 are the actions of the bars AC and AB respectively on the joint. [For clarity in the figures, the units (g N) have been omitted in Fig. 23.6.] Hence,

$$\frac{T_1}{\sin 150} = \frac{T_2}{\sin 90} = \frac{150]}{\sin 120}.$$

$$\therefore\ T_1 = 50\sqrt{3} \approx 87, \quad \text{and} \quad T_2 = 100\sqrt{3} \approx 173.$$

The forces exerted *by the bars on the joint* are therefore in the directions indicated by the arrows in Fig. 23.6 (i). The bar AB exerts a force T_2 on joint A in the direction shown and the bar AC exerts a force T_1 on the joint A in the direction shown. *Since these forces are equal and opposite to the forces exerted by the joints on the bars*, it follows that

AB is in compression with a stress $+100\sqrt{3}g$ N (a strut),
AC is in tension with a stress $-50\sqrt{3}g$ N (a tie).

We next analyse the equilibrium of joint B, choosing this joint because here the only unknowns *now* are the stresses in the rods BD, BC; for joint C there are three "unknowns".

Figure 23.6 (iii) shows the forces acting on joint B, where T_3 is the force exerted on the joint by the bar BD and T_4 is the force exerted on the joint by the bar BC. For this joint, the equations of equilibrium are,

$$T_4\frac{\sqrt{3}}{2}+120 = T_2\frac{\sqrt{3}}{2}, \quad \therefore\ T_4 = 20\sqrt{3}g \text{ N} \approx 35g \text{ N},$$

$$T_3 = \tfrac{1}{2}(T_2+T_4), \quad \therefore\ T_3 = 60\sqrt{3}g \text{ N} \approx 104g \text{ N}.$$

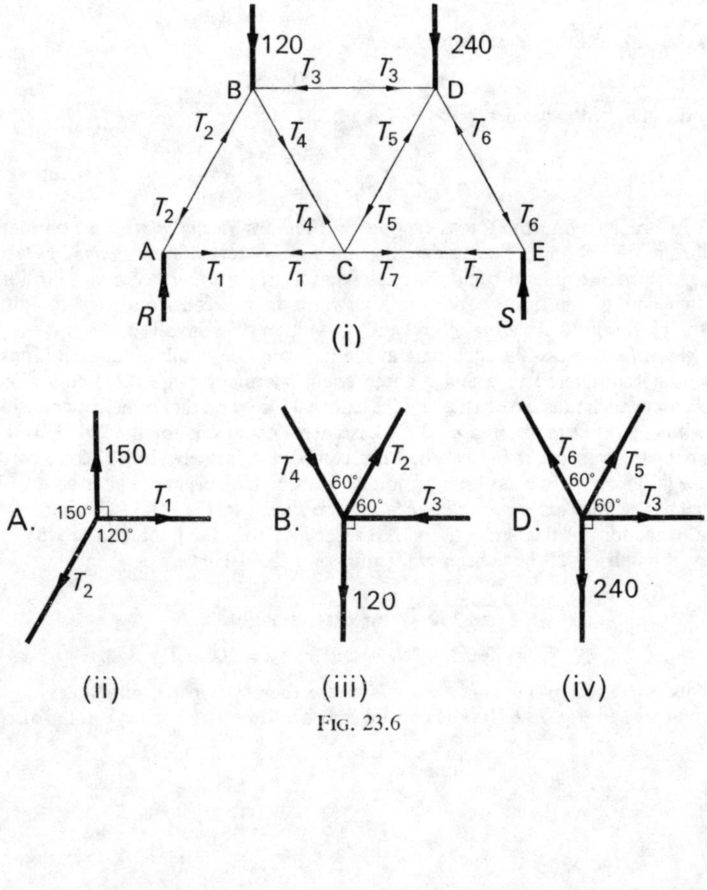

FIG. 23.6

Hence

BD is in compression with a stress of $60\sqrt{3}g$ N (a strut),
BC is in tension with a stress of $-20\sqrt{3}g$ N (a tie).

Figures 23.6 (iv) and (v) are respectively force diagrams for the joints D and E of the framework.

Hence, for the equilibrium of joint D,

$$T_5\frac{\sqrt{3}}{2}+T_6\frac{\sqrt{3}}{2} = 240, \quad \frac{1}{2}T_6 = \frac{1}{2}T_5+T_3.$$

$$\therefore\ T_5 = 20\sqrt{3}g \text{ N} \approx 35g \text{ N}, \quad T_6 = 140\sqrt{3}g \text{ N} \approx 242g \text{ N}.$$

For the equilibrium of joint E,

$$T_7 = T_6 \cos 60^\circ = 70\sqrt{3}g \text{ N} \approx 121g \text{ N}.$$

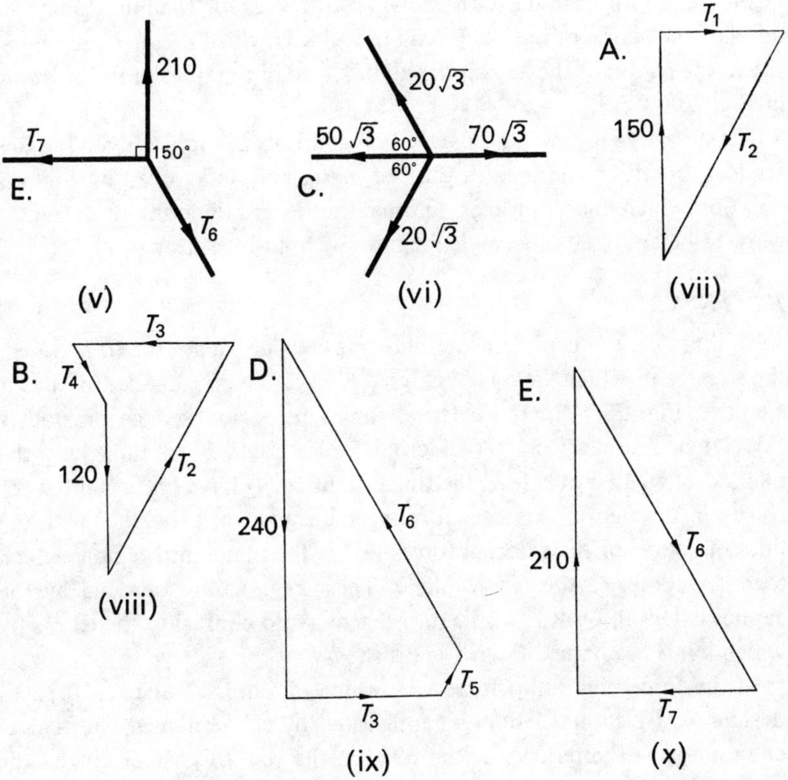

FIG. 23.6

DC is in compression with a stress of $+20\sqrt{3}g$ N (a strut),
DE is in compression with a stress of $+140\sqrt{3}g$ N (a strut),
CE is in tension with a stress of $-70\sqrt{3}g$ N (a tie).

Figure 23.6 (vi) shows the forces (already calculated) acting on the joint C and their evident equilibrium is a check on the preceding work.

23.4. Graphical Investigation of the Stresses in a Light Framework

Figures 23.6 (vii)–(x) are respectively polygons of forces for the joints A, B, D and E of the framework considered in the previous section. The action of the bar AB on joint A is deduced from Fig. 23.6 (vii) and the equal and opposite action of the bar AB on the joint B is one of the forces in Fig. 23.6 (viii). Similarly the polygon of forces for the joint D has as one side the action of the bar BD on the joint D which is equal and opposite to the action of the bar on the joint B, one of the sides of the polygon in Fig. 23.6 (viii).

The necessity to draw a separate polygon for each joint, involving the kind of repetition outlined in the last paragraph, is avoided by using a notation which enables forces, internal and external, acting on a framework to be analysed in a single diagram without repetition.

Bow's Notation

To illustrate the use of this notation we consider again the framework, the stresses in which we have analysed above. This framework is shown again in Fig. 23.7 (i), the external forces being marked as previously calculated. Alternatively the external forces could be obtained by the method of § 23.1. As before, the dimensions (g N) have been omitted for clarity in the figure. The bars forming the framework together with the lines of action of the external forces divide the plane into regions which together comprise the whole plane. These regions are denoted by the capital letters P, Q, R, . . ., V. In order to avoid confusion the letters by which joints are named are ringed as shown.

In the force diagram a force whose line of action divides two spaces designated by capital letters is represented by a line named with corresponding small letters. Thus the force in the rod AC which divides the spaces V and P is represented in the force diagram by the line vp.

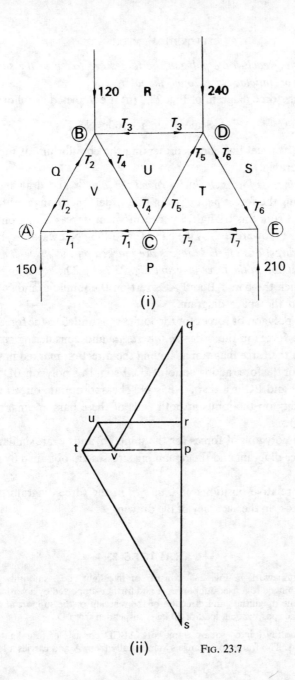

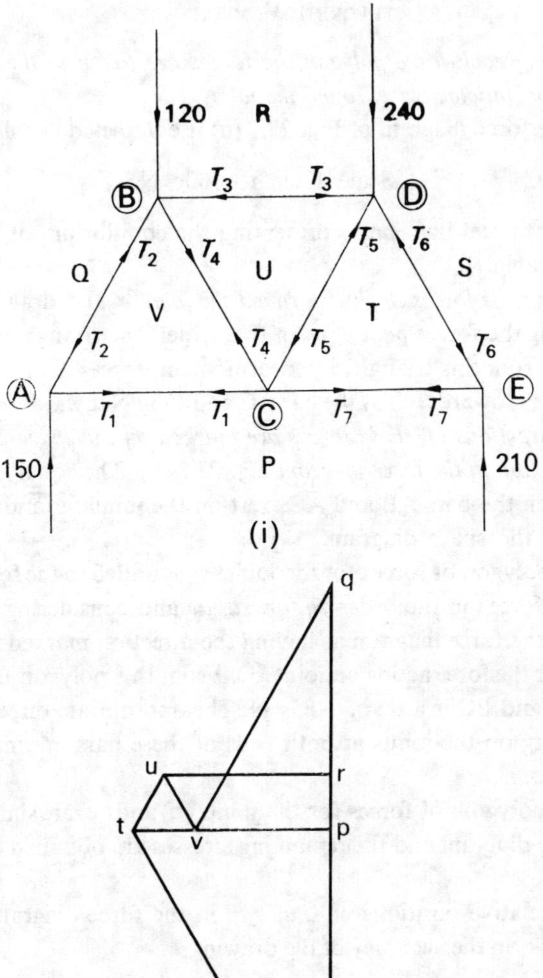

120
R
240
B
D
T_3
T_3
T_2
T_4
T_5
T_6
Q
U
S
V
T
T_2
T_4
T_5
T_6
A
E
T_1
T_1
C
T_7
T_7
150
P
210
(i)
q
u
r
t
v
p
s
(ii)

Fig. 23.7

In drawing each force polygon the forces are taken in the same order, clockwise or anticlockwise, round the joint.

Thus the force diagram of Fig. 23.7 (ii) is completed as follows:

Scale 1 cm to 100g N.

(a) The vertical line *sprq* representing the equilibrium of the external forces is drawn.

(b) *Taking the forces clockwise round the joint* (A), i.e. drawing the lines representing the forces *pq*, *qv*, *vp* in that order, the triangle of forces *pqv* is drawn. From this triangle, by measurement, forces acting on the joint (A) are 87g N towards (C) by the bar AC and 173g N towards (A) by the bar AB. *The directions of these forces are marked on the space-diagram Fig. 23.7 (i) but not on the force diagram Fig. 23.7 (ii).* The equal and opposite forces which the bars AB and AC exert on the joints (B) and (C) are also marked in the space diagram.

(c) The polygon of forces for the joint (B) is added to the force diagram taking the forces in the order *vq*, *qr*, *ru*, *uv* and considering *vq* which is already in the force diagram as having the direction marked in the space diagram for the force acting on joint (B). From this polygon BD is a strut of 104g N and BC is a tie of $-35g$ N. The appropriate directions of the forces acting on the joints at both ends of these bars are marked *in the space diagram.*

(d) The polygons of forces for the joints (D) and (E) are similarly added to the force diagram and the remaining stresses are obtained by measurement.

(e) The relative positions of *t*, *u*, *v*, *p* in the force diagram provide a partial check on the accuracy of the drawing.

EXERCISES 23.4

1. The framework in Fig. 23.8 consists of five light rods, smoothly jointed at A, B, C, D, hinged to a fixed support at A and further supported by a vertical reaction at B. Find the magnitude and direction of the reaction of the support at A and the stresses in the rods, when a load of 80 kg is suspended from D. (O.C.)

2. A smoothly jointed square framework ABCD consists of four light bars AB, BC, CD, DA. The framework hangs symmetrically from A and carries a load 4W at

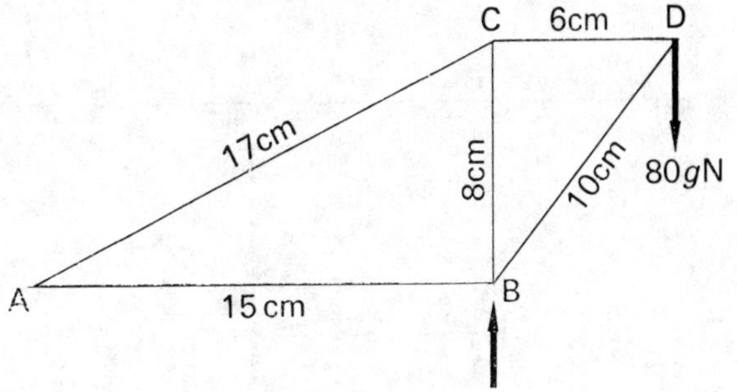

FIG. 23.8

the lowest point C, the square shape being maintained by a light strut joining B and D. Find the thrust exerted by this strut. (L.)

3. Figure 23.9 shows a framework consisting of six pin-jointed light rods AB, BC, CA, CD, DB, and BE, all in the same vertical plane and freely hinged at D, E to a vertical wall. A load of 200 kg is suspended from A. Find the stress in each rod, stating whether the rod is a tie or a strut. (N.)

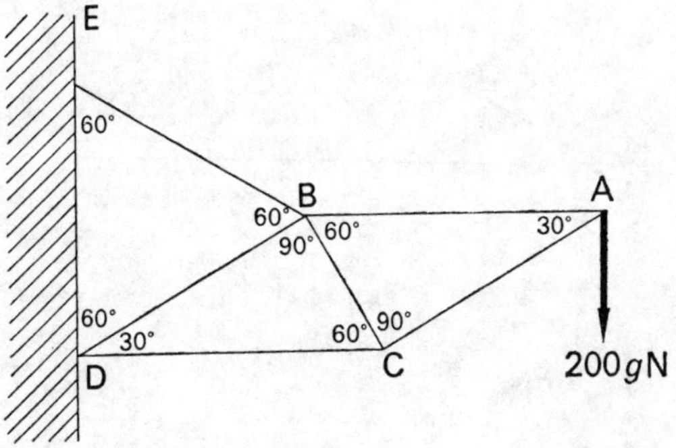

FIG. 23.9

4. Figure 23.10 represents a framework of nine smoothly jointed light rods which is supported in a vertical plane by vertical forces applied at the points A, D on the same level. The frame is loaded at E, F with masses of 60 kg and 30 kg respectively. If each of the triangles in the figure is isosceles and right-angled, find the vertical supporting forces at A, D and the stresses in the rods, stating whether they are ties or struts. (N.)

5. A freely jointed framework is in the form of a trapezium ABCD, with B joined to D, as in Fig. 23.11; AB = AD = BC, $\angle ADC = \angle BCD = 60°$, and the framework is freely supported in a vertical plane at C and D, with the rod CD horizontal. Loads of 500 kg and 300 kg hang from A and B respectively.

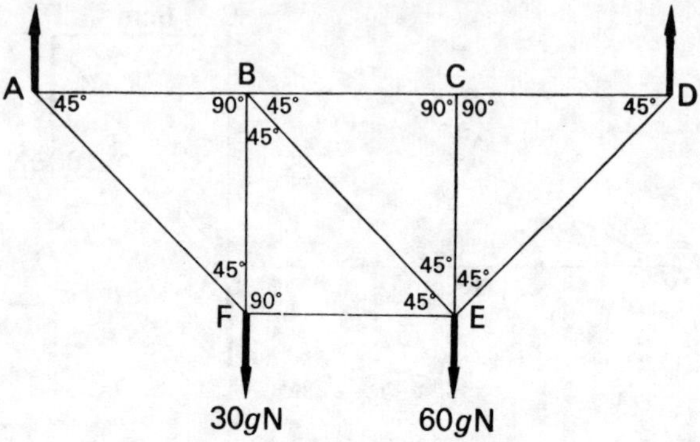

FIG. 23.10

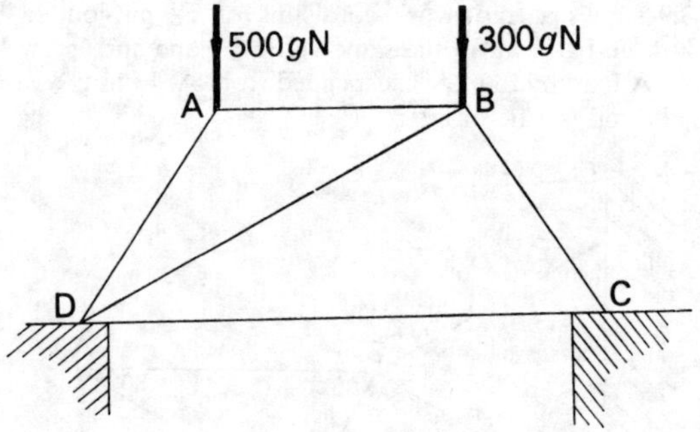

FIG. 23.11

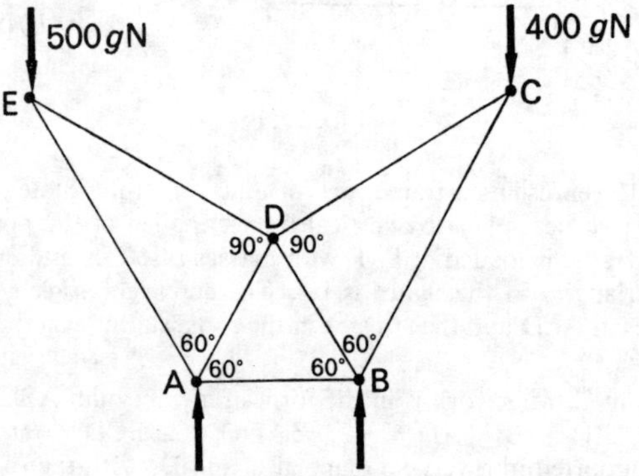

FIG. 23.12

Draw a force diagram, and determine the stresses in the rods, indicating which are in tension and which are in compression. (L.)

6. Figure 23.12 shows a framework of seven light freely jointed rods in equilibrium in a vertical plane with AB horizontal, supported by vertical forces at A and B and carrying vertical loads of 500 kg and 400 kg at E and C respectively.

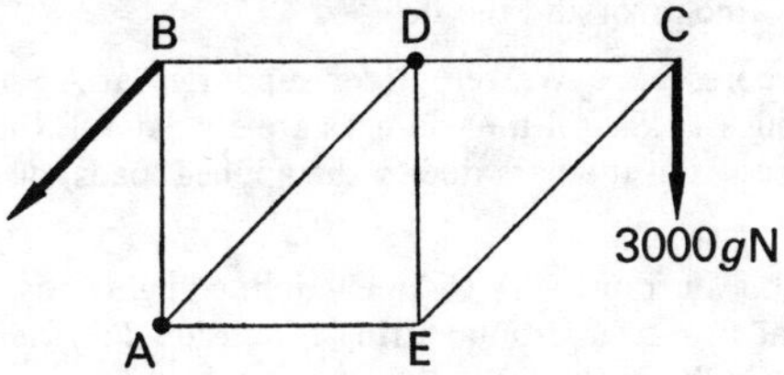

FIG. 23.13

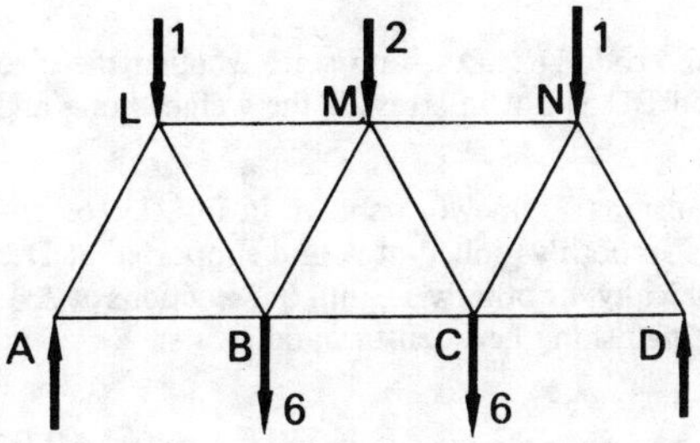

FIG. 23.14

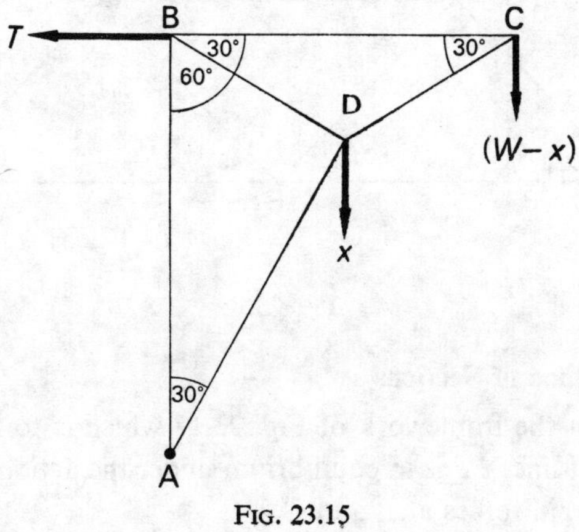

FIG. 23.15

Draw a force diagram and find the stresses in the rods, stating their nature. Find also the forces at A and B. (L.)

7. Figure 23.13 represents a smoothly jointed framework in which the lines are horizontal, vertical, or inclined at 45° to the vertical. The framework carries a load of 3000 kg at C, and is supported by a pivot at A and a tie at B. Draw a force diagram, and find the stress in each bar, stating whether they are tensions or thrusts. Also find the forces exerted by the pivot and the tie. (O.C.)

8. Figure 23.14 represents a Warren girder supported at A and D, and loaded as shown, the unit being 100 kg. All the triangles are equilateral. Find the forces on the supports and the stresses in the bars due to the applied loads, distinguishing between tensions and thrusts. (O.C.)

9. Figure 23.15 show a framework of freely jointed light rods. It is fixed by a joint at A and attached at B to a horizontal string of tension T; a weight $(W-x)$ is hung from C and x from D. Prove that

$$T = \frac{\sqrt{3}}{2}\left(W - \frac{1}{2}x\right),$$

find the stresses in the rods DC, DA, and state whether these rods are ties or struts.

Prove that the rod BD is not in stress if the weight hung at D is twice that at C. (O.C.)

10. The two-dimensional framework shown in Fig. 23.16 consisting of seven light, freely jointed rods, is smoothly pinned at A and supported at D by a reaction perpendicular to ED. Graphically, or otherwise, find the reactions at A and D and the stresses in the members, distinguishing between ties and struts. (L.)

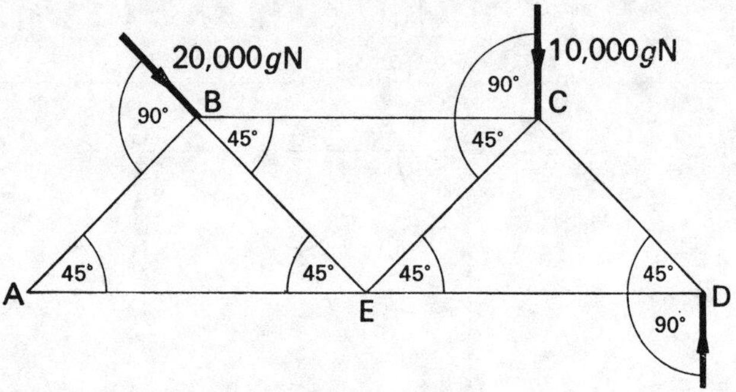

FIG. 23.16

23.5. The Method of Sections

That part of the framework of Fig. 23.17 which is to the right of the dotted straight line XY is in equilibrium under the action of,

(a) the external forces at B and C,

(b) the forces exerted by the bars on the joints at B, C and D and the equal and opposite forces exerted by the joints on the bars,

(c) the forces T_1, T_2, T_3 newtons exerted by the parts of the bars to the left of XY.

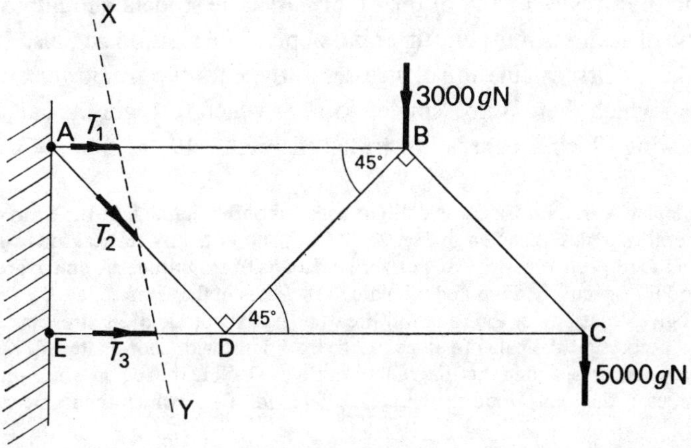

FIG. 23.17

These latter forces and the external forces at B and C are therefore in equilibrium, and *three independent equilibrium equations can be obtained by using an appropriate set of any of the usual equilibrium conditions.*

Thus, taking 1 unit as 1000*g* N, the sum of the moments about A is zero,

$$T_3 = 3\times 2+5\times 3 = 21,$$

the sum of the moments about D is zero,

$$T_1 = -3\times 1-5\times 2 = -13,$$

the sum of the vertical components is zero,

$$T_2/\sqrt{2}+3+5 = 0, \quad \therefore\ T_2 = -8\sqrt{2}.$$

These three forces T_1, T_2, T_3 are *forces exerted by the respective part bars* on that part of the framework to the right hand of the dotted line and they are equal and opposite to the forces *exerted on those part bars* by the joints at B and D. Therefore AB is a tie in tension $13{,}000g$ N, AD is a tie in tension $8000\sqrt{2}g$ N and ED is a strut in thrust $21{,}000g$ N.

This is the *method of sections*. In suitable cases it can be used to determine the stresses in three of the bars of a framework without previously finding the stresses in any of the other bars. The student should note that the line of sections must cut three bars only. The method can also be used to make the first calculation of stresses in the bars of a framework in some cases in which there is no "single" joint at which to begin the calculation or drawing. Such a case is illustrated in Fig. 23.19.

Example. A framework of seven light rods, smoothly jointed, in the form of three equilateral triangles as shown in Fig. 23.18 (i), is supported by vertical forces P and Q at A and C respectively with AC horizontal. Loads of magnitudes X and Y are placed at D and E respectively. Find and tabulate the stresses in the seven rods.

It is given that any of the rods will break if the magnitude of its stress exceeds the value T. Represent the pair of values (X, Y) by a point with coordinates X, Y referred to rectangular axes, and in this diagram indicate by shading the region which represents safe values of the loads. Find the greatest total load, $X+Y$, which the frame can bear. (N.)

Taking moments about C and A in turn for the equilibrium of the whole framework we find

$$P = \tfrac{1}{4}(3X+Y), \quad Q = \tfrac{1}{4}(X+3Y).$$

[Check, by vertical resolution, $P+Q = X+Y$.]

Now resolutions at A and C give [for the forces as marked in Fig. 23.18 (i)]

$$T_1 = \frac{1}{2\sqrt{3}}(3X+Y), \quad T_2 = \frac{1}{4\sqrt{3}}(3X+Y),$$

$$T_6 = \frac{1}{4\sqrt{3}}(X+3Y), \quad T_7 = \frac{1}{2\sqrt{3}}(X+3Y).$$

Then resolutions at D and E give

$$T_3 = \frac{1}{2\sqrt{3}}(Y-X), \quad T_4 = \frac{1}{2\sqrt{3}}(X+Y), \quad T_5 = \frac{1}{2\sqrt{3}}(X-Y).$$

A check can now be obtained by resolutions at B. A further check is available by taking a section through the rods AB, BD, DE and considering the equilibrium of the framework to the right of this section.

Clearly from the above results (taking X, Y to be both $\geqq 0$)

$$T_1 \geqq T_2, \quad T_7 \geqq T_6, \quad T_4 \geqq |T_3|, \quad T_4 \geqq |T_5|.$$

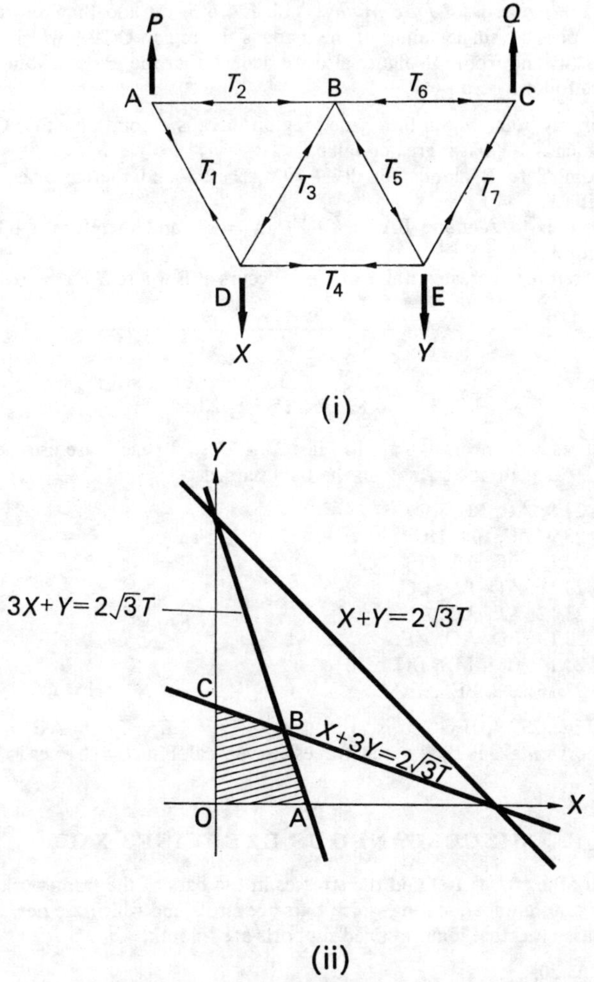

FIG. 23.18

Since the greatest permitted stress is T, we must therefore have (X, Y) satisfying the inequalities

$$3X+Y \leqq 2\sqrt{3}T, \quad X+3Y \leqq 2\sqrt{3}T, \quad X+Y \leqq 2\sqrt{3}T.$$

By addition, the first two of these inequalities imply $X+Y \leqq \sqrt{3}T$. Hence the greatest value of $X+Y$ is $T\sqrt{3}$.

Using the methods of *Pure Maths.*, Vol. I, § 5.6, we find that the region which represents possible single values of the loads is the region OCBA which is shaded in Fig. 23.18 (ii) and from this figure also we deduce that the greatest value of $X+Y$ is $\sqrt{3}T$. This follows because

(i) for any point within the shaded region there is a point on either CB or BA at which $X+Y$ has a greater value,
(ii) from C to B along CB, $d(X+Y)/dX = 2/3$ and therefore $X+Y$ increases with X,
(iii) from B to A along BA, $d(X+Y)/dX = -2$ and therefore $X+Y$ decreases with X,
(iv) therefore the greatest value of $X+Y$ occurs at B where $X+Y = \sqrt{3}T$.

EXERCISES 23.5

References in numbers 1–8 are to Figs. 23.8–23.16. In each case use the method of sections to calculate the stresses in the bars named.

1. Fig. 23.8; AC, BC, BD.
2. Fig. 23.9; BE, BD, DC.
3. Fig. 23.10; BC, BE, FE.
4. Fig. 23.11; AD, BD, BC.
5. Fig. 23.12; AE, AD, AB.
6. Fig. 23.13; BD, AD, AE.
7. Fig. 23.14; LM, MB, BC.
8. Fig. 23.16; BC, BE, AE.

9. In Fig. 23.19; FGCD is a square, FD = FE = FA = AG = GB = GC, EFGB is horizontal and the external forces are vertical. Find the stresses in the bars.

MISCELLANEOUS EXERCISES XXIII

In each of exercises 1–9 find the stresses in the bars of the framework referred to by the diagram number, stating which bars are struts and which are ties. In each case it may be assumed that joints at fixed supports are smooth.

1. Fig. 23.20.
2. Fig. 23.21.
3. Fig. 23.22.
4. Fig. 23.23. (Find the stresses in AB, AC only.)
5. Fig. 23.24.
6. Fig. 23.25.
7. Fig. 23.26.
8. Fig. 23.27.
9. Fig. 23.28.

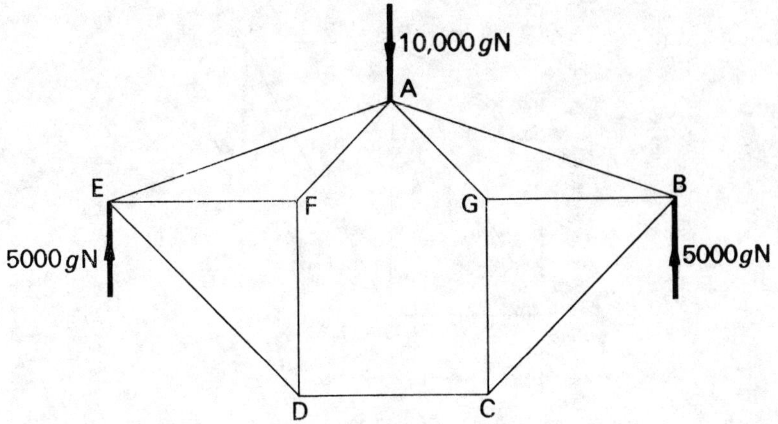

FIG. 23.19

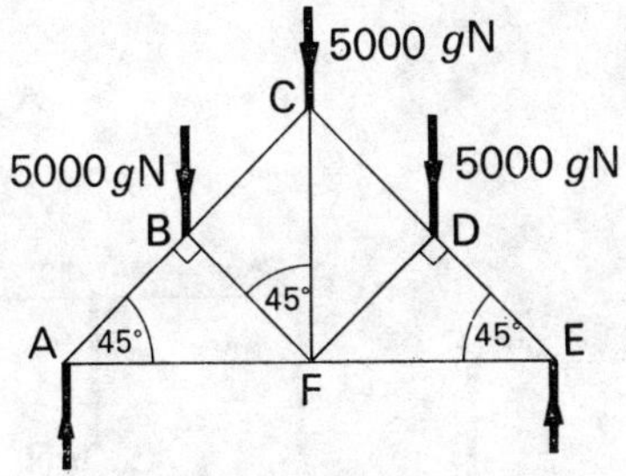

FIG. 23.20

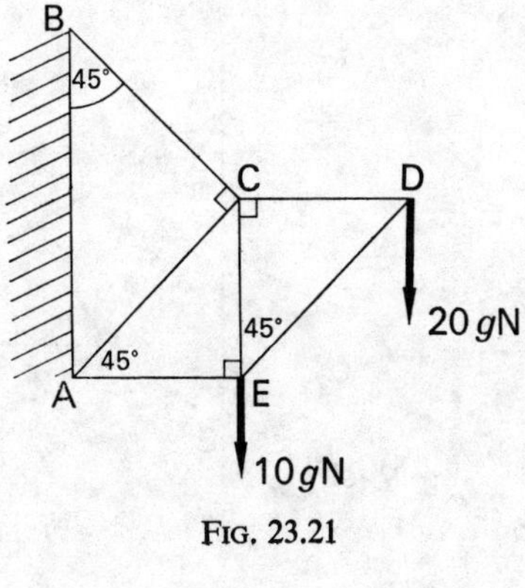

FIG. 23.21

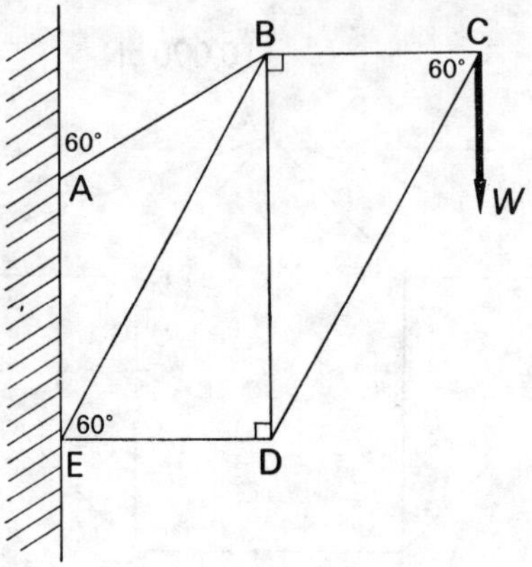

FIG. 23.22

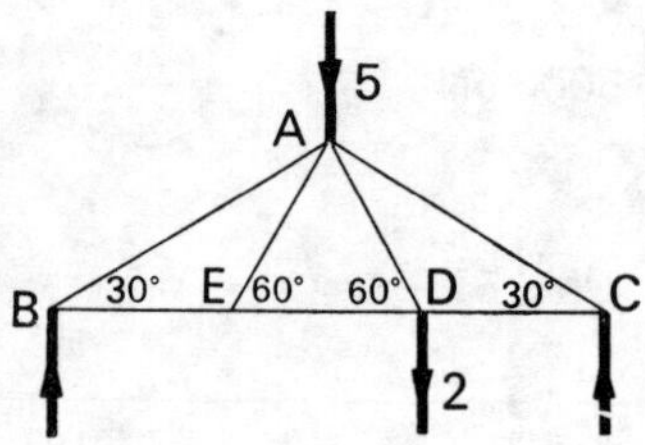

FIG. 23.23

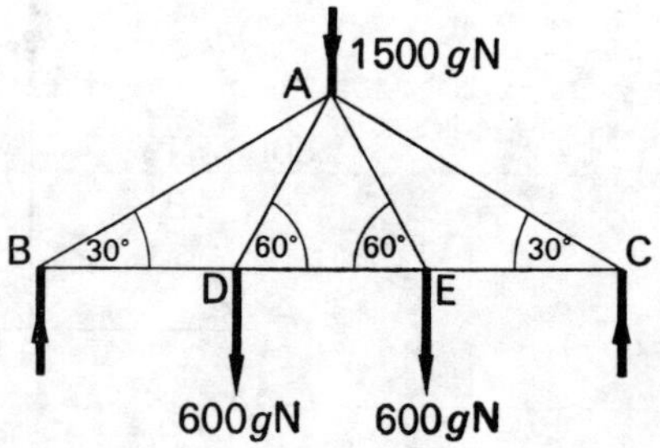

FIG. 23.24

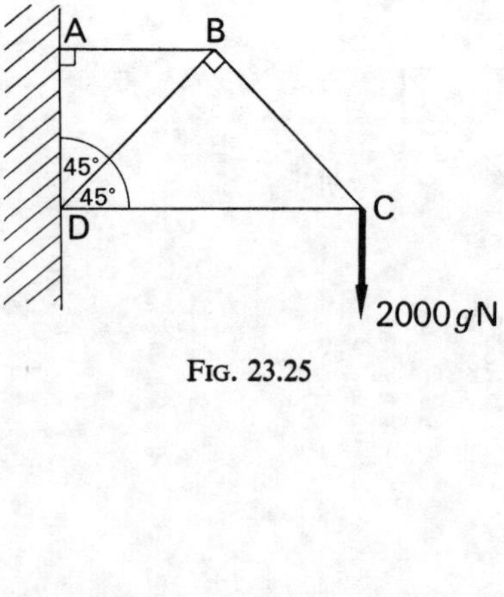

FIG. 23.25

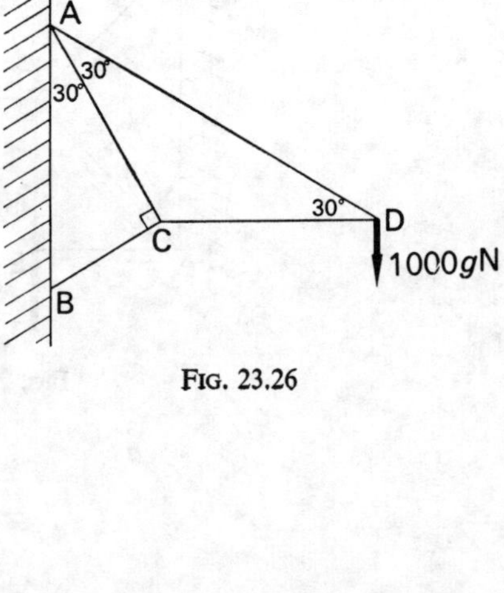

FIG. 23.26

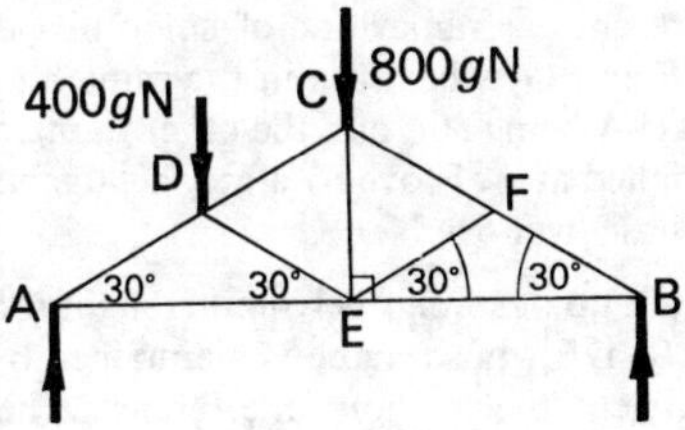

FIG. 23.27

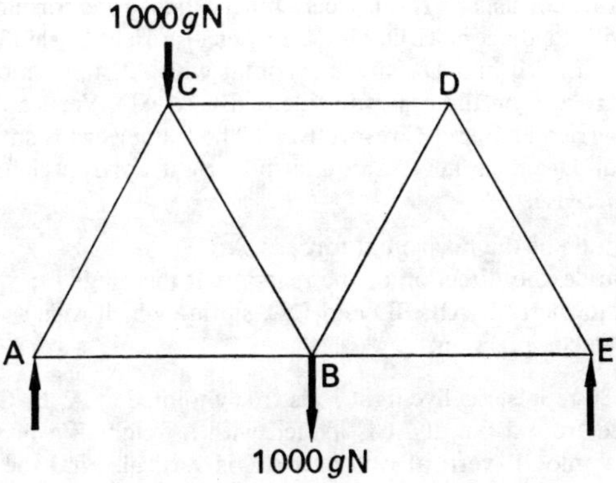

FIG. 23.28

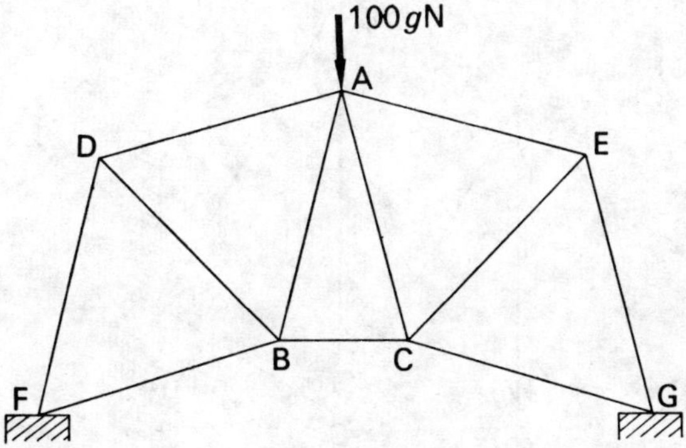

FIG. 23.29

10. Figure 23.29 represents a framework of smoothly jointed light rods, resting on smooth supports at F and G, which are in the same horizontal line. The triangle ABC is isosceles, the angle A being 30°, and the other triangles are equilateral. A vertical force of $100g$ N is applied at A. Prove by a graphical method or otherwise that the stress in the rod BC is a little over $63g$ N.

11. A framework is built up of seven freely jointed light rods. Five rods are the sides of a regular pentagon ABCDE whose shape is maintained by the two remaining rods BD and CE which cross each other without interference. The framework is suspended from A and carries loads of $10g$ N at each of the joints C and D. Find, graphically or otherwise, the magnitudes of the forces in the rods BD, CE and CD, stating which of these forces are tensile and which compressive.

12. A framework consists of seven freely hinged light rods forming the sides of a square ABCD, with its diagonal BD, and the sides of a right-angled isosceles triangle BCE with BE = CE. AB and DC are horizontal with AB uppermost. E lies in the plane of the square and on the opposite side of BC to AD. Vertical loads of $100g$ N and $150g$ N are carried at E and C respectively. The framework is smoothly hinged to a fixed support at D and is kept in equilibrium by a horizontal force at A. Find, graphically or otherwise,

(i) the magnitude of the horizontal force at A;
(ii) the magnitude and direction of the reaction at the hinge D;
(iii) the forces in the rods AB, BD and DC, stating which rods are in tension and which are in compression.

13. Figure 23.30 represents five light rods freely jointed at A, B, C, D. The framework is suspended from a pin at A, is loaded with a weight Wg N at B, the joint D presses against a smooth vertical wall and AC is vertical. Find the magnitude and direction of the reaction of the pin at A, and the stresses in the rods, distinguishing between com pression and tension.

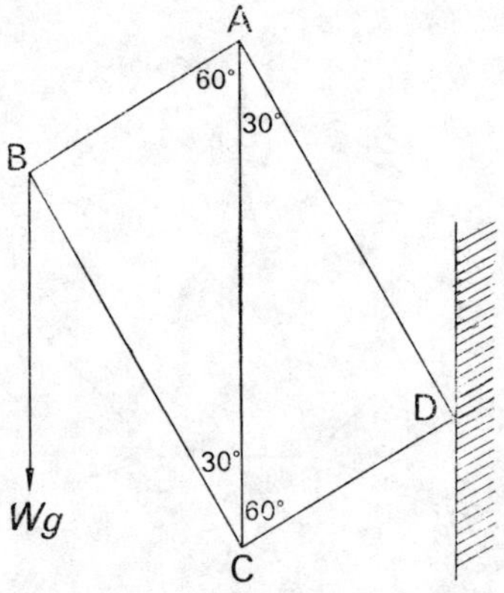

FIG. 23.30

14. A framework of light rigid smoothly jointed rods is arranged in a vertical plane as shown in Fig. 23.31, the complete triangles being equilateral and AH being parallel to BC. The points A, B are fixed so that AF, BE are horizontal, and loads of 10 kg are attached at C, D, E respectively. Find the stresses in HG, GC, CD.

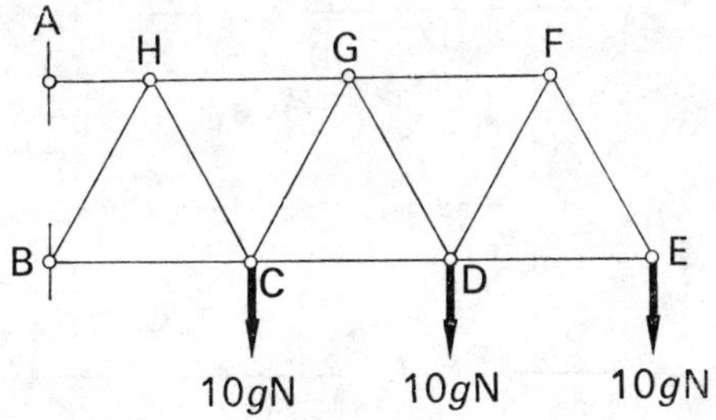

FIG. 23.31

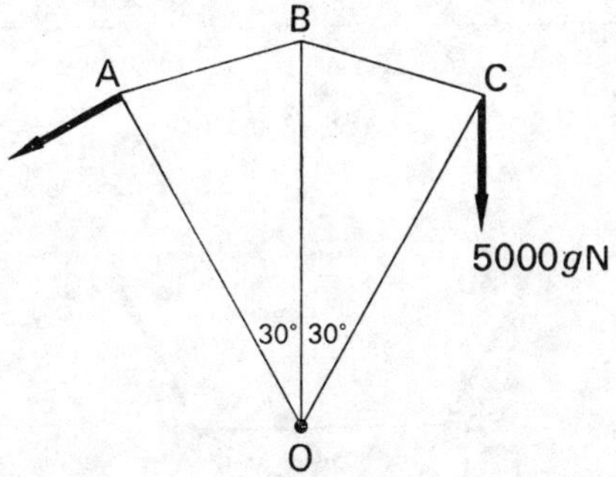

FIG. 23.32

15. The framework shown in Fig. 23.32 consists of five light rods freely hinged together. The two rods AB, BC are equal in length and so are the three rods OA, OB, OC, the angles AOB, BOC both being 30°. The frame is freely hinged to a fixed point O and stands in a vertical plane with the end A anchored by a light chain pulled in a direction perpendicular to the rod OA. Find graphically the stresses in the rods and the reaction at O when the rod OB is vertical and a load of 5000 kg is suspended at C.

16. The framework of light smoothly jointed rods shown in Fig. 23.33 carries loads of 1, 2, 3, 4 units at P, Q, R, S, is pivoted at O and supported in a vertical plane by a horizontal force at P. Find, graphically or otherwise, the forces at O and P and the stresses in QT, TU and UQ distinguishing ties from struts. (L.)

17. Five light rods AB, BC, CD, DA, AC are freely jointed together at their ends to form a quadrilateral frame ABCD stiffened by the diagonal rod AC. The rods AB, AD are equal in length, the angle BAD = 60° and the angles ABC, ADC are right

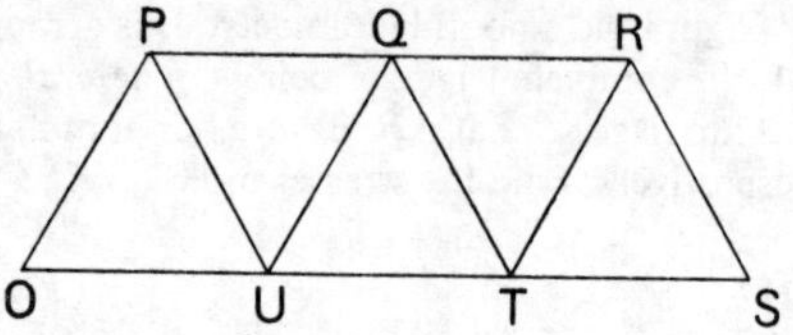

FIG. 23.33

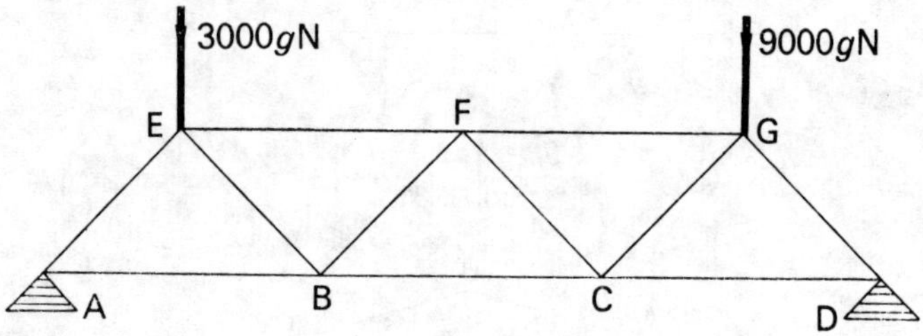

FIG. 23.34

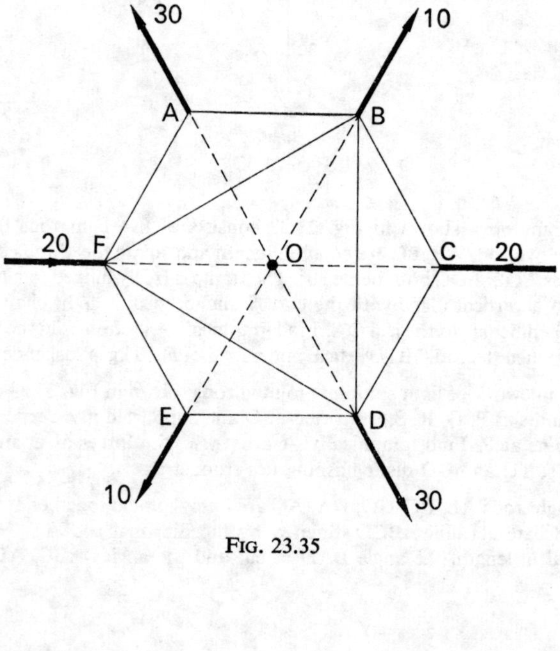

FIG. 23.35

angles. The frame hangs freely from A and supports loads of 200 kg and 300 kg at B and D. Find graphically the forces in the rods when the system is in equilibrium.

18. Six light rods of equal length are smoothly jointed together to form a regular hexagon OABCDE, and three other light rods join OB, OC, OD. Particles of weight w are attached to A and E. The system rests in a vertical plane with OC horizontal (A vertically above E), the point O being fastened to a fixed peg. The framework is kept in position by means of a string attached to B, whose line of action is along CB produced. Find the tension of the string.

Find the stresses in OA, OB, OC, OD, OE, and state whether these rods are struts or ties. (O.C.)

19. The light jointed framework shown in Fig. 23.34 has all its angles equal to 45° or 90°; it is supported at its ends with five of its bars horizontal, and it carries loads of 3000 kg and 9000 kg. Find the stresses in FB, FC, BC, indicating which are in tension and which are in compression.

20. Fig. 23.35 represents a freely jointed framework of six light rods in the shape of a regular hexagon ABCDEF, together with three other light rods BD, DF, FB. Forces of magnitude 30, 10, 20, 30, 10, 20 units are applied at the joints A, B, C, D, E, F respectively, in the directions indicated, their lines of action all passing through O, the centre of the hexagon. Find, graphically or otherwise, the forces in the rods BD, DF and FB, stating which rods are in tension and which in compression. (L.)

CHAPTER XXIV

CONTINUOUSLY DISTRIBUTED FORCES

24.1. Introduction—Shearing Force and Bending Moment

The action of one part of a body on another, as illustrated by the particular case of a rod fixed to a vertical wall, was discussed in § 20.2 where we concluded that this action could be reduced to a single force acting at a point in the plane of section and a couple. We now consider the more general case of a thin, nearly straight beam AB under the action of a set of external forces and couples which are all in a vertical plane containing AB (Fig. 24.1). [In this book we discuss only the forces involved and the

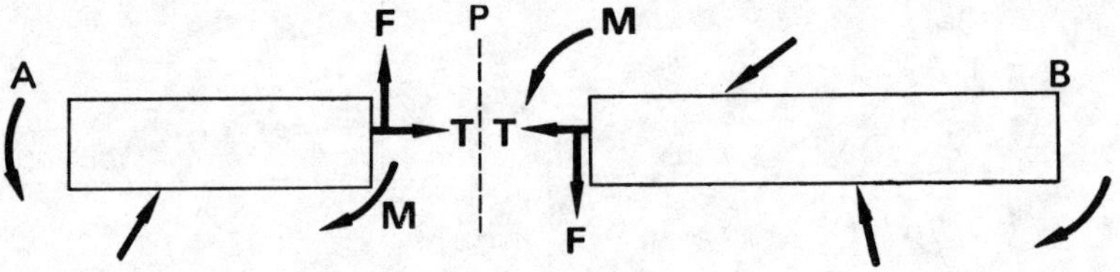

FIG. 24.1

resulting internal stress system of the beam. We do not discuss the change of shape of the beam resulting from these forces.] Each of the external forces acting on the beam may either be a continuously distributed force, as, for example, the weight of a heavy beam, or it may be concentrated at a certain point, as, for example, at a point where the beam is supported.

We represent the internal forces in the beam in the manner of Fig. 24.1 which shows the beam divided geometrically into two parts by a normal section at a point P, i.e. by a section whose plane is perpendicular to the tangent to the beam at P. (The shape of the beam was defined as *nearly straight.*) Since each portion of the beam is in equilibrium, the forces exerted across the section at P by the r.h. portion on the l.h. portion must balance the external forces on the l.h. portion. Similarly the forces exerted by the l.h. portion on the r.h. portion balance the external forces on the latter. In § 19.3 we showed that any coplanar set of forces is equivalent to a single force acting at an arbitrary point in the plane together with a couple. Therefore, in general, we can represent the action of one portion of the beam on another by a system of two component forces T and F at some point of the section together with a couple M, such that the whole system is in equilibrium with the external forces acting on the same part of the beam (Fig. 24.1).

The component F is called the *shearing force*, the component T is called the *tension*, and the couple M is called the *bending moment*. In the sign convention used in this book T, F, M are positive when they act in the direction shown in Fig. 24.1, i.e. T is positive when each portion of the beam is in tension, F is positive when it is upwards for the left-hand portion of the beam, and M is positive when it is clockwise for the left-hand portion of the beam. The law of action and reaction requires that the forces exerted across the section by the l.h. portion on the r.h. portion are as shown in Fig. 24.1 where they are positive.

Example 1. A uniform beam AB, of length 10 m and of mass 1000 kg, is supported at its extremities and loaded with 5000 kg at C and 2000 kg at D where AC = 2 m, DB = $2\frac{1}{2}$ m. Find the shearing force and the bending moment at G, the mid-point of AB.

The external forces acting on the beam are shown in Fig. 24.2 (i). Since the beam is in equilibrium, $R+S = 8000g$ N and (moments about B) $10R = 50{,}000g$ N,

$$\therefore\ R = 5000g \text{ N}, \quad S = 3000g \text{ N}.$$

The forces acting on the portion AG of the beam are shown in Fig. 24.2 (ii) where P is the mid-point of AG, F is the shearing force and M is the bending moment. Since no external force acting on AG has a component at right angles to F, there is no tension in AG. Then, for the equilibrium of AG,

$$F = 500g \text{ N},$$

and (moments about G) $$M = -8750g \text{ Nm}.$$

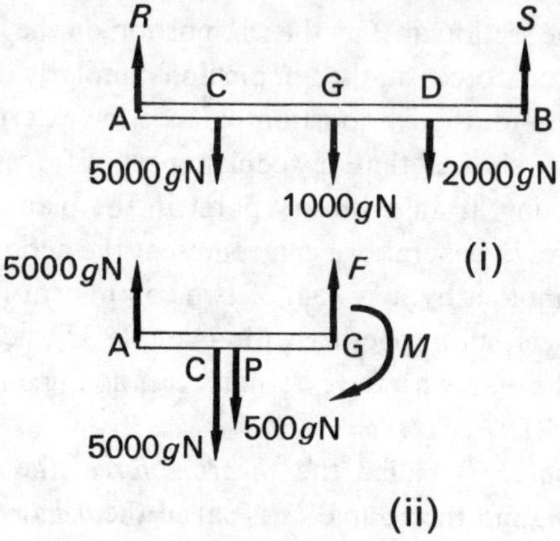

FIG. 24.2

Example 2. A uniform beam AB, of length $2a$ and weight W, is firmly clamped at A so that AB, which is straight, makes the angle θ with the horizontal at A and A is below B [Fig. 24.3 (i)]. Find expressions for each of the shearing force, the tension, and the bending moment at a point P of AB distance x from A.

The forces acting on the portion PB of the rod are shown in Fig. 24.3 (ii). These are the weight of PB, $W(2a-x)/(2a)$ acting through its mid-point G, the shearing force F,

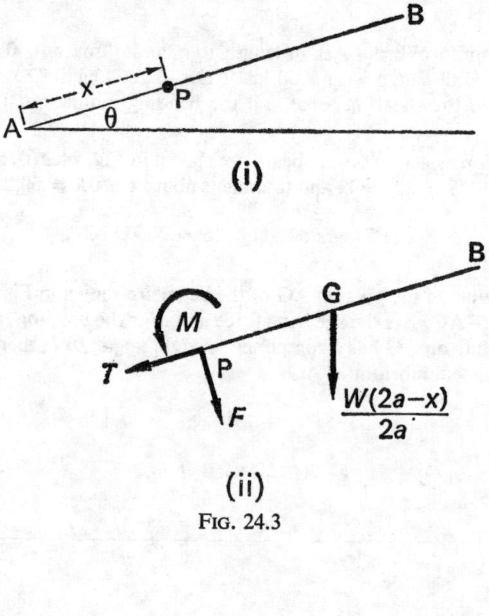

FIG. 24.3

the tension T and the bending moment M. Because this portion is in equilibrium

$$F = -\frac{W(2a-x)}{2a}\cos\theta,$$

$$T = -\frac{W(2a-x)}{2a}\sin\theta,$$

$$M = \frac{W(2a-x)^2\cos\theta}{4a}.$$

EXERCISES 24.1

In the exercises which follow the beams will be referred to as being horizontal or as being supported horizontally although there is in each case some bending of the beam which makes the description only approximately correct.

1. A uniform beam AB, of length 10 m and mass 60 kg, is fixed to a vertical wall at the end A and rests in a position with AB at right angles to the wall at A. Calculate the shearing force and the bending moment at a point P of the beam distant 4 m from A.

2. A uniform beam AB, of length 10 m and mass 40 kg, is supported horizontally at C and D where AC = 2 m, DB = 4 m. Calculate the shearing force and the bending moment at a point of the beam distant 3 m from A.

3. A uniform beam AB, of weight W and length $2l$, is supported horizontally at A and B. Find the shearing force and the bending moment at a point distance x from A and find the point of the beam at which the numerical value of the bending moment is greatest.

4. A uniform beam AB, of length 18 m and mass 90 kg, is loaded with 30 kg at its mid-point and 30 kg at B. The beam is supported horizontally at A and at C where BC = 6 m. Calculate the shearing force and the bending moment at a point 6 m from A.

5. A beam AB, of length 24 m, is supported horizontally at one end A and at a point C, 4 m from the other end B. The beam carries a load which is uniformly distributed along its length and which is equivalent to 2000 kg per metre run. The mass of the beam is small enough to be negligible compared with the load. Find the shearing force and the bending moment at a point of the beam distant x m from A and hence find the greatest shearing force and the greatest bending moment and the positions where they occur.

6. A beam AB of length $4a$ is to be supported horizontally at A and at a point C distant a from B. The beam is to carry loads, each of weight L, at D, where AD = a, and at B. The weight of the beam is sufficiently small to be negligible compared with its load. Calculate the bending moment at a point P of the beam between D and C and distant x from D. If the bending moment of the beam between D and C must not exceed Wa in magnitude, find the greatest possible value of L.

7. A uniform bar AB, of mass 32 kg and length 1·6 m, rests horizontally on two supports at its ends. A load of mass 8 kg is suspended from the bar at a point P, where AP = 0·4 m. Find, by calculation, at what point of the bar the shearing force is zero and evaluate the bending moment at this point.

8. A uniform beam AC projects 6 m horizontally from a wall to which it is fixed at A. The beam is of mass 10 kg/m and carries a load of 40 kg at B, 2 m from A, and a load of 30 kg at C. Calculate the shearing force and the bending moment at a section 4 m from A.

9. Figure 24.4 shows the forces acting in a vertical plane on a uniform beam AB, of mass W and length $2l$, which is clamped at A and which remains horizontal. Find expressions in terms of W, P and l for

(i) the force and the couple exerted on the beam at A,

(ii) the shearing force, the tension, and the bending moment at the mid-point G of AB.

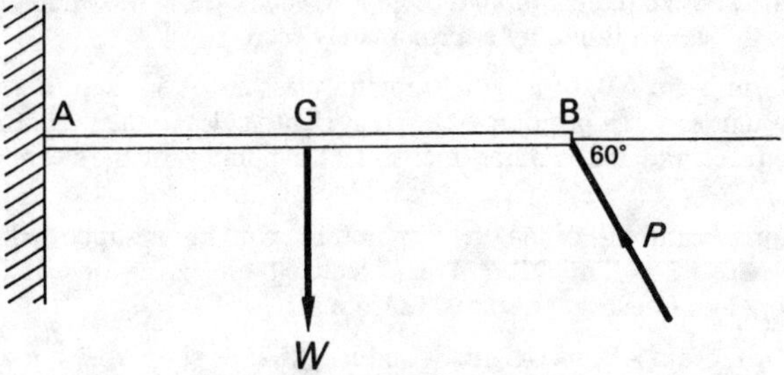

FIG. 24.4

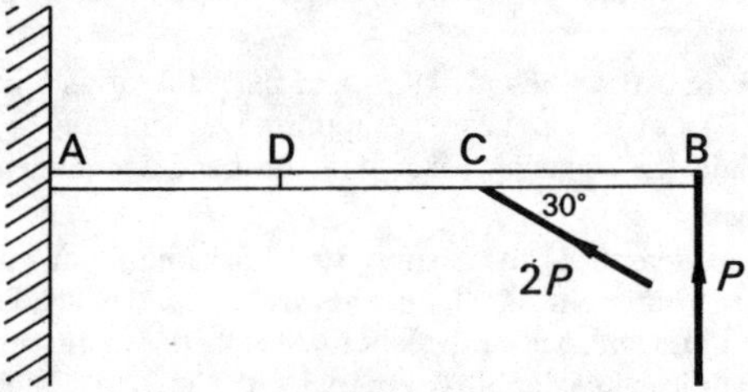

FIG. 24.5

10. In Fig. 24.5, AB represents a thin bar of length $3a$, clamped at A. The point C in AB is such that AC = $2a$. The bar is in equilibrium under the action of forces P at B perpendicular to AB and $2P$ at C making 30° with AB. The weight of the bar is negligible compared with the other forces. Calculate

(i) the shearing force at D in the bar, where AD = a,

(ii) the tension at D,

(iii) the bending moment at D.

24.2. Relations Between Bending Moment, Shearing Force and Loading

Figure 24.6 is a broken diagram of a straight horizontal beam AB on which there is a continuous vertical load of w per unit length. P and Q are points on AB so that AP $= x$ and AQ $= x+\delta x$. We assume that there are no concentrated external forces (loads, reactions at supports, clamping couples, etc.) acting on PQ. The internal forces and couples

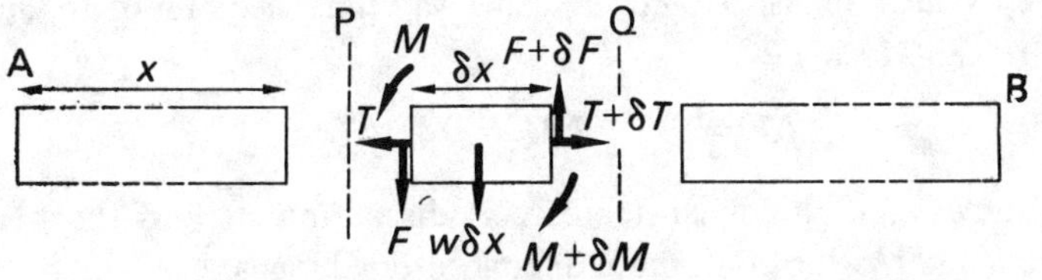

FIG. 24.6

acting on this element of the rod across each of the sections at P and Q are shown in the figure. These consist of the shearing force F, the tension T and the bending moment M at P and the corresponding quantities $F+\delta F$, $T+\delta T$, and $M+\delta M$ at Q (δF, δT, δM representing the changes in F, T, M resulting from the change δx in x).

Then, resolving horizontally and vertically and taking moments about P for the element PQ,

$$(T+\delta T)-T = 0,$$

$$F+\delta F-F-w\delta x = 0,$$

$$(M+\delta M)-M-(F+\delta F)\delta x+\tfrac{1}{2}w(\delta x)^2 = 0,$$

and from these equations we obtain

$$\frac{\mathrm{d}T}{\mathrm{d}x} = \lim_{\delta x\to 0}\frac{\delta T}{\delta x} = 0, \tag{24.1}$$

$$\frac{\mathrm{d}F}{\mathrm{d}x} = \lim_{\delta x\to 0}\frac{\delta F}{\delta x} = w, \tag{24.2}$$

$$\frac{\mathrm{d}M}{\mathrm{d}x} = \lim_{\delta x\to 0}\frac{\delta M}{\delta x} = \lim_{\delta x\to 0}(F+\delta F-\tfrac{1}{2}w\delta x) = F. \tag{24.3}$$

Equation (24.1) implies that if all the external forces act vertically then the tension T vanishes at all points of the beam.

Concentrated loads. If a concentrated load W acts at a point between P and Q, the set of forces acting is shown in Fig. 24.7. Here the increments ΔT, ΔF, ΔM may not tend to zero as $\delta x \to 0$. In fact, resolution and taking moments leads to

$\Delta T = 0$, $\Delta F = W + w\delta x$, $\Delta M = (F + \Delta F)\delta x$ + terms involving δx and higher powers of δx.

Hence, in the limit, as $\delta x \to 0$ in such a way that the point of application of W remains inside PQ,

$$\Delta F = W, \quad \Delta M = 0, \quad \Delta T = 0.$$

This shows that the shearing force is discontinuous and the bending moment and tension continuous at concentrated loads.

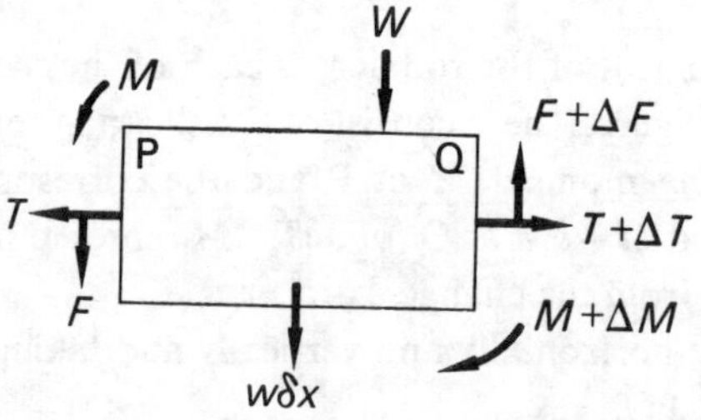

FIG. 24.7

Shearing Force and Bending Moment Diagrams

Example 1. *A uniform beam of length 2l and weight w per unit length supported at the same level at its ends.*

Figure 24.8 (i). Each of the reactions R and S at the supports is equal to lw.

Figure 24.8 (ii). If P is the point distant x from A, F is the shearing force at P and M is the bending moment there, then from the equilibrium of the portion AP of the beam.

$$F = w(x - l),$$
$$M = w(\tfrac{1}{2}x^2 - lx).$$

These expressions for F and M illustrate, in a particular case, the result $F = dM/dx$ obtained by general considerations above.

Figure 24.8 (iii) is the *shearing force diagram* (the F–x graph) and Fig. 24.8 (iv) is the *bending moment diagram* (the M–x graph) for the beam.

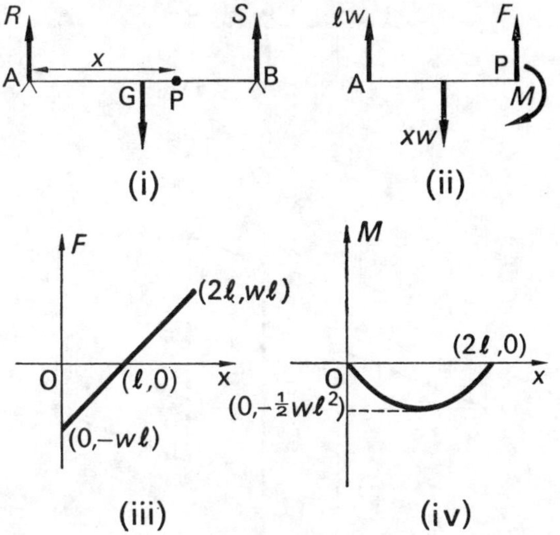

FIG. 24.8

Example 2. A uniform beam, of length $3a$ and weight w per unit length, is supported in a horizontal position by vertical forces at its points of trisection C, D and a load of $5wa$ is suspended from the mid-point G of the beam. Find the shearing force and bending moment at a point P where AP $= x$ and draw the shearing force and bending moment diagrams.

Figure 24.9 (i) shows typical positions, P_1, P_2, P_3, P_4 of P, one in each of the ranges of x given below. The conditions of equilibrium of that portion of the beam to the left of P lead to the results in the table. For example, suppose P lies in the second range $a < x < 3a/2$; vertical resolution and moments about P for the left-hand portion give

$$-wx+4wa+F = 0, \qquad -wx(\tfrac{1}{2}x)+4wa(x-a)+M = 0.$$

$$\therefore\ F = w(x-4a), \qquad M = \tfrac{1}{2}wx^2-4wa(x-a).$$

Range	F	M
$0 \leqq x < a$	wx	$\frac{1}{2}wx^2$
$a < x < 3a/2$	$w(x-4a)$	$\frac{1}{2}wx^2-4wa(x-a)$
$3a/2 < x < 2a$	$w(x+a)$	$\frac{1}{2}wx^2-4wa(x-a)+5wa(x-3a/2)$
$2a < x \leqq 3a$	$w(x-3a)$	$\frac{1}{2}wx^2-4wa(x-a)+5wa(x-3a/2)-4wa(x-2a)$

The shearing force and bending moment diagrams are shown in Figs. 24.9 (ii) and 24.9 (iii).

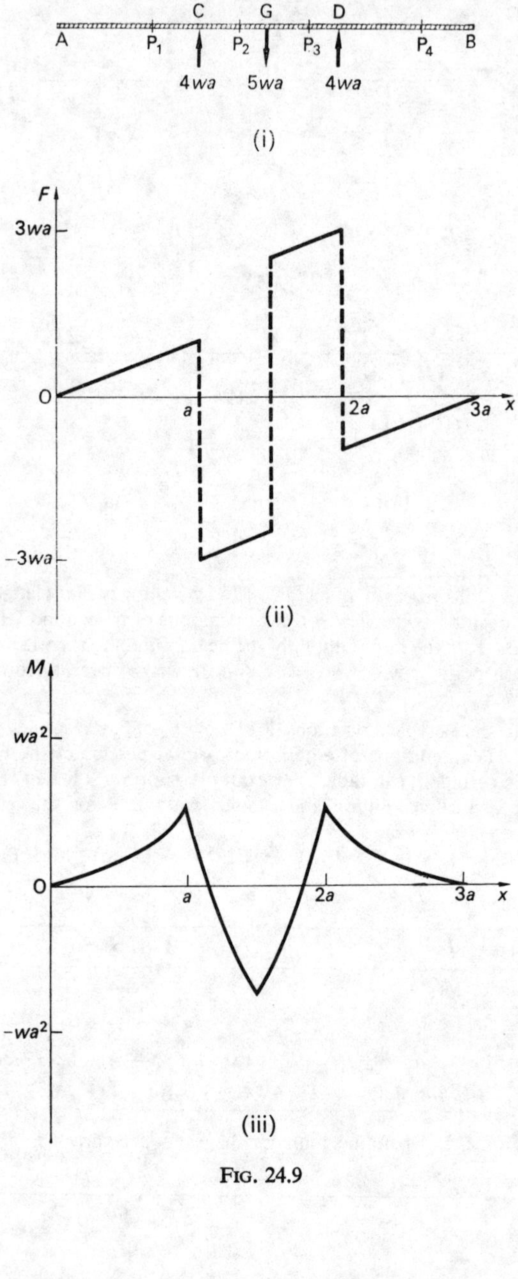
C G D
A P1 P2 P3 P4 B
4wa 5wa 4wa
(i)
F
3wa
-3wa
O
a
2a
3a
x
(ii)
M
wa2
-wa2
O
a
2a
3a
x
(iii)

FIG. 24.9

EXERCISES 24.2

In each of exercises 1–8 draw the shearing force diagram and the bending moment diagram for the horizontal beam AB loaded and supported as described.

1. Length $2l$, weight w per unit length, clamped at A.

2. Length $2l$, weight w per unit length, supported at A and C where AC $= l$.

3. Length $3l$, weight w per unit length, supported at C and D where AC $=$ CD $= l$.

4. Length 10 m, mass 200 kg, supported at A and B and carrying loads of 100 kg at C and 200 kg at D where AC $=$ CB $=$ 3 m.

5. Length 20 m, weight negligible, fixed at A and supported at its middle point, carrying a load of 30,000 kg at B.

6. Length l, weight negligible, carrying a load W at its mid-point and a load W at B.

7. Length $4l$, weight per unit length w, supported at A and B and carrying an evenly distributed load of $5w$ per unit length between C and D where AC $=$ DB $= l$.

8. Length $4l$, weight per unit length w, supported at A and B and carrying concentrated loads $20lw$ at C and D and also an evenly distributed load of $5w$ per unit length between C and D where AC $=$ DB $= l$.

9. A uniform beam AB, of length 20 m and of mass 100 kg, is supported at its ends so as to be horizontal, and a load of mass 200 kg is hung from it at a point distant 8 m from A. Draw the shearing force and bending moment diagrams and find the greatest numerical value of the bending moment.

10. A heavy uniform beam AB, 10 m long, is supported in a horizontal position by vertical forces applied to it at A and at the point C of the beam between B and the mid-point of the beam such that AC $= c$. Draw the shearing force and bending moment diagrams and find the value of c if M vanishes at the centre of the beam.

***11.** A uniform heavy rigid beam AB, of length $2l$ and weight W, rests in a horizontal position on two supports, one at the end B and the other at a point C between A and B, while from the free end A hangs a weight W.

For any given possible value c of AC obtain expressions for the shearing force and bending moment at any point X of the beam in terms of x the distance AX. Illustrate your results by a sketch and indicate points of zero and maximum bending moment.

Prove that when C is chosen so that the beam is about to turn round the support at that point, the greatest value of the bending moment is $\frac{9}{16}Wl$. (C.S.)

***12.** A uniform beam AE, of weight W and length $8a$, rests symmetrically on two supports B, D, which are in the same horizontal line and are at a distance $4a$ apart. A weight W is suspended from the beam at the point C such that BC $= a$, CD $= 3a$. Find the shearing force and bending moment at all points of the beam, and show that the maximum bending moment is $\frac{11}{16}aW$. (C.S.)

***13.** AFBCED is a light horizontal beam 12 m long, bearing equal loads W at A, B, C, D and supported at F and E. The lengths of AB, BC, CD are each 4 m, of AF 2 m and of ED 3 m. Find graphically the pressures on F and E, and obtain a diagram showing the distribution of the bending moment along the beam.

***14.** A uniform horizontal rod AB, of length $4l$ and of weight $4lw$, is smoothly hinged to a wall at B and rests across a smooth support at a point E distant $3l$ from B. A load of weight $4nlw$ is hung from A. Find the bending moment at any point of the rod distant x from A.

Show that, if the bending moment vanishes at a point between E and B, then n must be less than unity. (C.S.)

***15.** A uniform beam, of length $2a$ and weight $2wa$, rests on two supports at the same horizontal level at equal distances $a-b$ from its ends. Find the ratio b must have to a in order that the greatest absolute value of the bending moment shall be as small as possible. Show that for this ratio, the bending moments at the centre and the supports are numerically equal and of amount $wa^2(\frac{3}{2}-\sqrt{2})$. (C.S.)

24.3. A Uniform Flexible Inelastic String Hanging Under Gravity

We define a *flexible string* as a continuous line of particles in which the only action which one element can exert on a neighbouring element is a force (the tension) along the line joining the elements, i.e. along the tangent to the string. There is no couple and no transverse force; the string offers no resistance to bending. In this section we consider the equilibrium of such a string, fixed at its ends and hanging freely under gravity as shown in Fig. 24.10.

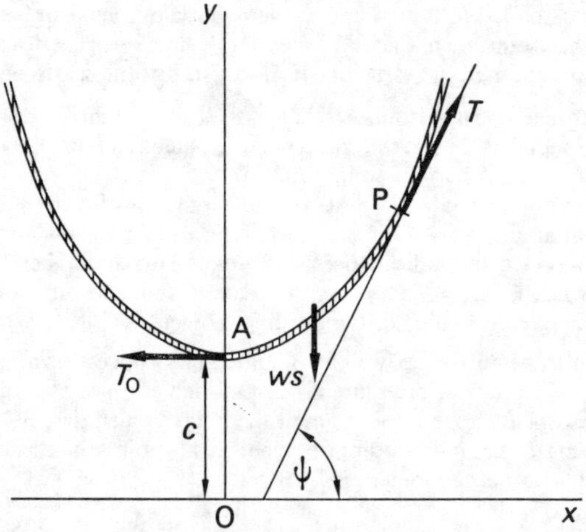

FIG. 24.10

In this figure A is the lowest point of the string, P is another point of the string and the tangent at P to the string makes an angle ψ with the horizontal. We suppose that the weight per unit length of the string is uniform and equal to w. Then the forces acting on the portion AP of the string are,

(i) its weight ws,

(ii) the tension T exerted by the part of the string to the right of P along the tangent to the string at P,

(iii) the tension T_0 exerted by the part of the string to the left of A, *horizontally* along the tangent to the string at A.

Then, for the equilibrium of this part of the string,

$$T_0 = T\cos\psi, \tag{24.4}$$

$$ws = T\sin\psi. \tag{24.5}$$

Equation (24.4) shows that the horizontal component of the tension is constant throughout the string. We write $T_0 = wc$, where c is constant. Then, by division,

$$s = c\tan\psi. \tag{24.6}$$

[Throughout the work which follows reference should be made to the authors' *Sixth Form Pure Mathematics*, Vol. II, Chap. XIV.] This equation (24.6) is the intrinsic equation of the curve of the string. The curve is called the *catenary* (Latin—*catena*, a chain).

We now select as axes of cartesian coordinates the vertical line through A as y-axis and the horizontal line at a distance c below A as x-axis. The x-axis is sometimes called the *directrix* of the catenary (not associated with the directrix of a conic), and c is called the *parameter* of the catenary.

In order to obtain y in terms of ψ for the catenary we use the relationship

$$\frac{dy}{d\psi} = \frac{dy}{ds}\cdot\frac{ds}{d\psi}.$$

But $\mathrm{d}y/\mathrm{d}s = \sin\psi$, and, from equation (24.6), $\mathrm{d}s/\mathrm{d}\psi = c\sec^2\psi$,

$$\therefore \frac{\mathrm{d}y}{\mathrm{d}\psi} = c\sec^2\psi\sin\psi = c\sec\psi\tan\psi.$$

$$\therefore y = \int c\sec\psi\tan\psi\,\mathrm{d}\psi.$$

$$\therefore y = c\sec\psi + A,$$

where A is constant. With the axes we have chosen, $y = c$ when $\psi = 0$. Therefore $A = 0$ and so

$$y = c\sec\psi. \tag{24.7}$$

Therefore, $$y^2 - s^2 = c^2(\sec^2\psi - \tan^2\psi),$$

i.e. $$y^2 = c^2 + s^2. \tag{24.8}$$

Also $$\frac{\mathrm{d}x}{\mathrm{d}\psi} = \frac{\mathrm{d}x}{\mathrm{d}s}\cdot\frac{\mathrm{d}s}{\mathrm{d}\psi}.$$

$$\therefore \frac{\mathrm{d}x}{\mathrm{d}\psi} = \cos\psi . c\sec^2\psi,$$

i.e. $$x = \int c\sec\psi\,\mathrm{d}\psi.$$

$$\therefore x = c\ln(\sec\psi + \tan\psi) + B,$$

where B is constant. [*Pure Mathematics*, Vol. I, eqn. (10.6).] We have chosen axes so that $x = 0$ when $\psi = 0$, $\therefore$ $B = 0$.

$$\therefore x = c\ln(\sec\psi + \tan\psi). \tag{24.9}$$

Also, $$\frac{\mathrm{d}y}{\mathrm{d}x} = \tan\psi = \sqrt{(\sec^2\psi - 1)} = \sqrt{\left(\frac{y^2}{c^2} - 1\right)}.$$

$$\therefore x = \int \frac{c\,\mathrm{d}y}{\sqrt{(y^2 - c^2)}} = c\cosh^{-1}\left(\frac{y}{c}\right) + K,$$

where K is constant, and from the condition $y = c$ when $x = 0$ it follows that $K = 0$.

$$\therefore y = c\cosh(x/c). \tag{24.10}$$

This is the cartesian equation of the catenary. The student will recognize, in the shape of the catenary, the shape of the curve $y = \cosh x$ discussed in *Pure Mathematics*, Vol. II, § 12.4.

From (24.8) and (24.10)

$$s = \sqrt{(y^2-c^2)} = \sqrt{\{c^2 \cosh^2 (x/c) - c^2\}},$$

$$\therefore\ s = c \sinh (x/c). \qquad (24.11)$$

[*Alternatively*, equations (24.10) and (24.11) can be obtained by writing equation (24.9) in the form

$$\sec \psi + \tan \psi = e^{x/c}$$

from which $$\sec \psi - \tan \psi = e^{-x/c}.$$

Then addition and subtraction lead to the equations

$$y = c \cosh (x/c), \quad s = c \sinh (x/c).]$$

From $T_0 = T \cos \psi$, we have

$$T = T_0 \sec \psi = wc \sec \psi,$$

$$\therefore\ T = wy. \qquad (24.12)$$

This equation shows that the tension at any point of the string is proportional to the ordinate at that point.

Example 1. A uniform heavy chain of length 32 m hangs symmetrically over two smooth pegs at the same level so that the lowest point of the portion of the chain between the pegs is 2 m below the level of the pegs. Find the length of either vertical portion of the chain and show that the distance between the pegs is 16 ln 2 m.

It is a characteristic of a chain hung freely over smooth pegs in this way that the ends of the vertical portions of the chain are on the x-axis (the directrix of the catenary). The reason for this is apparent in the work which follows.

If $2s$ m is the length of chain between the pegs, Fig. 24.11, the length of each vertical portion of the chain is $(16-s)$ m. The tension in the curved portion of the chain

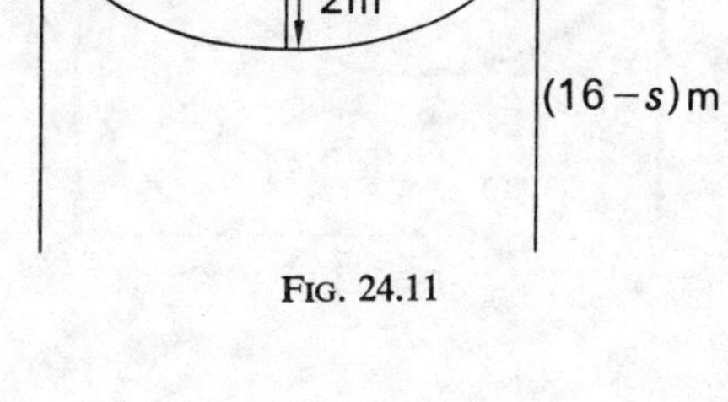

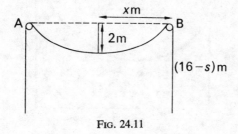

FIG. 24.11

at B is equal to the tension in the vertical portion of the chain at B, therefore

$$wy = w(16-s),$$

where y is the ordinate of B referred to the usual axes for the catenary and the weight of 1 metre of the chain is equal to the weight of w kilograms.

Thus, $$y = 16-s.$$

But also, $$y = 2+c$$

and $$y^2 = s^2+c^2,$$

where c m is the parameter of the catenary.

$$\therefore\ (16-s)^2 = s^2+(14-s)^2,$$

i.e. $$s^2+4s-60 = 0.$$

Therefore, since s is positive, $s = 6$, $c = 8$, and the length of the vertical portion of the chain is 10 m.

Also at B, $$y = c\cosh(x/c),$$

$$\therefore\ 10 = 8\cosh(x/8),$$

$$\therefore\ x = 8\cosh^{-1}\left(\frac{5}{4}\right) = 8\ln\left\{\frac{5}{4}+\sqrt{\left(\frac{25}{16}-1\right)}\right\} = 8\ln 2.$$

The distance between the pegs is $2x$ m $= 16\ln 2$ m.

Example 2. The ends of a uniform flexible chain of length 56 m are attached to two points A and B, where B is 14 m higher than A. The tension at B is 39/25 times the tension at A. If the lowest point C of the chain lies between A and B, find the lengths of chain CA and CB and show that the parameter c of the catenary in which the chain hangs is 15 m.

Let the ordinates of A and B referred to the usual axes be y_A and y_B, and let the tensions at A and B be T_A and T_B, Fig. 24.12.

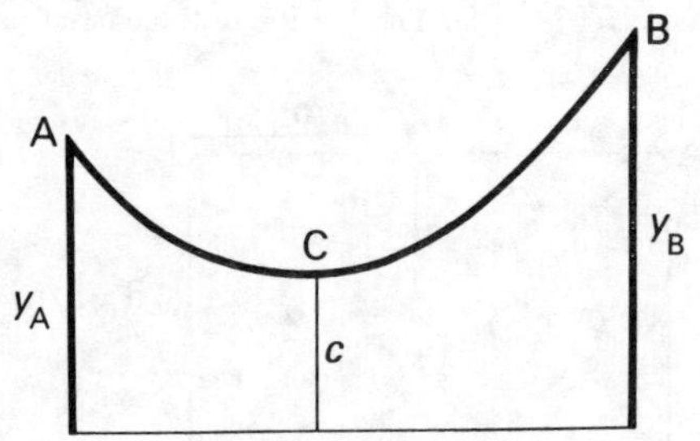

FIG. 24.12

At A, $$T_A = wy_A,$$

At B, $$T_B = wy_B = w(14+y_A),$$

$$\therefore \frac{y_A}{14+y_A} = \frac{25}{39}, \quad \therefore y_A = 25.$$

At A, $$s_A^2 = y_A^2 - c^2, \quad \therefore s_A^2 = 25^2 - c^2.$$

At B, $$(56-s_A)^2 = y_B^2 - c^2, \quad \therefore (56-s_A)^2 = 39^2 - c^2.$$

Hence, equating values of c^2, we find $s_A = 20$, $c = 15$.
AC is 20 m long, CB is 36 m long and the parameter of the catenary is 15 m.

Example 3. A uniform heavy flexible string AB, of length a and weight wa, will break if subjected to a tension greater than $3wa$. The string is attached to a fixed point at A and hangs in equilibrium under the action of a horizontal force nwa applied at B. If the string is about to break, show that (1) $n = 2\sqrt{2}$, (2) the tangent to the string at A makes an angle $\sin^{-1}(\frac{1}{3})$ with the horizontal, (3) the height of A above the level of B is $(3-2\sqrt{2})a$. (N.)

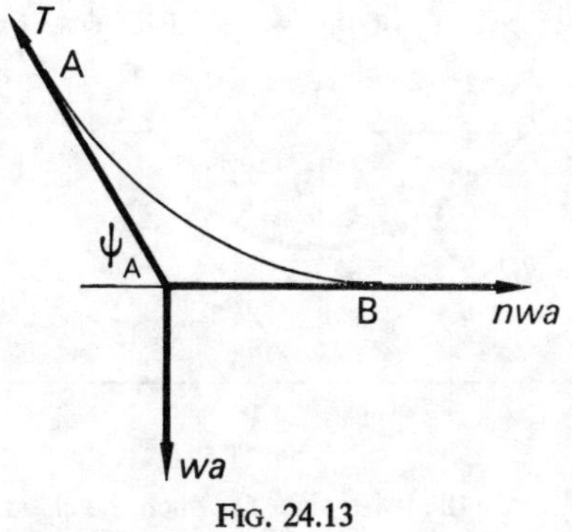

FIG. 24.13

From equation (24.12) the tension in the string is greatest at A and therefore, since the string is just about to break, the force acting on the string at A, equal and opposite to the tension in the string at A, is $3wa$. This force acts along the tangent to the string, Fig. 24.13.

The whole string is in equilibrium under the action of this force, the horizontal force nwa at B, and its weight wa. The lines of action of these three forces will therefore be concurrent as shown in Fig. 24.13.

From the triangle of forces,

$$(3wa)^2 = (wa)^2 + (nwa)^2$$

and hence $$n = 2\sqrt{2}. \qquad (1)$$

The tension at B is nwa; but, since the string is horizontal at B, the tension at B is $wy_B = wc$, where y_B is the ordinate of B and c is the parameter of the catenary.

$$\therefore \; cw = nwa.$$

$$\therefore \; c = 2a\sqrt{2}.$$

At A, since $T_A = 3wa$, $\quad \therefore \; y_A = 3a$

and since $y = c \sec \psi$, where ψ is the angle made by the tangent to the string with the horizontal,

$$3a = c \sec \psi_A, \quad \therefore \; \sec \psi_A = \frac{3}{2\sqrt{2}}, \quad \sin \psi_A = \tfrac{1}{3}. \tag{2}$$

The vertical distance of A above B is

$$y_A - c = 3a - 2a\sqrt{2} = (3-2\sqrt{2})a. \tag{3}$$

Example 4. The ends of a uniform chain, of length 24 m and mass 8 kg, are attached to two points in the same horizontal line, and the mid-point of the chain is 8 m below this line. Prove that the parameter of the catenary in which the chain hangs is 5 m and find the tension of the chain at its mid-point and at its ends. Show also, by the use of tables, that the distance apart of the two points of suspension is 16 m approximately.

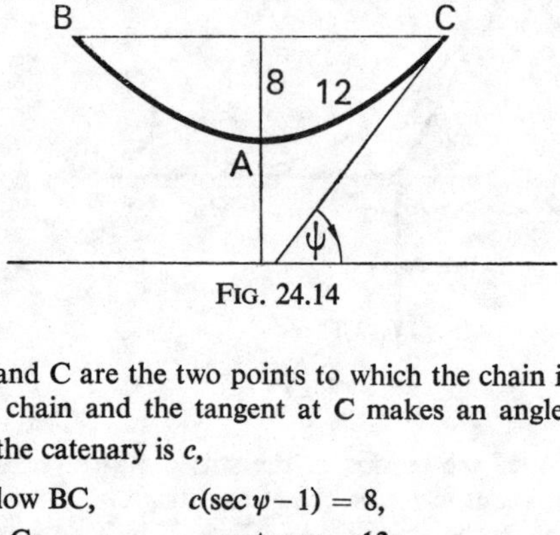

FIG. 24.14

In Fig. 24.14, B and C are the two points to which the chain is attached, A is the lowest point of the chain and the tangent at C makes an angle ψ with the x-axis. If the parameter of the catenary is c,

because A is 8 m below BC, $\quad c(\sec \psi - 1) = 8,$

because $s = 12$ m at C, $\quad c \tan \psi = 12,$

$$\therefore \; \frac{\sec \psi - 1}{\tan \psi} = \frac{2}{3}.$$

This equation reduces to $2 \sin \psi + 3 \cos \psi - 3 = 0$, $(\psi \neq 0)$,

and then to $\quad 6t^2 - 4t = 0,$

where $t = \tan \frac{1}{2}\psi$.

Hence $\quad \tan \frac{1}{2}\psi = \frac{2}{3}, \quad \tan \psi = \frac{12}{5}.$

Therefore $c = 12 \cot \psi = 5$ as required.

The tension at A is $wc = 1\frac{2}{3}g$ N.

The tension at each of B and C is (Tension at A) $\sec \psi = 4\frac{1}{3}g$ N.
The distance BC $= 2c \log (\sec \psi + \tan \psi)$ m

$$= 10 \ln \left(\frac{13}{5} + \frac{12}{5}\right) \text{ m} = 10 \ln 5 \text{ m} \approx 16 \text{ m}.$$

EXERCISES 24.3

1. A uniform flexible chain, of length $54a$, hangs over two small smooth pegs, the lengths of the vertical portions being $20a$ and $13a$ respectively. Show that the parameter of the catenary between the pegs is $12a$, and that the horizontal distance between the pegs is $12a \ln (9/2)$. (L.)

2. A uniform chain, of length 14 m and mass 28 kg, is attached at its ends to two fixed points A and B, B being 2 m above the level of A. The tension at A is equal to the weight of 26 kg. Show that the length of chain between A and the lowest point C (which lies between A and B) is 5 m, and find the tension at C. Show also that the horizontal distance between A and B is 12 ln 3 m.

3. A uniform chain, of length $2l$ and weight $2wl$, hangs in equilibrium with its ends attached to two points B and C at the same level. The depth of the middle point A of the chain below BC (the central sag) is k and the tangents to the chain at B and C are each inclined at an angle α to the horizontal. Show that $k = l \tan (\alpha/2)$.

If the tension at B is double the tension at A, show that $k = l/\sqrt{3}$. If now the distance BC is altered so that the central sag is halved, show that the tension at A is increased in the ratio 11/4. (N.)

4. A uniform heavy flexible string AB, of length $2a$, has its ends A, B attached to two light rings which can slide on a fixed straight horizontal wire. The coefficient of friction between each ring and the wire is $1/\sqrt{3}$. Show that, when equilibrium is limiting at A and B, the tangent to the string at A makes an angle $\frac{1}{3}\pi$ with the horizontal. Find the depth of the mid-point of the string below AB and show that the distance AB is

$$(2a/\sqrt{3}) \ln (2+\sqrt{3}). \qquad \text{(N.)}$$

5. A uniform heavy flexible string AB, of length $2l$, has its ends A, B attached to light rough rings which can slide on a fixed horizontal rod. The coefficient of friction between the ring and the rod is $1/\sqrt{3}$. Show that when equilibrium is limiting at both ends the depth of the mid-point M of AB below the rod is $l/\sqrt{3}$.

If a particle of the same weight as the string is now attached to M and the string takes up a new symmetrical position of limiting equilibrium, show that M falls a distance $l(3-\sqrt{7})/\sqrt{3}$. (L.)

6. The ends of a uniform string of length $2l$ are attached to small light rings which are threaded on a rough straight horizontal wire. Prove that the greatest possible distance between the rings in a position of equilibrium is $2l \tan \lambda \ln \cot \frac{1}{2}\lambda$, where λ is the angle of friction. (L.)

7. A uniform heavy chain AB is of length $8l$ and weight w per unit length. A smooth ring of weight wl fixed to the end A is free to slide on a fixed vertical wire, and the chain is slung over a smooth peg C so that a length $5l$ of the chain hangs vertically. Find the parameter of the catenary AC, and show that the distance of the peg C from the vertical wire is $3l \ln (\sqrt{10}-1)$. (L.)

8. A uniform chain of length 23 m is attached to a fixed point A and passes over a small smooth peg at B, the portion beyond B hanging vertically. If in the equilibrium position the catenary in which the chain hangs has its vertex between A and B and the tangents to the catenary at A and B make angles $\tan^{-1}(3/4)$ and $\tan^{-1}(12/5)$ respectively with the horizontal, find the parameter c of the catenary and the vertical and horizontal distances of B from A. (L.)

***9.** The ends of a uniform chain, of length $2l$ and weight $2wl$, are attached to two points A and B in the same horizontal line. To the middle point C of the chain is attached a particle of weight W. Show that in equilibrium each half of the chain is part of a catenary such that the length of arc from the vertex of the catenary to C is $W/2w$. If $W = 4wl$ and the depth of C below AB is $l/3$, show that the parameter of each catenary is

$$\frac{8\sqrt{7}}{3}l, \quad \text{and that the distance AB is} \quad \frac{16\sqrt{7}}{3}l \ln\left(\frac{8}{7}\right). \qquad \text{(N.)}$$

***10.** A uniform chain rests symmetrically over two smooth pegs A, B at the same level, so that the central portion forms a catenary with its vertex 2 m below AB and a 50 m length of the chain hangs freely outside each peg. Show that the total length of the chain is 128 m, and find the resultant thrust on the peg A if the linear density of the chain is $\frac{1}{2}$ kg/m.

24.4. The Tightly Stretched Wire

We consider a uniform wire of length $2l$ tightly stretched between two points A and B on the same horizontal level and distance $2a$ apart; k is the *sag* at the mid-point of the wire and c is the parameter of the catenary, Fig. 24.15. Since chord BC < arc BC, it follows from the right-angled triangle BCD that

$$k^2 = \text{BC}^2 - \text{BD}^2 < l^2 - a^2.$$

But $l-a$ is small and therefore

$$k \approx \sqrt{\{2l(l-a)\}}$$

is small compared with l.

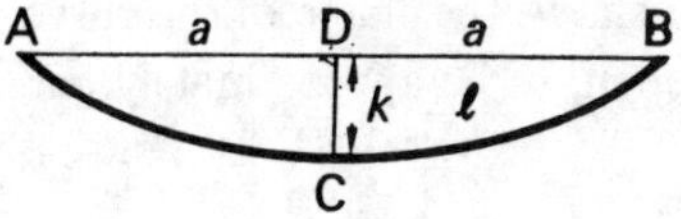

FIG. 24.15

Then, for the point B, from equation (24.10)

$$k+c = c \cosh (a/c),$$

and from equation (24.11)

$$l = c \sinh (a/c).$$

Hence
$$\left(\frac{k+c}{c}\right)^2 - \left(\frac{l}{c}\right)^2 = 1.$$

$$\therefore \; c = \frac{l^2}{2k} - \frac{k}{2}.$$

It follows that, since k is small compared with l or a, c is large and approximately equal to $l^2/(2k)$, and a/c is approximately equal to $2k/l$ and is therefore small. We now obtain a good approximation to l from the formula $l = c \sinh (a/c)$ by expanding $\sinh (a/c)$ and neglecting terms involving higher powers of a/c than the second. Thus,

$$l \approx c\left(\frac{a}{c} + \frac{a^3}{6c^3}\right),$$

i.e.
$$l \approx a + \frac{a^3}{6c^2}.$$

Also, if y_B is the ordinate at B,

$$y_B = c \cosh \frac{a}{c},$$

$$\therefore \; y_B \approx c\left(1 + \frac{a^2}{2c^2}\right),$$

$$\therefore \; y_B \approx c + \frac{a^2}{2c}.$$

(This approximation shows the shape of the curve, when the sag is small compared with the span, to be approximately parabolic.)

But
$$k = y_B - c,$$
$$\therefore\ k \approx \frac{a^2}{2c}.$$

The difference between the length and the span

$$2(l-a) \approx \frac{a^3}{3c^2} = \frac{8}{3}\left(\frac{a^2}{2c}\right)^2 \Big/ 2a \approx \frac{8}{3}\,\frac{k^2}{2a}.$$

Therefore, the difference between the length and the span

$$\approx (8/3)\{(\text{sag})^2/\text{span}\}.$$

EXERCISES 24.4

1. A uniform wire of length 102 m has a horizontal span of 100 m. Calculate an approximate value of the sag in the middle.

2. A uniform wire of mass 0·5 kg/m hangs from two points in a horizontal line and 20 m apart with a sag of 0·2 m. Calculate an approximate value for the maximum tension in the wire.

3. A tightly stretched telegraph wire has a span of 25 m. The wire is of mass 0·5 kg/m and the tension in the wire must not exceed a force equal to the weight of 300 kg. Calculate an approximate value for the least possible sag of the wire.

4. The sag of a telegraph wire stretched between two poles at a distance $2a$ apart is k. Show that the tension at each end of the wire is approximately

$$w\left(\frac{a^2}{2k}+\frac{7k}{6}\right),$$

where w is the weight per unit length of the wire. (L.)

24.5. A Uniformly Loaded Inextensible String

In Vol. I, § 2.11 we discussed the method to be used in problems concerning an inextensible string of negligible weight fixed at each end and loaded at points along its length. Here we investigate, by that method, the shape of a light string, *suspended from two points at the same level and loaded with a number of equal weights spaced so that the horizontal distances between the weights are equal.* We show that the points of suspension and the points of attachment of the weights all lie on a parabola.

Figure 24.16 shows four of the particles attached, as described, to the string at A, B, C and D. The parts of the string AB, BC, CD make angles θ_1, θ_2, θ_3 with the vertical. The coordinates of B, C, D referred to horizontal and vertical axes through A as origin are (x_1, y_1), (x_2, y_2), (x_3, y_3) respectively and $x_1 = x_2-x_1 = x_3-x_2 = a$.

Suppose the tensions in the strings AB, BC, CD are T_1, T_2, T_3 respectively. Then because the horizontal component of tension is constant throughout the string,

$$T_1 \sin \theta_1 = T_2 \sin \theta_2 = T_3 \sin \theta_3 = H \text{ (say)},$$

and by vertical resolution for the forces acting at each of the points B and C,

$$T_2 \cos \theta_2 - T_1 \cos \theta_1 = W,$$
$$T_3 \cos \theta_3 - T_2 \cos \theta_2 = W,$$

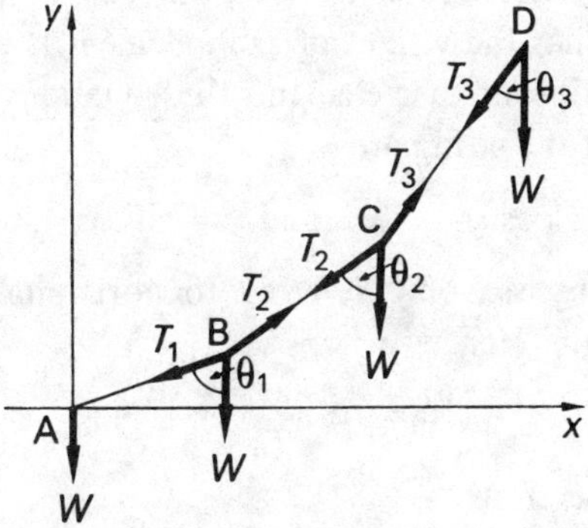

FIG. 24.16

where each of the weights is W. From these equations

$$\cot \theta_2 - \cot \theta_1 = \cot \theta_3 - \cot \theta_2 = W/H,$$

i.e. $$\frac{y_2-y_1}{a} - \frac{y_1}{a} = \frac{y_3-y_2}{a} - \frac{y_2-y_1}{a}$$

and this reduces to $$y_3 = 3(y_2-y_1).$$

Now, if the equation of the parabola through A(0, 0), B(a, y_1), C($2a$, y_2) is

$$y = Kx^2+Lx,$$

then
$$y_1 = Ka^2+La$$

and
$$y_2 = 4Ka^2+2La,$$

$$\therefore\ y_3 = 3(y_2-y_1) = 9Ka^2+3La,$$

i.e.
$$y_3 = Kx_3^2+Lx_3.$$

Therefore D lies on the parabola through A, B, C and similarly all the other points of the string at which weights are attached lie on this parabola.

A light string which supports a continuous load whose horizontal distribution is uniform is the limiting case of the uniformly loaded string when the distance between the loads is reduced indefinitely. Such a string will therefore hang in a parabola.

This result is obtained independently thus:
Referring to Fig. 24.10 and considering the string in that diagram as a string loaded so that the weight of each element is proportional to the horizontal projection of that element, the equations of equilibrium for the portion AP of the string are

$$T\cos\psi = T_0 \quad \text{and} \quad T\sin\psi = wx,$$

where x is the abscissa of P referred to horizontal and vertical axes through A as origin. Hence

$$\tan\psi = \frac{wx}{T_0} = \frac{\mathrm{d}y}{\mathrm{d}x}.$$

By integration, therefore,

$$y = \frac{wx^2}{2T_0}+K$$

where K is constant. But $x = 0$ when $y = 0$; therefore $K = 0$.
Therefore the equation of the curve is

$$y = \frac{wx^2}{2T_0},$$

which is the equation of a parabola.

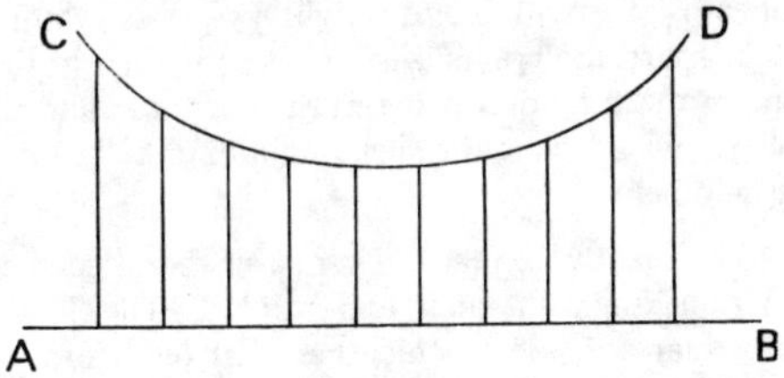

FIG. 24.17

The suspension bridge in which the weight of the horizontal roadway is large compared with the weights of the other parts affords an example of a chain loaded in this way. In Fig. 24.17 the horizontal roadway AB hangs by means of equally spaced vertical rods from the parabolic chain CD.

MISCELLANEOUS EXERCISES XXIV

***1.** A beam of material of uniform density ϱ is of the form of the solid of revolution obtained by the rotating of the straight lines

$$y = a \qquad (-2 \leqq x \leqq -1),$$
$$y = a(x+2) \qquad (-1 \leqq x \leqq 0),$$
$$y = a(2-x) \qquad (0 \leqq x \leqq 1),$$
$$y = a \qquad (1 \leqq x \leqq 2)$$

about the x-axis. The beam rests on two supports at the same horizontal level at the sections $x = -1$, $x = 2$. Determine the bending moment and shearing force at the central section and give a rough sketch of the bending moment distribution along the beam. (C.S.)

***2.** A uniform rigid beam AB, of weight W and length $2l$, is clamped at one end A so that the end is kept horizontal, and the beam is otherwise unsupported. A weight W is hung from the centre of the beam. Find the shearing stress and the bending moment at all points of the beam. (C.S.)

***3.** A heavy uniform horizontal beam of length $2l$ rests symmetrically on two supports which are at a distance $2a$ apart on a horizontal level. Illustrate, by a simple sketch, the value of the bending moment for every point of the beam.

If $a = (4-2\sqrt{3})l$, find the points on the beam where the bending moment is zero (C.S.)

***4.** A uniform bar AB, of length l and weight w per unit length, is attached to a fixed smooth hinge at A and is kept horizontal by a light chain of length $2l$ which joins B to the point vertically above, and distant $\sqrt{3}l$ from, A. Find the thrust, shearing force and bending moment at any point of the bar. (C.S.)

***5.** A uniform beam, of length $4l$ and weight $4wl$, rests symmetrically on two supports at a distance $2l$ apart, the points of support being in a horizontal line. A weight $4wl$ is placed on the beam at a point between the supports, and at a distance $l/2$ from one of them. Draw graphs showing the variation along the beam of the shearing force and of the bending moment. (C.S.)

***6.** ABC and ADC are two equal uniform thin bars, each weighing w per unit length and bent at right angles at their mid-points B, D. They are freely jointed at A and C to form a square of side a, which hangs at rest from a cord attached at A. Find the bending moment, the shearing force and the tension (i) at a point of CB distant x from C, (ii) at a point of BA distant ξ from B. (C.S.)

***7.** A uniform beam, of length $2l$ and weight $2W$, rests on two supports at the same level each at distance a from the mid-point of the beam. A weight W is suspended from each end and a weight $4W$ from the mid-point. Find the bending moment at any point along the beam and show that if a is greater than $(6-\sqrt{30})l$ the numerically greatest moment will occur at the mid-point. (C.S.)

8. Each end of a uniform chain, of length $4a$ and weight $8W$, is attached to a ring of weight W. The rings are threaded on a rough fixed horizontal bar and the coefficient of friction between each ring and the bar is 3/5. If the rings are in limiting equilibrium, prove that the sag in the chain is a and that the distance between the rings is $3a \ln 3$. (N.)

9. A uniform flexible chain, of length $2l$ and weight W, hangs from two fixed points H, K on the same level, so that the lowest point of the chain is at a depth h below the line HK. Show that the parameter of the catenary in which the chain hangs is given by $2hc = l^2-h^2$, and deduce that the tension at either point H or K is $\frac{1}{4}W(l/h+h/l)$. (L.)

***10.** A uniform heavy chain BC, of length $2l$ and weight w per unit length, hangs symmetrically over two fixed smooth pegs H, K at the same level, and the lowest point A of the portion of the chain between the pegs is at a depth $l/18$ below the level of the pegs. Find the lengths of the portions of the chain which hang vertically, and the distance between the pegs. Show further that the thrust on either peg is $\frac{1}{6}\sqrt{13}$ of the weight of the chain. (L.)

11. A uniform flexible string AB, of length l and weight wl, will break if subjected to tension in excess of $2wl$. It is fixed at B and is in equilibrium under the action of a horizontal force F at A. Show, if the string is just about to break, that $F = wl\sqrt{3}$ and find the horizontal and vertical distances of B from A. (L.)

***12.** A uniform flexible chain, of length $54a$, hangs over two small smooth pegs, the lengths of the vertical portions being $20a$ and $13a$ respectively. Show that the parameter of the catenary between the pegs is $12a$ and that the horizontal distance between the pegs is $12a \ln (9/2)$. (L.)

***13.** A uniform flexible string of length $4a$ and weight $4wa$ has one end attached to a fixed point A and passes over a smooth peg B fixed at the same level as A and distant $2a$ from it. A particle of weight wb is to be attached to the free end of the string so that there is an equilibrium position with a length a of the string hanging vertically from B and a length $3a$ in the form of a catenary between A and B. Using tables to obtain a graphical solution of the equation $2 \sinh u = 3u$, derive an approximation for the weight of the particle, determining the value of b/a correct to two significant figures. (N.)

***14.** One end of a uniform inextensible flexible string, of length l and total weight W, is fixed at ground level, and the other is attached to a flying kite of weight $4W$. The string at ground level makes an angle $\tan^{-1}\frac{4}{3}$ with the horizontal, and the resultant force exerted on the kite by the wind makes an angle $\tan^{-1}\frac{20}{3}$ with the horizontal. Find (i) the tension in the string at ground level, (ii) the height of the kite above the ground. [The effect of the wind on the string is to be neglected.] (C.S.)

***15.** A uniform chain AB of length $l = a+b$ hangs from the end B with a portion AP of length a resting on a smooth plane inclined at an angle α to the horizontal. Prove that the height of B above the level of A is h, where

$$h^2 = l^2 \sin^2 \alpha + b^2 \cos^2 \alpha. \qquad \text{(C.S.)}$$

16. A uniform chain of length l has one end fixed and the other end is held in position by a horizontal force equal to the weight of a length k of the chain. Prove that the vertical distance between the ends is $\sqrt{(l^2+k^2)}-k$, and find an expression for the horizontal distance.

If $k = l\sqrt{3}$, find the inclination of the chain to the horizontal at the fixed end. (L.)

17. A uniform string of length $2l$ is to have its ends attached to two pegs at the same level, so that the lowest point of the catenary in which it hangs may be at a distance h below the level of the pegs. Show that the distance between the pegs must be

$$\frac{l^2-h^2}{h} \ln \frac{l+h}{l-h}. \qquad \text{(L.)}$$

***18.** A uniform flexible chain, of length l and total weight wl, has one end A attached to a fixed point. The other end B is held in position by the application of a horizontal force P.

Prove that

$$P = w\frac{(l^2-h^2)}{2h},$$

and that the tension of the chain at A is

$$w\frac{(l^2-h^2)}{2h},$$

where h is the vertical distance A is above B. (C.S.)

***19.** A uniform chain, of length b and weight w per unit length, has one end free to slide on a smooth vertical wire and passes over a smooth peg at distance a from the wire, the whole system being in a vertical plane. To the other end of the chain is attached a weight nwa. Show that for equilibrium to be possible $n+b/a$ must be not less than e. (C.S.)

***20.** A uniform heavy chain is fixed at one end at a point A at distance d from the edge of a rough horizontal table and at the same height as the table. The chain lies in a vertical plane with a portion on the table. The coefficient of friction is $\frac{1}{2}$. Prove that equilibrium is possible only if the total length of the chain is greater than ed. The edge of the table is smooth. (O.S.)

CHAPTER XXV

*THE MOTION OF BODIES WITH VARIABLE MASS

*25.1. Introduction

In all problems considered so far in these volumes the bodies involved have been assumed to be of constant mass. This assumption in most cases allows of a close approximation to the correct equation of motion, but there are many cases in which the equation of motion would be appreciably altered if the assumption were not made, e.g. in a motor car, consumption of fuel and escape of exhaust gases with a velocity differing from that of the car, influence the equation of motion.

The advent of the jet engine and the rapid development of the large rockets required to put earth satellites and space probes into orbit have given rise to a variety of problems involving bodies of changing mass or bodies which pick up and eject the material of the medium through which they move. Here we are concerned primarily with the rectilinear motion of such a body but the methods are applicable to more complicated problems.

In these cases we do not write down the equations of motion of the separate parts of a system but consider the change in momentum of the system as a whole. The system in question consists of the body in motion, i.e. an aircraft or a rocket, together with any matter which is absorbed and any matter which is ejected in a short interval of time δt. At the beginning of this interval all these different parts of the system have their separate states of motion; at the end of the interval each part has, usually, a different state of motion. We use the fact that the change of linear momentum of the *whole* system in the interval δt is given by the impulse of the *external* forces acting on the *whole* system. Having written down the equation expressing this momentum balance for an interval of time δt, we obtain a differential equation by dividing by δt and then taking the limit as $\delta t \to 0$.

In solving these problems it is advisable in each case to proceed from first principles and derive the differential equation of the motion rather than to quote standard results.

*25.2. Rectilinear Motion of a Particle of Variable Mass—Rockets

We first discuss some examples concerning the motion of a particle of variable mass along a straight line.

1. A body falls under constant gravity picking up matter from rest as it falls, so that at time t its mass is m and speed v. Consider the system which consists of the body at a given instant and the material, of mass δm, which it picks up in the subsequent interval δt; this material is initially at rest. The initial momentum of the system is

$$p = mv + \delta m . 0.$$

Finally the body and the additional material are moving with velocity $v + \delta v$, and the final momentum is

$$p + \delta p = (m + \delta m)(v + \delta v).$$

The external force acting on the *whole* system throughout this interval is the total weight $mg + (\delta m)g$.

$$\therefore \ (m+\delta m)g\delta t = \delta p = (m+\delta m)(v+\delta v) - mv.$$

$$\therefore \ mg\delta t + g\delta m . \delta t = m\delta v + v\delta m + \delta m . \delta v.$$

$$\therefore \ mg + g\delta m = m\frac{\delta v}{\delta t} + v\frac{\delta m}{\delta t}.$$

$$\therefore \ \lim_{\delta t \to 0}(mg + g\delta m) = \lim_{\delta t \to 0} m\frac{\delta v}{\delta t} + \lim_{\delta t \to 0} v\frac{\delta m}{\delta t}.$$

$$\therefore \ mg = m\frac{dv}{dt} + v\frac{dm}{dt} = \frac{d}{dt}(mv). \tag{25.1}$$

If the matter picked up had been moving downwards with speed u, then in place of equation (25.1), the momentum balance would have been

$$(m+\delta m)g\delta t = \delta p = (m+\delta m)(v+\delta v) - (mv + \delta m . u)$$

and this leads to the differential equation

$$mg = m\frac{dv}{dt}+v\frac{dm}{dt}-u\frac{dm}{dt} = \frac{d}{dt}(mv)-u\frac{dm}{dt}. \qquad (25.2)$$

Note that equation (25.1) expresses the second law of motion in the form

rate of change of downward momentum = downward force

but equation (25.2) shows that this result must be modified when the additional mass is not picked up from rest.

2. A body moves vertically upwards under gravity so that at time t its mass is m and its speed is v. The body ejects material at the rate of k units of mass per second vertically downwards with a speed u *relative to the body*. In this case the system considered is the body and the material it ejects in the short interval δt. At the start of the interval the body has mass m and velocity v; at the end of the interval it has mass $m+\delta m$ (a mass $-\delta m = k\delta t$ having been ejected) with a velocity $v+\delta v$, and the ejected mass has a velocity between $v+\delta v-u$ and $v-u$. The upward momentum of the ejected mass therefore lies between $(-\delta m)(v-u)$ and $(-\delta m)(v+\delta v-u)$ and can be expressed as $-\delta m(v-u+\eta)$ where $\eta \to 0$ as $\delta t \to 0$. The external force acting on the whole system is the weight mg. The momentum equation is therefore

$$(m+\delta m)(v+\delta v)+(-\delta m)(v-u+\eta)-mv = -mg\delta t.$$

$$\therefore\ m\delta v+(u-\eta+\delta v)\delta m = -mg\delta t.$$

$$\therefore\ m\frac{\delta v}{\delta t}+(u-\eta+\delta v)\frac{\delta m}{\delta t} = -mg.$$

$$\therefore\ \lim_{\delta t\to 0} m\frac{\delta v}{\delta t}+\lim_{\delta t\to 0}\left\{(u-\eta+\delta v)\frac{\delta m}{\delta t}\right\} = -mg.$$

$$\therefore\ m\frac{dv}{dt}+u\frac{dm}{dt} = -mg, \qquad (25.3)$$

where $dm/dt = -k$.

In the following examples a wide variety of simple problems is considered. We repeat that in every case the student should derive the equations of motion from first principles as illustrated above.

Example 1. A spherical raindrop of initial radius a falls from rest under gravity. Its radius increases with time at a constant rate μ owing to condensation from a surrounding cloud which is at rest. Find the distance fallen by the raindrop after time t. (C.S.)

At time t the radius of the raindrop is r and its downward velocity is v. But equation (25.1) above holds and therefore

$$\frac{\mathrm{d}}{\mathrm{d}t}\left(\frac{4}{3}\pi r^3 \varrho v\right) = \frac{4}{3}\pi r^3 \varrho g, \tag{1}$$

where ϱ is the density. Also because of condensation

$$\frac{\mathrm{d}r}{\mathrm{d}t} = \mu.$$

$$\therefore\ r = a+\mu t.$$

Substitution in (1) gives

$$\frac{\mathrm{d}}{\mathrm{d}t}\{(a+\mu t)^3 v\} = (a+\mu t)^3 g.$$

Integration and use of the initial condition, $v = 0$ at $t = 0$, gives

$$(a+\mu t)^3 v = \frac{g}{4\mu}\{(a+\mu t)^4 - a^4\}. \tag{2}$$

If the distance fallen in time t is x, $v = \mathrm{d}x/\mathrm{d}t$ and (2) becomes

$$\frac{\mathrm{d}x}{\mathrm{d}t} = \frac{g}{4\mu}\left\{a+\mu t - \frac{a^4}{(a+\mu t)^3}\right\}.$$

Integration and use of the initial condition, $x = 0$ at $t = 0$, gives

$$x = \frac{g}{4\mu}\left\{at + \frac{1}{2}\mu t^2 + \frac{a^4}{2\mu(a+\mu t)^2} - \frac{a^2}{2\mu}\right\}. \tag{3}$$

[Note that the usual result of free fall without condensation can be obtained by letting $\mu \to 0$ in (2) and (3).]

Example 2. A rocket continuously ejects matter backwards with velocity c relative to itself. Show that if gravity is neglected the velocity v and total mass m of the rocket are related by the equation

$$m\frac{\mathrm{d}v}{\mathrm{d}t} + c\frac{\mathrm{d}m}{\mathrm{d}t} = 0.$$

Deduce that whatever the rate of burning of the rocket, v and m are related by the formula

$$v = c \ln (M/m),$$

where M is a constant.

Assuming that m decreases at a constant rate k, show that the distance the rocket travels from rest before the mass has fallen from the initial value m_0 to m_1 is

$$c(m_1/k)\{m_0/m_1-1-\ln(m_0/m_1)\}. \qquad \text{(C.S.)}$$

In this case the analysis of case (2) above is valid and the first equation follows at once from (25.3) on putting $g = 0$, $u = c$. The variables of this equation are separable,

$$\therefore\ c\int_{m_0}^{m}\frac{dm}{m} = -\int_{V}^{v} dv, \tag{1}$$

where m_0 is the initial mass and V is the initial velocity of the rocket.

$$\therefore\ v = V+c\ln(m_0/m).$$

But, since V is constant, we can write $V = c\ln(M/m_0)$, where M is constant and then

$$v = c\ln(M/m_0)+c\ln(m_0/m),$$

i.e.

$$v = c\ln(M/m). \tag{2}$$

If $V = 0$ and the rocket travels a distance x whilst the mass falls from m_0 to m, we can write (2) in the form

$$\frac{dx}{dt} = \frac{dx}{dm}\frac{dm}{dt} = c\ln\left(\frac{m_0}{m}\right). \tag{3}$$

But m decreases at a constant rate k and therefore $dm/dt = -k$.

$$\therefore\ \frac{dx}{dm} = -\frac{c}{k}(\ln m_0-\ln m).$$

Hence the distance travelled by the rocket before the mass has fallen from m_0 to m_1 is

$$X = -\frac{c}{k}\int_{m_0}^{m_1}(\ln m_0-\ln m)\,dm$$

$$= -\frac{c}{k}\Big[m\ln m_0-m\ln m+m\Big]_{m_0}^{m_1}$$

$$= -\frac{c}{k}(m_1\ln m_0-m_1\ln m_1+m_1-m_0)$$

$$= \frac{m_1c}{k}\left\{\frac{m_0}{m_1}-1-\ln\left(\frac{m_0}{m_1}\right)\right\}.$$

Note that here we have used m as the independent variable. We could have found x in terms of t by integrating (3) with $m = m_0-kt$ and finally eliminating t but in many problems of rocketry the mass ratio m_0/m_1 is of prime importance and it is very convenient to use m as the independent variable.

Example 3. A rocket in rectilinear motion is propelled by ejecting all the products of combustion of the fuel from the tail at a constant rate and at a constant velocity relative to the rocket. Show that, for a given initial total mass M, the final kinetic energy of the rocket is greatest when the initial mass of fuel is $(1-e^{-2})M$. (C.S.)

In this case, and again neglecting gravity, result (2) of example 2 above shows that the speed, when the initial mass M has fallen to λM $(\lambda < 1)$, is $c \ln (1/\lambda)$. Therefore the kinetic energy is

$$T = \tfrac{1}{2}\lambda M(-c \ln \lambda)^2 = \tfrac{1}{2}Mc^2\lambda(\ln \lambda)^2.$$

Consider

$$f(\lambda) = \lambda(\ln \lambda)^2.$$

Then

$$f'(\lambda) = (\ln \lambda)(\ln \lambda+2)$$

and therefore $f(\lambda)$ has a maximum when $\ln \lambda = -2$, i.e. when $\lambda = e^{-2}$. Therefore T is a maximum when the final mass of the rocket is $e^{-2} M$, i.e. when the initial mass of fuel is $(1-e^{-2})M$.

Example 4. A rocket of initial total mass M propels itself by ejecting mass at a constant rate μ per unit time with speed u relative to the rocket. If the rocket is at rest directed vertically upwards, show that it will not initially leave the ground unless $\mu u > Mg$, and assuming this condition to hold show that its velocity after time t is given by

$$-u \ln (1-\mu t/M)-gt.$$

Show also that when the mass of the rocket has been reduced to half the initial value, its height above ground level will be

$$\frac{uM}{2\mu}\{1-\ln 2-Mg/4\mu u\}. \qquad \text{(L.)}$$

In this case the equation of motion is given by (25.3) which takes the form

$$(M-\mu t)\frac{dv}{dt}-\mu u = -(M-\mu t)g,$$

i.e.

$$\frac{dv}{dt} = \frac{\mu u-(M-\mu t)g}{M-\mu t}. \qquad (1)$$

For the rocket to leave the ground initially we must have $dv/dt > 0$ at $t = 0$, i.e. $\mu u > Mg$. [If this condition is not satisfied the rocket will not lift off the ground until the r.h. side of (1) increases to zero, i.e. until $t = (Mg-\mu u)/(\mu g)$. It may even happen that, if the exhaust velocity is too low and/or the final mass of the rocket is too large, the rocket cannot leave the ground at all.]

Integration of (1) subject to the initial conditions $v = 0$ at $t = 0$ gives

$$v = \int_0^t \left\{\frac{\mu u}{M-\mu t}-g\right\} dt = \Big[-u \ln (M-\mu t)-gt\Big]_0^t$$

$$= -u \ln (1-\mu t/M)-gt.$$

Writing $v = \mathrm{d}x/\mathrm{d}t$ and integrating again we find the distance risen whilst the mass of the rocket is reduced to half its initial value, i.e. during a time $M/(2\mu)$, is

$$X = \int_0^X \mathrm{d}x = \int_0^{M/(2\mu)} \{-u \ln(1-\mu t/M) - gt\}\,\mathrm{d}t$$

$$= \left[-\mu t \ln\left(1-\frac{\mu t}{M}\right) + ut + \frac{uM}{\mu}\ln\left(1-\frac{\mu t}{M}\right) - \frac{1}{2}gt^2\right]_0^{M/(2\mu)}$$

$$= \frac{uM}{2\mu}\left(1-\ln 2 - \frac{Mg}{4\mu u}\right).$$

Example 5. A machine-gun of mass M_0 (without ammunition) stands on rough level ground (coefficient of friction μ) and fires bullets at the rate of mass m per second at a constant horizontal velocity u relative to the ground. The gun contains ammunition to fire for t_0 seconds. Assuming that the gun begins to recoil as soon as it is fired, find the speed of recoil immediately after the ammunition has been expended, and show that the whole time of recoil is

$$\frac{mt_0}{M_0}\left(\frac{u}{\mu g} - \frac{1}{2}t_0\right). \qquad \text{(O.S.)}$$

Here we establish the equation of motion from first principles.

Let the mass and speed of the gun and remaining ammunition at time t be M, v respectively as illustrated in Fig. 25.1(i). At time $t+\delta t$ the system is as illustrated in Fig. 25.1(ii) where a mass $-\delta M$ of bullet has been fired with speed u. [All velocities in the figures are shown *relative to the ground*.]

The change in momentum (from right to left) in time δt is

$$(M+\delta M)(v+\delta v) - (-\delta M)u - Mv$$

$$= M\delta v + (u+v)\delta M + \text{terms in } (\delta t)^2 \text{ etc.},$$

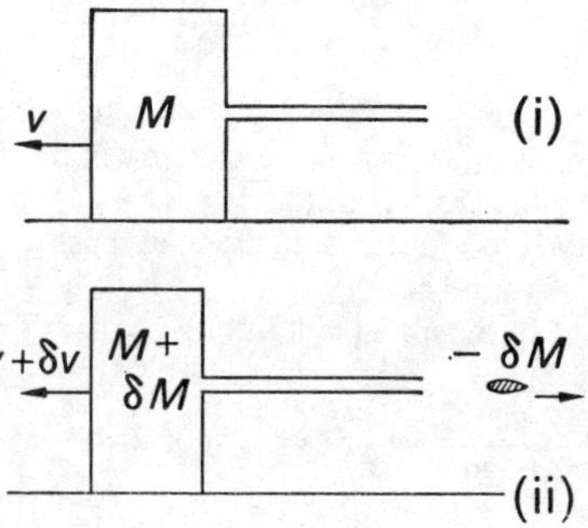

FIG. 25.1

and the impulse of the force of friction from left to right is

$$\mu Mg\delta t + \text{terms in } (\delta t)^2 \text{ etc.}$$

Therefore, to the first order in δt,

$$M\delta v + (u+v)\delta M = -\mu Mg\delta t.$$

Dividing by δt and letting $\delta t \to 0$,

$$M\frac{\mathrm{d}v}{\mathrm{d}t} + (u+v)\frac{\mathrm{d}M}{\mathrm{d}t} = -\mu Mg,$$

or

$$\frac{\mathrm{d}}{\mathrm{d}t}(Mv) = -\mu Mg - u\frac{\mathrm{d}M}{\mathrm{d}t}.$$

But $M = M_0 + mt_0 - mt$ and therefore

$$\frac{\mathrm{d}}{\mathrm{d}t}\{(M_0+mt_0-mt)v\} = -\mu(M_0+mt_0-mt)\,g + um.$$

Integrating gives

$$(M_0+mt_0-mt)v = umt - \mu M_0 gt - \mu mgt_0 t + \tfrac{1}{2}\mu mgt^2.$$

Therefore, at time t_0, i.e. when the ammunition is expended, the speed of recoil is

$$v_0 = \frac{umt_0 - \mu M_0 gt_0 - \frac{1}{2}\mu mgt_0^2}{M_0}.$$

After $t = t_0$ the only horizontal force acting on the gun is the force of friction which causes a retardation μg. Therefore the additional time before the gun comes to rest is $t_1 = v_0/(\mu g)$ and the whole time of recoil is

$$t_0 + t_1 = t_0 + \frac{umt_0 - \mu M_0 gt_0 - \frac{1}{2}\mu mgt_0^2}{M_0 \mu g}$$

$$= \frac{mt_0}{M_0}\left(\frac{u}{\mu g} - \frac{1}{2}t_0\right).$$

Example 6. Two buckets of water each of total mass M_0 are suspended at the ends of a cord passing over a smooth pulley and are initially at rest. Water begins to leak from a small hole in the side of one of the buckets at a steady slow rate of m units of mass per second. Establish the equations of motion, and prove that the velocity V of the bucket when a mass M_1 of water has escaped is given by

$$V = \frac{2M_0 g}{m}\ln\left(\frac{2M_0}{2M_0 - M_1}\right) - \frac{gM_1}{m}. \qquad \text{(C.S.)}$$

Suppose that at time t after release the mass of the leaking bucket is M and its upward velocity is v. Let T be the tension in the string at this instant. Then the equation of motion (downwards) of the other bucket is

$$M_0 g - T = M_0 \frac{dv}{dt}. \tag{1}$$

The change in momentum of the leaking bucket and its contents from time t to time $t+\delta t$ is

$$(M+\delta M)(v+\delta v)+(-\delta M)v - Mv$$
$$= M\delta v + \text{terms of order } (\delta t)^2 \text{ etc.}$$

Equating this to the impulse in time δt of the upward forces, i.e. to $(T-Mg)\delta t$+terms of order $(\delta t)^2$, leads to

$$M\frac{dv}{dt} = T - Mg. \tag{2}$$

Thus the usual equations of motion are unaffected by the leak. This is because the water which leaks out has no velocity *relative to the bucket* at the moment when it leaves the bucket.

Equations (1) and (2) give

$$\frac{dv}{dt} = \frac{(M_0-M)g}{M_0+M},$$

i.e.

$$\frac{dv}{dt} = \frac{mgt}{2M_0-mt}.$$

$$\therefore v = \int_0^t \frac{mgt}{2M_0-mt}\,dt$$

$$= g\int_0^t \left\{-1+\frac{2M_0}{2M_0-mt}\right\} dt$$

$$= g\left[-t-\frac{2M_0}{m}\ln(2M_0-mt)\right]_0^t.$$

$$\therefore v = g\left\{-t-\frac{2M_0}{m}\ln\left(1-\frac{mt}{2M_0}\right)\right\}.$$

The required result is obtained by writing $t = M_1/m$.

---

*25.3. The Rectilinear Motion of Chains

We conclude with some illustrative examples concerning the motion of a uniform chain. Although these problems are not of practical importance, they nevertheless give illustrations of fundamental dynamical principles.

In example 1 below the chain is constrained to move so that the motion is everywhere continuous but in examples 2, 3, 4, 5 discontinuities of velocities arise, impulsive forces act and the energy equation cannot be applied.

Example 1. A uniform chain AB, of mass m per unit length and length $3a$, hangs over a small smooth fixed pulley. The portion in contact with the pulley is constrained by a smooth semicircular guide, Fig. 25.2, to remain in contact with the pulley. The chain is released from rest with A, B at distances a, $2a$ respectively bellow the pulley and with the hanging portions vertical. At time t the end A has risen a distance x. Show that

$$a\dot{x}^2 = \tfrac{2}{3}gx(a+x).$$

Hence show that A reaches the pulley after a time

$$\sqrt{\{(3a)/(2g)\}}\ \ln(3+2\sqrt{2}).$$

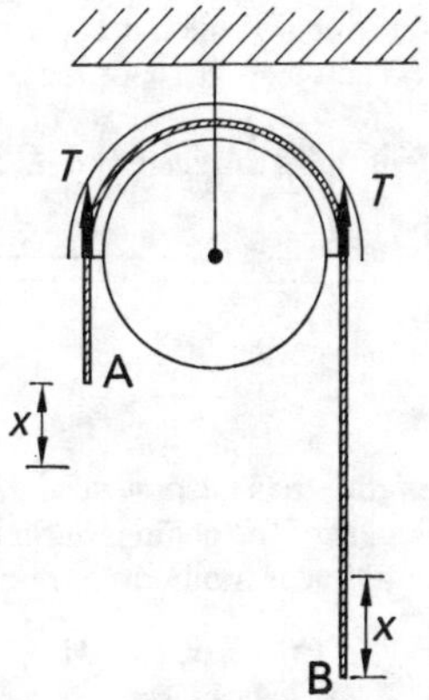

FIG. 25.2

For clarity, the size of the pulley in Fig. 25.2 has been magnified. Since the chain moves smoothly through the guide, energy is conserved. Potential energy, measured from the pulley as origin, has changed by the removal of a mass xm of the chain from one side of the pulley to the other, so that its centre of gravity is lowered by a distance

$$\left(2a+\frac{x}{2}\right)-\left(a-\frac{x}{2}\right) = (a+x).$$

The energy equation is therefore

$$\tfrac{1}{2}.3ma\dot{x}^2 = mgx(a+x).$$

$$\therefore\ a\dot{x}^2 = \tfrac{2}{3}gx(a+x).$$

$$\therefore\ \frac{\mathrm{d}x}{\mathrm{d}t} = \sqrt{\left\{\frac{2gx(a+x)}{3a}\right\}}.$$

Hence the time for x to increase from 0 to a is

$$t_0 = \sqrt{\left(\frac{3a}{2g}\right)}\int_0^a \frac{\mathrm{d}x}{\sqrt{(x^2+ax)}} = \sqrt{\left(\frac{3a}{2g}\right)}\int_0^a \frac{\mathrm{d}x}{\sqrt{\{(x+\frac{1}{2}a)^2-\frac{1}{4}a^2\}}}$$

$$= \sqrt{\left(\frac{3a}{2g}\right)}\left[\cosh^{-1}\left(\frac{x+\frac{1}{2}a}{\frac{1}{2}a}\right)\right]_0^a = \sqrt{\left(\frac{3a}{2g}\right)}(\cosh^{-1}3-\cosh^{-1}1)$$

$$= \sqrt{\left(\frac{3a}{2g}\right)}\ln(3+2\sqrt{2}).$$

Example 2. A mass M is attached to one end of a chain whose mass per unit length is m. The whole is placed with the chain coiled up on a smooth table and M is projected horizontally with velocity V. When a length x of the chain has become straight, show that the velocity of M is $MV/(M+mx)$. Calculate (a) the tension in the chain at this instant, (b) the time before a length l is dragged into motion.

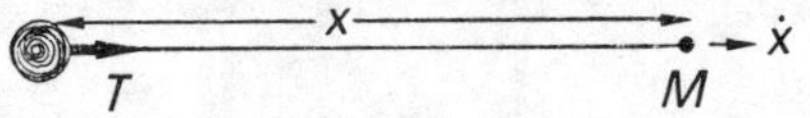

FIG. 25.3

Suppose that at time t a length x has become straight, Fig. 25.3, so that the velocity of the particle and the moving part of the chain is $\dot{x}$. Since no external horizontal forces act on the system, the horizontal linear momentum remains constant.

$$\therefore\ (M+mx)\dot{x} = MV \tag{1}$$

giving the required value of $\dot{x}$.

Note, however, that kinetic energy is not conserved in this case but reduced in the ratio $M/(M+mx)$. The loss in energy is due to the series of impulses which take place at the coil as the elements of the chain are suddenly jerked into motion by the tension T at the coil. We calculate T by considering the momentum given to the element of the chain dragged into motion in time δt. The impulse of T on the coil in time δt is $T\delta t$. The mome tum imparted to the element of length $\dot{x}\delta t$ dragged into motion in time δt is $m\dot{x}\delta t \times \dot{x}$.

$$\therefore\ T\delta t = m\dot{x}^2\delta t.$$

$$\therefore\ T = m\dot{x}^2. \tag{2}$$

Equations (1) and (2) give $T = M^2mV^2/(M+mx)^2$. Also from (1) we find the time before a length l of the chain is dragged into motion is

$$\frac{1}{MV}\int_0^l (M+mx)\,\mathrm{d}x = \frac{(M+\frac{1}{2}ml)l}{MV}.$$

Example 3. A mass M is fastened to a chain of mass m per unit length coiled up on a rough horizontal plane (coefficient of friction $= \mu$). The mass is projected from the coil with velocity V; show that it will be brought to rest in a distance

$$\frac{M}{m}\left\{\left(1+\frac{3mV^2}{2M\mu g}\right)^{1/3}-1\right\}. \qquad \text{(L.)}$$

In this case, as in example 2 above, the tension in the string, when the mass M has moved a distance x, is

$$T = m\dot{x}^2. \qquad (1)$$

The equation of motion of the chain is

$$(M+mx)\ddot{x} = -\mu(M+mx)g-T.$$

$$\therefore\ (M+mx)\ddot{x} = -\mu(M+mx)g-m\dot{x}^2,$$

i.e.

$$(M+mx)v\frac{\mathrm{d}v}{\mathrm{d}x}+mv^2 = -\mu(M+mx)g, \qquad (2)$$

where $v\ (=\dot{x})$ is the speed of the particle.

Writing (2) in the form

$$\frac{\mathrm{d}}{\mathrm{d}x}(v^2)+\frac{2mv^2}{(M+mx)} = -2\mu g, \qquad (3)$$

we see that the integrating factor (*Pure Maths.*, Vol. II, § 17.6) is

$$\exp\left\{\int\frac{2m\,\mathrm{d}x}{(M+mx)}\right\} = (M+mx)^2$$

and therefore (3) can be written

$$\frac{\mathrm{d}}{\mathrm{d}x}\{(M+mx)^2v^2\} = -2\mu g(M+mx)^2.$$

$$\therefore\ (M+mx)^2v^2 = -\frac{2\mu g(M+mx)^3}{3m}+\text{constant}.$$

The initial conditions give the constant as $M^2V^2+\frac{2}{3}\mu gM^3/m$. The system comes to rest when $v = 0$, i.e. when

$$\frac{2}{3}\mu g\left\{\frac{(M+mx)^3}{m}-\frac{M^3}{m}\right\} = M^2V^2.$$

This equation gives the required value of x.

Example 4. A uniform chain of length l and weight wl is suspended by one end and the other end is at a height h above a smooth inelastic table. Prove that if the upper end is let go the pressure on the table as the coil is formed increases from $2hw$ to $(2h+3l)w$. (C.S.)

Each element of the chain falls freely under gravity until it strikes the table. Suppose that at time t after the lower end strikes the table a length x of the chain rests on the table so that each element of the moving part of the chain has fallen a distance $h+x$ and is moving with speed $v = \sqrt{\{2g(h+x)\}}$. The momentum destroyed by impact with the table in time δt is

$$\frac{w}{g} v \times v\delta t = \frac{w}{g} v^2 \delta t$$

and therefore the force exerted by the moving chain on the table is wv^2/g. Further, the force on the table due to the stationary chain is wx. Therefore the total force exerted on the table is

$$P = \frac{w}{g} v^2 + wx,$$

i.e.

$$P = w(2h+3x).$$

Clearly, as x increases from 0 to l, P increases from $2hw$ to $(2h+3l)w$.

Example 5. A great length of uniform chain is coiled at the edge of a horizontal platform, and one end is allowed to hang over until it just reaches another platform distant h below the first. The chain then runs down under gravity. Prove that it ultimately acquires a finite terminal velocity V, that its velocity at time t is $V \tanh (Vt/h)$, and that the length of chain which has then run down is $h \ln \cosh (Vt/h)$. (C.S.)

We assume that the chain is constrained by a smooth guide at the edge of the upper platform. Fig. 25.4(i) so that the moving portion of the chain is vertical. If this were not the case, each element of the chain would be given a horizontal velocity when it was dragged into motion and the chain would run into a bight as illustrated in Fig. 25.4(ii).

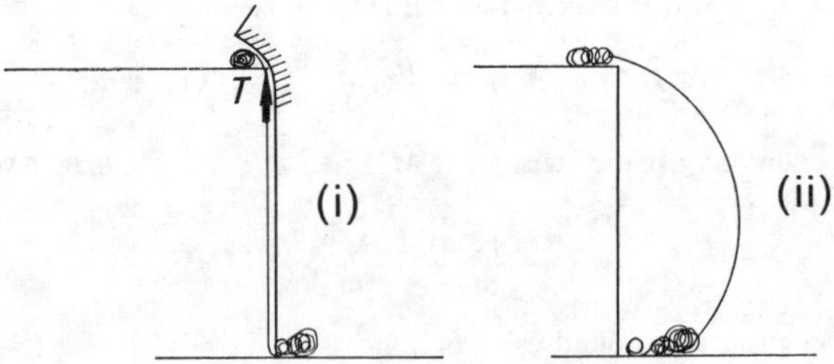

FIG. 25.4

Let x be the length of the string which has piled up on the lower platform at time t. Then the equations of motion at the upper coil and for the hanging portion are

$$T = m\dot{x}^2,$$
$$mh\ddot{x} = mhg - T$$

where m is the mass per unit length of the chain.

$$\therefore\ h\ddot{x}+\dot{x}^2 = gh,$$

i.e.
$$h\frac{d}{dx}(v^2)+2v^2 = 2gh,$$

where $v = \dot{x}$.

The solution of this equation (*Pure Maths.*, Vol. II, § 17.9) for which $v = 0$ when $x = 0$ is

$$v^2 = gh(1-e^{-2x/h}). \tag{1}$$

$$\therefore\ \frac{dx}{dt} = \sqrt{\{gh(1-e^{-2x/h})\}}.$$

$$\therefore\ t = \frac{1}{\sqrt{(gh)}}\int_0^x \frac{dx}{\sqrt{(1-e^{-2x/h})}} = \frac{1}{\sqrt{(gh)}}\int_0^x \frac{e^{x/h}\,dx}{\sqrt{(e^{2x/h}-1)}}$$

$$= \sqrt{\left(\frac{h}{g}\right)}\left[\cosh^{-1}(e^{x/h})\right]_0^x = \sqrt{\left(\frac{h}{g}\right)}\cosh^{-1}(e^{x/h}).$$

$$\therefore\ x = h \ln\cosh\{t\sqrt{(g/h)}\}, \tag{2}$$

$$\therefore\ v = \sqrt{(gh)}\tanh\{t\sqrt{(g/h)}\}. \tag{3}$$

Hence, as $t \to \infty$, $v \to \sqrt{(gh)}$ since $\tanh\{t\sqrt{(g/h)}\} \to 1$ as $t \to \infty$. Therefore the chain acquires a finite terminal velocity $V = \sqrt{(gh)}$ and the given results follow from (2) and (3). [Note that this conclusion could have been anticipated from (1) by letting $x \to \infty$.]

The energy of the moving chain is destroyed by impact with the lower plane, on which the force exerted is

$$mgx+mv^2.$$

---

* MISCELLANEOUS EXERCISES XXV

***1.** A spherical hailstone, falling under gravity in still air, increases its radius r by condensation according to the law $dr/dt = \lambda r$, where λ is constant. If air resistance is neglected, prove that the hailstone approaches a limiting velocity $g/(3\lambda)$. (L.)

***2.** A raindrop falls from rest through an atmosphere containing water vapour at rest. The mass of the raindrop, which is initially m_0, increases by condensation uniformly with time in such a way that after a given time T it is equal to $2m_0$. The motion is opposed by a frictional force $\lambda m_0/T$ times the velocity of the drop, where λ is a positive constant. Show that after time T the velocity is

$$\frac{gT}{2+\lambda}(2-2^{-(1+\lambda)}). \qquad \text{(C.S.)}$$

***3.** A small raindrop falling through a cloud acquires moisture by condensation from the cloud. When the mass of the raindrop is m, the rate of increase of mass per unit time is km, where k is small. The raindrop starts from rest. Prove that when it has fallen a distance h through the cloud, its velocity is given approximately by

$$v^2 = 2gh\left(1-\tfrac{2}{3}k\sqrt{\frac{2h}{g}}\right).$$

(The resistance of the cloud to the motion is to be neglected, and the cloud is assumed to be stationary and of infinite mass.) (C.S.)

***4.** A raindrop falls through a stationary cloud, its mass m increasing by accretion uniformly with the distance fallen, $m = m_0(1+kx)$. The motion is opposed by a resisting force $m_0k\lambda v^2$ proportional to the square of the speed v. If $v = 0$ when $x = 0$ prove that

$$v^2 = \frac{2g}{(3+2\lambda)k}\left\{1+kx-\frac{1}{(1+kx)^{2+2\lambda}}\right\}. \qquad \text{(C.S.)}$$

***5.** A small body is projected vertically upwards in a cloud, the velocity of projection being $\sqrt{(2gh)}$. During the ascent the body picks up moisture from the cloud, its mass at height x above the point of projection being $m_0(1+\alpha x)$, where α is a positive constant, and the added mass is picked up from rest. Prove that the greatest height reached is h', where

$$h' = \{\sqrt[3]{(1+3\alpha h)}-1\}/\alpha. \qquad \text{(L.)}$$

***6.** A particle of mass m is projected vertically upwards with initial velocity V in a dust-laden atmosphere. Dust becomes attached to the object at a rate of λv units of mass per unit time, where v is the speed of the particle. Show that, when the particle has risen through a height h,

$$3(m+\lambda h)^2v^2 = -2gh(\lambda^2h^2+3\lambda mh+3m^2)+3m^2V^2.$$

Prove that, if λ is small, the maximum height attained is reduced owing to the presence of the dust by an amount approximately equal to $\frac{1}{4}\lambda V^4/(mg^2)$. (O.S.)

***7.** A bucket is held under a tap from which J mass units of water per time unit emerge and fall freely. At the instant when the total mass of the bucket and the water in it is M, show that the force necessary to support the bucket is

$$Mg+Jv,$$

where v is the velocity with which the jet enters the water in the bucket, provided that the depth of water in the bucket increases at a negligible rate.

Show also, that, if the bucket is moving downwards with uniform velocity w, the upward force necessary is

$$Mg+(v-w)^2J/v. \qquad \text{(L.)}$$

*8. A machine-gun fixed to a truck running on smooth horizontal rails fires bullets at the rate of m kg/s in a direction parallel to the rails. The mass of the truck, machine gun and ammunition is M kg. The explosive in the cartridges is doing P joules of work per second. Prove that if the mass of the explosive used may be neglected and the mass of each individual bullet is very small compared with m and M, then the velocity of each bullet relative to the truck, immediately after firing, is $\sqrt{(2Pg/m)}$ m/s.

*9. A rocket driven car, of total initial mass M, loses mass at a constant rate m per unit time at constant ejection speed V relative to the car. If the total resistance to motion is kv when the velocity is v, show that the acceleration of the car along a straight horizontal road is

$$\frac{mV-kv}{M-mt}$$

at time t from the start, and hence that the speed from rest is then

$$\frac{mV}{k}[1-(1-mt/M)^{k/m}]. \qquad \text{(L.)}$$

*10. A train of mass M is moving with velocity V when it begins to pick up water from rest at a uniform rate. The power is constant and equal to H. If after time t a mass m of water has been picked up, find the velocity and show that the loss of energy is

$$\frac{m(Ht+MV^2)}{2(m+M)}. \qquad \text{(C.S.)}$$

*11. A mass m of water issues per unit time from a pipe with uniform velocity u, and strikes a pail which retains it, there being no elasticity. Initially the pail is at rest, and at a subsequent instant is moving in the direction of the stream with velocity V. Prove that

$$\frac{dV}{dt} = \frac{m(u-V)^3}{Mu^2},$$

and that the loss of energy up to this instant is

$$\tfrac{1}{2}MuV,$$

where M is the mass of the pail, and gravity is omitted from consideration. (C.S)

*12. An engine contains a quantity of fuel which is being steadily consumed at the rate of m units of mass per unit time, the products of combustion being ejected with the speed of the engine. There is a constant propulsive force $k\alpha^2$, and a resistance kv^2, where v is the velocity at time t. If at $t = 0$ the mass is M and the velocity is zero, prove that

$$v = \alpha\left\{\frac{M^\lambda-(M-mt)^\lambda}{M^\lambda+(M-mt)^\lambda}\right\},$$

where $\lambda = 2k\alpha/m$. (C.S.)

*13. A gun of mass M stands on a horizontal plane and contains shot of mass M'. The shot is fired at the rate of mass m per unit of time with velocity u relative to the ground. If the coefficient of friction between the gun and the plane is μ, show that the velocity of the gun backward by the time the mass M' is fired is

$$\frac{M'}{M}u - \frac{(M+M')^2 - M^2}{2mM}\mu g. \qquad \text{(C.S.)}$$

***14.** A body consists of equal masses M of inflammable ar d non-inflammable material. It descends freely under gravity from rest whilst the combustible part burns at the uniform rate of λM, where λ is a constant. If the burning material is ejected vertically upwards with a constant upward velocity u relative to the body, and the air resistance is neglected, show, from considerations of momentum, or otherwise, that

$$\frac{d}{dt}[(2-\lambda t)v] = \lambda(u-v) + g(2-\lambda t)$$

where v is the velocity of the body at time t.

Hence show that the body descends a distance

$$g/(2\lambda^2) + (1 - \ln 2)u/\lambda$$

before all the inflammable material is burnt. (L.)

***15.** Show that the average value $\bar{g}$ of the acceleration due to gravity over a vertical rise H from the surface of the Earth (radius R) is $gR/(R+H)$, where g is the value at the Earth's surface.

A rocket missile, starting from rest on the ground, attains a speed V after a vertical flight of duration T. The fuel is burnt at a constant rate, is ejected with velocity v_e relative to the rocket, and is exhausted at time T. Neglecting air resistance, and assuming constant gravity $\bar{g}$, prove that

$$V = -\bar{g}T - v_e \ln\{1 - (m_0/M_0)\},$$

where m_0 is the initial mass of fuel and M_0 the total initial mass of the missile. (L.)

***16.** If a rocket, originally of mass M, throws off every unit of time a mass eM with relative velocity V, and if M' be the mass of the case, etc., show that it cannot rise at once unless $eV > g$, nor at all unless

$$\frac{eMV}{M'} > g.$$

If it just rises vertically at once, show that its greatest velocity is

$$V \ln\frac{M}{M'} - \frac{g}{e}\left(1 - \frac{M'}{M}\right),$$

and that the greatest height it reaches is

$$\frac{V^2}{2g}\left(\ln\frac{M}{M'}\right)^2 + \frac{V}{e}\left(1 - \frac{M'}{M} - \ln\frac{M}{M'}\right). \qquad \text{(L.)}$$

***17.** A ball of mass m is projected at $t = 0$ with horizontal and vertical velocities u and v into a medium which deposits matter on the ball at a uniform rate k per unit time. Show that the equation of its path, under gravity, referred to rectangular axes through its initial position is

$$y = \frac{g}{4l^2}(1-e^{2lx/u})+\frac{2lv+g}{2lu}x,$$

where $l = k/m$. (O.S.)

***18.** A uniform fine chain of length $3l/2$ and mass $3ml/2$ hangs over a small smooth peg at a height l above a horizontal table. The chain is released from rest in the position in which it hangs in two vertical straight pieces with one end just touching the table. Show that when the other end is leaving the peg the force on the table is

$$mgl(4 \ln \tfrac{3}{2} - \tfrac{1}{2}). \quad \text{(C.S.)}$$

***19.** A uniform perfectly flexible chain is coiled at the edge of a table with one end just hanging over. Prove that, if a length x of the chain has fallen over the edge at time t after the start, then $6x = gt^2$. How much energy has been dissipated in this time? (C.S.)

***20.** A chain of length a is coiled up on a ledge at the top of a rough plane of inclination α to the horizontal, and one end is allowed to slide down. Prove that, if the inclination of the plane is double the angle of friction (λ), the chain will be moving freely at the end of a time $\sqrt{\{6a/(g \tan \lambda)\}}$. (C.S.)

***21.** A long chain AB of mass λ kg/m is laid upon the ground in a straight line. The end A is attached to a motor car which is then driven towards B with acceleration f m/s^2 so that the chain is doubled back on itself. Neglecting friction between the chain and the ground, calculate the tension at A after t seconds. Show that the kinetic energy of the chain is two-thirds of the work done by the car; explain why these quantities are not equal. (C.S.)

***22.** A rocket, free from all external forces, has at time t total mass $M(t)$ (including unburnt fuel) and speed $U(t)$, and is ejecting exhaust gases backwards at a speed $V(t)$ *relative* to itself. By using momentum conservation, or other basic dynamical principles, determine the equation of motion of the rocket.

Find the sum, $P(t)$, of the rate of increase of kinetic energy of the rocket and the rate of increase of the total kinetic energy of the exhaust gases. Show that

$$\dot{U}^2 = 2P\frac{d}{dt}(M^{-1}). \quad \text{(C.S.)}$$

CHAPTER XXVI

VECTOR ALGEBRA

26.1. The Concept of a Vector

Thus far in these volumes we have used the idea of a vector in the simplest possible way in order to study the fundamental vector quantities involved in Theoretical Mechanics (see Vol. I, § 2.1). In §§ 18.1, 18.2 we extended our use of vectors in order to examine, more thoroughly than we had done before, the uniplanar motion of a particle. In § 19.6 we introduced the idea of the moment of a force as a vector product. Here, § 26.3, we define a vector more precisely and introduce and illustrate the techniques of Vector Algebra.

The word *vector* denotes the important *abstract* idea of the combination of a magnitude and a specific direction. We deal here with vectors in three dimensions, i.e. with three components. As we have already seen, such a concept is exemplified in many physical quantities such as displacement, velocity, acceleration, momentum and force. However, a typical vector, which need not have a physical association, is a *directed segment of a line*, $\overrightarrow{AB}$. This is a section $\overrightarrow{AB}$ of a straight line, the length AB being the magnitude of the vector and the direction along the line from A to B being the direction of the vector. We shall consider the properties of this segment and assume that these properties also apply to all the quantities with magnitude and direction listed above.

[Not all directed magnitudes are vectors. It is matter for proof, which we shall not consider here, whether or not a physical quantity with a directed magnitude is a vector.]

We can consider three kinds of directed segments. The first kind occurs when the end A is "anchored" and $\overrightarrow{AB}$ becomes the *position vector* of B relative to the "origin" A. The second kind occurs when the segment can "slide" along the whole (infinite) length of a fixed straight line, provided that the "sense" or direction from A to B remains the same. This is a *line vector*, the most familiar example being a mechanical force which has magnitude and a line of action but has the same effect if applied at any point of this line. Third, the directed segment $\overrightarrow{AB}$ may not be restricted in any way; in this case it is called a *free vector*. A displacement is a common example of this third kind; the moment of a couple is another. For example, if A is one mile due north of B and C is one mile due north of D, the displacements from A to B and from C to D can be represented by the same free vector.

A free vector has only the attributes of magnitude and direction whereas the other types of vector specified above have restrictions placed upon them. Unless the context specifies otherwise, we shall use the word vector to denote a free vector.

26.2. Cartesian Coordinates and Components

The magnitude of a directed segment, its length, is a precisely determined quantity in any given case. To specify the direction of this directed segment we introduce a *rectangular frame of reference*. Whenever vectors are used, or vector equations stated, there is, as it were, a frame of reference in the background. An important advantage of a relationship expressed in vector form is that, although a frame of reference is needed against which to "see" the directions of vectors, the forms in which relations between vectors are stated are independent of any particular frame of reference. By choosing a suitable frame of reference in a given problem the relations can often be made to appear in a simple form. [See also *Pure Maths.*, Vol. II, Chap. XXI.]

A rectangular cartesian frame of reference consists of three mutually perpendicular straight lines through one point, the origin O. The reader can visualize such a frame by looking at the corner of a room where the intersections of two walls and the floor provide three lines which are (usually) at right angles to one another. The three lines are related by the right-hand rule. We label the axes Ox, Oy, Oz (or Ox_1, Ox_2, Ox_3) and they are *right-handed* if a rotation from Ox towards Oy takes a right-handed corkscrew along Oz; similarly, a rotation from Oy towards

Oz takes a right-handed corkscrew along Ox, and so on (Fig. 26.1). The reader should decide for himself which labellings of the edges of a room meeting at a corner provide r.h. axes. The labellings which do not do so give *left-handed axes.* So far we have considered axes which start from O and extend indefinitely away from O; these are, in fact, only the positive halves of the coordinate axes. If the lines are extended through O on the other sides, these extensions are the negative halves of the axes and we have a "positive sense" for each axis from the negative half towards the positive half. It is the "positive sense" of each axis which is related in the r.h. corkscrew rule with the "positive senses" of the other two axes. If A, B are two points on any one of the axes, we can say unambiguously whether B is on the positive or the negative side of A.

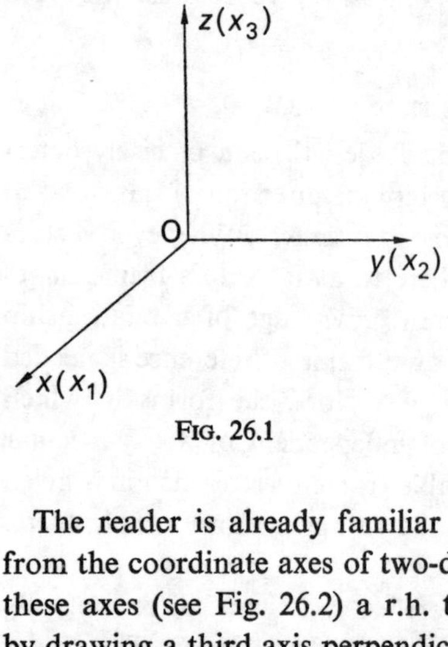

FIG. 26.1

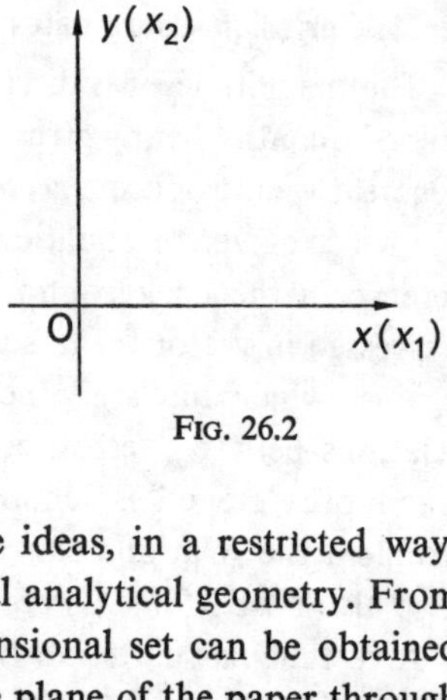

FIG. 26.2

The reader is already familiar with these ideas, in a restricted way, from the coordinate axes of two-dimensional analytical geometry. From these axes (see Fig. 26.2) a r.h. three-dimensional set can be obtained by drawing a third axis perpendicular to the plane of the paper through the origin towards the reader. (A left-handed set is produced by drawing the third axis away from the reader.)

The three coordinate axes which we denote by different letters of the alphabet or by suffixes, as convenient, define three *coordinate planes,* Oyz, Ozx, Oxy, or Ox_2x_3, Ox_3x_1, Ox_1x_2 (keeping the cyclic, right-handed order xyz or 123), which divide the space surrounding the origin into eight sections or *octants*. The position of a point P is specified by its perpendicular distances from each of the coordinate planes, i.e. the distance is measured parallel to an axis. This distance is measured *from* the plane *to* P; if this sense of measurement is in the positive sense of the corresponding axis, the *coordinate* of P is positive; if the sense is opposite to that of the corresponding axis, the coordinate of P is negative. The measured distance is the numerical value of the coordinate. Alternatively we say that a point with a positive (negative) coordinate lies on the positive (negative) side of the appropriate coordinate plane. The following coordinates give points which lie one in each of the octants

$$(1, 1, 1), \quad (-1, 2, 1). \quad (1, -3, 2), \quad (2, 1, -1), \quad (1, -1, -1),$$
$$(-3, 2, -3), \quad (-2, -4, 3), \quad (-1, -2, -3).$$

There is no commonly accepted order of numbering the octants as there is for the quadrants in two dimensions. The position of a point is denoted, in general, by (x, y, z) or by (x_1, x_2, x_3). *Unless otherwise stated we shall use right-handed cartesian axes of reference.*

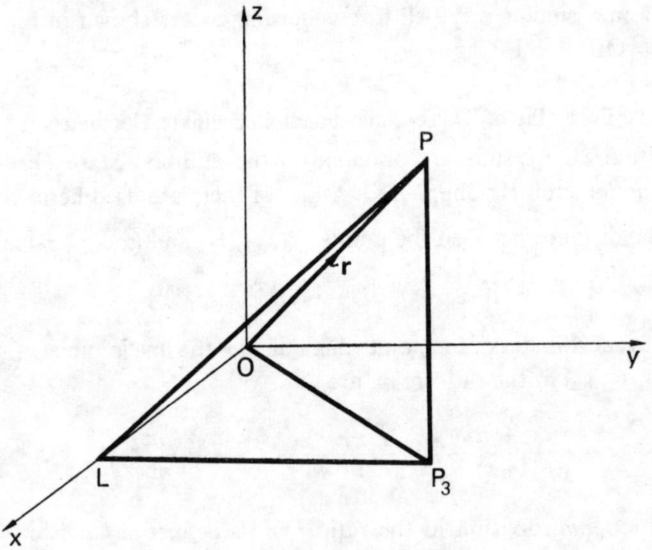

FIG. 26.3

Suppose a point P has coordinates (x, y, z). Then OP is the *position vector* of P. All information about the position of P is incorporated in the three coordinates of P; therefore we denote its position vector by the symbol $\mathbf{r}$ or sometimes $\mathbf{x}$ which stands for (x, y, z) or (x_1, x_2, x_3). The set (x, y, z) or (x_1, x_2, x_3) is sometimes called an *ordered set* because not only the value but also the position of a symbol in the set is significant. The position vectors of P and Q are the same if, and only if, P and Q are the same point. Hence, we say that the vectors $\mathbf{r}_p$, (x_p, y_p, z_p), and $\mathbf{r}_q$, (x_q, y_q, z_q), are equal if and only if

$$x_p = x_q, \quad y_p = y_q, \quad z_p = z_q. \tag{26.1}$$

The coordinates of P are called the *components* of the position vector of P. To find these components we must find the "orthogonal projections" of $\mathbf{r}$ on to the coordinate axes. We draw a plane through P (see Fig. 26.3) parallel to the plane Oyz, i.e. the plane LP_3P. Here P_3 is the foot of the perpendicular from P to the plane Oxy and P_3L is perpendicular to Ox. Then $|x|$ is the distance OL. The sign of x is positive or negative according as L is on the positive or negative side of O. We find y and z in a similar way. All three coordinates are shown in Fig. 26.3, viz. $x = OL$, $y = LP_3$, $z = P_3P$.

26.3. The Formulae of Three-dimensional Coordinate Geometry

The following results are obtained in the authors' *Sixth Form Pure Mathematics*, Vol. II, Chap. XXI. Many of them are used here.

1. The distance between the points (x_1, y_1, z_1) and (x_2, y_2, z_2) is

$$\sqrt{\{(x_1-x_2)^2+(y_1-y_2)^2+(z_1-z_2)^2\}}. \tag{26.2}$$

2. The coordinates of the point which divides the line joining (x_1, y_1, z_1) and (x_2, y_2, z_2) in the ratio $l : m$, are

$$\left(\frac{lx_2+mx_1}{l+m}, \quad \frac{ly_2+my_1}{l+m}, \quad \frac{lz_2+mz_1}{l+m}\right). \tag{26.3}$$

Here *external* division in the ratio $l : m$ is defined as division in the ratio $l : -m$.

3. The first degree equation

$$ax+by+cz+d = 0 \tag{26.4}$$

represents a plane.

4. The equation of the plane through the three points (x_1, y_1, z_1), (x_2, y_2, z_2), (x_3, y_3, z_3) is

$$\begin{vmatrix} x & y & z & 1 \\ x_1 & y_1 & z_1 & 1 \\ x_2 & y_2 & z_2 & 1 \\ x_3 & y_3 & z_3 & 1 \end{vmatrix} = 0. \tag{26.5}$$

5. The equations of the line through the points (x_1, y_1, z_1) and (x_2, y_2, z_2) are

$$\frac{x-x_1}{x_2-x_1} = \frac{y-y_1}{y_2-y_1} = \frac{z-z_1}{z_2-z_1}. \tag{26.6}$$

6. The equations of the line through (a, b, c) with direction ratios $l:m:n$ are

$$\frac{x-a}{l} = \frac{y-b}{m} = \frac{z-c}{n} \tag{26.7}$$

or

$$x = lt+a; \quad y = mt+b; \quad z = nt+c, \tag{26.8}$$

where t is a parameter.

The equations of a line through (a, b, c) with direction cosines $\cos\alpha$, $\cos\beta$, $\cos\gamma$ are

$$\frac{x-a}{\cos\alpha} = \frac{y-b}{\cos\beta} = \frac{z-c}{\cos\gamma}, \tag{26.9}$$

where $\cos^2\alpha+\cos^2\beta+\cos^2\gamma = 1$.

Thus (26.7) and (26.9) are equivalent forms where

$$\cos\alpha = \frac{l}{\sqrt{(l^2+m^2+n^2)}}; \quad \cos\beta = \frac{m}{\sqrt{(l^2+m^2+n^2)}};$$

$$\cos\gamma = \frac{n}{\sqrt{(l^2+m^2+n^2)}}.$$

7. The angle θ between two lines with direction cosines l_1, m_1, n_1 and l_2, m_2, n_2 is given by

$$\cos\theta = l_1l_2+m_1m_2+n_1n_2. \tag{26.10}$$

The two lines are therefore at right angles if

$$l_1l_2+m_1m_2+n_1n_2 = 0. \tag{26.11}$$

8. The direction ratios of a normal to the plane $a_1x+b_1y+c_1z+d_1 = 0$ are

$$a_1 : b_1 : c_1. \tag{26.12}$$

9. The acute angle between the planes

$$a_1x+b_1y+c_1z+d_1 = 0$$

and

$$a_2x+b_2y+c_2z+d_2 = 0$$

is θ, where

$$\cos\theta = \left|\frac{a_1a_2+b_1b_2+c_1c_2}{\sqrt{(a_1^2+b_1^2+c_1^2)}\sqrt{(a_2^2+b_2^2+c_2^2)}}\right|. \tag{26.13}$$

EXERCISES 26.3

1. Find the coordinates of the projection of the point $(-3, 2, 1)$ on (i) the plane Oxy, (ii) the play Ozx, (iii) the plane Oyz, (iv) the x-axis, (v) the y-axis, (vi) the z-axis.

2. Find the coordinates of the points which are symmetric with the point (a, b, c) relative to (i) the plane Oxy, (ii) the plane Ozx, (iii) the plane Oyz, (iv) the x-axis, (v) the y-axis, (vi) the z-axis, (vii) the origin.

3. If A$(-a, -a, -a)$, B$(a, -a, -a)$, C$(-a, a, -a)$, D(a, a, a) are four vertices of a cube, find its other vertices.

4. Given the points A$(1, -2, -3)$, B$(2, -3, 0)$, C$(3, 1, -9)$, D$(-1, 1, -12)$, find the distance between: (i) A and C, (ii) B and D, (iii) C and D.

5. Show that the triangle with vertices at A$(3, -1, 2)$, B$(0, -4, 2)$, C$(-3, 2, 1)$ is isosceles.

6. Show that the triangle with vertices at $A_1(3, -1, 6)$, $A_2(-1, 7, -2)$, $A_3(1, -3, 2)$ is right-angled.

7. Determine whether the triangle whose vertices are at $M_1(4, -1, 4)$, $M_2(0, 7, -4)$, $M_3(3, 1, -2)$ is obtuse-angled.

8. Show that the triangle whose vertices are at M(3, −2, 5), N(−2, 1, −3), P(5, 1, −1) is acute-angled.

9. Find the points on the x-axis whose distances from the point A(−3, 4, 8) are equal to 12.

10. Find a point on the y-axis which is equidistant from the two points A(1, −3, 7), B(5, 7, −5).

26.4. The Definitions of Vectors and Scalars

In § 26.2 we defined the position vector **r** of a point P to be the ordered set of the *components* (x, y, z). A free vector represented by the directed segment $\overrightarrow{AB}$ is similarly denoted by a single symbol **a** or **b** or **c**..., the symbols standing for the ordered sets of components (a_1, a_2, a_3) or (b_1, b_2, b_3) or (c_1, c_2, c_3).... These components are obtained by "projecting" the segment $\overrightarrow{AB}$ orthogonally onto the coordinate axes. For example, if A and B have coordinates (x_a, y_a, z_a) and (x_b, y_b, z_b) respectively, then

$$a_1 = x_b - x_a, \quad a_2 = y_b - y_a, \quad a_3 = z_b - z_a. \tag{26.14}$$

Equation (26.14) can be represented by the single vector equation $\mathbf{a} = \mathbf{r}_b - \mathbf{r}_a$ and gives an unambiguous method of obtaining the *components* of a vector or directed segment referred to an arbitrary frame of reference.

There are many quantities such as mass, energy, density, with numerical values, which are not associated with any direction. If the numerical value is unaltered by an arbitrary change of direction of the axes (or is *invariant* for a rotation of axes) the quantity is a *scalar*. Figure 26.3 suggests that, in general, the components of a vector are altered by a rotation of the axes but the magnitude (or length) of the directed segment is unaltered. Therefore the magnitude of a vector is a scalar.

Notation. We use Clarendon or bold-face letters, **a**, **b**, ..., **A**, **B**, ..., to denote vectors and the corresponding italic letters with suffixes 1, 2, 3, to denote the components. In writing manuscript it is customary to denote a vector by drawing a line under the appropriate symbol, thus $\underline{a}$ denotes **a**. Apart from one or two exceptions and commonly accepted symbols we denote the magnitude, which is *always positive*, either by the italic letter without a suffix or by the modulus sign as summarized in the table on page 760.

	Vector	*Components*	*Magnitude*
a		(a_1, a_2, a_3)	$\lvert\mathbf{a}\rvert = a = +(a_1^2+a_2^2+a_3^2)^{1/2}$
b		(b_1, b_2, b_3)	$\lvert\mathbf{b}\rvert = b = +(b_1^2+b_2^2+b_3^2)^{1/2}$
r	(position vector)	(x, y, z)	$\lvert\mathbf{r}\rvert = r = +(x^2+y^2+z^2)^{1/2}$
x	(position vector)	(x_1, x_2, x_3)	$\lvert\mathbf{x}\rvert = x = +(x_1^2+x_2^2+x_3^2)^{1/2}$
i	(unit vectors along	(1, 0, 0)	1
j	the directions of	(0, 1, 0)	1
k	the axes)	(0, 0, 1)	1
0	(the null vector)	(0, 0, 0)	0

The unit vectors **i, j, k** are to be regarded as free vectors which are not confined to pass through the origin nor to lie in the respective axes: they denote the positive *directions* of the axes only. In general, vectors with a circumflex accent, $\hat{\mathbf{a}}$, $\hat{\mathbf{b}}$, . . ., etc., are unit vectors, i.e. vectors with unit magnitude, and are used to denote directions. If $\hat{\mathbf{a}}$ is a unit vector in the direction of **a**, then $\hat{\mathbf{a}} = \mathbf{a}/\lvert\mathbf{a}\rvert$. The vector $\lambda\mathbf{a}$, where λ is a positive scalar, is defined to be a vector in the same direction as **a** and with magnitude $\lambda\lvert\mathbf{a}\rvert = \lambda a$. The vector $-\mathbf{a}$ has the same magnitude as **a** but the opposite direction.

26.5. The Addition and Subtraction of Vectors

The addition (or subtraction) of vectors is *defined* by the addition (or subtraction) of the components; if

$$\mathbf{c} = \mathbf{a} \pm \mathbf{b},$$

then

$$c_1 = a_1 \pm b_1, \quad c_2 = a_2 \pm b_2, \quad c_3 = a_3 \pm b_3. \tag{26.15}$$

This implies that $\mathbf{a}+\mathbf{b} = \mathbf{b}+\mathbf{a}$. The relation 26.15 is more familiar in its equivalent form of the "parallelogram law" of addition (usually in connection with forces), i.e. if $\overrightarrow{OA}$ and $\overrightarrow{OB}$ represent **a** and **b** respectively, then $\mathbf{c} = \mathbf{a}+\mathbf{b}$ is represented by $\overrightarrow{OC}$ where C is the fourth vertex of the parallelogram OACB. As long as we consider free vectors, either of the opposite sides OA, BC can represent **a**, and either of the opposite sides OB, AC can represent **b** in Fig. 26.4 (i). In this case the triangle OAC can be considered as a triangle of vectors and the relation $\mathbf{a}+\mathbf{b} = \mathbf{c}$ is represented by $\overrightarrow{OA}+\overrightarrow{AC} = \overrightarrow{OC}$. The addition of several vectors, in Fig. 26.4 (ii), leads to a "polygon law". It should be noted that Fig. 26.4 (i) is a plane figure but that usually the polygon of Fig. 26.4 (ii) is *not* a plane figure. For the two figures the relevant equations are

$$\text{(i)} \qquad \mathbf{c} = \mathbf{a}+\mathbf{b},$$

$$\text{(ii)} \qquad \mathbf{f} = \mathbf{a}+\mathbf{b}+\ldots+\mathbf{c}+\mathbf{d}. \tag{26.16}$$

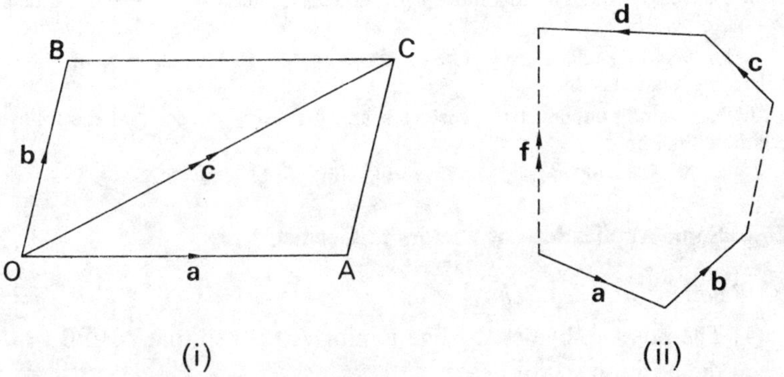

FIG. 26.4

The most important application of the polygon of vectors is the representation of a vector in terms of its components. In Fig. 26.3, OLP_3P is a polygon in which $\overrightarrow{OP} = \mathbf{r}$ represents the sum of three vectors $x\mathbf{i}$, $y\mathbf{j}$, $z\mathbf{k}$. Therefore

$$\mathbf{r} = x\mathbf{i}+y\mathbf{j}+z\mathbf{k}$$

or, for a free vector,

$$\mathbf{a} = a_1\mathbf{i}+a_2\mathbf{j}+a_3\mathbf{k}. \tag{26.17}$$

This expresses symbolically the relation between a vector and its components; but it should be noted that a feature of all vector relationships, e.g. equations (26.1), (26.14), (26.15), is that a single vector relation is equivalent to three equations between components.

EXERCISES 26.5

1. Given the vectors **a**, **b**, construct each of the following vectors: (i) $\mathbf{a}+\mathbf{b}$, (ii) $\mathbf{a}-\mathbf{b}$, (iii) $\mathbf{b}-\mathbf{a}$, (iv) $-\mathbf{a}-\mathbf{b}$.

2. Find the moduli of the sum and difference of the vectors $\mathbf{a} = (3, -5, 8)$ and $\mathbf{b} = (-1, 1, -4)$.

3. Given $|\mathbf{a}| = 13$, $|\mathbf{b}| = 19$, and $|\mathbf{a}+\mathbf{b}| = 24$, calculate $|\mathbf{a}-\mathbf{b}|$.

4. Given $|\mathbf{a}| = 11$, $|\mathbf{b}| = 23$, and $|\mathbf{a}-\mathbf{b}| = 30$, calculate $|\mathbf{a}+\mathbf{b}|$.

5. The vectors **a** and **b** are mutually perpendicular and $|\mathbf{a}| = 5$, $|\mathbf{b}| = 12$. Calculate $|\mathbf{a}+\mathbf{b}|$ and $|\mathbf{a}-\mathbf{b}|$.

6. The vectors **a** and **b** are inclined at an angle $\phi = 60°$ and $|\mathbf{a}| = 5$, $|\mathbf{b}| = 8$. Calculate $|\mathbf{a}+\mathbf{b}|$ and $|\mathbf{a}-\mathbf{b}|$.

7. What conditions must the vectors **a** and **b** satisfy in order that the following relations shall hold?

(i) $|\mathbf{a}+\mathbf{b}| = |\mathbf{a}-\mathbf{b}|$, (ii) $|\mathbf{a}+\mathbf{b}| > |\mathbf{a}-\mathbf{b}|$, (iii) $|\mathbf{a}+\mathbf{b}| < |\mathbf{a}-\mathbf{b}|$.

26.6. Some Applications of Vectors to Geometry

(a) *Relations Between Points*

(1) The point P divides the line joining A to B so that AP/PB $= l/m$. Then the position vector of P is

$$\mathbf{r}_P = \frac{m\mathbf{r}_A + l\mathbf{r}_B}{m+l}. \tag{26.18}$$

(If l/m is negative P does not lie between A and B.)

From Fig. 26.5

$$\mathbf{r}_P = \overrightarrow{OP} = \overrightarrow{OA} + \overrightarrow{AP} = \mathbf{r}_A + \overrightarrow{AP}.$$

Now AP/PB $= l/m$, and hence AP/AB $=$ AP/(AP+PB) $= l/(l+m)$.

$$\therefore \ \overrightarrow{AP} = \frac{l}{l+m}\overrightarrow{AB}.$$

But $\overrightarrow{OA} + \overrightarrow{AB} = \overrightarrow{OB}$.

$$\therefore \ \overrightarrow{AB} = \overrightarrow{OB} - \overrightarrow{OA} = \mathbf{r}_B - \mathbf{r}_A.$$

$$\therefore \ \overrightarrow{AP} = \frac{l}{l+m}(\mathbf{r}_B - \mathbf{r}_A).$$

$$\therefore \ \mathbf{r}_P = \frac{m\mathbf{r}_A + l\mathbf{r}_B}{l+m}.$$

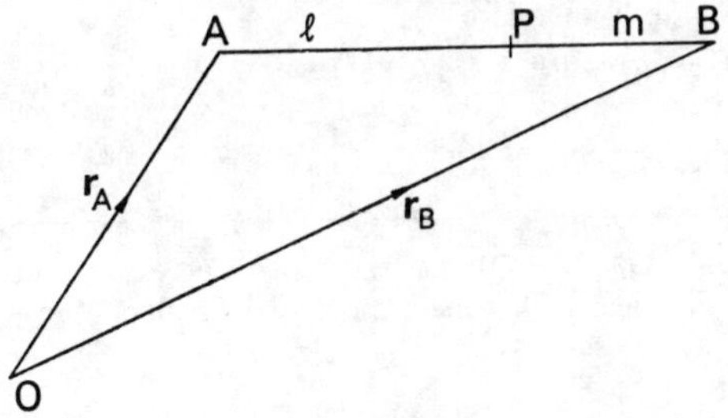

FIG. 26.5

The three component equations of (26.18) are, from equation (26.3),

$$x_p = \frac{mx_a+lx_b}{l+m}, \quad y_p = \frac{my_a+ly_b}{l+m}, \quad z_p = \frac{mz_a+lz_b}{l+m}.$$

Example 1. In a parallelogram ABCD, X is the mid-point of AB and Y divides BC in the ratio 1 : 2. If DX and AY intersect at R, calculate DR/DX and AR/AY.

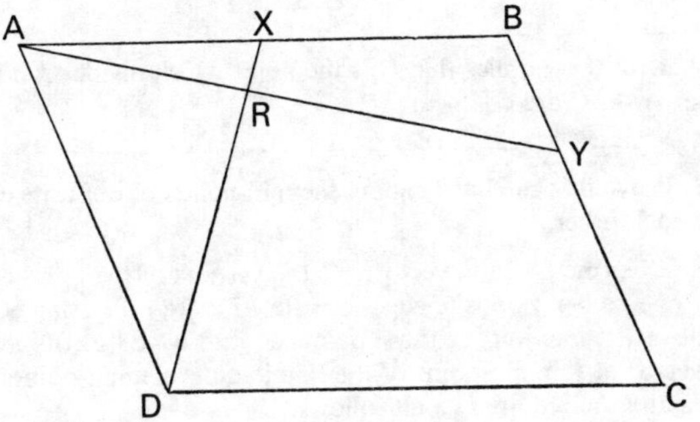

FIG. 26.6

We use the fact that:

If $\lambda\mathbf{a} = \mu\mathbf{b}$, $a \neq 0, b \neq 0$, then either **a** is parallel to **b** and $\lambda = \mu$ or $\lambda = 0$, $\mu = 0$.

With reference to Fig. 26.6, let $\overrightarrow{AB} = \mathbf{a}$, $\overrightarrow{AD} = \mathbf{b}$, $\overrightarrow{AR} = \lambda\overrightarrow{AY}$, $\overrightarrow{DR} = \mu\overrightarrow{DX}$.

Then $\quad \overrightarrow{AR} = \lambda(\overrightarrow{AB}+\overrightarrow{BY}) = \lambda(\mathbf{a}+\tfrac{1}{3}\mathbf{b})$,

$\quad \overrightarrow{DR} = \mu(\overrightarrow{DA}+\overrightarrow{AX}) = \mu(-\mathbf{b}+\tfrac{1}{2}\mathbf{a})$.

But $\quad \overrightarrow{AR}+\overrightarrow{RD} = \overrightarrow{AD}$.

$\therefore \; \lambda(\mathbf{a}+\tfrac{1}{3}\mathbf{b})-\mu(-\mathbf{b}+\tfrac{1}{2}\mathbf{a}) = \mathbf{b}$.

$\therefore \; (\lambda-\tfrac{1}{2}\mu)\mathbf{a} = (1-\mu-\tfrac{1}{3}\lambda)\mathbf{b}$.

But **a** is not parallel to **b**, therefore

$$(\lambda-\tfrac{1}{2}\mu) = 0, \quad (1-\mu-\tfrac{1}{3}\lambda) = 0.$$

Therefore $\lambda = \frac{3}{7}, \quad \mu = \frac{6}{7}$,

i.e. $\text{DR} = \frac{6}{7}\text{DX}, \quad \text{AR} = \frac{3}{7}\text{AY}.$

Example 2. If $\mathbf{a} = \overrightarrow{\text{OA}}$, $\mathbf{b} = \overrightarrow{\text{OB}}$, $\mathbf{c} = \overrightarrow{\text{OC}}$, then a necessary and sufficient condition for A, B, C to be collinear is that there should exist scalars λ, μ, ν such that

$$\lambda\mathbf{a}+\mu\mathbf{b}+\nu\mathbf{c} = \mathbf{0}, \tag{1}$$

where

$$\lambda+\mu+\nu = 0 \tag{2}$$

and not more than one of λ, μ, ν vanishes.

This condition is clearly necessary, i.e. if A, B, C are collinear then equations (1), (2) must be satisfied, for in this case by equation (26.18) **a**, **b**, **c** must be related by an equation of the form

$$(l+m)\mathbf{c} = m\mathbf{a}+l\mathbf{b},$$

whence the required condition follows.

Conversely, if

$$\lambda\mathbf{a}+\mu\mathbf{b}+\nu\mathbf{c} = \mathbf{0}$$

where $\lambda+\mu+\nu = 0$, then

$$\mathbf{c} = \frac{\lambda\mathbf{a}+\mu\mathbf{b}}{\lambda+\mu}.$$

By equation (26.18) this implies that C is the point which divides AB in the ratio μ/λ and hence that A, B, C are collinear.

Example 3. Prove that the lines joining the mid-points of opposite edges of a tetrahedron bisect each other.

Let **a**, **b**, **c**, **d**, be (the position vectors of) the vertices of the tetrahedron. Then the mid-points of one pair of opposite edges are $\frac{1}{2}(\mathbf{a}+\mathbf{b})$, $\frac{1}{2}(\mathbf{c}+\mathbf{d})$, using equation (26.18). The mid-point of the line joining these points is $\frac{1}{4}(\mathbf{a}+\mathbf{b}+\mathbf{c}+\mathbf{d})$. By symmetry this is the position vector of the mid-point of the line joining the mid-points of any pair of opposite edges and the required result follows.

Example 4. If the diagonals of a quadrilateral bisect each other it is a parallelogram.

Let the positions of the corners A, B, C, D be **a**, **b**, **c**, **d** respectively. The mid-points of the diagonals are $\frac{1}{2}(\mathbf{a}+\mathbf{c})$ and $\frac{1}{2}(\mathbf{b}+\mathbf{d})$. These are the same point.

$$\therefore\ \mathbf{a}+\mathbf{c} = \mathbf{b}+\mathbf{d} \quad \text{or} \quad \mathbf{a}-\mathbf{b} = \mathbf{d}-\mathbf{c},$$

i.e.

$$\overrightarrow{\text{BA}} = \overrightarrow{\text{CD}}.$$

This means that $\overrightarrow{\text{BA}}$ and $\overrightarrow{\text{CD}}$ have the same magnitude and direction, i.e. ABCD is a parallelogram.

Example 5. Find the position of the centre of mass of particles of masses m_i situated at the points $\mathbf{r}_i$, $(i = 1, 2, \ldots, n)$.

The centre of mass G_2 of m_1 and m_2 divides the line joining them in the ratio m_2/m_1; therefore its position vector is, from equation (26.18),

$$\frac{m_1\mathbf{r}_1+m_2\mathbf{r}_2}{m_1+m_2}.$$

The centre of mass of m_1+m_2 at G_2 and m_3 at $\mathbf{r}_3$ divides the line joining these points in the ratio $m_3/(m_1+m_2)$. This point G_3 has position vector

$$\frac{(m_1\mathbf{r}_1+m_2\mathbf{r}_2)+m_3\mathbf{r}_3}{(m_1+m_2)+m_3},$$

using equation (26.18) again.

This *suggests* that the centre of mass G_n of the n particles has position vector

$$\bar{\mathbf{r}} = \frac{m_1\mathbf{r}_1+m_2\mathbf{r}_2+\ldots+m_n\mathbf{r}_n}{m_1+m_2+\ldots+m_n}.$$

This result can easily be proved by mathematical induction; the proof is left as an exercise for the reader.

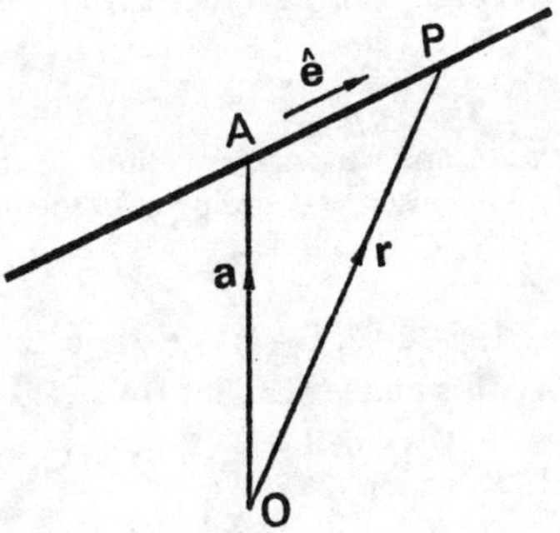

FIG. 26.7

(b) *The Equation of a Straight Line*

To reach a point on a straight line, a moving point, starting from the origin, can go from O to A, a point on the line, and then proceed along the line. Suppose $\mathbf{a}$ is the position of a point A on the line, $\hat{\mathbf{e}}$ is a unit vector along the direction of the line, and s is the distance AP (Fig. 26.7). Then the position vector of P is

$$\mathbf{r} = \mathbf{a}+s\hat{\mathbf{e}}. \tag{26.19}$$

This is the equation of a straight line in vectors. If we express this in terms of components, those of $\overrightarrow{OP}$ are (x, y, z) where

$$\frac{x-a_1}{l_1} = \frac{y-a_2}{l_2} = \frac{z-a_3}{l_3} = s. \tag{26.20}$$

Here (l_1, l_2, l_3), the components of $\hat{\mathbf{e}}$, are the *direction cosines* of the line. If $\mathbf{b}$, *not* a unit vector, is parallel to the line, then the displacement $\overrightarrow{AP}$ is a multiple of $\mathbf{b}$, and we can still write the equation of the line in the form

$$\mathbf{r} = \mathbf{a} + t\mathbf{b}, \tag{26.21}$$

where t is a parameter which varies as P moves along the line. This gives rise to

$$\frac{x-a_1}{b_1} = \frac{y-a_2}{b_2} = \frac{z-a_3}{b_3} (= t). \tag{26.22}$$

In equations (26.21), (26.22) the parameter t is *not* equal to the distance AP unless $|\mathbf{b}| = 1$.

Example. Find the vector and cartesian equations of the line through the points A$(1, -2, 1)$, B$(0, -2, 3)$. Find also the coordinates of the point in which this line cuts the plane Oyz.

The vector $\overrightarrow{AB} = (0-1,\ \ -2+2,\ 3-1) = (-1,\ 0,\ 2) = -\mathbf{i}+0\mathbf{j}+2\mathbf{k}$ is parallel to the line and the point A lies on the line. But $\overrightarrow{OA} = (1, -2, 1) = \mathbf{i}-2\mathbf{j}+\mathbf{k}$. Hence equation (26.21) becomes $\mathbf{r} = \overrightarrow{OA}+t\overrightarrow{AB} = \mathbf{i}-2\mathbf{j}+\mathbf{k}+t(-\mathbf{i}+0\mathbf{j}+2\mathbf{k})$. The corresponding cartesian equations [cf. equation (26.22)] are

$$\frac{x-1}{-1} = \frac{y+2}{0} = \frac{z-1}{2} (= t).$$

Here the zero in the denominator of the second ratio is to be interpreted as indicating that the numerator of this ratio vanishes also, i.e. for all points on the line, $y+2 = 0$.

The parametric equations of the line can be written

$$x = 1-t, \quad y = -2, \quad z = 1+2t.$$

This line meets the plane Oyz where $x = 0$, i.e. where $t = 1$. Hence the coordinates of the required point are $(0, -2, 3)$.

(c) *The Equation of a Plane*

Three or more vectors are said to be *coplanar* when they are all parallel to one plane. For example, the vectors $\mathbf{b} = \overrightarrow{AB}$, $\mathbf{c} = \overrightarrow{AC}$, $\mathbf{d} = \overrightarrow{AD}$ are coplanar if A, B, C, D all lie in one plane.

Provided that $\overrightarrow{AB}$ and $\overrightarrow{AC}$ are not parallel to each other and D lies in the plane ABC, then (Fig. 26.8)

$$\mathbf{d} = \overrightarrow{AD} = \overrightarrow{AK} + \overrightarrow{KD},$$

where $\overrightarrow{KD}$ is parallel to $\overrightarrow{AC}$. Hence,

$$\mathbf{d} = p\mathbf{b} + q\mathbf{c},$$

where the scalars $p = AK/AB$, $q = KD/AC$. This relation must be satisfied if **b**, **c**, **d** are coplanar. Conversely, if there are scalars p, q such that **d** can be expressed in terms of **b**, **c** in this manner, then **b**, **c**, **d** are coplanar.

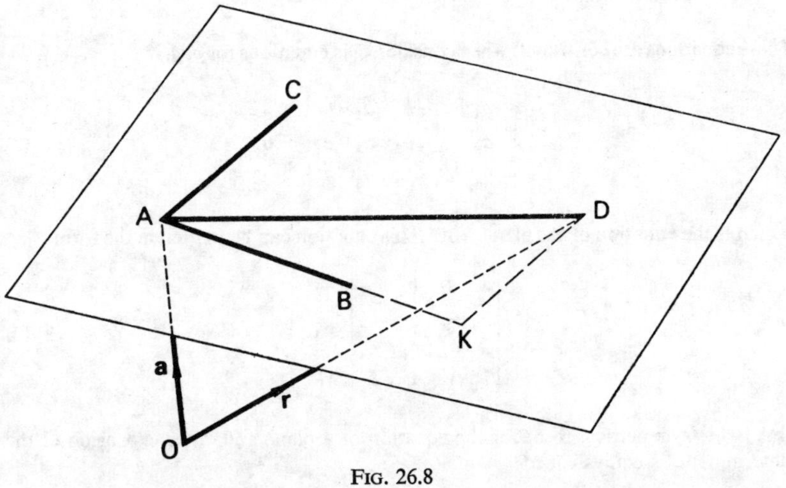

FIG. 26.8

The position of D in Fig. 26.8 can be varied by giving p, q different values so that an arbitrary point of the plane has position vector of the form

$$\mathbf{r} = \mathbf{a} + p\mathbf{b} + q\mathbf{c}, \tag{26.23}$$

where O is the origin of position vectors and $\overrightarrow{OD} = \mathbf{r}$. This is the equation of a plane in vector notation. If the plane passes through the origin, then $\mathbf{a} = \mathbf{0}$. Note that the vector equation of a two-dimensional locus, a plane, involves two parameters, whereas the vector equation of a one-dimensional locus, a line, involves one parameter only.

Example 1. Find the vector and cartesian equations of the plane through the three points A, B, C with position vectors **a**, **b**, **c**.

The vectors $\mathbf{b}-\mathbf{a}$ and $\mathbf{c}-\mathbf{a}$ both lie in the plane. Therefore equation (26.23) becomes, in this case,

$$\mathbf{r} = \mathbf{a}+p(\mathbf{b}-\mathbf{a})+q(\mathbf{c}-\mathbf{a}). \tag{1}$$

Writing $\mathbf{r} = x\mathbf{i}+y\mathbf{j}+z\mathbf{k}$, $\mathbf{a} = a_1\mathbf{i}+a_2\mathbf{j}+a_3\mathbf{k}$, etc., the components of equation (1) can be written

$$(x-a_1)+p(a_1-b_1)+q(a_1-c_1) = 0,$$
$$(y-a_2)+p(a_2-b_2)+q(a_2-c_2) = 0,$$
$$(z-a_3)+p(a_3-b_3)+q(a_3-c_3) = 0.$$

These equations are consistent, when considered as equations for p, q, if

$$\begin{vmatrix} x-a_1 & a_1-b_1 & a_1-c_1 \\ y-a_2 & a_2-b_2 & a_2-c_2 \\ z-a_3 & a_3-b_3 & a_3-c_3 \end{vmatrix} = 0 \tag{2}$$

which is the equation of the plane ABC. This equation can be written in the form

$$\begin{vmatrix} x & a_1 & b_1 & c_1 \\ y & a_2 & b_2 & c_2 \\ z & a_3 & b_3 & c_3 \\ 1 & 1 & 1 & 1 \end{vmatrix} = 0; \tag{3}$$

this is the symmetrical form for the equation of a plane and, after expansion of the determinant, is equivalent to

$$A_1x+B_1y+C_1z+D_1 = 0, \tag{4}$$

where A_1, B_1, C_1, D_1 are constants. Thus, the equation of a plane is linear in the coordinates (x, y, z) of a variable point P on the plane. Conversely one linear equation in (x, y, z) represents a plane.

Example 2. Find the equations of the line in which the plane through the points A(2, 0, 1), B(0, 4, 0), C(1, −1, 2) cuts the plane Ozx.

Substitution in either of equations (2) or (3) of example 1 above gives the equation of the plane ABC in the form

$$x+y+2z = 4.$$

This plane cuts the plane Ozx (on which $y = 0$) in the line

$$x+2z = 4, \quad y = 0.$$

This can be written

$$\frac{x}{2} = \frac{y}{0} = \frac{z-2}{-1},$$

so that the line has the vector equation

$$\mathbf{r} = 2\mathbf{k}+p(2\mathbf{i}-\mathbf{k}).$$

EXERCISES 26.6

1. In a triangle ABC, the point L divides AB in the ratio 2:1, and the point M divides AC in the ratio 1:2. The point O is the mid-point of LM and BO produced cuts AC at Q. Given that $\overrightarrow{AB} = \mathbf{a}$ and $\overrightarrow{AC} = \mathbf{b}$, show that

$$\overrightarrow{AO} = \tfrac{1}{3}\mathbf{a}+\tfrac{1}{6}\mathbf{b}, \quad \overrightarrow{BO} = \tfrac{1}{6}\mathbf{b}-\tfrac{2}{3}\mathbf{a},$$

and hence calculate BO/BQ and AQ/AC.

2. By vector methods:

(i) Prove that the medians of a triangle are concurrent and that each divides the other two in the ratio 2:1.

(ii) Prove that the centroid of three equal particles at the vertices of a triangle is at the meeting of the medians.

(iii) Prove that the four lines, each of which joins a vertex to the centroid of the opposite face of a tetrahedron, are concurrent. Prove also that the lines joining the mid-points of opposite pairs of edges are concurrent in the same point.

(iv) Find the centre of mass of four equal particles at the vertices of a tetrahedron.

3. The vectors **a** and **b** represent two sides $\overrightarrow{BC}$, $\overrightarrow{CA}$, of an equilateral triangle ABC. Find the vectors which represent (i) the third side, and (ii) the sides of the triangle DEF formed by the mid-points of the sides of ABC.

4. The sides AB, BC of a regular octagon ABCDEFGH are represented by vectors **a**, **b** respectively. Find the vectors which represent the remaining sides.

5. Three edges of a unit cube OA, OB, OC are represented by the vectors **i**, **j**, **k** respectively. Find the vectors which represent (i) the diagonal of the cube through O, (ii) the three remaining diagonals of the cube, and (iii) the diagonals OD, OE, OF of the three faces which pass through O.

6. Particles of masses 1, 2, 3 are situated at the corners A, B, C respectively of the cube of question 5; particles of mass 1 are situated at the remaining vertices of the cube. Find the position vector of the centre of mass of these particles.

7. Find the vector and cartesian equations of the line joining the points with position vectors $2\mathbf{i}-\mathbf{j}+2\mathbf{k}$ and $4\mathbf{i}-3\mathbf{j}+3\mathbf{k}$. Find also the position vector of the point where this line cuts the plane whose vector equation is

$$\mathbf{r} = 2\mathbf{i}+s\mathbf{j}+t\mathbf{k}. \quad \text{(L.)}$$

8. Find the equation of the plane which passes through the points (2, 2, 1), (2, 3, 2), (−1, 3, 0).

9. Show that the points (1, 0, 1), (3, 2, 0), (4, 4, 1), (2, 2, 2) are coplanar.

10. Find the cartesian equations of the line through the points (1, 2, 3), (2, 1, 5) and show that this line lies in the plane $x+3y+z-10 = 0$. (L.)

26.7. The Scalar Product

The scalar product of two vectors **a** and **b** is *defined* as the product of the moduli (lengths) of the vectors and the cosine of the angle between them. The scalar product is written **a . b** (to be read as **a** dot **b**). Thus

$$\mathbf{a}.\mathbf{b} = |\mathbf{a}|\,|\mathbf{b}|\cos\theta, \tag{26.24}$$

where θ ($\leqq \pi$) is the angle between the positive directions of **a** and **b**.

Clearly the scalar product is independent of the particular frame of reference used. Nevertheless, we can find an expression for **a . b** in terms of components. In Fig. 26.9, $a^2+b^2-2ab\cos\theta = \text{AB}^2$.

$$\therefore\ \mathbf{a}.\mathbf{b} = \tfrac{1}{2}(a^2+b^2-\text{AB}^2). \tag{26.25}$$

But
$$\overrightarrow{\text{AB}} = \mathbf{b}-\mathbf{a} = (b_1-a_1,\quad b_2-a_2,\quad b_3-a_3).$$

$$\therefore\ \text{AB}^2 = (b_1-a_1)^2+(b_2-a_2)^2+(b_3-a_3)^2.$$

Also
$$a^2 = a_1^2+a_2^2+a_3^2,\quad b^2 = b_1^2+b_2^2+b_3^2.$$

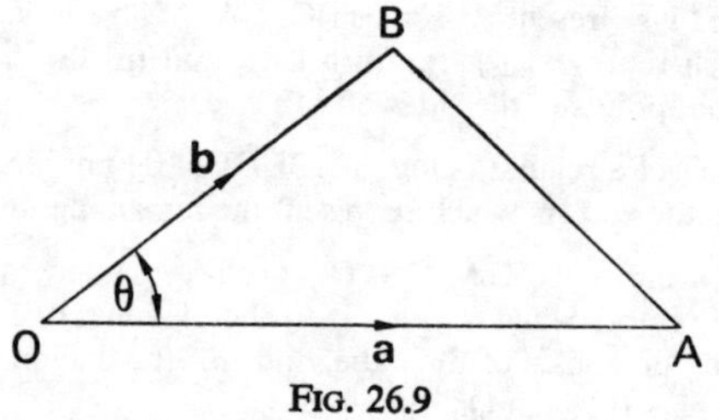

FIG. 26.9

Substitution in equation (26.25) leads at once to

$$\mathbf{a}.\mathbf{b} = a_1b_1+a_2b_2+a_3b_3. \tag{26.26}$$

The same form for this result is obtained whatever frame of reference is used.

Properties of the Scalar Product

(1) $$\mathbf{a}.\mathbf{b} = \mathbf{b}.\mathbf{a},$$

i.e. the scalar product of two vectors is *commutative*. This follows directly from (26.26).

(2) $$\mathbf{a}.(\mathbf{b}+\mathbf{c}) = \mathbf{a}.\mathbf{b}+\mathbf{a}.\mathbf{c},$$

i.e. the *distributive* law holds for scalar multiplication. Again this follows from equation (26.26) and can be generalized to

$$\left(\sum_{i=1}^{m} \mathbf{p}_i\right)\cdot\left(\sum_{j=1}^{n} \mathbf{q}_j\right) = \sum_{i=1}^{m}\sum_{j=1}^{n} \mathbf{p}_i.\mathbf{q}_j. \tag{26.27}$$

(3) If $\mathbf{a}.\mathbf{b} = 0$, then $|\mathbf{a}|\,|\mathbf{b}| \cos\theta = 0$. Hence, if neither of the vectors is a null vector, $\cos\theta = 0$, i.e. $\theta = \frac{1}{2}\pi$ and the vectors are perpendicular. A scalar product of vectors differs from the product of two numbers in that a scalar product may be zero although neither of the factors is zero.

(4) From equation (26.26)

$$\mathbf{a}.\mathbf{a} = a_1^2+a_2^2+a_3^2 = |\mathbf{a}|^2. \tag{26.28}$$

It is customary to write $\mathbf{a}.\mathbf{a} = \mathbf{a}^2$.

(5) With the usual notation for unit vectors along the coordinate axes

$$\mathbf{i}.\mathbf{i} = \mathbf{j}.\mathbf{j} = \mathbf{k}.\mathbf{k} = 1, \tag{26.29}$$
$$\mathbf{i}.\mathbf{j} = \mathbf{j}.\mathbf{i} = \mathbf{j}.\mathbf{k} = \mathbf{k}.\mathbf{j} = \mathbf{k}.\mathbf{i} = \mathbf{i}.\mathbf{k} = 0.$$

(6) If one of the vectors of a product is a unit vector, $\hat{\mathbf{b}}$ (see Fig. 26.10), then

$$\mathbf{a}.\hat{\mathbf{b}} = a\cos\theta = \mathrm{ON} \tag{26.30}$$

which is the orthogonal projection of $\mathbf{a}$ on to the direction $\hat{\mathbf{b}}$.

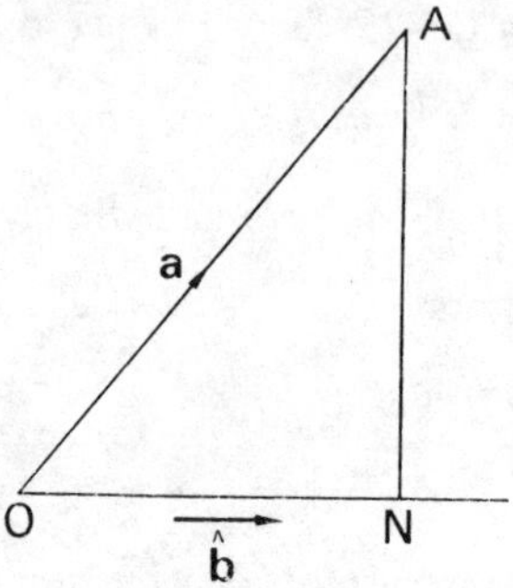

FIG. 26.10

(7) Another important set of relations is obtained from (26.30); if

$$\mathbf{a} = a_1\mathbf{i}+a_2\mathbf{j}+a_3\mathbf{k},$$

then

$$\mathbf{a}.\mathbf{i} = a_1, \quad \mathbf{a}.\mathbf{j} = a_2, \quad \mathbf{a}.\mathbf{k} = a_3 \tag{26.31}$$

and

$$\mathbf{a} = (\mathbf{a}.\mathbf{i})\mathbf{i}+(\mathbf{a}.\mathbf{j})\mathbf{j}+(\mathbf{a}.\mathbf{k})\mathbf{k}. \tag{26.32}$$

Equation (26.32) expresses analytically the method of obtaining the components of a vector by projection.

(8) If both the vectors in a scalar product are unit vectors, then $\hat{\mathbf{a}}.\hat{\mathbf{b}} = \cos\theta$, where θ is the angle between the directions $\hat{\mathbf{a}}$, $\hat{\mathbf{b}}$. Moreover, equation (26.32) shows that

$$\hat{\mathbf{a}} = \mathbf{i}\cos\theta_1+\mathbf{j}\cos\theta_2+\mathbf{k}\cos\theta_3,$$

i.e. the components of $\hat{\mathbf{a}}$ are "*direction cosines*", and

$$\hat{\mathbf{a}}^2 = \cos^2\theta_1+\cos^2\theta_2+\cos^2\theta_3 = 1. \tag{26.33}$$

This relation, (26.33), is the analogue of $\cos^2\theta+\cos^2(\frac{1}{2}\pi-\theta) = 1$ in two dimensions. The reader should note exactly where the angles θ_1, θ_2, θ_3 occur in Fig. 26.3. The angle θ_1 is xOP, $\theta_2 = y$OP, $\theta_3 = z$OP; all these angles lie in different planes. Unit vectors and their components, direction cosines, are extensively used in three-dimensional geometry to find angles. If two directions are given by

$$\hat{\mathbf{a}} = \mathbf{i}\cos\alpha_1+\mathbf{j}\cos\alpha_2+\mathbf{k}\cos\alpha_3, \quad \hat{\mathbf{b}} = \mathbf{i}\cos\beta_1+\mathbf{j}\cos\beta_2+\mathbf{k}\cos\beta_3,$$

then

$$\hat{\mathbf{a}}.\hat{\mathbf{b}} = (\mathbf{a}.\mathbf{b})/|\mathbf{a}|\,|\mathbf{b}| = \cos\theta$$
$$= \cos\alpha_1\cos\beta_1+\cos\alpha_2\cos\beta_2+\cos\alpha_3\cos\beta_3. \qquad (26.34)$$

If the two directions are perpendicular, then $\cos\theta = 0$, i.e.

$$\hat{\mathbf{a}}.\hat{\mathbf{b}} = 0 = \cos\alpha_1\cos\beta_1+\cos\alpha_2\cos\beta_2+\cos\alpha_3\cos\beta_3.$$

It is customary to denote the direction cosines of a line by (l, m, n). Thus, with $\theta_1, \theta_2, \theta_3$ defined as above, $l = \cos\theta_1$, $m = \cos\theta_2$, $n = \cos\theta_3$ and

$$l^2+m^2+n^2 = 1. \qquad (26.35)$$

Also from equation (26.34) the angle θ between the lines with direction cosines (l_1, m_1, n_1), (l_2, m_2, n_2) is given by

$$\cos\theta = l_1l_2+m_1m_2+n_1n_2. \qquad (26.36)$$

If l, m, n are proportional to f, g, h, so that

$$l = f/\sqrt{(f^2+g^2+h^2)}, \quad m = g/\sqrt{(f^2+g^2+h^2)}, \quad n = h/\sqrt{(f^2+g^2+h^2)},$$

then $f:g:h$ are called *direction ratios* of the line with direction cosines (l, m, n). For example, the line

$$\frac{x-2}{3} = \frac{y+1}{2} = \frac{z-4}{-5}$$

has direction ratios $3:2:-5$ and direction cosines

$$(3/\sqrt{38}, 2/\sqrt{38}, -5/\sqrt{38}).$$

Example 1. Find the projection of AB, where A is the point **a** and B is the point **b**, on a line in the direction $\hat{\mathbf{e}}$ whose components (direction cosines) are (l_1, l_2, l_3).

By equation (26.30) the projection is

$$\overrightarrow{AB}.\hat{\mathbf{e}} = (\mathbf{b}-\mathbf{a}).\hat{\mathbf{e}} = l_1(b_1-a_1)+l_2(b_2-a_2)+l_3(b_3-a_3).$$

Example 2. A line makes angles $\theta_1, \theta_2, \theta_3, \theta_4$ with the four diagonals of a cube. Prove that

$$\cos^2\theta_1+\cos^2\theta_2+\cos^2\theta_3+\cos^2\theta_4 = \tfrac{4}{3}.$$

Without loss of generality we take the edges of the cube to be of unit length. Choosing the coordinate axes Ox, Oy, Oz along three concurrent edges OA, OC, OG respectively of the cube, the position vectors of the corners are (see Fig. 26.11): O, **0**; A, **i**; B, **i**+**j**; C, **j**; D, **i**+**k**; E, **i**+**j**+**k**; F, **j**+**k**. Then $\overrightarrow{OE}$ is **i**+**j**+**k** and $OE^2 = 3$. Suppose the direction of the given line is $\hat{\mathbf{e}} = l_1\mathbf{i}+l_2\mathbf{j}+l_3\mathbf{k}$. Then

$$\cos\theta_1 = \overrightarrow{OE}.\hat{\mathbf{e}}/|\overrightarrow{OE}| = (l_1+l_2+l_3)/\sqrt{3}.$$

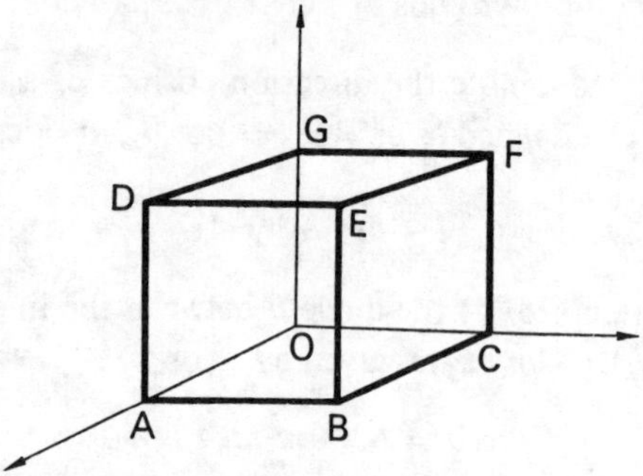

FIG. 26.11

Also $$\overrightarrow{AF} = -\mathbf{i}+\mathbf{j}+\mathbf{k}, \quad AF = \sqrt{3};$$

$$\therefore \cos\theta_2 = \overrightarrow{AF}.\hat{\mathbf{e}}/|\overrightarrow{AF}| = (-l_1+l_2+l_3)/\sqrt{3}.$$

Similarly $$\cos\theta_3 = (l_1-l_2+l_3)/\sqrt{3}, \quad \cos\theta_4 = (l_1+l_2-l_3)/\sqrt{3}.$$

$$\therefore \sum_{r=1}^{4}\cos^2\theta_r$$

$$= \tfrac{1}{3}[(l_1+l_2+l_3)^2+(-l_1+l_2+l_3)^2+(l_1-l_2+l_3)^2+(l_1+l_2-l_3)^2]$$

$$= 4(l_1^2+l_2^2+l_3^2)^2/3 = \tfrac{4}{3}.$$

Example 3. Find the cosines of the angles of the triangle with vertices

$$A(\mathbf{i}-\mathbf{k}), \quad B(2\mathbf{i}+\mathbf{j}+3\mathbf{k}), \quad C(3\mathbf{i}+2\mathbf{j}+\mathbf{k}).$$

The sides of the triangle are

$$\overrightarrow{BC} = (3\mathbf{i}+2\mathbf{j}+\mathbf{k})-(2\mathbf{i}+\mathbf{j}+3\mathbf{k}) = \mathbf{i}+\mathbf{j}-2\mathbf{k},$$

$\overrightarrow{CA} = -2\mathbf{i}-2\mathbf{j}-2\mathbf{k}$, $\overrightarrow{AB} = \mathbf{i}+\mathbf{j}+4\mathbf{k}$, whence $BC = \sqrt{6}$, $CA = \sqrt{12}$, $AB = \sqrt{18}$. Now the *interior* angle, A, of the triangle is, for example, given by

$$\cos A = -\frac{\overrightarrow{AB}.\overrightarrow{CA}}{AB.CA} = -\frac{(-2-2-8)}{\sqrt{18}.\sqrt{12}} = \sqrt{\left(\frac{2}{3}\right)}.$$

Similarly, $\cos B = 1/\sqrt{3}$, $\cos C = 0$.

The last result is verified by noting that

$$AB^2 = 18 \quad \text{and} \quad BC^2+CA^2 = 6+12 = 18 = AB^2.$$

Example 4. (a) If **A** and **B** are vectors given by $\mathbf{A} = 8\mathbf{i}+2\mathbf{j}-3\mathbf{k}$ and $\mathbf{B} = 3\mathbf{i}-6\mathbf{j}+4\mathbf{k}$, calculate $\mathbf{A}.\mathbf{B}$ and show that **A** and **B** are perpendicular.

(b) The edges OP, OQ and OR of a tetrahedron OPQR are the vectors **A, B** and **C** respectively. If OP and QR are perpendicular show that $\mathbf{A}.(\mathbf{B}-\mathbf{C}) = 0$. If also OQ and RP are perpendicular prove that OR and PQ are perpendicular. (L.)

(a) $\mathbf{A}.\mathbf{B} = 8.3-2.6-3.4 = 0$. But $|\mathbf{A}| \neq 0$, $|\mathbf{B}| \neq 0$, and $\mathbf{A}.\mathbf{B} = |\mathbf{A}|\,|\mathbf{B}| \cos\theta$; therefore **A** is perpendicular to **B**.

(b) $\overrightarrow{OP} = \mathbf{A}$ and $\overrightarrow{QR} = \overrightarrow{OR}-\overrightarrow{OQ} = \mathbf{C}-\mathbf{B}$. Since $\overrightarrow{OP}$ and $\overrightarrow{QR}$ are perpendicular

$$\mathbf{A}.(\mathbf{C}-\mathbf{B}) = 0. \tag{1}$$

Again $\overrightarrow{OQ} = \mathbf{B}$ and $\overrightarrow{RP} = \overrightarrow{OP}-\overrightarrow{OR} = \mathbf{A}-\mathbf{C}$.

$$\therefore \mathbf{B}.(\mathbf{A}-\mathbf{C}) = 0. \tag{2}$$

These two relations (1), (2) show that

$$\mathbf{A}.\mathbf{C} = \mathbf{A}.\mathbf{B} = \mathbf{B}.\mathbf{C}.$$

$$\therefore \mathbf{C}.(\mathbf{A}-\mathbf{B}) = 0.$$

But $\mathbf{C} = \overrightarrow{OR}$ and $\mathbf{A}-\mathbf{B} = \overrightarrow{OP}-\overrightarrow{OQ} = \overrightarrow{QP}$. Hence OR and QP are perpendicular.

The work done by a force

Suppose that a constant force **F** of magnitude F acts on a particle and that, while the force is acting, the particle undergoes a displacement from P to P′, Fig. 26.12, and the angle between PP′ and the direction of **F** is θ. Then *by definition* the work, W, done by the force is $F \cos\theta \times PP'$,

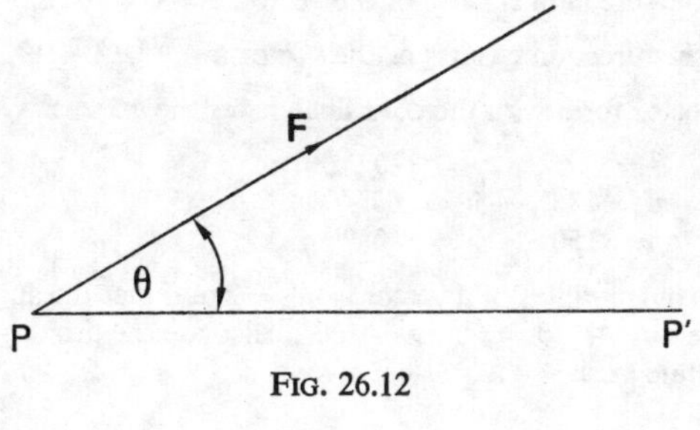

FIG. 26.12

i.e. the magnitude of the displacement multiplied by the resolute of **F** in the direction of the displacement. We can write this result in the form

$$W = \mathbf{F}.\mathbf{x},$$

where
$$\mathbf{x} = \overrightarrow{\mathrm{PP}'}.$$

Example. A particle acted upon by forces of 5 newtons in the direction of the vector $3\mathbf{i}+2\mathbf{j}-6\mathbf{k}$ and 3 newtons in the direction of the vector $2\mathbf{i}+\mathbf{j}-2\mathbf{k}$ is displaced from the point $\mathbf{i}+2\mathbf{j}+3\mathbf{k}$ to the point $5\mathbf{i}+4\mathbf{j}+\mathbf{k}$, the unit of distance being 1 m. Find the total work done by the forces.

Unit vectors along the lines of action of the forces, $\mathbf{F}_1$, $\mathbf{F}_2$, say, are

$$\tfrac{1}{7}(3\mathbf{i}+2\mathbf{j}-6\mathbf{k}). \quad \tfrac{1}{3}(2\mathbf{i}+\mathbf{j}-2\mathbf{k})$$

and so

$$\mathbf{F}_1 = \tfrac{5}{7}(3\mathbf{i}+2\mathbf{j}-6\mathbf{k}), \quad \mathbf{F}_2 = \tfrac{3}{3}(2\mathbf{i}+\mathbf{j}-2\mathbf{k}).$$

The displacement of the particle is

$$\mathbf{x} = (5\mathbf{i}+4\mathbf{j}+\mathbf{k})-(\mathbf{i}+2\mathbf{j}+3\mathbf{k}) = 4\mathbf{i}+2\mathbf{j}-2\mathbf{k}.$$

The work done by the forces in the displacement is

$$\mathbf{F}_1.\mathbf{x}+\mathbf{F}_2.\mathbf{x} = \tfrac{5}{7}(12+4+12)+(8+2+4) \text{ joules}$$
$$= 34 \text{ joules}.$$

EXERCISES 26.7

1. Find the scalar products of the following pairs of vectors:

(i) $3\mathbf{i}+2\mathbf{j}-\mathbf{k}$ and $2\mathbf{i}+3\mathbf{j}-2\mathbf{k}$,
(ii) $4\mathbf{i}-3\mathbf{j}+2\mathbf{k}$ and $-\mathbf{i}+2\mathbf{j}+3\mathbf{k}$,
(iii) $2\mathbf{i}+3\mathbf{j}+4\mathbf{k}$ and $2\mathbf{i}-4\mathbf{j}+2\mathbf{k}$.

2. Calculate the direction cosines of the vector $\mathbf{a} = (12, -15, -16)$.

3. Calculate the direction cosines of the vector $\mathbf{a} = (3/13, 4/13, 12/13)$.

4. Can any vector form with the coordinate axes the angles:

(i) $\alpha = 45°$, $\beta = 60°$, $\gamma = 120°$,
(ii) $\alpha = 45°$, $\beta = 135°$, $\gamma = 60°$,
(iii) $\alpha = 90°$, $\beta = 150°$, $\gamma = 60°$?

5. Given that the modulus of a vector is $|\mathbf{a}| = 2$ and that the angles which it makes with the axes are $\alpha = 45°$, $\beta = 60°$, $\gamma = 120°$, calculate the projections of the vector **a** on to the coordinate axes.

6. If A, B, C and D are four points whose coordinates are $(-2, 1, 1)$, $(3, 2, 2)$, $(1, 1, -2)$, and $(1, 2, 2)$ respectively, calculate the angle between $\overrightarrow{AB}$ and $\overrightarrow{CD}$.

7. Referred to a set of right-handed perpendicular axes with origin O the coordinates of two points P and Q are $P(5, -3, 4)$, $Q(1, 2, -2)$. Determine the direction cosines of $\overrightarrow{PQ}$ and the angle between $\overrightarrow{OP}$ and $\overrightarrow{PQ}$.

8. (a) Show that $\mathbf{A}.\mathbf{A}-\mathbf{B}.\mathbf{B} = (\mathbf{A}+\mathbf{B}).(\mathbf{A}-\mathbf{B})$, where $\mathbf{A}.\mathbf{B}$ denotes the scalar product of the vectors **A** and **B**. If $(\mathbf{C}-\mathbf{A}).\mathbf{A} = (\mathbf{C}-\mathbf{B}).\mathbf{B}$ prove that, in general, $\mathbf{A}-\mathbf{B}$ and $\mathbf{C}-\mathbf{A}-\mathbf{B}$ are perpendicular.

(b) Given that

$$\overrightarrow{OA} = \mathbf{A} = 2\mathbf{i}-3\mathbf{j}+\mathbf{k},$$
$$\overrightarrow{OB} = \mathbf{B} = \mathbf{i}+\mathbf{j}+\mathbf{k},$$
$$\overrightarrow{OC} = \mathbf{C} = 4\mathbf{i}+2\mathbf{j}-2\mathbf{k},$$

where **i**, **j**, **k** are mutually perpendicular unit vectors show that OA is perpendicular to OB and also to OC. (L.)

9. Use vector methods to find the angle between the diagonals of a cube.

10. Show that the line joining the points (1, 2, 3), (0, 1, 2) is perpendicular to the line joining the point (3, 2, 4) to (4, 5, 0).

11. In the plane of the triangle ABC squares ACXY, BCWZ are described, in the order given, externally to the triangle, on AC and BC respectively. Taking $\overrightarrow{CX} = \mathbf{b}$, $\overrightarrow{CA} = \mathbf{a}$, $\overrightarrow{CW} = \mathbf{q}$, $\overrightarrow{CB} = \mathbf{p}$, prove that $\mathbf{a}.\mathbf{p}+\mathbf{q}.\mathbf{b} = 0$. Deduce that $\overrightarrow{AW}.\overrightarrow{BX} = 0$, and state the geometrical meaning of this equation. (N.)

12. The line AB is the common perpendicular to two skew lines AP and BQ, and C and R are the mid-points of AB and PQ respectively. Prove, by vector methods, that CR and AB are perpendicular. (N.)

13. Show that the lines

$$l_1 : \mathbf{r} = (0, 1, 0)+s(1, -1, 1)$$
$$l_2 : \mathbf{r} = (1, -1, 0)+t(1, 1, 1)$$

have no point in common. If A lies on l_1, B lies on l_2 and AB is perpendicular to both l_1 and l_2, find the length of AB and the equation of AB. Find the cartesian equation of:

(i) the plane perpendicular to AB containing l_1,
(ii) the plane perpendicular to AB containing l_2. (N.)

14. The point of application of the force $\mathbf{F} = (-3, 2t, t^2)$ moves along the line $\mathbf{r} = \mathbf{a}+t\mathbf{b}$, where $\mathbf{a} = (5, 8, 4)$, $\mathbf{b} = (3, -4, 3)$. Determine the work done by **F** as t changes from 1 to 3. (N.)

26.8. The Vector Product

The vector product of two vectors **a** and **b** is discussed in § 19.6. This product is defined there as $\mathbf{a}\times\mathbf{b} = \hat{\mathbf{v}}ab \sin\theta$, where $\hat{\mathbf{v}}$ is the unit vector in the direction shown in Fig. 19.10 and is shown to be non-commutative and to obey the distributive law. We add here further properties of the vector product:

(1)
$$\mathbf{a}\times\mathbf{b} = -\mathbf{b}\times\mathbf{a}. \tag{26.37}$$

This follows directly from the definition because the direction of the rotation from **b** to **a** is opposite to that from **a** to **b**, and shows that the vector product is *non-commutative*.

(2) The distributive law

$$\mathbf{a}\times(\mathbf{b}+\mathbf{c}) = \mathbf{a}\times\mathbf{b}+\mathbf{a}\times\mathbf{c}. \tag{26.38}$$

and its generalized form

$$\left(\sum_{i=1}^{m}\mathbf{p}_i\right)\times\left(\sum_{j=1}^{n}\mathbf{q}_j\right) = \sum_{i=1}^{m}\sum_{j=1}^{n}\mathbf{p}_i\times\mathbf{q}_j \tag{26.38a}$$

can be shown to hold for vector products.

(3) If $\mathbf{a}\times\mathbf{b} = \mathbf{0}$, then $|\mathbf{a}|\,|\mathbf{b}|\sin\theta = 0$. Hence, if neither of the vectors is a null vector, $\sin\theta = 0$, i.e. $\theta = 0$ or π and the vectors are parallel.

(4) It follows directly from the definition that $\mathbf{a}\times\mathbf{a} = \mathbf{0}$.

(5) With the usual notation for unit vectors along the coordinate axes

$$\begin{gathered}\mathbf{i}\times\mathbf{i} = \mathbf{0}, \quad \mathbf{j}\times\mathbf{j} = \mathbf{0}, \quad \mathbf{k}\times\mathbf{k} = \mathbf{0},\\ \mathbf{i}\times\mathbf{j} = \mathbf{k} = -\mathbf{j}\times\mathbf{i}, \quad \mathbf{j}\times\mathbf{k} = \mathbf{i} = -\mathbf{k}\times\mathbf{j},\\ \mathbf{k}\times\mathbf{i} = \mathbf{j} = -\mathbf{i}\times\mathbf{k}.\end{gathered} \tag{26.39}$$

(6) When we express $\mathbf{a}\times\mathbf{b}$ in terms of components by use of equations (26.38a), (26.39) we see that

$$\begin{aligned}\mathbf{a}\times\mathbf{b} &= (a_1\mathbf{i}+a_2\mathbf{j}+a_3\mathbf{k})\times(b_1\mathbf{i}+b_2\mathbf{j}+b_3\mathbf{k})\\ &= \mathbf{i}(a_2b_3-a_3b_2)+\mathbf{j}(a_3b_1-a_1b_3)+\mathbf{k}(a_1b_2-a_2b_1).\end{aligned} \tag{26.40}$$

This is frequently written as a determinant

$$\mathbf{a}\times\mathbf{b} = \begin{vmatrix}\mathbf{i} & \mathbf{j} & \mathbf{k}\\ a_1 & a_2 & a_3\\ b_1 & b_2 & b_3\end{vmatrix} \tag{26.40a}$$

of which (26.40) is the expansion. Reversing the positions of the rows of this determinant changes the sign and shows the *non-commutative* property of the vector product $\mathbf{a}\times\mathbf{b}$.

Example 1. If $\mathbf{a} = 2\mathbf{i}-3\mathbf{j}+4\mathbf{k}$, $\mathbf{b} = 3\mathbf{i}+4\mathbf{j}-7\mathbf{k}$, then

$$\mathbf{a}\times\mathbf{b} = \begin{vmatrix} \mathbf{i} & \mathbf{j} & \mathbf{k} \\ 2 & -3 & 4 \\ 3 & 4 & -7 \end{vmatrix}$$

$$= 5\mathbf{i}+26\mathbf{j}+17\mathbf{k}.$$

Example 2.
$$\begin{aligned}(\mathbf{a}\times\mathbf{b})^2 &= |\mathbf{a}\times\mathbf{b}|^2 = a^2b^2\sin^2\theta = a^2b^2-a^2b^2\cos^2\theta \\ &= (a_1^2+a_2^2+a_3^2)(b_1^2+b_2^2+b_3^2)-(a_1b_1+a_2b_2+a_3b_3)^2 \\ &= \mathbf{a}^2\mathbf{b}^2-(\mathbf{a}.\mathbf{b})^2.\end{aligned}$$

But

$$\mathbf{a}\times\mathbf{b} = (a_2b_3-a_3b_2)\mathbf{i}+(a_3b_1-a_1b_3)\mathbf{j}+(a_1b_2-a_2b_1)\mathbf{k},$$

$$\therefore\ (\mathbf{a}\times\mathbf{b})^2 = (a_2b_3-a_3b_2)^2+(a_3b_1-a_1b_3)^2+(a_1b_2-a_2b_1)^2.$$

Hence

$$(a_1^2+a_2^2+a_3^2)(b_1^2+b_2^2+b_3^2)-(a_1b_1+a_2b_2+a_3b_3)^2$$
$$= (a_2b_3-a_3b_2)^2+(a_3b_1-a_1b_3)^2+(a_1b_2-a_2b_1)^2.$$

Since **a** and **b** are arbitrary vectors their components may have any values whatever. The last relation is known as *Lagrange's identity*.

Example 3. Find the unit vector perpendicular to both $2\mathbf{i}-\mathbf{j}+\mathbf{k}$ and $3\mathbf{i}+4\mathbf{j}-\mathbf{k}$.

The vector product of the two vectors has the required direction. Let

$$\mathbf{a} = (2\mathbf{i}-\mathbf{j}+\mathbf{k})\times(3\mathbf{i}+4\mathbf{j}-\mathbf{k}) = -3\mathbf{i}+5\mathbf{j}+11\mathbf{k}.$$

Hence the required unit vector is

$$\hat{\mathbf{a}} = \frac{\mathbf{a}}{|\mathbf{a}|} = \frac{-3\mathbf{i}+5\mathbf{j}+11\mathbf{k}}{(9+25+121)^{1/2}} = -\frac{3\mathbf{i}}{\sqrt{155}}+\frac{5\mathbf{j}}{\sqrt{155}}+\frac{11\mathbf{k}}{\sqrt{155}}.$$

Example 4. Find in standard form the equation of the line of intersection of the two planes

$$x+6y+z+15 = 0, \quad 3x+2y-z+1 = 0.$$

We solve this problem by two methods.

1. In vector notation the planes are given by

$$\mathbf{r}.(\mathbf{i}+6\mathbf{j}+\mathbf{k}) = -15, \quad \mathbf{r}.(3\mathbf{i}+2\mathbf{j}-\mathbf{k}) = -1.$$

The direction of the line of intersection of these planes is perpendicular to the two vectors which are normal to the planes, i.e. it is parallel to the vector product of these two (normal) vectors. Hence the line has the direction of the vector

$$(\mathbf{i}+6\mathbf{j}+\mathbf{k})\times(3\mathbf{i}+2\mathbf{j}-\mathbf{k}) = -8\mathbf{i}+4\mathbf{j}-16\mathbf{k}.$$

The unit vector in this direction is

$$(-2\mathbf{i}+\mathbf{j}-4\mathbf{k})/\sqrt{21}.$$

Either by inspection, or by finding the intersection with, say, $z = 0$, we must now find one point on the line. A trial shows that $2\mathbf{i}-3\mathbf{j}+\mathbf{k}$ (or $x = 2$, $y = -3$, $z = 1$) satisfies the equations of both planes. Hence, the equation of the line is

$$\mathbf{r} = (2\mathbf{i}-3\mathbf{j}+\mathbf{k})+\lambda(-2\mathbf{i}+\mathbf{j}-4\mathbf{k})$$

where λ is a variable scalar.

If we put $z = 0$ in the equations of the planes and solve for x, y we obtain

$$x = 3/2, \quad y = -11/4,$$

so that the equation of the line becomes

$$\mathbf{r} = (6\mathbf{i}-11\mathbf{j})/4+\mu(-2\mathbf{i}+\mathbf{j}-4\mathbf{k}).$$

(The variable μ is related to λ by $\mu = \lambda-1/4$.)

2. The second method regards the equations of the planes as simultaneous equations in x, y which we solve, finding x, y in terms of z. Thus we write the given equations in the form

$$\frac{x}{-6(z-1)-2(z+15)} = \frac{y}{3(z+15)+(z-1)} = \frac{1}{2-18}.$$

$$\therefore\ x = \tfrac{1}{2}z+\tfrac{3}{2}, \quad y = -\tfrac{1}{4}z-\tfrac{11}{4}.$$

This solution, in which z can be given any value, gives corresponding values of x, y, z for points on the line of intersection. We can obtain a vector form by writing

$$\mathbf{r} = x\mathbf{i}+y\mathbf{j}+z\mathbf{k} = z\left(\frac{\mathbf{i}}{2}-\frac{\mathbf{j}}{4}+\mathbf{k}\right)+\frac{3\mathbf{i}}{2}-\frac{11\mathbf{j}}{4},$$

Since z is arbitrary we write $z = -4\mu$ on the r.h. side and obtain

$$\mathbf{r} = \frac{3\mathbf{i}}{2}-\frac{11\mathbf{j}}{4}-\mu(2\mathbf{i}-\mathbf{j}+4\mathbf{k}),$$

as before.

The process of solving for x, y is equivalent to the operation of finding the vector product in the former method.

We now give some important applications of the vector product.

(a) *Plane Areas in Three Dimensions*

In *Pure Maths.*, Vol. II, § 11.11 we pointed out that a positive or negative sign can be given to the area of a triangle according to the sense of rotation in which its vertices are enumerated. Using vector products leads to the concept of the *vector area* of a triangle. The magnitude of the vector product $\overrightarrow{OA}\times\overrightarrow{OB}$ is OA . OB sin $\theta = 2\Delta$, where Δ is the area of the triangle OAB. Writing the vector product $\overrightarrow{OA}\times\overrightarrow{OB}$ gives a sense of rotation O → A → B around the triangle (see Fig. 26.13). This sense of rotation is linked by the r.h. corkscrew rule with the positive direction of $\overrightarrow{OA}\times\overrightarrow{OB}$. Therefore, we ascribe a vector area **S** to the triangle OAB given by

$$\mathbf{S} = \tfrac{1}{2}(\overrightarrow{OA}\times\overrightarrow{OB}). \tag{26.41}$$

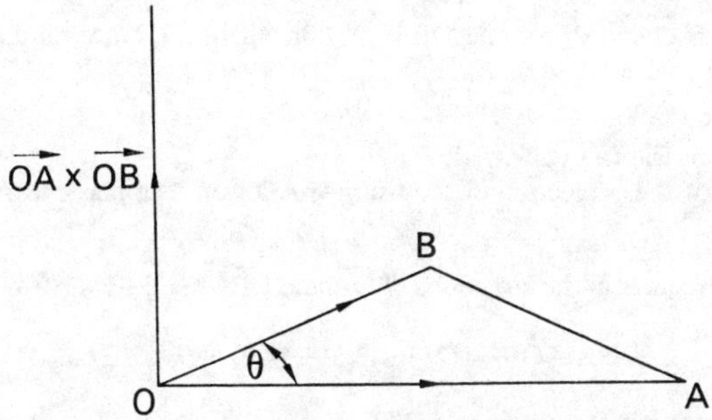

FIG. 26.13

In using a directed line segment as a vector we prescribe the positive sense along the line and obtain the components by orthogonal projection of the *line* segment on the *coordinate lines* (or axes) of the frame of reference. In representing a directed area by a vector the positive sense of rotation around the perimeter is prescribed and we obtain the components by orthogonal projection of the *area* segment on the *coordinate planes.* Our investigation has shown that the vector product gives the vector area **S** for the special shape of a triangle, in terms of the line segments which constitute two of its sides, by formula (26.41). Similarly if ABCD is a parallelogram its vector area is $\overrightarrow{AB}\times\overrightarrow{AD}$.

Example 1. If A, B are the points with position vectors $2\mathbf{i}-3\mathbf{j}+4\mathbf{k}$, $3\mathbf{i}+4\mathbf{j}-7\mathbf{k}$ respectively, then, by example 1, p. 779,

$$\overrightarrow{OA}\times\overrightarrow{OB} = 5\mathbf{i}+26\mathbf{j}+17\mathbf{k}.$$

The area of the triangle OAB is therefore

$$\tfrac{1}{2}\,|\,\overrightarrow{OA}\times\overrightarrow{OB}\,| = \tfrac{1}{2}\sqrt{(5^2+26^2+17^2)} = \tfrac{1}{2}\sqrt{(990)}.$$

Example 2. A triangle is projected orthogonally onto a plane which is perpendicular to the direction $\hat{\mathbf{n}}$; find the area of the projection.

Since no frame of reference is specified, we choose a frame such that the coordinate plane Oyz is parallel to the given plane. Then $\hat{\mathbf{n}} \equiv \mathbf{k}$. The area of the projected triangle is $S_3 = \mathbf{S}.\mathbf{k} = \mathbf{S}.\hat{\mathbf{n}}$. The last form does not involve the frame of reference and therefore is true in general. Hence the projected area is $\mathbf{S}.\hat{\mathbf{n}}$.

Example 3. If $\overrightarrow{OA} = 2\mathbf{j}+\mathbf{k}$ and $\overrightarrow{OB} = 2\mathbf{i}+3\mathbf{j}$, where **i**, **j**, **k** are mutually orthogonal unit vectors, calculate

(a) cos AOB,

(b) the area of the triangle OAB,

(c) the area of the projection of the triangle AOB on to a plane normal to the unit vector **k**. (L.)

(a) The unit vectors in the directions of $\overrightarrow{OA}$ and $\overrightarrow{OB}$ are $(2\mathbf{j}+\mathbf{k})/\sqrt{5}$ and $(2\mathbf{i}+3\mathbf{j})/\sqrt{13}$ respectively.

$$\therefore\ \cos AOB = (2\mathbf{j}+\mathbf{k}).(2\mathbf{i}+3\mathbf{j})/\sqrt{65} = 6/\sqrt{65}.$$

(b) The vector area of the triangle OAB is

$$\mathbf{S} = \tfrac{1}{2}(2\mathbf{j}+\mathbf{k})\times(2\mathbf{i}+3\mathbf{j}) = \tfrac{1}{2}(-3\mathbf{i}+2\mathbf{j}-4\mathbf{k}).$$

$$\therefore\ |\mathbf{S}| = S = \tfrac{1}{2}(9+4+16)^{1/2} = \tfrac{1}{2}\sqrt{29}.$$

(c) The area of projection is $\mathbf{S}.\mathbf{k} = -2$. (The negative sign means that the sense of rotation OAB on the projected figure is the negative sense, $Oy \rightarrow Ox$, in the plane $z = 0$.)

Example 4. A tetrahedron has its vertices at A(0, 0, 1), B(3, 0, 1), C(2, 3, 1), and D(1, 1, 2). Find the angles between the faces ABC and BCD, between the edges AB, AC, and between the edge BC and the face ADC. (L.)

The vectors representing the edges are

$$\overrightarrow{AB} = 3\mathbf{i},\quad \overrightarrow{AC} = 2\mathbf{i}+3\mathbf{j},\quad \overrightarrow{BC} = -\mathbf{i}+3\mathbf{j},\quad \overrightarrow{BD} = -2\mathbf{i}+\mathbf{j}+\mathbf{k}.$$

Therefore the vector areas of the faces ABC and BCD are, respectively,

$$\mathbf{S}_1 = \tfrac{1}{2}3\mathbf{i}\times(2\mathbf{i}+3\mathbf{j}) = \tfrac{9}{2}\mathbf{k},$$
$$\mathbf{S}_2 = \tfrac{1}{2}(-\mathbf{i}+3\mathbf{j})\times(-2\mathbf{i}+\mathbf{j}+\mathbf{k}) = \tfrac{1}{2}(3\mathbf{i}+\mathbf{j}+5\mathbf{k}).$$

The unit vectors normal to these faces are respectively

$$\mathbf{n}_1 = \mathbf{k} \quad \text{and} \quad \hat{\mathbf{n}}_2 = (3\mathbf{i}+\mathbf{j}+5\mathbf{k})/\sqrt{35}.$$

The angle α between the faces is given by

$$\cos\alpha = \hat{\mathbf{n}}_1.\hat{\mathbf{n}}_2 = 5/\sqrt{35} = \sqrt{(5/7)}.$$

Unit vectors along the edges AB, AC are respectively

$$\mathbf{i},\ (2\mathbf{i}+3\mathbf{j})/\sqrt{13}.$$

Therefore the angle β between the edges is given by

$$\cos\beta = \mathbf{i}.(2\mathbf{i}+3\mathbf{j})/\sqrt{13} = 2/\sqrt{13}.$$

The vector area of the face ADC is $\mathbf{S}_3 = \tfrac{1}{2}\overrightarrow{AD}\times\overrightarrow{AC} = \tfrac{1}{2}(\mathbf{i}+\mathbf{j}+\mathbf{k})\times(2\mathbf{i}+3\mathbf{j}) = \tfrac{1}{2}(-3\mathbf{i}+2\mathbf{j}+\mathbf{k})$, and the unit normal to this face is $\hat{\mathbf{n}}_3 = (-3\mathbf{i}+2\mathbf{j}+\mathbf{k})/\sqrt{14}$. The unit vector along BC is $(-\mathbf{i}+3\mathbf{j})/\sqrt{10}$, and therefore the angle between BC and the normal to ADC is γ where

$$\cos\gamma = (-\mathbf{i}+3\mathbf{j}).(-3\mathbf{i}+2\mathbf{j}+\mathbf{k})/\sqrt{140} = 9/\sqrt{140}.$$

Hence the angle between BC and the plane ADC is $\pi/2-\gamma$, i.e. $\sin^{-1}(9/\sqrt{140})$.

(b) *The Equation of a Plane*

In § 26.6 (c) the equation of a plane was obtained in the form

$$\mathbf{r} = \mathbf{a}+s\mathbf{b}+t\mathbf{c}. \tag{26.42}$$

The use of a vector product associates a plane area with a vector perpendicular to the plane. Suppose that $\hat{\mathbf{n}}$ is a unit vector normal to a plane (the unit normal) and $\mathbf{r}$ is the position vector of an arbitrary point P on the plane; N is the foot of the perpendicular from O to the plane. Figure 26.14, which is a section of a three-dimensional figure, indicates that

$$\mathbf{r}.\hat{\mathbf{n}} = p, \tag{26.43}$$

where p = ON is the perpendicular distance of O from the plane. If the sense O → N is the same as that of $\hat{\mathbf{n}}$, p is positive (or O is on the *negative*

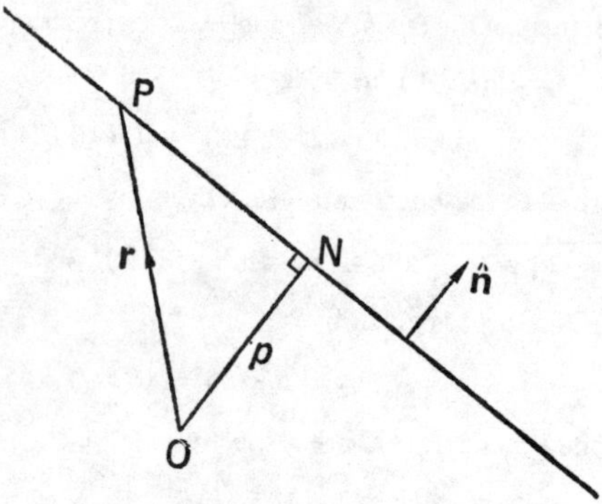

FIG. 26.14

side of the plane); if the sense O → N is opposite to that of $\hat{\mathbf{n}}$, then p is negative. Equation (26.43) is the *normal* form for the equation of a plane and, when expressed in cartesian components, becomes

$$lx+my+nz = p \tag{26.44}$$

where $\hat{\mathbf{n}} = \mathbf{i}l+\mathbf{j}m+\mathbf{k}n$, i.e. (l, m, n) are the direction cosines of the normal to the plane. If the direction ratios of the normal to the plane are $a:b:c$ so that $\mathbf{n} = a\mathbf{i}+b\mathbf{j}+c\mathbf{k}$, then equations (26.43) and (26.44) can be written

$$\mathbf{r}.\mathbf{n} = q, \tag{26.45}$$

$$ax+by+cz = q. \tag{26.46}$$

The connection between the forms (26.43) or (26.44) and the form (26.23) for the equation of a plane is obtained by the use of a vector product. In equation (26.23) the vectors **b** and **c** lie in the plane so that the vector product

$$\mathbf{n} = \mathbf{b}\times\mathbf{c} \quad \text{or} \quad \hat{\mathbf{n}} = (\mathbf{b}\times\mathbf{c})/(bc \sin \theta) \tag{26.47}$$

is normal to the plane because the vector product is perpendicular to both **b** and **c** by definition. Therefore,

$$\mathbf{r}.\mathbf{n} = \mathbf{a}.\mathbf{n}+s(\mathbf{b}.\mathbf{n})+t(\mathbf{c}.\mathbf{n}) = \mathbf{a}.\mathbf{n},$$

i.e.

$$\mathbf{r}.\mathbf{n} = q,$$

since $\mathbf{b}.\mathbf{n} = 0 = \mathbf{c}.\mathbf{n}$ and we have written $\mathbf{a}.\mathbf{n} = q$. Division by $|\mathbf{n}| = bc \sin \theta$ gives the form (26.43).

Example. Find the perpendicular distance from a point A, position vector $\mathbf{r}_0$, to the plane $\mathbf{r}.\hat{\mathbf{n}} = p$. Interpret the sign of the result and express the distance in terms of cartesian coordinates.

The equation of the plane through A parallel to the given plane is $(\mathbf{r}-\mathbf{r}_0).\hat{\mathbf{n}} = 0$. The equations of the planes are therefore $\mathbf{r}.\hat{\mathbf{n}} = \mathbf{r}_0.\hat{\mathbf{n}}$ and $\mathbf{r}.\hat{\mathbf{n}} = p$. Therefore (see Fig. 26.15), OM $= \mathbf{r}_0.\hat{\mathbf{n}}$ and ON $= p$. Hence the required perpendicular distance is

$$\text{MN} = \text{ON}-\text{OM} = p-\mathbf{r}_0.\hat{\mathbf{n}}. \tag{1}$$

MN is positive if it is drawn in the positive sense of $\hat{\mathbf{n}}$.

The cartesian form of equation (1) is

$$\text{MN} = p-(lx_0+my_0+nz_0),$$

where (l, m, n) are the direction cosines of the normal $\hat{\mathbf{n}}$ and (x_0, y_0, z_0) are the coordinates of A.

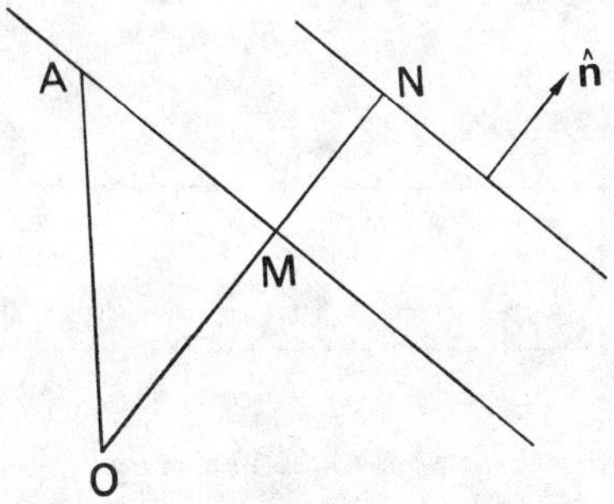

FIG. 26.15

Using the notation of equations (26.45) and (26.46) the perpendicular distance of the point $\mathbf{r}_0$ from the plane $\mathbf{r}.\mathbf{n} = q$ is easily shown to be

$$(q-\mathbf{r}_0.\mathbf{n})/|\mathbf{n}| = \{q-(ax_0+by_0+cz_0)\}/\sqrt{(a^2+b^2+c^2)}.$$

(c) *The Moment of a Force*

In elementary two-dimensional mechanics the moment of a force about a point (or, more precisely, the turning-moment of the force about an axis through that point perpendicular to the plane containing the force and the point) is defined as the product pF, where F is the magnitude of the force and p is the perpendicular distance of its line of action from the point. This moment is represented by twice the area of the triangle OAB, which has O as a vertex and its base AB, of length F, on the line of action of the

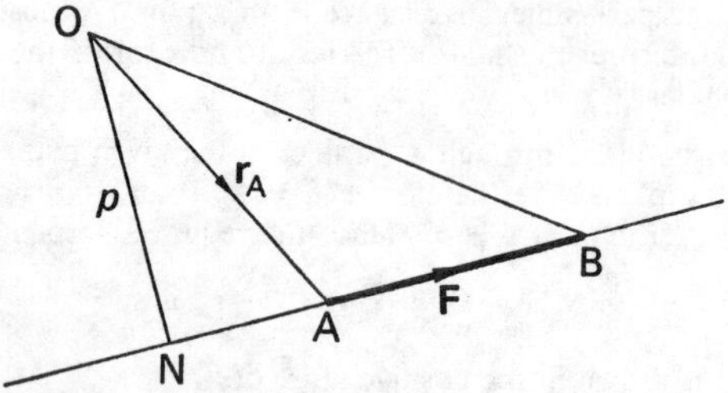

FIG. 26.16

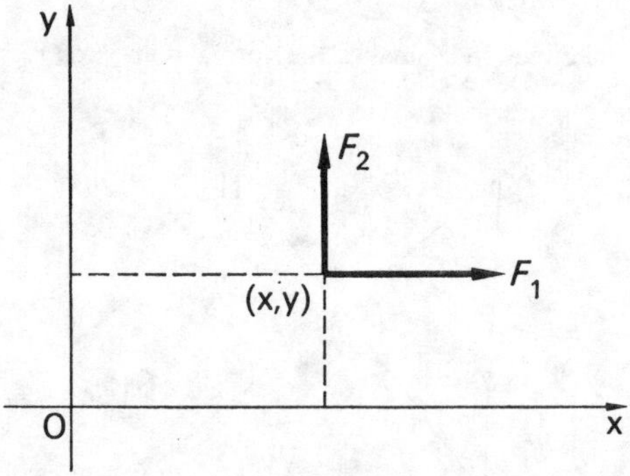

FIG. 26.17

force. We now extend this definition to three dimensions. Suppose that (Fig. 26.16) O represents the origin of position vectors and **F** is an arbitrary force (line-vector). If $\mathbf{r}_A$ is the position vector of any point A on the line of action then the vector $\mathbf{M} = \mathbf{r}_A \times \mathbf{F}$ is twice the vector area of the triangle OAB. The magnitude of $\mathbf{r}_A \times \mathbf{F}$ is the turning-moment of **F** about an axis through O perpendicular to OAB. We notice that $\mathbf{r}_A$ may be replaced by the position vector **r** of any other point on the line of action, for

$$\mathbf{r} = \mathbf{r}_A + t\mathbf{F},$$

and

$$\mathbf{r} \times \mathbf{F} = (\mathbf{r}_A + t\mathbf{F}) \times \mathbf{F} = \mathbf{r}_A \times \mathbf{F} = \mathbf{M}. \tag{26.48}$$

Let us consider the turning-moment of **F** about the axis Oz. The component, F_3, parallel to this axis will have no turning-moment. The remaining two components will give a turning-moment (see Fig. 26.17)

$$xF_2 - yF_1$$

about Oz, where $(x, y, 0)$ are the coordinates of the point of intersection of **F** with Oxy. This turning-moment is the component M_3 of the vector **M** in equation (26.48).

Thus, by using a vector product we introduce the *vector moment of a force about a point*, which has been defined in such a way that its component in any direction is the turning-moment of the force about a line through the point drawn in the given direction. In general, the turning-moment L of **F** about a line through **a** drawn in a direction $\hat{\mathbf{l}}$ is defined by

$$L = \{(\mathbf{r}-\mathbf{a})\times\mathbf{F}\}.\hat{\mathbf{l}} \tag{26.49}$$

where **r** is any point on the line of action of **F**. As is usual with vector products the order of the factors in (26.48) or (26.49) is important; the position vector of a point on the line of action of **F** comes before **F** in equation (26.48).

Example. A force **F** has components $(7, 2, -3)$ and acts through the point B $(4, 2, 6)$; a line l passes through the point A $(1, 2, 4)$ and has direction ratios $(2, 3, -2)$. Find the moment of **F** about l.

The moment of **F** about **A** is

$$\mathbf{M} = \overrightarrow{\mathrm{AB}}\times\mathbf{F} = (3\mathbf{i}+0\mathbf{j}+2\mathbf{k})\times(7\mathbf{i}+2\mathbf{j}-3\mathbf{k}) = (-4\mathbf{i}+23\mathbf{j}+6\mathbf{k}).$$

A unit vector along the direction of the line l is $\hat{\mathbf{l}} = (2\mathbf{i}+3\mathbf{j}-2\mathbf{k})/\sqrt{17}$.

Hence the moment **F** about l is $\mathbf{M}.\hat{\mathbf{l}} = 49/\sqrt{17}$.

EXERCISES 26.8

1. If $\mathbf{A} = \mathbf{i}-2\mathbf{j}$ and $\mathbf{B} = 2\mathbf{i}+5\mathbf{j}-4\mathbf{k}$ find a unit vector perpendicular to the plane of **A** and **B**.

2. The vertices O, P, Q, R of a tetrahedron have coordinates (0, 0, 0), (2, 1, 1), (1, 2, 2) and (0, 0, 3) respectively, referred to rectangular cartesian axes. Find by vector methods

(i) the angle between the planes OPR, OQR,
(ii) the angle between the line OP and the plane PQR,
(iii) the area of the face PQR. (L.)

3. Referred to a set of right-handed perpendicular axes with origin O the coordinates of three points A, B, C are (1, 2, −1), (2, 4, 1), (−1, 3, 4) respectively. Find (i) the cosine of the angle between AB and AC, and (ii) the area of the triangle ABC. (L.)

4. A, B and C are points with coordinates (1, 2, 3), (2, 4, 1) and (3, 3, 1) respectively, referred to a right-handed system of rectangular axes. Find the scalar product $\overrightarrow{AB} . \overrightarrow{AC}$ and the components of the vector product $\overrightarrow{AB} \times \overrightarrow{AC}$. Hence find the angle between $\overrightarrow{AB}$ and $\overrightarrow{AC}$ and the area of the triangle ABC.

5. Prove, by the use of vectors, that the lines joining the mid-points of opposite sides of a skew quadrilateral (i.e. whose sides do not lie in one plane) bisect each other.

If **a, b, c, d** are the sides of a skew quadrilateral taken in order, show that the area of the parallelogram formed by the mid-points of the sides is equal to the magnitude of

$$\tfrac{1}{4}(\mathbf{c}\times\mathbf{b}+\mathbf{d}\times\mathbf{c}+\mathbf{d}\times\mathbf{b}).$$

6. Find the equation of the plane which goes through the point (3, −2, −7) and is parallel to the plane given by $2x-3z+5 = 0$.

7. Find the equation of the plane which goes through the point (2, 1, −1) and has a normal vector $\mathbf{n} = (1, -2, 3)$.

8. Find the equation of the plane which goes through the origin and has a normal vector $\mathbf{n} = (5, 0, -3)$.

9. The point $P(2, -1, -1)$ is the foot of the perpendicular from the origin on to a certain plane. Find the equation of the plane.

10. Find the equation of the plane which goes through the two points (2, −1, 3), (3, 1, 2) and which is parallel to the vector $\mathbf{a} = (3, -1, -4)$.

11. The points P, Q, R have coordinates (1, 1, 1), (1, 3, 2), (2, 1, 3) respectively, referred to rectangular axes Oxyz. Calculate the products $\overrightarrow{PQ} . \overrightarrow{PR}$, $\overrightarrow{PQ} \times \overrightarrow{PR}$ and deduce the values of the cosine of the angle QPR and the area of the triangle PQR. (N.)

12. If **p** and **q** are non-null vectors such that the vector product $\mathbf{p}\times\mathbf{q} = \mathbf{0}$, show that $\mathbf{p} = \lambda\mathbf{q}$ where λ is a scalar.

Three vectors **a, b, c** are such that

(i) $\mathbf{b}\times\mathbf{c} = \mathbf{c}\times\mathbf{a} \neq \mathbf{0}$,

prove that

(ii) $\mathbf{a}+\mathbf{b} = k\mathbf{c}$,

where k is a scalar. If also

(iii) $\mathbf{a}\times\mathbf{b} = \mathbf{b}\times\mathbf{c} = \mathbf{c}\times\mathbf{a} \neq \mathbf{0}$

prove that

(iv) $\mathbf{a}+\mathbf{b}+\mathbf{c} = \mathbf{0}$.

Give geometrical interpretations of equations (iii) and (iv). (N.)

13. (i) Define the scalar and vector products of two vectors **a**, **b** in terms of a, b and the angle θ between the vectors, explaining carefully any sign conventions used.

Deduce the formula

$$|\mathbf{a}\times\mathbf{b}|^2 = a^2b^2-(\mathbf{a}\cdot\mathbf{b})^2.$$

(ii) Find the most general form for the vector **u** when

$$\mathbf{u}\times(\mathbf{i}+\mathbf{j}+2\mathbf{k}) = \mathbf{i}-\mathbf{j}. \qquad \text{(N.)}$$

14. Three vectors **a**, **b** and **c** are such that $\mathbf{a} \neq \mathbf{0}$ and

$$\mathbf{a}\times\mathbf{b} = 2\mathbf{a}\times\mathbf{c}.$$

Show that

$$\mathbf{b}-2\mathbf{c} = \lambda\mathbf{a},$$

where λ is a scalar.
Given that

$$|\mathbf{a}| = |\mathbf{c}| = 1, \quad |\mathbf{b}| = 4,$$

and the angle between **b** and **c** is $\cos^{-1}(\frac{1}{4})$, show that

$$\lambda = +4 \quad \text{or} \quad -4.$$

For each of these cases find the cosine of the angle between **a** and **c**. (N.)

15. Calculate the moment about the point C (1, 1, 1) of a force of 5 newtons acting along the line $\overrightarrow{AB}$, where A, B are the points (2, 3, 4), (3, 5, 6) respectively, the distances being measured in metres. (N.)

26.9. Triple Products

(a) *The Triple Scalar Product*

This is the scalar product of a vector **a** and the vector product $\mathbf{b}\times\mathbf{c}$, i.e. $\mathbf{a}\cdot\mathbf{b}\times\mathbf{c}$ or $\mathbf{b}\times\mathbf{c}\cdot\mathbf{a}$. Because the vector product is non-commutative

$$\mathbf{a}\cdot\mathbf{b}\times\mathbf{c} = -\mathbf{a}\cdot\mathbf{c}\times\mathbf{b} = -\mathbf{c}\times\mathbf{b}\cdot\mathbf{a}. \qquad (26.50)$$

Using formulae (26.39) and (26.40) we find

$$\mathbf{a}\cdot\mathbf{b}\times\mathbf{c} = \mathbf{a}\times\mathbf{b}\cdot\mathbf{c} = \begin{vmatrix} a_1 & a_2 & a_3 \\ b_1 & b_2 & b_3 \\ c_1 & c_2 & c_3 \end{vmatrix} = \Delta. \qquad (26.51)$$

We can form similar triple scalar products from the same three vectors using $\mathbf{c}\times\mathbf{a}$ with **b**, and $\mathbf{a}\times\mathbf{b}$ with **c** and we find that all the possible triple scalar products formed when the cyclic order of the factors **a**, **b**, **c** is maintained are equal to Δ. Those in which the cyclic order is reversed are equal to $-\Delta$. (This corresponds to one of the properties of a determinant.) The complete list of products is

$$\begin{aligned}\Delta &= \mathbf{a}\times\mathbf{b}\,.\,\mathbf{c} = \mathbf{b}\times\mathbf{c}\,.\,\mathbf{a} = \mathbf{c}\times\mathbf{a}\,.\,\mathbf{b}\\ &= \mathbf{a}\,.\,\mathbf{b}\times\mathbf{c} = \mathbf{b}\,.\,\mathbf{c}\times\mathbf{a} = \mathbf{c}\,.\,\mathbf{a}\times\mathbf{b}\end{aligned} \tag{26.52}$$

and

$$\begin{aligned}-\Delta &= \mathbf{a}\times\mathbf{c}\,.\,\mathbf{b} = \mathbf{b}\times\mathbf{a}\,.\,\mathbf{c} = \mathbf{c}\times\mathbf{b}\,.\,\mathbf{a}\\ &= \mathbf{a}\,.\,\mathbf{c}\times\mathbf{b} = \mathbf{b}\,.\,\mathbf{a}\times\mathbf{c} = \mathbf{c}\,.\,\mathbf{b}\times\mathbf{a}\end{aligned} \tag{26.53}$$

These formulae show that the positions of the "dot" and "cross" product signs within the triple product may be interchanged.

We now give a direct geometrical interpretation of the triple scalar product. Suppose that the three vectors **a**, **b**, **c** represent three concurrent edges of a parallelepiped, Fig. 26.18. Then the vector product $\mathbf{b}\times\mathbf{c}$ represents the vector area of one face and the triple product $\mathbf{a}\,.\,\mathbf{b}\times\mathbf{c}$ gives the volume of the parallelepiped. If **a** points towards the positive side of the face OBC the volume is positive. The other triple products with the same cyclic order give the volume of the same figure, the evaluation starting with a different face. Reversal of the cyclic order changes the sign of the volume because it interchanges the positive and negative sides of the face OBC (or of whichever face is being used). This result is also stated by saying that, if $\mathbf{a}\,.\,\mathbf{b}\times\mathbf{c}$ is positive, then the three vectors form a *right-handed* triad; if $\mathbf{a}\,.\,\mathbf{b}\times\mathbf{c}$ is negative, they form a *left-handed triad.* The vectors **a**, **b**, **c** form a right-handed triad if the figure OABC can be continuously deformed, by altering the angles at O by amounts less than $\frac{1}{2}\pi$ without altering the sense of any of the vectors, so that OA, OB, OC coincide with the positive directions of a r.h. rectangular frame of reference.

If the triangle OBC is taken as the base of a tetrahedron whose opposite vertex is A, then the volume of the tetrahedron is

$$V = \tfrac{1}{3}\mathbf{a}\,.\,[\tfrac{1}{2}(\mathbf{b}\times\mathbf{c})] = \tfrac{1}{6}(\mathbf{a}\,.\,\mathbf{b}\times\mathbf{c}). \tag{26.54}$$

The same considerations apply to the sign of this volume as to the volume of the parallelepiped. If the points A, B, C, D have coordinates

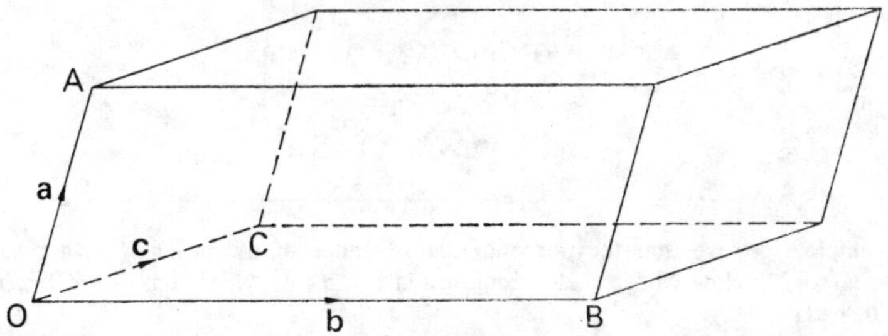

FIG. 26.18

(x_1, y_1, z_1), (x_2, y_2, z_2), (x_3, y_3, z_3), (x_4, y_4, z_4) respectively, then the volume of the tetrahedron ABCD is

$$V = \tfrac{1}{6}\overrightarrow{AB}.\overrightarrow{AC}\times\overrightarrow{AD} = \frac{1}{6}\begin{vmatrix} x_2-x_1 & y_2-y_1 & z_2-z_1 \\ x_3-x_1 & y_3-y_1 & z_3-z_1 \\ x_4-x_1 & y_4-y_1 & z_4-z_1 \end{vmatrix}, \qquad (26.54a)$$

i.e.

$$V = \frac{1}{6}\begin{vmatrix} 1 & x_1 & y_1 & z_1 \\ 1 & x_2 & y_2 & z_2 \\ 1 & x_3 & y_3 & z_3 \\ 1 & x_4 & y_4 & z_4 \end{vmatrix} \qquad (26.54b)$$

where, in each case, the numerical value of the determinant gives the scalar volume of the tetrahedron.

Example 1. The edges OP, OQ, OR of a tetrahedron OPQR are the vectors **A**, **B** and **C** respectively, where $\mathbf{A} = 2\mathbf{i}+4\mathbf{j}$, $\mathbf{B} = 2\mathbf{i}-\mathbf{j}+3\mathbf{k}$ and $\mathbf{C} = 4\mathbf{i}-2\mathbf{j}+5\mathbf{k}$. Evaluate $\mathbf{B}\times\mathbf{C}$ and deduce that OP is perpendicular to the plane OQR.

Write down the length of OP and the area of the triangle OQR and hence the volume of the tetrahedron. Verify your result by evaluating $\mathbf{A}.(\mathbf{B}\times\mathbf{C})$. (L.)

$$\mathbf{B}\times\mathbf{C} = (2\mathbf{i}-\mathbf{j}+3\mathbf{k})\times(4\mathbf{i}-2\mathbf{j}+5\mathbf{k}) = \mathbf{i}+2\mathbf{j} = \tfrac{1}{2}\mathbf{A}.$$

Now $\mathbf{B}\times\mathbf{C}$ is perpendicular to the plane OQR; therefore the vector **A**, and hence also OP, are perpendicular to the plane OQR.

The length $OP = |\overrightarrow{OP}| = |\mathbf{A}| = 2\sqrt{5}$. Also $|\mathbf{B}\times\mathbf{C}| = \sqrt{5}$ so that the area of the triangle OQR is $\frac{1}{2}\sqrt{5}$. Hence the volume of the tetrahedron is

$$\tfrac{1}{3}\text{OP}.(\text{area OQR}) = \tfrac{1}{3}(2\sqrt{5})(\tfrac{1}{2}\sqrt{5}) = \tfrac{5}{3}.$$

Also

$$\mathbf{A}.\mathbf{B}\times\mathbf{C} = \begin{vmatrix} 2 & 4 & 0 \\ 2 & -1 & 3 \\ 4 & -2 & 5 \end{vmatrix} = 10.$$

$$\therefore\ V = \tfrac{1}{6}(\mathbf{A}.\mathbf{B}\times\mathbf{C}) = \tfrac{5}{3}.$$

Example 2. Prove that the perpendicular distance of the point A with position vector $\mathbf{a}$ from the line whose vector equation is $\mathbf{r} = \mathbf{b}+\lambda\hat{\mathbf{e}}$, where $\hat{\mathbf{e}}$ is a unit vector, is $|(\mathbf{a}-\mathbf{b})\times\hat{\mathbf{e}}|$.

Find the shortest distance from A (1, 3, −2) to the line joining (2, 1, −2) and (−1, 1, 2). (L.)

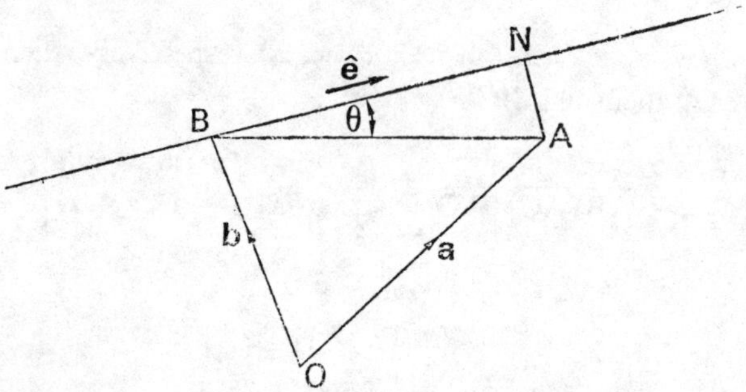

FIG. 26.19

Suppose O is the origin of position vectors, Fig. 26.19, and B is the point with position vector $\mathbf{b}$ so that $\overrightarrow{OB} = \mathbf{b}$. Then $\overrightarrow{BA} = \mathbf{a}-\mathbf{b}$ and the required perpendicular distance AN is BA $\sin\theta$. But $|\overrightarrow{BA}\times\hat{\mathbf{e}}| = |\overrightarrow{BA}|\,|\hat{\mathbf{e}}|\sin\theta = \text{BA}\sin\theta$.

$$\therefore\ \text{AN} = |(\mathbf{a}-\mathbf{b})\times\hat{\mathbf{e}}|. \qquad (1)$$

The line joining the points (2, 1, −2), (−1, 1, 2) has equations

$$\frac{x-2}{-3} = \frac{y-1}{0} = \frac{z+2}{4} \qquad (2)$$

or, expressed in suitable vector form, $[\hat{\mathbf{e}} = (-3\mathbf{i}+4\mathbf{k})/5]$,

$$\mathbf{r} = 2\mathbf{i}+\mathbf{j}-2\mathbf{k}+\lambda(-3\mathbf{i}+4\mathbf{k})/5.$$

Hence, using equation (1), the perpendicular distance

$$\begin{aligned}\text{AN} &= |\{(\mathbf{i}+3\mathbf{j}-2\mathbf{k})-(2\mathbf{i}+\mathbf{j}-2\mathbf{k})\}\times(-3\mathbf{i}+4\mathbf{k})/5| \\ &= |(8\mathbf{i}+4\mathbf{j}+6\mathbf{k})/5| = \tfrac{1}{5}\sqrt{116}.\end{aligned}$$

This result can be obtained by other methods (see *Pure Maths.*, Vol. II, Chap. XXI).

(b) *The Triple Vector Product*

The vector product of $\mathbf{a}$ and $\mathbf{b}\times\mathbf{c}$, i.e. $\mathbf{a}\times(\mathbf{b}\times\mathbf{c})$, is a triple vector product. The position of the brackets in this expression is very important. The vector $\mathbf{a}\times(\mathbf{b}\times\mathbf{c})$ is perpendicular both to $\mathbf{a}$ and to $\mathbf{b}\times\mathbf{c}$; since it is perpendicular to $\mathbf{b}\times\mathbf{c}$ it lies in the plane of $\mathbf{b}$ and $\mathbf{c}$. On the other hand $(\mathbf{a}\times\mathbf{b})\times\mathbf{c}$, being perpendicular to $\mathbf{a}\times\mathbf{b}$, lies in the plane of $\mathbf{a}$ and $\mathbf{b}$. These are in general different planes. Hence $\mathbf{a}\times(\mathbf{b}\times\mathbf{c}) \neq (\mathbf{a}\times\mathbf{b})\times\mathbf{c}$.

The formula for expanding $\mathbf{a}\times(\mathbf{b}\times\mathbf{c})$ can be obtained by writing out components and rearranging the expressions. The result is

$$\mathbf{a}\times(\mathbf{b}\times\mathbf{c}) = \mathbf{b}(\mathbf{a}\,.\,\mathbf{c})-\mathbf{c}(\mathbf{a}\,.\,\mathbf{b}). \tag{26.55}$$

Formula (26.55) can be established by the use of components as follows. Choose the coordinate axes so that Ox is directed along $\mathbf{a}$, and the plane of Oxy is the plane of $\mathbf{a}$ and $\mathbf{b}$. Then we can write

$$\mathbf{a} = a_1\mathbf{i},\quad \mathbf{b} = b_1\mathbf{i}+b_2\mathbf{j},\quad \mathbf{c} = c_1\mathbf{i}+c_2\mathbf{j}+c_3\mathbf{k}.$$

$$\therefore\ \mathbf{b}\times\mathbf{c} = b_2c_3\mathbf{i}-b_1c_3\mathbf{j}+(b_1c_2-b_2c_1)\mathbf{k},$$

$$\therefore\ \mathbf{a}\times(\mathbf{b}\times\mathbf{c}) = (a_1b_2c_1-a_1b_1c_2)\mathbf{j}-a_1b_1c_3\mathbf{k}.$$

But

$$\begin{aligned}(\mathbf{a}\,.\,\mathbf{c})\,\mathbf{b}-(\mathbf{a}\,.\,\mathbf{b})\,\mathbf{c} &= a_1c_1\mathbf{b}-a_1b_1\mathbf{c}\\ &= (a_1b_2c_1-a_1b_1c_2)\mathbf{j}-a_1b_1c_3\mathbf{k}.\end{aligned}$$

However, a relation between vectors is independent of any particular frame of reference and hence, since $\mathbf{a}\times(\mathbf{b}\times\mathbf{c})$ and $(\mathbf{a}\,.\,\mathbf{c})\,\mathbf{b}-(\mathbf{a}\,.\,\mathbf{b})\,\mathbf{c}$ have the same components referred to the frame chosen above, equation (26.55) follows at once.

Example 1. Find the vector $\mathbf{x}$ which satisfies the equations

$$\mathbf{x}\times\mathbf{a} = \mathbf{b},\quad \mathbf{x}\,.\,\mathbf{c} = p$$

in which p is a given scalar and $\mathbf{a}.\mathbf{c} \neq 0$. (L.)

Taking the vector product of the first equation with $\mathbf{c}$ gives

$$(\mathbf{b}\times\mathbf{c}) = (\mathbf{x}\times\mathbf{a})\times\mathbf{c} = \mathbf{a}(\mathbf{x}\,.\,\mathbf{c})-\mathbf{x}(\mathbf{a}\,.\,\mathbf{c}) = p\mathbf{a}-\mathbf{x}(\mathbf{a}\,.\,\mathbf{c}).$$

$$\therefore\ \mathbf{x} = (p\mathbf{a}-\mathbf{b}\times\mathbf{c})/(\mathbf{a}\,.\,\mathbf{c}).$$

Example 2. Find the vector $\mathbf{x}$ and the scalar λ which satisfy the equations

$$\mathbf{a}\times\mathbf{x} = \mathbf{b}+\lambda\mathbf{a}, \quad \mathbf{a}\,.\,\mathbf{x} = 2,$$

where

$$\mathbf{a} = \mathbf{i}+2\mathbf{j}-\mathbf{k}, \quad \mathbf{b} = 2\mathbf{i}-\mathbf{j}+\mathbf{k}. \qquad \text{(L.)}$$

The given equations are equivalent to four scalar equations which have the three components of $\mathbf{x}$ and λ as the unknowns.

Taking the vector product of the first equation with $\mathbf{a}$ gives

$$\mathbf{b}\times\mathbf{a}+\lambda(\mathbf{a}\times\mathbf{a}) = (\mathbf{a}\times\mathbf{x})\times\mathbf{a} = \mathbf{x}\mathbf{a}^2-\mathbf{a}(\mathbf{x}\,.\,\mathbf{a}).$$

$$\therefore\ \mathbf{x} = \frac{\mathbf{b}\times\mathbf{a}+2\mathbf{a}}{\mathbf{a}^2}.$$

In the special case given

$$\mathbf{x} = \frac{(-\mathbf{i}+3\mathbf{j}+5\mathbf{k})+2(\mathbf{i}+2\mathbf{j}-\mathbf{k})}{6} = \frac{1}{6}(\mathbf{i}+7\mathbf{j}+3\mathbf{k}).$$

Taking the scalar product of the first equation with $\mathbf{a}$ gives

$$0 = \mathbf{a}\,.\,\mathbf{a}\times\mathbf{x} = \mathbf{a}\,.\,\mathbf{b}+\lambda\mathbf{a}^2.$$

$$\therefore\ \lambda = -\frac{\mathbf{a}\,.\,\mathbf{b}}{\mathbf{a}^2} = -\frac{(2-2-1)}{6} = \frac{1}{6}.$$

EXERCISES 26.9

1. A tetrahedron has its vertices at the points O (0, 0, 0), A (1, 1, 2), B $(-1, 2, -1)$, and C $(0, -1, 3)$. By consideration of the vector product $\overrightarrow{AC}\times\overrightarrow{AB}$, or otherwise, determine

(i) the area of the face ABC and (ii) the unit vector normal to the face ABC. Hence, or otherwise, determine the volume of the tetrahedron. (L.)

2. Find the volume of the tetrahedron whose vertices are the points $(1, 3, -1)$, $(2, 2, 3)$, $(4, 2, -2)$, $(3, 7, 4)$. (L.)

3. Show that the points $(3, 4, 0)$, $(-1, -2, -2)$, $(2, 8, 3)$, $(-5, 3, 3)$ are coplanar and find the equation of their plane. (L.)

4. Find the shortest distance between a diagonal of a rectangular parallelepiped, of edges a, b, c, and the edges which do not meet that diagonal. (L.)

5. Find the perpendicular distance from the point $(2, 2, 1)$ to the line of intersection of the two planes

$$2x-y-z = 3, \quad 3x-y-3z = 4. \qquad \text{(L.)}$$

6. The coordinates of the four points A, B, C, D are respectively $(1, 2, 1)$, $(-1, 0, 2)$, $(2, 1, 3)$ and $(3, -1, 1)$. Find the shortest distance between the lines AB and CD. (L.)

7. Show that the shortest distance between the lines

$$\frac{x+4}{3} = \frac{y-3}{-2} = \frac{z+6}{5}$$

and $x-2y-z = 0$, $x-10y-3z = -7$, is $\frac{1}{2}\sqrt{14}$ and find the coordinates of its end points. (L.)

8. Solve the following equations for **x**.

(i) $\mathbf{x}\times\mathbf{a} = \mathbf{b}$, where $\mathbf{a}.\mathbf{b} = 0$.

(ii) $\lambda\mathbf{x}+\mathbf{x}\times\mathbf{c} = \mathbf{a}$.

(iii) $a\mathbf{x}+(\mathbf{x}.\mathbf{u})\mathbf{v} = \mathbf{w}$,

considering the cases in which $a+\mathbf{u}.\mathbf{v}$ is not zero and is zero separately. (L.)

26.10. Applications to Kinematics

In §§ 18.1, 18.2 we defined and discussed derivatives of vectors w.r. to the time and in particular the velocity and acceleration of a point moving in a plane. Here, using scalar and vector products, we use and extend the results of those sections to the kinematics of a lamina and of a particle moving in a plane. [Also, in § 18.2 we obtained formulae for the components of velocity and acceleration of a point in terms of different representations of its position, arriving at results (18.9)–(18.16).]

1. *Differentiation of a Unit Vector*

If **a** is a vector whose magnitude, a, is constant but whose direction may depend upon t, then $a^2 = \mathbf{a}^2 = \mathbf{a}.\mathbf{a}$. Hence

$$0 = \frac{\mathrm{d}(a^2)}{\mathrm{d}t} = \frac{\mathrm{d}}{\mathrm{d}t}(\mathbf{a}.\mathbf{a}) = \frac{\mathrm{d}\mathbf{a}}{\mathrm{d}t}\cdot\mathbf{a}+\mathbf{a}\cdot\frac{\mathrm{d}\mathbf{a}}{\mathrm{d}t} = 2\mathbf{a}\cdot\frac{\mathrm{d}\mathbf{a}}{\mathrm{d}t}. \tag{26.56}$$

Therefore the vectors **a** and $\mathrm{d}\mathbf{a}/\mathrm{d}t$ are perpendicular.

If **a** is a unit vector in *two* dimensions, we can write

$$\hat{\mathbf{a}} = \mathbf{i}\cos\theta+\mathbf{j}\sin\theta.$$

$$\therefore \frac{\mathrm{d}\hat{\mathbf{a}}}{\mathrm{d}t} = -\mathbf{i}\dot{\theta}\sin\theta+\mathbf{j}\dot{\theta}\cos\theta = \dot{\theta}\hat{\mathbf{b}}, \tag{26.57}$$

where $\hat{\mathbf{b}} = -\mathbf{i}\sin\theta + \mathbf{j}\cos\theta = \mathbf{i}\cos(\theta+\frac{1}{2}\pi)+\mathbf{j}\sin(\theta+\frac{1}{2}\pi)$. Therefore $\hat{\mathbf{b}}$ is another unit vector obtained by rotating $\hat{\mathbf{a}}$ through one right angle in the positive sense. If $\mathbf{k}$ is a unit vector perpendicular to the plane of $\mathbf{i}$, $\mathbf{j}$ and forms a r.h. set with them, we can also write eqn. (26.57) in the form

$$\frac{d\hat{\mathbf{a}}}{dt} = \dot{\theta}(\mathbf{k}\times\hat{\mathbf{a}}). \tag{26.58}$$

2. *Angular Velocity*

In Vol. I, § 13.2 we defined the angular velocity and the angular acceleration of a straight line rotating in a plane about a fixed point in that plane, and in Chapter XVI we extended these ideas to the uniplanar motion of a lamina.

If one point of the lamina is fixed in position, the only motion possible is one of rotation about an axis perpendicular to its plane passing through that point. The most general motion of the lamina can be specified by the motion of an arbitrary point A and the rotation of the lamina about A. The rotation is specified by the angular velocity of the lamina which is, by definition, the rate of increase of the angle between a line fixed in the lamina and a line fixed in space. Choosing different lines in the lamina or in space merely alters the angle by a constant and does not affect the rate of increase of that angle and so leads to a unique value for the angular velocity. Hence we refer to the *angular velocity of the lamina* without specifying an origin.

If one point of the lamina is fixed at O, any other point P can only have a transverse velocity $r\dot{\theta}$ (OP $= r$), since the lamina is rotating about O. This is conveniently expressed by means of vectors if we introduce a *unit* vector $\mathbf{k}$ perpendicular to the plane of the lamina; then

$$\mathbf{v} = \dot{\theta}(\mathbf{k}\times\mathbf{r}), \tag{26.59}$$

where $\mathbf{r}$ is the position vector $\overrightarrow{OP}$. If we specify the motion of the lamina by giving the velocity $\mathbf{v}_A$ of a point A, then the velocity of any other point P relative to A is given by (26.59) [the motion of P relative to A being in a circle with A as centre] and the actual velocity of P is

$$\mathbf{v} = \mathbf{v}_A + \dot{\theta}(\mathbf{k}\times\mathbf{r}), \tag{26.60}$$

where $\mathbf{r} = \overrightarrow{AP}$.

Results (26.58)–(26.60) *suggest* (but do not prove) that a rotation about an axis with angular velocity ω can be associated with a vector angular velocity $\boldsymbol{\omega}$ directed along the axis where $|\boldsymbol{\omega}| = \omega$, see Fig. 26.20.

Example. A rigid body is rotating about a fixed axis with angular velocity ω which is represented by a vector $\boldsymbol{\omega}$ directed along the axis of rotation such that $\omega = |\boldsymbol{\omega}|$. Show that the velocity of a point P, whose position vector is $\mathbf{r}$ w.r. to an origin O on the axis of rotation, is $\mathbf{v} = \boldsymbol{\omega} \times \mathbf{r}$.

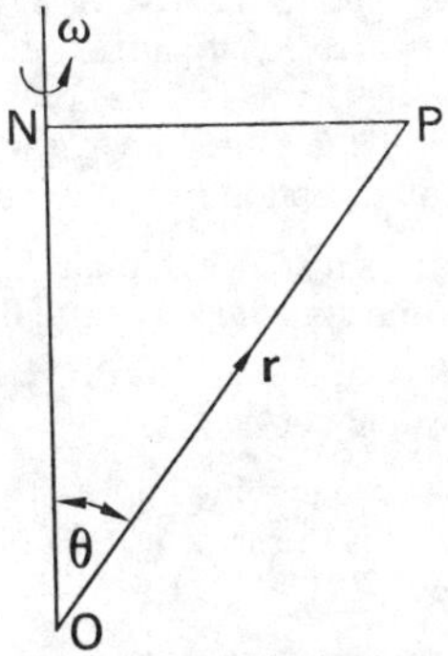

FIG. 26.20

The speed of P (Fig. 26.20) is ωPN $= \omega r \sin\theta$, and is perpendicular to the plane OPN and is directed into the plane of the diagram.

The vector $\boldsymbol{\omega} \times \mathbf{r}$ has magnitude $\omega r \sin\theta$ and is perpendicular to the plane OPN and is directed into the plane of the diagram. Hence, the velocity vector $\mathbf{v}$ and the vector $\boldsymbol{\omega} \times \mathbf{r}$ have identical magnitude and direction.

$$\therefore \; \mathbf{v} = \boldsymbol{\omega} \times \mathbf{r}.$$

For a discussion of the application of vector methods to the dynamics of a rigid lamina the reader should consult more advanced works, e.g. Plumpton and Chirgwin, *A Course of Mathematics for Engineers and Scientists*, Vol. III, §§ 7.4, 7.5.

MISCELLANEOUS EXERCISES XXVI

1. Three points A, B and C have position vectors $\mathbf{i}+\mathbf{j}+\mathbf{k}$, $\mathbf{i}+2\mathbf{k}$ and $3\mathbf{i}+2\mathbf{j}+3\mathbf{k}$ respectively, relative to a fixed origin O. A particle P starts from B at time $t=0$, and moves along BC towards C with constant speed 1 unit per sec. Find the position vector of P after t seconds (a) relative to O and (b) relative to A.

If the angle PAB $= \theta$, find an expression for $\cos\theta$ in terms of t. (L.)

2. Distances being measured in kilometres and speeds in km/h, a motor boat sets out at 11 a.m. from a position $-6\mathbf{i}-2\mathbf{j}$ relative to a marker buoy, and travels at a steady speed of magnitude $\sqrt{53}$ on a direct course to intercept a ship. The ship maintains a steady velocity vector $3\mathbf{i}+4\mathbf{j}$ and at 12 noon is at a position $3\mathbf{i}-\mathbf{j}$ from the buoy. Find the velocity vector of the motor boat, the time of interception, and the position vector of the point of interception from the buoy. (L.)

3. Masses $m_1, m_2, \ldots, m_n$ are situated at points $P_1, P_2, \ldots, P_n$ and O is a fixed origin. If the centre of mass of the system is G, write down the equation which gives $\overrightarrow{OG}$ in terms of m_i and $\overrightarrow{OP_i}$ $(i = 1, 2, \ldots, n)$. Prove that the position of the centre of mass is independent of the origin chosen.

Show also that, if the particles are moving under the action of forces $\mathbf{F}_1, \mathbf{F}_2, \ldots, \mathbf{F}_n$ respectively, the acceleration of G is the same as that of a particle of mass $(m_1+m_2+ +\ldots+m_n)$ acted on by a force $\mathbf{F}_1+\mathbf{F}_2+\ldots+\mathbf{F}_n$. (N.)

4. A particle of mass m is moving so that its position vector $\mathbf{r}$, at time t, is given by

$$\mathbf{r} = \{a\sin(\omega t+\alpha),\quad b\sin(\omega t+\beta),\quad c\sin(\omega t+\gamma)\}$$

where $a, b, c, \omega, \alpha, \beta$ and γ are constants. Write down the values of $\dot{\mathbf{r}}$ and $\ddot{\mathbf{r}}$ and show that:

(i) the angular momentum $\mathbf{r}\times m\dot{\mathbf{r}}$ of the particle about the origin O is a constant vector,

(ii) the kinetic energy of the particle has the form $k-\frac{1}{2}m\omega^2\mathbf{r}^2$ where k is a constant,

(iii) $\ddot{\mathbf{r}} = -\omega^2\mathbf{r}$.

Deduce from (i) that the particle moves in a plane containing the origin. (N.)

5. A particle of mass m moves so that its position vector $\mathbf{r}$ at time t with respect to an origin O is given by

$$\mathbf{r} = (t^2-1)\,\mathbf{i}+2t\mathbf{j}.$$

Calculate the angular momentum, $\mathbf{h}$, of the particle about O at time t, and its derivative $d\mathbf{h}/dt$.

Find also the force $\mathbf{F}$ acting on the particle and its moment about O.

(The moment of the force about O is defined as $\mathbf{r}\times\mathbf{F}$ and the angular momentum about O as $\mathbf{r}\times m\mathbf{v}$, where $\mathbf{v}$ is the velocity of the particle.) (N.)

6. If $\mathbf{p}$ is a unit vector of varying direction prove that

$$\mathbf{p}\cdot\frac{d\mathbf{p}}{dt}$$

is zero. Hence show that the component of

$$\frac{d^2\mathbf{p}}{dt^2}$$

in the direction of **p** is $-v^2$, where **v** is the vector

$$\frac{d\mathbf{p}}{dt}. \qquad \text{(N.)}$$

7. A unit vector $\hat{\mathbf{r}}$ rotates in the xy plane. At time t the vector makes an angle θ with the axis Ox, the positive sense of measurement of θ being the sense of rotation from Ox to Oy through one right angle. Show that

$$\frac{d\hat{\mathbf{r}}}{dt} = \hat{\boldsymbol{\theta}}\frac{d\theta}{dt},$$

where $\hat{\boldsymbol{\theta}}$ is a unit vector perpendicular to $\hat{\mathbf{r}}$, and specify the sense of $\hat{\boldsymbol{\theta}}$. Obtain a similar result for $d\hat{\boldsymbol{\theta}}/dt$.

A point P moves on a circle of radius a and centre O; at time t the radius OP makes an angle θ with a fixed radius of the circle. Find, in terms of θ and its time derivatives and of a, the components of the acceleration of P along and perpendicular to $\overrightarrow{\text{OP}}$.

(N.)

8. (a) A cube has opposite faces ABCD and EFGH whose vertices are the points **0**, **j**, **j**+**k**, **k** and **i**, **i**+**j**, **i**+**j**+**k**, **i**+**k** respectively. Prove that the mid-points of HE, EA, AB and BC are four consecutive vertices of a regular hexagon. Find a unit vector which is normal to the plane of the hexagon.

(b) Two unit vectors **a** and **b** contain an angle $\cos^{-1}\frac{3}{5}$ and **c** is a unit vector perpendicular to both of them. Express the unit vectors that are equally inclined to **a**, **b** and **c** in the form $x\mathbf{a}+y\mathbf{b}+z\mathbf{c}$. (N.)

9. Define the scalar product **a** . **b** and the vector product **a**×**b** of the two vectors **a** and **b**. The points A, B, C have coordinates (2, 1, 2), (9, 1, 4), (7, 2, 3) respectively referred to a right-handed orthogonal frame Oxyz with unit vectors **i**, **j**, **k** directed along the axes Ox, Oy, Oz respectively. Calculate $\overrightarrow{\text{AB}}$, $\overrightarrow{\text{AC}}$ in terms of **i**, **j**, **k** and deduce the values of $\overrightarrow{\text{AB}}\,.\,\overrightarrow{\text{AC}}$ and $\overrightarrow{\text{AB}}\times\overrightarrow{\text{AC}}$.

Hence, or otherwise, find

(i) the cosine of the acute angle between AB and AC;
(ii) the area of the triangle ABC;
(iii) the cosine of the acute angle between the plane of the triangle ABC and the plane $z = 0$. (L.)

10. A tetrahedron OABC has its vertices at the points O (0, 0, 0), A (1, 2, −1), B (−1, 1, 2) and C (2, −1, 1) in a rectangular coordinate system. Write down vector expressions for $\overrightarrow{\text{AB}}$, $\overrightarrow{\text{AC}}$ and $\overrightarrow{\text{BC}}$ and evaluate

$$\overrightarrow{\text{AB}}\,.\,\overrightarrow{\text{AC}}, \quad \overrightarrow{\text{AB}}\times\overrightarrow{\text{AC}}, \quad \overrightarrow{\text{OA}}\times\overrightarrow{\text{BC}} \quad \text{and} \quad \overrightarrow{\text{OA}}\,.\,\overrightarrow{\text{AB}}\times\overrightarrow{\text{AC}}.$$

Hence, or otherwise, find

(i) the angle BAC,
(ii) the area of triangle ABC,
(iii) a unit vector which is perpendicular to both $\overrightarrow{OA}$ and $\overrightarrow{BC}$,
(iv) the shortest distance between OA and BC,
(v) the volume of the tetrahedron. (L.)

11. (i) The point A lies at the extremity of the position vector **a** measured from an origin O. Show that the position vector of any point P lying on the line through A parallel to a vector **b** may be expressed as

$$\mathbf{r} = \mathbf{a} + p\mathbf{b},$$

where p is a scalar parameter, and explain the geometrical significance of p.

(ii) Show that the component of the vector **a** parallel to the vector **b** is **c** where

$$b^2\mathbf{c} = (\mathbf{a}\,.\,\mathbf{b})\mathbf{b}.$$

(iii) The vector **c** and the scalar λ satisfy the equations

$$\mathbf{a}\times\mathbf{c} = \lambda\mathbf{a} + \mathbf{b},$$
$$\mathbf{a}\,.\,\mathbf{c} = 1,$$

where $\mathbf{a} = \mathbf{i}+2\mathbf{j}$, $\mathbf{b} = 2\mathbf{i}+\mathbf{j}-2\mathbf{k}$. Find the value of λ, and express **c** in terms of **i**, **j** and **k**. (L.)

12. The points A, B, C have coordinates (1, 1, 1), (2, 3, 4), (3, 2, 2) respectively referred to an orthonormal system of axes $Oxyz$. Find the equation of the plane ABC. If the vectors $\overrightarrow{OA}$, $\overrightarrow{OB}$ are denoted by **a**, **b** respectively, find $\mathbf{a}.\mathbf{b}$ and show that $\mathbf{a}\times\mathbf{b} = \mathbf{i}-2\mathbf{j}+\mathbf{k}$, where **i**, **j**, **k** are unit vectors in the directions Ox, Oy, Oz.

Hence, or otherwise, find

(i) the cosine of the angle AOB,
(ii) the area of the triangle OAB.

Show that the area of the orthogonal projection of the triangle OAB on the plane of ABC is $\sqrt{(7/5)}$ units of area. (L.)

13. The points A, B, C, D have cartesian coordinates (1, 2, −1), (2, 0, 3), (3, 1, 1), (4, −4, 2) respectively. Show that the planes which bisect the line segments AB, BC, CD respectively at right angles have the equations

$$2x-4y+8z-7 = 0,$$
$$x+y-2z+1 = 0,$$
$$2x-10y+2z-25 = 0.$$

If O_1 and O_2 are the circumcentres of the triangles ABC, BCD, respectively, show that the equations of the normals to the planes ABC, BCD at O_1 and O_2, respectively, can be written in vectorial form as

$$2\mathbf{r} = \mathbf{i}-3\mathbf{j}+\lambda_1(2\mathbf{j}+\mathbf{k}),$$
$$2\mathbf{r} = 16\mathbf{i}+9\mathbf{k}+\lambda_2(3\mathbf{i}+\mathbf{j}+2\mathbf{k}),$$

where λ_1 and λ_2 are scalar parameters.

Hence show that the coordinates of the centre of the sphere which passes through the points A, B, C, D are $(\frac{1}{2}, -\frac{5}{2}, -\frac{1}{2})$. (L.)

14. Define the vector product $\mathbf{a}\times\mathbf{b}$ of two vectors $\mathbf{a}$ and $\mathbf{b}$.

The coordinates of the three points A, B and C referred to rectangular axes $Oxyz$ are $(4, 7, -4)$, $(0, -2, 1)$ and $(1, 3, -2)$, respectively. Find

(i) the unit vector $\hat{\mathbf{e}}_1$ along $\overrightarrow{OA}$;

(ii) a unit vector $\hat{\mathbf{e}}_2$ perpendicular to $\overrightarrow{OA}$ and $\overrightarrow{OB}$;

(iii) a unit vector $\hat{\mathbf{e}}_3$ perpendicular to $\hat{\mathbf{e}}_1$ and $\hat{\mathbf{e}}_2$;

(iv) $\hat{\mathbf{e}}_1 . \hat{\mathbf{e}}_2 \times \hat{\mathbf{e}}_3$.

Express $\overrightarrow{OC}$ in the form $\lambda\hat{\mathbf{e}}_1+\mu\hat{\mathbf{e}}_2+\nu\hat{\mathbf{e}}_3$ and find the coordinates of D referred to $Oxyz$ if

$$\overrightarrow{OD} = 4\hat{\mathbf{e}}_1+3\hat{\mathbf{e}}_2+\hat{\mathbf{e}}_3. \qquad \text{(L.)}$$

15. Forces $\mathbf{i}+3\mathbf{j}$, $-2\mathbf{i}-\mathbf{j}$, $\mathbf{i}-2\mathbf{j}$ act through the points with position vectors $2\mathbf{i}+5\mathbf{j}$, $4\mathbf{j}$, $-\mathbf{i}+\mathbf{j}$ respectively. Prove that this system of forces is equivalent to a couple, and calculate the moment of this couple. (L.)

16. A particle of mass m moves in a horizontal plane under the action of a variable force $\mathbf{F}$ so that the position vector of the particle at time t is $\mathbf{r} = 4 \cos kt\, \mathbf{i}+3 \sin kt\, \mathbf{j}$, where k is a constant. Find

(a) the period of the motion,

(b) the greatest magnitude of $\mathbf{F}$.

If the force $\mathbf{F}$ ceases to act when $t = \pi/(3k)$, find the position vector of the particle when $t = 4\pi/(3k)$. (L.)

17. A man bicycling at a constant speed u finds that when his velocity is $u\mathbf{j}$ the velocity of the wind appears to be

$$\tfrac{1}{2}v_1(\mathbf{i}-\sqrt{3}\mathbf{j}),$$

where $\mathbf{i}$ and $\mathbf{j}$ are unit vectors in the east and north directions respectively: but when his velocity is $\frac{1}{2}u(-\sqrt{3}\mathbf{i}+\mathbf{j})$ the velocity of the wind appears to be $v_2\mathbf{i}$. Prove that the true velocity of the wind is

$$\tfrac{1}{6}\sqrt{3}u(\mathbf{i}+\sqrt{3}\mathbf{j}),$$

and find v_1 and v_2 in terms of u. (L.)

18. A red ball is stationary on a rectangular billiard table OABC. It is then struck by a white ball of equal mass and equal radius with velocity

$$u(-2\mathbf{i}+11\mathbf{j}),$$

where $\mathbf{i}$ and $\mathbf{j}$ are unit vectors along OA and OC respectively. After impact the red and white balls have velocities parallel to the vectors $-3\mathbf{i}+4\mathbf{j}$, $2\mathbf{i}+4\mathbf{j}$ respectively. Prove that the coefficient of restitution between the two balls is $1/2$. (L.)

19. (a) If $\mathbf{u} = a\mathbf{i}+b\mathbf{j}+c\mathbf{k}$, where $\mathbf{i}$, $\mathbf{j}$, $\mathbf{k}$ are mutually perpendicular unit vectors, show that $a = \mathbf{u}.\mathbf{i}$, $b = \mathbf{u}.\mathbf{j}$ and $c = \mathbf{u}.\mathbf{k}$.

If $\mathbf{u} = (1/\sqrt{3})(\mathbf{i}+\mathbf{j}+\mathbf{k})$, $\mathbf{v} = \sqrt{(\frac{2}{3})}(\mathbf{i}-\frac{1}{2}\mathbf{j}-\frac{1}{2}\mathbf{k})$ and $\mathbf{w} = (1/\sqrt{2})(\mathbf{j}-\mathbf{k})$, show that $\mathbf{u}$, $\mathbf{v}$ and $\mathbf{w}$ are mutually perpendicular unit vectors and express $\mathbf{i}$ in the form

$$p\mathbf{u}+q\mathbf{v}+r\mathbf{w}.$$

(b) Prove that, when a particle moves in a plane, the radius of curvature, ϱ, of its path is given by $\varrho = v^3/|\mathbf{v}\times\mathbf{f}|$, where $\mathbf{f}$, $\mathbf{v}$ are the acceleration and velocity vectors and v is the magnitude of $\mathbf{v}$.

Given that at a certain instant $\mathbf{v} = 4\mathbf{i}-3\mathbf{j}$, $\mathbf{f} = 3\mathbf{i}+4\mathbf{j}$, find the value of ϱ. (N.)

20. (i) Define the scalar and vector products of two vectors $\mathbf{a}$, $\mathbf{b}$ in terms of a, b and the angle θ between the vectors, explaining carefully any sign conventions used.

Deduce the formula

$$|\mathbf{a}\times\mathbf{b}|^2 = a^2b^2-(\mathbf{a}.\mathbf{b})^2.$$

(ii) Find the most general form for the vector $\mathbf{u}$ when

$$\mathbf{u}\times(\mathbf{i}+\mathbf{j}+2\mathbf{k}) = \mathbf{i}-\mathbf{j}. \qquad \text{(N.)}$$

21. Express as an equation involving a determinant the condition that the vector $(x\mathbf{i}+y\mathbf{j}+z\mathbf{k})$ can be expressed in terms of the vectors $(a\mathbf{i}+b\mathbf{j})$, $(b\mathbf{j}+c\mathbf{k})$. (L.)

22. The unit vectors $\mathbf{i}$, $\mathbf{j}$, $\mathbf{k}$ are drawn from the origin O along the axes Ox, Oy, Oz respectively. Write down the position vector of the centre of mass of a system of three particles of masses m_1, m_2, m_3 placed at the points $\mathbf{i}$, $\mathbf{j}$, $\mathbf{k}$ respectively.

A uniform solid sphere with centre O has radius a. Find the position vectors with respect to O of the centres of mass of

(a) the hemisphere for which x is positive,

(b) the octant for which x, y, z are positive. (L.)

23. If the points A, B, C have position vectors $\mathbf{a}$, $\mathbf{b}$, $\mathbf{c}$ from an origin O, show that the equation

$$\mathbf{r} = t\mathbf{a}+(1-t)\mathbf{b},$$

where t is a parameter, represents the straight line AB, and find the equation of BC.

Find the equation of the straight line joining L the mid-point of OA to M the mid-point of BC. Find also the position vector of the point in which the line LM meets the straight line joining the mid-point of OB to the mid-point of AC. (L.)

24. From a point whose position vector from the origin is $\mathbf{s}$, the perpendicular is drawn to a plane. If this perpendicular is represented by the vector $\mathbf{p}$, find, in scalar product form, the vector equation of the plane.

From the point $\mathbf{s}_1 = \mathbf{i}+\mathbf{j}+\mathbf{k}$ the perpendicular drawn to a plane π_1 is $\mathbf{i}-\mathbf{j}+\mathbf{k}$. From the point $\mathbf{s}_2 = 3\mathbf{i}-\mathbf{j}-\mathbf{k}$ the perpendicular drawn to a plane π_2 is $\mathbf{i}+2\mathbf{j}+\mathbf{k}$. Find the equation of a plane π_3 containing the line of intersection of the planes π_1 and π_2 and passing through the mid-point of the line joining $\mathbf{s}_1$ to $\mathbf{s}_2$. Find also the length of the perpendicular from the origin on to the plane π_3. (L.)

25. Points A, B, C have position vectors **a, b, c** and λ, μ, ν are variable parameters subject to the condition $\lambda+\mu+\nu = 1$. If the points are not collinear prove that the plane ABC is represented by the equation $\mathbf{r} = \lambda\mathbf{a}+\mu\mathbf{b}+\nu\mathbf{c}$.

Prove that the equation of the line of intersection of the two planes

$$\mathbf{r} = \lambda_1\mathbf{i}+2\mu_1\mathbf{j}+3\nu_1\mathbf{k}, \quad \lambda_1+\mu_1+\nu_1 = 1$$

and

$$\mathbf{r} = 2\lambda_2\mathbf{i}+\mu_2\mathbf{j}+2\nu_2\mathbf{k}, \quad \lambda_2+\mu_2+\nu_2 = 1,$$

can be written in terms of a single parameter t as

$$6\mathbf{r} = (3+t)\mathbf{i}+4t\mathbf{j}+9(1-t)\mathbf{k}. \qquad \text{(L.)}$$

26. Sketch the curves given by the equations

$$\mathbf{r} = 2\cos p\,\mathbf{i}+2\sin p\,\mathbf{j},$$
$$\mathbf{r} = q\mathbf{i}+(q^2+c)\mathbf{j},$$

where c is a scalar constant.

Determine the range of values of c for which the curves meet in four distinct real points. Find in vector form the equations of the two parallel straight lines each of which passes through two of the four points of intersection, given that the position vector of one point of intersection is $\mathbf{r} = 2\mathbf{i}$. (L.)

27. (i) Find the vector equation of the line joining the points with position vectors $5\mathbf{i}-2\mathbf{j}+\mathbf{k}$ and $2\mathbf{i}-7\mathbf{j}-4\mathbf{k}$. Find the position vector of the point where this line meets the plane $\mathbf{r} = -\mathbf{i}+p\mathbf{j}+q\mathbf{k}$.

(ii) Prove that the position vector of the point dividing the line joining the points with position vectors **a, b** in the ratio $m:l$ is $(l\mathbf{a}+m\mathbf{b})/(l+m)$.

P, Q, R are points on the sides BC, CA, AB respectively of the triangle ABC which divide them internally so that BP : PC = 2 : 3, CQ : QA = 3 : 4, AR : RB = 2 : 1. Prove vectorially that AP, BQ, CR are concurrent. (L.)

28. Find the shortest distance between the straight lines with vector equations

$$\mathbf{r} = -3\mathbf{i}+5s\mathbf{j}+\mathbf{k}, \quad \mathbf{r} = 3\mathbf{i}-2\mathbf{j}+\mathbf{k}+t(-\mathbf{i}+2\mathbf{j}-\mathbf{k}). \qquad \text{(L.)}$$

29. The position vector of the point P at time t is

$$a\tan t\,\mathbf{i}+a\sec t\,\mathbf{k},$$

where a is a positive constant and $0 \leq t < \pi/2$. Show that the velocity and the acceleration of P when $t = 0$ are at right angles to each other.

If A is the point with position vector $a\mathbf{j}$, obtain the vector equation of the straight line AP at time t. The point Q divides AP internally in the ratio $\cos t : (1-\cos t)$. Show that the acceleration of the point Q is constant in magnitude and is always directed towards a fixed point. (L.)

30. The position vectors of the vertices A, B, C, D of a tetrahedron ABCD are **a, b, c, d** respectively relative to an origin **O**. Forces $\lambda\overrightarrow{AB}$, $\lambda\overrightarrow{AC}$, $\lambda\overrightarrow{AD}$, $\mu\overrightarrow{OB}$, $\mu\overrightarrow{OC}$,

$\mu\overrightarrow{OD}$, where λ and μ are constants, act along the lines AB, AC, AD, OB, OC, OD respectively. Find the resultant of this system of forces.

If $\lambda = 2$, $\mu = 3$, $\mathbf{a} = 15\mathbf{i}+5\mathbf{j}$, $\mathbf{b} = \mathbf{i}-5\mathbf{k}$, $\mathbf{c} = 3\mathbf{i}+2\mathbf{j}-3\mathbf{k}$, $\mathbf{d} = -4\mathbf{i}-8\mathbf{j}+2\mathbf{k}$, find the moment of the couple required to maintain equilibrium if the tetrahedron is smoothly hinged along the edge BC. (L.)

31. The position vectors of the vertices B and C of a triangle ABC are respectively $8\mathbf{i}+3\mathbf{j}+5\mathbf{k}$ and $6\mathbf{i}+4\mathbf{j}+9\mathbf{k}$. Two forces $3\mathbf{i}+2\mathbf{j}+\mathbf{k}$ and $4\mathbf{i}+5\mathbf{j}+6\mathbf{k}$ act along AB and AC respectively. A third force $\mathbf{F}$ acts through A. If the system of forces is in equilibrium, find

(a) the magnitude of the force $\mathbf{F}$,

(b) the position vector of A,

(c) the equation of the line of action of $\mathbf{F}$ in vector form. (L.)

32. (i) The following forces act through the centre of a uniform sphere: $\mathbf{F}_1$ of magnitude $9g$ N in the direction of the vector $\mathbf{i}+2\mathbf{j}-2\mathbf{k}$, $\mathbf{F}_2$ of magnitude $7g$ N in the direction of the vector $6\mathbf{i}+3\mathbf{j}-2\mathbf{k}$, $\mathbf{F}_3$ and the sphere's own weight, $5g$ N in the direction $-\mathbf{k}$. The centre of the sphere starts from rest at A (4, 3, 2) and is moved by this system of forces to B (8, 7, 6) in one second. Given that the unit of length is 1 metre, find the work done by each of the forces $\mathbf{F}_1$ and $\mathbf{F}_2$ as the centre of the sphere moves from A to B. Find also the magnitude and direction of the force $\mathbf{F}_3$ and of the resultant of the system.

(Take $g = 9{\cdot}8$ m/s²)

(ii) A small ring is threaded on to a smooth wire in the form of the helix

$$\mathbf{r} = a\cos p\,\mathbf{i}+a\sin p\,\mathbf{j}+ap\,\mathbf{k}.$$

Find the work done by the variable force $\mathbf{P} = \lambda(y\mathbf{i}+x\mathbf{j}+z\mathbf{k})$ as the ring moves along the wire from the point $(a, 0, 0)$ to the point $(0, a, \frac{1}{2}\pi a)$. (L.)

33. A force of magnitude $\sqrt{6}$ N acts along the line

$$\mathbf{r} = (s-4)\,\mathbf{i}+(s+1)\,\mathbf{j}+(2s+3)\,\mathbf{k}$$

and a second force of magnitude $\sqrt{14}$ N acts along the line

$$\mathbf{r} = (t-7)\,\mathbf{i}+(2t-3)\,\mathbf{j}+(2-3t)\,\mathbf{k}.$$

Show that these two lines meet and find the position vector of their point of intersection P.

Find the magnitude of the resultant of these two forces and the vector equation of its line of action. If these two forces act on a particle of mass 2 kg which is initially at rest at P, find the velocity vector and the position vector of the particle after 4 seconds. (L.)

34. Particles A and B start simultaneously from points which have position vectors $-11\mathbf{i}+17\mathbf{j}-14\mathbf{k}$ and $-9\mathbf{i}+9\mathbf{j}-32\mathbf{k}$ respectively. The velocities of A and B are constant and represented by $6\mathbf{i}-7\mathbf{j}+8\mathbf{k}$ and $5\mathbf{i}-3\mathbf{j}+17\mathbf{k}$ respectively. Show that A and B will collide.

A third particle C moves so that its velocity relative to A is parallel to the vector $2\mathbf{i}+3\mathbf{j}+4\mathbf{k}$ and its velocity relative to B is parallel to the vector $\mathbf{i}+2\mathbf{j}+3\mathbf{k}$. Find the velocity of C and its initial position if all three particles collide simultaneously. (L.)

35. Two identical smooth spheres are moving on a horizontal table with velocity vectors $3\mathbf{i}+4\mathbf{j}$ and $-\mathbf{i}+\mathbf{j}$ and collide when the line joining their centres is parallel to the vector $\mathbf{i}$. If the coefficient of restitution between the spheres is $\frac{1}{2}$, find the velocity vectors of the spheres after impact. Find also the ratio of the magnitudes of the velocities, before and after impact, of the spheres relative to each other. If, at this instant of impact, the centres of the spheres are 2 units of distance apart, find the distance between their centres 1 unit of time later. (L.)

36. The equation of the path of a particle P is

$$\mathbf{r} = \mathbf{i}t+\mathbf{k}t^2,$$

where t is the time. Show that the acceleration of P is constant.

The velocity of another particle Q relative to P is $(\mathbf{i}-\mathbf{j})$ and when $t = 0$, $\overrightarrow{PQ} = \mathbf{j}$. Find the equation of the path of Q and the time at which Q is nearest to P. (L.)

37. At time $t = 0$ two particles A and B leave the point $\mathbf{i}+2\mathbf{j}$, the velocity vector of A being $\mathbf{i}+4\mathbf{j}+\mathbf{k}$ and the velocity of B relative to A being of magnitude $\sqrt{90}$. A third particle C leaves the point $4\mathbf{i}+3\mathbf{k}$ at time $t = 0$ with velocity vector $2\mathbf{i}-\mathbf{j}+3\mathbf{k}$. If the particles travel with constant velocity and if B collides with C, find the initial velocity vector of B. Find also the value of t at the instant when the collision takes place.

If the particles B and C coalesce on collision and then move in a direction perpendicular to the velocity of A, find the ratio of the masses of the particles B and C. (L.)

38. The velocity vectors of the particles P_1, P_2 are

$$u_1\mathbf{i}+v_1\mathbf{j}, \quad u_2\mathbf{i}+v_2\mathbf{j}$$

respectively. Their relative velocity has the same magnitude as that of the velocity of P_1. If the velocity of one particle is reversed, the magnitude of the relative velocity is doubled. Find the ratio of the speeds of P_1 and P_2 and the sine of the angle between their directions. (L.)

39. If $\mathbf{u} = 3\mathbf{i}+4\mathbf{j}+5\mathbf{k}$ is the position vector of a point P, find the magnitude of $\mathbf{u}$ and calculate to the nearest degree the angles made by $\mathbf{u}$ with the unit vectors $\mathbf{i}$, $\mathbf{j}$, $\mathbf{k}$. Find also the unit vector in the same direction as $\mathbf{u}$.

Show that the equation

$$\mathbf{r} = 4(\mathbf{i}\cos p+\mathbf{j}\sin p),$$

where p is a parameter, represents a circle. Find the position vectors of the points on this circle which are nearest to and farthest from the point P. (L.)

40. A particle is moving in a horizontal circle on the smooth inner surface of the paraboloid

$$\mathbf{r} = 2ap\cos\theta\,\mathbf{i}+2ap\sin\theta\,\mathbf{j}+ap^2\,\mathbf{k},$$

where **k** is a unit upward vertical vector, and p and θ are parameters. Find the time of one revolution.

If the particle is brought to rest, and then released, and if its maximum speed thereafter is v, show that the magnitude of its initial acceleration on release was

$$gv/(v^2+2ga)^{1/2}. \qquad \text{(L.)}$$

41. A particle of mass 3 units is acted on by the forces

$$\mathbf{F}_1 = 2\mathbf{i}+3\mathbf{j}, \quad \mathbf{F}_2 = 3\mathbf{j}+4\mathbf{k}, \quad \mathbf{F}_3 = \mathbf{i}+2\mathbf{k},$$

and initially it is at rest at the point $\mathbf{i}-\mathbf{j}-\mathbf{k}$. Find the position and the momentum of the particle after 2 seconds. Find also the work done on the particle in this time. (L.)

ANSWERS TO THE EXERCISES

EXERCISES 15.3 (p. 417)

1. $4M(a^2+b^2)/3$. **2.** $5Mr^2/4$. **3.** $Ma^2/3$.
4. $5Ma^2/3$. **5.** $M(3b^2+3c^2-a^2)/12$.
6. $2M(a^5-b^5)/\{5(a^3-b^3)\}$.
7. $M\{(r^2/4)+(l^2/3)\}$. **8.** $1{\cdot}5$ kg m^2.
10. (i) $16Ml^2/3$; (ii) $56Ml^2/3$.
13. $\sqrt{\{(4b^2-a^2)/72\}}$, **14.** $l/\sqrt{2}$.
15. (i) $196{\cdot}8$ kg m^2; (ii) $31{\cdot}4$ kg m^2.

EXERCISES 15.4 (p. 424)

1. $\sqrt{(2gl)}$. **2.** $6\frac{1}{3}\,g$ N.
3. 2 radians/s; $9{\cdot}78$ kg m^2; $3{\cdot}26$ J.
4. $\frac{1}{2}Ma^2$; $Ma\pi n^2/(7200\,F)$.
5. $3Ma^2/2$; $\sqrt{\{g/(3a)\}}$. **6.** $2\sqrt{g}$ radians/s $\approx 3{\cdot}1$ radians/s.
11. $2{\cdot}32$ radians/s. **12.** $\frac{1}{2}Ma^2$.
13. $9mga/(2\pi)$. **14.** $\sqrt{\{21g/(20a)\}}$. **15.** $mMg/(M+2m)$.

EXERCISES 15.5 (p. 431)

1. $2\pi\sqrt{\{7a/(3g)\}}$.
2. $4ma^2/3$; $4\pi\sqrt{\{a/(3g)\}}$; $3g/(8\pi^2)$ m $\approx 0{\cdot}37$ m.
4. $2\pi\sqrt{\{(5l\sqrt{2})/(3g)\}}$. **5.** $\frac{2}{3}\pi\sqrt{(14a/g)}$.
6. (i) Ma^2; (ii) $\frac{1}{2}Ma^2$.
9. $a\sqrt{2}$; $2\pi\sqrt{\{(2a\pi)/[g\sqrt{(\pi^2+4)}]\}}$; $\sqrt{\{[2g\sqrt{(\pi^2+4)}]/(\pi a)\}}$.
11. $x+a^2/(3x)$; $x = a/\sqrt{3}$.
12. (i) $2a/3$; (ii) $(a\sqrt{5})/3$; $2\pi\sqrt{(2a/g)}$.
14. $2\pi\sqrt{\{(9a^2+2x^2)/(gx)\}}$; $3a/\sqrt{2}$.
15. $m(a+12x^2)\dot{\theta}^2-mg(a+24x)\cos\theta = \text{constant}$; $2\pi\sqrt{\{[2(a^2+12x^2)]/[(a+24x)g]\}}$.
16. $\frac{2}{3}\pi\sqrt{(14a/g)}$. **17.** $2\pi\sqrt{\{a/(g\sqrt{3})\}}$.
18. 3. **19.** $2\pi\sqrt{\{(I+ml^2)/[(Mh+ml)g]\}}$.
20. (ii) $2\pi\sqrt{\{(2a\sqrt{2})/(3g)\}}$.

EXERCISES 15.6 (p. 438)

4. $kmg/(1+2k)$. **7.** $2g/15 \approx 133$ cm/s^2; $8{\cdot}1\times 10^{-3}$ J, 110 cm/s^2.
8. $3M : (2M+m)$.

EXERCISES 15.7 (p. 442)

4. $\sqrt{\{12g(\sin\theta+\cos\theta-1)/(23a)\}}$; $12mg/23$.
6. $\frac{3}{4}mg \sin\theta\,(3\cos\theta-2)$, $\frac{1}{4}mg(1-3\cos\theta)^2$.
7. $\frac{1}{4}mg\cos\theta$.

EXERCISES 15.8 (p. 451)

1. $\frac{1}{2}M\sqrt{(3ga/2)}$.
3. $3\sqrt{\{g/(8a)\}}$.
4. $M\omega/(M+2m)$; $\cos^{-1}\{1-(aM^2\omega^2)/[4mg(M+2m)]\}$.
5. $mv/\{(16M+3m)a\}$; None.
6. (i) $Px/(MK^2)$.
7. $\sqrt{\{[2g(M+2m\sin^2\alpha)]/[Ma(1+\cos\alpha)]\}}$.
8. $6u/(7a)$.
10. $\sqrt{\{3g/(2a)\}}$; $\cos^{-1}(\frac{3}{4})$.
12. $2\sqrt{(g/a)}$.
13. $7\Omega/16$.
14. $\frac{1}{3}\Omega$.

MISCELLANEOUS EXERCISES XV (p. 454)

1. $2\pi\sqrt{\{5l/(3g)\}}$; $5l/3$.
4. $2\pi\sqrt{\{3a/(2g)\}}$.
6. $\sqrt{\{6ga(\sqrt{2}-1)\}}$.
7. (i) $3Ma^2/7$; (ii) $43Ma^2/35$.
8. $12g/5$, $6g/5$.
9. Nt/R; $N(N-R)t^2/(2IR)$; Nt/R.
10. $(5a\sqrt{2})/6$.
11. $\frac{1}{2}mg$, $(mg\sqrt{3})/8$.
14. $(mg\sin\theta)/10$, $mg(14\cos\theta-9\cos\alpha)/5$.
15. $(2\sqrt{3}-1)\sqrt{\{3g/(2a)\}}$.
18. $6mg/5$, $2mg/5$.
20. A line in the plane ABC and parallel to AB distant AB/$\sqrt{3}$ from C.

EXERCISES 16.2 (p. 464)

1. Space-centrode (part of) circle centre O radius $2a$, ($x^2+y^2 = 4a^2$); body-centrode (part of) circle of radius a and centre the mid-point of AB.
2. I is fixed coinciding with O; the space and body-centrodes are points also coinciding with O.
3. As for 2 above.

4. Space-centrode is parabola focus O directrix Px; body-centrode is parabola focus A, directrix the line through O parallel to the rod.
5. If $(x, 0)$, $(0, y)$ are the coordinates of A, B respectively, then $\dot{x} = \omega y$, $\dot{y} = -\omega x$ so that both A and B move with simple harmonic motion along the axes; I lies on OC produced so that OI = 2OC. [See Chapter XIV, equation (14.1a).]

MISCELLANEOUS EXERCISES XVI (p. 482)

1. $7\dot{x}^2 = 10gx \sin \alpha$; acceleration $= (5g \sin \alpha)/7$; time $= \sqrt{\{14x/(5g \sin \alpha)\}}$, velocity $= \sqrt{\{(10gx \sin \alpha)/7\}}$; 18 m.
2. (i) 0·005 kg m²; (ii) 0·1225 kg m²; $g/7$ m/s² $\approx$ 1·4 m/s².
3. $(v\sqrt{82})/20$ at $\tan^{-1}(\frac{4}{5})$ with BA and towards the side of AB from which the particle came.
4. $[(M+m'+nm)ga^2 \sin \alpha]/[2Ma^2+m'(\frac{1}{2}b^2+a^2)+(nm/3)(4a^2+ab+b^2)]$.
5. $\sqrt{\{3g/(10a)\}}$; $9g/(20a)$; $R_B = 9mg/50$, $R_A = 49mg/100$.
10. When the disc has rotated through the angle θ,

$$\tfrac{1}{2}m\{k^2+a^2(\tfrac{5}{4}-\sin \theta)\}\,\dot{\theta}^2 - mga \sin \theta = \tfrac{1}{2}m[k^2+(5a^2/4)]\,\omega^2.$$

12. Reel, $ga_2k_1^2/(k_1^2k_2^2+a_2^2k_1^2+a_1^2k_2^2)$; Pulley, $ga_1k_2^2/(k_1^2k_2^2+a_2^2k_1^2+a_1^2k_2^2)$.
14. $2\mu gx(a-y)^2 = aV^2(a-2y)$.
15. The centre of mass of the system has a constant horizontal component of velocity $\frac{1}{2}\sqrt{(ag)}$ and the rod oscillates through an angle $2\cos^{-1}(7/12)$; when the angular velocity of the rod vanishes the speed of the ring is $\frac{1}{2}\sqrt{(ag)}$.
18. Tension $= [g(1+\sin \alpha)]/[(1/m)+(1/M)+(a^2/Mk^2)]$;
acceleration $= g\{[(1/M)+(a^2/Mk^2)] \sin \alpha-(1/m)\}/[(1/m)+(1/M)+(a^2/Mk^2)]$.
20. Angular acceleration $= \mu a(g \cos \alpha+(P/M) \sin \alpha)/k^2$; linear acceleration $= P(\cos \alpha-\mu \sin \alpha)/M-g(\mu \cos \alpha+\sin \alpha)$.
22. $2a^2\omega^2(\mu \cos \alpha-\sin \alpha)/\{(7\mu \cos \alpha-2 \sin \alpha)^2 g\}$;
$2\omega(\mu \cos \alpha-\sin \alpha)/(7\mu \cos \alpha-2 \sin \alpha)$.
24. $\sqrt{(42ag)}$. **25.** $(l^2+3a^2)\omega/(4l^2)$.

EXERCISES 17.1 (p. 491)

1. -4; 6. **2.** $s = e^{v^2/(2k)}$.
3. $-3/2$; $\frac{2}{3}(1-e^{-3})$. $[s = \frac{2}{3}(1-e^{-3t})$.]
5. 5. **6.** $e^{1/10}$; 100 ln 100 $\approx$ 460. $[v = e^{t/100}$.]
7. $10(e^{1/5}-1)$, $[v = 10(e^{t/5}-1)]$; $10(5e^{1/5}-6)$. $[s = 10(5e^{t/5}-t-5)$.]
8. $v = (V/s)\sqrt{(s^2-a^2)}$; $f = a^2V^2/s^3$.
9. $A = 1/80$ m⁻¹ s, $B = 1/80^2$ m⁻¹; $x = 6400 \ln \{(80+t)/80\}$; $v = 80e^{-x/6400}$.
10. $10\{\sqrt{(8/3)}-1\}$ m. $[3x^2 = v^2-100$.]
11. $x = 20(3+2e^{2t/5})/(3+e^{2t/5})$; 2; (5/2) ln 3.
12. (i) 8; (ii) 4; (iii) 1.
14. $v = (50+2x)/5$.
15. (i) $dv/dt = -kv^3$; (ii) $dv/dx = -kv^2$.

EXERCISES 17.2 (p. 505)

1. $50\,000/(147)\{\frac{5}{3}\ln(\frac{5}{2})-1\}$ m $\approx$ 180 m.
2. $v(10) = 3{\cdot}5$ m/s; $v(20) = 10{\cdot}5$ m/s; $v(30) = 8{\cdot}75$ m/s. $v_{\max} = 11{\cdot}9$ m/s.
3. 40 km/h; $0{\cdot}225$ m/s^2.
4. 8 kg m/s.
5. $2{\cdot}5$ m.
9. $(P-R)(a-x)/a$.
10. $62{\cdot}5$ m; $69\frac{4}{9}$ J.
11. $\frac{1250}{49}\{25\ln(\frac{5}{3})-10\}$ m $\approx$ 71 m.
14. $u/(1+uRt)$.
16. $V\sqrt{(16/7)}$.
19. $\frac{1}{2}mV^2-\{(mg)/(2k)\}\ln[1+k(V^2/g)]$.
20. 10 m/s.

EXERCISES 17.3 (p. 511)

4. $50/3$ m/s $\approx$ 60 km/h; $10\{\frac{2500}{27}\ln 4-\frac{875}{18}\}$ m $\approx$ 800 m.
5. $85{\cdot}4$ s.
6. $\frac{800}{3}\ln(\frac{512}{387})$ m $\approx 74{\cdot}6$ m; $2{\cdot}44$ kW approx.
9. $a = 1000/7$, $b = 8/7$.

EXERCISES 17.4 (p. 515)

1. $a\dot{\theta}^2 = 2g\sin\theta$; $T = 3mg\sin\theta$.
3. A leaves the cylinder at once.
5. $r = a\sqrt{(5-4\cos\theta)}$.

EXERCISES 17.5 (p. 524)

1. $\sqrt{2}e^{-\pi/4}$, damped oscillatory.
2. $x = 4e^{-1} \approx 1{\cdot}5$, $\dot{x} = -2e^{-1} \approx -0{\cdot}74$; asymptotic to origin.
3. $x = -2e^{-\pi/2}$, $\dot{x} = 0$; damped oscillatory.
4. $x = 2e^{-t}-e^{-2t}$.
5. If AP $= (1+x)$ m, $\ddot{x}+8\dot{x}+32x = 0$;
$x = e^{-4t}(A\cos 4t+B\sin 4t)$; $\text{AP}_{\max} = \{1+(ue^{-\pi/4}\sqrt{2})/8\}$ m.
6. $x = (u/2k)\,e^{-kt}\sin 2kt$; $2ku\,e^{-\pi/2}$.
8. $x = 0{\cdot}245+\frac{1}{10}e^{-2t}(3\cos 6t+\sin 6t)$; $\pi/3$.
9. $\ddot{x}+2\lambda n\dot{x}+n^2x = 0$; $x = \{u\,e^{-\lambda nt}\sin[nt\sqrt{(1-\lambda^2)}]\}/[n\sqrt{(1-\lambda^2)}]$.
11. $s = (\lambda/6)(2\sin t+\sin 2t)$.
12. For $0 \leqslant t \leqslant \pi/\omega$, $x = \frac{1}{2}c(2\sin\omega t-\sin 2\omega t)$;
for $\pi/\omega \leqslant t \leqslant 2\pi/\omega$, $x = -c\sin 2\omega t$.
13. When spring is compressed by an amount $a/3$.
14. $x = V(8-9e^{-nt}+e^{-3nt})/(6n)$; $3amn^2x$.

MISCELLANEOUS EXERCISES XVII (p. 527)

1. $\frac{1}{2}m\{a-b-b\ln(a/b)\}$; acc $= -g(v^2+b)/b$; $R(v) = mgv^2/b$.
2. $M(2v^3+V^3)/(6PV)$.
3. $a(v^2+V^2)/(MV^2)$.
4. 80 m/s; 3200 ln (4/3) m; 40 ln 3 s.
11. (i) $(\mathrm{d}v/\mathrm{d}t) = k(V-v)$; (ii) $v(\mathrm{d}v/\mathrm{d}s) = k(V-v)$; $v = V(1-\mathrm{e}^{-kt})$; $ks = V\ln[V/(V-v)]-v$.
14. $1{\cdot}5\times10^6h^2MV^2/\{p(p-v)\}$ joules.
15. 4 m/s.
20. 4624 N.
21. $\frac{1}{2}a$, $\frac{1}{4}a(1+\sqrt{5})$.
24. $U/\sqrt{2}$.
26. $\mathrm{e}^{-2kx}\{\dot{x}^2-(\omega^2/2k^2)(2kx+1)\} =$ constant.
27. $\ddot{x}+k\dot{x}+\omega^2x = F\cos pt$.
28. $x = [F/(\omega^2+a^2)]\{1-\mathrm{e}^{-at}(\cos\omega t+(a/\omega)\sin\omega t)\}$; ultimately rests where $x = F/(\omega^2+a^2)$.
29. $(\sin\omega t)/(2k\omega)-\{\mathrm{e}^{-kt}\sin[t\sqrt{(\omega^2-k^2)}]\}/[2k\sqrt{(\omega^2-k^2)}]$.
30. $a\coth\{\pi/(6\sqrt{3})\}$.

EXERCISES 18.2 (p. 543)

1. $y = ux/v-gx^2/(2v^2)$.
2. $(x-2y)^2-2u^2(x-y) = 0$.
3. $x^2+y^2 = a^2$ (described in the clockwise direction).
4. $x^2/a^2+y^2/b^2 = 1$ (described in the counter-clockwise direction).
5. $y^2 = 4k^2x$.
6. $xy = 1$ (a rectangular hyperbola).
7. $\int_0^1 \sqrt{\{2(t^2+2t+2)\}}\,\mathrm{d}t = \{2\sqrt{5}-\sqrt{2}+\ln(\sqrt{10}+2\sqrt{2}-2-\sqrt{5})\}/\sqrt{2}$.
8. $\omega ab/\mathrm{OP}$.

EXERCISES 18.3 (p. 549)

1. $2mg$. **3.** $\sqrt{(2g)}$; $mg/\sqrt{2}$.
4. (i) $mg\cos\alpha\{1+2\ln(2\cos\alpha)\}$.
8. $\frac{1}{2}mg\cos\psi(3\cos\psi-2)$.
10. $mg(2+3\cos\theta)$ on the bead towards O.

EXERCISES 18.4 (p. 558)

1. $mg\sin\omega t$.
6. Taking axes Oxy, along and perpendicular to the initial position of AB, $v_A = \{\frac{1}{2}v\sin\theta, \frac{1}{2}v(1+\cos\theta)\}$, $v_B = \{-\frac{1}{2}v\sin\theta, \frac{1}{2}v(1-\cos\theta)\}$.

EXERCISES 18.5 (p. 566)

1. $\beta = (\pi - 2\alpha)/4$; $V^2/\{g(1+\sin\alpha)\}$.
2. $\tan^{-1}\{\sqrt{[(r+h)/(r-h)]}\}$.
5. $\sqrt{[g\{b+\sqrt{(a^2+b^2)}\}]}$; $\tan^{-1}\{[b+\sqrt{(a^2+b^2)}]/a\}$.

MISCELLANEOUS EXERCISES XVIII (p. 567)

5. $(V/\omega)\sinh\omega t$. **9.** $\sqrt{(2ga\sin\theta)}$; $\{3mg\sin\theta\cos\theta, mg(1+3\sin^2\theta)\}$.
10. $a(\frac{1}{2}\pi+\sqrt{3})$; 60°. **12.** $\{u/3, u/\sqrt{3}\}$.
13. The string rotates with constant angular velocity $\sqrt{(g/l)}$ and the centre of the string describes a parabola.
14. $\{5\sqrt{(g/h)}\}/2^{7/4}$.
17. $T = 2ml\omega^2/3$; $R = 2m\omega^2(a+\frac{2}{3}l)\sinh\omega t$.
20. $x = a\cos nt+(u/n)\sin nt$, $y = b\cos 2nt+(v/2n)\sin 2nt$.

EXERCISES 19.3 (p. 583)

1. 5 N at $\tan^{-1}(\frac{3}{4})$ with AB; $3a$ m.
2. $\sqrt{73}$ N at $65\frac{1}{2}°$ with AB cutting BC internally at X, where BX : XC = 5 : 3.
3. 1 N parallel to AB, on the opposite side of AB to C, and distant $3\sqrt{3}$ m from AB.
4. $P\sqrt{5}$. **5.** $a/\sqrt{3}$.
6. Force of 60 N at 60° with AB, couple in sense of CBA and moment $105\sqrt{3}$ Nm.
7. $\sqrt{3}$ N.
8. $\sqrt{6}$ N at 45° with BC, cutting BC internally at X where BX/CX = $2\sqrt{3}-1$.
9. Force of $\sqrt{(92-40\sqrt{3})}$ N at $\tan^{-1}[(3\sqrt{3}-2)/(7-2\sqrt{3})]$ with AB, couple in sense ABC of moment $9a\sqrt{3}/2$ Nm.
10. A force of magnitude M/a parallel to BC cutting AB produced at X where BX = $a\sqrt{2}$; $-3M/2$, $-\frac{1}{2}M$.
11. $X = 6$ N, $Y = 3\frac{1}{5}$ N, $(11\frac{1}{4}, 0)$, $(0, -6)$, [$G = 36$ Nm].
12. $P = 1$, $Q = 4$; $19\sqrt{3}/2$ Nm.
13. 11 N along AD.
14. Force of 10 newtons making angle $\tan^{-1}(\frac{3}{4})$ with AD, couple of moment 16 joules in sense ABC; cuts AD produced $\frac{2}{3}$ m from D making angle $\tan^{-1}(\frac{3}{4})$ with AD produced.
15. 1 : 2.
16. Force $k\overrightarrow{CB}$ and couple of moment $2k\Delta$ABC in sense ABC; kCB parallel to CB meeting BA produced at X where AX = AB.
18. P, $-\frac{1}{2}P$, $\sqrt{3}P/2$.
19. $20/\sqrt{3}$ N parallel to the $(-10, -10)$ side.
20. $10a$ units in sense ADC; $3\sqrt{2}$ units along CA.

21. $4\sqrt{13}$ units. **22.** $M\sqrt{10}/(4a)$.
23. $X = \{(M_3-M_1)a+(M_1-M_2)b\}/(ac)$, $Y = (M_1-M_2)/a$;
$R = \sqrt{(X^2+Y^2)}$; $M_1+Xy-Yx = 0$.
24. $2\Delta ABC$; $h/(k-1)$.
25. $X = 4$, $Y = -8\sqrt{3}$, $G = 18a\sqrt{3}$.

EXERCISES 19.5 (p. 588)

7. $\sqrt{7}FG$.

MISCELLANEOUS EXERCISES XIX (p. 592)

2. $p = 5$, $q = 6$, $r = 10$; 3 newtons parallel to BA; 8 m from D.
3. The point X in BC produced where BX $= 7a/2$; the resultant is of magnitude $2P\sqrt{2}$ and acts along the line XY, where Y lies on BA produced and BY $= 7a/2$.
6. $2\sqrt{5}$ units; $2x-y-4 = 0$.
7. $2P$; 60°; AO $= 2\frac{1}{2}a$, OB $= 4\frac{1}{2}a$; $\frac{5}{2}aP\sqrt{3}$.
9. (i) A force kb through B parallel to AC; (ii) a force $2k\,\overrightarrow{BX}$, where X is the mid-point of AC.
10. $(P-R)y-(Q-S)x+(P+Q+R+S)a = 0$.
11. (i) $2\sqrt{2}:3$; $-\sqrt{2}/3$.
12. $P = -\sqrt{2}$, $Q = \sqrt{2}$; $2\sqrt{2}$ newtons along DB.
13. $p = -(2q+r)$, $s = 4q+3r$.
14. $P\sqrt{5}$. **15.** $2F$. **16.** $Q = \frac{1}{2}P$, $R = \frac{1}{2}P\sqrt{5}$.
17. OBA. **19.** $39a\sqrt{3}/2$.
20. $13P$; mid-point of AB.

EXERCISES 20.1 (p. 603)

1. $3T\cos\alpha\,\operatorname{cosec}\beta$; $T\cos\alpha$, $3T\cos\alpha\cot\beta$.
6. $5(1+\sqrt{2})\,g$ N vertically.
7. $\mu Mg(\sqrt{2}-1)$. **8.** $Mg(2-\sqrt{3})$.

EXERCISES 20.4 (p. 616)

2. 60°; $\frac{1}{2}W\sqrt{7}$ at $\tan^{-1}(2/\sqrt{3})$ to horizontal.
3. (i) $W\sec\beta$; (ii) $F = W\tan\beta$, $R = 2W$.
9. $1-(\sqrt{2})/3$. **10.** Horizontal $6W/17$, vertical $7W/17$.
13. $(g\sqrt{2})/3$ Nm.
14. $\tan^{-1}(2\mu) \geqq \theta \geqq \tan^{-1}\{2/(3\mu')\}$.

16. (i) $R = 3W$, $F = 5W/(2\sqrt{3})$; (ii) $X = 5W/(2\sqrt{3})$, $Y = 2W$; (iii) $\mu \geqq 5/(6\sqrt{3})$.
18. At B, $\frac{1}{2}W\sqrt{17}$ at $\tan^{-1} 4$ with horizontal; at C, $\frac{1}{2}W\sqrt{5}$ at $\tan^{-1} 2$ with horizontal.
20. C.
24. $\frac{1}{2}a(w \cos \theta + 4P \sin \theta)$.

MISCELLANEOUS EXERCISES XX (p. 621)

1. $(n+1)a/n$; $\frac{1}{3}(n+1)W$.
3. $x = 28/11$, reaction $5\frac{1}{2}g$ N; $2g$ Nm.
5. At P, $\tan \theta$; at Q, $\tan \varphi$.
8. At B, P horizontally, W vertically downwards; at A, P horizontally, $2W$ vertically upwards.
9. $4W/5$ along $\overrightarrow{AB}$.
11. $\frac{1}{2}W \tan \beta$, W.
13. $W/(2\sqrt{3})$.
17. $[(4\lambda)/\pi] - [W/(2\sqrt{3})]$.

EXERCISES 21.1 (p. 627)

1. (a) $\frac{1}{2}km$; (b) $-\frac{1}{2}km$; (c) $-km(\sqrt{2}-1)$.
3. $\frac{1}{2}kmr^2$. **4.** $\frac{1}{2}mga$. **6.** $11mga/12$.

EXERCISES 21.3 (p. 636)

1. $Wl(2\mu \sin \theta - \cos \theta)$.
6. $\sin^{-1} \{h \sin 2\alpha)/(3c)\}$.

EXERCISES 21.5 (p. 650)

1. $P\delta(2l \cos \theta - nl \cot \theta) - W\delta(l \sin \theta)$
$= l\{P(n \operatorname{cosec}^2 \theta - 2 \sin \theta) - W \cos \theta\}\delta\theta$; $\frac{5}{8}$.
2. $W(b - a\sqrt{2})/(a\sqrt{2})$.
5. A thrust $11W/24$.
6. $W\sqrt{(\frac{13}{12})}$ at $\tan^{-1} [1/(2\sqrt{3})]$ with the horizontal.
7. Horizontal $W\sqrt{15}/8$; vertical $15W/8$.
8. BC exerts a horizontal force $W/(2\sqrt{3})$ in sense CF on CD; ED exerts an upward force W and a horizontal force $W/(2\sqrt{3})$ in sense ED on CD.
10. $l > a$; $[W \sec \alpha\sqrt{\{l^2 - 4a(l-a) \sin^2 \alpha\}}]/(l-a)$.

MISCELLANEOUS EXERCISES XXI (p. 652)

17. A horizontal force $\frac{1}{2}W \tan \psi$.

EXERCISES 22.2 (p. 670)

4. Stable with BC above the pegs.
7. Stable.
9. If θ is the angle between AB and the upward vertical, $\theta = 0, \pi$ unstable, $\theta = \pm\pi/3$ stable.
10. If θ is the angle between the rod and the vertical, $\theta = 0, \pi$, unstable; $\theta = \frac{1}{3}\pi$, stable.
11. Stable.
12. Diagonal vertical, stable.
15. Unstable.
16. $\frac{1}{2}Wl \sin \varphi$.
18. $\theta = 0$ unstable, $\theta = 2\cos^{-1}(\frac{3}{4})$ stable, $\theta = \pi$ unstable. [The string is slack in the position $\theta = \pi$.]
19. $\cos^{-1}\{(a \sin \alpha \cos^2 \alpha)/c\}$.
20. When $5\lambda > 2W$, $\theta = 0$ unstable and $\theta = \cos^{-1}\{(2W+\lambda)/(6\lambda)\}$ stable; when $5\lambda < 2W$, $\theta = 0$ (only) stable.

EXERCISES 22.3 (p. 677)

4. $\sin^{-1}(1/2\sqrt{3})$, unstable.

EXERCISES 23.1 (p. 684)

1. 2·2P; passes through the mid-point of AB and cuts DA produced where AX = 0·45a.
2. 82 N, 2·5 m from D in CD produced.
3. Between B and D, 0·72 m from D.
4. 3·9 N; 0·07 m.
5. 2·4P, at about 38° with BC; cuts BC at 0·8BC from B.
6. 0·35 m from D in AD produced.
7. String at Q, 0·07g N; string at P, 0·03g N.
8. 80 Nm in the sense PQRS.

EXERCISES 23.4 (p. 692)

1. 32g N vertically downward; BD+100g N; AB+60g N; CD−60g N; BC+32g N; AC−68g N.
2. 4W.
3. AB−$200\sqrt{3}g$ N, AC+400g N, BC−$[(400\sqrt{3})/3]g$ N, BE−$\frac{1400}{3}g$ N, BD−$\frac{200}{3}g$ N, DC+$[(800\sqrt{3})/3]g$ N.

4. At A, $40g$ N; at D, $50g$ N; AB$+40g$ N; BC$+50g$ N; CD$+50g$ N; AF$-40\sqrt{2}g$ N; BF$+10g$ N; FE$-40g$ N; BE$-10\sqrt{2}g$ N; CE no stress; DE$-50\sqrt{2}g$ N.
5. AB$+[(500\sqrt{3})/3]g$ N; BC$+[(700\sqrt{3})/3]g$ N; CD$-[(700\sqrt{3})/6]g$ N; DB$-100g$ N; AD$+[(1000\sqrt{3})/3]g$ N.
6. AB$+300\sqrt{3}g$ N; BC$+400\sqrt{3}g$ N; CD$-300g$ N; DB$-200\sqrt{3}g$ N; DA$-100\sqrt{3}g$ N; DE$-500g$ N; AE$+500\sqrt{3}g$ N; At A, $600g$ N; at B $300g$ N.
7. EC$+3000\sqrt{2}g$ N; DC$-3000g$ N; DE$-3000g$ N; AE$+3000g$ N; AD$+3000\sqrt{2}g$ N; BD$-6000g$ N; AB$+6000g$ N; force at A $3000\sqrt{13}g$ N at $\tan^{-1}(\frac{3}{2})$ with AE; force at B $6000\sqrt{2}g$ N.
8. At A, $800g$ N; at D, $800g$ N; AB$-[(800\sqrt{3})/3]g$ N; AL$+[(1600\sqrt{3})/3]g$ N; LB$-[(1400\sqrt{3})/3]g$ N; LM$-500\sqrt{3}g$ N; MB$+[(200\sqrt{3})/3]g$ N; BC$-[(1600\sqrt{3})/3]g$ N; then symmetry.
9. $+2(W-x)$, $+[(\sqrt{3})/2](2W-x)$.
10. $17{,}000g$ N at 146° anticlockwise with AD; $14{,}600g$ N; BC$+19{,}000g$ N; CD$+21{,}000g$ N; DE$-12{,}500g$ N; CE$-6500g$ N; BE$+6500g$ N; BA$+13{,}500g$ N; AE$-24{,}000g$ N.

EXERCISES 23.5 (p. 700)

1–8. See answers to Ex. 23.4.
9. AE$+(30\sqrt{3}-50)\times 1000g$ N; EF$+(10\sqrt{3}-15)\times 1000g$ N; ED$-(30\sqrt{2}-15\sqrt{6})\times 1000g$ N; AF$+(20\sqrt{3}-30)\times 1000g$ N; FD$+(30-15\sqrt{3})\times 1000g$ N; DC$-(30-15\sqrt{3})\times 1000g$ N; then symmetry.

MISCELLANEOUS EXERCISES XXIII (p. 700)

1. AB$+(7{\cdot}5)/\sqrt{2}$; BC$+5\sqrt{2}$; AF$-7{\cdot}5$; BF$+(2{\cdot}5)\sqrt{2}$; CF$-5(\times 1000g$ N); then symmetry.
2. CD-20; DE$+20\sqrt{2}$; CE-30; AE$+20$; CB$-25\sqrt{2}$; CA$+5\sqrt{2}$ (g N).
3. CD$+2W/\sqrt{3}$; BC$-W/\sqrt{3}$; BD$-W$; DE$+W/\sqrt{3}$; BE$+4W/\sqrt{3}$; AB$-2W$.
4. AB$+6\frac{1}{3}$; AC$+7\frac{2}{3}$.
5. AB$+2700g$ N; AD$-400\sqrt{3}g$ N; BD$-[(2700\sqrt{3})/2]g$ N; DE$-[(2300\sqrt{3})/2]g$ N; then symmetry.
6. AB-4; BD$+2{\cdot}8$; BC$-2{\cdot}8$; DC$+2{\cdot}0$ ($\times 1000g$ N).
7. AC$+0{\cdot}87$; BC$+1{\cdot}5$; AD-2; CD$+1{\cdot}73$ ($\times 1000g$ N).
8. CE-2; EF no stress; AD$+14$; DC$+10$; AE$-12{\cdot}1$; DE$+4$; EB$-8{\cdot}7$; CF$+10$; BF$+10$ ($\times 100g$ N).
9. AB$-7{\cdot}2$, BE$-4{\cdot}33$, BC$-2{\cdot}89$, BD$-8{\cdot}66$, DE$+8{\cdot}66$, DC$+8{\cdot}66$, AC$+14{\cdot}4$ ($\times 100g$ N).
11. BD, CE each$+27{\cdot}5$; CD-31 (g N).
12. (i) $300g$ N; (ii) $50\sqrt{61}$ (≈ 390) g N at $\tan^{-1}(\frac{5}{6})$ ($\approx 40°$) with horizontal and towards E; (iii) AB$-300g$ N, BD$+250\sqrt{2}$ (≈ 354) g N, DC$+50g$ N.

13. $(2/\sqrt{3})Wg$ N at 60° with the horizontal; AB$-\frac{1}{2}Wg$ N.
AD$+(W/2\sqrt{3})g$ N, AC$-Wg$ N, BC$+(W3\sqrt{2})g$ N, CD$+\frac{1}{2}Wg$ N.
14. HG$-20\sqrt{3}\,g$ N; GC$+[(40\sqrt{3})/3]\,g$ N; CD$+[(40\sqrt{3})/3]\,g$ N.
15. OC+5; OB+1·34; OA+0·67; BC−2·6; AB−2·6;
reaction at O, $5\sqrt{7}$ at $\tan^{-1}[(5\sqrt{3})/3]$ with the horizontal ($\times 1000\,g$ N).
16. Force at O, 28·4 units at $20\frac{1}{2}°$ with OS; force at P, $[(46\sqrt{3})/3]$ units;
QT$-[(14\sqrt{3})/3]$; TU$-[(4\sqrt{3})/3]$; UQ$+6\sqrt{3}$.
17. AB−1·7; AC−1·2; AD−2·7; BC+1·2; DC+1·2 ($\times 100\,g$ N).
18. $T = w\sqrt{3}/3$; OA$+[(2\sqrt{3}w)/3]$; OB$-w/2$; OC$+[(w\sqrt{3})/6]$; OD$+(w/2)$;
OE$-[(2\sqrt{3}w)/3]$.
19. FB$+\sqrt{2}$; FC$-\sqrt{2}$; BC−6 ($\times 1000\,g$ N).
20. BD$-[(80\sqrt{3})/3]$ units; DF$+[(18\sqrt{3})/3]$ units; FB$+[(70\sqrt{3})/3]$ units.

EXERCISES 24.1 (p. 711)

1. $-36\,g$ N; $108\,g$ Nm.
2. $2g$ N; $8\,g$ Nm.
3. $F = W(x-l)/(2l)$, $M = -Wx(2l-x)/(4l)$; at the centre.
4. $F = 15\,g$ N; $M = 0$.
5. For $0 < x < 20$, $F = (10x-96)/5\times 1000\,g$ N, $M = (5x^2-96x)/5\times 1000\,g$ Nm; for $20 < x \leqq 24$, $F = (2x-48)\times 1000\,g$ N, $M = (x-24)^2\times 1000\,g$ Nm;
$F_{max} = 20\frac{4}{5}\times 1000\,g$ N at C; $M_{max} = 92\frac{4}{25}\times 1000\,g$ Nm at $9\frac{3}{5}$ m from A.
6. $\frac{1}{3}L(2x-a)$; $3W$.
7. 0·7 m from A; $-8{\cdot}1\,g$ Nm.
8. $-50\,g$ N; $80\,g$ Nm.
9. At A, force with components $\frac{1}{2}P$ in direction AB, $(W-\frac{1}{2}P\sqrt{3})$ vertically upwards, couple $(W-P\sqrt{3})l$ anticlockwise; at G, shearing force $\frac{1}{2}(P\sqrt{3}-W)$ tension $-\frac{1}{2}P$, bending moment $\frac{1}{4}(W-2P\sqrt{3})l$.
10. (i) $2P$; (ii) $-P\sqrt{3}$; (iii) $-3Pa$.

EXERCISES 24.2 (p. 717)

9. $1200\,g$ Nm. **10.** $6\frac{2}{3}$ m.
11. For $0 < x < c$, $F = W(2l+x)/(2l)$, $M = Wx(4l+x)/(4l)$,
for $c < x < 2l$, $F = W(2l+x)/(2l) - 3Wl/(2l-c)$,
$M = Wx(4l+x)/(4l) - 3Wl(x-c)/(2l-c)$.
12. For $0 \leqq x < 2a$, $F = Wx/(8a)$, $M = Wx^2/(16a)$;
$2a < x < 3a$, $F = Wx/(8a) - 5W/4$, $M = Wx^2/(16a) - 5W(x-2a)/4$;
$3a < x < 6a$, $F = Wx/(8a) - W/4$, $M = Wx^2/(16a) - W(x+2a)/4$;
$6a < x < 8a$, $F = Wx/(8a) - W$, $M = Wx^2/(16a) - W(x-4a)$.
13. $R(E) = 16W/7$, $R(F) = 12W/7$.
14. $4nlwx + \frac{1}{2}wx^2$ for $0 \leqq x \leqq l$;
$4nlwx + \frac{1}{2}wx^2 - 8(2n+1)wl(x-l)/3$ for $l \leqq x \leqq 4l$.
15. $2-\sqrt{2}$.

EXERCISES 24.3 (p. 725)

2. $24\,g$ N. **4.** $a/\sqrt{3}$. **7.** $3l$.
8. $c = 4$; $5\frac{2}{5}$ m, $4 \ln 10$ m.
10. $40\,g$ N at $\tan^{-1}(\frac{4}{3})$ below horizontal.

EXERCISES 24.4 (p. 728)

1. $5\sqrt{3}$ m $\approx 8{\cdot}7$ m. **2.** $125\,g$ N.
3. $0{\cdot}13$ m.

MISCELLANEOUS EXERCISES XXIV (p. 731)

1. $F = -10\pi\varrho g a^2/9$, $M = -73\pi\varrho g a^2/36$.
2. If x is the distance from A,
for $0 < x < l$, $F = -W(4l-x)/(2l)$, $M = 2W(l-x)+Wx^2/(4l)$,
for $l < x < 2l$, $F = -W(2l-x)/(2l)$, $M = W(l-x)+Wx^2/(4l)$.
3. At the ends and at the two points each distant $(2-\sqrt{3})l$ from the centre.
4. If x is the distance from B,
$T = wl/(2\sqrt{3})$, $F = \frac{1}{2}w(l-2x)$, $M = \frac{1}{2}wx(l-x)$.
6. (i) $M = wx(a+x)/(2\sqrt{2})$, $F = w(a+2x)/(2\sqrt{2})$, $T = w(2x-a)/(2\sqrt{2})$;
(ii) $M = -w\xi(a-\xi)/(2\sqrt{2})$, $F = w(a-2\xi)/(2\sqrt{2})$, $T = w(a+2\xi)/(2\sqrt{2})$.
7. If x is distance from one end,
for $0 \leqq x \leqq l-a$, $M = Wx(2l+x)/(2l)$,
for $l-a \leqq x \leqq l$, $M = Wx(2l+x)/(2l)-4W(x-l+a)$,
then symmetry.
10. Each $13l/18$; $(4l/3) \ln (3/2)$.
11. $\frac{1}{2}l\sqrt{3} \ln 3$, $(2-\sqrt{3})l$.
13. The solution of $2 \sinh u = 3u$ is $u \approx 1{\cdot}62$, $(u = a/c)$; $wb \approx 0{\cdot}62wa$.
14. (i) $25W/16$; (ii) $7l/8$, $(c = 15l/16)$.
16. $k \ln [\{k+\sqrt{(k^2+l^2)}\}/l]$; $\pi/6$.

MISCELLANEOUS EXERCISES XXV (p. 747)

19. $\frac{1}{2}m(gx^2-x\dot{x}^2) = mg^3t^4/216$, where m is the mass per unit length.
21. $3\lambda f^2t^2/16$ newtons; energy is continually lost as the chain is jerked into motion.

EXERCISES 26.3 (p. 758)

1. (i) $(-3, 2, 0)$; (ii) $(-3, 0, 1)$; (iii) $(0, 2, 1)$; (iv) $(-3, 0, 0)$; (v) $(0, 2, 0)$; (vi) $(0, 0, 1)$.
2. (i) $(a, b, -c)$; (ii) $(a, -b, c)$; (iii) $(-a, b, c)$; (iv) $(a, -b, -c)$; (v) $(-a, b, -c)$; (vi) $(-a, -b, c)$; (vii) $(-a, -b, -c)$.

3. $(a, a, -a)$, $(a, -a, a)$, $(-a, a, a)$, $(-a, -a, a)$.
4. (i) 7 units; (ii) 13 units; (iii) 5 units.
7. The angle $M_1M_3M_2$ is obtuse.
9. (5, 0, 0) and (−11, 0, 0).
10. (0, 2, 0).

EXERCISES 26.5 (p. 762)

2. $|\mathbf{a}+\mathbf{b}| = 6$, $|\mathbf{a}-\mathbf{b}| = 14$.
3. 22. **4.** 20. **5.** $|\mathbf{a}+\mathbf{b}| = |\mathbf{a}-\mathbf{b}| = 13$.
6. $|\mathbf{a}+\mathbf{b}| = \sqrt{129}$, $|\mathbf{a}-\mathbf{b}| = 7$.
7. (i) Vectors **a** and **b** must be perpendicular; (ii) the angle between **a** and **b** must be acute; (iii) the angle between **a** and **b** must be obtuse.

EXERCISES 26.6 (p. 769)

1. $BO/BQ = \frac{2}{3}$, $AQ/AC = \frac{1}{4}$.
2. (iv) The meeting point of the lines joining the mid-points of opposite edges.
3. $-(\mathbf{a}+\mathbf{b})$; (ii) $-\frac{1}{2}\mathbf{a}$, $-\frac{1}{2}\mathbf{b}$, $\frac{1}{2}(\mathbf{a}+\mathbf{b})$.
4. $\overrightarrow{CD} = \sqrt{2}\mathbf{b}-\mathbf{a} = -\overrightarrow{GH}$; $\overrightarrow{DE} = \mathbf{b}-\sqrt{2}\mathbf{a} = -\overrightarrow{HA}$; $\overrightarrow{EF} = -\mathbf{a}$; $\overrightarrow{FG} = -\mathbf{b}$.
5. (i) $\mathbf{i}+\mathbf{j}+\mathbf{k}$; (ii) $-\mathbf{i}+\mathbf{j}+\mathbf{k}$, $\mathbf{i}-\mathbf{j}+\mathbf{k}$, $\mathbf{i}+\mathbf{j}-\mathbf{k}$;
(iii) $\mathbf{j}+\mathbf{k}$, $\mathbf{k}+\mathbf{i}$, $\mathbf{i}+\mathbf{j}$.
6. $(4\mathbf{i}+5\mathbf{j}+6\mathbf{k})/11$.
7. $\mathbf{r} = 2\mathbf{i}-\mathbf{j}+2\mathbf{k}+t(2\mathbf{i}-2\mathbf{j}+\mathbf{k})$; $(x-2)/2 = (y+1)/(-2) = (z-2)/1$;
$2\mathbf{i}-\mathbf{j}+2\mathbf{k}$.
8. $2x+3y-3z-7 = 0$. **10.** $(x-1)/1 = (y-2)/(-1) = (z-3)/2$.

EXERCISES 26.7 (p. 776)

1. (i) 14; (ii) −4; (iii) 0.
2. $\frac{12}{25}$, $-\frac{3}{5}$, $-\frac{16}{25}$. **3.** $\frac{3}{13}$, $\frac{4}{13}$, $\frac{12}{13}$.
4. (i) Yes; (ii) no; (iii) yes.
5. $\sqrt{2}$, 1, −1.
6. $\cos^{-1}[5/(3\sqrt{51})]$.
7. $(-4/\sqrt{77}, 5/\sqrt{77}, -6/\sqrt{77})$; $\cos^{-1}(-59/\sqrt{3850})$.
9. $\cos^{-1}(\frac{1}{3})$.
11. AW and BX are perpendicular.
13. $AB = 1/\sqrt{2}$; $\mathbf{r} = \frac{1}{4}(5, -1, 5)+t(1, 0, -1)$; (i) $x-z = 0$;
(ii) $x-z-1 = 0$.
14. −24 units of work.

EXERCISES 26.8 (p. 787)

1. $(8\mathbf{i}+4\mathbf{j}+9\mathbf{k})/\sqrt{161}$.

2. (i) $\cos^{-1}(\frac{4}{5})$; (ii) $\frac{1}{3}\pi$; (iii) $3/\sqrt{2}$. **3.** (i) $10/(3\sqrt{30})$; (ii) $\frac{1}{2}\sqrt{170}$.

4. 8; $-2\mathbf{i}-2\mathbf{j}-3\mathbf{k}$; $\cos^{-1}(8/9)$; $\frac{1}{2}\sqrt{17}$.

6. $2x-3z-27 = 0$. **7.** $x-2y+3z+3 = 0$.

8. $5x-3z = 0$. **9.** $2x-y-z = 4$.

10. $9x-y+7z-40 = 0$.

11. $\overrightarrow{PQ}.\overrightarrow{PR} = 2$; $\overrightarrow{PQ}\times\overrightarrow{PR} = 4\mathbf{i}+\mathbf{j}-2\mathbf{k}$; $\cos Q\hat{P}R = 2/5$; $\Delta PQR = \frac{1}{2}\sqrt{21}$ units^2.

12. (ii) No two of **a**, **b**, **c** are parallel; (iv) **a**, **b**, **c** are the sides of a triangle.

13. (ii) $-\mathbf{k}+t(\mathbf{i}+\mathbf{j}+2\mathbf{k})$, where t is an arbitrary parameter.

14. $\pm\frac{1}{4}$.

15. $\frac{5}{3}(-2\mathbf{i}+\mathbf{j}+0\mathbf{k})$ [in newton metres].

EXERCISES 26.9 (p. 794)

1. (i) $\frac{1}{2}5\sqrt{3}$ sq. units; (ii) $(-\mathbf{i}+\mathbf{j}+\mathbf{k})/\sqrt{3}$; $\frac{5}{3}$ cub. units.

2. 12 cub. units **3.** $5x-7y+11z+13 = 0$.

4. $bc/\sqrt{(b^2+c^2)}$, $ca/\sqrt{(c^2+a^2)}$, $ab/\sqrt{(a^2+b^2)}$.

5. $\sqrt{(\frac{5}{7})}$. **6.** $\frac{7}{3}$.

7. $(2, -1, 4)$, $(\frac{7}{2}, 0, \frac{7}{2})$.

8. (i) $\mathbf{a}\times\mathbf{b}/\mathbf{a}^2+p\mathbf{a}$, where p is a variable scalar;
(ii) $\{\lambda^2\mathbf{a}+(\mathbf{a}.\mathbf{c})\mathbf{c}+\lambda(\mathbf{c}\times\mathbf{a})\}/\{\lambda(\lambda^2+\mathbf{c}^2)\}$;
(iii) $\{a\mathbf{w}+(\mathbf{v}\times\mathbf{w})\times\mathbf{u}\}/\{a(a+\mathbf{u}.\mathbf{v})\}$ when $a+\mathbf{u}.\mathbf{v} \neq 0$;
$p\mathbf{v}+\mathbf{w}/a$, where p is a variable scalar, when $a+\mathbf{u}.\mathbf{v} = 0$.

MISCELLANEOUS EXERCISES XXVI (p. 798)

1. (a) $\mathbf{i}+2\mathbf{k}+\frac{1}{3}t(2\mathbf{i}+2\mathbf{j}+\mathbf{k})$;
(b) $-\mathbf{j}+\mathbf{k}+\frac{1}{3}t(2\mathbf{i}+2\mathbf{j}+\mathbf{k})$;
$\cos\theta = (6-t)/\sqrt{\{6(3t^2-2t+6)\}}$.

2. Velocity $7\mathbf{i}+2\mathbf{j}$, time $12-30$, position $4\frac{1}{2}\mathbf{i}+\mathbf{j}$.

4. $\dot{\mathbf{r}} = \omega\{a\cos(\omega t+\alpha), b\cos(\omega t+\beta), c\cos(\omega t+\gamma)\}$,
$\ddot{\mathbf{r}} = -\omega^2\{a\sin(\omega t+\alpha), b\sin(\omega t+\beta), c\sin(\omega t+\gamma)\}$.

5. $\mathbf{h} = -2m(t^2+1)\mathbf{k}$; $d\mathbf{h}/dt = -4mt\mathbf{k}$;
$\mathbf{F} = 2m\mathbf{i}$; $\mathbf{r}\times\mathbf{F} = -4mt\mathbf{k}$.

7. $d\hat{\boldsymbol{\theta}}/dt = -\hat{\mathbf{r}}\, d\theta/dt$; $(-a\dot{\theta}^2, a\ddot{\theta})$.

8. (a) $(1/\sqrt{3})(\mathbf{i}+\mathbf{j}-\mathbf{k})$; (b) $\pm(5/\sqrt{114})(\mathbf{a}+\mathbf{b}+8\mathbf{c}/5)$.

9. $\overrightarrow{AB} = 7\mathbf{i}+2\mathbf{k}$, $\overrightarrow{AC} = 5\mathbf{i}+\mathbf{j}+\mathbf{k}$;
$\overrightarrow{AB}.\overrightarrow{AC} = 37$; $\overrightarrow{AB}\times\overrightarrow{AC} = -2\mathbf{i}+3\mathbf{j}+7\mathbf{k}$;
(i) $\cos\theta = 37/(3\sqrt{159})$; (ii) $\frac{1}{2}\sqrt{62}$ units^2; (iii) $7/\sqrt{62}$.

10. $\overrightarrow{AB} = -2\mathbf{i}-\mathbf{j}+3\mathbf{k}$, $\overrightarrow{AC} = \mathbf{i}-3\mathbf{j}+2\mathbf{k}$, $\overrightarrow{BC} = 3\mathbf{i}-2\mathbf{j}-\mathbf{k}$; $\overrightarrow{AB}.\overrightarrow{AC} = 7$;
$\overrightarrow{AB}\times\overrightarrow{AC} = 7(\mathbf{i}+\mathbf{j}+\mathbf{k})$; $\overrightarrow{OA}\times\overrightarrow{BC} = -4\mathbf{i}-2\mathbf{j}-8\mathbf{k}$; $\overrightarrow{OA}.\mathrm{AB}\times\overrightarrow{AC} = 14$;
(i) $\pi/3$; (ii) $(7\sqrt{3})/2$; (iii) $(1/\sqrt{21})(2\mathbf{i}+\mathbf{j}+4\mathbf{k})$; (iv) $\sqrt{(7/3)}$; (v) $7/3$.
11. $\lambda = -(\mathbf{a}.\mathbf{b})/\mathbf{a}^2 = -\frac{4}{5}$;
$\mathbf{c} = \{-\mathbf{a}\times\mathbf{b}+(\mathbf{a}.\mathbf{c})\mathbf{a}\}/\mathbf{a}^2 = \frac{1}{5}(5\mathbf{i}+3\mathbf{k})$.
12. $\mathbf{a}.\mathbf{b} = 9$; (i) $\sqrt{(27/29)}$; (ii) $\frac{1}{2}\sqrt{6}$.
14. (i) $\frac{1}{9}(4\mathbf{i}+7\mathbf{j}-4\mathbf{k})$; (ii) $\frac{1}{9}(\mathbf{i}+4\mathbf{j}+8\mathbf{k})$; (iii) $\frac{1}{9}(8\mathbf{i}-4\mathbf{j}+\mathbf{k})$;
(iv) 0; $\overrightarrow{OC} = \frac{1}{3}(11\hat{\mathbf{e}}_1-\hat{\mathbf{e}}_2-2\hat{\mathbf{e}}_3)$; (3, 4, 1).
15. $10\mathbf{k}$, i.e. 10 units anticlockwise.
16. (a) $2\pi/k$; (b) $4mk^2$; $2(1-\pi\sqrt{3})\,\mathbf{i}+\frac{3}{2}(\pi+\sqrt{3})\,\mathbf{j}$.
17. $v_1 = u/\sqrt{3}$, $v_2 = 2u/\sqrt{3}$.
19. (a) $p = \mathbf{i}.\mathbf{u} = 1/\sqrt{3}$, $q = \mathbf{i}.\mathbf{v} = \sqrt{(2/3)}$, $r = \mathbf{i}.\mathbf{w} = 0$.
(b) $\varrho = 5$.
20. (a) (ii) $\mathbf{u} = \lambda\mathbf{i}+\lambda\mathbf{j}+(2\lambda-1)\mathbf{k}$, where λ is arbitrary.
21. $\begin{vmatrix} a & 0 & x \\ b & b & y \\ 0 & c & z \end{vmatrix} = 0.$
22. $(m_1\mathbf{i}+m_2\mathbf{j}+m_3\mathbf{k})/(m_1+m_2+m_3)$;
(a) $(3a/8)\mathbf{i}+0\mathbf{j}+0\mathbf{k}$; (b) $(3a/8)(\mathbf{i}+\mathbf{j}+\mathbf{k})$.
23. $\mathbf{r} = \frac{1}{2}\lambda\mathbf{a}+\frac{1}{2}(1-\lambda)(\mathbf{b}+\mathbf{c})$; $\frac{1}{4}(\mathbf{a}+\mathbf{b}+\mathbf{c})$.
24. $\mathbf{r}.\mathbf{p} = \mathbf{p}.\mathbf{s}+\mathbf{p}^2$; $x-4y+z = 2$, $\frac{1}{3}\sqrt{2}$.
26. $-2 > c > -17/4$; $\mathbf{r} = t\mathbf{i}$, $\mathbf{r} = s\mathbf{i}-\mathbf{j}$.
27. $\mathbf{r} = 5\mathbf{i}-2\mathbf{j}+\mathbf{k}+t(3\mathbf{i}+5\mathbf{j}+5\mathbf{k})$; $-\mathbf{i}-12\mathbf{j}-9\mathbf{k}$.
28. $3\sqrt{2}$.
29. $\mathbf{r} = \lambda a\tan t\,\mathbf{i}+a\{(1-\lambda)\,\mathbf{j}+\lambda\sec t\,\mathbf{k}\}$
30. $(\lambda+\mu)(\mathbf{b}+\mathbf{c}+\mathbf{d})-3\lambda\mathbf{a}$; $270\mathbf{i}-300\mathbf{j}-150\mathbf{k}$, magnitude $60\sqrt{3}$ units.
31. (a) $7\sqrt{3}$; (b) $2\mathbf{i}-\mathbf{j}+3\mathbf{k}$; (c) $\mathbf{r} = 2\mathbf{i}-\mathbf{j}+3\mathbf{k}+t(\mathbf{i}+\mathbf{j}+\mathbf{k})$.
32. (i) 12 J, 28 J; $\mathbf{F}_3 = (31\mathbf{i}+31\mathbf{j}+97\mathbf{k})$ N, magnitude $11\sqrt{51}$ N, direction $\mathbf{i}+\mathbf{j}+7\mathbf{k}$; resultant $40(\mathbf{i}+\mathbf{j}+\mathbf{k})$, magnitude $40\sqrt{3}$ N, direction $\mathbf{i}+\mathbf{j}+\mathbf{k}$;
(ii) $a^2\lambda\pi^2/8$.
33. $-6\mathbf{i}-\mathbf{j}-\mathbf{k}$; $2\mathbf{i}+3\mathbf{j}-\mathbf{k}$, $\mathbf{r} = -6\mathbf{i}-\mathbf{j}-\mathbf{k}+t(2\mathbf{i}+3\mathbf{j}-\mathbf{k})$; $\mathbf{v} = 4\mathbf{i}+6\mathbf{j}-2\mathbf{k}$, $\mathbf{r} = 2\mathbf{i}+11\mathbf{j}-5\mathbf{k}$.
34. A, B collide at $\mathbf{i}+3\mathbf{j}+2\mathbf{k}$ after 2 seconds; $\mathbf{v}_C = -6\mathbf{i}-25\mathbf{j}-16\mathbf{k}$ initially at $(13\mathbf{i}+53\mathbf{j}+34\mathbf{k})$.
35. $2\mathbf{i}+\mathbf{j}$, $0\mathbf{i}+4\mathbf{j}$; $5/\sqrt{13}$; 5 units.
36. $\mathbf{r} = \mathbf{i}2t+\mathbf{j}(1-t)+\mathbf{k}t^2$; after $\frac{1}{2}$ second.
37. $\mathbf{v}_B = 5\mathbf{i}-3\mathbf{j}+6\mathbf{k}$; $t = 1$; equal, 1:1.
38. $\sqrt{2}$; $\sqrt{(7/8)}$.
39. $|\mathbf{u}| = 5\sqrt{2}$; 65°, 56°, 45°; $(3\mathbf{i}+4\mathbf{j}+5\mathbf{k})/(5\sqrt{2})$; $\pm(12\mathbf{i}+16\mathbf{j})/5$.
40. $2\pi\sqrt{(2a/g)}$.
41. $\mathbf{r} = 3(\mathbf{i}+\mathbf{j}+\mathbf{k})$; $m\mathbf{v} = 6(\mathbf{i}+2\mathbf{j}+2\mathbf{k})$; 54 units.

INDEX